PETROGRAD

1917

0   ¼   ½   ¾   1 mile

Legend:
1. Russkii Reno factory
2. Novyi Lessner factory
3. Moskovsky Regiment
4. Meeting place of Sixth Congress
5. Erikson factory
6. Grenadersky Bridge
7. First Machine Gun Regiment
8. Sukhanov apartment
9. Elizarova apartment
10. Grenadier Regiment
11. Bolshevik headquarters, Vyborg District
12. Trud printing press
13. Mikhailovsky Artillery School
14. Crosses Prison
15. Metallist factory
16. Samsonevsky Bridge
17. Cirque Moderne
18. Kshesinskaia Mansion
19. Kronwerk Arsenal
20. Peter and Paul Fortress
21. Stock exchange
22. Petersburg University
23. *Aurora*
24. Finliandsky Regiment
25. 180th Infantry Regiment
26. Franco-Russian shipyard
27. Second Baltic Fleet Detachment
28. Keksgolmsky Regiment
29. Central telegraph office
30. Petrograd telegraph agency
31. Post office
32. War Ministry
33. Admiralty
34. Palace Square
35. St. Isaac's Cathedral
36. General Staff headquarters
37. Petrograd telephone station
38. Winter Palace
39. Pravda editorial offices and printing plant
40. Pavlovsky Regiment
41. War Memorial Field
42. Kazan Cathedral
43. City Duma
44. State Bank
45. Mariinsky Palace
46. Priboi publishing house
47. Litovsky Regiment
48. Fourteenth Cossack Regiment
49. Preobrazhensky Regiment
50. Sixth Engineer Battalion
51. Volynsky Regiment
52. Taurida Palace
53. Smolny
54. First Reserve Infantry Regiment
55. Bonch-Bruevich apartment
56. Znamensky Square
57. First and Fourth Cossack Regiments
58. Semenovsky Regiment
59. Petrograd electric station
60. Egersky Regiment
61. Petrogradsky Regiment
62. Izmailovsky Guards Regiment
63. Harbor Canal
64. Putilov factory

The Bolsheviks Come to Power

By the Same Author

PRELUDE TO REVOLUTION
*The Petrograd Bolsheviks
and the July 1917 Uprising*

THE BOLSHEVIKS COME TO POWER

The Revolution of 1917 in Petrograd

ALEXANDER RABINOWITCH

W · W · Norton & Company · Inc · New York

Library of Congress Cataloging in Publication Data

Rabinowitch, Alexander.
  The Bolsheviks come to power.

  Bibliography: p.
  Includes index.
  1. Leningrad—History—1917–1921. 2. Russia—
History—Revolution, 1917–1921. 3. Kommunisticheskaia
partiia Sovetskogo Soiuza—History. 4. Lenin,
Vladimir Il'ich, 1870–1924. I. Title.
DK265.8.L4R27 1976   947'.45'0841   76–20756
ISBN 0–393–05586–8

Maps by Harold K. Faye

For Ellen and Misha

Contents

List of Illustrations   ix

Acknowledgments   xi

Note on Transliteration, Dates, and Terminology   xiii

Introduction   xv

1 · THE JULY UPRISING   1

2 · THE BOLSHEVIKS UNDER FIRE   17

3 · PETROGRAD DURING THE REACTION   39

4 · THE INEFFECTIVENESS OF REPRESSION   51

5 · THE BOLSHEVIK RESURGENCE   83

6 · THE RISE OF KORNILOV   94

7 · KORNILOV VERSUS KERENSKY   110

8 · THE BOLSHEVIKS AND KORNILOV'S DEFEAT   129

9 · THE QUESTION OF A NEW GOVERNMENT   151

10 · "ALL POWER TO THE SOVIETS!"   168

11 · LENIN'S CAMPAIGN FOR AN INSURRECTION   191

12 · OBSTACLES TO AN UPRISING   209

13 · THE GARRISON CRISIS AND THE MILITARY
REVOLUTIONARY COMMITTEE   224

14 · ON THE EVE   249

15 · THE BOLSHEVIKS COME TO POWER   273

16 · EPILOGUE   305

Notes   315

Selected Bibliography   358

Index   379

Illustrations

Soldiers and cossacks celebrating during the February days   page xix

Members of the first Provisional Government (*Hoover Institution Archives*) page xxii

Members of the new coalition cabinet formed following the April crisis (*Hoover Institution Archives*)   page xxviii

The Presidium of the First All-Russian Congress of Workers' and Soldiers' Deputies (*Hoover Institution Archives*)   page xxxi

Demonstration sponsored by the First All-Russian Congress of Soviets (*Staatsbibliothek, Berlin*)   page xxxii

July 4, 1917, in Petrograd   page 11

Cartoon, "Lenin in the Role of Nicholas II"   page 37

Cartoon, "A High Post for the Leaders of the Rebellion"   page 18

Soldiers of the First Machine Gun Regiment (*Museum of the Revolution, USSR*)   page 29

Cartoon, "The Arrest of Alexandra Kollantai"   page 31

The funeral of seven cossacks killed during the July days (*Hoover Institution Archives*)   page 41

Kerensky departing for the front (*Staatsbibliothek, Berlin*)   page 56

Street scene in Petrograd, 1917 (*The National Archives*)   page 8

The Bolshoi Theater (*Hoover Institution Archives*)   page 112

Kerensky addressing military personnel (*Hoover Institution Archives*)   page 116

General Lavr Kornilov and Boris Savinkov arrive for the Moscow State Conference (*From* White Against Red *by Dimitry V. Lehovich, courtesy of Mr. Lehovich*)   page 114

V. N. Lvov (*Hoover Institution Archives*)   page 122

Factory workers gathered for a political meeting   page 155

Map of Kornilov affair   page 147

The Petrograd Soviet of Workers' and Soldiers' Deputies   page 161

Lenin's resolution endorsing insurrection (*Radio Times Hulton Picture Library*)   page 207

Military school cadets in the Winter Palace (*Collection Viollet*)   page 283

Workers in a Petrograd factory (*Staatsbibliothek, Berlin*)   page 264

Smolny during the October days (*Staatsbibliothek, Berlin*)   page 267

The Women's Batallion on the Palace Square (*Radio Times Hulton Picture Library*)   page 255

Petrograd during the October days   page 281

Soldiers operate the main Petrograd telephone station (*Radio Times Hulton Picture Library*)   page 270

Kerensky and aides in the Winter Palace (*Radio Times Hulton Picture Library*)   page 271

Lenin's manifesto of October 25 (*Staatsbibliothek, Berlin*)   page 275

Barricades near St. Isaac's Cathedral (*Staatsbibliothek, Berlin*)   page 280

The cruiser *Aurora* on the Neva   page 286

The Bolshevik Central Committee, elected at the Sixth Congress (*From* Velikii oktiabr' . . . albom) [see Bibliography]   page 58

Key members of the Bolshevik Military Organization (*From* Velikii oktiabr' . . . albom)   page 73

Members of the Bolshevik Petersburg Committee in 1917 (*From* Velikii oktiabr' . . . albom)   page 65

Members of the Bolshevik Kronstadt Committee (*From* Velikii oktiabr' . . . albom)   page 145

The *Rabotnitsa* editorial board (*From* Velikii oktiabr' . . . albom)   page XXIX

Members of the Military Revolutionary Committee (*From* Velikii oktiabr' . . . albom)   page 238

The First Council of People's Commissars (*From* Velikii oktiabr' . . . albom)   page 307

Acknowledgments

This book could not have been completed without the generous support of several funding institutions. A postdoctoral fellowship from the National Endowment for the Humanities enabled me to begin research at the Hoover Institution, Stanford, California, in 1967. Grants from the International Research and Exchanges Board and the American Council of Learned Societies made it possible to spend the fall semester 1970–1971 gathering material in Moscow and Leningrad as a participant in the Senior Scholars' Exchange between the United States and the USSR, and the remainder of the year finishing research and drafting the initial chapters in Washington, D.C. Summer faculty fellowships from Indiana University and its Russian and East European Institute allowed me to devote summers to work on the book. The bulk of the manuscript was completed in 1973–1974 at the Institute for Advanced Study, Princeton, New Jersey, where my stay was supported partially by a grant from the National Endowment for the Humanities.

It is a pleasure to acknowledge my debt to the staffs of the Lenin Library and the Fundamental Library of the Social Sciences in Moscow; the Saltykov-Shchedrin Library and particularly the Academy of Sciences Library in Leningrad; the Hoover Institution; the Indiana, Columbia, Georgetown, and Stanford university libraries; the New York Public Library; and the Library of Congress. I am especially grateful to Anna M. Bourguina of the Hoover Institution for help in obtaining several important sources unavailable elsewhere.

In the Soviet Union my work was enriched by consultations with Academician P. V. Volobuev. Professors George F. Kennan, Carl Kaysen, and Robert C. Tucker helped make my year at the Institute for Advanced Study one of the most memorable and without doubt the most productive of my life. Margaret Van Sant at the Institute for Advanced Study and Deborah Chase and Nancy Maness of the Indiana University Department of History and Russian and East European Institute, respectively, somehow managed to maintain good humor throughout the arduous task of typing the chapters.

I am grateful to Indiana University Press for permission to quote from my study *Prelude to Revolution: The Petrograd Bolsheviks and the July 1917 Uprising*, and to James L. Mairs and Emily Garlin, my editors at Norton, for their help in preparing the present book for publication.

The greatest debt that I have incurred is to my wife, Janet Rabinowitch. A constant source of intellectual stimulation and encouragement, she went over successive drafts with an experienced editorial eye and made countless suggestions for improvement. Whatever merits this book may possess are due in no small part to her interest and patience.

Special thanks are also due my colleague Stephen F. Cohen; his invariably sound advice and perceptive criticism were of enormous benefit at every stage of my work. Leopold Haimson, who has been the source of inspiration for a whole generation of American students of Russian labor history, shared useful thoughts relating to this study during several discussions in the spring of 1974. I owe much to them, as well as to John M. Thompson, George F. Kennan, William G. Rosenberg, S. Frederick Starr, Stephen Soudakoff, and Donald Raleigh, who read and commented on some or all of the chapters. Their suggestions have been invaluable in revising the manuscript. I alone, of course, bear responsibility for the remaining shortcomings.

Note on Transliteration, Dates, and Terminology

The system of transliteration employed in this work is the one used by the Library of Congress, with some simplifications. When appropriate, proper names are spelled in their more customary English forms.

All dates are given according to the Julian calendar, in use in Russia until 1918, rather than the Gregorian calendar of the West. In 1917 the former was thirteen days behind the latter.

As used in this book, "soviet" or "soviets" refers to the elected councils of workers', soldiers', and peasants' deputies, representative revolutionary organizations that sprang up throughout Russia in 1917, rather than to people or institutions of the USSR, the most common current meaning of these words. The term "Soviet" refers more specifically to the central institutions of the soviets in 1917, usually the Central Executive Committee of the All-Russian Congress of Soviets of Workers' and Soldiers' Deputies and the Executive Committee of the All-Russian Congress of Peasants' Deputies. The two All-Russian Executive Committees often met and acted jointly.

Introduction

Hundreds of books have been written about the October 1917 revolution in Russia. Why should anyone want to produce still another? During the years since I began working on the present book, this question has been asked of me many times.

My interest in studying and writing about the October revolution stems partly from that event's inherent drama and monumental historical significance. In Russia in 1917 the ultraradical Bolshevik party emerged from obscurity to direct the overthrow of the Western-style Provisional Government and to establish the first national communist political system. These events occurred during the eight months that followed the collapse of the centuries-old tsarist regime, in the third year of Russia's catastrophic involvement in a devastating European war. Russia was then the third largest country in the world, with a population of more than 165 million occupying an area three times as large as the continental United States and bigger than China and India together. I have long felt that existing accounts of this seminal chapter in modern Russian and, indeed, in world history do not do it justice.

Further stimulating my attraction to 1917 Russia as a subject for research and writing is the failure of existing works to answer many key questions relating to the October revolution and, most importantly, to explain satisfactorily why things turned out as they did. Many books on the revolution are memoirs written by participants in the events described; these personal recollections, though often valuable and fascinating, inevitably present a one-sided view of the revolution, either passionately sympathetic or profoundly hostile, depending on which side of the political fence the author was on in 1917.

Historians in the Soviet Union have produced an avalanche of studies on 1917. Many of these works, particularly those written in the relatively free 1920s and during the Khrushchev period, contain a wealth of illuminating factual data from previously untapped archives. But the requirement that writers in the Soviet Union conform to officially prescribed interpretations of history, influenced strongly by contemporary political considerations, limits the overall value of their work.

Outside the Soviet Union several monographs on important aspects of the revolution have appeared in recent years; foremost among these are the works of Oliver H. Radkey, William G. Rosenberg, Ronald G. Suny, Marc Ferro, George Katkov, and Rex Wade.[1] Nonetheless we still do not have a reliable history of the Provisional Government or of the Russian economy in the revolutionary period. We know little about the impact of millions of war-weary soldiers on Russian politics in 1917, or about the development of the revolution in provincial areas, or, for that matter, about the role of the peasantry or of the growing Russian working class in the revolution's course. In fact, the only broadly focused Western investigation of the October revolution based on intensive research in primary sources remains the first volume of William Henry Chamberlin's *The Russian Revolution, 1917–1921*.[2] Pioneering in its time and still of great value, Chamberlin's study was written in the early 1930s, before a large body of source material germane to an understanding of the revolution became readily accessible to Western scholars.

In this book, I have elected to focus attention on the revolution in Petrograd[3] for several related reasons. First, Petrograd was, after all, the capital. In the Russian empire, with its long tradition of strong, arbitrary rule from the center, the political situation in Petrograd, especially control of the institutions and symbols of national power, was of immense significance in determining the course of the revolution throughout the country. In addition to being the governmental hub, Petrograd, with a war-inflated population of 2.7 million in 1917, was the country's most important commercial and industrial center. For this reason and also because so much more information is available on Petrograd than on other major Russian cities in 1917, analysis of political, social, and economic developments there provide particularly worthwhile insights into the course of the revolution in urban Russia generally. Finally, because in 1917 the national headquarters of the Bolshevik Party and the center of Bolshevik activities were in Petrograd, it is there that one can best study both the party's operations from top to bottom and the way in which the Bolsheviks interacted with the masses.

But isn't Petrograd the one Russian city that has been treated extensively in Western literature on the revolution, one might fairly ask. True enough. Yet, despite all that has been written about 1917 in general and "Red Petrograd" in particular, we still do not have a full, reliable account of the revolution there. Two relatively recent studies, Sergei Melgunov's *The Bolshevik Seizure of Power*[4] and Robert V. Daniels's *Red October*,[5] while very useful, are limited in that both center chiefly on the period just before, during, and—in the case of Melgunov—right after the Provisional Government's overthrow; major developments in the summer and early fall of 1917, an appreciation of which is essential for an understanding of what happened in October, receive scant attention. Moreover, the political behavior of Petrograd workers, soldiers, and sailors, and its impact on the course of the revolution, are not taken into account, the events of October being presented largely as a disorganized struggle between two similarly indecisive and inept combatants—the Kerensky government and the Bolshevik leadership.

If the present book helps to fill this deficiency in Western historiography and, in so doing, stimulates readers to view the events of 1917 with new perspective, it will have accomplished its purpose. My primary aim has been to reconstruct, as fully and accurately as possible, the development of the "revolution from below" and the outlook, activity, and situation of the Bolshevik party organization in Petrograd at all levels between February and October 1917. In the process I have tried to clarify the vital relationship between these two central aspects of the revolution and the eventual Bolshevik success.

Extensive research along these lines has prompted me to question many of the basic assumptions of historians in both the Soviet Union and the West regarding the character and sources of strength of the Bolshevik Party in 1917 and, indeed, the very nature of the October revolution in Petrograd. Historians in the Soviet Union have stressed historical inevitability and the role of a tightly knit revolutionary party led by Lenin in accounting for the outcome of the October revolution, while many Western scholars have viewed this event either as an historical accident or, more frequently, as the result of a well-executed coup d'état without significant mass support; I find, however, that a full explanation of the Bolshevik seizure of power is much more complex than any of these interpretations suggest.

Studying the aspirations of factory workers, soldiers, and sailors as expressed in contemporary documents, I find that these concerns corresponded closely to the program of political, economic, and social reform put forth by the Bolsheviks at a time when all other major political parties were widely discredited because of their failure to press hard enough for meaningful internal changes and an immediate end to Russia's participation in the war. As a result, in October the goals of the Bolsheviks, as the masses understood them, had strong popular support.

In Petrograd in 1917 the Bolshevik Party bore little resemblance to the by-and-large united, authoritarian, conspiratorial organization effectively controlled by Lenin depicted in most existing accounts. To be sure, the party's course toward an early socialist revolution was strongly influenced by Vladimir Ilich Lenin. Born in Simbirsk in 1870, the son of a school inspector of minor nobility, Lenin, a lawyer by profession, had entered the Russian social democratic movement in the 1890s and quickly committed himself to the goal of organizing the Russian working class into a political force capable of leading the struggle to overthrow the tsarist autocracy. In

1903, almost singlehandedly, he had precipitated the famous split of the Russian Social Democratic Workers' Party into its radical Bolshevik and moderate Menshevik factions, chiefly over the issue of the nature and objectives of a Marxist revolutionary party in Russia. In the repressive conditions then prevailing, Lenin had sought the creation of a tightly knit, centrally directed organization of disciplined, militant revolutionaries, rather than the more democratic mass workers' party envisioned by the Mensheviks.[6] Only a highly professional party, Lenin then reasoned, would be capable of fulfilling revolutionary tasks and of protecting Russian social democracy from decimation by the authorities and from reformism.

In 1905 Lenin had modified the classic Marxist blueprint for a two-stage revolution, generally viewed by Russian social democrats as applicable to Russia, when he suggested that following the overthrow of the tsar, a "revolutionary democratic dictatorship of the proletariat and peasantry" might pave the way for a socialist revolution without an extended period of liberal government and capitalist industrial development.

After the outbreak of World War I, within all the major Russian socialist groups there had emerged "defensist" factions, which supported the Russian war effort, and "internationalist" factions, which condemned the military struggle in Europe and called for the arrangement of an immediate peace without victors or vanquished. At this time, Lenin had once again set himself squarely apart from most of his fellow socialists by rejecting support for his nation's war effort and proposing instead the fomenting of social revolution in all the warring countries as an immediate social democratic slogan. Subsequently, he had constructed a bold if coolly received theory to show that with the eruption of the war, the capitalist system had reached its highest, "imperialist," stage, a critical situation in international economic affairs that would inevitably precipitate an international socialist revolution.[7]

By the beginning of 1917, as the result of rapidly worsening economic conditions, staggering military reverses and horrendous personnel losses, and historically unprecedented governmental incompetence and mismanagement, the old regime was bankrupt among virtually all segments of the Russian population. On February 23, International Women's Day, disturbances that broke out among long lines of housewives waiting in the bitter cold to buy bread touched off massive demonstrations calling for the overthrow of the monarchy and an end to the war. A week later Tsar Nicholas II was forced to abdicate.

Lenin, who had been in exile abroad for close to a decade, was then in Zurich, Switzerland. Most of what he knew about the revolution in those early weeks he gleaned from conservative European newspapers, an obvious handicap but not one to prevent him from attempting to direct the activities of his followers in Russia. Reading accounts of Russian developments in the London Times, Le Temps, and the Neue Zürcher Zeitung, Lenin quickly concluded that while the workers had led the struggle during the February

Soldiers and cossacks celebrating during the February days in Petrograd.

days, the bourgeoisie had taken advantage of the situation to consolidate its own political power in Petrograd. To judge by his writings of March 1917, he seems not to have appreciated the degree to which socialist leaders in Petrograd had cooperated with liberals in the formation of the Provisional Government, or the extent to which the population at large, at least for the moment, acquiesced in this development. Lenin assumed that revolutionary Russian workers, having helped bring down the regime of Nicholas II, would instinctively see that a bourgeois government would do no more than the tsarist regime to fulfill their keenest aspirations. Moreover, following three years of the most terrible warfare in history, the end of which was not yet in sight, Lenin was obsessed by the thought that all of the major European countries were on the threshold of socialist revolution and that a proletarian insurrection in Russia would be the spark that would spur desperate, peace-hungry workers everywhere to rise against their governments. Thus in his initial directives to the party leadership in Petrograd, partially contained in his "Letters from Afar," he insisted on the necessity of arming and organizing the masses for the imminent second stage of the revolution, which would overthrow the "government of capitalists and large landowners."[8]

Returning to Petrograd on April 3, Lenin declared publicly that the February revolution had not solved the Russian proletariat's fundamental problems, that the working class of Russia could not stop halfway, and that in alliance with the soldier-masses the Russian proletariat would turn the bourgeois democratic revolution into a proletarian socialist revolution.[9]

The Petrograd Bolshevik organization in 1917 included many leaders whose views differed significantly from Lenin's; Bolsheviks of varying persuasions had important influence in determining the party's policies, contributing ultimately to its success. There were, among others, "moderate" or "right" Bolsheviks, who consistently rejected almost all of Lenin's fundamental theoretical and strategic assumptions. Their best known and most articulate spokesman was the thirty-four-year-old, Moscow-born Lev Kamenev, a Bolshevik since 1903. Kamenev did not accept the idea that the bourgeois democratic revolution in Russia was complete. Believing that the Russian working class was still relatively weak, rejecting the supposition that all Europe was on the verge of revolt, and convinced that neither the Russian peasantry nor the foreign bourgeoisie would permit the victory of socialism in Russia, the mild-mannered Kamenev, from the time of his return to Petrograd from Siberia in mid-March 1917, advocated vigilant socialist control over the Provisional Government rather than the latter's removal. In succeeding months, as the Russian revolution deepened, Kamenev spoke out for the creation of an exclusively socialist government; this was to be a broad coalition made up of all major socialist groups, which would retain its mandate only until the establishment of a democratic republic by a Constituent Assembly. On the war issue, Kamenev called for support of the Russian war effort pending conclusion of a negotiated peace, a position closer to that of most moderate socialists than to Lenin's.

Among Petrograd Bolsheviks in 1917 there were many other independent-minded leaders who, while sharing Lenin's theoretical assumptions regarding the possibility of a socialist revolution in Russia, often disagreed with him on tactical questions. Foremost of these was the legendary Lev Trotsky, then thirty-eight, who had first gained both international fame and enormous stature among the Petrograd masses as the bold and courageous chairman of the St. Petersburg Soviet during the revolution of 1905. A brilliant writer, Trotsky was a tireless and spellbinding public speaker justly considered one of the greatest orators of modern times.[10]

The general direction of Bolshevik activity in 1917 was set by the Seventh All-Russian Party Conference in April and the Sixth Bolshevik Party Congress of late July and early August; between such national assemblies it was determined primarily by majority vote of a democratically elected party Central Committee. At the same time, amid the chaotic, locally varying, constantly fluctuating conditions prevailing in Russia in 1917, the Central Committee, at the top of the Bolshevik organizational hierarchy, was simply unable to control the behavior of major regional organizations. Except in a broad, general way, it rarely tried. In Petrograd, important auxiliary arms such as the Petersburg Committee,[11] which directed party work in the capital, and the Military Organization,[12] responsible for the conduct of revolutionary activity among troops, were relatively free to tailor their tactics and appeals to suit local conditions. When necessary, they staunchly protected their prerogatives.

Beyond this, in 1917 Lenin's prerevolutionary conception of a small, professional, conspiratorial party was discarded and the doors opened wide to tens of thousands of new members who were by no means without influence, so that to a significant degree the party was now both responsive and open to the masses.

This is not to minimize Lenin's importance in the development of the revolution. It is almost as difficult for me as it has been for virtually all of my predecessors who have written about the revolution to envision the triumph of the Bolsheviks in Lenin's absence. For all the lively debate and spirited give-and-take that I find to have existed within the Bolshevik organization in 1917, the Bolsheviks were doubtless more unified than any of their major rivals for power. Certainly this was a key factor in their effectiveness. Nonetheless, my research suggests that the relative flexibility of the party, as well as its responsiveness to the prevailing mass mood, had at least as much to do with the ultimate Bolshevik victory as did revolutionary discipline, organizational unity, or obedience to Lenin.

I should add that in attempting to reconstruct the events with which this book deals, I have tried to let the facts speak for themselves; it is left for the reader to judge whether my conclusions are warranted by the evidence.

When Lenin returned to Petrograd in April 1917 and sounded the call for immediate social revolution, moderate socialists and Bolsheviks alike were unresponsive to his militant appeals. These were still the euphoric first weeks following the February revolution. The patriotic, liberal democratic Provisional Government, which was to rule until a representative Constituent Assembly could be popularly elected to establish a permanent political system, appeared to have the blessings and good wishes of practically everyone. Included in this government were some of the most talented and best known figures in the Russian liberal movement. The new prime minister was Prince Georgii Lvov, a much respected, progressive zemstvo leader (the zemstvos were institutions of limited local self-government created in 1864). Foreign minister and dominant figure in the government was Pavel Miliukov, a professor of history and the leading spokesman of the Kadets (Constitutional Democrats, the main Russian liberal party); alongside him in the cabinet were other prominent Kadets such as Nikolai Nekrasov, Andrei Shingarev, and Alexander Manuilov, ministers of transportation, agriculture, and education, respectively. The key Ministry of War was headed by the powerful industrialist and founder of the right-liberal Octobrist Party, Alexander Guchkov; as chairman of the Central War Industries Committee, Guchkov had already acquired considerable experience in helping to direct the war effort. The minister of finance was a self-made

М. Нар. Пр. Мануиловъ. Мин. Юст. Керенскій. Мин. Зем. Шингаревъ.

Мин. Фин. Терещенко.

Об.-Пр. Св. Син. Вл. Львовъ.

Мин. Ин. Д. Милюковъ. Пр. Сов. Мин. Мин. Вн. Д. Г. Е. Львовъ. Военн. Мин. Гучковъ.

М. Т. и Пр. Коноваловъ.

Мин. Пут. С. Некрасовъ.

1-ое ВРЕМЕННОЕ ПРАВИТЕЛЬСТВО.

Members of the first Provisional Government, formed at the beginning of March 1917. Bottom row, left to right: A. I. Konovalov, P. N. Miliukov, G. E. Lvov, A. I. Guchkov, N. V. Nekrasov. Top row: M. I. Tereshchenko, A. A. Manuilov, A. F. Kerensky, A. I. Shingarev, V. N. Lvov.

tycoon, Mikhail Tereshchenko. The new minister of justice was the young lawyer Alexander Kerensky. Prior to the revolution Kerensky had made a name as the flamboyant defense attorney in widely publicized political trials and as an outspoken leftist deputy in the Third and Fourth Dumas.

The long-time American consul general in St. Petersburg, John Harold Snodgrass, no doubt expressed the views of most contemporary observers when he commented in the *New York Times* of Sunday, March 25, 1917: "Nowhere in their country could the Russian people have found better men to lead them out of the darkness of tyranny. . . . Lvov and his associates are to Russia what Washington and his associates were to America when it became a nation."

Of course most friends of Russia abroad believed that because the new ministers had been selected by the Duma, the pale copy of a Western-style parliament that had been established in tsarist Russia following the revolution of 1905, they could speak for the entire population. This was not an altogether valid assumption. The Fourth Duma, in session in 1917, had been elected in 1912 under regulations that excluded the bulk of the population from the franchise. During the February days there also sprang up in Petrograd a soviet (council) of workers' and soldiers' deputies modeled after spontaneously created organs that had had a brief existence in Russia during the revolution of 1905. In the spring and summer of 1917, soviets were established in each of the districts of Petrograd, and, concomitantly, similar institutions of grass roots democracy came into being in cities, towns, and villages throughout Russia. In May an All-Russian Congress of Peasants' Soviets was convened in Petrograd, and in June representatives of workers' and soldiers' soviets gathered in the capital for their first nationwide congress. These national conventions formed permanent All-Russian Executive Committees (the Central Executive Committee of the All-Russian Congress of Soviets of Workers' and Soldiers' Deputies, and the Executive Committee of the All-Russian Congress of Peasants' Deputies), which, taken together, were numerically more representative and, by virtue of the loyalty that they commanded among factory workers, peasants, and particularly soldiers, potentially more powerful than the Provisional Government.

Until the fall of 1917 the central organs of the All-Russian Soviets were dominated by leaders of the moderate socialist parties—the social democratic Menshevik Party and the neopopulist Socialist Revolutionary Party (SRs). These leaders contented themselves with acting as guardians of the revolution and demonstrated no interest in challenging the Provisional Government as the lawful supreme political authority. This was, at least in part, for doctrinal reasons; the Mensheviks remained committed to the orthodox Marxist assumption that a "bourgeois revolution," which the overthrow of the autocracy appeared to represent, had necessarily to be followed by an indefinite period of bourgeois democratic rule. For their part, SRs in the Executive Committees, while not prevented by ideology from taking power into their own hands, shared with many Mensheviks the conviction that collaboration with military commanders and commercial and industrial groups was absolutely essential for Russia's survival in the war and as a bulwark against counterrevolution.

The situation that confronted Lenin upon his return to Russia in April, therefore, differed disappointingly from what he had anticipated. Among workers and soldiers, Bolshevik influence was relatively weak. The Mensheviks and SRs had overwhelming majorities in the soviets, which Lenin now considered the embryonic institutions of a workers' government. Under moderate socialist direction the soviets supported the Provisional Government and, pending arrangement of a negotiated peace, endorsed the Russian defense effort. If that were not sufficient cause for discouragement, the influence of moderately inclined Bolsheviks led by Kamenev had created a strong mood of compromise toward the government and of support for reconciliation with the Mensheviks within Lenin's own party.[13]

In adapting his goals to fit the prevailing situation and to make them palatable to the majority of his party, Lenin hewed a thin line; while scaling down his immediate objectives and accepting concessions to the moderates, he nonetheless retained the core of his radical program and his tactical flexibility. In regard to the possibility of forming a unified social democratic party, Lenin was intransigent; alliance with the Mensheviks, he argued, would associate the Bolshevik Party with the Russian defense effort and thus destroy its capacity to lead the world revolutionary struggle. To all who would listen, Lenin declared categorically that he would strike out on his own if his followers insisted on reunification and if they declined actively to oppose the government's war effort. Almost exclusively because of Lenin's interference, discussions regarding unification between the Mensheviks and Bolsheviks quickly broke down;[14] still, a strong attraction for political cooperation with other socialist groups lingered among the Bolsheviks throughout 1917.

Lenin also refused to alter his theoretical analysis of the revolution. In a summation of his views published in the party's main newspaper, *Pravda*, on April 7—the celebrated "April Theses"—he defined the situation in Russia as the transition between the first, "bourgeois democratic," stage of the revolution and the second, "socialist," stage. He still insisted that the Provisional Government should not be supported in any way and that the party's goal was the transfer of power to the soviets. Yet Lenin's message no longer included an immediate call to arms. As long as the masses retained faith in the bourgeoisie, Lenin explained, the party's primary task was to expose the fraudulence of the Provisional Government and the errors of the Soviet leadership. The party would patiently have to convince the masses that the Provisional Government could not bring peace and that the soviets were the only truly revolutionary form of government.[15]

In part because of these modifications and in part because of an energetic lobbying campaign, Lenin was able quickly to win a significant portion of the Bolshevik leadership to his side. This initial success is mirrored in the proceedings of the Bolshevik Petersburg Committee during April as well as in the results of the First Bolshevik Petrograd City Conference, where Lenin won his initial victories over the right. Meeting from April 14 to 22, the conference adopted by a decisive vote of thirty-seven to three a resolution written by Lenin condemning the Provisional Government and calling for the *eventual* transfer of power to the soviets.[16]

At the All-Russian Bolshevik Party Conference, which opened in Petrograd on April 24, Lenin won further victories. The conference resolution on the war reflected Lenin's uncompromising repudiation of the conflict and the Russian defense effort. In its resolution on the government question, the conference condemned the Provisional Government as an instrument of the bourgeoisie and an ally of counterrevolution, and suggested that, for self-protection, the proletariat would have to organize and arm.[17]

Still, at the April Conference the Kamenev faction argued loud and long for its position, not without significant results. The influence of the moderates is reflected in the fact that five of their number were elected to the nine-man Central Committee,[18] insuring the moderation of that body from late April through July. The moderate point of view was also evident in the major conference resolutions.[19]

Moreover, in part due to the influence of the moderates, full discussion of some of the fundamental theoretical assumptions underlying Lenin's program, most importantly his concept of imperialism as the highest stage of capitalism, was postponed.[20]

Taken together, the April Conference resolutions pointed the party vaguely toward the socialist revolution while leaving unanswered the crucial questions "How?" and "When?" While the ultimate goal of transferring power to the soviets was implicit in several of the resolutions, for the time being the party was to concentrate on "the prolonged task of building up the class consciousness of the proletariat," "mobilizing it into opposition to the wavering policies of the petty bourgeoisie," and "increasing and consolidating Bolshevik strength in the soviets."

The dominant view among Bolshevik leaders from all over Russia drawn together for the April Conference was that these tasks would not be accomplished overnight. Yet in the weeks that followed, among workers, soldiers, and sailors in the capital, support for the repudiation of the Provisional Government and the transfer of state power to the soviets grew with astonishing speed. This was partly because of widespread disenchantment with the results of the February revolution. Deteriorating economic conditions had helped trigger the upheaval in the first place. To Petrograd, in particular, the war brought critical shortages of housing, food, clothing, fuel, and raw materials. Some of the shortages stemmed from a halt in the flow of foreign commodities, such as coal from England and cheap cotton from the United States; most, however, were the result of domestic shipping and distribution problems. Russia's internal water transport and railway systems were simply inadequate to meet both civil and military needs. In the case of grain, peasants, finding it impossible to procure manufactured goods, refused to part with their produce for rapidly depreciating paper money. As the scarcity of goods increased, the gap between wages and the rising cost of living widened. Petrograd's roughly 390,000 factory workers, of whom approximately a third were women, were hardest hit by the resulting inflation. Despite a significant increase in nominal wages between the outbreak of the war and the beginning of 1917 (by as much as 260 percent), real wages declined to about a third of prewar levels, largely as a result of drastic increases in the price of consumer necessities.[21]

The February revolution did not alleviate these difficulties; on the contrary, administrative confusion increased in March and April, and this, in addition to the continued deterioration of transportation, led to a significant worsening of the supply situation. The increased shortages of raw materials and fuel that now developed forced factory owners to curtail production further and led to extensive additional layoffs. Simultaneously, delivery of foodstuffs also continued to decline; attempts by the government to introduce an effective food pricing and rationing system failed to ease the strains caused by these shortages. In the spring of 1917 workers in a number of industries had received substantial wage increases. However, skyrocketing prices quickly offset these gains, so that by early summer Petrograd factory workers, generally speaking, were economically little better off than they had been in February.[22]

To the 215,000 to 300,000 soldiers of the war-inflated Petrograd garrison, and also to the sailors and soldiers from the nearby Kronstadt naval base, who numbered around 30,000, the fruits of the February revolution were similarly disappointing. In normal times the guards regiments, which formed the backbone of the garrison, had been specially trained units recruited almost exclusively from the peasantry; this traditional core had been squandered in the campaigns of 1914–1916 on the battlefields of East Prussia and Galicia. Consequently, by 1917 most of the troops stationed in and around Petrograd, including those in regiments of the guard, were poorly trained wartime recruits, still predominately of peasant background. Military discipline was foreign to these soldiers; a high percentage had had their fill of duty at the front. The decisive moment of the February revolution had occurred when garrison units, one after another, joined rebelling townspeople.

After the collapse of the old regime, soldiers and sailors had removed officers who openly opposed the revolution as well as those with reputations for particular severity. Initially, they had hailed the changes in the armed forces brought about by the revolution. Among the most important of these was the formation of democratically elected army and navy committees with broad but vaguely defined administrative authority in all military units (the creation of such committees was initially sanctioned by the Petrograd Soviet in its famous Order Number One,[23] issued on March 1). Enlisted personnel watched suspiciously for any sign of a return to the old order and awaited the compromise peace they felt confident would be negotiated by the Petrograd Soviet. The Provisional Government's patriotic declarations and obvious overriding concern with halting the further development of the revolution and improving Russia's military preparedness were to them understandably disturbing.[24]

For these reasons, by the late spring of 1917 rapidly growing numbers of Petrograd workers and soldiers and Baltic Fleet sailors viewed the Provisional Government increasingly as an organ of the propertied classes, opposed to fundamental political change and uninterested in the needs of ordinary people. On the other hand, the soviets were contrasted more and more positively with the Provisional Government and viewed as genuinely democratic institutions of popular self-rule. The divorce between the orientation of the government and the mood and aspirations of the Petrograd masses had been reflected initially on April 20 and 21, when thousands of workers, soldiers, and sailors, carrying banners emblazoned with slogans such as "Down with Miliukov!" "Down with Annexationist Politics!" and even "Down with the Provisional Government!" took to the streets to protest

Members of the new coalition cabinet formed following the April crisis: Bottom row, left to right: A. I. Konovalov, A. A. Manuilov, F. I. Rodichev, V. N. Lvov, I. V. Godnev. Middle row: A. I. Shingarev, M. I. Tereshchenko, G. E. Lvov, N. V. Nekrasov, P. N. Pereverzev. Top row: M. I. Skobelev, V. M. Chernov, A. F. Kerensky, I. G. Tsereteli, A. V. Peshekhonov.

Miliukov's obvious intention of pursuing the war to a "victorious conclusion." Significantly, the crowds ended these demonstrations only at the request of the Petrograd Soviet, after openly ignoring government orders to disperse.[25]

In the wake of this April crisis, two of the ministers most closely associated with the government's unpopular foreign and military policies, Miliukov and Guchkov, left the cabinet. In this first political shake-up after the February revolution, several key moderate socialist leaders from the Petrograd Soviet were prevailed upon to accept ministerial posts. The Georgian Menshevik Iraklii Tsereteli, the passionate tribune of the Social Democratic fraction in the Second Duma before his arrest, imprisonment, and Siberian exile, and, for much of 1917, probably the single most authoritative official in the Soviet, became minister of posts and telegraph. (Tsereteli was the acknowledged head of the Menshevik-SR bloc and originator of many of its policies.) The titular head and main theoretician of the SRs, Viktor Chernov, became minister of agriculture. A close associate of Tsereteli's, Mikhail Skobelev, was named minister of labor. Aleksei Peshekhonov, founder and leader of the Popular Socialist Party, became minister of food supply. Pavel Pereverzev, another SR, took the post of minister of justice, while Kerensky became war and naval minister.

These personnel changes, however, did not significantly alter the government's orientation. The cabinet was now split between liberals, determined to delay fundamental reforms until the convocation of the Constituent Assembly and concerned in the meantime almost exclusively with restoring governmental authority, strengthening the fighting capacity of the army, and pursuing the war to a victorious conclusion and moderate socialist Soviet leaders, anxious to respond to popular demands for immediate reform and hopeful of taking the lead in bringing about the early conclusion of the war on the basis of no annexations and no indemnities. Consequently, the first coalition, formed at the beginning of May, was potentially even less capable of marshaling an attack on national problems than its predecessor. While unable to reach a consensus on domestic matters, in the realm of foreign policy the government chose simultaneously to upgrade the combat readiness of the armed forces in preparation for a summer offensive and to encourage negotiations aimed at achieving a compromise peace.

Once they had joined the first coalition, the moderate socialists became identified in the popular mind with the shortcomings of the Provisional Government. Only the Bolsheviks, among the major Russian political groups, remained untainted by association with the government and were therefore completely free to organize opposition to it, a situation of which the party took maximum advantage.

By the eve of World War I, the Bolsheviks had achieved considerable success in weaning Petrograd factory workers away from the more moderate Mensheviks.[26] Much of this gain was probably lost during the war, when thousands of experienced workers were shipped to the front and when the Bolshevik organization in Petrograd was decimated by arrests. Beginning soon after the February revolution, working through institutions such as the Bolshevik Military Organization, neighborhood party committees, district soviets, the trade union movement, factory-shop committees,[27] and other nonparty mass organizations, the Bolsheviks concentrated on increasing their influence among military personnel and factory workers. In the Petrograd Soviet, at endless rounds of political rallies, and in the pages of the mass-circulation party publications *Pravda*, *Soldatskaia pravda*, and *Rabotnitsa*[28] they trumpeted their programs and articulated what they perceived to be the most strongly felt aspirations of the masses. To the peasant-soldiers of the garrison, the Bolsheviks proclaimed: If you don't want to die at the front, if you don't want the reinstitution of tsarist discipline, if you want better living conditions and the redistribution of farmland, power must be transferred to the soviets. Of particular interest to workers, the Bolsheviks demanded tight soviet control over all phases of the economy, higher wages, an eight-hour working day, worker control in the factories, and an end to inflation. Heaping blame for unresolved problems

The *Rabotnitsa* editorial board. Bottom row, left to right: A. M. Kollontai, L. N. Stahl. Second row: A. I. Elizarova, V. M. Bonch-Bruevich. Third row: K. I. Nikolaeva, P. F. Kudelli, K. N. Samoilova.

upon "greedy capitalists and landlords," the Bolsheviks raised the ugly specter of counterrevolution should the soviets not assume governmental authority.

The results of these efforts were quickly apparent. In February there had been about two thousand Bolsheviks in Petrograd. At the opening of the April Conference party membership had risen to sixteen thousand. By late June it had reached thirty-two thousand, while two thousand garrison soldiers had joined the Bolshevik Military Organization and four thousand soldiers had become associated with "Club Pravda," a "nonparty" club for military personnel operated by the Military Organization.[29] (The influence of the party was particularly strong in several powerful military units quartered in working-class districts of the capital and at Kronstadt, where in mid-May the local soviet passed a resolution rejecting the authority of the Provisional Government.)

In Petrograd, by late spring, imposing numbers of impatient, Bolshevik-influenced workers, soldiers, and sailors, on the one hand, and the Provisional Government and moderate socialist leadership of the Soviet, on the other, were on a collision course; the former demanded the transfer of governmental power to the Soviet, while the latter insisted that such a step would invite disaster. This situation was highlighted in early June when the Bolshevik Military Organization, spurred on by its restless new rank-and-file converts in the garrison, proposed that the party organize an antiwar, antigovernment mass protest march during the meetings of the First All-Russian Congress of Soviets of Workers' and Soldiers' Deputies (the congress met in Petrograd from June 3 to June 24). The party Central Committee accepted the proposal and scheduled the demonstration for June 10. The idea struck a responsive chord. Because the core of the demonstration appeal was opposition to the launching of a new offensive against the Germans and Austrians and a call for the transfer of power to the SR-Menshevik–controlled Soviet, rather than to the Bolshevik Party itself, even nominal supporters of the moderate socialist parties were enticed into the movement.[30]

The Congress of Soviets, which had just passed a resolution pledging full cooperation and support to the government, viewed the proposed march as a repudiation of its policies, which indeed it was, and as a clear-cut threat to the coalition. On June 9 congress delegates resolved to take whatever steps were necessary to prevent the march; a three-day ban on demonstrations was issued, delegates were dispatched to workers' districts and military barracks, and maximum pressure was brought to bear on Bolshevik leaders to rethink their plans. At the eleventh hour, partly because of this opposition, the Bolshevik Central Committee aborted the march.

The unpopularity of the congress's stand among Petrograd workers and soldiers was reflected in an incident that occurred shortly afterward. On June 12, alarmed by the apparent restlessness of workers and soldiers in the capital and convinced that they would respond to appeals from the majority socialists as readily as to those of the Bolsheviks, the Congress of Soviets scheduled a mass march of its own for June 18. This demonstration was intended to serve as a gesture of conciliation to the Bolsheviks and as a means of channeling widespread unrest into the expression of support for the congress's policies. Though the Mensheviks and SRs worked feverishly to insure the success of the march, their plans backfired. On the appointed

Members of the Presidium of the First All-Russian Congress of Workers' and Soldiers' Deputies. Left to right: M. I. Skobelev, N. S. Chkheidze, G. V. Plekhanov, and I. G. Tsereteli.

day, the moderate socialist Soviet leadership watched long columns of workers and soldiers, representing virtually all of Petrograd's factories and military regiments, over 400,000 strong, parade by, holding aloft crimson banners bearing the slogans: "Down with the Ten Minister-Capitalists!" "Down with the Politics of the Offensive!" "All Power to the Soviets!" The sea of Bolshevik banners and placards, all contemporary observers agreed, was broken only occasionally by slogans endorsed by the congress.

This clear indication of the divergence between popular opinion in Petrograd and the behavior of the government and the Soviet leadership created strains among the moderate socialists; militant left factions began to emerge within both the Menshevik and SR organizations. Still, if disenchantment with the Provisional Government and support for the Bolshevik program were already far advanced in the capital, the same was not true in most of the provinces and at the front. The probable correlation of forces in the country at large was mirrored in the makeup of the First Congress of Soviets: in attendance were 533 registered Mensheviks and SRs, and 105 Bolsheviks.[31]

In these circumstances, with the moderate socialists stubbornly resisting all pressures to create a soviet government, Lenin cautioned his associates against deluding themselves that power might be transferred to the soviets peacefully. At the same time, he was adamant about keeping a tight reign in the short run on politically impatient elements within the Petrograd Bolshevik organization and on local workers and soldiers generally, while working to expand support for the party's program among peasants in the countryside and soldiers at the front.

This was by no means a simple task. The party's rapid growth since February had flooded its ranks with militants who knew next to nothing about Marxism and who were united by little more than overwhelming impatience for immediate revolutionary action. The problem had arisen initially

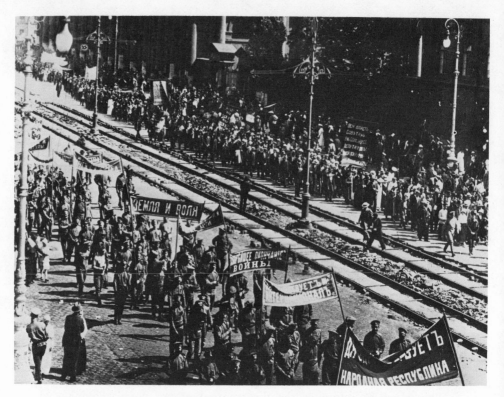

The mass demonstration sponsored by the First All-Russian Congress of Soviets on June 18. "The sea of Bolshevik banners and placards . . . was broken only occasionally by slogans endorsed by the congress."

in April during the mass protests against Miliukov. Rank-and-file party members from garrison regiments and factories undoubtedly helped provoke the street demonstrations in the first place, although the Central Committee did not become involved until after the movement was well underway; subsequently, the top party leadership endorsed the demonstrations. Impulsive elements in the Petrograd party organization and in the Bolshevik Military Organization, responsive to their militant constituents and fearful of losing ground to the anarchists, took a significantly more radical tack; some officials of the Petersburg Committee prepared and widely circulated a leaflet appealing, in the party's name, for the immediate overthrow of the Provisional Government and the arrest of cabinet ministers.[32] Similarly, during preparations for the abortive June 10 demonstration these same elements had laid plans on their own to seize vital public services and munitions stores.[33]

The beginning of the long-anticipated Russian offensive on June 18 compounded the problem of controlling unrest in Petrograd. Ordered to the front in support of the attack, thousands of garrison soldiers, including many members of the Bolshevik Military Organization, insisted that the Provisional Government be overthrown without further delay.

During the second half of June, Lenin devoted much attention to restraining those of his followers who were bent on immediate action.[34] At the same time he worked on a draft program for the approaching party congress, scheduled for July 26. By the end of the month Lenin was exhausted from the unaccustomed exertions and strains of the preceding weeks. On June 27, accompanied by his sister Maria, he left Petrograd for a few days of rest at the country cottage of Vladimir Bonch-Bruevich in the village of Neivola, in Finland. There he spent several days relaxing in the summer sun and strolling and swimming at a nearby lake.

This pleasant interlude was interrupted on the early morning of July 4 by the news that a mass insurrection had broken out in the capital. The alarming information was conveyed to Lenin by Maximilian Saveliev, who had been sent from Petrograd the previous evening on behalf of the Bolshevik Central Committee. The situation in the capital was critical, and it was evident that the party was deeply involved. Crucial decisions had to be made. Without delay, Lenin caught an early-morning train to Petrograd.[35]

The Bolsheviks Come to Power

·1·

THE JULY UPRISING

Still some twenty-five miles from the capital, the mud-spattered, dark green carriages of the Finnish railway train wound their way through pine- and fir-covered, boulder-strewn hills broken here and there by clusters of tidy log cottages. It was the first run of the morning. Seated on hard benches smooth from wear, in a dilapidated carriage occupied mainly by respectably dressed summer residents of the Finnish countryside commuting to work in Petrograd, Lenin, his younger sister Maria, and his comrades Bonch-Bruevich, an authority on Russian religious sects who had been active in the Russian Social Democratic Party from its earliest years, and Saveliev, the university-educated son of a minor noble, also a long-time party member, talked together animatedly. About nine o'clock the train crossed the Sestra River, a narrow, meandering stream that served as a boundary between Finland and Russia; minutes later it slowed to a stop at the small border station of Beloostrov.

Up the track a machinist uncoupled the locomotive, which, chugging and hissing rhythmically, moved off slowly to take on wood and water. Conversation between Lenin and his companions was interrupted at this point by an officious border inspector who popped into their compartment and commanded sharply, "Documents! Show your documents! Have them ready!" Many years later Bonch-Bruevich recalled his uneasiness as he and his friends handed their papers to the waiting inspector. Lenin was traveling on his own passport. Would the name "Ulianov" arouse suspicion? The inspector stamped all four passports with only a perfunctory glance and hurried on.[1]

During the twenty-minute stopover at Beloostrov, Bonch-Bruevich rushed off to fetch the morning papers, while Lenin, Saveliev, and Maria Ilinichna ordered coffee at the station buffet. Bonch-Bruevich soon returned with several late editions, and Lenin pounced on them for news of the uprising in Petrograd. Prominent stories in almost all the papers carried details of the previous day's events. From all indications it appeared that the movement of armed soldiers and factory workers into the streets had been triggered in mid-afternoon by soldiers of the several-thousand-man First Machine Gun Regiment. One or two machine gunners had been dispatched to each major factory and military unit, where, more often than not, their appeals for insurrection had been greeted with enthusiasm. By early evening upper-class citizens had disappeared from downtown streets, and thousands of soldiers in full battle dress and workers carrying banners, many of the latter accompanied by their families, were demonstrating outside the Mariinsky and Taurida palaces, headquarters of the Provisional Government and the Soviet respectively, demanding the transfer of power to the Soviet. According to these accounts, large groups of rebelling workers and soldiers had gone out of their way to parade past Bolshevik headquarters in the Kshesinskaia mansion, a sign of Bolshevik involvement in preparation of the uprising and of the authority of the party among the Petrograd masses.

Insurgents in motorcars commandeered on the streets and in military trucks bristling with machine guns and decorated with red banners had been observed weaving about the city all evening unhindered. There were numerous reports of random rifle and machine gun fire in widely scattered areas; the extent of casualties was as yet unknown. At rail stations long lines of alarmed, well-dressed Petrograders queued up for tickets and prepared to leave the city. With the consent of the guards on duty, insurgent forces had taken control of the psychologically and strategically important Peter and Paul Fortress. According to last-minute dispatches, a group of rebel soldiers had made an unsuccessful attempt to capture War Minister Kerensky. In addition, the left appeared to have secured a major victory in the Workers' Section of the Petrograd Soviet, which on the previous evening had broken with the leadership of the central Soviet organs by endorsing the idea of transferring power to the soviets and forming a commission to help give the mass movement a peaceful and organized character.[2]

At the start of the trouble the government and the Soviet had appealed to soldiers and workers not to go into the streets; after it was clear that this effort had failed, the commander of the Petrograd Military District, General Petr Polovtsev, a youthful but tough and already much decorated cavalry officer, had urgently called on units of the garrison to restore order in the streets. However, troops not participating in the uprising were ignoring his directives. Late in the evening Polovtsev had published a ban on further demonstrations of any kind. Meanwhile, both the cabinet and the All-Russian Executive Committees had been meeting in emergency session on and off throughout the night in connection with the expanding crisis.

In these early reports there was little consensus about what had sparked the uprising. One of the day's featured stories was that several Kadets had resigned from the cabinet because of differences with socialist ministers over government policy toward the Ukraine.[3] Some observers took it for granted that the developing insurrection was directly related to the apparent breakup of the coalition. Thus a correspondent for the Kadet newspaper *Rech'* suggested that the latter development had provided the opportunity for soldiers in a *few* military regiments and workers in *some* factories to demonstrate their preference for the transfer of "all power to the soviets."[4] Other observers attributed the disruptions to dissatisfaction among garrison troops with brutal measures adopted by military authorities to deal with front-line units that refused to advance against the enemy.[5]

Despite differences as to the precise issue that had triggered the movement to overthrow the government, virtually all commentators seemed agreed that the Bolsheviks, more than any other political group, were to blame for the trouble. A writer for *Izvestiia*, the newspaper of the Central Executive Committee and the Petrograd Soviet, concluded that a part of the Petrograd proletariat and garrison had come into the streets with arms in hand under the influence of "totally irresponsible Bolshevik agitation." In his view, the Bolsheviks were attempting to make use of genuine dissatisfaction and unrest among the proletarian and soldier masses for their own purposes.[6] An editorial in *Birzhevye vedomosti*, a nonparty liberal daily, put the matter more directly. "What is this?" queried the writer rhetorically. "The realization of the unfulfilled Bolshevik lust of June 10? An armed uprising against the Provisional Government and the majority of the organized democracy?"[7] Years later Bonch-Bruevich recalled that during the trip back to Petrograd Lenin was alarmed most of all by the fury toward the Bolsheviks that was sharply reflected in the July 4 papers.[8]

The third warning bell, announcing the train's impending departure, interrupted Lenin's thoughts. Gulping his coffee and grabbing up the papers, he bounded after his associates, who were hurrying back to their compartment. Once again settled in his seat, Lenin fell silent, absorbing the rest of the day's important news.

On this summer morning the papers reported more than the usual upset over the increasingly critical shortages of food and fuel. On July 2 the minister of food supply, Peshekhonov, had summoned representatives of the Central Petrograd Food Supply Board so that they could be apprised of the growing emergency. The report of a board staff member spelled out the dimensions of the existing food supply breakdown in the Petrograd area. It revealed that even with a reduction in rations, grain reserves would barely last until September. The Food Supply Board had recently purchased 100,000 poods (a pood equals thirty-six pounds) of rice in Vladivostok, but deliveries to Petrograd were delayed by shipping difficulties. Milk deliveries had fallen sharply, largely because of currency problems with Finland, Petrograd's main source of dairy products. Supplies of feed grain and hay reaching Petrograd were a scant third of the necessary minimum. Deliveries of eggs and vegetables were also sharply reduced, in part because authorities in several provinces were not permitting outbound shipments.[9]

There was news that the Committee on Fuel Supply had dispatched an emergency report to the mayor of Petrograd characterizing the situation with regard to wood supplies as catastrophic. The report placed the blame for this shortage on disruptions on rail lines, the overload of the Petrograd rail head, and difficulties with river transport caused by labor problems and by bad weather. It implied that unless immediate measures to eliminate supply and distribution problems for wood were undertaken, increasing numbers of plants and factories would be forced to shut down for lack of fuel.[10] A related report indicated that the growing fuel emergency had impelled officials of the Moscow Stock Exchange to forward an urgent memorandum to the Ministry of Trade and Industry in Petrograd. The stock exchange officials warned that the shutdown of many factories in the course of the summer because of lack of fuel and raw materials was already certain. These officials strongly supported factory owners who insisted on their financial inability to keep on the payroll the many thousands of employees who would soon be forced out of work. In addition, they predicted that massive labor unrest in major industrial areas was inevitable unless the government mobilized unemployed workers for jobs in agriculture and provided adequate relief benefits. The memorandum urged that the government inform the public of the nature and causes of the developing situation so that laid-off workers would not hold factory owners responsible for their situation.[11]

The main government committees charged with organizing elections to the Constituent Assembly and preparing a land reform program for its adoption were continuing their deliberations. The previous day the Elections Committee had spent many hours debating how members of the armed forces would be represented in the assembly. Meanwhile, the Land Reform Committee heard reports from representatives of local land committees on developments in the provinces. The delegate from Penza Province reported that local peasants were putting the principle of socialization of the land into practice spontaneously by seizing and dividing up land according to a labor norm. Efforts by authorities to protect private property were useless, he maintained. No official would dare take action against the peasants for fear of reprisal. A representative from Poltava Province declared that the peasants were demanding socialization of the land and were awaiting the implementation of this action through proper legislative procedures. "It is clear to me," he went on, "that to avoid land seizures it is necessary for the government to prepare laws on the leasing of land, the prohibition of land purchases and sales, and the conservation of forests. Any delay in the publication of such regulations will make peasants apprehensive that land reform will never come." A speaker from the Don Region declared that the population of his area was demanding the expropriation of private landholdings without compensation. The Petrograd Soviet's representative on the committee berated the Provisional Government for allowing individual ministries to pursue directly conflicting policies in the countryside. He was particularly critical of the Ministry of the Interior, which, he said, condemned as criminal and anarchical every action taken by the local land reform committees, set up by the Ministry of Agriculture.[12]

It was reported that a day-long strike of Petrograd lumber workers had been settled. Postal and telegraph workers, however, threatened a walkout beginning at 8:00 P.M. on July 4. Clerks and loaders at the main post office were already refusing to work or to allow postmen to make deliveries as the result of a dispute over fringe benefits and a monthly pay raise. At the same time, employees of hotels and rooming houses had joined a citywide waiters' strike. Like the waiters, they were calling for an end to hourly wages and demanding instead compensation based on a percentage of revenue in addition to their regular base salary. In the face of the walkout some restaurant owners were inviting their customers into the kitchen to serve themselves.[13]

The major news item from abroad was that in Berlin, Bethmann-Holweg had resigned as chancellor and had been replaced by George Michaelis.[14] Because of the former chancellor's apparent readiness to entertain the possibility of a negotiated compromise peace, German annexationist and military circles had for many months been applying pressure on Bethmann-Holweg to give up his post; his ultimate departure and the appointment of Michaelis, a nonentity selected by General Ludendorff, were striking indications of the military high command's decisive hold over German politics.

From Dvinsk came a detailed account of a visit to the northern front on July 1 and 2 by Minister of Labor Skobelev and Vladimir Lebedev, acting naval minister.[15] The two were hastily dispatched to the front in the wake of reports that sizable numbers of Fifth Army troops were refusing to obey their commanders' orders and remained adamantly opposed to engaging the enemy. This was the period between the start of the long-awaited and loudly trumpeted Kerensky offensive, launched on June 18, and the decisive German counterattack, begun on July 6. The main thrust of the initial Russian attack had taken place on the southwestern front. At first it had been modestly successful. (When word of the Russian advance reached Petrograd, the nationalist press was jubilant.) Yet within days the demoralized condition of the army at the front became evident, as units that had been persuaded to move into the attack at its start now refused to fight further. By July 4 even the inflated official military dispatches could not hide the fact that the initial breakthrough had bogged down and that Russian forces, under attack everywhere, were suffering heavy losses.

On the northern front, the advance was not due to begin until July 8. A few miles from the front lines, as bands blared, soldiers lined up smartly for review and roared their approval as Skobelev trooped the line. Many of these soldiers had seen action and been wounded in earlier campaigns.

Since the February revolution they had been reading *Pravda, Soldatskaia pravda, Okopnaia pravda,* [16] and the countless other revolutionary antiwar publications with which the Bolsheviks had inundated the battle zones; by now they were preoccupied with thoughts of peace and land and a more equitable political and social order. The objectives of the war were incomprehensible to most of the soldiers, and they were angered by the knowledge that while the Soviet was trying to arrange a just peace, the government was preparing to launch a new offensive. As a result, the soldiers' antagonism toward their officers mounted sharply. Some units were even becoming distrustful of their own elected committees, which, dominated by Mensheviks and SRs, by and large supported the government's military policies. Nevertheless, while their generals beamed encouragement, the ranks cheered Skobelev. He implored them to give their all for a free Russia, and they responded: "Right you are! We are ready to die for liberty! We will do our duty to the end!" The soldiers waved banners bearing the slogans "To the Attack!" and "Down with Cowards!" A group hoisted Lebedev and Skobelev to their shoulders and conveyed them to their motorcar. Yet barely a week later, when the order to attack was given, the same soldiers would throw down their weapons and stumble pell-mell from the battlefield.

The train carrying Lenin and his companions began slowing down. At the northernmost outskirts of Petrograd it passed the lush gardens of the Forestry Institute and crossed Sampsonevsky Prospect, which ran southward through the Vyborg District, Petrograd's large industrial ghetto. The crowded, soot-blackened factories, grimy, vermin-infested, multilevel barracks, and rundown workers' shanties that the train was now passing had provided fertile ground for the spread of revolutionary ideas during the first great spurt of Russian industrial development in the last decades of the tsarist regime. Embittered students from the Forestry Institute had joined their fellows at St. Petersburg University in the outburst of student unrest that had shaken the Russian government at the end of the 1890s, and they were to be found alongside industrial workers manning the barricades in 1905, July 1914, and February 1917. In October 1905 police had directed a hail of bullets at a crowd of workers demonstrating near the southern end of Sampsonevsky Prospect, at the corner of Botkinskaia Street. Just a short distance away, separated by narrow, muddy, refuse-ridden alleys, were three of Petrograd's larger factories—the Erikson, Novyi Lessner, and Russkii Reno plants. Major political strikes had taken place at the Erikson telephone and electrical factory in 1905, 1912, 1914, and 1916. In 1913 the Novyi Lessner machine factory had been the scene of one of the longest and most famous strikes in Russian labor history, lasting 102 days. A pitched battle between Reno auto factory workers and soldiers and the police in

October 1916 was one of the first signs of the impending storm that culminated a few months later in the fall of the tsar. Now, as Lenin's train moved sluggishly past and drew to a noisy stop at the Finland Station, all three factories were again shut down. Workers from the Reno, Erikson, and Novyi Lessner plants had been among the first to take to the streets the day before.

As Lenin strode from the train, the scene at the Finland Station was very different from the one which had greeted him in April. Then, returning from exile, he had been met by crowds of workers and soldiers. There had been banners and flowers, a band, and an honor guard of sailors. Even the leadership of the Soviet had made its appearance; Nikolai Chkheidze, chairman of the Petrograd Soviet, had been among those welcoming Lenin in what formerly had been the imperial waiting room. On that occasion Lenin had driven to Bolshevik headquarters perched atop an armored car, accompanied by an imposing procession of party functionaries, workers, and soldiers. Now, as Bonch-Bruevich hastened off in search of a taxi, there were no bands or welcoming speeches. An acrid odor of steam, stale food, and sweat permeated the humid summer air. Porters hustled about their tasks. From a booth draped in bunting, an elderly matron with pince-nez gesticulated wildly as she exhorted passersby: "Support our revolutionary soldiers! Sign your liberty loan pledges here!" On the square outside, throngs of workers and soldiers milled about, preparing to renew their demands for immediate peace and the transfer of power to the soviets.

During the more than two hundred years since its founding by Peter the Great, the Russian imperial capital, like prerevolutionary Paris, had become divided into sharply defined socioeconomic districts. Generally speaking, the central sections of the city, encompassing the southern parts of Vasilievsky Island and the "Petersburg side" on the right bank of the Neva, and much of the left bank extending from the river to the Obvodny Canal, were the domain of the upper and middle classes, while most factory workers lived and worked in the outer industrial districts. The central sections boasted the luxurious rococo and neoclassical palaces of the royal family and high aristocracy, the massive edifices that served as headquarters for imperial officialdom, the imposing Isaac and Kazan cathedrals, and the granite river and canal embankments which together made Petrograd one of Europe's most beautiful capitals. Here, too, were centers of Russian culture such as the Royal Mariinsky Theater, home of the opera and the famed imperial ballet; the Royal Alexandrinsky Theater, where the best in European drama and comedy alternated with the classics of Gogol, Turgenev, and Tolstoy; and the Petersburg Conservatory, on whose stage the most accomplished musicians of the time performed. Also located in this central area on the left bank of the Neva were the capital's banks, offices, and

Street scene in Petrograd, 1917.

better residential neighborhoods, which changed in character as one went further from the Admiralty—the hub of the city—from aristocratic palaces through professional apartment houses to the tenements of the lower middle class. Originating at the Admiralty and dominated by its needle spire was Nevsky Prospect, Petrograd's broadest and finest avenue, with the city's most fashionable shops, while across the Neva, to the north, the embankment at the eastern end of Vasilievsky Island was lined by the distinctive buildings of St. Petersburg University, the Russian Academy of Sciences, and the Academy of Fine Arts, three symbols of Russian intellectual and artistic achievement, and by the columned façade of the Stock Exchange.

The major factories of Petrograd were located in the districts surrounding this central area—in the Narva, Moscow, and Alexander Nevsky districts on the left bank of the Neva, and in the more remote areas of Vasilievsky Island and the Okhta and Vyborg districts on its right bank.

On the Petersburg side, surrounded by a formal garden and protected by a high, ornate, wrought-iron fence, was the spacious and elegant Kshesinskaia mansion, the former residence of Mathilde Kshesinskaia, prima ballerina of the Mariinsky Ballet and reputed to have been the mistress of Tsar Nicholas II. Kshesinskaia had fled the mansion during the February days, after which it had been taken over by soldiers of an armored car division quartered nearby. In early March, the Bolsheviks, then operating out of two cramped rooms in the attic of the Central Labor Exchange, requested and received permission from the soldiers to make the building their headquarters.[17] In short order, the Central Committee, the Petersburg

Committee, and the Bolshevik Military Organization were comfortably established in different parts of the mansion.

From the Bolsheviks' point of view, the Kshesinskaia mansion was ideally situated. A stone's throw from the Peter and Paul Fortress and the Cirque Moderne, a cavernous concert and assembly hall now the scene of frequent political rallies, it was also close to many military barracks as well as to the teeming factories in the Vyborg District. The move to the Kshesinskaia mansion coincided with the party's spurt in membership and popularity following the February revolution. The new headquarters, over which flew the red standard of the Central Committee, soon became a magnet for disgruntled workers, soldiers, and sailors. The mansion's spacious basement housed the Military Organization's Club Pravda, while the grounds outside the building became the scene of round-the-clock rallies. Each day from early morning until late at night, Sergei Bagdatiev,[18] or Moisei Volodarsky,[19] or another of the party's more popular agitators could be seen atop a rostrum overlooking the street haranguing crowds of passersby. Approximately once a week, elected representatives of party committees in the various districts of the capital assembled at the Kshesinskaia mansion for business meetings. It was to a stunned late-night gathering of some three hundred party leaders in the ornate, white-columned drawing room that Lenin had first personally outlined his new program upon his return to Petrograd on the night of April 3. Several weeks later the mansion was the meeting-place for the Bolsheviks' April Conference.

Not everyone was quite as pleased by this arrangement as were the Bolsheviks. By late spring, Kshesinskaia was determined to get her house back, evidently more for the purpose of expelling the Bolsheviks than out of any desire to return to it herself. In late April and May she badgered both the government and the Petrograd Soviet about evicting the Bolsheviks, and ultimately she took the matter to court. Subsequently, a justice of the peace had given the party twenty days to vacate the mansion,[20] but the Bolsheviks on various pretexts had delayed the move. It was to this beehive of radicalism that many of the demonstrating soldiers and workers came on the evening of July 3. While thousands of marchers chanting "All Power to the Soviets!" waited impatiently for instructions, party leaders from the Military Organization and the Petersburg Committee, gathered in the mansion's master bedroom, debated what action to take and ultimately agreed to support openly and lead the movement on the streets.

Lenin hastened to the Kshesinskaia mansion around midday on July 4. He had hardly been briefed on the latest events when some ten thousand Bolshevik-led sailors from Kronstadt, most of them armed and battle-hungry, surrounded the building, demanding his appearance. At first Lenin declined, asserting that his refusal to appear would express his opposition to the demonstration. But at the insistence of Kronstadt Bolshevik leaders, he ultimately acquiesced. As he stepped out on the second-floor balcony to address the sailors, he grumbled to some Military Organization officials, "You should be thrashed for this!"[21]

Lenin's ambivalent comments on this occasion reflected his dilemma. He voiced a few words of greeting, expressed certainty that the slogan "All Power to the Soviets" would triumph in the end, and concluded by appealing to the sailors for self-restraint, determination, and vigilance. Years later one of Lenin's listeners recalled that for many of the sailors, Lenin's emphasis on the necessity of a peaceful demonstration was unexpected. Anarchists among them and some Bolsheviks as well were unable to see how a column of armed men, eager for battle, could restrict itself to an armed demonstration.[22]

Lenin now found himself in an untenable situation. The previous day's developments had reconfirmed that among workers and soldiers in the capital, the Provisional Government had little support. The Soviet leadership, however, was still determined not to yield to mass pressure. Majority socialists remained convinced that neither the provincial population nor the army at the front would support a transfer of power to the soviets, and that in any case it was necessary for "all the vital forces of the country" to work together in the interest of the war effort and the survival of the revolution. They feared that by breaking with the liberals and the business and industrial circles who supported them they would run the risk of weakening the war effort and enhancing the likelihood of a successful counterrevolution.

Because of the Soviet's refusal to take power, the slogan "All Power to the Soviets" was, at least for the time being, tactically bankrupt from the Bolsheviks' point of view. The choice now facing the party was whether to attempt to seize power by force or to mount an effort to end the demonstrations. In weighing these alternatives Lenin considered the potential reaction of the provinces and the front to be of decisive importance. In this regard the situation was no doubt fluid and unclear, but the immediate indications were not very promising. Bolshevik support continued to be weak among the peasantry, while many soldiers were still loyal to the Soviet leadership.

On the afternoon of July 4 the extent of support for direct revolutionary action in the capital itself was by no means certain. The Kronstadt sailors were present in force and spoiling for a fight—en route from the Kshesinskaia mansion to the Taurida Palace they engaged in a confused gun battle with snipers firing from upper-story windows and rooftops on Nevsky Prospect, and broke into scores of houses and apartments, terrorizing the occupants. But some of the troops who had participated in the demonstrations the previous evening had already wearied of the event, while other garrison units still refused to take sides. Moreover, the possibility of the Bolsheviks seizing power independently of and in opposition to the Soviet had never been presented to the workers and soldiers; indeed, while there is

July 4, 1917 in Petrograd. Demonstrators on Nevsky Prospect scatter in confusion after being fired upon.

evidence that this contingency had been considered by a few top party officials before July (specifically by Lenin and by leaders of the Bolshevik Military Organization),[23] it had not been discussed within the party leadership generally. So the potential reaction to a call to battle even of many Bolshevik leaders, not to speak of their followers, was impossible to gauge.

All this suggested the advisability of a quick retreat. Yet that alternative also had drawbacks. The party was already compromised. The Bolsheviks' program and agitational work had obviously helped inspire the street movement. Banners carried by the demonstrators bore Bolshevik slogans. Pressured by its garrison converts, the Bolshevik Military Organization, without authorization from the Central Committee, had helped organize the movement in the first place. To be sure, on the afternoon of July 3 the Central Committee had made genuine attempts to hold back the movement. However, only a few hours later, with the demonstration already in progress, the leadership of the Military Organization and the Petersburg Committee, followed belatedly by the Central Committee, had reversed the party's earlier stand and publicly endorsed the demonstrations. Subsequently the Military Organization took full control of the movement and began mobilizing the most formidable and broadest possible military support. The organization had, among other things, summoned reinforcements from the front, dispatched armored cars to seize key posts and bridges, and sent a company of soldiers to occupy the Peter and Paul Fortress.[24]

There is no published record of the deliberations of the Bolshevik leadership on July 4; given the circumstances, it is doubtful that any record was kept. Mikhail Kalinin, a ranking Bolshevik participant, later recalled that at this point Lenin's mind was open on the question of whether the movement in the streets was the beginning of the seizure of power; Lenin did not exclude the possibility of throwing regiments into battle in favorable circumstances or, alternatively, of ultimately retreating with as few losses as possible.[25] As he pondered how the party might extricate itself from its exposed position, Lenin almost certainly received conflicting advice. Right Bolsheviks on the Central Committee, in view of their tactical stance on the development of the revolution and their opposition to measures risking a decisive rupture with the moderate socialists, must have been strongly opposed to seizing power in defiance of the All-Russian Executive Committees.[26]

Other authoritative figures who probably appealed for caution on this occasion were Trotsky and Grigorii Zinoviev. Among associates in the party, the curly-haired, pudgy Zinoviev, the son of a Jewish dairyman, was known primarily for his talents as a writer and party organizer. During the decade before the revolution, Zinoviev was probably Lenin's closest assistant and political confidant. Zinoviev returned to Russia with Lenin in April 1917 and subsequently became an editor of *Pravda* and a prominent member of the Bolshevik fraction in the Petrograd Soviet. Thirty-four years old in 1917, Zinoviev was often given to alternate fits of elation and depression. An internationalist on the war issue and receptive in theory to the possibility of an early socialist revolution in Russia, in political behavior Zinoviev nonetheless tended to be vastly more cautious than Lenin. In early June, for example, he firmly opposed the organization of a mass demonstration on the grounds that such action would herald a new stage in the revolution for which the Bolsheviks were unprepared. At the afternoon Central Committee meeting on July 3, both Zinoviev and Trotsky supported the demands of Kamenev and others that the party mobilize its forces to restrain the masses. At a subsequent meeting of party officials late that night, after assuring themselves that there was nothing the Bolsheviks could do to prevent a continuation of the protest the next day, Zinoviev and Trotsky took the side of those who argued that the party should endorse and control the movement. At the same time, they were adamant in their insistence that the demonstrations be peaceful.[27]

Some of the Petersburg Committee members who had favored applying pressure on the All-Russian Executive Committees in the past were probably cool to the idea of escalating the action on July 4. In June the volatile Volodarsky, for one, had supported the organization of mass demonstrations as a means of disrupting the war effort, of retaining the loyalty of the increasingly impatient working-class population, and, if possible, of forcing the majority socialists to form an all-socialist government. In Volodarsky's view, the best interests of the revolution demanded the creation of a soviet government in which a broad coalition of left socialist groups would work together. As an active member of the Petrograd Soviet with close ties to both workers and soldiers, however, Volodarsky was keenly aware of the loyalty of those groups to the Soviet; he would not have advocated overthrowing the Provisional Government against the will of the Soviet leadership.

Among the Petrograd Bolsheviks there were also militants who on the afternoon of July 4 probably argued for decisive military action. One of the most influential of these ultraradical local leaders was the Latvian Martin Latsis, representative of the powerful Vyborg District Bolshevik organization. In the course of preparations for the abortive June 10 demonstration Latsis had taken steps to insure that the marchers would be fully armed; along with the Central Committee's equally aggressive Ivar Smilga, a Lithuanian, Latsis had urged that the party be ready to "seize railroad stations, arsenals, banks, the post office, and telegraph."[28] During the period of rising unrest on the eve of the July days, he was critical of the party for playing the role of "fireman" among the masses, and on the night of July 3, after the uprising had begun he objected to the Central Committee's determination to avoid decisive confrontation with the government.

Top Military Organization figures, among them Nikolai Podvoisky and Vladimir Nevsky, both long-time Bolsheviks, were similarly inclined. A veteran of street combat against government authorities in 1905, Podvoisky, thirty-seven years old in 1917, had the reputation of an ultraradical. In the days immediately after the overthrow of the tsar, Podvoisky reportedly was the first to declare that "the revolution is not over; it is just beginning." Nevsky, from Rostov-on-the-Don, had at one time been a brilliant student in the Natural Sciences Faculty at Moscow University (in the 1920s he would distinguish himself as an historian of the Russian revolutionary movement). Along with Podvoisky, he had been active in the earliest Bolshevik fighting squads and military organizations. In memoirs relating to his activity in 1917, Nevsky invariably boasted about the independence and radicalism of the Military Organization leadership at this time and about its active involvement in the organization of the July uprising. According to him, on July 4 Military Organization leaders waited for a signal from the Central Committee "to carry the affair to its conclusion."[29]

Several hours after Lenin's return to Petrograd, word reached the Kshesinskaia mansion of two new factors that were ultimately of decisive importance. First, it was learned that the helplessness of the government, the unwillingness of garrison units to come to the rescue of the government or the Soviet, the threat posed by the arrival of the Kronstadt sailors at the Taurida Palace, and expanding anarchy and bloodshed in the streets had impelled the All-Russian Executive Committees to call for troops from the front to reestablish order. In response to this appeal Menshevik and SR-controlled army committees on the northern front were already forming composite detachments for immediate dispatch to the capital. Second, word was leaked to the Bolsheviks that high-level government officials were attempting to mobilize garrison troops against the Bolsheviks by accusing Lenin of having organized the July uprising at the behest of enemy Germany.

The charge that Lenin was a German agent was not new. The rightist press had been leveling such accusations since his return to Russia through Germany. (Lenin's known opposition to the war effort made him particularly vulnerable to this charge.) Apparently the Provisional Government had begun investigating the possibility of Bolshevik collusion with the enemy in late April after a German agent, one Lieutenant Ermolenko, had turned himself in to the Russian General Staff and had alleged in the course of interrogation that Lenin was one of many German agents then operating in Russia. This occurred about the time of the April crisis, just when the Bolsheviks were becoming a serious nuisance to the Provisional Government. Members of the cabinet were inclined, quite likely, to believe these allegations; in any case, the prospect of discrediting the Bolsheviks in the eyes of the masses had great appeal. And so three cabinet members —Kerensky, Nekrasov, and Tereshchenko—were assigned to facilitate the inquiry. Several intelligence agencies in Petrograd and at the front became involved; indeed a special counterespionage bureau attached to the Petrograd Military District seems to have devoted most of its attention to building a case against the Bolsheviks. Among other things, this agency monitored the party's communications and kept its leaders under surveillance, all with the enthusiastic support of the minister of justice, Pavel Pereverzev. Only the counterespionage bureau, he is reported to have declared, could save Russia.[30]

It is now known that during World War I the Germans expended a substantial sum for the purpose of disrupting Russian internal affairs and that a portion of this money was funneled to the Bolsheviks.[31] Relevant sources suggest, however, that most Bolshevik leaders, not to speak of the party's rank and file, were unaware of these subventions. While Lenin seems to have known of the German money there is no evidence that his policies or those of the party were in any way influenced by it.[32] Ultimately, this aid did not significantly affect the outcome of the revolution. As for the July events, the charge that the uprising was instigated by Lenin in cooperation with the Germans was obviously groundless; from mid-June on, as we have seen, Lenin had worked with energy to prevent an insurrection from breaking out.

At the time of the July days the official investigation of Lenin's German connections, such as they were, was incomplete. But with the government apparently on the verge of being overthrown, officials of the counterespionage bureau decided to act with all deliberate speed. They concocted a plan to use the bits and pieces of incriminating evidence already collected to convince representatives of previously neutral garrison units not only that the Bolsheviks were recipients of German funds, but also that the street demonstrations were being directed by the Germans. If the plan worked, they reasoned, garrison units would provide the troops necessary to defend the government, restore order, and arrest the Bolsheviks. The scheme was presented to Pereverzev, and he gave it his approval. Defending his decision several days later, the minister of justice explained: "I felt that releasing this information would generate a mood in the garrison that would make continued neutrality impossible. I had a choice between a proposed definite elucidation of the whole of this grand crime's roots and threads by some unspecified date or the immediate putting down of a rebellion that threatened the overturn the government."[33]

Thus, late on July 4 the counterespionage bureau invited representatives of several garrison regiments to General Staff headquarters, where they were briefed on the case against Lenin. All witnesses agreed that these representatives were genuinely shocked by the disclosures; for their part, officials of the bureau were so encouraged by the apparent potency of their case that they decided to make portions of the evidence available to the press. Because officials of the counterespionage bureau were concerned that accusations against Lenin coming directly from a government agency would be suspect, two "outraged citizens"—Grigorii Aleksinsky, a former Bolshevik representative in the Duma, and V. Pankratov, an SR—were hastily recruited to prepare a statement on the charges for immediate circulation to newspapers.[34]

It should be emphasized that the actions of the counterespionage bureau, the minister of justice, and later Aleksinsky and Pankratov were taken without the sanction of the full cabinet. As it turned out, at the time of the July uprising ministers Nekrasov, Tereshchenko, and Lvov felt strongly that while the Bolsheviks were indeed receiving money from the Germans, the evidence against Lenin then in the hands of the government was inconclusive, and that premature disclosure would prevent any possibility of ever substantiating it.[35] During the evening of July 4 Lvov had personally appealed to all newspapers to withhold publication of the charges against Lenin.[36] Of course, the information already passed to regimental representatives could not be prevented from spreading throughout the garrison. And the impact of the disseminated charges, together with rumors of massive troop movements from the front, was decisive. At 1:00 A.M., July 5, previously neutral regiments began marching to the Taurida Palace, where the All-Russian Executive Committees were in session, to proclaim their loyalty to the Soviet and the government. The immediate crisis having passed, the Executive Committees quickly adopted a resolution pledging support to what remained of the Provisional Government. The resolution also called for the convocation in two weeks of a meeting with representatives of provincial soviets for the purpose of reaching a final decision regarding the composition of a future cabinet and the question of establishing a soviet government.[37]

These developments late on July 4—that is, the dispatch of loyal troops from the front and the abrupt shift in the mood of a number of garrison regiments—were, of course, fully as damaging for the Bolshevik cause as they were providential for the Provisional Government. By late evening, the effect of both factors on the mood of previously passive garrison units was already becoming apparent. In these circumstances there wasn't time even to gauge the mood of the provinces. At two or three o'clock in the morning, July 5, a gathering of Central Committee members took stock of the developing situation and resolved to call on workers and soldiers to terminate the street demonstrations.

The party's retreat was made public in an unobtrusive back-page announcement in *Pravda* on July 5. "It has been decided to end the demonstrations," the announcement explained, "because the goal of presenting the slogans of the leading elements of the working class and the army has been achieved." This explanation was transparently false; the goal of the radical elements in the Petrograd garrison and of the Bolshevik extremists who had triggered the July uprising in the first place had been the overthrow of the Provisional Government. In belatedly supporting the movement, most party leaders probably held out the hope that the pressure of the streets would be enough to force the All-Russian Executive Committees to take power into their own hands. As it turned out, neither the extremists' aims nor the more limited hopes of party moderates were realized. The impatient workers, soldiers, and sailors of Petrograd who until now had flocked behind the Bolsheviks emerged from the July experience compromised and, temporarily at least, demoralized. At the same time the resolve of the government, of all moderate and conservative political groups, and of the well-to-do classes generally, to restore order at whatever cost and to have done with extremists once and for all was greatly intensified. Whether this defeat for the left would be decisive remained to be seen. In the meantime, isolated and exposed, the Bolsheviks were forced to turn to the unenviable task of somehow explaining their role in the unsuccessful insurrection, defending themselves against treason charges, and generally protecting themselves from the inevitable onslaught of reaction.

·2·

THE BOLSHEVIKS
UNDER FIRE

The attack on the Bolshevik Party in the wake of the July days was launched by *Zhivoe slovo*, a reactionary, scandalmongering boulevard newspaper aptly characterized by Lenin as a "yellow, base, dirty little rag."[1] *Zhivoe slovo* stood for law, order, and strong rule at home, and unrelenting war to total victory against the Central Powers. It regarded as archenemies socialists generally and the extremist Bolsheviks in particular. One can easily imagine with what glee *Zhivoe slovo*'s editors received the Aleksinsky-Pankratov charges on the evening of July 4. Interpreting subsequent efforts by Prince Lvov and others to delay their publication as proof that radicals in the highest levels of government were part of the nefarious plot to sell out Russia to the foreign foe, they published the sensational statement in full on the morning of July 5, prefaced by a front-page banner headline: "Lenin, Ganetsky, and Kozlovsky German Spies!" (Iakov Ganetsky and Mechislav Kozlovsky were Bolsheviks through whom German money had allegedly been funneled to the party.)

The Bolsheviks promptly protested. A short note in *Pravda* on July 5, written even before *Zhivoe slovo* reached the streets, warned readers that hostile circles might be planning a campaign to slander the Bolshevik leadership. Immediately after the appearance of the Aleksinsky-Pankratov statement, Lenin dashed off several scathing newspaper essays vehemently denying the charges against him and attempting to rebut them.[2] Simultaneously, other top Bolshevik leaders implored Soviet officials to protect them from being crucified by the press. In response, the Central Executive Committee issued an appeal urging the public to refrain from commenting on the accusations against the Bolsheviks until a special committee of inquiry to be set up by the Soviet had had time to conduct a thorough investigation.[3] Once *Zhivoe slovo* had opened the floodgates, however, neither the protests of the Bolsheviks nor the entreaties of Soviet leaders

ВЫСОКІЙ ПОСТЪ ДЛЯ ВОЖДЕЙ МЯТЕЖА

ЛЕНИНЪ ХОЧЕТЪ ЗАНЯТЬ ВЫСОКІЙ ПОСТЪ?.. ЧТО-ЖЪ? МѢСТО ДЛЯ НЕГО ГОТОВО!!!

Cartoon from *Petrogradskaia gazeta*, July 7, 1917, labeled "A High Post for the Leaders of the Rebellion." The caption reads: "Lenin wants a high post? . . . Well? A position is ready for him!!!" (An exact copy, redrawn for this volume.)

could prevent the eruption of an ugly scandal concerning the Bolsheviks' alleged German ties. By midday on July 5 Petrograd buzzed with rumors that "Lenin is a provocateur." The statement by Aleksinsky and Pankratov was immediately reproduced as a leaflet and within hours copies were being handed out by the hundreds on street corners. By the next day many Petrograd newspapers were treating the charges as established fact and openly competing with one another to produce sensational accounts of Bolshevik treachery.

Newspaper headlines on July 6 and 7 convey the ferocity of this campaign. "A Second and Great Azevshchina," proclaimed a headline in the rightist *Malenkaia gazeta*, its editor recalling the scandal that had rocked the Russian revolutionary movement in 1908 when it was revealed that the Socialist Revolutionary Party leader Evno Azev was working for the police. The editor of a popular nonparty daily, *Petrogradskii listok*, did not dig as far back for his headline. "Horrors!" he captioned his story in reference to July 4, when both the government and the Soviet were at the mercy of rioting workers and soldiers. "Petrograd was seized by the Germans."

Accusations against the Bolsheviks made on July 9 by the venerable Georgii Plekhanov, father of the Russian social democratic movement and

editor of the newspaper *Edinstvo*, were no less explicit.[4] In response to a
government telegram published the previous day, which declared, "It has
been definitely established that German agents took part in organizing the
July disturbances," Plekhanov observed: "If the government is convinced of
this, the riots cannot be treated as if they were merely the regrettable result
of tactical confusion. . . . Apparently, the disruptions . . . were an in-
tegral part of a plan formulated by the foreign enemy to destroy Russia.
Therefore stamping them out must be a constituent part of any plan for
Russia's national defense." Concluded Plekhanov: "The revolution must
crush everything in its way immediately, decisively, and mercilessly."

One of the most widely circulated post–July days indictments of the Bolsheviks was written by the famous old populist Vladimir Burtsev. Notorious years earlier for his relentless pursuit of police spies in revolutionary
organizations, Burtsev was, in 1917, an ultranationalist close in political
outlook to Plekhanov. On July 6, in an open letter subsequently printed in
many Petrograd papers, he joined the onslaught against the Bolsheviks. As
to whether or not Lenin was a German agent, Burtsev commented:
"Among the Bolsheviks, provocateurs and German agents have played and
continue to play a great role. In regard to the Bolshevik leaders about whom
we are now asked, we can say: No, they are not provocateurs. . . . [But]
thanks to them—to Lenin, Zinoviev, Trotsky, etc.— during those damna-
ble days, July 3, 4, and 5, William II achieved what he had previously only
dreamed about. . . . In those days Lenin and his comrades cost us no less
than a major plague or cholera epidemic."[5]

Rech', the organ of the Kadets, was relatively cautious in its treatment of
the Aleksinsky-Pankratov accusations. While affirming the principle that
the Bolsheviks ought not to be judged guilty until the charges against them
had been proven, writers for *Rech'*, in their insistence on strong measures
against the left, tacitly accepted the validity of the charges.[6] A front-page
account of the scandal in the right Menshevik *Den'* on July 6 was similarly
circumspect.

It bears recording that, unlike *Edinstvo* and *Den'*, several moderate
socialist papers in Petrograd (*Izvestiia*, *Golos soldata*, and *Volia naroda*, for
instance) heeded the admonitions of the Central Executive Committee to
refrain from commenting, directly or indirectly, on the merits of the
treason charges against Lenin and his followers. This provided the party
scant relief, however. For with the lone exception of Maxim Gorky's *Novaia
zhizn'*, the entire socialist press rejected Bolshevik claims that the July
movement had been spontaneous and called for decisive measures to deal
with extremism as insistently as did liberal and rightist papers.

Typical of anti-Bolshevik editorials appearing in moderate socialist papers
in the aftermath of the July days was one in *Izvestiia*, the main organ of the
Central Executive Committee, on July 6:

According to *Pravda*, the goals of the July 3–4 demonstrations have been achieved. [In reality] what did the demonstrations and the Bolsheviks (the official leaders of the demonstrations) accomplish? They [the demonstrations] caused the deaths of four hundred workers, soldiers, sailors, women, and children. . . . They resulted in the wrecking and looting of private apartments [and] stores. . . . They brought about a weakening of our forces at the front. ; . . They engendered dissension, . . . shattering united revolutionary action, which is the main source of the revolution's strength. . . . During July 3–4 the revolution was dealt a terrible blow. . . . If this defeat is *not* fatal for the entire revolutionary cause, the disorganizing tactics of the Bolsheviks will be least responsible for this.

A similarly hostile editorial, "To the Pillory," appeared in *Golos soldata*, a military-oriented organ of the Central Executive Committee, on July 6. "Gentlemen from *Pravda*," observed its author. "You could not have been unaware of what your appeals for a 'peaceful demonstration' would lead to. . . . You slandered the government; you lied and cast aspersions on the Mensheviks, SRs, and soviets; you created panic, frightening people with the specter of the still unreal danger of the Black Hundreds. . . . And now, according to the custom of all cowards, you are covering your tracks, hiding the truth from your readers and followers." A day earlier, a writer for the right SR paper *Volia naroda* had declared emphatically: "The Bolsheviks are openly acting contrary to the will of the revolutionary democracy. The revolutionary democracy [i.e., the socialist parties, soviets, trade unions, cooperatives, etc.] has enough power to force everyone to obey its will. It must do this. . . . In these feverish days, any procrastination might prove fatal."

The Provisional Government had contemplated the use of force to suppress militant leftist groups for the first time after the April crisis. During the late spring and early summer, mounting pressure for such action had been exerted by the military high command and by conservative and liberal political circles thoroughly alarmed by expanding anarchy at home as well as by apparent chaos among soldiers at the front. Prior to the July days, however, the government's capacity to move against the extreme left was limited by its lack of authority among the Petrograd masses and by the reluctance of many deputies in the central Soviet organs to countenance repression so long as any hope remained that such measures could be avoided.[7]

The July uprising strengthened the determination of the government to take whatever action was necessary to prevent similar outbreaks in the future; at the same time, a number of factors militated against the Soviet's continued opposition to the application of force against the left. For one thing, as we shall see, the July experience triggered an indiscriminate reaction against all leftist groups, moderate socialists included, thus putting the Soviet, as well as the Bolsheviks, on the defensive. Of course, the capacity of the Soviet leadership to influence the government's behavior was closely related to the authority that the Soviet enjoyed among the masses. Following the July uprising, workers, sailors, and soldiers in the capital were confused and dispirited. Whom they would follow in the future remained to be seen, but in the short run the Soviet's power base was, at best, uncertain. Meanwhile, troops dispatched from the front to the capital provided the government, at long last, with a sizable military force upon which it could depend.

Further decreasing the likelihood that the Soviet would interfere in the Provisional Government's adoption of repressive measures was the fact that the events of July 3–5 persuaded heretofore wavering Soviet deputies of the need to act quickly and decisively to restore order and, in this connection, to take a firm stand against the Bolsheviks. While reluctantly acknowledging the necessity of repression, most moderate socialists did not give up striving for reform and immediate peace. They insisted that repression be kept to a minimum, and, most important, that "exceptional measures" be taken only against individuals accused of specific crimes, not against "whole groups." In contrast to the liberals, the Mensheviks and SRs were genuinely alarmed by the danger that the reactionary wave following the July days posed for the revolution. But their response to the threat of counterrevolution (like their earlier response to attacks from the extreme left) was to rally more closely behind the government and to insist on coalition with the liberal parties.

It is ironic that the Soviet leadership had become most receptive to closer cooperation with the government at a time when the latter was in a shambles. It will be recalled that three Kadet ministers withdrew from the cabinet on the night of July 2. They were followed into retirement three days later by Pereverzev, who resigned in the wake of criticism of his unauthorized release of the Aleksinsky-Pankratov documents. Prince Lvov himself left the government on July 7 after socialist ministers presented him with a list of "general principles" intended as the basis of a political program for a new coalition. Modeled after proposals for reform adopted by the First All-Russian Congress of Soviets, these principles were simply too radical for Lvov. Unable to accept them, he resigned. The remaining cabinet members now named Kerensky acting prime minister and entrusted him with the formation of a new government.

Simultaneously, most of the measures rejected by Lvov were incorporated into a "Declaration of Principles" released for publication in the cabinet's name on July 8. Among other things, this declaration pledged the government to arrange an Allied conference in August for the purpose of working out the details of a compromise peace proposal, and to take all steps necessary to insure that elections to the Constituent Assembly would be held on September 7. The declaration acknowledged the importance of adopting, "at the earliest possible moment," local government reforms based on the principle of universal, direct, and secret suffrage, and promised the abolition of estates and of civil ranks and orders. Moreover, it pledged the government to the preparation of an overall plan for regulating the national economy and to the immediate passage of meaningful labor legislation. Finally, it committed the government to the preparation, for submission to the Constituent Assembly, of a basic land reform program transferring all land into the hands of the peasantry (to judge by Lvov's statements to the press at the time, this endorsement of revolutionary changes in landholding was what disturbed him most of all). In deference to the liberals, the declaration made no reference to the dissolution of the Duma and the State Council, or to the immediate declaration of a republic—two demands that had been endorsed by the Congress of Soviets and that were included in the original list of principles drawn up by the socialist ministers.[8]

As the price of their participation in a new coalition, the Kadets now demanded that the government disavow the declaration of July 8. Confident that the bulk of the population shared their view that the July days had discredited the moderate socialists along with the Bolsheviks, and consequently that a propitious moment for the reestablishment of order and the preeminence of the government had finally arrived, the Kadets were adamant in demanding that in the future socialist ministers maintain complete independence from the Soviet. In internal affairs they insisted that the government abjure consideration of any further social reforms (in keeping with this position they demanded that Chernov be replaced as minister of agriculture because of his role in facilitating land reform); moreover, they called for an end to pluralism in governmental authority, i.e., to the political and administrative authority of soviets and committees. On the war issue, the Kadets insisted that the government be guided by the principle of total commitment to the Allies and that it take all steps necessary to reestablish traditional military discipline and to build a strong army. Negotiations aimed at somehow squaring these demands with the declaration of July 8 were naturally tortured and acrimonious; while they dragged on, Russia, more than ever, was without effective national leadership.[9]

Meanwhile, the initially successful offensive at the front had been turned into a most terrible rout of the Russian armies by the Germans, who launched a massive, devastating counterattack against the Russian Eleventh Army on the southwestern front. Boris Savinkov, government commissar for the southwestern front, now telegraphed Petrograd:

> The German offensive . . . is developing into an unprecedented disaster. . . . Most units are in a state of rapidly spreading disintegration.

There can be no talk of authority or discipline. . . . Some units are withdrawing from their positions on their own, without even waiting for the enemy to approach. There were cases when orders for immediate reinforcements were debated in meetings for hours, with the result that these reinforcements were as much as a day late. . . . Long columns of deserters stretch for hundreds of versts [a verst equals six-tenths of a mile] to the rear. . . . Let the entire country know the truth of what is happening here.[10]

Even before receipt of this oppressive news, the All-Russian Executive Committees had gathered in joint session on the night of July 7–8 to discuss the latest developments, the most important being the behavior of the Bolsheviks, the sudden explosion of counterrevolutionary sentiment, and the breakup of the cabinet. This meeting culminated in the passage of a resolution that characterized the July movement as "an adventurous, abortive armed uprising" by "anarcho-Bolshevik elements." While stressing that "exceptional measures" could be taken only against individuals, this resolution explicitly recognized the responsibility of the government to assure the protection of revolutionary freedoms and the maintenance of order. At the same time, it strongly endorsed immediate passage of the reform legislation called for by the Congress of Soviets.[11]

For most moderate socialists, word of the debacle at the front appeared to reinforce strongly the need for the creation of a representative national government powerful enough to halt expanding anarchy. A joint emergency meeting of the All-Russian Executive Committees was hurriedly convened late on the night of July 9–10, soon after the situation at the front became known. Here, bitterness toward the Bolsheviks for subverting the policies of the Soviet majority, as well as support for the creation of a strong revolutionary dictatorship, reached a new peak; a succession of speakers lashed out at the Bolsheviks for, among other things, precipitating an assault on the Soviet during the July days, being responsible for the conditions that had triggered counterrevolutionary activity, and, perhaps worst of all, contributing mightily to the collapse of the armed forces.

The influential Menshevik Fedor Dan spoke for the entire moderate socialist bloc on this occasion. A physician by profession and, along with Lenin, a veteran of the first major social democratic organization established in St. Petersburg, among Menshevik leaders in 1917 Dan was slightly left of center. After the abortive June 10 demonstration, for example, he had strongly opposed Tsereteli on the question of applying sanctions against the Bolsheviks and their followers, believing that the Bolshevik threat was exaggerated and that precipitous action against the extreme left would only undermine further the position of the government and strengthen Lenin's hand. Now, his usually mild face taut with anger, dressed in a shapeless military surgeon's uniform, he proposed that, in view of the prevailing civil and military emergency, the Provisional Government immediately be proclaimed a "government to save the revolution," and, moreover, that it be vested with comprehensive powers to restore organization and discipline in the army, wage a decisive struggle against any and all manifestations of counterrevolution and anarchy, and promulgate the reform program embodied in the cabinet declaration of July 8. The Executive Committees subsequently adopted a resolution to this effect by an overwhelming vote.[12] "Let the government crush all anarchical outbursts and all attempts to destroy the gains of the revolution with an iron hand," declared a proclamation announcing this decision to the Russian public. "Let [the government] carry out all those measures required by the revolution."[13]

It is worth noting that the Menshevik-Internationalists and Left SRs (the extreme left groups within the Menshevik and SR camps), not to speak of the Bolsheviks, did not support the political resolution passed by the All-Russian Executive Committees on July 9, in effect a blank check for a government whose makeup and program were at this point completely unclear.

Bearded, frail Iulii Martov, his voice hoarse from endless speech-making, pince-nez drooping slightly on his nose, spoke for the Menshevik-Internationalists. The son of a russified, liberally inclined Jewish intellectual, Martov, in his mid-forties in 1917, had been propelled into the revolutionary movement by the injustices of Jewish life in tsarist Russia, by the fiercely repressive environment and virulent anti-Semitism he experienced in school, and by progressive ideas and "forbidden books" which he first encountered at home. Already a committed social democrat in the early 1890s and revered among his associates for his intellect, personal courage, high principles, and honesty, Martov had broken with Lenin, earlier a close friend and collaborator, at the time of the Bolshevik-Menshevik split in 1903. From then on he had been the Mensheviks' most prestigious and widely respected political figure. Following the outbreak of World War I, Martov had led the fight of Menshevik "internationalists" for an immediate, negotiated, compromise peace. Upon returning to Russia from exile abroad in early May 1917, he opposed the established Menshevik policies of limited support for the war and of participation in the government and headed a largely independent internationalist faction within the loosely structured Menshevik organization. Convinced that continued coalition government would lead to the destruction of the revolution, at the height of the July days Martov came out for the formation of an all-socialist government "capable of moving the revolution forward." Now, slightly less than a week later, he insisted emotionally that the Soviet's program for saving the country could not be realized if there were enemies on the left.

Martov went on to read a Menshevik-Internationalist declaration expressing the view that the Provisional Government's foreign and domestic policies, because they were neither consistent nor sufficiently revolutionary, had contributed significantly to the crisis facing Russia. The declaration concluded that the revolutionary democracy (i.e., the whole spectrum of democratic institutions and socialist parties) could save the country and the revolution only if the divisions that had already appeared in its ranks were not exacerbated, if all the powers of a revolutionary government were concentrated on combating the mounting threat of counterrevolution, and if decisive steps toward reform could convince the army that in rebuffing the enemy it was shedding blood for land, freedom, and an early peace.[14] A few days later, at a plenary session of the Executive Committees on July 17, after the Kadets had made plain their terms for entry into the government, Martov insisted that the soviets had no choice but to assume full governmental power. "Either the revolutionary democracy will take responsibility for the revolution upon itself," he declared, "or it will lose the ability to influence the revolution's fate."[15]

Events would soon show that Martov's vision of a revolutionary soviet government uniting all socialist elements, carrying out a broad program of reform, vigorously challenging the counterrevolution, and striving in every way to arrange an immediate compromise peace corresponded quite closely to the aspirations of the politically conscious Petrograd masses. We shall see, for example, that precisely these goals were expressed in the discussions and resolutions of most district-level soviets in the aftermath of the July days. Within the SR-Menshevik leadership at this time, however, Martov's views were shared by a relatively small minority. Discussion of political issues at the Executive Committees plenum on July 17 culminated in an endorsement of the position adopted by the Executive Committees on July 9.[16]

In view of the commitment of most Mensheviks and SRs to the Provisional Government and to coalition politics, it is not surprising that in negotiations to form a new cabinet the moderate socialists ultimately gave up considerable ground to the Kadets. These negotiations took place on July 21 and 22, after Kerensky, frustrated in his previous efforts to create a new government, abruptly tendered his resignation, which the remaining ministers refused to accept. Instead, they met with representatives of the various competing political parties, central Soviet organs, and Provisional Committee of the State Duma and agreed to give Kerensky complete freedom in forming a government. Armed with this mandate, Kerensky proceeded at this point to engage ministers on a nonrepresentative basis. Under this mutually acceptable arrangement, cabinet members would not act as representatives of their respective parties and socialist ministers would no longer be formally responsible to the Soviet. Although individual ministers might support the declaration of July 8, the cabinet as a whole would not be pledged to it. In practice this meant that the Soviet's leverage over the government was further reduced, while the principles put forward by the socialists, even in the scaled-down version of July 8, were no longer a part of the government's program.

On this basis, the second coalition, headed by Kerensky and composed of eight socialists and seven liberals, came into being. The most influential figures in the new cabinet were Kerensky (in addition to becoming prime minister, he retained the War and Naval Ministry) and two of his close associates, Nikolai Nekrasov (deputy prime minister and minister of finance) and Tereshchenko (foreign affairs). To almost everyone's surprise, Chernov managed to remain the minister of agriculture. Among those missing from the new cabinet was Tsereteli; in ill health and overwhelmingly tired of cabinet politics, he now opted to concentrate his energies on the affairs of the Soviet.[17]

The government crackdown on the Bolsheviks began very early on the morning of July 5 with the dispatch of a large detachment of military school cadets to raid the *Pravda* editorial offices and printing plant. The cadets arrived at their destination only a little too late to catch Lenin, who had left the premises moments earlier. A few members of the *Pravda* staff were beaten up and arrested during the raid. The cadets made a thorough search of the press, in the course of which they wrecked furniture and equipment and dumped bales of freshly printed newspapers into the nearby Moika Canal. Featured accounts of this episode in many Petrograd newspapers the next day triumphantly disclosed that the cadets had turned up a letter in German from a German baron; the letter was said to have hailed Bolshevik activity and expressed the hope that the party would acquire predominant influence in Petrograd. "German Correspondence Found" was the way a headline in *Malenkaia gazeta* summed up this discovery.[18]

On July 4 the cabinet specifically authorized the command of the Petrograd Military District to remove the Bolsheviks from the Kshesinskaia mansion. Before dawn on July 6 a full-scale attack force commanded by A. I. Kuzmin and composed of the Petrogradsky Regiment; eight armored cars; one company each from the Preobrazhensky, Semenovsky, and Volynsky guards regiments; a detachment of sailors from the Black Sea Fleet; some cadet detachments; students from the Aviation Academy; and a front-line bicycle brigade—all supported by heavy artillery—prepared to storm the Bolshevik headquarters. Warned of the impending attack, some second-level party leaders at the mansion seriously contemplated resistance and even began preparations in this regard. But in the end it was recognized that the situation was hopeless, and the Bolsheviks made a successful dash to the Peter and Paul Fortress, then still occupied by friendly forces.[19]

In the Kshesinskaia mansion, Kuzmin's troops seized a substantial quantity of arms and arrested seven Bolsheviks who were working frantically to complete the evacuation of party files. Moreover, they discovered in an attic some pogromist Black Hundred leaflets, evidently left there in tsarist times. (The Black Hundreds were extreme rightist groups that organized pogroms in late tsarist Russia.) To *Petrogradskaia gazeta*, this find indicated that the Bolsheviks were in league with the extreme right, as well as with the Germans. A headline in the paper on July 7 read: "Lenin, William II, and Dr. Dubrovin [a notorious member of the extreme right] Working Together! It Is Proved the Leninists Organized the Uprising in Association with the Black Hundreds!"

In the early afternoon of July 6 government troops reoccupied the Peter and Paul Fortress, one of the last strongholds of leftist resistance. By then, several of the military units dispatched from the northern front had reached the capital. The bicyclists, an armored car division, and the second squadron of the Little-Russian Dragoons had arrived in the morning, in time to participate in the taking of the Kshesinskaia mansion and the Peter and Paul Fortress. The Fourteenth Mistavsky Hussar Regiment, in full battle dress, reached Petrograd in the early evening. Preceded by standard-bearers holding aloft a red banner with the legend "We Have Come to Support the All-Russian Executive Committees of Soldiers', Workers', and Peasants' Deputies," the regiment marched off to the General Staff building to report to the government.[20] The minister of agriculture, Viktor Chernov, welcomed some of the troops on the Palace Square. "It makes me sad to speak of why you have come," he said. "But I believe this will be your first and last such visit. . . . We hope and believe that [in the future] no one will dare act contrary to the will of the majority of the revolutionary democracy."[21]

Between July 6 and 12 the cabinet issued a series of hastily formulated directives aimed at restoring order and punishing political troublemakers. At a marathon session the night of July 6–7 it was decreed that "all organizers and leaders of the armed movement against the government established by the people and all those making appeals and instigations in support of it should be arrested and brought to trial as traitors to their nation and the revolution."[22] Simultaneously, the government published new penal regulations which included the following: (1) Anyone guilty of making public appeals for murder, plundering, robbery, pogroms, and other heinous crimes, as well as for violence against any part of the population, is to be punished by confinement in a prison or fortress for no longer than three years; (2) those guilty of making public appeals for disobedience of lawful government directives are to be punished by confinement in a fortress for not more than three years or by incarceration in a prison; anyone guilty of inciting officers, soldiers, and other military personnel to disobey the laws in effect under the new democratic system in the army, or the directives of military authorities consistent with them, is to be punished according to regulations pertaining to acts of treason.[23]

Kerensky, named prime minister on July 7, had not been in Petrograd at the height of the July days, having left the capital for a tour of the front late on the afternoon of July 3. While at the front, he had received detailed reports on the developing crisis in the capital. In response, he shot off a telegram to Lvov demanding that "traitorous actions be decisively suppressed, insurgent units disarmed, and all instigators of insurrections and mutineers brought to trial."[24] While at the front, moreover, Kerensky was shown the latest issue of *Tovarishch*, a Russian-language propaganda weekly published by the Germans for circulation among enemy troops. An article in this issue suggested to Kerensky that the Germans had known in advance of the insurrection in the capital; naturally, this reinforced his belief that Lenin was a German agent.[25]

Incensed to the point of distraction, Kerensky boarded a train to return to the capital on the morning of July 6; at the railway depot in Polotsk, the carriage in which he was sleeping was partially wrecked by a bomb.[26] Although physically unharmed, Kerensky was understandably unnerved by the incident. It is not surprising that, upon his arrival in Petrograd on the evening of July 6, he was fuming and champing at the bit to have done with the Bolsheviks. From this time on, Kerensky stood at the forefront of cabinet ministers speaking out for a tough policy toward the extreme left. Addressing a crowd of soldiers and workers from a windowsill of the General Staff building a short while later (as two officers held his legs to prevent a fall), he pronounced: "I will not allow anyone to encroach upon the triumphs of the Russian revolution." With voice rising to fever pitch, he shouted: "Damnation to those traitors who abandon their brothers who are shedding blood at the front. Let those who betray their country in its days of trial be damned!"[27] In an interview with the Associated Press several days later, after he had been officially installed as prime minister, Kerensky declared with equal vigor: "[Our] fundamental task is the defense of the country from ruin and anarchy. My government will save Russia, and if the motives of reason, honor, and conscience prove inadequate, it will beat her into unity with blood and iron."[28]

First and foremost, the July insurrection was, of course, a garrison mutiny. At its July 6–7 session, the cabinet ordered that nonmilitary units participating in the July uprising be disarmed and dissolved, their personnel to be transferred at the discretion of the war and naval ministers. A detailed plan supplementing this order bore Kerensky's handwritten notation: "Agreed, but I demand that this be carried out forcefully, without deviation." About the same time, Kerensky issued a strong condemnation of the Kronstadt sailors, implying that they were acting under the influence of "German agents and provocateurs." All commands and ships of the fleet were ordered to turn over to the authorities in Petrograd for investigation and trial "all suspicious persons calling for disobedience to the government and agitating against the offensive."[29]

Steps aimed at halting the disintegration of the army at the front were also initiated at this time. Thus military commanders were authorized to fire on Russian units fleeing the field of battle on their own. Bolshevik

Soldiers of the First Machine Gun Regiment after being disarmed on July 8, 1917.

newspapers were banned from all theaters of military operations. Political meetings among front troops were strictly forbidden. Most significant, the government decreed the reinstitution of capital punishment for military offenses in the battle zones, simultaneously authorizing the creation of ad hoc "military revolutionary" courts with authority to impose the death sentence.[30]

To prevent rebel workers and sailors caught in the central sections of Petrograd from fleeing to the comparative safety of the left-bank factory districts, the drawbridges over the Neva were kept open. At the same time, the country's borders were sealed, to keep "German agents" from escaping abroad. Street assemblies were temporarily banned. The ministers of war and of the interior were empowered to shut down newspapers encouraging disobedience of military authorities or appealing for violence; by virtue of this order, the Bolshevik papers *Pravda, Soldatskaia pravda, Okopnaia pravda,* and *Golos pravdy* were closed. In a move obviously directed primarily toward disarming workers, all civilians in the capital were ordered to turn over to the government all weapons and military supplies in their possession; failure to hand over arms was to be considered theft of public property and prosecuted accordingly.[31]

On July 7 the cabinet made N. S. Karinsky, prosecutor of the Petrograd court of appeals, responsible for investigating all matters relating to the organization of the July uprising; in view of this, the All-Russian Executive Committees agreed to drop the Soviet's planned independent inquiry into the insurrection.[32] Even before the prosecutor's office was able to launch its investigation, however, the authorities in Petrograd had begun rounding up key Bolsheviks. The cabinet specifically ordered the arrest and detention of

Lenin, Zinoviev, and Kamenev. As we shall see, Lenin and Zinoviev immediately went underground (as did Nevsky and Podvoisky, the two top Military Organization officials). Only Kamenev did not flee—he was arrested and jailed on July 9.

Two days earlier the government had incarcerated members of two large naval delegations dispatched from Helsingfors to Petrograd by the leftist-dominated Central Committee of the Baltic Fleet (Tsentrobalt); among the arrested sailors were such influential "fleet" Bolsheviks as Pavel Dybenko and Nikolai Khovrin. A week later Vladimir Antonov-Ovseenko, another key Helsingfors Bolshevik, was also imprisoned. One of several suspicious characters in a car full of workers detained by a cossack patrol at this time was Sergei Bagdatiev, an Armenian by background who had once been a candidate for the Bolshevik Central Committee. On the afternoon of July 4, Bagdatiev was reported cruising around Petrograd atop an armored car, waving a rifle and crying out to gaping onlookers to "arrest the ministers." Upon interrogation following his arrest, Bagdatiev modestly admitted to being one of the organizers of the uprising. Newspaper accounts of his capture were very definite about two things: that Bagdatiev was a German spy and that he was a Jew. To *Malenkaia gazeta*'s man-on-the-scene, Bagdatiev's "outward appearance, his hooked nose, his short reddish beard," and the fact that he was "masquerading in a democratic workman's shirt" were dead giveaways. Noted the reporter, "Bagdatiev speaks Russian well with barely a trace of a Jewish accent."[33]

Flavian Khaustov, an editor of *Okopnaia pravda* and the focus of a widespread manhunt since his escape from the Crosses Prison (an ancient jail in the Vyborg District built in the form of two crosses) on June 18, was now recaptured, picked up leaving a theater at the Luna Park amusement center, evidently on a tip from an informer.[34] Taking leftist leaders from the Kronstadt naval base into custody was infinitely more difficult for the government. In response to a telegram from Kerensky demanding that "counterrevolutionary instigators" be turned over to the government at once, the Executive Committee of the Kronstadt Soviet wired back: "Inasmuch as no one knows of any 'counterrevolutionary' instigators in Kronstadt, it will be impossible to conduct arrests." Specifically directed to turn over several key Bolshevik leaders (Fedor Raskolnikov, Semion Roshal, and Afanasii Remnev), the Kronstadt Soviet persisted in its refusal to cooperate with the government. Only after the naval base was threatened with blockade and bombardment was it agreed that all of the sought-after Kronstadters, except for Roshal (who had disappeared), would turn themselves in.[35] Subsequently, Roshal also surrendered; encountering Raskolnikov in the Crosses shortly afterward, he explained, "After your arrest, it seemed awkward to hide."[36]

Alexandra Kollontai, an internationally prominent Bolshevik, was in

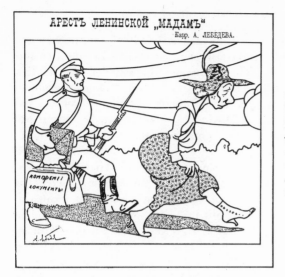

АРЕСТЪ ЛЕНИНСКОЙ „МАДАМЪ"

Карр. А. ЛЕБЕДЕВА.

Cartoon by A. Lebedev depicting the arrest of Alexandra Kollontai, from *Petrogradskaia gazeta*, July 16, 1917. The caption reads: "The Arrest of That Lenin 'Woman!' " The valise is marked "compromising documents." (An exact copy, redrawn for this volume.)

Stockholm during the July days. After the German-agent scandal broke, the Swedish press made life miserable for her, implying that she was abroad to arrange for further German subsidies. Consequently, she hurried back to Petrograd. She later described her reception at the Swedish-Finnish border on July 13. Some Russian officers boarded the train at Torneo and took her into custody. Word of her arrest spread through the station, and crowds soon formed on the platform chanting "German spy! Betrayer of Russia!" A dining car steward with a napkin tucked under his arm chased after her screaming: "It's the spy Kollontai! You belong on the scaffold with the betrayers of Russia." After the train had left Torneo, Kollontai and her guards made their way to the dining car, but revolutionary Russia's self-appointed guardian was still on duty. Barring the way, he blurted, "The spy Kollontai . . . won't eat anything in my dining car." Adding that "spies should be given only bread and water," he stubbornly refused to serve even that.[37]

As arrests of suspected leftists mounted, few non-Bolsheviks challenged the government. Among those who did were Martov; Trotsky; and Anatolii Lunacharsky, a playwright, Marxist philosopher, and powerful revolutionary tribune who at this time was a member of the Interdistrict Committee. At a Central Executive Committee meeting on July 17, for example, Trotsky staunchly defended the behavior of the Bolsheviks throughout the July days and mocked the idea of Lenin's being a German agent. "Lenin has been struggling for the revolution for thirty years," observed Trotsky. "I have been fighting against the oppression of the popular masses for twenty years. We cannot but be filled with hatred toward German militarism. Anyone who says differently does not know what a revolutionary is."[38]

To help the Bolshevik cause, Trotsky agreed to defend Raskolnikov in court. In mid-July he sent a letter of protest on the Bolsheviks' behalf to the government in which he declared: "In principle, I share the views of Lenin, Kamenev, and Zinoviev. . . . My relation to the events of July 3–4 was exactly the same as theirs. . . . There is no logical reason for ordering that Lenin, Zinoviev, and Kamenev be arrested and not me."[39] The government could not ignore such a challenge. Orders for the arrest of Trotsky, and Lunacharsky as well, were issued by Karinsky's office on the morning of July 23. Lunacharsky was picked up at his apartment a short while later. Trotsky, unaware that the authorities were on the lookout for him, called Karinsky that evening to discuss Raskolnikov's defense. When Trotsky inquired whether it would be all right for him to appear in court as Raskolnikov's lawyer, Karinsky replied: "I'll let you know. Where can you be reached?" "At Larin's," responded the unsuspecting Trotsky. Within an hour a squad of soldiers knocked at Larin's door and hustled Trotsky away.[40]

A warrant for Lenin's arrest was issued by the prosecutor of the Petrograd court of appeals on the evening of July 6. At once, a detachment of soldiers and officers from the Preobrazhensky Guards Regiment, commanded by the head of the counterintelligence bureau, Boris Nikitin, rushed to Lenin's last-known residence—the apartment of his oldest sister, Anna Elizarova. Although Lenin was not there at the time, Nikitin, who had been impatient to get his hands on the Bolshevik leader for months, was in no mood to come away empty-handed. While Nadezhda Krupskaia, Lenin's wife, looked on enraged, Nikitin supervised an inch-by-inch search of the apartment, confiscating papers and documents that seemed in any way suspicious. A reporter for *Petrogradskaia gazeta* who appeared at the apartment house early the next morning recorded Lenin's neighbors' reactions to the latest events. All voiced indignation at the idea of having harbored an enemy agent and agreed that the tenants of Number 24 had a lot of money (the word "German" was left unspoken). "You can see for yourself, buildings like this with a grand staircase and mahogany floors are not at all common in Petrograd," pointed out the custodian. "Lenin almost always travels by automobile," he added. "Lenin and his wife have better linens than anyone else," confided a female tenant. "Workers don't rent in this building," her companion chimed in. As the reporter prepared to leave, the custodian produced a petition demanding that the residents of Number 24 be evicted immediately. Already embellished with several signatures, the petition proclaimed: "We do not want such dangerous neighbors as Lenin and his family."[41]

Lenin learned of the warrant for his arrest and of the search at Elizarova's at the apartment of Sergei Alliluev (Stalin's future father-in-law), Lenin's fifth hiding-place in three days.[42] As he moved from hideout to hideout, Lenin weighed the pros and cons of surrender. Within his immediate entourage, opinion on the proper course to follow was sharply divided. Apparently, Kamenev, Trotsky, Lunacharsky, and Viktor Nogin, along with a significant number of Moscow Bolsheviks, felt that the Soviet could be relied on to assure Lenin's personal safety, and that under the Soviet's protection he would receive a fair and open trial which could be used as a forum for exposing the rottenness of the existing regime. They consequently urged that Lenin submit to the authorities.[43]

Several Petrograd party leaders, whose overriding concern seems to have been the negative impact of Lenin's flight on factory workers and soldiers, were of like mind. Volodarsky expressed this view during an intraparty debate over the issue of Lenin's appearance in court: "This question is just not as simple as it seems. Up to now we have been able to capitalize on all developments. The masses have understood us. But in this thing [Lenin's going underground] they don't."[44] Dmitrii Manuilsky, who, like Volodarsky, had particularly close ties to workers and soldiers, commented: "The question of Lenin and Zinoviev appearing for trial can't be looked at exclusively from the point of view of their personal safety. It is necessary to consider the problem from the perspective of the interests of the revolution and the interests and dignity of the party. We are forced to deal with the masses and can all observe the trump the bourgeoisie will play when the subject of our comrades ducking trial arises. . . . We must make a Dreyfus case out of the proceedings against Lenin."

According to the Bolshevik trade union leader Alexander Shliapnikov, the friendly advice of many comrades that Lenin submit to trial greatly upset Lenin's sister Maria, who favored her brother's attempting to reach Sweden.[45] Many other Bolshevik leaders, a majority of those participating in the Sixth Party Congress, which met in Petrograd at the end of July, also feared for Lenin's safety in the event that he turned himself in. They contended that the proceedings against Lenin were part of a plot by the party's class enemies to destroy the Bolsheviks and that in the prevailing climate Lenin could not receive a fair trial, indeed, that he would probably be assassinated before his case reached court. Thus, in the immediate aftermath of the July days these leaders urged that Lenin go into hiding. Subsequently, amid a storm of criticism from both inside and outside the party, they staunchly defended Lenin's behavior. As late as the end of July, Stalin occupied a middle position in this argument, contending that Lenin and Zinoviev ought not turn themselves in while the political situation was still fluid, but implying that the two should submit if a government with some degree of integrity was established that would guarantee Lenin's safety.[46]

At the outset, Lenin apparently leaned toward submission to the authorities.[47] On the afternoon of July 7 he dashed off a note protesting the search of his sister's apartment and expressing his readiness to present himself for arrest if his detention was sanctioned by the Central Executive Committee.[48] Sergei Ordzhonikidze, a long-time Georgian Bolshevik recently arrived in Petrograd, and Nogin were sent to the Taurida Palace with this message and with oral instructions to negotiate the terms of Lenin's imprisonment. They were to obtain from V. A. Anisimov, an official of the Bureau of the Central Executive Committee, ironclad guarantees of Lenin's safety and the promise of a quick, fair trial. The two met with Anisimov later that afternoon. While unable to give any absolute guarantees, Anisimov evidently assured them that the Soviet would do what it could to protect Lenin's rights. According to Ordzhonikidze, after this weak response even Nogin was uneasy about Lenin's fate were he to turn himself in.[49]

These apprehensions were immediately conveyed to Lenin. At the same time, Lenin also learned of the All-Russian Executive Committees' decision to abort their inquiry into the July days, and this information appears to have had a bearing on his thinking. At any rate, on July 8 Lenin made a firm decision not to surrender. In a letter that he now prepared for publication he explained:

> We have changed our plan to submit to the government because . . . it is clear that the case regarding the espionage of Lenin and others has been intentionally constructed by the forces of counterrevolution. . . . At this time there can be no guarantee of a fair trial. The Central Executive Committee . . . formed a commission to look into the espionage charges and under pressure from the counterrevolution this commission has been dissolved. . . . To turn ourselves in to the authorities now would be to put ourselves into the hands of the Miliukovs, Aleksinskys, Pereverzevs —that is, into the hands of dyed-in-the-wool counterrevolutionaries for whom the charges against us are nothing more than an episode in the civil war.[50]

On July 9, under cover of darkness, Lenin left the Alliluevs and, together with Zinoviev, fled to the village of Razliv near the small resort town of Sestroretsk, on the Gulf of Finland twenty miles northwest of the capital.[51] Lenin remained there until August 9, when he moved to Finland. At first he and Zinoviev ensconced themselves in the loft of a barn on the property of a Sestroretsk factory worker and long-time Bolshevik, Nikolai Emelianov. But since there was some danger of being spotted in this refuge by curious villagers, the fugitives soon moved to an isolated straw hut on the bank of a neighboring lake. Years later Zinoviev remembered that one day he and Lenin were frightened by the sound of gunfire nearby. As the two hid in some bushes, Lenin whispered, "The only thing left now is to die properly."[52] The shots, it turned out, had been fired by passing hunters. By and large, such unnerving incidents were not repeated. Until rain and cold made their hut uninhabitable in August, attacks by mosquitoes were the fugitives' greatest logistical problem. At Razliv Lenin rested, swam, and went for long walks. According to Alexander Shotman, who, along with Eino Rakhia and Ordzhonikidze, maintained communications between Lenin and the party leadership in Petrograd, Lenin was most of all concerned with receiving up-to-date newspapers from Petrograd. He pounced on each fresh batch of papers as soon as it arrived. Seated on the grass, he would mark up the papers and begin scribbling comments in his notebooks. During this period Lenin wrote regularly for the Bolshevik press, prepared pamphlets and draft resolutions for consideration by his colleagues in Petrograd (most importantly for an expanded Central Committee meeting on July 13 and 14 and for the Sixth Congress), and worked on a major theoretical treatise, *The State and Revolution.* [53]

Throughout this time criticism of Lenin's behavior and speculation in the press concerning his whereabouts continued. On July 7 *Zhivoe slovo* triumphantly headlined the erroneous news that Lenin had fallen into government hands, having been caught during the raid on the Kshesinskaia mansion. The same day, *Petrogradskaia gazeta*, not to be outdone, supplied its readers with further details. Basing its report on information from Mathilde Kshesinskaia's lawyer, who had rushed to inspect his client's home as soon as it was liberated, the paper revealed that some soldiers from the Volynsky Regiment had recognized Lenin, who was trying to pass as a sailor.

On July 13 Lenin's flight was the center of attention at a meeting of the All-Russian Executive Committees. [54] Coming in the wake of news of still more disasters at the front and increasingly unrestrained activity on the part of rightist organizations hostile to the revolution, this meeting quickly turned into yet another public demonstration of the Soviet's commitment to the Provisional Government and its hostility toward the Bolsheviks. More a political rally than a business session, the meeting began with Kerensky, just back from another trip to the front, delivering an impassioned plea for the Soviet's support and for a decisive break with Bolshevism. This was Kerensky's first appearance in the Taurida Palace since his accession to the post of prime minister, and the galleries were packed for the occasion. Waves of applause greeted the prime minister's appeal, as well as Chkheidze's response: "No sacrifice is too great for the defense of the revolution!" According to news accounts, Kerensky sprang from his chair at this point and embraced Chkheidze. Applause and shouts of "Long live the republic!" and "Three cheers for the motherland!" reverberated in the hall.

As soon as he could be heard above the noise, Fedor Dan rushed forward to speak. "We have already done what Kerensky asks us to do," he declared. "Not only have we delegated full support to the Provisional Government, we insist that the government make use of its power." Dan now proposed a bluntly worded majority-socialist–sponsored resolution accusing the Bolsheviks of crimes against the people and the revolution. The resolution branded Lenin's evasion of arrest "absolutely intolerable," insisted that the Bolshevik fraction initiate a discussion of its leaders' behavior, and provided for the suspension from membership in the Executive Committees of all persons under indictment. In vain Nogin protested. "You are being asked to adopt a resolution regarding the Bolsheviks before they have been tried," he warned. "You are asked to place outside the law the leaders of the fraction that prepared the revolution together with you." Dan's resolution carried by an overwhelming margin, and as the meeting went on, the condemnation of the Bolsheviks became even harsher. To roars of approval and stormy applause from the floor and the gallery, A. A. Bulat, a Trudovik,[55] delivered an emotional speech attacking remarks in defense of the Bolsheviks made by the trade union official David Riazanov moments earlier. Riazanov had drawn a parallel between the Provisional Government's demands for Lenin and the tsarist government's insistence, in June 1907, that the Duma cooperate in placing members of its Social Democratic Party fraction under arrest. Turning first to Tsereteli and then to members of the Bolshevik fraction, Bulat declaimed: "You have the gall to make such an analogy! . . . [You say] now the demand is for Lenin, then it was for Tsereteli. . . . Let me compare how Tsereteli acted then with how Lenin is behaving now. On this very platform Tsereteli came forward and declared for all to hear: We stand for an end to the present regime, for the destruction of the tsarist system, and for the creation of a democratic republic. . . . How is Lenin behaving? The only thing to say to him is 'gutless Lenin!' "

Reports of this sensational meeting appeared in the press on July 14, and on that day as well *Petrogradskaia gazeta* had some fresh news regarding Lenin's location. "Lenin Tracks Found!" proclaimed its headline. "The hiding-place in which Lenin is staying has been definitely established. . . . Lenin fled to Kronstadt through Lisy Nos."[56] The next day *Zhivoe slovo* disclosed that summer residents in Lisy Nos had seen a man resembling Lenin in sailor's clothes get out of a big car and board a cutter bound for Kronstadt on July 5. "At the present moment Lenin is in Stockholm," announced *Gazeta-kopeika* on July 15, quoting "an absolutely impeccable source." On July 15 *Birzhevye vedomosti*, citing "semi-official sources," maintained that Lenin had indeed been in Stockholm. However, with the help of the German ambassador to Sweden and the "not unknown Ganetsky-Furstenberg," he had already resettled in Germany. Finally, on August 8 *Zhivoe slovo* revealed that information placing Lenin in Germany had been planted by the Bolsheviks themselves to throw authorities off the track. "Lenin is actually only a few hours from Petrograd, in Finland," explained the report with somewhat greater accuracy. "Even his house number is known. But making an arrest won't be easy. . . . Lenin has a powerful, highly armed bodyguard."

Reading such farfetched reports in his hut at Razliv, Lenin often became convulsed with laughter.[57] But for the most part, during the remainder of July and the beginning of August the Petrograd newspapers must have been anything but pleasant reading. Maria Sulimova, a Bolshevik staff worker

ЛЕНИНЪ ВЪ РОЛИ НИКОЛАЯ II

НА УЛИЦАХЪ ПЕТРОГРАДА 3, 4, 5, 6 и 7 ІЮЛЯ.
Ленинъ:—Мнѣ не жаль русской кров и...; Лишь бы золото въ карманахъ звенѣло.

Cartoon from *Petrogradskaia gazeta*, July 8, 1917, headed "Lenin in the Role of Nicholas II." The caption reads: "On the streets of Petrograd 3, 4, 5, 6, and 7 July. Lenin: 'I don't mind spilling Russian blood . . . so long as there's gold jingling in my pockets.' " (An exact copy, redrawn for this volume.)

with whom Lenin stayed on July 6, recalls that when she brought Lenin up to date on the news, he reflected: "You, comrade Sulimova, they might arrest. But me, they will hang." Lenin expressed similar apprehension in a note he scribbled to Kamenev: *"Entre nous,* if they do me in, please publish my notebook, 'Marxism and the State.' "[58]

The memoirs of Shotman and Zinoviev provide valuable glimpses into Lenin's state of mind during this period. Shotman remembered that for a time Lenin exaggerated the scope and impact of the reaction and was pessimistic about the short-term prospects for revolution in Russia. There was no use talking further about a Constituent Assembly, Lenin felt, because the "victors" would not convene it; the party ought therefore to marshal what strength it had left and go underground "seriously and for a long time." The dismal reports that Shotman initially passed to Lenin in Razliv reinforced these convictions; it was several weeks before the news began to improve.[59]

Lenin's pessimism in the wake of the July days is confirmed by Zinoviev. Writing in the late twenties, he recalled that at the time Lenin assumed that a longer and deeper period of reaction lay ahead than actually turned out to be the case.

Even socialist newspapers were full of outlandish stories about the conspiracy of July 3–5 and about Lenin himself. Such a sea of lies and slander was never thrown at any other man in the world. Lenin's espionage, his connections with the German General Staff, his receipt of funds, etc., were the subjects of articles, poems, and cartoons. It is difficult to transmit the feeling we experienced when it became clear that the "Dreyfus" case was a reality, that lies and slander were being spread in millions of copies and circulated to every village, to every workshop. . . . But although the lies kept snowballing, there was no way to respond. The enemy became ever more insolent and inventive. . . . Already the slander had spread to the far corners of the country and throughout the world. . . . These were dark, difficult days.[60]

·3·

PETROGRAD
DURING THE REACTION

The great contrast between the political atmosphere prevailing in Petrograd before the July crisis and the dominant mood in its aftermath was nowhere more evident than in an event of otherwise minor importance—the government-sponsored funeral of seven cossacks killed fighting insurgents at the height of the July days.[1]

Saturday, July 15, was the day designated by the Provisional Government to pay tribute to the slain cossacks; several days before, government officials, the central Soviet organs, the Provisional Committee of the State Duma, and the Petrograd City Duma (municipal council) began working to stimulate public interest in the event, viewed by its sponsors as yet another means of further discrediting the Bolsheviks and demonstrating support for law and order. On behalf of the City Duma, Grigorii Shreider, the mayor of Petrograd, appealed to "all those loyal to the revolution and all those infused with its spirit" to pay homage to the fallen cossacks. Meanwhile, the Central Executive Committee directed that every factory in the capital appoint a thirty-man delegation to participate in the funeral. Fearing a repetition of the June 18 fiasco, the committee ordered workers not to carry banners or placards.

To judge by press accounts of the funeral itself, efforts to mobilize a big crowd for the occasion were highly successful. *Golos soldata* reported that by early morning Nevsky Prospect had already taken on "a very special appearance." Although few shops opened for business, people were everywhere about. The crowds were packed tightest in the area near St. Isaac's, Petrograd's largest cathedral, where the main services were to take place. Crowds also lined the route along which the cortege was to travel, from the cathedral to the Alexander Nevsky monastery where the dead cossacks were to be interred.

Throughout the previous night townspeople, along with relatives and friends of the slain cossacks, had waited in long lines outside St. Isaac's for their turn to pay their last respects. Inside the vast candle-lit cathedral the dead cossacks lay in state in open, white caskets, while stern-faced cossacks stood guard over their fallen comrades. Once admitted to the cathedral, many of the mourners remained there for the rest of the night, so that by early morning the church was filled to capacity and further entry was barred except to invited dignitaries. These began to arrive well before the requiem service was scheduled to start. Representatives of the various diplomatic missions in Russia, among them David Francis of the United States, Joseph Noulens of France, and George Buchanan of England, each accompanied by a military attaché in dress uniform, took their places alongside members of the Russian cabinet, the majority socialist leadership of the Soviet, officials of the zemstvo and city administrations, representatives of the merchant and industrial estates, emissaries from each cossack force in Russia and from every unit in the Petrograd garrison, and delegations from major factories in the capital as well as from a host of lesser groups and organizations.

Shortly before 10:00 A.M., Kerensky appeared in the cathedral. Reportedly looking pale and nervous (he was just then at a most difficult juncture in his efforts to form a government), he watched as the former court cappella, the combined St. Isaac's and Kazan cathedral choirs, and the personal choir of the metropolitan filed to places reserved for them. The cathedral became hushed as the archbishop of Petrograd, followed by the exarch of the Georgian Orthodox Church and the members of the Holy Synod, ascended the platform before the altar to begin the requiem. At the start of the service, a procession of dignitaries laid wreaths of bright summer flowers at the foot of the caskets. Among the first to come forward was a delegation of cossacks bearing a floral tribute inscribed: "To those who loyally did their duty and died at the hands of German agents." They were followed by the Kadet leaders Fedor Rodichev, Pavel Miliukov, and Vasilii Maklakov, who carried a large wreath beribboned in green and bearing the legend: "To the loyal sons of free Russia who fell in the struggle against traitors to their country." An approving observer from *Zhivoe slovo* reported that when the hundreds of voices of the combined choirs broke the silence to entone a solemn hymn, the entire congregation dropped to its knees. In this moving service the prominent Kadet Ariadna Tyrkova professed to have heard the voice of Russia itself.

The requiem lasted nearly three hours. At its close, guards replaced and screwed down the casket lids. The caskets were then carried by selected high officials to the square outside the cathedral, where cossack and dragoon units, regiments of the Petrograd garrison, several military bands, and a detachment of trumpeters were massed for the procession to the Alexander Nevsky Monastery. As the first of the caskets, borne by cabinet ministers led by Kerensky, appeared from inside the cathedral, the commander of the Petrograd Military District ordered: "Present arms!" Regimental banners fluttered in a soft breeze from the Neva while a single trumpeter played taps. Then the air was rent by the loud boom of ceremonial cannon at the Peter and Paul Fortress. The polished sabers of the cossacks gleamed in the bright sun, and at an officer's command a forest of bayonets rose and sprang back in salute. Kerensky stepped forward. "Citizens!" he thundered,

> Citizens, we are sharing a rare, sad, historical moment. . . . Every one of us must bow before the heroes who fell on the streets of the capital in the struggle for our homeland, for freedom, and for the honest name of a Russian citizen. On behalf of the government, I say to you that the Russian state is going through a terrible moment. It is closer to destruction than ever before in its history. . . . Before all of you I openly declare that all attempts to foment anarchy and disorder regardless of where they come from will be dealt with mercilessly. . . . Before the bodies of the fallen, I beseech you to swear that along with us you will work to save the state and freedom.

Raising his right hand, Kerensky shouted, "I pledge this!" There was a brief silence, then thousands of hands shot into the air and a roar erupted from the crowd: "We swear it!" Those nearest Kerensky lifted him on to their shoulders and carried him to a waiting automobile.

The cortege started forward. The bells of St. Isaac's tolled as the bands played the majestic anthem "How Glorious Is Our God in Zion." Leading

The funeral of seven cossacks killed in Petrograd during the July days. Government ministers and State Duma deputies follow the caskets.

the procession were the trumpeters, who were followed by a cossack squadron carrying pikes tied with black bunting; priests in flowing black robes bearing tall crosses, church banners, and incense burners; several rows of choirboys; high dignitaries of the church; and the St. Isaac's and metropolitan's choirs. The remains of the slain cossacks were borne on seven horse-drawn gun carriages. A riderless horse ambled behind each of the first six carriages. Seated in the saddle of the mount behind the last carriage was a thin-faced boy of about ten—the son of the slain cossack —wearing the distinctive dark blue uniform trimmed with maroon of the Don Cossacks. Bringing up the rear of the long cortege were government and Soviet officials, followed by the delegations that had attended the ceremony and seemingly endless ranks of military troops.

As the head of the procession turned from Morskaia Street into Nevsky Prospect, bells at several neighboring churches began to toll, adding their peals to those from St. Isaac's. When the procession reached the Kazan Cathedral itself, it halted for a brief service, a procedure that was repeated in front of the Znamensky Church. With these interruptions, the cortege did not reach its destination until late afternoon. Remarkably, the time passed without incident.

Observers of the cossacks' funeral could not but have contrasted that occasion with the antigovernment demonstrations of the preceding months. On July 15 there were few workers to be seen, and, as one reporter noted, "the military bands did not play the 'Marseillaise' once all the way to the cemetery." A commentator in *Rech'* on July 16 expressed great pleasure at what this outpouring of public sympathy for the slain cossacks suggested about the apparent transformation in the popular mood. "The days July 3–5 had thrust all the stench stored up over many months into the streets and revealed in all its horror and repulsiveness where the unrestricted sway of 'insurgent lackeys' and 'drunk helots' led," he wrote. "July 15 demonstrated what a healthy core had made its appearance, once the logic of the revolution caused this shady scum to be expelled." The cossacks' funeral was thus both a sad and a joyous occasion, the writer in *Rech'* concluded—sad for the losses mourned and joyous because Russia could now embark on a period of "national rejuvenation."

What was most astounding about the post–July days reaction in Petrograd was how quickly the prevailing political climate appeared to have shifted. One newspaper reporter observed at the time, "The difference in mood between July 4 and 5 is so enormous, it is misleading to refer to it as a change—it is as if one had suddenly been transported from one city to another and found oneself amidst different people and different moods."[2] Many years later the left Menshevik Vladimir Woytinsky remembered July 5, when the streets of Petrograd became the scene of "a counterrevolutionary orgy" and "the debauchery of the Black Hundreds threatened to destroy the victory over the insurgents," as one of the saddest days of his life.[3]

As early as July 6 the All-Russian Executive Committees warned that the illegal arrests and the violent acts carried out in retaliation against the intimidation of July 3–4 constituted a grave threat to the revolution (that is, to the repudiation of tsarism and to the establishment of a permanent democratic political system). A session of the Petrograd City Duma on July 7 was continually interrupted by reports of trouble throughout the city. A Menshevik deputy declared, "Citizens who look like workers or who are suspected of being Bolsheviks are in constant danger of being beaten." "Quite intelligent people are conducting ultra–anti-Semitic agitation," volunteered another deputy. Responding to such reports, the City Duma deputies agreed to prepare a public condemnation of street violence. Published the next day, the statement cautioned the public against falling prey to "irresponsible agitators who, placing all the blame for the calamities being endured by the country on either the Jews, the bourgeoisie, or the workers, are instilling extremely dangerous thoughts in the minds of the aroused masses."[4]

In the Petrograd press of this period there appeared a rash of reports regarding a sudden burst of activity on the part of extreme rightist groups. Among these organizations, apparently one of the most active was a group called Holy Russia, which, according to a story in *Izvestiia*, operated out of a book store on Pushkin Street.[5] Holy Russia published its own one-page weekly newspaper, *Groza* (Thunderstorm), which heaped blame for all of Russia's ills on non-Russians, especially Jews, as well as on socialists, liberals, the bourgeoisie, and the proletariat. According to *Groza*, only Tsar Nicholas II was capable of furnishing bread and peace to the Russian people; only he could save the country from total ruin.[6] There were also frequent press reports of pogromist street agitation. *Petrogradskii listok*, for example, carried an account of a street-corner rally at which several speakers appealed to listeners to "smash the Jews and the bourgeoisie because they are responsible for the murderous war." One speaker put particular emphasis on "Jewish domination of the central organs of the Russian democracy." The assembled crowd would not disperse until broken up by a detachment of soldiers and militiamen.[7]

At about this time several local Bolshevik Party offices were raided and wrecked. During the afternoon of July 9, for instance, soldiers raided party headquarters in the Liteiny District. The same evening Bolshevik headquarters in the Petrograd District was attacked by "one hundred military school cadets arriving in four trucks and an armored car." Three party members in the headquarters were arrested and some money was seized by the cadets. Coming across the rubles, one of the cadets inquired incredulously, "Is this German money?"[8] Not only Jews and Bolsheviks but also nonparty labor organizations and Menshevik and SR groups felt the impact of this kind of action. Thus the Trud publishing house, which printed much trade union as well as exclusively Bolshevik material, was wrecked on July 5. A few days later the headquarters of the metalworkers' union, the largest labor union in Russia, was also raided.[9] A local Menshevik office that happened to adjoin the Bolshevik headquarters in the Petrograd District was wrecked when the latter was raided on July 9.[10] Office personnel had already left for the day.

During these days several moderate socialist officials were less successful in escaping blows aimed primarily at the Bolsheviks. Thus a Trudovik representative on the Central Executive Committee was badly beaten and briefly jailed for publicly urging that people refrain from referring to Lenin as a spy until his case had been properly investigated.[11] And on July 5 Mark Liber, one of the most influential Mensheviks in the Soviet and an arch-critic of the Bolsheviks as well, was arrested by soldiers who mistook him for Zinoviev.[12]

During these same days, Iurii Steklov (a prominent radical Social Democrat with close ties to Bolshevik moderates) encountered such difficulties not once, but three times. The night of July 7 his apartment was raided by a detachment from the Petrograd Military District. Steklov immediately phoned Kerensky, who arrived on the scene and persuaded the soldiers to leave Steklov alone. Later, however, a crowd of private citizens and soldiers, indignant that the first raiding party had come away empty-handed, gathered at Steklov's door bent on lynching him. Once more, Kerensky was summoned, and again he hurried over and freed Steklov, this time seeing to it that Steklov left the premises. Evidently in part to avoid such harassment, Steklov left the capital the next afternoon for a few days at his summer home in Finland. Yet this proved no escape. Steklov's cottage neighbored that of Bonch-Bruevich, where Lenin had been staying on the eve of the July days. During the night of July 10 military cadets, looking for Lenin and not finding him at Bonch-Bruevich's, moved on to search Steklov's home, grabbed Steklov, and forced him to return to Petrograd. In reference to such incidents the *Izvestiia* of the Moscow Soviet commented ruefully, "The cadets are not very knowledgeable about our differences."[13]

On July 18 the Provisional Committee of the Duma held a sensational, widely publicized meeting, yet another barometer of the times. During the February days, deputies to the State Duma had created the Provisional Committee to help restore order. Along with the Executive Committee of the Petrograd Soviet, this committee had played a prominent role in the formation of the first Provisional Government. Subsequently, relatively little was heard from the Provisional Committee; its fifty or sixty active members, headed by Mikhail Rodzianko, seemed content to hold periodic unofficial discussions of governmental problems and, with less frequency, to issue pronouncements on political questions about which they felt strongly. During the early summer, however, as liberal and conservative members of the committee reacted to attacks from the left and to the government's obvious incapacity to deal with outstanding problems, the committee's meetings and pronouncements became increasingly militant. In the wake of developments in June and July, more than a few deputies became convinced that the Duma's complicity in the overthrow of the old regime had been a tragic error and that the Russian state was on the brink of destruction. Quite a number of deputies now also came to believe that the Duma, Russia's sole legally elected representative body, was duty bound to try to save the country by helping to create a powerful government free of leftist influence.

This view was forcefully expressed on July 18 at a meeting of the Provisional Committee convened to formulate a public declaration on the existing political situation and, more fundamentally, to discuss the Duma's course of action.[14] At this meeting, two rightist deputies, A. M. Maslenikov and Vladimir Purishkevich, the latter best known for his involvement in the assassination of Rasputin, went furthest in attacking the prevailing situation.

Maslenikov placed most of the blame for the tragedies befalling Russia on the leaders of the Soviet, whom he called "dreamers," "lunatics passing themselves off as pacifists," "petty careerists," and "a group of fanatics, transients, and traitors." (Maslenikov implied that those involved were mostly Jews, and he made no distinction between moderate socialists and Bolsheviks.) To the approval of many deputies, he proposed that the full Duma be convened in official session and demanded that all cabinet members report to it for a complete accounting. The Duma could then determine how the government should be reconstructed and what policies it should follow. "The State Duma is a trench defending the honor, the dignity, and the existence of Russia," he concluded. "In this trench we will either win or die."

Purishkevich voiced complete agreement with Maslenikov and expressed particular bitterness toward all those who continued to concern themselves with the defense of the revolution at a time when, in his words, "Every patriot ought to be shouting from every rooftop: 'Save Russia, save the motherland!' She is poised on the edge of ruin more because of internal enemies than because of the foreign foe." According to Purishkevich, what the country needed most was a strong voice to sound the alarm about the misfortunes befalling Russia, as well as liberal use of the noose. "If a thousand, two thousand, perhaps five thousand scoundrels at the front and several dozen in the rear had been done away with," he declared, "we would not have suffered such an unprecedented disgrace." To restrict hanging to the front, he contended, referring to the reimposition of the death penalty there, made no sense at all; rather, "it is necessary to eradicate the sources of trouble, not merely its consequences." Like Maslenikov, Purishkevich viewed the activity of the Soviet as wholly pernicious and looked to the Duma "to speak out sternly and powerfully and to mete out proper punishment to all who had earned it." "Long live the State Duma," shouted Purishkevich emotionally toward the end of his speech. "It is the only organ capable of saving Russia. . . . And let all the sinister forces that cling to the Provisional Government be destroyed. . . . These forces are led by people who have nothing in common with the peasantry, the soldiers, or the workers, and who fish in troubled waters alongside provocateurs maintained by the German emperor."

Despite the strong rhetoric by Maslenikov and Purishkevich, the public appeal for firm government (free of Soviet influence) and for total commitment to the war effort that the Provisional Committee subsequently adopted was moderate in tone. Moreover, the committee rejected the notion of attempting to convene the full Duma "to mete out punishment"; a majority of the deputies apparently agreed with Miliukov's conclusion that such a step was inappropriate.

Nonetheless, for the left and especially for the Bolsheviks these were indeed difficult days, subsequently remembered by many revolutinary veterans as perhaps the roughest in the history of the party. In some early memoirs of this period, Alexander Ilin-Zhenevsky, an editor of *Soldatskaia pravda*, recorded the problems he encountered searching for a press willing to print Bolshevik publications. Sent away with insults wherever he went, often even before identifying himself, he recalled wondering whether one could tell a Bolshevik by his looks.[15] The Kronstadt Bolshevik Ivan Flerovsky described a walk that he and Lunacharsky had taken together on July 5. On Nevsky Prospect, just below the Anichkov Bridge, Flerovsky was "grabbed by a fellow wearing a cross of St. George in his lapel who was screaming, 'Here they are . . . anarchists . . . this one is from Kronstadt!' " A hostile mob at once surrounded Flerovsky and Lunacharsky and dragged them off to General Staff headquarters. In his memoirs Flerovsky relates in some detail the harrowing moments that ensued. The square separating the headquarters from the Winter Palace was in use at the time as a staging and billeting area for military forces mobilized by the government to restore order. It was crammed with pup tents, machine guns, artillery pieces, and stacked rifles. As Flerovsky and Lunacharsky were led through the area, crowds of milling, restless soldiers shook their fists menacingly and shouted obscenities at the pair of "German agents."[16]

Bolshevik newspapers of the post–July days period contain numerous accounts of the indignities suffered by suspected leftists. On July 14, for example, *Proletarskoe delo*[17] printed an anguished letter from two imprisoned sailors, Aleko Fadeev and Mikhail Mikhailov:

> On July 7 at 9:00 A.M. we set out to return to our units in Kronstadt when we were suddenly apprehended by a detachment of cadets and taken to General Staff headquarters. . . . While we were being led through the streets, the intelligentsia pounced on us, determined to kill us. Some of the attackers said scandalous things about us, that we were German agents.

. . . When we passed the naval staff building, even the doorman there begged our guard to line us up on the bank and shoot us. . . . Just as we arrived at headquarters . . . another convoy drew up with ten people under arrest. All had been beaten up and blood was streaming from their faces.

Many of those detained in this way were questioned and soon released. Some, however, spent weeks and even months in prison. Trotsky, who was imprisoned in the Crosses, described his encounters with some of these prisoners. One worker, Anton Ivashin, was beaten up and arrested in a public bath. Ivashin came to grief when, overhearing some dragoons newly arrived from the front talking about how the Petrograd garrison was receiving money from the Germans, he interrupted his scrubbing to inquire whether the soldiers had actually seen any evidence. He was immediately hauled off to jail. Another of Trotsky's fellow prisoners, Ivan Piskunov, was arrested for an equally careless remark. Chancing to come upon a street rally and hearing a soldier affirm that six thousand rubles had been found in the pockets of a rebel soldier killed in the July days, he barely managed to blurt, "That can't be!" before he was pummelled and dragged away.[18] While there were frequent incidents of this kind during the post–July days reaction, what seems most remarkable is that only one Bolshevik, Ivan Voinov, a twenty-three-year-old helper in the *Pravda* circulation room, was killed. On July 6, Voinov was arrested while distributing copies of *Listok pravdy*. While he was being transported for interrogation, one of his captors struck him on the head with a saber; the young Bolshevik died instantly.[19]

It is difficult to estimate the number of Bolsheviks incarcerated in the aftermath of the July uprising, in part because many of those arrested were soon released and hence are not counted in available published sources, and also because political prisoners were held in many places of detention scattered throughout the capital. Roughly thirty "politicals," among them Petr Dashkevich, Nikolai Krylenko, I. U. Kudelko, Mikhail Ter-Arutuniants, Osvald Dzenis, Nikolai Vishnevetsky, and Iurii Kotsiubinsky, all military officers and the cream of Military Organization unit-level garrison leadership, were held in the First District Militia headquarters. Ilin-Zhenevsky, who often passed the building, later recalled seeing the familiar faces of his former close associates peering through the barred windows of their cells; catching sight of him, they would smile and wave.[20]

About 150 prisoners, a large percentage of them Kronstadt sailors indiscriminately rounded up in the streets, were held in the Second District Militia headquarters. The Crosses held 131 "politicals," many of whom were suspected extreme leftists netted in the streets, often merely for a loose word. In the Crosses, too, were some of the government's most prized prisoners—including Trotsky, Kamenev, Lunacharsky, Raskolnikov, Vasilii Sakharov, Roshal, Remnev, and Khaustov; some of the soldiers of the First Machine Gun Regiment who had initially triggered the July days; and Antonov-Ovseenko, Dybenko, and Khovrin of Tsentrobalt. Female prisoners, including the notorious Kollontai, were jailed in the Vyborg District hard-labor prison for women; twenty Bolsheviks were kept in the Transfer Prison; and over a dozen party members, presumably those requiring medical treatment, were held in the Nikolaevsky Military Hospital.[21]

The regime in these places of detention varied considerably. Nonetheless, except perhaps for the food, conditions in all of them were a good deal less oppressive than in tsarist days. While the staff in most prisons included a significant percentage of holdovers from before the February revolution, even these veterans now tended to be relatively lenient. Raskolnikov recalled that many of his guards at the Crosses were cautious toward, indeed even fearful of, "politicals." After all, following the February revolution, yesterday's high officials suddenly turned up in jail, while some of the previous inmates instantly became cabinet ministers. Prison personnel were naturally wary of such a turnabout happening again.[22]

Bolsheviks in common cells holding several inmates were also relatively well off. The prisoners who suffered most in the aftermath of the July days were those held in the Second District Militia headquarters, where overcrowding was a problem, and those particularly notorious figures, among them Raskolnikov, Trotsky, Kamenev, and Lunacharsky, who were initially kept in solitary confinement in the Crosses.[23]

Treatment of the imprisoned Bolsheviks shifted with the prevailing political winds. Thus the going was roughest for "politicals" just after the July days, when the Provisional Government appeared potentially strong and when it seemed as if the Bolsheviks were permanently crushed. When the fortunes of the party began to recover, the prison regime became noticeably freer. After a few weeks, Raskolnikov, for one, was removed from solitary confinement and was amazed to find that the doors to cells in the Crosses were now kept open throughout the day. "With the beginning of this open-door policy," he wrote, "individual cells were transformed into Jacobin clubs. Moving from one cell to another in noisy groups, we argued, played chess, and shared what we read in the papers." Recalling significant differences of opinion among his fellow prisoners, Raskolnikov observed that while all prisoners had faith in the ultimate triumph of the proletariat, in contrast to prerevolutionary days—when political prisoners were, typically, ideologically well-grounded, professional revolutionaries—a significant number of his comrades in the Crosses were youthful, recent converts to the Bolshevik cause. As a consequence, there were frequent, fierce debates about revolutionary tactics between impatient hotheads who believed the party had made a grievous error in not trying to take power in July, and older, experienced, more disciplined Bolsheviks who defended the tactics of the Central Committee. When Raskolnikov insisted that power could not be seized until a majority of workers supported the Bolsheviks, the hotheads countered that an energetic revolutionary vanguard could seize power on its own in the interest of the working class. Raskolnikov adds that while Trotsky had fully supported the cautious policy of the Central Committee during the July days, now, sitting in jail, he occasionally had second thoughts. "Perhaps we should have given it a try. What if the front had supported us? Then everything would have turned out differently." But these impetuous thoughts inevitably gave way very quickly to a more logical analysis of the prevailing correlation of forces.[24]

Almost all jailed rebels were allowed writing materials, and many took advantage of lax security to send petitions, articles, and messages to the world outside. Some prisoners, Roshal for one, used this time to begin writing memoirs. Among the inmates of the Crosses, the most prolific author appears to have been Trotsky. Taking time out only for daily walks, he remained rooted to his desk, writing political pamphlets and preparing daily articles for the Bolshevik press.

A week after his arrest, Kamenev drew up a personal appeal to the Central Executive Committee for help in expediting the proceedings against him:

> I turned myself over to the courts because I had faith . . . that the authorities would present the accusations against me without delay and that I would have full opportunity to explain myself. Instead, a whole week has gone by and I still have not seen a single representative of the court authorities. . . . Meanwhile my being locked up has deprived me of the ability to wage a public struggle against the vile slander concerning my connection with German money. . . . I want to think that the Soviet will not force me to acknowledge that those of my comrades who failed to obey its directives [to submit to the authorities] acted more wisely than I.[25]

Somewhat later, a group of political prisoners identifying themselves only as "soldiers thrown into prison" formulated an appeal to "comrade cyclists and soldiers of other military units that have arrived from the front": "You, dear comrades, know that our comrade workers and soldiers have been in Petrograd prisons without trials for more than a month. . . . Do you know that many of our comrade soldiers and workers are charged with being traitors merely because they had the courage to call themselves Bolsheviks? It is painful for us if you are aware of this and remain silent . . . [but] we do not believe this to be the case. . . . We believe you are already on our side, that you sympathize with us, and that you will come to help us."[26] There is no record of any response to such appeals.

Naturally, Bolsheviks who still had their freedom did what they could to help arrested comrades, mobilizing public concern for their plight and maintaining the strongest possible pressure upon the government to release them. The Bolshevik Petersburg Committee created a special organization, the "Proletarian Red Cross," to collect funds for prisoners and their families; mutual aid organizations were also established at the district level.[27]

After several weeks of detention and increasing signs of a possible rightist coup, the patience of some prisoners reached the breaking point, despite improving conditions of confinement. What appears to have oppressed prisoners most was the government's desultoriness in handling their cases—in particular, in questioning and formally indicting them. Condemnation as German agents also enraged each and every prisoner, including the usually very controlled Trotsky. "Within our stone cells this slander pressed in on us like a wave of suffocating gas," one prisoner subsequently related.[28]

The inmates' growing frustration was reflected in their increasingly bitter letters and declarations, which appeared prominently in the leftist press. On August 2 political prisoners in the Second District Militia headquarters hit on a new way to protest their treatment, declaring a hunger strike. This action ended three days later, after representatives of the Central Executive Committee guaranteed that the prisoners' cases would be attended to without further delay and that individuals against whom there were no specific charges would soon be released.[29] Beginning in mid-August, inmates at the Second District Militia headquarters were gradually freed, and in due course this success stimulated a wave of hunger strikes at other prisons. In time these protests would arouse the sympathy of a major segment of the Petrograd population. For the moment, however, only a very small percentage of jailed Bolsheviks were actually set free.

·4·

THE INEFFECTIVENESS
OF REPRESSION

Viewing the apparent swing in sentiment against the Bolsheviks and the seemingly decisive steps taken by the Provisional Government to restore order in the immediate wake of the July uprising, many contemporary observers were inclined to believe, wishfully no doubt, that the Bolsheviks had incurred a fatal defeat. As one newspaper editor wrote confidently at the time: "The Bolsheviks are compromised, discredited, and crushed. More than that, they have been expelled from Russian life, their teaching has turned out to be an irreversible failure, and has scandalized itself and its believers before the world and for all time."[1] And as another writer, a Kadet, put it: "The Bolsheviks are hopelessly compromised. . . . Bolshevism has died a sudden death. . . . [It] has turned out to be a bluff inflated with Germany money."[2]

With the benefit of hindsight, one can see that those who facilely wrote off Bolshevism as a potent political force in the mid-summer of 1917 failed completely to take account of the basic concerns and great potential power of the Petrograd masses and of the enormous attraction that a revolutionary political and social program like that of the Bolsheviks held for them. At the same time, such people were obviously misled by the torrent of tough-sounding decrees emanating from the Winter Palace; they read into the actions of the Provisional Government a singleness of purpose and degree of strength and effectiveness that it simply did not possess. Kerensky's flaming hard-line rhetoric notwithstanding, almost none of the major repressive measures adopted by the cabinet during this period either was fully implemented or successfully achieved its objectives. The policy of getting arms and ammunition out of the hands of civilians, for example, encountered early obstacles and was not pursued for long. Similarly, only the First Machine Gun Regiment, the 180th Infantry Regiment, and the Grenadier Regiment, among the many units of the Petrograd garrison in which Bolsheviks had a strong foothold, were effectively disarmed. While considerable numbers of personnel from radicalized units were transferred to the front in late July and August, none of these units, contrary to the original intention, were completely liquidated. As for the government's avowed aim of arresting and quickly bringing to trial leaders and supporters of the July insurrection, although many Bolsheviks were jailed after the rebellion's collapse, most of the Petrograd party organization's roughly thirty-two thousand members were not disturbed by the authorities. Those leftists actually jailed were not formally indicted for some time, if at all, and the October revolution intervened before any of them were brought to trial.

Various factors contributed to this state of affairs. The Provisional Government's fundamental weakness and lack of credibility among the masses were probably the main reasons for its lack of success in disarming civilians. The official justification for requisitioning weapons was that soldiers under attack at the front badly needed them; actually, the government's main concern in taking this action was to lessen the danger of renewed civil strife by confiscating hand guns, rifles, and machine guns which workers had acquired during the February days and which they had used in July to terrorize the government and the Soviet. The central Soviet organs endorsed this effort. But most factory workers, suspicious of the government's intentions and alarmed over what they perceived to be the mounting danger of counterrevolution, would have none of it. Although some civilians obediently turned in weapons immediately after publication of government orders to this effect, it soon became apparent that most workers possessing arms were unwilling to surrender them peacefully. Government troops consequently raided factories and offices of leftist supporters in which arms were believed to be hidden. More often than not these fishing expeditions failed to turn up weapons, and they were discontinued toward the end of July. Their main result was to exacerbate relations between factory workers and the authorities.

That many strongly Bolshevik-influenced military units managed to avoid disarmament was probably partly a result of the fact that they publicly repudiated their previous behavior and adopted fervent pledges of loyalty to the new Kerensky regime as soon as the latter's plans concerning the garrison became known. That the government's plan of transferring Bolshevized troops out of the capital was only partially realized was in part because front commanders had headaches enough as it was and were understandably reluctant to accept such unreliable reinforcements. Additionally, making a fair determination of which troops among the 215,000 to 300,000 soldiers of the Petrograd garrison actually deserved to be punished by shipment to the front was no easy matter. Even in the most belligerent regiments, only a very small proportion of soldiers had consciously acted to overthrow the government in July. The command of the Petrograd Military District was disorganized, and inevitably many largely blameless units were summarily punished by shipment out of the capital, while some troops that had mutinied in July were still in Petrograd in October.

The fact that only a small percentage of Bolshevik leaders were arrested after the July days was due partly to the All-Russian Executive Committees' stubborn insistence that action be taken only against individuals, not against whole political groups. Of course, the Provisional Government did not contain any Cavaignacs; this was in part because cabinet ministers were justifiably apprehensive about the government's ability to control the massive protest that an officially sponsored, indiscriminate attack on the left was bound to stimulate. To be sure, at the height of the reaction that followed the July days, some leftist institutions were subjected to military attack. Present-day Soviet historians view these assaults as part of a deliberate, all-out campaign by the government to crush the entire Bolshevik organization and the militant labor movement generally. Yet this interpretation does not withstand careful scrutiny. When each of the major post-July military attacks on the left is examined closely, one finds that with a few exceptions (among the most prominent of which were the government's raids on the Kshesinskaia mansion and the offices of *Pravda*), this or that attack on a district Bolshevik committee or nonparty labor organization or factory either was directly connected to government attempts to confiscate weapons or was undertaken at the initiative of some zealous, anonymous, second-level official, often a holdover from the tsarist regime, without the approval of higher authorities.

This was the case with the July 9 raid on Bolshevik headquarters in the downtown Liteiny District. Several days before this attack, the Liteiny District Committee had unwittingly moved into new quarters in a building also housing a regional counterintelligence office. As far as the personnel in this office were concerned, every Bolshevik was a German agent; acting on their own, they picked the next Sunday to forcibly evict their new neighbors.[3] Similarly, the same day's raid on Bolshevik Party headquarters in the Petrograd District, which ended with the wrecking of a neighboring Menshevik office, was initiated and led by junior officers attached to the Petrograd Military District. Probing by reporters later revealed that the attack force did not have a warrant, and spokesmen for the government and even General Polovtsev himself denied prior knowledge of the operation.[4]

Raids in the suburb of Sestroretsk at this time were also apparently the result of an excess of zeal on the part of lower-level military personnel. When members of a local hunting club at Sestroretsk took some pot shots at camping soldiers, the soldiers jumped to the conclusion that factory workers were responsible and reported as much to the headquarters of the Petrograd Military District. General Polovtsev responded by ordering his troops to disarm some worker detachments known to exist in the Sestroretsk factory. Although this occurred before publication of the Provisional Government's orders regarding the turning in of weapons, the commander of the force sent to the Sestroretsk factory announced that all weapons in the hands of civilians, regardless of whether or not they belonged to the worker detachments, were to be confiscated. Moreover, despite the fact that large quantities of arms and ammunition were turned in, government troops arrested seven leftist organizers and searched and wrecked scores of private apartments and labor organization offices in the town of Sestroretsk itself.[5] Evidently because General Polovtsev could not or, more likely, would not control the frequent excesses of his subordinates, he was relieved of command at the Central Executive Committee's insistence on July 13.[6]

Why it took so long to indict Bolsheviks arrested after the July uprising and why not one was tried are complex questions. There is, first of all, the problem of why the government did not actively prosecute cases in connection with the German-agent charges. Several related factors may have been responsible for this. Though it is now evident that funds from German sources were funneled to the Bolsheviks during the revolutionary period, we know that at the time of the July uprising, the government's case was far from complete. Then, too, Lenin—the central figure in the alleged conspiracy—was never caught. Many of those arrested after the July days were picked up and imprisoned merely for a loose word; prosecuting them could have led only to embarrassment for the government.

Charges of complicity in organizing an insurrection leveled against many jailed lower-level Bolshevik leaders, particularly those from the Military Organization, were based on significantly more solid grounds; published portions of the official inquiry into the background and development of the July uprising indicate that the government had gathered a good deal of persuasive evidence of the significant role played by activists from the Military Organization and the Petersburg Committee in its organization and expansion.[7] Why some of these people were not speedily brought to trial is a real puzzle. Part of the explanation may be that their cases became swamped among the many more altogether flimsy ones being pursued at the same time. In addition, many of those Bolsheviks whose important roles in organizing the July uprising could be established most definitely were also accused of the much more difficult to substantiate charge of having conspired with the Germans. No doubt this affected the disposition of their cases.

More fundamentally, what the available evidence reveals most clearly is that the harassed Provisional Government, only five months old, was simply ill-equipped to deal effectively with a judicial problem of this nature and magnitude. In the aftermath of the February days, institutions and procedures had been established to investigate and prosecute officials of the old regime. Not until after the July days, however, was the Provisional Government forced to address itself to the problem of handling a major popular rebellion—appropriate procedures had to be established on a piecemeal, ad hoc basis. Within the cabinet, differences of opinion regarding which statutes of the tsarist criminal code were applicable to the existing situation caused delays. Moreover, while the government had the good judgment to concentrate overall responsibility for investigating and prosecuting accused insurgents in the hands of a single authority (N. S. Karinsky, prosecutor of the Petrograd court of appeals), several subordinate military and civil agencies were also necessarily involved. Coordination between these agencies was either very poor or nonexistent; this caused further confusion and delay.

Then, too, it is well to remember that in the aftermath of the July days, the work of the Provisional Government and of its individual departments was especially disorganized. In retrospect, it is obvious that the government's most crucial problem, if it was to survive, was somehow to ease mass unrest and to deal decisively with the extreme left. But to the harried men of the Provisional Government, this was by no means apparent. As we have seen, from July 2, when the first coalition collapsed, until July 23, when Kerensky finally succeeded in putting together a full cabinet, Russia was without a properly functioning government. It appeared that the Bolsheviks were permanently suppressed and most of Kerensky's time was understandably taken up by political discussions aimed at forming a new coalition and planning for the stabilization of the front. After all-night negotiating sessions in the Winter Palace, Kerensky would leave Petrograd for Mogilev, Pskov, or some other front-line location to consult with his military commanders.

During this period individual ministers were shuffled from cabinet post to cabinet post like cards in a deck. This was the case in the Interior Ministry and the Ministry of Justice, the departments most intimately involved in proceedings relating to the "affair of July 3–5." After Lvov's resignation on July 8, Tsereteli became interior minister; on July 24, he was replaced by Nikolai Avksentiev, who served until the end of August, when he, too, stepped down. At the Ministry of Justice, Ivan Efremov replaced the departed Pereverzev on July 11. In the cabinet announced on July 23, Alexander Zarudny became minister of justice; Zarudny was replaced by Pavel Maliantovich on September 25. The result of these continual ministerial changes was chaos; it could not have been otherwise.

Meanwhile, public demands to do something about imprisoned leftists mounted—from liberals and conservatives, anxious to expose the Bolsheviks fully and without delay, and from socialists, equally determined that the Bolsheviks be either properly indicted and tried or set free. Evidently in the hope of silencing these critics, Karinsky on July 21 released a report on the progress of his inquiry. This report assigned exclusive blame for stimulating, organizing, and directing the July uprising to the Bolsheviks. As regards charges of espionage against the party, the report concluded that, among others, Lenin, Zinoviev, Kollontai, Sakharov, Raskolnikov, and

Kerensky departing for the front.

Roshal had entered into an agreement with Russia's enemies "to assist in the disorganization of the Russian army and the rear . . . ; for this purpose, with the money received from these states they organized an armed insurrection against the existing order."[8] In his report, Karinsky provided only the weakest circumstantial evidence to support these charges, making frequent allusions to more substantial proof which could not then be made public. Predictably, the report triggered an outcry from the left. As *Novaia zhizn'* put it: "It is difficult to understand why instead of an objective account of what happened we get what amounts to an indictment. . . . The conclusions do not follow from the premises. . . . The portions of the report dealing with treason are so ambiguous and superficial, it is staggering to think that they could have been released by the prosecuting authority."[9]

In view of the tendentious nature of Karinsky's report, Martov recommended to the Central Executive Committee that the government be prevailed upon to permit arrested leftists to defend themselves during investigative proceedings. He also urged that an attempt be made to have representatives of the Central Executive Committee included in the government's commission of inquiry. A measure of the great upset triggered by Karinsky's action is the fact that despite dislike for the Bolsheviks and fundamental loyalty to the government, a majority of committee members immediately accepted both recommendations. They also adopted a public statement in which they strongly protested the publication of materials from the preliminary investigation of the July 3–5 cases before the completion of the investigation and condemned "this clear violation of the law" as an ominous sign that the new court system had inherited the worst features of the old tsarist courts. Meanwhile, many of the jailed Bolsheviks had yet even to be formally questioned, and to workers and soldiers their plight became a *cause célèbre*. Whatever opportunity may have existed in the immediate aftermath of the July days to decisively scandalize the Bolsheviks and their cause quickly passed, and the government was forced gradually to release those Bolsheviks in its hands.

The overall ineffectiveness of the government's post–July days attempts to suppress and discredit the Bolsheviks becomes apparent when one examines the condition and activities of the Bolshevik Central Committee, the Petersburg Committee, and the Military Organization during the second half of July and in early August. Of the nine-man Central Committee elected at the April Conference, for example, only Kamenev was behind bars. The necessity of remaining under cover put a severe crimp in the work of Lenin and Zinoviev; still, neither was entirely lost to the party. Zinoviev maintained and indeed soon increased his journalistic endeavors, while Lenin, by means of frequent written dispatches from Razliv and Finland, continued to exert an influence on the formation of Bolshevik policy.[10] Moreover, Iosif Stalin and Iakov Sverdlov, along with the Moscow leaders Felix Dzerzhinsky, Andrei Bubnov, Grigorii Sokolnikov, and Nikolai Bukharin, all of whom were elected to the Central Committee at the end of July, filled the gap left by the absence of top Petrograd Bolshevik officials in jail or in hiding.[11]

Under the coolheaded leadership of Sverdlov, an indefatigable young administrator from the Urals who headed the party secretariat, the Central Committee quietly set itself up for business in a modest apartment outside the center of town. In the mid-1920s, when public criticism of higher party organs was still tolerated, Ilin-Zhenevsky recalled the operation of the Central Committee in this period with undisguised nostalgia:

> Just about every day I used to go [to Central Committee headquarters] . . . and I frequently encountered a serene family scene. Everyone sits at the dining table and drinks tea. On the table, a large samovar steams cozily. L. R. Menzhinskaia [one of the secretaries], a towel over her shoulder,

The Bolshevik Central Committee, elected at the Sixth Congress. Surrounding Lenin in the circle from left to right: Ia. M. Sverdlov, L. D. Trotsky, G. E. Zinoviev, I. V. Stalin, L. B. Kamenev, M. S. Uritsky, A. S. Bubnov, G. Ia. Sokolnikov, F. E. Dzerzhinsky. Behind the circle, bottom row: V. P. Nogin, V. P. Miliutin; second row: A. A. Ioffe, N. N. Krestinsky; third row: I. T. Smilga, F. A. Sergeev; fourth row: E. D. Stasova, G. Lomov, A. I. Rykov, N. I. Bukharin, S. G. Shaumian, A. M. Kollontai. Missing from the picture are Ia. A. Berzin and M. F. Muranov. Ioffe, Stasova, and Lomov were Central Committee candidates.

rinses glasses, wipes them, and pours tea for each arriving comrade. . . . Involuntarily, a comparison with the present headquarters of the Central Committee comes to mind. [We have] a gigantic building with a labyrinth of sections and subsections. Bustling about on every floor are an enormous number of employees, feverishly completing urgent tasks. Naturally, with its functions so expanded today, there is no possibility of the Central

Committee operating in any other way. Still, there is a certain sadness in the fact that the time when simple and unpretentious, yet profoundly comradely and united effort was possible, has gone and will never come again.[12]

During the first weeks following the July uprising, the closure of *Pravda* handicapped the Central Committee's work; not until early August was it able to resume publication of a regular newspaper.[13] Nonetheless, even in mid-July, while the reaction in Petrograd held full sway, Sverdlov felt confident enough of the future to cable party committees in the provinces that "the mood in Piter is hale and hearty. We are keeping our heads. The organization is not destroyed."[14]

On July 13, less than two weeks after the July uprising, the Central Committee managed to convene a secret two-day strategy conference in Petrograd. Bringing together members of the Central Committee, officials of the Military Organization, and representatives of party committees from Petrograd and Moscow,[15] this meeting had as its central purpose the evaluation of changes in the political situation caused by the July uprising and formulation of appropriate tactical directives for the guidance of subordinate party organizations throughout Russia. The conference's importance is attested to by the fact that Lenin prepared, expressly for its consideration, a set of theses on tactics, in which he departed sharply from his pre-July tactical stance.[16] In these theses Lenin argued that the counterrevolution, fully supported by the Mensheviks and SRs, had managed to take full control of the government and the revolution. Not only the moderate socialist parties but also the Soviet had become "mere fig leaves of the counterrevolution."

The perspective for the future outlined by Lenin flowed directly from this assessment of the prevailing situation. Now that the counterrevolution had consolidated itself and the soviets were powerless, there was no longer, in his estimation, any possibility that the revolution might develop peacefully. The party's pre-July orientation toward transfer of power to the soviets and the chief Bolshevik slogan, "All Power to the Soviets," had to be abandoned. The only tactical course left to the party was to prepare for an eventual armed uprising and transfer of power to the proletariat and poorer peasantry. (In conversations with Ordzhonikidze at this time, Lenin spoke of the possibility of a popular rising by September or October and of the need to focus Bolshevik activity in the factory-shop committees. The factory-shop committees, Lenin is quoted by Ordzhonikidze as saying, would have to become insurrectionary organs.)[17]

In order to appreciate the response of participants in the July 13–14 Central Committee conference to Lenin's directives, it is well to bear in mind the following factors. First, while there is evidence that by mid-June (i.e., prior to the July days) Lenin had given up whatever hope he may have had for the transfer of power to the soviets without an armed struggle, it appears that he shared his views in this regard with only a very few closest associates.[18] To the party at large, his efforts to prevent a premature rising during the second half of June conveyed the impression that events had moderated his outlook; thus the ideas expressed in the theses came as a shot out of the blue. Second, the course now envisioned by Lenin inevitably reopened intraparty disputes over fundamental theoretical assumptions which had been papered over at the April Conference and which were to have been thrashed out at the approaching party congress. Finally, as we shall see, Lenin's assessment of the prevailing situation ran counter to the mood and views of many Bolshevik leaders, who, unlike Lenin, could evaluate the impact of the reaction personally and were in touch daily with leaders of left Menshevik and SR factions and the Petrograd masses generally.

No official record of the deliberations of the Bolshevik leadership on July 13–14 has been published. From related contemporary documents we know that Lenin's ideas were the subject of fierce debate.[19] Volodarsky, of the Petersburg Committee, and Nogin and Rykov, from Moscow, took issue with Lenin on "every key issue touched on in the theses."[20] There is also evidence that Zinoviev, who was as vehemently opposed to Lenin's course as were Volodarsky, Nogin, and Rykov, but who was not at the conference, made his views known to the participants in writing.[21] Sverdlov, Viacheslav Molotov, Stalin's future foreign minister, who was then a dour-faced political activist in his mid-twenties, and Saveliev probably spearheaded the fight for the adoption of Lenin's course. When the theses were put to a vote, they were decisively rejected, ten of the fifteen party officials attending the conference voting against them.[22]

The basic differences in outlook between Lenin and the conference majority were reflected in the resolution that the conferees went on to adopt. In contrast to Lenin's view that the moderate socialists had completely sold out to the government and that state power was effectively in the hands of counterrevolutionary capitalists and large landowners, this resolution, while acknowledging that the Kerensky government was a dictatorship, implied that it was not yet fully "under the thumb of the counterrevolution." According to the resolution, the dictatorship of Kerensky, Tsereteli, and Efremov represented (1) the peasant petty bourgeoisie and the portion of the working class that had not yet become disillusioned with petty bourgeois democrats, and (2) the bourgeois and landowning classes. These two sides, the resolution indicated, were still engaged in bargaining with one another. With regard to the Mensheviks and SRs, the resolution stated that by their cowardice and betrayal of the proletariat they were constantly strengthening the position of classes hostile to the revolution. But there was no suggestion that the Mensheviks and SRs were irretrievably lost to the revolutionary cause; in line with this view, the resolution was silent about the need to withdraw the slogan "All Power to the Soviets." Declaring simply that the Kerensky government was incapable of providing solutions to the basic problems of the revolution, the resolution pointed to the need for placing power in the hands of *revolutionary proletarian and peasant soviets* which would take decisive steps to end the war, put a stop to compromises with the bourgeoisie, transfer land to the peasants, establish workers' control in industry and the distribution of goods, and destroy strongholds of the reaction. (Subsequently, Volodarsky remembered that this qualification of the slogan "All Power to the Soviets" was the only concession that he and his followers made to those who demanded that the slogan be scrapped altogether.)[23]

The tasks of the party in the prevailing circumstances, the resolution stated, were to expose each and every sign of counterrevolution, effectively to criticize the reactionary policies of petty bourgeois leaders, to strengthen the position of the revolutionary proletariat and its party wherever possible, and to prepare the forces necessary for a decisive struggle to fulfill the Bolshevik program, if the development of the political crisis in the country permitted this, on a genuinely mass scale.[24] It was a formulation that could mean almost anything. The resolution said nothing about the end of the peaceful period in the development of the revolution or about the need to prepare for an armed uprising. Implicit was the assumption that the party would continue to devote considerable attention to work in the soviets. When this resolution is compared with the course Lenin was advocating, one of the things that emerges most distinctly is the reluctance of its authors to give up the hope of cooperating with other socialist elements to establish a soviet government. This mood is also mirrored in the decision, taken as the July 13–14 meeting adjourned, to invite "internationalists" to participate in the coming party congress with a consultative vote, and even to invite the SRs, presumably to gain a sense of where they stood.[25]

When Lenin learned, on July 15, what had transpired at the Central Committee conference, he reacted with anger and alarm. The current situation was not unlike the one he had encountered at the time of his return to Russia in early April. Once again, he had to counteract a strong impulse within Bolshevik ranks to forego radical revolutionary action and to work closely, if not to merge, with more moderate political groups. Now, however, he was forced to reorient his party's policies from a remote hiding-place twenty miles from Petrograd, without benefit of a regular newspaper.

Lenin responded to the rejection of his theses by the Central Committee conference in a long essay, "On Slogans."[26] Pointedly observing at the outset of this essay that "all too often in the past when history has made a sharp turn, even progressive parties have been unable to adapt quickly to new situations and have repeated slogans that were valid before but had now lost all meaning," he insisted that the slogan "All Power to the Soviets," while valid during the period from February 27 to July 4, had patently lost its usefulness after that date. "Unless this is understood," he warned, "it is impossible to understand anything about the urgent questions of the day." Lenin went on to suggest that the thinking of his adversaries in the party who believed that the SRs and Mensheviks might yet rectify their errors was "childishly naïve," if not "simply stupid." "The people must be told the whole truth," he insisted, "namely that power is in the hands of a military clique of Cavaignacs . . . that power must be overthrown." He added: "Soviets may appear in this revolution, but *not* the present soviets. . . . The present soviets have failed. . . . [They] are like sheep brought to the slaughterhouse, bleating pitifully under the knife." Declaring toward the close of "On Slogans" that "a new cycle [in the class struggle] is beginning, one that does not involve the old classes, old parties, and old soviets," he insisted that the party "start looking forward instead of backward" and operate with "new, post-July class and party categories."

For the time being, however, Lenin was on the outside looking in. The Central Committee conference resolution was the national leadership's main political evaluation and official pronouncement on tactics between the April Conference and the Sixth Congress. It was quickly reproduced as a leaflet, 340 bundles of which were rushed to subordinate Bolshevik organizations throughout the country. The resolution was duly published in each of the party's main provincial organs and served as a guide for resolutions on the political situation and tactics adopted at precongress party conferences and meetings that took place during the second half of July throughout Russia.[27]

The experience of the Bolshevik Petersburg Committee during this same period confirms that the damage done to the Bolsheviks during the reaction following the July days was comparatively superficial and easily overcome. Composed of close to fifty elected district committee representatives who met weekly to discuss important policy issues, the Petersburg Committee was directed by a six-man Executive Commission, no members of which were arrested after the July days. The Petersburg Committee's work was momentarily thrown into disarray by the loss of offices and records in the Kshesinskaia mansion. "We lost just about everything—our documents, accounts, quarters—literally everything!" a member of the Executive Commission dejectedly reported at the time.[28] Still, contact between the commission and district party committees was never seriously disrupted. A temporary home for the Petersburg Committee was quickly found in the relatively safe Vyborg District, where as early as July 7 party workers were turning out revolutionary leaflets on a dilapidated hand press left from tsarist days.[29]

During the first weeks after the July uprising, the problem that seems to have troubled Petersburg Committee officials most was what effect the latest events, and particularly the charges of espionage against the top party leadership, would have on the Bolsheviks' influence and following among the Petrograd masses. An initial answer to this question came at the first full post–July days gathering of the Petersburg Committee on July 10,[30] and at a session of the Second City Conference of Petrograd Bolsheviks on July 16. (The Second City Conference began on July 1 and was suspended on July 3 because of the July uprising; the conference was resumed on July 16.) At both meetings representatives from each district in the capital delivered personal reports on conditions in their areas. These reports indicated that among factory workers, resentment toward the party was limited from the outset and in any case it did not last long.

More precisely, to judge by the reports of July 10, employees of factories situated in relatively prosperous, not primarily industrial neighborhoods of the capital seemed to be genuinely hostile to the Bolsheviks in the wake of the July days. In these areas, there were frequent instances of Bolsheviks being insulted by fellow workers and of their actually being hounded out of workshops. The representative of the Nevsky District, for one, termed the attitude of workers towards Bolsheviks there "pogromist." According to him, better-known party members were "hunted." Moreover, offices belonging to the party were continually in danger of pillage by street crowds. The representative of the Porokhovsky District, one of six Bolsheviks thrown out of his factory a day or two after the July days, complained of "slanders" against the Bolsheviks and of their being "under surveillance." He stated quite bluntly that workers in his district were "a stagnant swamp." Reviewing late developments in the Kolpinsky District, another speaker reported that the sympathy of workers there had turned away from the Bolsheviks as soon as the July demonstrations had ended.

These firsthand reports suggested that in addition to engendering bitterness toward the Bolsheviks among undetermined numbers of Menshevik, SR, and nonaffiliated workers, the July events seriously undermined the faith of at least some factory-level Bolshevik organizers in their own higher party leadership. Latsis, of the Vyborg District, reported on one shocking sign of such a development at the Metallist factory. With almost eight thousand workers, this plant was among the largest industrial establishments in Petrograd. Before July, its flourishing three hundred-member collective had been a bright spot among Petrograd party organizations at the factory level. Latsis reported that after a military raid on the Metallist factory earlier that day, leaders of all political organizations represented there had gathered to discuss the latest developments. In the course of this discussion, Mensheviks and SRs had heaped blame on the Bolsheviks for having provoked the rise of the reaction. Under this pressure, the Bolsheviks present evidently swore to behave with greater restraint in the future. Worse yet from the party's point of view, the Metallist factory Bolsheviks adopted a formal resolution pledging support to the Soviet and placing their organization under the Soviet's full control. Immediately published in many papers, this remarkable resolution also demanded that the Bolshevik Central Committee and the Petersburg Committee divest themselves of authority and turn themselves in to the courts to demonstrate publicly that "one hundred thousand Bolshevik workers are not German agents."[31]

Such indications of shattered loyalty must have been profoundly disturbing to Petersburg Committee members. More significant, nonetheless, was that among party members, strong reactions to the July events, like the one at the Metallist factory, were quite rare. Indeed, judging by the district reports of July 10, Petersburg Committee members were, if anything, relieved that matters were not significantly worse. To be sure, those present agreed that the influx of newcomers to the party had stopped. But the one development that all feared most—mass defections—had not materialized. A party organizer from Vasilevsky Island transmitted the news that while Bolsheviks in factories under his jurisdiction were sometimes attacked, there was no sign that these assaults were affecting the party's numerical strength. With obvious satisfaction he also reported that SRs in one large factory had adopted a resolution in which they declared, "If you arrest the Bolsheviks, go ahead and arrest us too." The representative of the Narva District, which contained the giant Putilov factory, insisted that pogromist agitation had an impact only in the most backward factories and that "the street press is not believed." Latsis, in his report on the all-important Vyborg District, was similarly encouraging. "There is no mass exodus from the party," he stated; "resignations are strictly of an individual character." He also indicated that in factories where workers had had an opportunity to assemble for political meetings, one could detect a desire for all revolutionary groups to pull together.

At the Second City Conference on July 16 the report from the Nevsky District was still dismal. Vasilii Vinokurov related instances of individual Bolsheviks being beaten by fellow workers who wanted them to withdraw from the party. He noted that in his district a patriotic, pogromist, anti-Bolshevik wave was still very much on the rise.

Elsewhere, however, developments were significantly more encouraging. Speaking for the Executive Commission, Volodarsky was able to inform conference delegates that "reports reaching us show that the spirit [of workers] is good everywhere." The spokesman for the Porokhovsky District concluded that the pogromist mood there was already dwindling; as nearly as he could tell, flight from the party was limited to "chance elements that don't even pay dues." A Narva District Bolshevik leader affirmed confidently that the spirit of factory workers was "respectable" and that "work is progressing normally." The representative from Vasilevsky Island went so far as to term the mood of workers in his locale "bright." He added that while "some politically backward female workers are fearful," "in other places the mood is even better than it was before the July days." As on July 10 he noted that decreases in party strength were inconsequential—a slip-

Members of the Bolshevik Petersburg Committee in 1917 (incomplete). Bottom row, left to right: L. M. Mikhailov, V. M. Molotov. Second row: M. P. Tomsky, G. F. Fedorov, V. V. Shmidt, V. N. Zalezhsky, G. I. Boky, M. I. Kalinin, I. A. Rakhia. Third row: N. I. Podvoisky, K. I. Shutko, N. K. Antipov, N. P. Komarov, V. I. Nevsky, M. Ia. Latsis. Fourth row: N. F. Sveshnikov, P. A. Zalutsky, V. Volodarsky, S. N. Ravich, S. P. Prokhorov, S. V. Kosior. Fifth row: N. A. Kubiak, L. R. Menzhinskaia, A. V. Shotman, V. Slutskaia, I. K. Naumov, I. M. Moskvin. Sixth row: P. L. Pakhomov, M. M. Kharitonov, G. K. Krela, A. K. Skorokhodov, B. P. Pozern, E. P. Pervukhin, G. N. Pylaev.

page of one hundred out of a total party membership of four thousand in the district.

On July 10 the representative of the Petersburg District had reported the mood in his district as "unstable"; now, despite the fact that the local Bolshevik committee was without a headquarters, the mood, he said, was "good." The representative of the First City District proudly related that "there were more people than usual at our last meeting." Latsis remained uneasy about the situation in the Metallist factory, but to him sentiment everywhere else in the Vyborg District appeared to be "swinging in the Bolsheviks' favor." He commented, "If fewer people are entering the party, it is because our staff has been disorganized." Equally significant, he again suggested that in the face of attacks by the counterrevolution, workers were exhibiting a desire to forget past differences and close political ranks.

Apart from attempting to ascertain the effects of the July events on the stature of the party among the masses, delegates to the Second City Conference were most concerned about formulating an appropriate program of action for the future. With several of the most prominent Central Committee members temporarily unavailable, the obligation to present the Central Committee's position on this issue fell to Stalin, then thirty-eight years old. Temperamental, coarse, and overbearing, an undistinguished theoretician, writer, and public speaker, Stalin was overshadowed as a revolutionary leader in 1917 by Lenin, Trotsky, and even Zinoviev, Kamenev, and Lunacharsky. This was probably the primary reason he was not sought by the government after the July uprising. Evidently largely because of his Georgian background, Stalin was recognized as the party's leading authority on the nationalities question. On occasion he also represented the Central Committee in the Executive Committee of the Petrograd Soviet and in the Central Executive Committee. Apart from that, he seems to have spent most of his time assisting with the editing of *Pravda* and doing day-to-day administrative chores.

Initially, Stalin's views on the development of the revolution corresponded closely to those of Kamenev, but after Lenin's return to Russia he swung sharply leftward. By the middle of June he could be counted among the ultramilitants within the Bolshevik leadership. (As a gesture of protest against cancellation of the June 10 demonstration he, along with Smilga, submitted his resignation to the Central Committee; it was subsequently rejected.)

The honor of representing the Central Committee at the Second City Conference was a mixed blessing for Stalin since, as was soon apparent, the views embodied in the Central Committee conference resolution described above did not fully represent his own thinking. His task was further complicated by the fact that some delegates were already aware of and sympathetic to Lenin's views on the prevailing situation and the appropriate course for the party, and anxious that they be given a hearing. In these circumstances, Stalin adopted an ambiguous, sometimes contradictory, middle-of-the road tactical stance, unsatisfactory to practically everyone.

Thus in his main report, "On the Current Moment," using words that might have been borrowed from Lenin, Stalin announced that the peaceful period in the development of the revolution had ended, that the counter-revolution had emerged triumphant in the wake of the July days, and that the Central Executive Committee had aided and abetted this development and was now powerless. In amplifying these statements, however, Stalin differed with Lenin in defining "the triumph of the counterrevolution"; he also departed from Lenin in his views on the nature and condition of the Provisional Government, the character and attitudes of the petty bourgeoisie, the significance of the July experience for the development of the revolution, and the prospects for the immediate future. According to Stalin, the Provisional Government was greatly influenced, but certainly not controlled, by the counterrevolution. The petty bourgeoisie still wavered between "the Bolsheviks and the Kadets." The political crisis of which the July days was a part had not ended. The country was engulfed in a period of "sharp conflicts, clashes, and collisions" during which the immediate goal of workers and soldiers would remain the exclusion of capitalists from government and the creation of a "petty bourgeois and proletarian democracy." In this situation, Stalin further explained, the main job of the party would be to urge "restraint, fortitude, and organization on the masses," to rebuild and strengthen Bolshevik organizations, and "not to neglect [activity in] legal institutions."[32]

In short, while Lenin called on the party to break decisively with more moderate political groups and to point the masses toward an armed seizure of power independently of the soviets, Stalin's main emphasis was on the need for restraint and consolidation. Yet if in this sense his ideas were less than satisfactory to those sympathetic to Lenin's views, Stalin's statements regarding the triumph of the counterrrevolution and the powerlessness of the Central Executive Committee, as well as his assertion that the immediate course of the revolution was bound to be violent, were understandably vexing to people sharing the outlook of the Central Committee conference majority. Moreover, Second City Conference delegates across the board were apparently troubled by Stalin's failure to discuss the future of the soviets (the foremost question on everyone's mind) and by his relatively passive view of the party's future political role among the masses.

This predominantly negative reaction to Stalin's remarks was revealed during the heated debate that followed the speech. Taking part in this argument were, among others, S. D. Maslovsky, Vasilii Ivanov, Moisei Kharitonov, Gavril Veinberg, Viacheslav Molotov, Anton Slutsky, and Maximilian Saveliev. Maslovsky began the discussion by inquiring to what extent the party ought to promote conflicts with the government and whether it would assume direction of armed protests in the future. To this Stalin replied noncommittally, "We can expect that these actions will be armed, and we must be ready for anything." Ivanov then asked what the party's attitude was toward the slogan "All Power to the Soviets," implying that the slogan had reached a dead end. Pinned down, Stalin answered that from now on "we speak the language of the class struggle—all power to the workers and poorer peasants, who will pursue revolutionary politics."[33]

Kharitonov, a long-time Bolshevik and former émigré, criticized Stalin for not touching on the international situation as it affected the development of the revolution in Russia. "We have been saying that if there is no revolution in the West our cause is lost," he declared. "Well, the West European revolution did not come to our aid in time, and our revolution could not expand further." Nonetheless, Kharitonov was not without optimism for the future. Scoffing at Stalin's suggestion that the counterrevolution was victorious in Petrograd, he insisted that from the time of the February revolution there had been a gradual shift of power to the soviets, which would continue. "There were moments when we had to fear the dispersal of the soviets," he said, referring to the days immediately preceding. "But this time has definitely passed." He added: "Without the soviets our bourgeoisie would not be able to retain power for more than a few days."[34]

When his turn to speak came, Volodarsky seconded Kharitonov's contention that Stalin exaggerated the strength of the counterrevolution. "People who claim the counterrevolution is victorious are making judgments about the masses on the basis of their leaders," he explained, with both Stalin and Lenin in mind. "While the [top Menshevik-SR] leaders are shifting rightward, the masses are moving leftward. Kerensky, Tsereteli, and Avksentiev are caliphs for an hour. . . . The petty bourgeoisie will swing to our side. Bearing this in mind, it is clear that the slogan 'All Power to the Soviets' is not obsolete,"·he concluded. Added Veinberg: "The present government won't be able to do a thing about the economic crisis; the soviets and political parties will swing leftward. The majority of the democracy is grouped around the soviets and so rejecting the slogan 'All Power to the Soviets' can have very harmful consequences."[35]

Among those now venturing opinions on "the current moment," Molotov, Saveliev, and Slutsky came closest to expressing Lenin's sentiments. Molotov insisted that before the latest events "the soviets could have taken power without violence had they desired to do so. . . . They didn't. [Instead] the developments of July 3 and 4 impelled the soviets on a counterrevolutionary course. . . . Power has slipped out of the hands of the Soviet into the hands of the bourgeoisie. We can't fight for soviets that have betrayed the proletariat. Our only solution lies in the struggle of the proletariat accompanied by those strata of the peasantry capable of following it."

For his part, Slutsky chastised Volodarsky for shutting his eyes to the counterrevolution's great success. "If we think of the term counterrevolution as meaning transfer of power to a specific group, a change in which the group previously in power can't get it back," he explained, "then what we are witnessing is plainly the trimph of the counterrevolution." Obviously not completely familiar with Lenin's thinking, however, he added that "no one is suggesting that we should simply throw away the 'All Power to the Soviets' slogan like worthless rubbish."

"At a time when the workers' revolution is expanding and the soviets are struggling against it," contended Saveliev, "the slogan 'All Power to the Soviets' just sows confusion." "We have two choices," he declared. "Either we expand the revolution or we stop. The party of the proletariat cannot stop. The winner will be up to history. The revolution goes on, and we are headed for the final assault."[36]

After everyone wishing to do so had spoken out, Stalin read the resolution of the Central Committee conference in its entirety. A proposal that a committee be established to revise the resolution as a whole failed by a narrow margin of three votes, after which the resolution was considered point by point. Early in this phase of the discussion an unidentified delegate from the Vyborg District requested, to no avail, that the chair read Lenin's theses (this despite the fact that copies of both "The Political Situation" and "On Slogans" were in the possession of the chairman).[37]

As each point in the resolution was reached, one of the "Leninists," either Molotov, Slutsky, or Saveliev, rose to propose amendments in line with the theses. Either because defending the Central Committee resolution was uncomfortable for Stalin or because supporters of the resolution were dissatisfied with Stalin's earlier performance, Volodarsky rebutted these amendments. In response to a delegate's protest that Volodarsky had no right to the floor inasmuch as he had not been the main speaker, the chair ruled that Volodarsky "represents the conference at which the resolution was originally adopted." At one point in the torrid parliamentary battle over amendments, after Slutsky tried unsuccessfully to insert a clause in the resolution declaring that the counterrevolution had triumphed, Volodarsky blurted out in exasperation: "We are witnessing an attempt, at whatever the cost, to muscle through points that have already been rejected. The whole crux of our argument [i.e., with Lenin] is whether we are witnessing a temporary or a decisive victory of the counterrevolution." Retorted Saveliev: "I sense a flippant attitude toward Lenin's theses here."[38]

All told, Molotov, Slutsky, and Saveliev introduced some eighteen amendements to the resolution read by Stalin, all but one of which were rejected. As a result, in most respects the resolution that the conference ultimately passed was a copy of the one adopted by the Central Committee conference.

The bitterness that the controversy over a new tactical course engendered at this time was revealed in the voting. Twenty-eight delegates came out in favor of the resolution, with three against and twenty-eight abstentions. Justifying their abstentions, some delegates from the Moskovsky District explained that they were not voting because of the "inadequacy of the resolution." Molotov declared that he was abstaining because "at such a crucial time it is impossible to adopt a vague resolution." Finally, Viktor Narchuk, speaking for eleven delegates from the Vyborg District, explained that his group had decided to abstain because "the conference had not heard Lenin's theses and because the resolution was defended by someone other than the main speaker."[39]

The Bolshevik agency damaged most severely after the July uprising was undoubtedly the Military Organization. From the time of its formation, the Military Organization's chief purposes were to win the support of the soldiers of the Petrograd garrison and to organize them into a disciplined revolutionary force. By midsummer considerable progress had been made in regard to the first objective. Several thousand soldiers had joined either the Military Organization itself or Club Pravda, party cells had been established in most garrison units, and in several units Bolshevik influence was paramount. Plans formulated by the government in the wake of the July days to disarm and dissolve Bolshevized regiments that had been actively involved in the uprising were only partially realized; still, a high percentage of the party's most experienced and effective unit-level leaders were now jailed, the immensely popular *Soldatskaia pravda* was silenced, and links between the Military Organization's top leadership and the troops were temporarily severed. Bolsheviks were effectively excluded from military barracks and, generally speaking, the party's operations in the garrison were all but halted.

More markedly than in the case of workers, soldiers of the Petrograd garrison appear to have turned against the Bolsheviks after the July experience. This was probably in part because a relatively higher percentage of soldier-Bolsheviks were undisciplined, politically inexperienced newcomers whose loyalties to the party were tenuous. In addition, however strong their desire for peace, soldiers tended to be more patriotic than workers and were consequently more likely to be swayed by the charge that the Bolsheviks were working for the Germans. Then too, as suggested earlier, garrison soldiers hoped, not without foundation, that by repudiating the Bolsheviks they might avoid transfer to the front. For these reasons and probably for others as well, units of the garrison immediately after the July days often conducted their own political housecleaning, isolating known Bolsheviks from contact with troops and in some cases turning them in to the authorities.

On July 10, for example, at a meeting of soldiers' committees in the First Reserve Infantry Regiment, it was agreed to arrest leading Bolsheviks in the unit and to draw up a list of personnel guilty of making appeals for radical action, presumably for use by the government. A formal resolution that these committees adopted two days later declared that chief responsibility for the behavior of the First Reserve Infantry Regiment on July 4 rested with the Bolsheviks Vasilii Sakharov and Ivan and Gavril Osipov, and a soldier of unknown party affiliation, Eliazar Slavkin. The resolution accused the four of carrying on dangerous agitation and making inflammatory speeches that hypnotized the troops; moreover, on July 4 they had allegedly committed a "vile provocation" by erroneously reporting that mass action had been authorized by the Soviet.[40]

At the same time, garrison units anxious to clear themselves of charges of involvement in the July days adopted fervent pledges of support to the government and the Executive Committees. Typical of such resolutions was one adopted at a mass meeting of soldiers from the Litovsky Guards Regiment on July 9:

> Having consciously refrained from taking part in the armed movement of July 3 and 4, we condemn this action as dangerous and shameful to the revolutionary cause. . . . We call on everyone to obey the firm will of the Executive Committees and the Provisional Government. . . . We appeal to our garrison comrades to join their powerful voices to our resolution, in so doing expressing the unified and conscious will of the garrison, which is directed toward defending liberty from attacks by German agents who are allied with counterrevolutionaries and who make use of the ignorance and backwardness of certain segments of the soldiers and worker masses.[41]

As if assaults by the authorities and harsh criticism by garrison soldiers were not enough, in mid-July the Military Organization was also forced to endure attacks from embittered elements within the Bolshevik Party itself. Among top Bolshevik officials, the value of maintaining a distinct military arm had been the subject of continued controversy from the time that Social Democratic military organizations were first formed after the 1905 revolution. Supporters of military organizations contended that regular military forces were a key factor in every modern revolution. Moreover, they argued that the situation and concerns of soldiers and sailors differed so markedly from those of civilian elements of the population that military organizations possessing a great degree of autonomy and independence were an absolute necessity if the former were to be won to the side of the revolution, making possible its success. On the other hand, critics of military organizations argued that the potential costs of such organs in terms of duplication of effort and loss of control far outweighed whatever benefits might be derived from them. It is not surprising, then, that the apparent involvement of the Bolshevik Military Organization in the preparation of the July uprising without authorization from the Central Committee intensified criticism of the organization; officials of the Petersburg Committee, as well as elements of the national party leadership, evidently took part in these attacks on the Military Organization.[42]

Despite the danger of detection, Podvoisky, then sought by the authorities, was forced to appear and defend the Military Organization at the Second City Conference on July 16 and at the Sixth Party Congress on July

28.[43] Moreover, at the Sixth Congress the Military Organization was the subject of a formal inquiry by a specially organized military section. Boris Shumiatsky, a delegate to the Sixth Congress from the mid-Siberian Bureau of the party and evidently a member of the section, subsquently related that at the congress, Bukharin, Kamenev, and Trotsky (the last two presumably by written messages or through intermediaries) insisted on the necessity of dissolving the Military Organization on the grounds that it overlapped the work of regular party organs. According to Shumiatsky, a majority of the military section rejected this position, acknowledging the necessity of maintaining a special Military Organization under the Central Committee. In the published materials on the Sixth Congress, the debate and decision concerning the Military Organization's status are reflected in the military section's final communique, which, among other things, announced the adoption of the following resolution by a vote of eight to four: "Because of a whole series of peculiarities in living conditions and in professional and organizational matters [pertaining to] the existence and work of party members in the armed forces, the section sanctions the existence below the Central Committee, under its constant and direct supervision, of a special Military Organization to direct the everyday work of the party in the armed forces."[44]

Despite the authorities' active search for them, the Military Organization's most important officials, Nevsky and Podvoisky, managed to evade arrest following the July days. Although Podvoisky was twice detained by military patrols, he was able to conceal his identity. Nevsky, who had incurred a minor bullet wound in the leg during a shooting incident on July 4, fled to the provinces. Shortly after Nevsky's return to Petrograd in mid-July, officials of the Military Organization still at large, among them Podvoisky, Nevsky, Ilin-Zhenevsky, and Mikhail Kedrov, met secretly at the apartment of Genrikh Yagoda to assess their losses and discuss future strategy. According to Ilin-Zhenevsky, participants in this meeting agreed for the time being to try "to combine underground activity with legal work," that is, to maintain a central headquarters under cover and, as feasible, to resume open organization and agitational activity among the troops.[45]

One of the goals set by Military Organization officials at this meeting was to resume, as quickly as possible, publication of a Bolshevik newspaper for soldiers, along the lines of the now illegal *Soldatskaia pravda*. During the third week of July Podvoisky finally found a press willing to produce such a paper, and the first issue appeared on July 23. The new organ, *Rabochii i soldat*, was to be edited by Podvoisky, Nevsky, and Ilin-Zhenevsky, and managed by Kedrov and Yagoda.[46] All appeared to be going well with the paper until complications arose at a Central Committee meeting on August 4. This was the first meeting of the new Central Committee elected by the Sixth Congress. Since the committee did not yet have a paper to replace *Pravda*, it decided to appropriate *Rabochii i soldat*. Moreover, obviously

Key members of the Bolshevik Military Organization. Top row, left to right: P. V. Dash-kevich, N. I. Podvoisky, V. I. Nevsky. Second row: V. R. Menzhinsky, S. N. Sulimov, A. F. Ilin-Zhenevsky, M. S. Kedrov, E. F. Rozmirovich. Third row: A. D. Sadovsky, K. N. Orlov, N. V. Krylenko, N. K. Beliakov, K. A. Mekhonoshin. Fourth row: R. F. Sivers, S. M. Dimanshtein. Fifth row: F. P. Khaustov, S. M. Nakhimson.

mindful of the organizational control problems experienced in June and July, it resolved that for the time being, neither the Petersburg Committee nor the Military Organization would be permitted to publish a separate paper.[47]

The Central Committee went on to stipulate that the editorial board of

Rabochii i soldat would be composed of Stalin, Sokolnikov, and Miliutin from its own membership and one representative each from the Military Organization and the Petersburg Committee, subsequently designated as Podvoisky and Volodarsky, respectively. This arrangement was profoundly distasteful to Military Organization officials, who were accustomed to working on their own, were jealous of their prerogatives, and were convinced, as Podvoisky put it at the time, that "a combined news organ" could neither fulfill the objectives of the Military Organization nor meet the needs of the soldier masses among whom the Military Organization conducted propaganda and agitation.[48] The fate of *Rabochii i soldat* was sealed on August 10 when a particularly inflammatory editorial provided the Provisional Government with an excuse to shut down the paper. Hurriedly, the Central Committee now made new publishing arrangements. Without clearance from the Central Committee, the Military Organization did the same. Thus, on August 13, for the first time since the July days, two Bolshevik papers, the Central Committee's *Proletarii* and the Military Organization's *Soldat*, appeared on Petrograd newsstands.

When the Central Committee got wind of the Military Organization's independent action, it determined to take over *Soldat* as well and directed Stalin to inform Podvoisky of this decision. Moreover, to prevent the Military Organization from embarking on further publishing ventures, Smilga was ordered to appropriate, for use by the Central Committee, funds in the Military Organization's possession that had been earmarked for the publication of *Rabochii i soldat*.[49] Stalin and Smilga apparently carried out their duties with firmness and dispatch, for on August 16 the Central Committee received two sharply worded appeals from the Military Organization's All-Russian Bureau.[50] The first appeal insisted on the Military Organization's right to publish a separate newspaper, in terms which indicated that it would not be easy to get the Military Organization leaders to back down; the second protested "the unprincipled way, violating the most elementary principles of party democracy," in which Stalin and Smilga had dealt with the Military Organization and demanded that the Central Committee establish a more workable relationship with the bureau of the Military Organization so that the latter might carry out its responsibilities.[51]

There is evidence that around this time the Central Committee established another special commission to inquire into the Military Organization's affairs, primarily with relation to the organization of the July uprising and the publication of *Rabochii i soldat* and *Soldat*.[52] Indeed, Nevsky related that Military Organization leaders were now subjected to a party "trial," during the course of which Bubnov, Dzerzhinsky, Menzhinsky, and Sverdlov were delegated to oversee various aspects of the Military Organization's activities.[53] It is impossible to determine from existing evidence the relationship of this "trial" to the work of the military section at the Sixth Congress. In any case, the Military Organization was evidently cleared of most charges against it, perhaps partly as a result of Lenin's intervention. Nevsky quotes Sverdlov as having told him that when Lenin learned that Sverdlov had been delegated to acquaint himself with the Military Organization, Lenin's advice was: "To acquaint yourself is necessary. It is necessary to help them, but there should be no pressure and no reprimands. To the contrary, they should be supported. Those who don't take risks never win. Without defeats there can be no victories."[54]

The published minutes of a meeting of the Central Committee on August 16 indicate that after listening to the Military Organization's two appeals, the committee reaffirmed the Military Organization's subordinate position within the party hierarchy, bluntly declaring that according to party statutes the Military Organization could not exist as an independent political center. Yet, having delivered this rebuke, the committee agreed to let the Military Organization continue publishing *Soldat*, with the proviso that a member of the Central Committee with the right of veto be included on its editorial board. Simultaneously it delegated Sverdlov and Dzerzhinsky to conduct discussions with the Military Organization bureau to establish a proper relationship between it and the Central Committee, and to keep tabs on *Soldat*.[55]

While the Military Organization leadership was fighting to preserve its status within the party organization, the Bolshevik position among soldiers of the garrison had improved considerably. Significantly, the regeneration of support for the party program that now occurred began in military units heretofore relatively free of Bolshevik influence. As Menzhinskaia enthusiastically reported in a letter of July 17 from the Central Committee to the Moscow Region bureau: "The mood is shifting in our favor in those regiments in and around Piter where up to now we have not had much success. Among soldiers, Kerensky's latest decrees, especially his reinstitution of the death penalty, have caused a terrible stir and explosion of hostility toward officers."[56]

Brief published summaries of post–July days meetings between high officials of the Military Organization and representatives of Bolshevik collectives in the Petrograd garrison confirm that government repression and the threat of counterrevolution helped the Military Organization overcome some of the worst effects of its unsuccessful insurrection by late July and the beginning of August. Delegate reports at the first of these gatherings on July 21 revealed that the events of early July had initially caused great confusion among the troops and had adversely affected their attitudes toward Bolsheviks.[57] At the next Military Organization meeting a week later, delegates remained dispirited and very much concerned about persecution of party members; nonetheless they were agreed that the negative impact of the July experience on soldiers who were sympathetic to Bolshevism was minimal.[58]

By August 5 the same unit representatives were proudly describing mass meetings organized in the garrison to protest repression and the continued existence of the Duma and State Council; they also indicated that Military Organization membership was again on the increase.[59] Finally, at the Military Organization meeting on August 12 most unit representatives were of the mind that sympathy for the Bolshevik cause in the garrison was expanding "even more rapidly than before." Apparently, some of them averred candidly that this was the result less of Military Organization efforts than of the actions of the government and the moderate socialists. After hearing out these representatives, the Military Organization secretary recorded that the success of the Bolsheviks was due "not to agitation, which is still difficult to conduct, but to new punishment regulations, the repression of revolutionary soldiers, and temporizing on the part of the 'defensists.' "[60]

The fact that repressive measures undertaken by the Kerensky administration had the entirely unintended effect of heightening popular suspicion of the government and of impelling the Petrograd masses to put aside past political differences and to unite more closely in defense of the revolution is clearly reflected in numerous documents of the time. Among the richest and most valuable of these documents are the voluminous protocols and resolutions of the Petrograd district soviets for 1917.[61]

As will be recalled, soviets came into being in each district of the capital soon after the February revolution. Often created upon the initiative of workers and soldiers themselves, these soviets first sprang up in heavily industrial sections of the city. The Vyborg and Peterhof district soviets, for example, were founded during the February days. A local soviet was formed in the Vasilevsky Island District in March. Subsequently, similar bodies were created in the central city, so that by the end of May a network of over a dozen district and subdistrict soviets blanketed Petrograd and its environs.

As in the case of the Petrograd Soviet, during this first period after the collapse of the tsarist order the strongest political groups in the district soviets were the Mensheviks and SRs. Yet, in part because the majority socialist leadership on the national level did not attach much importance to work in such organs, the district soviets were never dominated by middle-class intellectuals and political parties, as were the Petrograd Soviet and the All-Russian Executive Committees. Readily accessible to ordinary workers and soldiers, the district soviets busied themselves mainly with immediate local concerns, such as food supply, the maintenance of public order, labor disputes, and social welfare, taking time to discuss only those broader national issues about which their constituencies were generally aroused. For these reasons, the proceedings of the district soviets are a more reliable gauge of the shifting moods and concerns of the Petrograd masses than are the deliberations of the Petrograd Soviet or the All-Russian Executive Committees.

One of the most striking observations that emerges from study of the district soviets between late April and early August is the divergence that developed during this time between the political outlook of the district soviets, on the one hand, and the central Soviet organs, on the other. In mid-July, for example, when the All-Russian Executive Committees were pledging their unlimited support to the Kerensky regime, most district soviets were becoming overwhelmingly suspicious of the government, increasingly exasperated with the temporizing of national Menshevik and SR leaders, and, gradually, more strongly attracted to the idea of creating a revolutionary soviet government. (Just as Volodarsky had argued at the Second City Conference, while the moderate socialist leadership shifted rightward, the masses were moving leftward.)[62]

The divergence of views between the district soviets and the national Soviet leadership, particularly the feeling of the former that the Petrograd Soviet was not devoting enough attention to the concerns of the district soviets, was reflected in the activation in mid-July and August of an organization known as the Interdistrict Conference of Soviets. Initially formed during the April crisis but quiescent during most of June and the first half of July, the Interdistrict Conference was an assembly of district soviet representatives, two from each local soviet in Petrograd, which met, as the need arose, to coordinate the activities of individual district soviets and, increasingly, to bring the combined pressure of all district soviets to bear on the central Soviet organs.[63]

A second feature that emerges from study of the Petrograd district soviets during the summer of 1917 is the expanding influence within them of leftist groups such as the Menshevik-Internationalists, the Interdistrict Committee, and the Bolsheviks. In April, for example, the Bolsheviks had been strongly influential only in the Vyborg and Kolpinsky district soviets. Initially, a large majority of the Interdistrict Conference members were Mensheviks and SRs, and its first chairman was the Menshevik Anisimov. By midsummer, however, in addition to the Vyborg and Kolpinsky district soviets, the Vasilevsky Island, Kolomensky, and First City district soviets, geographically scattered throughout the capital, were frequently passing Bolshevik-sponsored resolutions.

Nonetheless, with the possible exception of the Vyborg District Soviet, it appears that none of these soviets were effectively controlled by the Bolsheviks. The Mensheviks and SRs, more accurately their Menshevik-Internationalist and Left SR offshoots, retained influence in most district soviets at least until the late fall of 1917, and even those local soviets in which the Bolsheviks had majorities preserved their essentially democratic character. In early August a Menshevik-Internationalist, Alexander Gorin, was elected chairman of the Interdistrict Conference. Under his direction a compatible coalition of Bolsheviks, Menshevik-Internationalists, and Left SRs steered the assembly along an independent, revolutionary course.[64]

The protocols and resolutions of the Petrograd district soviets lend support to the idea that immediately after the July days anti-Bolshevik feeling on the part of workers and soldiers in some areas of the capital ran high. On July 13, for instance, the Okhtinsky District Soviet, located on the right bank of the Neva, adopted a resolution endorsing the condemnation of the Bolsheviks and the unqualified pledge of support to the government that the All-Russian Executive Committees had issued a few days earlier.[65] At about the same time, the highly independent Rozhdestvensky District Soviet, just across the river, passed a resolution declaring that the events of July 3 and 4 "force the whole conscious organized revolutionary democracy to fear for the fate of the Russian revolution. An irresponsible minority, injecting the uneducated masses with slogans abhorrent to the representatives of the all-Russian democracy, is unconsciously but definitely leading us to civil war. . . . We declare that responsibility for the bloodshed on the streets of Petrograd on July 3–4 falls completely on those irresponsible persons and parties who consciously or unconsciously continually pursued politics that disorganized the force of the revolution."[66]

Apparently, only the consistently militant Vyborg District Soviet attempted to buck the tide at this juncture, publicly continuing to call for transfer of power to the soviets and attempting to defuse criticism of the Bolsheviks. For example, on July 7, the day the All-Russian Executive Committees first endorsed repressions by the government, the Vyborg District Soviet defiantly insisted that the effective solution of the government crisis, the regulation of the shattered economy, and the promulgation of reforms were dependent on the transfer of power to the soviets.[67]

What the relevant documents indicate most clearly is that in the aftermath of the July uprising, most district soviets were not interested in either condemning or defending the Bolsheviks. Their primary concern was with such matters as the government's effort to disarm workers and to transfer radicalized soldiers from the capital, the reinstitution of capital punishment at the front, the apparently indiscriminate attacks on the left, and the resurgence of the extreme right. Each of these developments was perceived by almost every district soviet as a serious threat to the revolution.

The Interdistrict Conference met for the first time in a month and a half on July 17, partly to discuss the question of whether or not district soviets should cooperate with the government in the campaign to confiscate arms from the population. This meeting opened with appeals by soldiers from the front that the deputies endorse this campaign in the interest of national defense. The soldiers added that they were all dedicated to defending the revolution and hence that their demands ought not to be interpreted as hostile to workers. In response, a highly skeptical deputy observed diplomatically that while workers might be willing to trust the composite detachment that had just arrived from the front, there was no way of predicting what might happen tomorrow. Workers had no assurance that someone else might not take advantage of their helplessness. "Entire caches of arms are still in the hands of the Black Hundreds and nothing is being done about it," another deputy interjected angrily at this point. Someone else then suggested that while workers might be prevailed upon to turn in machine guns, bombs, and perhaps even rifles, under no circumstances would they part with their revolvers. Ultimately, the conference effectively evaded cooperation with the government and for all intents and purposes thwarted any significant coordinated effort by district soviets to help disarm workers by voting to leave the matter up to the discretion of each district soviet.[68]

A few district soviets subsequently agreed to help disarm workers. On July 28, for example, after listening to a plea for aid in procuring arms by a Don Cossack, the Admiralty District Soviet passed a resolution declaring that military weapons were completely unnecessary for personal defense and that in view of the government's frequent appeals, retaining them was a crime against liberty and the Russian army.[69] However, there were almost no factories and few workers in the Admiralty District, an area in central Petrograd with numerous military-administrative agencies and army barracks. District soviets in heavily working-class sections of the city, reflecting the mood of their constituencies, tended to view with the greatest suspicion the efforts of the government to confiscate weapons.

Thus on July 20, after listening to some front representatives and discussing the arms question at length, the relatively moderate Petrograd District Soviet, while endorsing the turning in of rifles and machine guns, declared firmly that the confiscation of revolvers and sidearms would be considered "a counterrevolutionary assault on the working class" which it would be necessary to oppose by every possible means.[70] When the Peterhof District Soviet considered the question of disarming workers on July 29, deputies protested that it was not the workers who should be disarmed but "the counterrevolutionary and hooligan elements that have been shooting from rooftops and windows of houses . . . and that have come out openly and brazenly against the revolution and its triumphs."[71] Obviously, the government would get little help from the Peterhof Soviet in taking arms from workers. As nearly as one can tell, this was the position of all but a few district soviets.

The Provisional Government's restoration of the death penalty met with similar hostility from the district soviets. Typifying their response to this step was the following declaration by the Rozhdestvensky District Soviet, in which the Bolsheviks were still a small minority:

> One of the dearest victories of the Great Russian Revolution, the abolition of capital punishment, has been eliminated by a stroke of the Provisional Government's pen. . . . In the name of "saving the revolution," military courts knowing only one sentence, execution, will be convened.

And soldiers designated for the roles of executioners will hurriedly drag their worried sick, condemned comrades, tormented by three years of slaughter . . . into an isolated corner and shoot them like dogs for no other reason than because they were unwilling to selflessly sacrifice their lives for their class enemies. . . .

The result is a gross absurdity: a free country has eliminated the death penalty for high-ranking criminals, all those Nikolais, Sukhomlinovs, Shturmers, Prokopovichs, etc. [the last three were former tsarist ministers] but retains it for soldiers oppressed by three years of senseless carnage. . . .

It is a crime to kill tormented and desperate people, crazed by recognition of the futility of their suffering and unable to see the end of this endless war. It is a crime to be silent about this reactionary, impulsive step by the Provisional Government against one of the most priceless triumphs of the revolution. . . .

Down with Capital Punishment!

Down with Legalized Murder!

Long Live the Revolutionary International![72]

At its meeting on July 17, responding to scores of alarming reports of counterrevolutionary "excesses" in every district, the Interdistrict Conference adopted a resolution declaring that unmistakable indications of "an enlivened, actively organizing counterrevolutionary movement" had been reflected in the events of July 3–5 and the immediately succeeding days. The resolution called on the Petrograd Soviet to display energy and firmness in exposing counterrevolutionary cells and to insist that the government take decisive steps to combat the counterrevolution. It also demanded, among other things, a full investigation of all improper raids and arrests and the immediate release of political prisoners against whom substantial charges had not yet been made.[73]

One can easily imagine the dismay of district soviet deputies two days later upon reading detailed press accounts of the Duma Provisional Committee's sensational meeting of July 18. At an emergency session of the Interdistrict Conference on July 21 every deputy taking the floor insisted on the immediate dissolution of the Provisional Committee. Indeed, several speakers advocated immediate, concrete measures to insure that this was accomplished. A spokesman for the Rozhdestvensky District Soviet, for one, proposed that the conference march en masse to the Taurida Palace in order to make their views known to the Central Executive Committee; this suggestion was accepted with the proviso that in addition to demanding the dissolution of the Duma, the district soviet deputies also insist on the restoration of full rights to democratic committees in the army, the rehabilitation of the leftist press, the halting of attempts to disarm workers, the immediate release of all political prisoners not yet charged with specific violations of the law, the prosecution of Purishkevich and Maslenikov, rescission of the policy of breaking up regiments of the Petrograd garrison, and the immediate abolition of capital punishment at the front.[74]

At the same time, individual district soviets responded to the pleas of Purishkevich and Maslenikov for "liberal use of the noose" against the left with protest declarations of their own. Typical of these public statements was the following one passed by unanimous vote in the Vyborg District Soviet:

> The Soviet of Workers' and Soldiers' Deputies of the Vyborg District, having learned of the private meeting of members of the former State Duma and of their emergence on the national political arena, considers that the Duma, as an institution of the old autocratic system, . . . is subject to immediate dissolution. The soviet insists that the Provisional Government issue a decree dissolving this counterrevolutionary institution and categorically protests against the Black Hundred Duma members who had the audacity to stand up and refer to revolutionary organs as a handful of fanatics, transients, and traitors. . . . The soviet demands a decisive struggle against counterrevolutionary elements and, in particular, against former members of the State Duma and believes that they should be made to stand trial for insulting the entire democracy, represented by the soviet.[75]

Significantly, by the end of July even relatively moderate district soviets were more concerned with consolidating all leftist groups, including the Bolshevik Party, in defense of the revolution than with penalizing the Bolsheviks for their behavior weeks earlier. To formerly hostile deputies in the district soviets, the Bolsheviks now appeared as simply the left flank of the revolution, which was threatened with destruction.

This spirit of letting bygones be bygones, and alarm in the face of the counterrevolution, emerged at the Interdistrict Conference's emergency meeting of July 21. In a stirring appeal for the unification of all democratic forces to combat the advancing counterrevolution, Viktor Rappaport, a Menshevik-Internationalist, voiced the view that while the counterrevolution had begun with attacks on the Bolsheviks, blows against leftist groups close to the Bolsheviks could also be expected. "The counterrevolution is mobilizing," Rappaport declared, "and we cannot afford to dissipate our resources."

Judging by their subsequent comments, most of the assembled district soviet spokesmen shared this sentiment. A three-man committee, including one member of the Interdistrict Committee (Manuilsky) and two Menshevik-Internationalists (Gorin and Rappaport) was appointed to draw up a declaration on the counterrevolution and the existing political situation for consideration by each district soviet and, ultimately, for transmittal to the Central Executive Committee. In the document drawn up by this committee (the Interdistrict Conference's first public statement on broad national issues), the July uprising was characterized as "a spontaneous act of military units and workers," the direct result of the political crisis partly caused by the Kadets. According to the declaration, the counterrevolution had utilized the events of July 3–4 for an open assault on the revolutionary democracy in general and its left flank in particular. Meanwhile, the post–July days persecution of the Bolsheviks had divided the forces of the revolution, isolating its left flank. The breakup of regiments loyal to the revolution, mass arrests, the destruction of the labor press had all served simply to weaken the revolutionary democracy. Expressing the opinion that another coalition government would lead only to a deepening of the existing political crisis and would open the doors more widely to the advancing counterrevolution, the declaration concluded that only a strong revolutionary government, composed exclusively of elements from the revolutionary democracy and conducting internal and foreign policies according to the program outlined by the Congress of Soviets, could save Russia and the revolution.[76]

Reflected in this declaration was the desire, articulated by Martov in the Executive Committees at this time, to unite all genuinely revolutionary elements in an exclusively socialist, soviet government which would combat the counterrevolution, pursue a meaningful reform program, and work for an immediate peace. This strong impulse to band together in defense of the revolution was also vividly expressed in a resolution, supported by the Bolsheviks and passed on August 1, by deputies of the Narva District Soviet:

> In view of the extreme dangers threatening our country from both within and without, we . . . believe that disorganization in the ranks of the revolutionary democracy . . . is intolerable and harmful. Furthermore, we believe that all political groupings and multifarious shades of opinion come from "above." The majority of those "below" don't understand, don't know, indeed can't even comprehend . . . all of their disputes. We appeal . . . to all who are participating in the common revolutionary struggle and who value our newly won freedom . . . to respond to our call. We recommend that they rally around the Soviet of Workers' and Soldiers' Deputies as the highest organ of the democracy. We propose that those above find a common language so that united we can struggle against the enemies of the revolution.[77]

·5·

THE BOLSHEVIK
RESURGENCE

On the night of July 26, in a spacious private assembly hall in the heart of the Vyborg District, some 150 Bolshevik leaders from all over Russia gathered for the opening of the party's long-awaited Sixth Congress.[1] This national assembly of Bolshevik officials began with the election of Lenin, Trotsky, Kamenev, Kollontai, and Lunacharsky to the posts of honorary congress co-chairmen and ended, fifteen sessions and eight days later, with the singing of the "Internationale." In the interim, the delegates listened to formal greetings and statements of encouragement from the Petrograd Trade Union Soviet, the American Socialist Workers' Party, "jailed soldiers and officers of the Petrograd garrison," twenty-one military regiments in Riga, several thousand Putilov factory workers, three Petrograd district soviets, the Muslim social democratic organization in Baku, and more than a dozen other various and sundry labor organizations and political institutions. The delegates received detailed, firsthand status reports from representatives of the Central Committee, the Petersburg Committee, the Military Organization, and the Interdistrict Committee (which now formally merged with the Bolshevik Party), as well as from emissaries of nineteen major provincial party organizations. Most important, they hammered out official positions on the question of Lenin's refusal to submit to the authorities[2] and on broad political problems such as the war issue and the current Russian economic and political situation. Finally, lest the assembled delegates had overlooked anything, they reconfirmed all of the resolutions adopted by the April Conference.

The work of the Sixth Congress proceeded in an atmosphere of extreme tension, heightened periodically by rumors that the Kerensky administration was on the verge of raiding and dispersing the congress. These rumors acquired increased credibility on July 28, the third day of the congress, when the government published a decree authorizing the ministers of the interior and of war to ban any assemblies or congresses deemed harmful to the war effort or to the security of the state.[3] Following this, the congress' meeting-place was quietly switched to an out-of-the-way workers' club belonging to the Interdistrict Committee, in the Narva District, on the southwest outskirts of the capital. Roughly simultaneously, party officials supervised election of a smaller congress which, meeting separately, agreed on a public manifesto to be issued in the event that the congress was actually broken up, and hurriedly elected a new Central Committee to direct Bolshevik activities until the next national party congress.[4]

The mood of the embattled delegates in these trying circumstances was vividly reflected in the emotional reception which they gave to a speech by Iurii Larin, a Menshevik-Internationalist who a few weeks after the congress joined the Bolshevik Party. Of this moment Ilin-Zhenevsky subsequently wrote: "I remember the enthusiasm that seized the congress when the chairman [Iakov Sverdlov] announced that one of the leaders of the Menshevik-Internationalists, Comrade Larin, wanted to greet the delegates. . . . To thunderous applause, barely hobbling along on a paralyzed leg and shaking all over with nervousness, Larin moved slowly down the aisle to the speakers' platform. The nearer he approached to it, the louder the applause became."[5]

Larin's remarks to the delegates were, in part, an earnest appeal for revolutionary unity. "When you are being attacked, it is the obligation of every honest internationalist to be with you," he said. "The time has come to build a united revolutionary Social Democratic Party" and "to transfer power into the hands of the revolutionary democracy." At the same time, Larin's talk was a warning against resorting to violent revolutionary action. He affirmed bluntly:

> Among us are some who are apprehensive about your overly great permissiveness toward the Military Organization. We know that during the movement of July 3–5, the Military Organization was calling for immediate action at the very same time that the political powers of the party were agitating against a coming out.
>
> I heard comrades say that the soviets of workers' and soldiers' deputies have adopted a reactionary position and so "Down with the soviets, we will build our own organization"; this is precisely the kind of dangerous road along which we would not be able to accompany you. . . . Our task is not to destroy the soviets and not to create new organizations, but to bring about changes in the composition of the present soviets. . . . We are opposed to rash methods. The soviets are elective institutions.[6]

Obviously, much of Larin's speech conflicted with Lenin's position. Yet the official congress protocols indicate that the applause following his remarks was as tumultuous as it had been before them. Again, Ilin-Zhenevsky commented on the episode: "To get a feeling of what occurred at the congress when [Larin] finished his speech, you have to imagine the atmosphere of persecution and repression in which our party found itself. At this moment every expression of sympathy and support was especially valued. It seemed that Comrade Martov and with him all that was alive and talented within the Menshevik fraction would return to our united Social Democratic ranks."[7]

Principally because of problems in arriving at a consensus on fundamental theoretical issues and also because of dificulties caused by the absence from the congress of Lenin, Trotsky, Kamenev, and other key party leaders, the delegates agreed toward the end of their deliberations to postpone once again the adoption of a new party program. Hence, to the extent that fundamental theoretical questions relating to the development of the revolution were argued out at the congress, this was done mainly in the course of debate on "the current political situation." The working sessions of July 30–31, during which this debate took place, were undoubtedly the most important of the entire congress. With Lenin out of action, Trotsky had been slated to deliver the main speech and to present a draft resolution on "the current political situation";[8] when Trotsky was arrested two days before the start of the congress, Stalin was hastily recruited to perform this task.

It is noteworthy that on this occasion supporters of the tactical program advocated by Lenin left very little to chance. Kronstadt Bolsheviks had run off copies of "On Slogans" for every delegate, and these were distributed shortly before Stalin's speech.[9] And, very likely as a result of lobbying efforts by the "Leninists," Stalin's remarks to the Sixth Congress on the prevailing situation and course for the future paralleled Lenin's views much more closely than had Stalin's speeches at the Second City Conference.

This is not to suggest that Stalin's position now coincided with Lenin's in every respect. During a discussion early in the congress, for example, Stalin declared that "at the present time, where state power lies is unclear."[10] And at another point in the congress, Stalin, discussing the soviets, showed that he was much less negatively inclined toward them than was Lenin.[11] Still, in his main speech on the current political situation, Stalin characterized the Provisional Government as a puppet manipulated by the counterrevolution. He was critical of "comrades who feel that because capitalism is poorly developed in Russia, the goal of a socialist revolution is utopian," contending that "the demand that Russia should delay socialist changes until [the revolution in] Europe began is rank pedantry."[12] Subsequently, echoing Lenin, Stalin declared that the peaceful stage of the revolution was over and insisted that the old slogan "All Power to the Soviets" had to be dropped.

Upon completing his speech, Stalin put before the congress a ten-point draft resolution, "On the Current Political Situation," which, one is tempted to surmise, was written for the most part by Lenin.[13] The first seven points of this resolution defined the course of the Russian revolution through the July days in terms very similar to those in Lenin's theses. "At the decisive points, namely at the front and in Petersburg," this portion of the resolution stated, "state power is in the hands of the counterrevolutionary bourgeoisie, supported by the military clique of the army high command." Points eight through ten of the resolution dealt with the condition and role of the soviets and the party's immediate tactical program in a manner also strongly reminiscent of Lenin, point eight suggesting directly that the existing soviets were bankrupt and a liability. The peaceful progress of the revolution and the nonviolent transfer of power to the soviets had become impossible, and the most appropriate slogan for the party was the complete liquidation of the counterrevolutionary bourgeoisie. Points nine and ten affirmed that the success of the next revolution would depend on how quickly and thoroughly the majority of the people learned the futility of hopes for compromise with the bourgeoisie; however, the text implied that the proletariat, particularly the workers of Petrograd, would be compelled to seize power at the first opportunity (i.e., when political, economic, and military conditions had become sufficiently catastrophic), regardless of whether or not the mass of the population had come to recognize the necessity of a new revolution through their own experience.

As at the Second City Conference, arguments relating to the current political situation in general and the Stalin resolution in particular centered chiefly on the seminal issue of the practical future of the soviets, heretofore the focal point of every delegate's political activity and hopes.[14] Konstantin Iurenev, a close associate of Trotsky, began the debate by asking skeptically: "Up to now we have been consolidating our forces around one organ—the soviets; in what form are we to consolidate our forces now?" Iurenev also wondered why the slogan "All Power to the Soviets" was necessarily inappropriate for a violent stage in the revolution. The Stalin resolution proposed, he concluded, "that we adopt a course that would be disastrous for our revolutionary gains. . . . If we adopt it, we will be headed in the direction of isolating the proletariat from the peasantry and the broad masses of the population. . . . Paragraphs eight to ten must be drastically revised."[15]

Volodarsky rushed to the speaker's platform after Iurenev had stepped down. "They tell us that since the peaceful period of the revolution has ended, the slogan 'All Power to the Soviets' is outdated. Is this really so?" he demanded, "Do we need to maintain the slogan 'All Power to the Soviets' in the same form as before July 3–5? Certainly not! But you can't throw out the baby with the bath water. We must simply modify our slogan 'All Power to the Soviets' roughly as follows: 'All power to the proletariat, supported by the poorer peasantry and revolutionary democracy organized in the soviets of workers', soldiers', and peasants' deputies.' "[16]

Alesha Dzhaparidze, leader of the Bolshevik organization in Baku who had been elected a candidate member of the Central Committee the previous day, spoke out in the same vein. At the time of the July days the Bolsheviks had been making significant strides in building support in the Baku Soviet, and Dzhaparidze was critical of Stalin for, as he put it, "equating soviets [in the provinces] with the Central Executive Committee." "If earlier the provincial soviets expressed the Central Executive Committee's views, they don't now," he said. "While we are living through a period of counterrevolution we must fight for the soviets and, as revolutionary defenders of the idea of [rule by] the soviets, we will acquire commanding importance in them."[17]

"After July 4 there was a change in the tactics of the proletarian party," Manuilsky pointed out. The party "found it necessary to shift from offense to the defense of positions won in the revolution. With this disadvantageous correlation of forces, to introduce maximalist slogans, as the left wing of our party is now doing, is to adopt tactics of desperation. Fixing mistrust upon the soviets, we risk facilitating their eviction from the Taurida Palace and the Smolny Institute. We have to recognize that in Russia 90 percent of the population is petty bourgeois, and consequently tactics which isolate the proletariat from the petty bourgeoisie must be acknowledged to be harmful."[18]

Fifteen congress delegates took the floor during this debate, most of them using every second of their allotted fifteen minutes of speaking time. Of these delegates, eight expressed themselves in favor of retaining the slogan "All Power to the Soviets," one (Bukharin) took an intermediate position,[19] and six sided with Stalin. Among the most eloquent of those who took Stalin's position was Sokolnikov. Like Stalin, he pointed to the expansion of the counterrevolution after the July days. And he went on: "Before, we stood for the transfer of all power into the hands of the soviets. . . . [But] this is no longer a possibility. Heretofore the soviets were revolutionary organs and we could present them as organs of power. They stopped being revolutionary organs the moment artillery was moved against the working class."

In his comments, Sokolnikov seemed not to exclude the possibility that the soviets might be rejuvenated, in particular that they might again become organs of insurrection. In this sense his assessment of the prevailing situation differed from Lenin's. Nonetheless, Sokolnikov shared with Lenin the view that a popular mass uprising was next on Russia's revolutionary agenda. "We must explain [to the masses] that the main issue is not the soviets but organizing the masses for an uprising," he declared. At this point the audience burst into applause. He continued: "It is necessary to attract the peasant masses away from the petty bourgeois leaders, explaining to them that land will be transferred to them only with the support of a proletarian rising. . . . For the peasant masses, the road to a socialist revolution lies in support of the proletarian avant-garde."[20]

Ivar Smilga, earlier far and away the most militantly inclined member of the Central Committee, echoed Sokolnikov. Quoting extensively from "On Slogans," he declared, "Not only Volodarsky, but even an old social democrat like Nogin is mistaken; power is in the hands of a military clique. In order for power to come into the hands of those classes which will work for the expansion of the revolution, it is necessary to overthrow the existing government." Expressing the view that the soviets had "committed suicide" by rejecting power when they could have had it, he suggested that conditions for a new revolutionary eruption were developing rapidly and that the Bolsheviks would be obliged to take the initiative when the explosion came. "No one has the right to deprive us of this initiative if fate gives us another chance to stand at the head of the movement," he insisted. "Comrade Iurenev talks of caution," he added. "Let me remind him of Danton's words: 'In revolution, one needs boldness, boldness, and more boldness!' "[21]

One of the last to take the floor during the Sixth Congress debate over the current political moment was the newly elected Central Committee member from Moscow, Andrei Bubnov. Taking issue with Nogin, who had attempted earlier to minimize the significance of differences that had emerged over the issue of defining the current moment, he insisted that these were quite serious, mirroring the fundamental differences of opinion over the development of the revolution at the April Conference. Bubnov then went on to defend the arguments of the left. "The soviets have no power now," he affirmed. "They are rotting—there can be no illusions about this. . . . If, previously, we spoke of the 'transfer of power,' that term is now obsolete. We must build up our strength for the decisive battle, for the seizure of power. The slogan of transferring power to the soviets has to go."[22]

On the afternoon of July 31, as soon as arguments on the current political situation were completed, Dzhaparidze moved that the Stalin resolution not be put to an immediate vote and, instead, that a committee be formed to draw up a new one. As provided for in Dzhaparidze's motion, the work of this committee was to be guided both by the Stalin resolution and by a statement on the current moment, embodying the views of the moderates, which had been adopted a few days earlier by Moscow Bolsheviks.[23] Congress delegates, while accepting the idea of postponing a vote on the current moment and of having a committee study the problem further, stipulated that the Stalin resolution be the basis for the resolution which this committee would draft.[24]

Subsequently elected to the resolutions committee were Stalin, Sokolnikov, Bubnov, Miliutin, and Nogin, and two representatives of the Moscow Regional Bureau, Bukharin and Georgii Lomov. These seven delegates spent many hours attempting to resolve differing assessments of the prevailing situation, possibly receiving some advice from Lenin in Razliv. The resolution which they formulated and which was adopted by unanimous vote of the congress with four abstentions on August 3 was a compromise between the two contending sides.[25] Apart from omitting some particularly hostile references to the Mensheviks and SRs, the first half of this resolution, which defined the course of the revolution through the July days, followed Stalin's draft resolution almost verbatim. The committee resolution affirmed that the peaceful transfer of power to the soviets had become an impossibility and substituted the slogan "Complete Liquidation of the Dictatorship of the Counterrevolutionary Bourgeoisie" for the slogan "All Power to the Soviets."

At the same time, an entirely new section, taken straight from the statement of the Moscow Bolsheviks, was introduced into the committee resolution; this section specified that the party was to take upon itself the role of "leading fighter against the counterrevolution," protecting mass organizations in general and the soviets in particular from counterrelutionary attacks. In these organs, the party was to work with all possible energy to strengthen the position of "internationalists," consolidating around itself all elements dedicated to the struggle against the counterrevolution. Hence, for the foreseeable future, the central focus of the party's activities was still to be the soviets and, indeed, the possibility of working with majority socialists in defense of the revolution was, for practical purposes, left open. Moreover, missing entirely from the resolution adopted by the congress were explicit references to a "new revolution" as well as suggestions regarding the possibility that the seizure of power by the Bolsheviks might precede their acquisition of majority support in the country. The concluding paragraphs of the resolution stated simply that the proletariat was to avoid succumbing to provocations and was to direct its energies toward the organization and preparation of its forces for the moment when the national crisis and deep mass upsurge had created propitious conditions for the urban and rural poor to support the struggle of workers against the bourgeoisie. At this juncture, the task of these classes would be to take power into their own hands.[26]

What then was the significance of the programmatic decisions of the Sixth Congress? Officially, the slogan "All Power to the Soviets" was now withdrawn. It is missing from all official Bolshevik Party documents throughout the month of August. Beyond this, however, the decisions seem to have had little practical impact. The party remained pointed in the direction of a socialist revolution, as it had been since April. This course had received solid endorsement by the congress. But the crucial questions of "How?" and "When?" were still left vague. Intraparty programmatic differences were not resolved. As Bubnov explained in a report on the work of the Sixth Congress to a meeting of the Moscow Regional Bureau: "At the congress, as at the April Conference, there emerged two points of view, two tendencies, which . . . were not brought out definitely enough and which remained in concealed form."[27] Furthermore, the party's decisions notwithstanding, many mass organizations in Petrograd continued to view the creation of a revolutionary soviet government as the solution to their most pressing problems.[28] At the time of the Kornilov affair in late August, the goal of an exclusively socialist regime had come to be nearly universally shared by Petrograd workers and soldiers, and the Bolsheviks themselves were forced to formally resurrect their old rallying cry, "All Power to the Soviets!"

While bitterness and hostility toward the Bolsheviks on the part of Petrograd workers and soldiers evaporated within a few weeks after the July uprising, by early August there were numerous unmistakable signs that with its apparatus intact, the Bolshevik Party had embarked on a new period of growth.

This resurgence was reflected in the frequently voiced complaints by local Menshevik and SR leaders of numerous defections to the Bolsheviks.[29] It was mirrored as well in Bolshevik gains in strictly local balloting in Kronstadt[30] and in scattered elections for the Petrograd Soviet. Factory workers and garrison soldiers could recall their representatives in the Soviet whenever they saw fit, and during the first half of August Bolshevik supporters in several Petrograd industrial plants took advantage of growing dissatisfaction with the policies of the central Soviet organs to substitute Bolsheviks for deputies advocating the programs of the moderate socialists.[31]

The Bolsheviks did not obtain a majority in the Petrograd Soviet itself until the beginning of September; however, an early indication that the Mensheviks and SRs were in for difficulties there came on August 7, at the first meeting of the Workers' Section since the July days. According to an agenda prepared by the Soviet leadership on that day, the Workers' Section was to discuss some organizational questions and also to make preparations for a conference on national defense scheduled to open in the capital the next day. But Bolshevik representatives in the section, supported by the Left SRs, would have none of this. They demanded that the meeting immediately discuss the plight of arrested "internationalists" and the government's decision to restore the death penalty at the front. In a vote on this proposal, a majority supported the Bolsheviks. The deputies next listened to an impassioned appeal on behalf of imprisoned leftists by the indefatigable Volodarsky, as well as a defense of the authorities by Dan and Gots. By an overwhelming margin, they then voted for a Bolshevik resolution specifying that the arrest and persecution of comrades belonging to the extreme left represented "a blow to the revolutionary cause, a shameful stain" which served only the interests of the counterrevolution. The resolution demanded, among other things, the immediate release of all those arrested after the July days who were not yet formally charged, early public trials for those indicted, and prosecution of all officials responsible for "illegally depriving citizens of their liberty."[32] The deputies even named a special commission to express sympathy and support personally to "Trotsky, Lunacharsky, Kollontai, and other political prisoners." Moreover, they adopted a resolution by Martov condemning the restoration of capital punishment as a measure having openly counterrevolutionary aims. This resolution lambasted the Central Executive Committee for not opposing capital punishment and demanded that the Provisional Government rescind the measure.[33]

Citywide elections held on August 20 for a new Petrograd City Duma provided even more tangible evidence of the rapid Bolshevik recovery. Attaching considerable significance to these elections, the Bolsheviks had devoted some attention to them even before the July days. The July defeat served simply to fortify their determination to make a good showing. As an editorial in *Rabochii i soldat* on August 9 put it: "This will be the first important engagement of the class struggle in the completely changed post–July 3–5 circumstances. . . . If the Kadets win [the election] the revolution will have been dealt a mighty blow. . . . If the defensists win, we will have the same mess as before. . . . The victory of our party would be the first triumph of the revolution over the counterrevolution."

From August 12 to 15 the attention of all political groups in Petrograd was focused on the Moscow State Conference.[34] In the last few days before the Duma elections, however, the competition for votes became more feverish. Leading Kadets such as Miliukov, Shingarev, Nabokov, and Tyrkova now took to the stump. Miliukov, referring to district duma elections held in May in which Kadets had done poorly, declared that citizens of Petrograd now had the opportunity to "retake examinations" they had failed earlier when they entrusted control of local dumas to parties that "occupied themselves with various fantasies."[35]

The Bolsheviks had laid ambitious plans for their campaign, and as the day of reckoning approached, party officials nervously took stock of all that remained undone.[36] Still, party workers had managed to organize an impressive number of political rallies and meetings and to inundate working-class districts of the capital with campaign leaflets. The party's efforts had received a great boost with the appearance of *Soldat* and *Proletarii* just as the campaign became intense. Moreover, worsening economic conditions and the unpopular policies of the government and the majority socialists obviously worked to the Bolsheviks' advantage, a situation which they exploited to the fullest. "Each worker and soldier is going to have to decide for himself whether he wants workers to wallow in the mud and stench of the ghettos, without schools or light, without adequate transportation facilities," declared an editorial in *Soldat* on election eve. "If this is what he wants then he should vote for our opponents. On the other hand, if he wants those streets in the working-class suburbs that are now breeding places for disease to be sanitary, if he wants to see them paved and lighted and surrounded by schools and gardens, let him vote for the Bolsheviks." The same day's issue of *Proletarii* claimed: "Only our party is striving for fundamental, radical changes in city government. Only our party favors shifting the entire tax burden from the poor to the rich."[37]

Most of all, the party sought to capitalize on popular fears regarding the dangers of counterrevolution by associating all the Bolsheviks' rivals with the assaults of the extreme right. As an editorial in *Soldat* on August 19 put it, in these elections soldiers and workers would have to decide whether they wanted their city run by "those who join with the capitalists and land-owners in issuing penal laws against workers [and] in decreeing capital punishment—who complain about higher wages for labor, decide on mass layoffs, and keep comrades locked up in prison, driving them to hunger strikes and death." This same theme was emphasized in a long, front-page appeal for votes on election day by Stalin in *Proletarii*. Wrote Stalin:

> The Party of People's Freedom [the Kadet Party] defends the interests of large landowners and capitalists. The Party of People's Freedom insisted on the offensive at the front . . . and worked for the triumph of the coun-terrevolution. . . . A vote for the party of Miliukov is a betrayal of one-self, of one's wife and children, and of one's brothers in the rear and at the front. . . . [The Mensheviks and SRs] defend the interests of secure petty proprietors in the cities and in the countryside. . . . To vote for these parties means to vote for a union with the counterrevolution against work-ers and poorer peasants. . . . [It means] to endorse arrests in the rear and capital punishment at the front.[38]

Inasmuch as the objective of the campaign was to mobilize the broadest possible support, the Bolshevik campaign literature of the time contained few references to potentially divisive aspects of the party's theoretical and tactical program. Even the term "Bolshevik" seems to have been used spar-ingly, perhaps because of the danger that it was still tainted by the German-agent charges. Every vote for "List 6," the list of "Social-Democratic Internationalists," was billed simply as "a blow for the revolu-tion against the counterrevolution." Trumpeted *Proletarii* on August 15, and again on August 18 and 19:

> Every worker, peasant, and soldier must vote for our list because only our party is struggling staunchly and bravely against the raging counter-revolutionary dictatorship of the bourgeoisie and large landowners. [Only our party] is fighting the reimposition of capital punishment, the destruc-tion of worker and soldier organizations, and the suppression of all the freedoms won with the blood and sweat of the people. You must vote for our party because it alone is struggling bravely with the peasantry against large landowners, with workers against factory owners, with the oppressed everywhere against the oppressors.

After the balloting for the City Duma, it took several days to tabulate the final vote. When the results were in, the Bolsheviks, showing surprising strength in every section of the capital, received 183,624 votes, giving them sixty-seven seats in the new Duma. The Bolshevik tally was second only to that of the SRs, who received 205,659 votes and seventy-five seats; this represented an improvement of 14 percent over the Bolsheviks' performance in the district duma elections of late May. The Kadet vote was 114,483 votes, giving them forty-two seats, while the Mensheviks trailed with 23,552 votes and eight seats.[39]

What did the vote mean? Some contemporary observers were inclined to ignore the Bolshevik success altogether. Thus, by not very deft manipulation of the figures, a writer for the Kadet paper *Rech'* claimed that the election results revealed growing support for Kadet positions among "true residents of Petrograd."[40] Significantly more forthright was a postelection analysis by a political observer for *Novaia zhizn'*. This writer stated directly that the elections had been a "striking and incontrovertible victory" for the Bolsheviks. The success of the party, he explained, was a reflection of the extremely tense mood of workers and substantial numbers of soldiers, and their alienation from the policies of the Soviet majority and the new course of the government. The victory was "undoubtedly facilitated by the unpardonable persecution of [Bolshevik] leaders, which inevitably began with great pomp and always burst like a soap bubble." "The repression of the extreme left served only to increase its popularity among the masses," he added. "The Bolshevik press was closed, the party's agitation was constrained—but the enforced silence was the most eloquent propaganda."[41]

Like *Rech'*, the Menshevik *Rabochaia gazeta* was at first inclined to minimize the import of the impressive Bolshevik vote. An initial account of the election in *Rabochaia gazeta* suggested that the Bolshevik total had been greatly inflated by the votes of rightists whose aim was to magnify the red threat in order to justify their own political program.[42] The very next day, however, the same paper reassessed the election and arrived at conclusions very similar to those of *Novaia zhizn'*. Commented *Rabochaia gazeta*: "One must conclude that the Bolshevik triumph was enormous, greatly exceeding the expectations of the Bolsheviks themselves. For this Bolshevik success, we are indebted to the inadequacy of creative work on the part of the democracy, which has not given the masses any concrete results; we are also indebted to the system of repression—chaotic, hasty, at times ridiculous and senseless—which . . . clothed the Bolsheviks in a halo of suffering, destroying the impact which the criminal action of July 3–5 had had on the worker and soldier masses."[43]

·6·

THE RISE OF KORNILOV

For Russian liberals and conservatives who had prematurely celebrated the demise of Bolshevism and the turn toward firm government and order in the wake of the July uprising, developments in the second half of July and the first weeks of August were shattering. During this troubled time all Petrograd newspapers were filled with indications of the deepening political and social crisis engulfing Russia. Each day brought fresh reports of expanding anarchy and violence among land-hungry peasants in the countryside; disorders in the cities; the increasing militancy of factory workers; the government's inability to resist movements toward complete autonomy on the part of the Finns and Ukrainians; the continuing radicalization of soldiers at the front and rear; catastrophic breakdowns in the production and distribution of essential supplies; skyrocketing prices; and the resurgence and expanding influence of the Bolsheviks, who, alone among the major political groups, appeared to profit from these difficulties and who, after the Sixth Congress, appeared to be waiting impatiently for an early opportunity to organize an armed insurrection.

In mid-August a series of explosions and fires of unknown origin ripped through a number of factories engaged in war work.[1] The food situation in Petrograd, already alarming, suddenly became desperate,[2] primarily because of continuing chaos in domestic railway and water transport systems. On August 21 there came perhaps the blackest news of all—the Germans had occupied the city of Riga, a vital seaport on the Baltic. Now hordes of anxious citizens, at least those who were financially able to do so, made hurried preparations to abandon Petrograd in expectation of further civil disorders and an early enemy assault on the capital. A sudden dramatic rise in the number of houses and apartments advertised for rent bore eloquent testimony to the prevailing panic.

No one was more troubled by these ominous signs of continuing political, social, and economic disintegration than Kerensky. Yet fearful that naked repression untempered by reform would arouse the Soviet and bring the Petrograd masses into the streets once again, and unable to unite his cabinet behind a reform program of any kind, he was incapable of significantly influencing the course of events. In view of the resulting paralysis of national leadership, increasing numbers of industrial and business figures, representatives of gentry interests, military officers—in short, a broad specturm of liberal, not to speak of conservative, opinion—and even Allied representatives in Russia concluded that the second coalition government was no more viable than the first. For these groups, the lone remaining hope of restoring order at the front and arresting chaos in the rear seemed to be an alliance of antisocialist liberal and conservative forces and the establishment of a strong dictatorship dedicated to the task of eliminating conflicting sources of political authority (most importantly, the Soviet), bridling the revolution, and marshaling the Russian population in defense of the motherland.

By August 1917 this orientation was shared by most Kadets and by such important centrist political pressure groups as the All-Russian Union of Trade and Industry and the Union of Landowners, both based in Moscow.[3] It has recently been shown that while a minority of Kadet leaders responded to the events of late July and August by calling for continued support of coalition government and close cooperation with moderate socialists in the satisfaction of mass demands for reform, the main body of the party, headed by Miliukov, shifted decisively rightward.[4] At the same time, Kadets of this persuasion tended, by and large, to shy away from direct participation in preparations for a coup d'état (this appears to have been the position of the All-Russian Union of Trade and Industry and the Union of Landowners as well). Believing that any effort to establish a dictatorship not endorsed by both the cabinet and the Soviet would most likely fail, for the time being they sought simply to exert pressure, both within and outside the government, for the most forceful measures possible to restore law and order and the fighting capacity of the armed forces.[5]

Other sizable center and rightist political groups, impatient with Kerensky at this time, had no such reservations about how a dictatorship should be established. Predictably, among the most prominent of these more militant groups were various organizations representing military officers. Embittered elements of the officer corps had first begun to consider possibilities for a military dictatorship as early as April 1917; subsequently their number grew rapidly, and representatives of a host of military organizations began swarming around army headquarters in Mogilev like bees in a hive, concocting elaborate schemes to halt and reverse the changes wrought by the February revolution. In July and August the most important of these militant pressure groups representing officers were the Union of Officers of the Army and Navy, whose Central, or "Main," Committee was permanently headquartered in Mogilev, and the Military League and the Union of Saint George Cavaliers, both based in Petrograd.[6]

Among civilian organizations of similar orientation functioning during the summer of 1917, the Society for the Economic Rehabilitation of Russia and the Republican Center were probably the most prominent. The Society for the Economic Rehabilitation of Russia, first formed in April 1917 and headed by Alexander Guchkov and Aleksei Putilov, initially united influential figures in the fields of business, industry, and insurance to finance the preparation and dissemination of anti-Bolshevik propaganda and to support candidates for election to the Constituent Assembly.[7] But as the political crisis in Russia deepened, the society began to work closely with top military personnel and to devote increasing attention to the support of preparations for the establishment of a military dictatorship. The evolution of the Republican Center was similar. Founded in May under the auspices of the powerful Siberian bank by conservative business and military leaders to support a propaganda campaign aimed at "braking the spontaneous [revolutionary] movement,"[8] the Republican Center soon acquired an active military section. Headed by Colonel L. P. Desimeter and including representatives of all of the more important militant officer groups operating at the time, this organ concerned itself almost exclusively with technical preparations for the seizure of power.

It remains to be recorded that during the spring and summer of 1917 these military and civilian rightist organizations considered several prominent military figures for the post of dictator, among them Generals Alekseev and Brusilov and Admiral Kolchak.[9] By late July, however, the obvious favorite had become General Lavr Kornilov, the newly appointed commander-in-chief of the Russian army. Short, lean, noticeably bandy-legged in stature, straightforward and tough in manner, Kornilov was distinguished by his narrow beard, his thick, graceful mustache, and the slanted eyes and high cheekbones of his Mongolian forebears. Born into the family of a cossack officer in 1870 and raised in a remote corner of Siberia, Kornilov received a narrowly military education and began his professional career as an explorer of Chinese Turkestan and the eastern provinces of Persia. He saw action in Manchuria in the Russo-Japanese War and served from 1907 to 1911 as military attaché in the Russian legation in Peking. During the first months of World War I he advanced rapidly in rank, and early in 1914 he received command of an infantry division. Shortly thereafter, in the spring of 1915, the bulk of his division was annihilated by Austrian forces; Kornilov himself was captured while wandering in the woods and subsequently spent close to a year in a Hungarian prison camp.[10]

An impression of Kornilov's state of mind during his confinement was recorded by General E. I. Martynov, who shared quarters with the general in captivity and under whom Kornilov had served in Manchuria. According to Martynov, during those months of rising popular indignation against the tsarist regime in Russia, Kornilov, gnawed by thwarted ambition, passed the hours of enforced leisure engrossed in books about Napoleon, a pastime which only caused him further frustration. Martynov maintained that at that time Kornilov was sympathetic to the Black Hundreds. Reading in the Austrian press of the struggle between progressive Duma leaders and the Russian government, Kornilov talked incessantly of the pleasure he would derive from hanging "all those Guchkovs and Miliukovs."[11]

In July 1916, Kornilov, disguised as an Austrian soldier, managed to escape and returned to Russia. Largely because of publicity in the Russian press, thirsting for triumphs, however small, during this militarily bleak period, Kornilov became a national hero overnight. Kornilov's escape, more than anything else, fostered the aura of courage and bravery which surrounded him by the time of the February revolution; apart from this, his military record was undistinguished, a fact that once prompted General Brusilov to comment brusquely: "He was the commander of a mounted partisan detachment and nothing more."[12]

After the February events, Kornilov made a rapid, if superficial, adjustment to the changed political atmosphere. Appointed commander of the Petrograd Military District at the urging of Duma leaders in search of a well-known and authoritative figure to help restore order and calm,[13] Kornilov commented to reporters upon his arrival in the capital on March 5 that the revolution "insures victory over the enemy."[14] Shortly afterward, having paid a dutiful call on the Executive Committee of the Petrograd Soviet, Kornilov set off for Tsarskoe Selo to arrest the Empress Alexandra. Yet for all this outward display of revolutionary zeal, Kornilov remained very much an officer of the old school; national political issues interested him only insofar as they affected the primary task of restoring the army. He was described by Martynov as "an absolute ignoramus in the realm of politics" and by General Alekseev, who also knew him well, as "a man with a lion's heart and the brains of a sheep."[15]

Kornilov understood very little about the conflicting concerns of the various political groups and classes within Russian society. He drew little distinction, for example, between the moderate socialist leadership of the Petrograd Soviet, which, while working for a negotiated compromise peace, nonetheless steadfastly supported the Russian defense effort, and the Bolsheviks, who condemned the war and the defense effort altogether. After all, was not the Soviet responsible for initiating the breakdown of traditional military discipline in the armed forces and for all those meddlesome committees and political commissars? During the height of the April protests, Kornilov, his patience exhausted, had called out his artillery with the intent of using it against demonstrating workers and soldiers, but this order was immediately countermanded by the Petrograd Soviet.[16] In response, Kornilov abruptly resigned his command and departed for the southwestern front, bristling with antagonism toward the Soviet, and hostility and bitterness toward the Provisional Government for what he considered its spinelessness in dealing with Russia's "internal enemies."

From this moment, Kornilov was understandably suspect in Soviet circles, while among workers and soldiers in Petrograd his name was fast becoming synonymous with repression and counterrevolution. At the same time, Kornilov's tough approach to the problem of controlling civil disorder attracted the attention of conservatives, who began to look upon him as the potential strongman to head a more authoritarian government. Indeed, members of an embryonic Petrograd rightist organization formed in mid-March by Vasilii Zavoiko and E. P. Semenov began to focus on Kornilov as a potential dictator in April.[17] At that time, a member of the Zavoiko-Semenov circle initiated discussions with Kornilov, who expressed his willingness to work with the group. In order to maintain a liaison after the general's unexpected departure for the front, Zavoiko himself enlisted in the army and became Kornilov's orderly.[18]

Zavoiko, a shady character later universally condemned as a political intriguer of the worst sort, quickly acquired enormous influence over Kornilov.[19] The general subsequently testified that Zavoiko's services to him were mainly literary. "Since Zavoiko wielded a skillful pen," he affirmed, "I had him draw up orders and papers requiring a particularly strong, artistic style."[20] It is obvious however, that the functions performed by Zavoiko went significantly beyond those of a literary nature. The relationship was defined more accurately by Martynov: "With such a flimsy store of knowledge, Kornilov was in need of guidance, and Zavoiko became his personal guide, one would say mentor, on all state matters."[21] From the moment of his appointment to Kornilov's staff, Zavoiko fed Kornilov's anxieties about the government in Petrograd, nurtured his superior's personal ambitions, worked unceasingly to further Kornilov's popularity as a potential national leader, and, as time went on, stood at the center of all the political intrigues constantly swirling around the general.

The beginning of the June offensive found Kornilov in command of the Eighth Army on the southwestern front. When the Germans reinforced Austrian troops there and launched a powerful counterattack, the Eighth Army was soundly battered. But for a short time—between June 23 and 29—Eighth Army forces made some gains, taking the ancient Galician town of Halicz, moving on toward Kalusz, and in the process capturing some twelve thousand enemy soldiers and two hundred artillery pieces ("Kornilov's trophies," they were proudly dubbed by the press). This occurred at a time when the Russian advance in other areas had been reversed, and jingoistic papers in Petrograd reacted jubilantly. More than any other officer, Kornilov received personal credit for Russia's short-lived military successes. Subsequently, in no small part because of Zavoiko's talents as a publicity agent, Kornilov attracted wide notice for his "willingness to trade space for lives" and, even more, for his insistence that spontaneously retreating soldiers be fired upon as a means of restoring discipline. At the same time, the Russian commander-in-chief, General Brusilov, and, of course, the Bolsheviks were made to bear the onus for Russia's defeats.

All this publicity increased Kornilov's popularity with the right; it also brought the general's qualities to the attention of Maximilian Filonenko, a right SR and government commissar with the Eighth Army, and Boris Savinkov, commissar for the southwestern front and ultimately a figure of no small historical importance. Savinkov was a revolutionary extremist who turned rabid chauvinist under the impact of the Great War. Political conspirator *par excellence*, Savinkov had been one of the most flamboyant and notorious figures in the famous terrorist SR Battle Organization between 1903 and 1905. He had, in fact, taken a prominent part in the sensational killings of numerous tsarist officials, among them Nicholas II's hated minister of the interior, Viacheslav Plehve, and the Grand Duke Sergei. After 1905, Savinkov spent much of his time abroad where he busied himself writing a number of popular novels once uncharitably described by Woytinsky as "a mixture of pulp magazine technique with revolutionary yarns and a cheap imitation of Dostoevsky generously spiced with eroticism imported from France."[22] At the outbreak of World War I, Savinkov enlisted in the French army, and in April 1917 he returned to Russia and placed himself at the disposal of the Provisional Government. In the early summer, Savinkov, who was close to Kerensky, then minister of war, was appointed government representative on the southwestern front.

As a front commissar, Savinkov had witnessed firsthand the virtual disintegration of Russian combat units. On July 9, in great anguish, he had apprised Kerensky by telegraph of the horrors then unfolding.[23] In his approach to the problem of the army, Savinkov naturally differed from those who repudiated in toto the changes in the armed forces wrought by the revolution. Rather, he emphasized the crucial role of civil commissars in overseeing the behavior of officers and in smoothing relations between them and the mass of radicalized soldiers.[24] With somewhat less vigor, he defended the role of democratic committees, albeit with strictly limited and well-defined competence. Nonetheless, Savinkov was also a strong advocate of severe measures to restore order at home and on the front—an outlook which Filonenko shared.[25] There is some evidence that in late July Savinkov had sounded out Miliukov about the possibility of establishing a military dictatorship;[26] at the same time, both he and Filonenko began to look to Kornilov for leadership in halting the flood of desertions from the front and for help in pressuring Kerensky to acquiesce in the creation of an authoritarian regime.

One of Kerensky's first actions upon becoming prime minister on July 8, instigated quite likely by Savinkov and Filonenko, was the appointment of Kornilov as commander of the southwestern front. Here enemy pressure was greatest and the disintegration of Russian units most advanced. Kornilov wasted no time in reinforcing his reputation for iron firmness. On the day he assumed command, in a telegram to Kerensky drafted by Zavoiko, Kornilov demanded the authorization of capital punishment for fleeing soldiers in terms so threatening that Savinkov was forced to intercede and insist the message be revised.[27] The next day, without waiting for Kerensky's reply, Kornilov ordered his subordinate commanders to use machine guns and artillery on units falling back without orders.[28]

Kerensky did not need Kornilov's warning to appreciate the gravity of Russia's military situation and the need for drastic measures to halt the waves of Russian soldiers now rushing pell-mell from the battlefield. On July 9, even before receipt of Kornilov's first telegram, Kerensky had issued orders to all commanders to fire on units retreating without authority. Three days later, upon Kerensky's recommendation, the Provisional Government officially reinstituted the use of capital punishment to maintain discipline at the front. Nonetheless, evidence of Kornilov's effort at applying pressure on the government was leaked to the press, quite likely by the resourceful Zavoiko. Accounts in nationalist papers in Petrograd conveyed the impression that Kornilov was pushing the government to authorize stern measures to restore discipline in the army (this was true), while Kerensky was acting reluctantly in response to this pressure (this was not the case at all). As a result, in rightist circles, Kornilov's stock soared while the government's took a corresponding plunge. Among the masses, meanwhile, Kornilov's image as perhaps the foremost symbol of counterrevolution was significantly reinforced.

On July 16, Kerensky, accompanied by Foreign Minister Tereshchenko and by Savinkov and Filonenko, met at General Staff headquarters (Stavka) in Mogilev with the Russian military high command. This emergency council was organized at Kerensky's behest to evaluate jointly the military situation on all fronts in the wake of the enemy's successful counteroffensive and to consider ways of halting the disintegration of the army. Because of the particularly unstable situation on the southwestern front, Kornilov had been directed to remain at his post and to telegraph a report to the conference, but most of the other top Russian generals were present, among them the commander-in-chief, General Brusilov; General Denikin, western front commander; General Klembovsky, from the northern front; and Generals Ruzsky and Alekseev, both temporarily unassigned.[29] Not unexpectedly, these officers vented their bitterness at the changes that the revolution had brought to the army. One after the other they blasted the Soviet and the Provisional Government in general, as well as Kerensky personally, for having directly facilitated the army's ruin. At the core of the generals' complaints were incompetent commissars and constantly proliferating, power-seeking committees, which, they felt, had subverted the authority of officers and continually interfered with military operations. As one of the front commanders declared: "There cannot be dual authority in the army. The army must have one head and one authority." General Brusilov articulated the seminal importance the generals obviously attached to the army's restoration: "There is only one reason for all the difficulties that the Provisional Government has experienced in Petrograd and for all the disasters within Russia—namely, the absence of an army."[30]

Implicit in the generals' comments was their conviction that the government's permissiveness was primarily to blame for the army's troubles and, concomitantly, that the imposition of strict discipline in the ranks, along with appropriate legal and administrative sanctions, would alone restore the fighting capacity of the army; the generals made it clear that if Kerensky were unwilling to act decisively in this regard without further delay, they would be compelled to take matters into their own hands. The longest, most impassioned speech was delivered by General Denikin, a dashing, young, much-decorated hero of the early war years, who followed his indictment of Kerensky and postrevolutionary conditions in the army with a series of blunt demands for immediate implementation by the government, which subsequently received strong support from most of his colleagues. Denikin insisted on complete freedom of action for the generals in all military matters. He called for the immediate abolition of commissars and democratic committees, the revocation of the Declaration of Soldiers' Rights,[31] the restoration in full of the traditional authority of officers, the reintroduction of capital punishment and the use of special military courts to reimpose discipline among units in the rear, and the total prohibition of political activity in the army—in sum, not only a return to the old order among troops in battle zones, but the extension of repressive measures to military forces everywhere in Russia. Beyond this, Denikin demanded the formation of special punitive units for use by commanders to impose their authority by force when necessary.

One of the participants in the July 16 council at Stavka recorded that Kerensky listened to Denikin's indictment in stunned silence, hunched over a table, his head buried in his arms, and that Tereshchenko was moved to tears by the oppressive report.[32] "If one may say so, Denikin was the hero of the occasion," General Alekseev later recorded appreciatively in his diary.[33] Compared with Denikin's bombast, Kornilov's report to the council was relatively mild, no doubt partly because Zavoiko was away at the time and Savinkov and Filonenko had had some influence in its preparation.[34] That Kornilov was basically in sympathy with Denikin is attested to by a telegram that Kornilov dispatched to him immediately upon receiving the text of Denikin's speech: "I would sign such a report with both hands. . . ."[35]

Kornilov's telegraphed report, while affirming the need for the traditional prestige and disciplinary authority of officers to be restored, for strict curbs on political activity in the armed forces, and for the extension of capital punishment and special courts to the rear, at the same time implied that commanders were to some degree responsible for breakdowns in order and discipline. Indeed, Kornilov called for a purge of the officer corps. In contrast to the other generals' blanket condemnation of commissars and committees, Kornilov's report was silent on the problem of civil interference in military matters. Beyond this, Kornilov actually proposed expanding the role of commissars (an unmistakable mark of Savinkov's influence). Finally, while insisting on the necessity of defining precisely and limiting narrowly the democratic committees' sphere of competence, Kornilov, unlike his fellow commanders, did not call for their immediate elimination.[36]

In the course of the train trip back to Petrograd after the July 16 council at Stavka, Kerensky, coaxed by Savinkov and Filonenko, apparently made up his mind to remove Brusilov and promote Kornilov to the post of commander-in-chief; two days later these changes were announced. At the same time, Kerensky named General Vladimir Cheremisov to replace Kornilov as commander of the southwestern front. Savinkov was to recall much later that he and Filonenko had urged Brusilov's removal because of his inability to cope with the crisis in the army and had pushed Kornilov as his replacement because of the firmness and coolness under pressure exhibited by the latter during his tenure (one week!) as southwestern front commander.[37] This may well be true—at the time, Savinkov and Filonenko were preoccupied with finding a leader who would apply force decisively and unflinchingly against recalcitrant troops. It is harder to understand why, in view of his own personal political ambitions, Kerensky accepted their recommendation. At precisely this time, the new prime minister was engaged in a desperate effort to defend himself against attacks from both the extreme left and right and to piece together a second centrist, liberal-socialist coalition; his prospects for success in this venture were, as yet, uncertain. By now, Kornilov, by virtue of his growing popularity among liberals and conservatives had become a powerful political figure and a natural rival to Kerensky.

Kerensky subsequently claimed that his elevation of Kornilov was dictated by the latter's merits as a commander in the field[38] and by his enlightened position on reform in the army, particularly his view of the future role of political commissars and democratic committees.[39] Yet this explanation does not ring true. Kornilov's achievements on the battlefield were undistinguished, and, the July 16 telegram notwithstanding, his predilection for the application of massive military force to curb disorder at home and at the front was a matter of record. It was probably Kornilov's reputation for severity and toughness, rather than his alleged readiness to accommodate revolutionary change, that now made him attractive to Kerensky. What the army needed, Kerensky appears to have concluded, was a strong personality at its head. On this he was basically in agreement with Savinkov and Filonenko. To the new prime minister, anxiously working to consolidate his political position, the selection of Kornilov had the added advantage of being extremely popular with disgruntled liberals and conservatives and with the nonsocialist press in Petrograd.[40]

It is also well to keep in mind that Kerensky's options in the matter of a new commander were quite limited. That the ineffective Brusilov had to go was by now universally acknowledged. Yet judging by the proceedings of the council at Stavka, most senior Russian commanders were at least as reactionary and personally antagonistic to Kerensky as Kornilov. Kerensky might have considered two relatively junior officers who were not invited to Stavka on July 16: Kornilov's replacement as commander of the Eighth Army, General Cheremisov, and the commander of the Moscow Military District, General Verkhovsky. However, precisely because they rejected the idea that repressive measures alone could restore discipline in the army, and because they were willing to work with committees and commissars and to purge the officer corps of ultrareactionaries, Cheremisov and Verkhovsky were suspect among many of the elements whose support Kerensky sought to win. As to the danger of independent political action by Kornilov, Savinkov (who now stepped up to the post of deputy minister of war) and Filonenko (who was simultaneously named commissar at staff headquarters) doubtless expected that since they had been able to moderate Kornilov's behavior in the past, it would be possible to continue to do so; very likely they transmitted this assurance to Kerensky.

It immediately became apparent to Kerensky that controlling Kornilov, surrounded in Mogilev by right extremists, would not be easy. The day after his appointment (July 19), in a bluntly worded telegram drafted by Zavoiko and leaked at once to the press, Kornilov made his assumption of command of the army contingent upon Kerensky's acceptance of a series of demands altogether as ominous as those voiced by Denikin at the Stavka council. Kornilov insisted that, as commander-in-chief, he would not be subject to regulation of any kind and that he would be responsible "only to [his] conscience and to the people as a whole." He demanded total independence in regard to operational directives and appointments of commanders. Special courts and the application of capital punishment to enforce discipline were to apply to soldiers in the rear as well as those at the front. Kornilov further demanded government acceptance of all the other recommendations he had made to the Stavka council.[41] Additionally, on July 20 the new commander-in-chief wired Kerensky insisting that the appointment of Cheremisov as commander of the southwestern front be rescinded.[42]

There is evidence that after receiving these telegrams, Kerensky began to have second thoughts about the appointment of Kornilov as supreme commander and seriously considered dropping the idea.[43] Yet he was now in an extremely awkward position. Kornilov's appointment had been made public, and, thanks to Zavoiko, the general's "conditions" were also widely known. The Kadets, all other liberal and conservative groups, and the nonsocialist press had already formed in solid ranks behind Kornilov. Their attitude was expressed by *Novoe vremia* on July 20: "It was difficult, in fact probably impossible, to find a more suitable general and supreme comman-der in these days of mortal danger being experienced by Russia. The Provi-sional Government was forced to choose between meetings at the front, the disintegration of the army, the destruction of southern Russia—and the sav-ing of the state. And it found in itself the courage and decisiveness to make the choice." A break with Kornilov at this point probably would have put an end to the delicate negotiations then underway to form a new coalition government with the Kadets. And so a compromise of sorts was hastily arranged between Kornilov and Kerensky. Kornilov, for his part, pledged responsibility to the government and dropped his insistence on the im-mediate implementation of his other conditions. The government, in turn, committed itself to giving the demands of the generals a sympathetic hear-ing and to acting on them with all deliberate speed. Kerensky also agreed to find another post for Cheremisov; although this concession was of no appar-ent import at the time, Kerensky was ultimately to pay very dearly for it.[44]

General Kornilov subsequently made two trips from Mogilev to Petro-grad in an effort to persuade the cabinet to implement his recommendations. The first visit took place on August 3. On this occasion Kornilov brought along a formal proposal (another example of Zavoiko's writing talent) em-bodying most of the demands for the repression of troops at the front and rear and for the restoration of officers' authority that had been made by Denikin and Kornilov at the Stavka council, as well as the conditions pressed by Kornilov on July 19. Although Kornilov no longer insisted on un-limited authority for himself in the August 3 proposal, he now reversed his earlier stand regarding the future role of commissars, calling for strict limi-tation, rather than expansion, of their authority.[45] He also envisioned a narrower, more tightly controlled role for democratic committees then he had suggested in his memo of July 16. Still, as Kerensky later acknowl-edged, he, Savinkov, and Filonenko were ready, in principle, to support all these measures. They found Kornilov's formal proposal so crude in style and potentially inflammatory in language, however, that all three agreed the document could not be submitted even to a closed session of the cabinet. Filonenko was therefore assigned to rework the proposal in more diplomatic terms for presentation to the government by Kornilov on August 10.[46] While given an audience by the cabinet before leaving the capital on August 3, Kornilov did not mention his recommendations for reform, restricting his comments to general observations on prevailing conditions in the army.

When the Petrograd press got wind of the contents of Kornilov's proposal[47] the news set off a fierce and prolonged public controversy be-tween the center and right, staunchly supportive of Kornilov and his pro-gram, and the moderate and extreme left, united once again in opposition (particularly to the extension of capital punishment to the rear and the curbing of democratic committees). In an antagonistic front-page editorial on August 4, *Rabochaia gazeta*, for example, lashed out at the Kadets (and indirectly at Kornilov) for advocating a return to the ways of the old regime, complaining that it was precisely this traditionally severe discipline that had made the old army a reliable instrument of the autocracy. "Kadets," the editorial demanded, "tell us directly, which people do you have in mind as military dictators—whom are you preparing for the part of Napoleon?" Among rank-and-file workers, soldiers, and sailors, the alarm over Kornilov's program rekindled the still-smoldering protest against the restoration of capital punishment at the front. Thus, on August 7, it will be recalled, the Workers' Section of the Petrograd Soviet adopted a strongly worded resolution demanding that capital punishment be rescinded.[48]

At about this time, it appeared that General Cheremisov, in Petrograd for reassignment, was in close touch with moderate socialist leaders. *Izvestiia*, on August 4, carried accounts of the press conferences held the previous day by General Kornilov, following his meeting with the cabinet, and by General Cheremisov. In response to reporters' questions, Kornilov had once again emphasized the importance of immediate authorization by the government of broader repressive measures and deprecated the future role of democratic committees. In contrast, the burden of Cheremisov's comments was that repressive measures alone, "not even mass executions," could restore discipline—that it would be impossible to do so as long as the soldiers did not understand and accept the necessity, obligation, and duty of carrying on the war. In the task of raising the consciousness of the troops, Cheremisov attached great importance to joint efforts by officers and democratic committees. *Izvestiia* pointedly contrasted the two statements: "Today we bring you accounts of two conferences, with General Kornilov and with General Cheremisov, on the same subject. But just take note of how they differ. At the same time that the first stubbornly insists on all out repressive measures . . . and completely disregards the importance of army organizations, the second puts the center of gravity in the struggle with disintegration in the army on the joint work of the officer staff with organizations of soldiers. . . . The sympathy of the democracy is not on the side of Kornilov."[49]

By the second week in August, rumors, not without some foundation, were circulating in the capital that Kerensky had suggested to those around him that Kornilov would not work in the post of commander-in-chief and that Cheremisov might be a suitable replacement. When word of Kerensky's wavering reached Mogilev, Kornilov and his entourage were naturally alarmed. The campaign of liberal and conservative groups on Kornilov's behalf was intensified; nonsocialist papers featured daily pledges of support for Kornilov from organizations such as the Union of Officers, the Union of Cossack Troops, and the Union of Saint George Cavaliers.

Between August 8 and 10, Moscow was the scene of a widely publicized

Conference of Public Figures attended by several hundred specially invited leaders of business, industry, agriculture, the professions, the army, and liberal and conservative political groups. The primary purpose of the conference was the adoption of mutually acceptable positions on major issues for presentation to the broader Moscow State Conference, due to open on August 12.[50] Among the delegates were the wealthy industrialists Riabushinsky, Tretiakov, Konovalov, and Vishnegradsky; a large group of Kadets, led by Miliukov; and a host of top military leaders, including Generals Alekseev, Brusilov, Kaledin, and Iudenich. On August 9 these dignitaries interrupted their consideration of broad political issues to adopt a pledge of confidence in Kornilov. This declaration, dispatched to Kornilov and widely circulated the same day, affirmed that all attacks on Kornilov's authority in the army and in Russia were "treachery" and that "all thinking Russia" looked to Kornilov with hope and faith." "May God help you," the resolution concluded, "in your great task of reconstructing a powerful army and saving Russia."[51]

While the public furor over Kornilov raged on, Filonenko busied himself with the revision of Kornilov's August 3 proposal for consideration by the cabinet on August 10. Not content merely to recast the document in more moderate language, he introduced some sweeping recommendations for drastic controls over rail lines and factories. Thus, he added a provision that all railroads be placed under martial law; failure on the part of rail workers to fulfill directives was to carry the same penalty as a soldier's refusal to obey orders at the front—that is, summary execution. To implement these measures, he recommended that military revolutionary courts be set up at major railway depots. A further provision added by Filonenko called for the country's coal mines and all factories engaged in defense work (practically speaking, this could be interpreted to include almost all factories) to be placed under military control. In these enterprises, strikes, lockouts, political meetings, and, in fact, assemblies of any kind were to be prohibited for the duration. Employees would be assigned minimum mandatory work quotas; workers not meeting their quotas would be dismissed summarily and dispatched to the front. "These measures," injected Filonenko at the end of the revised draft, "must be adopted and put into practice immediately with iron decisiveness and consistency."[52]

Savinkov, fully sympathetic to Filonenko's recommendations, pleaded with Kerensky to support them within the cabinet, and even resigned when the prime minister demurred. Kerensky initially rejected Savinkov's resignation, later accepted it, and ultimately, partly because of pressure from Kornilov, prevailed upon Savinkov to return to his post.[53] Kerensky himself has acknowledged that to halt the slide of industry and transport into absolute chaos, he would gladly have taken the lead in implementing the steps envisioned by Filonenko. Within liberal and conservative circles, of course, and even among members of the cabinet, the need for such extreme measures had already been widely discussed. In view of the storm from the left that Kornilov's more limited August 3 program had provoked, however, Kerensky was understandably apprehensive about the probable impact of Filonenko's amendments on the leadership of the Soviet, not to mention the workers and soldiers. His conclusion seems to have been that such measures would have brought a decisive rupture with the Soviet, a bloody confrontation of uncertain outcome with the Bolshevik-led masses, and at the very best, the establishment of an authoritarian government completely at the mercy of the military. Unlike large numbers of former moderates, Kerensky paused, for the moment, on the brink of such a drastic course.

Kornilov, warned by members of his entourage in Mogilev of plots being hatched against him in Petrograd, tried to beg off coming to the capital on August 10. This was completely agreeable to Kerensky, who, although quite willing to use Kornilov to carry out repression at the front, was understandably nervous about the general's popularity with the right and his potential influence on national politics. Savinkov and Filonenko, to the contrary, were determined to employ pressure from Kornilov to force Kerensky's acceptance of the revised Kornilov program. They therefore persuaded the commander-in-chief not to cancel his trip. Kornilov remained wary, however, taking with him to Petrograd a bodyguard of Turkoman soldiers armed with machine guns. Shortly after Kornilov's train left Mogilev for the capital, a telegram from Kerensky reached Stavka informing the commander-in-chief that the government had not called him, did not insist on his coming, and, in view of the strategic situation, could not take responsibility for his departure from the front.[54]

Arriving in Petrograd, Kornilov was met at the train by Filonenko and Savinkov, who brought with them the revised report. Giving the document his hasty approval, the general set off at once for the Winter Palace. Petrograd newspapers the following day carried detailed accounts of his colorful motorcade. Strict military security was observed along the route. Kornilov's car, moving slowly through the streets, was guarded by grim-faced, scarlet-robed Turkoman soldiers jogging alongside, their curved swords dangling unsheaved from their belts; it was preceded and followed by open-top automobiles filled with more Turkomans, armed with machine guns. When the procession neared the Winter Palace, Kerensky, at an upper-story window, watched in amazement and disbelief as the Turkomans jumped from the cars and dashed to the entrance. Emplacing a machine gun in the main vestibule, they took up positions beside it, prepared, if the need arose, to rescue their commander by force.[55]

Such was the extraordinary prelude to a short, predictably icy encounter between Kerensky and Kornilov which served only to exacerbate their differences and complicate their relations. At the outset, Kornilov formally presented his revised and expanded program, with which Kerensky, as we know, was already familiar. The prime minister's response was reportedly

noncommittal, although he may have conveyed the impression that the recommendations were acceptable in principle, which was actually the case.[56]
Kornilov, who had risked the trip to Petrograd in the conviction that the
situation brooked no further delay, was ill-disposed to let the matter drop;
he demanded that the cabinet meet that evening to discuss his proposals.
Kerensky declined to call a full cabinet meeting, arranging instead an informal session to which he invited only his two closest supporters in the
cabinet, Nekrasov and Tereshchenko. Excluded were four Kadet ministers
who were geared for a decisive struggle on behalf of Kornilov's program
and seven moderate socialist ministers who were certain to be unalterably
opposed. The upshot of this gathering on the evening of August 10 was that
while Kerensky, Tereshchenko, and Nekrasov registered their willingness to
support before the full cabinet Kornilov's recommendations relating to the
restoration of the army (in substance the recommendations Kornilov first
brought to Petrograd on August 3), they firmly insisted on laying aside the
new provisions dealing with controls over railways and factories added by
Filonenko.[57]

One can well imagine Kornilov's frustration as he left Petrograd for
Mogilev late on the night of August 10. His encounters with the prime
minister on August 3 and 10 had strengthened his disdain for Kerensky
personally. Worse, an incident which had occurred during his meeting with
the cabinet on August 3 aroused Kornilov's fears that politics in Petrograd
had degenerated to such a point that German agents had direct pipelines
into the highest level of government. While Kornilov was delivering his
report on the state of the army, Kerensky had quietly cautioned him against
being too precise about actual conditions. After the meeting Savinkov explained to the general that while there was no evidence that any ministers
were leaking information directly to the enemy, some cabinet members
were in close touch with members of the All-Russian Executive Committees, among whom were persons suspected of having German ties.[58] Kornilov must have been genuinely appalled by this incident, which no doubt
strengthened his misgivings about Kerensky's government. But above all,
his two unsuccessful attempts to get his emergency proposals before the
cabinet confirmed his suspicions, initially awakened during his tenure as
commander of the Petrograd Military District and constantly fed by the
rightist elements surrounding him at Stavka, that the Provisional Government was too weak and divided to act decisively and that independent
military intervention might well be called for if the authoritarian regime
necessary to take the country in hand was ever to be established.[59]

On August, 6, three days after his first visit to the capital, Kornilov
initiated a request that the Petrograd Military District, heretofore under the
control of the Ministry of War, be placed under his direct command. Justified by the likelihood that the Petrograd area would soon be in the zone of
military operations, this change, if accepted, would greatly strengthen

Kornilov's hand in a military clash with the government or the left. At the same time Kornilov ordered substantial troop dispositions obviously aimed at their possible use in Petrograd.[60] To the delight of the right extremists, who had long since been preparing for a coup, such preparations were intensified after Kornilov's second visit to Petrograd. In a conversation with his chief of staff, General Lukomsky, on August 11, Kornilov explained that these actions were necessary because a Bolshevik rising was to be expected and it was "high time to hang the German agents and spies headed by Lenin" and to "disperse the Soviet of Workers and Soldiers in such a way that it would not reassemble anywhere." Commenting to Lukomsky on his appointment of the ultraconservative General Krymov as commander of the troops being concentrated around Petrograd, Kornilov expressed pleasure that Krymov would not hesitate, if necessary, "to hang the entire Soviet membership."[61]

Of course, all this does not necessarily mean that Kornilov was now irrevocably committed to direct military action against the government. In view of the unpopularity of the steps envisioned in Kornilov's program among the Petrograd masses and their likely response to its implementation, the troop dispositions made by Kornilov during the first half of August were advisable whether the army ultimately acted alone or in cooperation with Kerensky. It appears that Kornilov, unlike many of his supporters, still held out some hope that the government would take stock of its situation and submit to his authority peacefully.[62] Lukomsky recalls that Kornilov commented to him on August 11 that "he was not planning to move against the government—that he hoped it would be possible to reach agreement with it."[63] Nonetheless, it also appears clear that Kornilov was now prepared to act independently, should this prove necessary.

·7·

KORNILOV
VERSUS KERENSKY

The deepening hostility between Kerensky and Kornilov, the increasing polarization of Russian society, and Kerensky's weakness in the prevailing situation became most apparent during the Moscow State Conference held August 12 to 14. Originally conceived by Kerensky in late July to familiarize authoritative political figures from all over Russia with the country's grave problems and to mobilize their support for the programs of the newly created second coalition, this conference had no actual legislative function. Among its close to twenty-five hundred participants, "the flower of the Russian population,"[1] were the members of Kerensky's cabinet, top-ranking military officers, deputies from all four State Dumas, and members of the Executive Committees of the All-Russian Congress of Workers' and Soldiers' Deputies and the All-Russian Congress of Peasants' Deputies. Present as well were representatives of trade unions, municipal councils, institutions of higher learning, cooperatives, provincial zemstvos, and various and sundry congresses and committees relating to business, industry, and the armed forces.[2]

Politically, the delegates were split between liberals and conservatives, by and large staunchly supportive of Kornilov and of stringent measures to restore order, and moderate socialists, who recognized the need for firm government but continued to insist on tempering repression with at least modest steps toward reform. The first group had a slight majority; noted one observant reporter, "Representatives of the bourgeoisie seem to overwhelm democratic elements; morning coats, frock coats, and starched shirts predominate over the side-fastening Russian blouses."[3]

There were practically no spokesmen for the extreme left. The Bolshevik Central Committee initially had planned that party representatives in the All-Russian Executive Committees would accompany their colleagues to Moscow; the Bolshevik delegates would formally repudiate the conference at the first opportunity and then stage a walkout.[4] When this intention became known, however, the majority socialist Soviet leadership required that all members of the Soviet conference delegation agree in advance not to speak out at the conference without specific authorization; for practical purposes, Bolsheviks going to the Moscow Conference with the Soviet delegation were given the choice of accepting the positions of the majority or risking expulsion from the Executive Committees.[5] Given these circumstances, the party elected to absent itself from the conference altogether.

The Moscow State Conference convened in an atmosphere of tension. For several days prior to August 12, Moscow had been rife with rumors that troops loyal to Kornilov were converging on the city and that Kornilov and his supporters were about to make a move against the government. Conference delegates arrived in Moscow to find the streets plastered with posters hailing Kornilov; a publicity brochure lauding the "first people's commander-in-chief" circulated widely.[6] Kornilov himself was not scheduled to make an appearance at the conference until August 14. Nonetheless, so great was the fear of a rightist coup as the conferees assembled that on August 12 the Moscow Soviet formed a six-man Provisional Revolutionary Committee to help assure proper protection for the government and the Soviet. The seriousness with which the possibility of an attack by the right was taken at this time is indicated by the fact that the Moscow Bolsheviks Viktor Nogin and Nikolai Muralov, along with two Mensheviks and two SRs, took an active part in the Provisional Revolutionary Committee's work.[7]

In anticipation of the conference the extreme left–oriented Bolshevik Moscow Regional Bureau took the lead in organizing a wildcat protest strike for August 12, the opening day; the strike was subsequently endorsed by trade union leaders, by the more conservative Bolshevik Moscow Committee, and by representatives of Moscow district soviets and district Bolshevik committees.[8] By a vote of 312 to 284, however, a joint meeting of the Moscow Workers' and Soldiers' Soviets opposed such action.[9] Nonetheless, on the appointed day employees in most Moscow factories did not report for work; many congregated instead at protest meetings. Restaurants and coffeehouses were shut down, streetcars ceased operation, and, for the most part, cab drivers were nowhere about.[10] Even employees at the buffets in the Bolshoi Theater, where the conference met, went out on strike, forcing conference delegates to serve their own refreshments. That evening all Moscow was dark as employees of the gas works stayed away from their jobs.[11]

The impact of the strike bore witness to the power and sentiment of the working classes and the resurgence of Bolshevik influence. A writer in the *Izvestiia* of the Moscow Soviet, whose editorial line reflected the views of the majority socialists, conceded with embarrassment that it was "time to realize that the Bolsheviks are not irresponsible groups but one of the ele-

The Bolshoi Theater, scene of the Moscow State Conference.

ments of the organized revolutionary democracy behind whom stand the broad masses, not always disciplined but, on the other hand, wholly committed to the cause of the revolution."[12]

To judge by formal deliberations at the conference, this message was lost on most delegates. At one of the early sessions, when Miliukov cautioned that the demands outlined by Kornilov should not serve as cause for suspicion and voiced great fear that the government was not making sufficient provision for the restoration of order and the security of property,[13] the Bolshoi exploded with shouts of "Right you are!," loud bravos, and waves of applause. A similar outburst of unrestrained enthusiasm occurred in the right half of the hall when the cossack leader General Aleksei Kaledin declared that "the survival of the state requires the continuation of the war to a victorious conclusion above all," and that "the entire life of the country and all the actions of the Provisional Government must be subordinated to this fundamental assumption." Kaledin outlined a series of basic principles upon which the government should act which, in essence, paralleled Kornilov's program. Amid shouts of "Exactly!" from the right and agonized cries of "No!" from the left, Kaledin declared that "the usurpation of state power by central and local committees and by the soviets must be brought to an end immediately and abruptly."[14]

When the brilliant orator Vasilii Maklakov, one of the founders of the Kadet Party, took the podium and implored the government "to rely and believe in those at the front" and "to find the courage to take the daring steps necessary to lead the country forward [because] the judgment day is approaching," the right delegates again stood and cheered.[15] But when Chkheidze read aloud the All-Russian Executive Committees' platform,[16] which went a long way toward meeting liberal and conservative demands for emphasis on law and order and universal sacrifice in the interest of national defense, and embodied only the most modest concessions to mass demands,[17] these delegates sat scowling in their seats.

Trying to walk a tightrope between the left and right, Kerensky in his opening address refrained from commitment to a specific program of action and, typically sought salvation in strong words. Turning to the left, he thundered: "Let everyone who has already tried to use force of arms against the power of the people know that such attempts will be crushed with blood and iron." Turning next to the right, he roared with equal vigor (in obvious reference to Kornilov and his supporters): "At the same time let those who think the time is ripe to overthrow the revolutionary government with bayonets, be even more careful. I can make anyone serving me with ultimatums obey the will of the supreme power and myself as its head."[18] Kerensky's frenzied address, at times seemingly uncontrolled and uncomfortably theatrical, lasted close to two hours. Miliukov later described the event: "By the expression of his eyes, which he focused on the imagined enemy, by the tense gesturing of his arms, by the intonation of his voice which rose to a scream for extended periods of time, then subsided to a tragic whisper, by his measured phrases and calculated pauses, he appeared to want to scare somebody and to create an impression of force and power. . . . In actuality he only engendered pity."[19]

Kornilov arrived in Moscow by train on the afternoon of August 13. At the Alexandrovsky (now the Belorussian) Station his followers staged a carefully orchestrated welcome which contrasted sharply with the cool reception accorded government ministers upon their arrival in Moscow two days earlier.[20] As the moment for Kornilov's arrival approached, an honor guard and band from the Alexandrovsky Military Academy and a detachment from the Women's Cadet Academy posted themselves on the platform. Also on hand to greet the "first people's commander-in-chief" were a throng of "ladies in gaily colored dresses," bemedaled officers by the dozen, conservative and liberal leaders participating in the state conference, a coterie of municipal authorities, and enthusiastic official deputations from all the patriotic organizations supporting Kornilov. The Moscow Women's Battalion of Death stood at attention on a viaduct overlooking the station, while a mounted cossack detachment was arrayed on the square outside.

As the train slowed to a halt, Kornilov's red-robed Turkoman guards, sabers bared, leaped to the platform and posted themselves in two ranks. While the band played a fanfare and a loud cheer issued from the crowd, Kornilov, resplendent in full-dress uniform, appeared on the steps of his coach. Waving and smiling, he bounded to the platform and made his way through the lines of Turkomans toward the waiting dignitaries. As he passed, the ladies pelted him with flowers, distributed moments earlier by some young officers.

In a brief welcoming speech, the right Kadet Fedor Rodichev conveyed

The "first people's commander-in-chief," General Lavr Kornilov, and Boris Savinkov, front commissar and deputy minister of war, arrive for the Moscow State Conference.

the mood of the moment. "You are now the symbol of our unity," he entoned. "We are unified, indeed all Moscow is unified in confidence in you. . . . Save Russia and a thankful people will crown you."[21] To be sure, at least a few of Rodichev's listeners must have observed, as one reporter commented, that there were no common citizens or regular soldiers on hand, but this circumstance, not surprisingly, seems to have escaped the general's notice.

Shortly after his arrival, Kornilov, seated in an open automobile at the head of a long motorcade, made a pilgrimage to the sacred Iversky shrine, where the tsars traditionally worshiped when they visited Moscow. After prostrating himself before the "miraculous" Iversky icon of the Madonna, Kornilov returned to his railway carriage. There, during the remainder of the evening and the following day, he received a stream of visitors, including a group of influential Kadets, led by Miliukov; the financiers Aleksei Putilov and A. I. Vishnegradsky; the notorious Purishkevich; and Generals Verkhovsky, Kaledin, and Alekseev. Verkhovsky, who, as commander of the Moscow Military District, had formal responsibility for providing security to the Moscow Conference, called on Kornilov to dissuade him from participating in any conspiracy against the government. After the visit he commented that Kornilov's supporters misunderstood the prevailing situation and the mood of the masses to such a degree that "they seem like people who have just dropped from the moon."[22] Kadets who visited Kornilov, reflecting continued nagging doubt about the efficacy of a unilateral coup, may also have urged restraint upon the general. Miliukov, for one, subsequently claimed to have warned Kornilov that a clash with Kerensky was untimely because the prime minister still had a following in the provinces.[23] On the other hand, numerous civil and military figures sought out Kornilov in Moscow expressly to pledge their unqualified support. Most tangibly, Putilov and Vishnegradsky, representing the Society for the Economic Rehabilitation of Russia, agreed to provide the commander-in-chief with a substantial subsidy to help finance the establishment of an authoritarian, exclusively nonsocialist regime.[24]

Kerensky, for his part, was becoming increasingly apprehensive about Kornilov's scheduled address to the Moscow Conference on August 14. Would the general try to use the assembly to apply pressure on the government to adopt his proposals, or, worse still would he attempt to stampede the conference into supporting his personal ambitions? In an effort to dissuade Kornilov from taking any action and to convince him to restrict his remarks at the conference to military operations and the situation at the front, Kerensky dispatched his minister of transport, Petr Iurenev, to see Kornilov on the evening of the thirteenth. Dissatisfied with Kornilov's response to Iurenev, Kerensky himself telephoned the general later that evening with the same admonition, and he repeated his plea at the Bolshoi Theater the next morning, as Kornilov was about to mount the podium. The general's reply was enigmatic: "I will give my speech in my own way."

To Kerensky's immense relief, Kornilov's address was relatively mild. Still, it was a hollow victory for Kerensky. As far as Kornilov was concerned, Kerensky's strictures were further confirmation, if more were needed, of the prime minister's weakness.[25] Moreover, as the right roared its approval, Kornilov was followed to the rostrum by speaker after speaker whose expressed aversion to the changes wrought by the revolution and fundamental hostility toward the Provisional Government were by no means similarly restrained.

The Moscow Conference ended on the night of August 15; as a device for uniting diverse elements of Russian society behind the Provisional Government, it had been a total failure. Kerensky came away from the ordeal with an increased awareness of his own isolation. "It is hard for me," he anguished aloud at the time, "because I struggle with the Bolsheviks of the left and the Bolsheviks of the right, but people demand that I lean on one or the other. . . . I want to take a middle road, but nobody will help me."[26] Kerensky left Moscow with an inflated sense of support for a rightist program. The end of the Moscow Conference coincided with the spreading wave of industrial fires, followed a few days later by the sudden fall of Riga;[27] quite apart from the pressure of Kornilov's supporters, these developments impelled Kerensky to reconsider the question of stricter civil and military controls. From this reevaluation, Kerensky finally seems to have concluded that something on the order of the major curbs on political freedom and the thoroughgoing repression embodied in Kornilov's proposal of August 10 could no longer be delayed, even if such action precipi-

Kerensky addressing a crowd of military personnel.

tated a decisive break with the Soviet and the masses. On August 17, with a
heavy heart, one must assume, he gave Savinkov assurances to this effect
and instructed him to draft specific decrees for action by the cabinet.[28]

Yet, if Kerensky had now moved distinctly closer to Kornilov politically,
there remained a crucial difference between the two men which goes far
toward explaining the events that followed: Kerensky and Kornilov each
viewed himself (and not the other) as the strongman in a new authoritarian
government. More than ever, each was contemptuous toward and apprehensive of the other. Kerensky was determined to use Kornilov for his
own ends, while Kornilov harbored similar intentions regarding Kerensky.
Meanwhile, spurred by the Moscow Conference, preparations for a coup by
rightist groups at home and at the front were reaching a climax. The stage
was set for a final, decisive confrontation.

In the wake of the Moscow Conference, Kornilov continued preparations
to concentrate an imposing array of troops from the front around Petrograd.
The main units directed toward the capital were the First Don Cossack
Division and the Ussuriisky Mounted Division, both belonging to
Krymov's Third Cavalry Corps.[29] The Russian military high command regarded these forces as among the most disciplined and politically reliable in
the entire army; during the first half of August these units had begun to
move from reserve positions on the Rumanian front to the Nevel–
Novosokolniki–Velikie Luki region, roughly three hundred miles
from Petrograd on the direct rail line. Around August 20, the First Don
Cossack Division was transferred to the Pskov area, half the remaining distance to the capital. Simultaneously, the equally crack Savage Division, so
called because it was comprised primarily of mountain tribesmen from the

northern Caucasus whose ferociousness and cruelty in combat were legendary, was attached to the Third Corps and shipped from the southwestern front to Dno, just east of Pskov.[30] Cossack and shock units stationed along the Baltic were earmarked for an eventual role in the pacification of the capital as well. On August 25, General A. M. Dolgorukov, commander of the Finnish-based First Cavalry Corps, was called to Stavka in connection with plans to have one of his main elements, the Fifth Cossack Division, advance on Petrograd from the north, while units of the Third Corps were moving in on the capital from the south. Among other troop relocation orders emanating from Stavka at this time was a directive to the Reval "Shock Battalion of Death" to proceed to Tsarskoe Selo.[31]

As nearly as one can piece together from scattered, sometimes contradictory evidence, an elaborate scheme for a rightist putsch in Petrograd to coincide with the approach of front troops was worked out by the Main Committee of the Union of Officers and the Military Section of the Republican Center and Military League.[32] This plan appears to have been linked to a series of fund-raising rallies scheduled by the Soviet leadership in Petrograd for Sunday, August 27, the six-month anniversary of the February revolution. The conspirators evidently assumed that the rallies would be accompanied by disorders which could be used as a pretext for proclaiming martial law, wrecking Bolshevik organizations, dispersing the Soviet, and establishing a military dictatorship. To insure that the occasion would not pass without suitable disturbances, the rightist press was to whip up political tension in the capital, while agitators posing as Bolsheviks were to circulate in factories, rousing workers. The conspirators also agreed that as a last resort they would stage a leftist rising themselves; at this point, the military forces converging on the capital would be called in to help restore order and establish a strict new regime.[33]

As the day designated for action neared, the Main Committee of the Union of Officers, under a variety of pretexts, concentrated inordinate numbers of pro-Kornilov officers in Petrograd. On August 22 the army chief of staff instructed infantry, cavalry, and cossack division headquarters on all fronts to send three officers to Mogilev, ostensibly for orientation in the handling of newly developed English trench mortars. Actually, upon their arrival at Stavka these officers were briefed and sent on almost immediately to Petrograd.[34]

To what extent the government was aware of these activities is unclear. In early August Kerensky had received an alarming report on the work of the Union of Officers from the SR Central Committee.[35] After the Moscow State Conference, the prime minister's apprehension regarding conspiracies being hatched against him at Stavka became obsessive; at his insistence, the government resolved to forbid the Union of Officers from using staff funds to finance its activities, to remove the union's Main Committee from Mogilev, and to arrest some of its most active members.[36] The extent of

Kornilov's personal involvement in and commitment to the realization of his extreme supporters' plans is also difficult to ascertain. Could Kornilov's apparent preparations to intervene directly in national politics and his support of rightist activity in the capital have stemmed from a sincere belief, encouraged by the conspirators with whom he was surrounded, that the Bolsheviks were on the verge of staging a popular rising which the government would be unable to quell? The evidence on this point is inconclusive. There are indications that even now Kornilov held out hope that ultimately Kerensky would recognize the need for a tougher government free of Soviet influence and would cooperate in its establishment.

Kornilov's hope that Kerensky might prove cooperative was strengthened to some extent by discussions at Mogilev between the general and the deputy minister of war, Savinkov, representing the prime minister, during the afternoon and evening of August 23 and the following morning.[37] These conversations touched on a number of sore points between Kornilov and Kerensky. A central issue was what was to be done about those provisions of Kornilov's program relating to the rear that had been rejected by Kerensky on August 10. By this time, the civil control decrees that Kerensky had asked Savinkov to prepare on August 17 had been drafted. In sum, they embodied many of Kornilov's demands; Kornilov evidently expressed approval of the decrees, and Savinkov voiced confidence that they would be adopted "in the next few days." How the government would respond to the storm of popular protest these decrees were certain to trigger was a matter of mutual concern. Savinkov suggested, no doubt wishfully, that the Bolsheviks and perhaps also the Soviet would rebel against them and that the government would deal mercilessly with such opposition. To strengthen the government's hand as it embarked on this tough new course, Savinkov proposed that the Third Corps be dispatched to the capital and placed at the War Ministry's disposal. He insisted, however, that for "political reasons" the reactionary General Krymov be removed as commander of the Third Corps, and that a regular cavalry unit be substituted for the Savage Division prior to the Third Corps's move to the capital.[38]

Kornilov agreed to these conditions at the time, although subsequently he simply ignored them. In effect, the government was sanctioning troop dispositions which the commander-in-chief had initiated some weeks earlier on his own. It was decided that Kornilov should notify Savinkov by telegraph two days before the Third Corps was in place. The government would then declare martial law in Petrograd, after which the new regulations would be issued.[39]

Savinkov and Kornilov tentatively reached this understanding at their first meeting on the afternoon of August 23, despite the fact that the meeting had evidently gotten off to an unpromising start. Kornilov had complained about Soviet socialists in the cabinet and had heaped abuse on Kerensky personally. Savinkov noted later that Kornilov declared directly that the Provisional Government was, quite simply, "incapable of adopting a firm course," that "for every step in this direction, it was necessary to pay with a portion of the fatherland."[40] But after Kornilov had read Savinkov's draft decrees and received authorization to send troops to Petrograd, his mood warmed considerably.[41] Thus, when Savinkov attacked the Union of Officers and asked Kornilov to prevent his staff from aiding it materially and to make the Main Committee transfer its operations to Moscow, Kornilov agreed to do so.

Still another potentially sticky issue now tentatively settled was whether the government or the General Staff would have primary command authority over the Petrograd Military District. In a telegram to Kerensky on August 19, Kornilov had reaffirmed his desire to have troops of the Petrograd garrison placed under his direct command. Cabling the government to report on the fall of Riga a few days later, he had reiterated this demand.[42] At the same time, Kornilov also insisted that more garrison troops be shipped to defense positions on the northern front. The removal of radicalized soldiers from the capital had been, of course, one of the government's goals since the July days. Consequently, the cabinet had responded with alacrity to Kornilov's demand, and the level of transfers between the capital and the front had increased significantly towards the end of August. Placing all garrison soldiers under Kornilov's control, however, was quite another matter; Kerensky later remarked that if this had been done, "we could have been eaten alive at any moment."[43] Hence, Savinkov, in Mogilev, was under instructions to persuade Kornilov to accept command of the Petrograd Military District, minus those troops actually in the city and its immediate suburbs. When this issue was raised midway in the Savinkov-Kornilov talks, Kornilov agreed to Savinkov's proposal with little argument.

At the close of their discussions, Savinkov questioned General Kornilov about his attitude toward the government. In response, Kornilov, with dubious sincerity, pledged loyalty to Kerensky.[44] Still, Savinkov's visit may have led Kornilov to conclude that events were finally bringing Kerensky around to his own point of view and hence that it might not be necessary to utilize force against the government. In any case, Kornilov had every reason to be relieved and encouraged—if there were further problems in establishing a strong national government in Petrograd, in which the influence of Soviet socialists would be eliminated and the army would have the leading voice, reliable troops under the uncompromising Krymov soon would· be in a position to deal with them. The meetings in Mogilev must also have been reassuring to Savinkov: Kornilov and Kerensky, it seemed, were finally about to act in concert to reestablish order—the goal that Savinkov had sought all along. There appeared to be hope that the threat of Bolshevism and meddling by the Soviet would soon be ended and that Russia could proceed with the primary task of restoring the war effort.

On the evening of August 24, shortly after Savinkov's departure for Petrograd, General Krymov received instructions from Kornilov to push on to Petrograd upon receiving word of a "Bolshevik rising." He then left Mogilev to be with his soldiers.[45] The following day the Third Corps was placed on alert, and Krymov drafted a directive to be distributed by the corps upon its entry into the capital. In this order, Krymov placed the entire Petrograd Military District, including Finland and Kronstadt, under strict martial law. A curfew was imposed between 7:00 P.M. and 7:00 A.M. With the exception of groceries and pharmacies, all commercial enterprises were ordered closed. Strikes and meetings of any kind were forbidden. Civilians possessing firearms were to turn them in immediately. Strict censorship of all periodicals was proclaimed. Persons caught violating any of these regulations (with the exception of the censorship rule) were to be shot. "I warn everybody," Krymov cautioned in the directive, "that by the instructions of the commander-in-chief, the troops will not fire into the air."[46]

That night, August 25, Krymov received supplementary orders to begin his move northward on the morrow. In this connection, the northern-front commander, General Klembovsky, was instructed that the Ussuriisky Mounted Division, still in the Velikie Luki region, was to be placed aboard trains which would proceed to the capital via Pskov, Narva, and Krasnoe Selo. Simultaneously, the other main elements of the Third Corps—the Savage Division at Dno and the First Don Cossack Division at Pskov—were to embark for the suburban towns of Tsarskoe Selo and Gatchina, respectively. Moreover, each of the major units of the Third Corps received specific assignments in connection with the military occupation of Petrograd. The Savage Division, in spite of Kornilov's promise to Savinkov that it would not be sent to Petrograd, was to occupy the Moscow, Liteiny, Alexander Nevsky, and Rozhdestvensky districts; disarm workers and all troops of the Petrograd garrison, except the personnel of cadet academies; organize guard and patrol duty; assume responsibility for guarding prisons; take charge of railroad stations; and, utilizing whatever force was required, crush any and all disturbances and incidents of disobedience. At the same time, Kornilov dispatched the prearranged telegram to Savinkov: "The corps will be in place in the suburbs of Petrograd by evening of August 28. I request that Petrograd be proclaimed under martial law on August 29."[47]

In Petrograd at this time, while Savinkov was preparing to bring his new civil control decrees to a vote in the cabinet, right extremists, either oblivious to the arrangements worked out between Savinkov and Kornilov or simply ignoring them, doggedly continued to set the stage for a putsch. The rightist press trumpeted daily warnings of left-inspired "massacres" which, allegedly, would take place on the twenty-seventh. In the Soviet, majority socialists and Bolsheviks alike were troubled by a rash of reports of insurrectionary appeals to workers made by "strangers in soldiers' tunics."

At this juncture, there occurred a startling series of events which shattered all illusions that Kornilov and Kerensky would work together, and simultaneously undermined preparations for a putsch. It began with a meeting at the Winter Palace on August 22 between Kerensky and Vladimir Nikolaevich Lvov, a well-meaning though naïve and muddleheaded busybody who had been a liberal deputy in the Third and Fourth Dumas and had served without distinction as chief procurator of the Holy Synod in the first and second post-February cabinets. Lvov shared the conviction of many industrial, business, and agrarian leaders in Moscow, with whom he had ties, that Russia's survival was dependent on the creation, by peaceful means, of a law-and-order–directed "national cabinet" which would include representatives of all major patriotic groups. Unlike many of Kornilov's avid supporters, however, Lvov retained a measure of respect for Kerensky, with whom he had become acquainted in the Duma and the cabinet. He assumed that both Kerensky and Kornilov were working selflessly toward the same end—the establishment of an authoritarian regime. Hearing with alarm of the preparations afoot at Stavka to seize power, Lvov thought it his duty to do what he could to help avert a clash between the prime minister and the commander-in-chief. Casting himself in the role of intermediary between the two men, Lvov hastened to Petrograd, where he gained an interview with Kerensky on the evening of August 22.[48] Affirming mysteriously that he had come on behalf of "certain groups with significant strength," Lvov painted a bleak picture of the government's situation and volunteered to sound out key political figures, presumably starting with Kornilov, regarding the basis upon which a "national" government might be formed.

If one is to believe Lvov's memoir account of this conversation, Kerensky responded by giving him full authority to conduct political negotiations on his behalf, even suggesting his willingness to step down as prime minister.[49] Kerensky later denied vehemently Lvov's version of the conversation and suggested a different interpretation: suspecting from the start that Lvov was involved in a conspiracy and seeing in his proposal an opportunity to smoke out his enemies' intentions, he had not opposed Lvov's undertaking informal soundings—nothing more.[50] The more plausible of the two accounts, it would seem, is Kerensky's. There is no other evidence that Kerensky was at any time genuinely willing to share power with Kornilov; moreover, in view of Kerensky's continuing obsession with conspiracies against him, the use of Lvov for intelligence purposes had a certain logic. As to Lvov's version, it is difficult to say whether, in his enthusiasm, he misunderstood Kerensky, or whether, carried away by self-importance and a sense of urgency, he consciously exceeded his authority and then sought to conceal that fact.[51]

At any rate, Lvov left Petrograd at once, and, after stopping briefly in Moscow, where he circulated word that Kerensky was amenable to the reconstruction of the government, the creation of a "national cabinet," and, if

V. N. Lvov.

necessary, his own resignation, he boarded the next available train to Mogilev, arriving at Stavka on August 24. From the outset of his conversations with Kornilov, Lvov very likely conveyed the impression that he had been empowered by Kerensky to help form a new cabinet with or without Kerensky's participation. Meeting with Kornilov initially on the evening of August 24, he invited the general to state his position on the character and makeup of a new government. Kornilov's initial response to this approach was noncommittal, in part, no doubt, because he had not yet consulted Zavoiko. It is clear, however, that to Kornilov, and, even more, to extremists like Zavoiko, Lvov's appearance at Stavka, coming as it did on the heels of Savinkov's visit, was a further indication of Kerensky's weakness and readiness to compromise.[52] Significantly, Zavoiko and other rightist leaders in Mogilev now began intense, open discussions of candidates for ministerial posts in a new government.

Kornilov, accompanied this time by Zavoiko, did not mince words when he made his demands known to Lvov at their second meeting, on August 25. Petrograd would have to be placed under martial law, he stated. The commander-in-chief of the army, "whoever he might be," would have to be given supreme civil, as well as military, authority everywhere in the country. In the new government, Kornilov went on, there would be room for Kerensky as minister of justice and Savinkov as minister of defense. For their own protection, he urged that both men come to Mogilev no later than August 27. According to Lvov, when Kornilov mentioned Kerensky as a possible minister of justice, Zavoiko, "in a tone that teachers use toward pupils," bluntly rejected the idea, proposing instead that Kerensky be named deputy prime minister.[53]

That these terms did not strike Lvov as outlandish testifies strongly to his simplemindedness. He responded by suggesting only that leading Kadet, business, and industrial figures be invited to Mogilev to participate in the formation of a new cabinet. Nevertheless, some remarks made by Zavoiko as Lvov was about to board the train for the return trip to Petrograd raised doubts in his mind about Kerensky's probable fate in the event that he actually placed himself in Stavka's hands; Zavoiko had said casually: "Kerensky is needed as a name for the soldiers for ten days or so, after which he will be eliminated."[54]

Late on the afternoon of the twenty-sixth, weary but apparently undeflated by the results of his negotiations, Lvov was back in the Winter Palace to report to Kerensky. Shortly before Lvov was admitted to see the prime minister, Savinkov had confidently assured Kerensky that Kornilov would support him in every way possible. This helps explain Kerensky's reaction when Lvov officiously enumerated Kornilov's terms, insisted that they be brought before the government at once, and compassionately implored Kerensky to quickly set as much distance as possible between himself and Petrograd in the interest of sparing his life! Thinking Lvov was joking, the prime minister erupted in laughter. "This is not a time for jokes," Lvov interjected, begging Kerensky to yield to Kornilov.

Kerensky was later to acknowledge that at this point he found himself pacing back and forth in his study, unable to absorb what was happening. In a state of shock, he suggested that his visitor put Kornilov's demands in writing, which Lvov promptly did.[55] Moreover, seeking further confirmation of Kornilov's treachery and a firmer basis upon which to initiate action against him, Kerensky arranged to converse directly with Kornilov by teleprinter. What followed was at once one of the most tragic, ludicrous, and by now familiar moments in 1917 Russian politics. The episode is sufficiently illuminating to warrant its reproduction in some detail. To converse directly with Kornilov, it was necessary to utilize the communications equipment in the War Ministry. Lvov agreed to meet Kerensky there at half-past eight. Lvov was late for the appointment, but this did not deter the prime minister, now close to hysteria; he put through the call to Kornilov and simply pretended that Lvov was by his side:

KERENSKY: "Good day, General. V. N. Lvov and Kerensky at the apparatus. We beg you to confirm the statement that Kerensky is to act according to the communication made to him by Vladimir Nikolaevich."

KORNILOV: "Good day, Alexander Fedorovich; good day, Vladimir Nikolaevich. Confirming again the description of the present situation of the country and the army as it appears to me which I requested V. N. to convey to you, I declare again that the events of the past days and of

those that I can see coming imperatively demand a definite decision in
the shortest possible time."

KERENSKY: "I, Vladimir Nikolaevich, ask you whether it is necessary to act
on that definite decision which you asked me to communicate privately
to Kerensky. Without your personal confirmation, Alexander
Fedorovich hesitates to give me his full confidence."

KORNILOV: "Yes, I confirm that I asked you to convey to Alexander
Fedorovich my urgent plea that he should come to Mogilev."

KERENSKY: "I, Alexander Fedorovich, understand your answer as
confirmation of the words conveyed to me by V. N. To do that and
leave here today is impossible. I hope to depart tomorrow. Is it necessary for Savinkov to go?"

KORNILOV: "I beg urgently that Boris Viktorovich shall come with you.
What I said to V. N. refers in equal degree to Savinkov. I beg you
earnestly not to put off your departure later than tomorrow. Believe me,
only my recognition of the responsibility of the moment makes me so
persistent in my request."

KERENSKY: "Shall we come only in case of an outbreak, of which there are
rumors, or in any case?"

KORNILOV: "In any case."

KERENSKY: "Good-by. We shall soon see each other."

KORNILOV: "Good-by."[56]

One can easily imagine the unrestrained glee at Stavka that must have
followed this conversation; hopes were raised that Kerensky would submit
without a struggle to the construction of a new government under Kornilov.
Meanwhile, Kerensky's worst fears seemed about to materialize. Although
the conversation by teleprinter had verified concretely only that Kornilov
wanted Kerensky and Savinkov to come to Mogilev, Kerensky now concluded that he had been double-crossed and that Stavka was bent on dis-
pensing with him entirely. A jumble of thoughts rushed through his mind.
He had shifted, during the past week, to a rightward course which, if fully
revealed, would be gravely compromising in the eyes of the moderate
socialists. Would it be realistic, then, to rely on their support in a conflict
with Kornilov? And how would the volatile Petrograd masses, the very
elements he had hoped to suppress, react to this new crisis? No doubt they
could be mobilized to fight Kornilov. But would this not lead naturally to a
rejuvenation of the left? In combating Kornilov would he not be defeating
himself and dealing a further blow to hopes of restoring order and the
fighting capacity of the army?

With such considerations in mind, Kerensky seems to have concluded
that the wisest course of action was to forestall Kornilov's sympathizers in
the cabinet from attempting to compromise with the general at his expense
and to keep the left uninformed about the developing crisis, while at the
same time removing Kornilov as commander-in-chief before the Third

Corps reached the outskirts of Petrograd. In fact, for almost twenty-four hours Kerensky's imbroglio with Kornilov was not disclosed to the press or even to the Soviet leadership.

Late on the night of August 26, after having Lvov arrested and locked in a back room of the Winter Palace, Kerensky consulted with Nekrasov, his closest associate, as well as with Savinkov and other high officials of the War Ministry. He then interrupted a cabinet meeting in the Malachite Room (it is ironic that the ministers were in the process of discussing Savinkov's decrees) and broke the news of Kornilov's "treachery." As proof, he read aloud the tape of his conversation with the general and circulated it for all to see. Kerensky next requested his fellow ministers to grant him unlimited authority to deal with the emergency as he saw fit. He observed that the developing situation might require a "restructuring of the cabinet"; in view of what was to follow, it appears that Kerensky was considering the possible creation of a Directory (a powerful national executive body composed of less than a half-dozen top leaders, like the one that existed in France from 1795 to 1799). Information about what happened next is murky. Apparently the Kadets Kokoshkin and Iurenev, long since disgruntled with Kerensky's leadership and apprehensive that he would misuse "extraordinary powers," vehemently expressed their opposition, threatening to resign if his proposal were granted. The majority of the cabinet, however, supported the prime minister, and to give him a completely free hand in forming a new government they dutifully tendered their resignations. Kerensky apparently accepted the resignations but requested the cabinet members to remain at their posts as "acting ministers" pending construction of a new government. Only Kokoshkin refused to stay on.[57]

This last official meeting of the second coalition dragged on until close to 4:00 A.M. (August 27). Upon its conclusion, Kerensky dispatched a terse telegram to Kornilov commanding him to yield his post to the chief of staff, General Lukomsky, and to proceed at once to Petrograd. Upon reception of the cable in Mogilev four hours later, a dumbfounded Lukomsky immediately wired back: "It is too late to halt an operation started with your approval. . . . In order to save Russia, you must go along with Kornilov. . . . Kornilov's dismissal would bring horrors the likes of which Russia has never seen. . . . I cannot accept General Kornilov's post."[58]

Lukomsky's response, of course, dashed Kerensky's hope of quickly removing Kornilov and preventing the conflict from erupting openly. Moreover, the front troops dispatched by Kornilov were continuing their advance toward Petrograd. Hence by midday, August 27, Kerensky had begun to make plans for the defense of the capital; in this connection he ordered that Petrograd be placed under martial law and that Savinkov, who could be counted on to struggle with the extreme left as well as with Kornilov, be installed as governor-general of Petrograd in overall charge of military preparations. Kerensky also prepared a public announcement on

the crisis, the release of which was delayed several hours while first Savinkov, and then Maklakov, tried unsuccessfully, over the teleprinter, to persuade Kornilov to step down.[59] In the meantime, Kerensky sought to divert
Kornilov's troops from the capital. "I order that all echelons moving toward
Petrograd and its outskirts be stopped and redirected to their previous
stations—Petrograd is completely calm and no insurrections are expected,"
stated the cable which he now sent to, among others, the commanders of
the northern front and the Third Corps, and Kornilov.[60]

The order fell on deaf ears. And so in the early evening Kerensky's announcement was made public and a copy sent to Kornilov. All things considered, the proclamation was relatively restrained. The movement of hostile troops from the front toward the capital was not mentioned. The public
was simply informed that Kornilov had dispatched Lvov to the Provisional
Government with a demand for the surrender of all civil and military
power, that this act reflected a desire on the part of certain circles to "establish a regime opposed to the conquests of the revolution," and that in view
of this the government had empowered Kerensky to take prompt and reso-
lute countermeasures. Among these, it was announced, were the firing of
Kornilov and the proclamation of martial law in Petrograd.[61]

As the poet Zinaida Gippius speculated in her diary at the time,
Kornilov's initial reaction to this announcement "must have been that
someone had gone completely mad; the next moment he must have been
enraged."[62] Kornilov had neither sent Lvov nor, to his mind, threatened the
government. Late that night Zavoiko drafted an impassioned, if typically
ineptly worded, response which was sent to all military commanders and
read immediately to reporters; it stated in part:

> The first portion of the Minister-President's telegram is full of lies. It
> was not I who sent Vladimir Lvov to the Provisional Government but he
> who came to me as the envoy of the Minister-President. . . . Thus a great
> provocation has taken place which jeopardizes the fate of the motherland.
>
> People of Russia! Our great motherland is dying. The hour of her death
> is near. Forced to speak openly, I, General Kornilov, declare that under
> the pressure of the Bolshevik majority in the Soviets, the Provisional Gov-
> ernment acts in complete harmony with the plans of the German general
> staff and simultaneously with the forthcoming landing of the enemy forces
> on the coast of Riga; it is killing the army and undermines the very founda-
> tion of the country.
>
> The heavy sense of the inevitable ruin of the country commands me in
> this ominous moment to call upon all Russian people to come to the aid of
> the dying motherland. . . .
>
> I, General Kornilov, son of a cossack peasant, declare to all and each
> that I want nothing for myself, except the preservation of a Great Russia,
> and I vow to bring the people by means of victory over the enemy to a

Constituent Assembly, where they themselves will decide their fate and choose their new form of government. . . .

> August 27, 1917
> General Kornilov[63]

After issuing this declaration of war, Kornilov instructed his subordinates to continue the movement of troops along the rail lines to Petrograd. For the time being, the general's confidence that troops of the Third Corps would follow their commanders appeared justified. On August 27 echelons of the Savage Division boarded trains at Dno to begin their advance on the capital; the next morning lead elements of the division neared Vyritsa. Meanwhile, the Ussuriisky Mounted Division, having reached Pskov, was continuing on to Narva-Iamburg, while the First Don Cossack Division had moved from Pskov to Luga.[64]

A significant portion of the military high command now quickly registered solidarity with Kornilov. Among those to do so were Generals Klembovsky and Baluev, commanders of the northern and western fronts, respectively; General Shcherbatov, deputy commander of the Rumanian front; and General Denikin, commander of the southwestern front. The latter wired Kerensky:

> At a conference with members of the Provisional Government on July 16, I pointed out that by virtue of a whole series of military enactments, the government had ruined and corrupted the army and trampled our campaign banners in the mud. . . . Today I received word that General Kornilov, proposing certain demands which could still save the country and the army, is being removed from the post of commander-in-chief. Viewing this as the government's return to its former policy of the systematic destruction of the army and, consequently, of the country, it is my duty to inform the government that I will not join it in this course.[65]

The Main Committee of the Union of Officers circulated telegrams to all army and naval headquarters proclaiming that the Provisional Government "could no longer remain at the head of Russia" and urging officers everywhere to be "tough and unflinching" in their support of Kornilov.[66]

On August 28 prices on the Petrograd stock exchange shot upward in anticipation of a victory by Kornilov. To many government officials, Kerensky's situation appeared hopeless. Typical of the ominous reports which were now in circulation was a telegram to Tereshchenko from the Foreign Ministry's representative in Mogilev, Prince Grigorii Trubetskoi. Reported Trubetskoi: "A sober appraisal of the situation forces us to admit that the entire commanding personnel, the overwhelming majority of the officers, and the best combat units in the army will follow Kornilov. In the rear, the entire Cossack host, the majority of the military schools, and the best combat units will go over to Kornilov's side. Added to this physical strength is the superiority of the military organization over the weakness of the government organs. . . . The majority of the popular and urban masses have grown indifferent to the existing order and will submit to any cracking of the whip."[67]

Subsequent events would reveal how mistaken was this estimate of the situation. Almost from the start of the Kornilov crisis, socialist leaders, with a better sense of the mass mood, were confident that the forces bent on the creation of a strong military dictatorship would ultimately be rebuffed.[68] It even may be, as Sukhanov recalls, that among some political leaders with close ties to workers and soldiers, news of Kornilov's advance brought a sense of "relief, . . . excitement, exultation, and the joy of liberation." Hopes were raised that "the [revolutionary] democracy might take new heart, and the revolution might swiftly find its lawful course."[69] But this mood was scarcely Kerensky's. As Kornilov's columns, led by Krymov, appeared to have Petrograd in a vise, and as the forces of the right and left seemed poised for a head-on clash, the prime minister finally grasped the depth of his own isolation. Caught between two fires and expecting reprisals regardless of who won, Kerensky despaired; it appeared virtually certain that his political career was at an end.

·8·

THE BOLSHEVIKS
AND KORNILOV'S DEFEAT

Petrograd awoke to near-perfect weather on Sunday, August 27, the day designated for celebrating the six-month anniversary of the February revolution. It was seasonably warm and the air was crystal clear. Placards in bold type, prominently displayed throughout the city, reminded citizens of the fund-raising rallies scheduled that day in the capital's largest meeting and concert halls. The morning papers contained no hint of the open struggle that had erupted between Kornilov and Kerensky. The front page of *Izvestiia* was given over to an appeal for donations for the Soviet's upkeep: "The duty of every worker, soldier, and peasant, the duty of every responsible citizen in these critical black days, is to support the legitimate organ of the all-Russian revolution," admonished the headline. For the second consecutive day *Rabochii* cautioned workers and soldiers not to respond to provocative appeals for revolutionary action. "Sinister people are circulating rumors of a rising set for today and allegedly being organized by our party," the paper warned. "The Central Committee implores workers and soldiers not to yield to provocations, to maintain restraint and calm, and not to take part in any action today."

Most of the top Soviet leadership spent Sunday morning circulating through the districts of Petrograd, making speeches at fund-raising rallies. Toward midday, garbled rumors of the rift between Kornilov and Kerensky began to circulate through the Smolny Institute, the former exclusive boarding school for daughters of the nobility which since early August had been serving as central headquarters of the Soviet.[1] The gravity of the emergency facing the government did not become apparent to Soviet deputies until mid-afternoon. At that point, leaders of the various parties represented in the Soviet began rounding up their colleagues for emergency fraction meetings. But it was not until eleven-thirty that evening, more than twenty-four hours after Kerensky had concluded that Kornilov was intent on overthrowing the government, that the All-Russian Executive Committees convened in a closed joint plenary session to consider the crisis.

With interruptions, the Executive Committees, gathered in the majestic, high-ceiling assembly hall of Smolny, deliberated through the night and well into the morning of August 28. Two difficult, interrelated problems confronted the deputies. In the first place, in view of the apparent alliance and subsequent conflict between Kerensky and Kornilov, the foundering of the second coalition, and Kerensky's intention of establishing a Directory, the Soviet needed to adopt a position regarding the future of the Provisional Government. In addition, the deputies were forced to cope with the more immediately pressing task of helping to organize the military defense of the capital.

Debate on the government question was heated. A spokesman for the Bolsheviks, Sokolnikov, took the position that the revolutionary democracy could have no confidence in the existing government, implying that it should be removed immediately. "The Provisional Government created conditions for counterrevolution," he asserted; "only the realization of a decisive program—a republic, peace, and bread—can instill in the masses confidence in the government." Yet, for the time being, the Bolsheviks did not offer a formal resolution on the government question. The moderate socialists, for their part, accepted at face value Kerensky's version of his differences with Kornilov, namely, that at hand was a carefully planned conspiracy against the revolution and the legitimate government. In these circumstances, they saw no choice but to support the prime minister. Thus, S. L. Vainshtein, on behalf of the Mensheviks, declared early in the proceedings: "We must acknowledge that the only person who can form a government at this time is Comrade Kerensky. An attack has been made on Kerensky and the Provisional Government, and if they should fall, the revolutionary cause will be lost."

The Executive Committees at first emphatically rejected an oblique suggestion by the SR representative, V. N. Rikhter, that it might be necessary to go along with Kerensky on the creation of a Directory; a majority was obviously more sympathetic to Martov's claim that "all directories spawn counterrevolution." The deputies passed a resolution stipulating that the form of government was to remain unchanged and granting Kerensky authority to fill the vacancies in the cabinet left by the withdrawal of the Kadets with "democratic elements." At the same time, they agreed to work for the convocation at an early date of yet another "state conference," this one to be made up exclusively of representatives of those democratic organizations which had supported the Soviet's platform at the Moscow State Conference. It was understood that this conference would reevaluate the government question and also that the Provisional Government would be responsible to it until the convocation of the Constituent Assembly. Significantly, the Bolsheviks abstained rather than vote against the resolution calling for retention of a coalition under Kerensky, and they actually sided with the Mensheviks and SRs on the question of convening another state conference, requiring only that the assembly be "revolutionary," i.e., composed entirely of socialist groups.

During a break in the Executive Committees' deliberations, members of the Presidium made a brief trip to the Winter Palace to inform the government of the preceding decisions. Kerensky, however, was adamant about the immediate creation of an all-powerful six-man Directory. Only a government small in number and totally unified in outlook, he contended, would be capable of acting swiftly and decisively enough to deal effectively with the attack from the right. Upon the delegates' return to Smolny, Kerensky's posture triggered a fresh round of acrimonious debate. Speaking for the Bolshevik fraction, Lunacharsky, for one, ignoring the decisions of the Sixth Congress, proclaimed that "the moment has come for the Soviet to create a national government." He introduced a resolution branding as counterrevolutionary both the Kornilov movement and the Provisional Government and calling for the creation of a government of workers, peasants, and soldiers (interpreted by Lunacharsky's listeners to mean transfer of all power to the soviets). This government would decree a "democratic republic" and speed convocation of a Constituent Assembly.[2] Evidently this proposal was not put to a vote.

As night turned to morning the existing danger to the revolution was presented to the deputies in ever more alarming terms. Many now learned for the first time of the immediate military threat posed by Krymov's advancing Third Corps and also of the fact that generals on several fronts were openly siding with Kornilov. In this tension-charged atmosphere, wild rumors acquired instant credence: "There is fighting in Luga!" "The rail station at Dno has been blown up!" "Soldiers loyal to Kornilov are even now disembarking at the Nikolaevsky Station!" Under the pressure of such reports the bleary-eyed deputies gradually swung to Kerensky's side, ultimately adopting a resolution proposed by Tsereteli pledging full support to the prime minister. The resolution left the form of government completely up to him, provided only that he pursue the struggle against Kornilov with vigor. Notably, even the Bolsheviks, while vehemently protesting the granting of such prerogatives to Kerensky, nonetheless announced that if the government were genuinely committed to fighting the counterrevolution, they would "form a military alliance with it."[3]

Addressing themselves to the immediate military threat, officials of the Soviet issued emergency appeals and instructions to key institutions and groups—to army and front committees, provincial soviets, postal-telegraph and railroad workers, and soldiers of the Petrograd garrison. According to the Soviet's directives, orders emanating from Stavka were not to be obeyed, the movement of counterrevolutionary forces was to be watched closely and impeded, correspondence and communications between elements hostile to the revolution were to be disrupted, and orders of the Soviet and the Provisional Government were to be carried out without hesitation.[4] To help organize and direct the struggle against Kornilov's forces, the Executive Committees created an extraordinary military defense organ—the Committee for Struggle Against the Counterrevolution—which began to function on the afternoon of August 28.

As first envisioned, the Committee for Struggle Against the Counterrevolution was to include, among others, three Menshevik representatives, three SRs, and even three Bolsheviks, the presence of the latter signifying grudging acknowledgement of the stature and growing influence of the Bolsheviks among the masses. But would the Bolsheviks really join actively with the moderate socialists and the government in the fight against Kornilov? As counterrevolutionary forces approached and the capital braced for battle, this was a crucial question in the minds of moderate socialist leaders. The Menshevik-Internationalist Sukhanov later pointed out the importance of the Bolsheviks at this time.

> The committee, making defense preparations, had to mobilize the worker-soldier masses. But the masses, insofar as they were organized, were organized by the Bolsheviks and followed them. At that time, theirs was the only organization that was large, welded together by an elementary discipline, and linked with the democratic lowest levels of the capital. Without it, the committee was impotent. Without the Bolsheviks, it could only have passed the time with appeals and idle speeches by orators who had lost their authority. With the Bolsheviks, the committee had at its disposal the full power of the organized workers and soldiers.[5]

For the Bolsheviks, mapping a suitable program of action during the Kornilov crisis was no simple matter. Although several top officials jailed in July had already been freed (Kamenev, for instance), Trotsky, who was soon to play a decisive role in the party's fortunes, was still languishing in prison. Lenin and Zinoviev remained underground, the former hiding in Finland, the latter in a Petrograd suburb. Lenin dispatched directives relating to the struggle against Kornilov to his colleagues in Petrograd as quickly as he could, but his instructions, written on August 30, did not reach the capital until the first days of September, well after the crisis had passed.[6] To be sure, the party leadership had as a practical guide the bitterly debated resolutions on tactics adopted four weeks earlier by the Sixth Congress. But, as we have seen, these were highly ambiguous: while the congress's statement "On the Political Situation" encouraged collaboration with all elements dedicated to fighting counterrevolution, the resolution "On Unification," which expressly declared that the Mensheviks had "deserted to the camp of the enemy of the proletariat for good," seemed to preclude cooperation in any form between Bolsheviks and moderate socialists.[7] Did this mean that the party could not join with the Mensheviks and SRs, not to speak of the government, in defense measures against Kornilov, but rather that it would have to strike out on an entirely independent revolutionary course?

On the night of August 27–28, Petrograd Bolshevik leaders had every reason to suppose that Lenin's assessment of the situation would conform to the views expressed in "On Unification." Apart from his unequivocal pronouncements of mid-July and his instructions to the Sixth Congress, of direct relevance were supplementary instructions to the Bolshevik Central Committee and an article, "Rumors of a Conspiracy," which Lenin wrote on August 18–19.[8] He had been prompted to prepare these statements after reading in *Novaia zhizn'* of August 17 a report of collaboration between Bolsheviks and moderate socialists in the Provisional Revolutionary Committee organized by the Moscow Soviet during the Moscow State Conference.[9] From this dispatch, Lenin correctly surmised that to ward off an expected counterrevolutionary military attack, Moscow Bolsheviks had allied closely with local Mensheviks and SRs. This news had enraged Lenin—here was further evidence of the reluctance of many of his most influential associates to break decisively with the Mensheviks and SRs and, to the contrary, of their inclination toward working with "compromisers" in pursuit of common goals. Lenin was apprehensive that such predilections within the party would hamper the prospect of its acting boldly to take power at an opportune moment; hence, he attacked the Moscow Bolsheviks unmercifully.

Starting from the assumption that the Provisional Government and the majority socialists were no less hostile to the revolution than "Kornilov and his cossacks," Lenin contended that the counterrevolutionary scare of mid-August had been artfully contrived by the Mensheviks and SRs to hoodwink the masses into believing that they were champions of the revolution.

> The political scheme of the Menshevik and defensist traitors is as clear as can be. . . . It is hard to believe that among the Bolsheviks there are fools and scoundrels who would enter into a bloc with the defensists now. . . . The congress resolution ["On Unification"] being what it is, any Bolshevik who came to terms with the defensists . . . would, of course, be expelled immediately and deservedly from the party. . . . Even in the event that a counterrevolutionary attack appeared genuine, not a single honest Bolshevik who had not taken leave of his senses completely would agree to any bloc. . . . In these circumstances a Bolshevik would say "our workers and soldiers will fight the counterrevolutionary troops." . . . They will do so not to defend the government . . . but independently, to protect the revolution as they pursue their own aims. . . . A Bolshevik would tell the Mensheviks: "We shall fight, of course, but we refuse to enter into any political alliance whatever with you [and] reject expression of the least confidence in you."

In the instructions appended to "Rumors of a Conspiracy," Lenin requested that the Central Committee launch an official inquiry into the behavior of local Bolshevik leaders during the Moscow State Conference and demanded that any party officials found guilty of participating in a bloc be removed from the Central and Moscow committees. Implying that the popular protest stimulated by the Moscow Conference indicated that an uprising on the order of the July days was not far off and that when this occurred the party would have to take power into its own hands, he insisted, "It is absolutely essential to have people at the helm in Moscow who will not swerve to the right, who will not form blocs with the Mensheviks, and who will understand the new tasks of the party and the new slogan of seizing power."[10]

Information on the initial responses of top Bolshevik leaders in Petrograd to news of Kornilov's attack on the Provisional Government is fragmentary; it appears that not until August 30 did the Central Committee meet as a body to take account of the latest developments.[11] The Bolshevik fractions in the All-Russian Executive Committees, among whom were several Central Committee members, first met in connection with the developing crisis on the early evening of August 27. They probably caucused again after midnight during an extended break in the Executive Committees' deliberations. It is well to bear in mind that within the party Soviet fractions, the influence of moderates such as Kamenev was strong throughout the summer of 1917. The right wing of the party had rejected Lenin's radical revolutionary course at the April Conference and later, with less energy, at the Sixth Congress. It did so again the night of August 27–28. At the start of the All-Russian Executive Committees' meeting just described, Bolshevik spokesmen did not present a formal resolution on the government question. Subsequently the party supported the Mensheviks and SRs in calling for another broad national conference to reassess the political situation. After Kerensky's firmness on the matter of establishing a Directory became known, Lunacharsky insisted not only that the Soviet break decisively with the government, but that it take upon itself the responsibility for forming a new government. His resolution, envisioning the declaration of a democratic republic and the immediate convocation of a Constituent Assembly, was fully consistent with the theoretical outlook of the moderates. Worse yet from the point of view expressed in "Rumors of a Conspiracy," in the heat of the moment a Bolshevik representative actually had offered a formal alliance with the government in defense of the revolution.

At about the time the Bolshevik Soviet fractions first met at Smolny, the Petersburg Committee was in emergency session across the city in the Narva District.[12] Ironically, the meeting had been scheduled three days earlier at the insistence of Bolshevik militants from the Vyborg District, disgruntled by what they perceived to be the failure of higher party bodies to respond adequately to the growing threat of counterrevolution. It began

with a report on the latest developments by the Central Committee's Andrei Bubnov. A revolutionary activist since his student days in Ivanovo-
Voznesensk and a veteran of some thirteen arrests and five prison terms,
the thirty-four-year-old Bubnov was a relatively recent arrival in Petrograd,
having moved from Moscow to the capital after his election to the Central
Committee at the Sixth Congress. In Moscow Bubnov had been associated
with a group of young radicals centered in the party's Moscow Regional
Bureau.[13] In early October he would appear before the Petersburg Committee to support Lenin's plea for organization of an immediate armed uprising, against advocates of more cautious tactics.[14] And to the thirty-six
local party officials assembled on the night of August 27 he proposed a
significantly more independent, militant course than that being pursued by
party leaders at Smolny. Obviously familiar with Lenin's "Rumors of a
Conspiracy," he warned the Petersburg Committee against repeating the
mistakes of some Moscow Bolsheviks during the Moscow State Conference
and collaborating with the Mensheviks and SRs. In Moscow, he observed,
"first the government turned to us for help and then we were spat upon."
Totally rejecting Bolshevik participation in mutual-defense organs of any
kind, he insisted that "there must be no interaction with the Soviet majority." Instead, he urged that the Bolsheviks work to control the actions of the
masses themselves while pursuing their own interests and helping neither
Kerensky nor Kornilov.[15]

When Bubnov had finished, Kalinin challenged the idea that the party
had little stake in the outcome of the conflict between the government and
the general staff, contending that if Kornilov appeared on the verge of defeating Kerensky, the Bolsheviks would have to intervene on Kerensky's
side. Disagreeing with Kalinin's moderate stance, a succession of speakers
vented their hostility to the moderate socialists and the government, as well
as to Kornilov. In their frustration, these speakers also lashed out at higher
party authorities—at Bolshevik moderates in the Executive Committees for
an excess of "defensism," at the leadership of the Military Organization for
elusiveness, and at the Central Committee for "operating in a fog" during
the July crisis. The Central Committee as well as the Executive Commission
of the Petersburg Committee were chided for "cooling" the masses too long,
for acting arbitrarily and independently, and for a "philistine outlook." On
the other hand, somewhat contradictorily, the two party committees came in
for criticism for not exerting enough leadership, particularly for devoting
insufficient attention to keeping lower party bodies and the masses abreast
of changes in the political situation. Observed the Vyborg District's always
irreverent Latsis, "recently the Bolshevik central organs have made one apprehensive about the future of the party."

Midway in the meeting sentiment against the Executive Commission was
so strong that it appeared the entire commission might be ousted on the
spot; ultimately, it was agreed that new elections for the commission would

be held at the next meeting. Although a few Petersburg Committee members must have been wondering privately whether it was not high time to organize a mass armed uprising, it is apparent that, to the bulk of the committee, discussions along this line were, as Kalinin said, "nonsense." At one caustic moment in the debate, an unidentified district committee representative abruptly shifted attention to practical matters. "We have vermicelli here," he shouted. "Consideration of the current moment is mixed up with pot shots at the Executive Commission! Let's get down to concrete defense measures!"

Despite these recriminations, there was little doubt within the Petersburg Committee about the necessity of drawing upon the full resources of the party and rallying mass organizations, as well as workers, soldiers, and sailors generally, for a life-and-death struggle against Kornilov. Committee members now turned their attention to preparations for battle. It was belatedly acknowledged, even by Bubnov, that for "purposes of information" the party would have to maintain contact with the defense organ established by the leadership of the Soviet. An emergency communications network was established, with representatives from each district to be stationed at Petersburg Committee headquarters and round-the-clock watches to be maintained at the headquarters of district and factory-shop committees. The Executive Commission was made responsible for preparing leaflets calling workers and soldiers to arms, and for contingency military planning. It was decided that all party agitators would be mobilized for action in working-class districts the next day. Most important, individual Bolsheviks were designated to coordinate defense preparations with those of major mass organizations in the capital. In short, though fully conscious of the differences between their own goals and those of Kerensky, and also wary of close collaboration with the moderate socialists, members of the Petersburg Committee joined their efforts with those of other left groups and directed their organizational talents and vast resources and energy to the fight against Kornilov.

There are some signs that during the Kornilov emergency the impulse for an immediate rising against the Provisional Government, as well as against Kornilov, may have been stronger within the Bolshevik Military Organization than within the Petersburg Committee. The relative militancy of at least a segment of the Military Organization is reflected in a one-page extra edition of *Soldat* which appeared on August 29 and in several editorials in the regular August 29 edition.[16] The lead editorial in the August 29 extra edition portrayed the situation in the following terms:

> The conspiracy is revealed. . . . The terrible thing is not so much the two Savage Divisons located at Dno . . . [but] the powerful military machine which is in Kornilov's hands and which he can employ against the revolution by means of crude provocations. We witnessed how this can be done in Petrograd. Why did Kornilov need malicious rumors about distur-

bances allegedly being prepared by the Bolsheviks on the half-year anniversary of the revolution? This was [Kornilov's] work. If the provocation
had been successful, if shots had again been heard on Petrograd streets,
neither Kerensky nor the Soviet leaders would have hesitated for a moment appealing to Kornilov for help, and he would have appeared here at
the head of his Chetniks and Ingushes as an angel of mercy. . . .

The power of the counterrevolution is simply enormous, and very
nearly its most important source of strength lies in the readiness of the
government to yield to Kornilov rather than permit the full development of
the revolution. Only the full development of the revolution, only a consistently revolutionary government, will not make a deal with Kornilov or the
Kadets or the Germans. The full development of the revolution means
transfer of all power into the hands of the revolutionary workers and
poorer peasantry and the waging of an uncompromising struggle against all
enemies of the people.

Exactly as is the case here now, when the enemy stood at the walls of
Paris in 1871 the bourgeoisie preferred to deal with the enemy rather than
compromise with the workers. The workers overthrew the bourgeoisie,
took power into their own hands, and yielded only because they were
ousted by the overwhelming force of government troops. They were defeated because they were isolated.

Now the situation is different. The workers' revolution, the government
of the revolutionary people, the dictatorship of the working class and
poorer peasantry, will not disappear without a trace in a country in the
sixth month of revolution. Revolutionary Petrograd, as revolutionary Paris
never did, will carry with it the entire country. And there is no other way
out.

As nearly as one can tell, Military Organization militancy during the
Kornilov crisis did not go beyond such journalistic endeavor. On the night
of August 28, Military Organization leaders met with their representatives
in most units of the garrison. Sverdlov, who had been appointed by the
Central Committee to oversee Military Organization operations after the
July uprising, chaired the meeting. In the resolution adopted by the assembled soldier-Bolsheviks, "compromisers in the Soviet" were blamed for
facilitating the consolidation of the counterrevolution. The resolution called
for the formation of a "people's government," but, by implication, "compromisers" could be included in this government. As a sign that the moderate socialist majority in the Soviet was genuinely ready to break with the
counterrevolutionary bourgeoisie, the resolution demanded, among other
things, the liberation of Bolsheviks jailed following the July uprising, the
arrest of counterrevolutionary officers, the preparation of the Petrograd
garrison for battle, and, with participation by representatives of soldier
organizations, the formulation of plans for defeating and suppressing
counterrevolutionary forces. The resolution also advocated the arming of
the workers and the abolition of capital punishment at the front.[17]

After their meeting, the Military Organization representatives returned to their respective units and did not reassemble until the crisis was over. The relevant sources furnish very little evidence of further activity on the part of the Military Organization or its bureau, as independent organizations, in the struggle against Kornilov.[18] This does not mean, however, that members of the Military Organization were not of key importance at this time. Rather, what appears to have happened is that in the sudden emergency occasioned by the advance of Kornilov's forces, Military Organization leaders, like their counterparts in the Petersburg Committee, channeled much of their effort to help defend the revolution through specially created organs such as the Committee for Struggle, other nonparty mass organizations, and the soviets. Working within these institutions, Bolshevik Military Organization members played a prominent role in helping to mobilize and arm large numbers of workers, soldiers, and sailors, and giving programmatic and tactical direction to their efforts. The party's official stance in the crisis was summed up in a policy directive which the Central Committee cabled to twenty key provincial Bolshevik committees on August 29: "In the interest of repulsing the counterrevolution, we are working in collaboration with the Soviet on a technical and informational basis, while fully retaining our independent political position. . . ."[19]

Ad hoc revolutionary committees similar to the Committee for Struggle had been created all over Russia during the February revolution; on a more limited scale such institutions had reappeared at the time of the June and July crises and during the counterrevolutionary scare of mid-August. The vast majority of these committees remained in existence for only a short time, which distinguished them in part from the more permanent soviets. Uniting representatives of all left groups, such ad hoc committees filled the need for authoritative military-revolutionary organizations capable of acting expeditiously in emergencies. In response to the Kornilov crisis, revolutionary committees sprang up like mushrooms after a late summer rain; between August 27 and 30 more than 240 of them were formed in various parts of Russia, often by urban and rural soviets.[20] In the Petrograd area alone, in addition to the Committee for Struggle, established by the All-Russian Executive Committees on the night of August 27–28, ad hoc committees to mobilize and organize the masses, procure weapons and ammunition, assure the maintenance of essential services, and in general to direct and coordinate the defense of the revolution were hastily created by the Petrograd Soviet; the Interdistrict Conference; several district soviets; and naval soviets in Reval, Helsingfors, and Kronstadt.

In part because of the isolation and lack of authority of the Provisional Government within those sectors of the Russian population most hostile to Kornilov, and no doubt also because many high government officials were secretly sympathetic to Kornilov and hence, at best, passive in the campaign against him,[21] the Committee for Struggle, above all its Military Section, willy-nilly became the national command post for combating the right. As formed on August 28, the committee was composed of three representatives each of the Bolsheviks, Mensheviks, and SRs, five representatives each from the All-Russian Executive Committees; and two representatives each from the Central Trade Union and Petrograd Soviets; a representative of the Interdistrict Conference was added to the committee the next day. In addition to its Military Section, the Committee for Struggle had a political commissariat and an information section.[22] The committee issued a constant stream of emergency bulletins which, through the Petrograd telegraph agency, gave wide publicity to appeals and directives from the government, soviets, and other mass organizations, and kept citizens everywhere abreast of late political and military developments. The committee also facilitated the distribution of arms and ammunition to garrison units in need of reinforcement, initiated steps to protect food supplies, dispatched a number of influential soviet officials to meet and harangue enemy forces, and, in the meantime, working through rail and communications workers' unions, sought to disrupt Kornilov's advance toward the capital.[23]

Nonetheless, the decisive moments of the Kornilov emergency occurred so quickly that effective coordination of the campaign against the right, even in the Petrograd area, proved impossible. It was also unnecessary. Spurred by the news of Kornilov's attack, all political organizations to the left of the Kadets, every labor organization of any import, and soldier and sailor committees at all levels immediately rose to fight against Kornilov. It would be difficult to find, in recent history, a more powerful, effective display of largely spontaneous and unified mass political action.

The initiative, energy, and authority of the Petrograd Interdistrict Conference of Soviets[24] during the Kornilov days emerge with particular clarity from the relevant documents. As early as August 24, the conference (still directed by the Menshevik-Internationalist Alexander Gorin but strongly influenced by the Bolsheviks), fearful that an attack by the counterrevolution was imminent, had passed a resolution which demanded that the government immediately declare Russia a democratic republic and announce that Russian war aims (presumably as defined by the Petrograd Soviet in March) were immutable. The resolution insisted on the immediate breakup of counterrevolutionary headquarters and formal recognition of the authority of democratic committees within the army, demanded an end to the persecution of leftists, and called for the immediate formation of a "Committee of Public Safety" and fighting squads of workers and unemployed to defend the revolution.[25]

Consequently, the Interdistrict Conference was fully primed to take prompt action when, a few days later, Kornilov's intentions were disclosed. At an emergency session of the conference on August 28, the assembled district soviet representatives voted to delegate a representative to the

Committee for Struggle and to each of its sections, to remain in permanent session, to take the lead in organizing an armed workers' militia under the political responsibility of the Interdistrict Conference and district soviets, to impose control by district soviets over the actions of local government commissars, to send out roving patrols charged with detaining counter-revolutionary agitators, and to establish close contact between soviets and dumas in all districts.[26] These were not mere statements of intent: the Interdistrict Conference at once dispatched to all district soviets in and around Petrograd specific directives relating to the recruitment, organization, and arming of a workers' militia.[27] For the duration of the Kornilov emergency, the Interdistrict Conference's offices at Smolny and the headquarters of each district soviet became directing centers for the preservation of revolutionary order and for mass action against the counterrevolution.[28]

The activities of the Peterhof District Soviet are illustrative of the initiatives taken by other district soviets. On August 28 Mikhail Bogdanov, a Bolshevik construction worker who represented the Peterhof Soviet in the Interdistrict Conference, reported to his soviet, erroneously as it turned out, that loyalist forces in Luga were suffering reverses. Bogdanov also informed the Peterhof deputies of the Interdistrict Conference's plans for the organization of a workers' militia. Bogdanov's listeners responded to this news by quickly agreeing to arrange factory meetings where measures for coping with the existing emergency would be discussed and to form a "Central Revolutionary Committee" to organize and direct a "Red Guard."[29]

The following morning a proclamation from "the Peterhof Central Revolutionary Committee, the Peterhof District Soviet, and factory-shop committees in the Peterhof District" was posted throughout the district. It announced that "military conspirators, headed by the traitor General Kornilov and supported by the blindness and lack of political consciousness of some divisions, are moving toward the heart of the revolution—Petrograd." Counterrevolutionary supporters, this proclamation continued, "are attempting to stab in the back revolutionary forces defending Petrograd, circulating provocatory rumors and appeals aimed at stimulating panic among the populace, and bringing workers into the streets prematurely." "Don't be taken in by such provocations," the proclamation warned. "Don't permit drunkenness. . . . Rely on your own power to maintain revolutionary order. Don't undertake mass action in the absence of our call. . . . Let us concentrate all our power on the fight against the counterrevolution. . . . Maintain calm, restraint, and discipline." At the direction of the Peterhof Central Revolutionary Committee, large numbers of factory workers were armed and sent to dig trenches, erect barricades, and string barbed wire along the southern approaches to the city; simultaneously, other workers were made responsible for keeping tabs on the activities of potential rightist supporters, protecting factories, and helping to preserve order.[30]

Other organizations, among them the Petrograd City Duma, the Petrograd Trade Union Soviet,[31] the Central Soviet of Factory-Shop Committees, and individual trade unions and factory committees, were similarly active in the struggle against Kornilov. On August 28 an emergency session of the City Duma, in which the Bolsheviks were now the second largest party, voted to prepare appropriate appeals to Kornilov's troops and to the population of Petrograd. The deputies also formed a commission to work with the authorities in assuring the procurement and distribution of adequate food supplies and selected a team of deputies to go to Luga to win over Kornilov's troops.[32]

On August 26 the Petrograd Trade Union Soviet and the Central Soviet of Factory-Shop Committees, meeting jointly, had endorsed the Interdistrict Conference's call for a "Committee of Public Safety" to help organize the defense of the capital. Now, at an unscheduled session on August 28, the Petrograd Trade Union Soviet's Executive Commission, in which Bolshevik influence was strong, responded to an invitation to appoint a representative to the Committee for Struggle by choosing the Bolshevik Vasilii Shmidt for the post. The next morning, after hearing an alarming report on food supply stocks in the capital from the head of the food supply administration, the full Trade Union Soviet formed a food supply commission of its own composed of representatives from the transport workers' union; the flour mill workers' union; restaurant, food store, and food industry workers; and the Trade Union Soviet.[33] On August 29 the Central Soviet of Factory-Shop Committees met with factory-shop committee representatives from industrial plants throughout the capital to evaluate preparations for battle and to help coordinate the distribution of arms to workers. That evening the Trade Union Soviet and the Central Soviet of Factory-Shop Committees held a joint session. After hearing a progress report by Shmidt on the work of the Committee for Struggle, the participants in this meeting agreed to support it in every way possible and to coordinate their own defense efforts with those of the committee. They also voted to insist on the liberation of revolutionaries still in jail and on the adoption of decisive measures to suppress the rightist press and arrest counterrevolutionaries. Moreover, after reevaluating the question of distributing arms to workers, they enthusiastically endorsed such action.[34]

The Petrograd Union of Metalworkers, which, as spokesman for over 200,000 workers, was far and away the most powerful labor union in Russia, allocated fifty thousand rubles from its treasury, as well as the services of its large, experienced staff, to the Committee for Struggle. The Left SR–controlled chauffeurs' union announced that the government could count on all of the transport and maintenance services it could provide, while the printers' union, dominated by Mensheviks, ordered typesetters to boycott presses that published newspapers supporting Kornilov.[35]

Of the individual trade unions, the most important during the Kornilov crisis was, inevitably, the Union of Railway Workers. On August 28 and 29 the Soviet Central Executive Committee had warned rail personnel that it was their responsibility to prevent needless bloodshed. Rail workers were directed to monitor the progress of military forces being moved toward Petrograd, to obey without hesitation orders of the government and soviet in regard to the holding up and redirection of these troops, and to ignore instructions coming from Kornilov. An analogous telegram was dispatched at about the same time by Kerensky to supervisors on all rail lines in the rear and at the front and to all rail committees. Significantly earlier, on August 27, the All-Russian Executive Committee of Railway Workers (customarily designated by its Russian acronym, Vikzhel) had formed a special bureau for struggle against Kornilov's forces.[36] On August 28 Vikzhel sent telegrams to key points along the entire Russian rail network directing that "suspicious telegrams" be held up and that Vikzhel be kept informed of the size and destination of all suspect military forces traveling on rail lines. Rail personnel were authorized to interrupt the movement of counterrevolutionary forces by any and all means, including withholding rail cars, absenting themselves from their posts, and, if need be, dismantling tracks and blocking the right of way. They were also encouraged to halt shipment of provisions to areas occupied by Kornilov's supporters. Implementation of these directives began immediately.[37]

Within hours after public announcement of the Kornilov emergency, alarm whistles were sounded in factories throughout Petrograd. Acting on their own, without instructions from higher authorities, workers reinforced security around plant buildings and grounds and began to form fighting detachments. On August 28–29 long lines of workers could be seen in the factory districts, waiting to enroll in these detachments, referred to with increasing frequency as "Red Guards."[38] To help arm these recruits, personnel in the cannon shops at the Putilov factory speeded production of a variety of weapons which were dispatched directly to the field without even a test-firing; metalworkers simply accompanied their products and adjusted the weapons on the spot. The factory committee at the sprawling Sestroretsk weapons factory funneled a few thousand rifles and limited quantities of ammunition to the newly formed workers' Red Guards. Other weapons were obtained from the arsenal in the Peter and Paul Fortress and from garrison soldiers, but the demand for arms far outran the supply. During the Kornilov days, many of the newly recruited Red Guards received training in the handling of arms from soldiers assigned to this task by the Bolshevik Military Organization. After a hasty indoctrination, Red Guards were dispatched, some to man hurriedly constructed defense fortifications in the southern Narva and Moscow districts and on the Pulkovo heights, others to lay barbed wire, dig trenches, or help tear up track along the rail lines leading to the capital, and still others to meet General Krymov's advancing troops.

Most soldiers in the partially dismantled Petrograd garrison responded to the crisis with equal dispatch. Soon after news of Kornilov's ultimatum to the government began to circulate on August 27, unit committees and hastily organized mass meetings of soldiers in military barracks throughout the capital and its suburbs had passed resolutions condemning the counterrevolution and voicing their readiness to help defend the revolution. Garrison soldiers strengthened communications with neighboring military units and with such institutions as the Committee for Struggle, the Soldiers' Section of the Petrograd Soviet,[39] district soviets, and the Bolshevik Military Organization. Garrison units suspended leaves, increased the number of soldiers assigned to guard duty, took stock of existing supplies of arms and ammunition, and formed delegations of agitators and composite fighting detachments for service at the front.

The Litovsky Guards Regiment declared in a resolution of August 28: "All troops not involved in work details or without valid medical excuses are required to participate in the detachment [now] being formed. Officers and men refusing to do their duty will be subject to revolutionary trial." The Sixth Engineers quickly organized a six-hundred-man detachment to aid in the construction of defense fortifications. The Petrograd Carters' Battalion pledged the five hundred carts at its disposal to help supply military units defending the Soviet. Between the night of August 28 and the following evening, detachments of armed soldiers from all the guards and reserve infantry regiments and numerous artillery and technical units in the capital, often accompanied by their officers, moved out to Gatchina, Tsarskoe Selo, Krasnoe Selo, and other strategic points, established themselves in trenches—some of which had been dug hours earlier by factory workers —and nervously awaited the enemy. (Within the Petrograd garrison, only cossack troops and military school cadets did not join at once in the campaign against the counterrevolution; the former remained neutral, while the latter sided openly with Kornilov.)[40]

Baltic Fleet installations dealt with the emergency in much the same way. On August 28 the Soviet in Reval, meeting with the Executive Committee of the Estonian Soviet and with army and fleet committees and representatives of the major socialist parties, organized a United Executive Committee to direct the fight against the counterrevolution; among other things, this organization brought garrison and naval units in the Reval area to battle readiness and instructed revolutionary forces to occupy key rail points nearby. In Helsingfors on the same day a joint emergency meeting of the Regional Executive Committee of the Army, Fleet, and Workers in Finland; the Executive Committee of the Helsingfors Soviet; members of Tsentrobalt; the Regional Committee of Finnish Peasant Soviets; and representatives of local army and ship committees (altogether some six hundred leftist political leaders, soldiers, sailors, and workers) began with the passage of a resolution branding Kornilov and his supporters "traitors to the revolution and the state," and demanding the transfer of governmental power to "the revolutionary democracy" and the immediate shutdown of all bourgeois newspapers and presses. The meeting culminated in the creation of a revolutionary committee with unrestricted powers to prevent counter-revolutionary action and to maintain order in Finland. Launching operations promptly, this committee helped to paralyze the activities of several large Finnish-based cossack and cavalry units which Kornilov had counted upon for support and dispatched a composite fifteen-hundred-man combat force from Vyborg to Petrograd. "Comrades! A terrible hour has struck —the revolution and all its achievements are in the gravest danger," began the Helsingfors Revolutionary Committee's proclamation of its supreme political authority in Finland. "The time has come when the revolution and the country need your strength, your sacrifices, perhaps your lives; because of this the revolutionary committee appeals to all of you to come to the defense of the revolution and freedom with closed ranks, . . . to deal a crushing blow to the counterrevolution, nipping it in the bud."

Initially, word of the Kornilov crisis was brought to Kronstadt during the night of August 27 by some sailors from the cruiser *Aurora*, then undergoing capital repairs in Petrograd. The Executive Committee of the Kronstadt Soviet (under its newly elected chairman, Lazar Bregman, a Bolshevik) immediately took control of all communications facilities, weapons stores, and private and port vessels; dispatched commissars to military headquarters and nearby naval forts at Ino and Krasnaia Gorka; and created a "Military-Technical Committee." This committee, which included the overall commander of all the Kronstadt naval units, the Kronstadt fort commander, the head of the Kronstadt militia, and representatives of all major parties in the Executive Committee, assumed, for practical purposes, full command authority over all military elements in Kronstadt. After receiving an urgent request for troop support from the Committee for Struggle, the Military-Technical Committee shot back a demand for the release of "our comrades, the finest fighters and sons of the revolution who are at this minute languishing in prison"; at the same time it declared unequivocally that the entire Kronstadt garrison, "as one man," was ready to come to the defense of the revolution. Three thousand well-armed sailors, a high percentage of whom had been to Petrograd last as participants in the July uprising, departed for the capital in the early morning of August 29. After disembarking at the quays along Vasilevsky Island, they were dispatched to help protect rail stations, bridges, the main post office, the telegraph and telephone station, the Winter Palace, and other key government buildings.[41]

The overwhelming superiority of the left over the pro-Kornilov forces was quickly evident. Steps taken by the moderate socialists and Bolsheviks to insure that factory workers would not be deceived by rightist agitators achieved their aim. Petrograd newspapers during the Kornilov days con-

Members of the Bolshevik Kronstadt Committee. Bottom row, left to right: B. A. Zhem-chuzhin, I. D. Sladkov, F. F. Raskolnikov, S. G. Roshal. Second row: B. A. Breslav, I. P. Flerovsky, S. Pelikhov, L. N. Stahl, A. M. Liubovich. Third row: D. N. Kondakov, V. I. Deshevoi, S. L. Entin, L. A. Bregman, P. I. Smirnov, I. N. Kolbin.

tained reports of scattered rightist agitation among the masses, but in no case did these incidents lead to the large-scale civil disorders hoped for by the conspirators. After the crisis erupted on August 27, conducting open counterrevolutionary agitation anywhere in Petrograd became very hazard-ous. In addition, swift action by rail and telegraph workers initially pre-vented rightist leaders in the capital from establishing communications with advancing counterrevolutionary forces.

Within units of the Petrograd garrison, the relatively few officers with the temerity to register sympathy for Kornilov, or even reluctance to oppose him, were simply ignored, to be dealt with when time permitted. In the Helsingfors area some officers suspected of harboring counterrevolutionary sentiments were lynched. In Vyborg, several high-level officers who refused to acknowledge the authority of a commissar sent to their unit by the Helsingfors revolutionary committee were immediately arrested; a mob of soldiers later broke into their place of detention and killed them. Aboard the battleship *Petropavlovsk*, based in Helsingfors, the entire crew participated in a vote to decide whether or not to execute four young officers who declined to pledge their allegiance to "democratic organizations." Sentiment was overwhelmingly against the officers and they were slaughtered, the firing squad carrying out the sentence having been selected by lot.[42]

On August 29 fourteen officers allegedly connected with the Kornilov conspiracy were rounded up in the Hotel Astoria, in the center of Petrograd. That day as well, a number of the junior officers who had been temporarily transferred from the front to Petrograd, supposedly for "training in the handling of newly developed English trench mortars," were discovered and detained aboard trains bound for the capital. It appears that most rightist leaders in Petrograd, among them Colonel V. I. Sidorin (chief liaison officer between Stavka and conspiratorial groups in the capital), Colonel Desimeter (head of the Republican Center's Military Section), and P. N. Finisov (a vice-president of the Republican Center) spent much of their time on August 27 and 28 simply waiting for word of Krymov's whereabouts; they passed the intervening hours downing quantities of vodka in private rooms at two popular Petrograd nightspots—the Malyi Iaroslavets and Villa Rode. On the evening of the twenty-eighth, Desimeter and Finisov set off toward Luga to locate Krymov. Sidorin remained behind to supervise the concoction of a "Bolshevik riot" upon receipt of a coded message from Desimeter: "Act at once according to instructions." Such a signal was dispatched to Sidorin on the morning of August 29 and was received in Petrograd that evening; but by that time the futility of the rightist cause was obvious. Sidorin reportedly was pressured out of proceeding with a simulated rising by General Alekseev, who threatened suicide unless the conspirators' plans were aborted.[43] In the end, Sidorin simply disappeared, allegedly taking with him a considerable sum of money put up by Putilov and the Society for the Economic Rehabilitation of Russia to finance a military coup.[44]

As for the forces under General Krymov's command, it will be recalled that on August 27 Kornilov directed elements of the Third Corps to continue their advance toward Petrograd and to occupy the city. The next day troop trains carrying these forces were strung out for hundreds of miles along the major rail lines leading to the capital—the Savage Division on the Moskovsko–Vindavo–Rybinskoi line between Dno and Vyritsa, the Ussuriisky Mounted Division on the Baltic line between Reval and Narva and

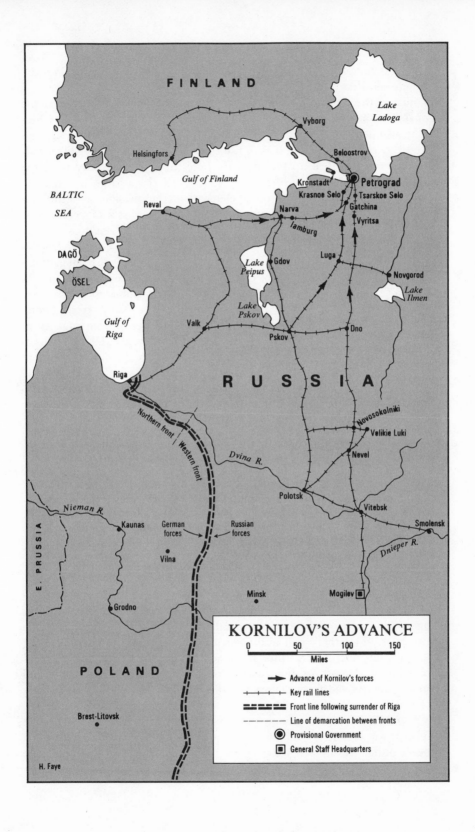

FINLAND

Lake
Ladoga

Vyborg

Helsingfors

Beloostrov

BALTIC
SEA

Gulf of Finland

Kronstadt

Krasnoe Selo

Petrograd

Tsarskoe Selo

Reval

Narva

Gatchina

Vyritsa

Iamburg

DAGÖ

Lake
Peipus

Gdov

Luga

Novgorod

ÖSEL

Lake
Ilmen

Gulf of
Riga

Valk

Lake
Pskov

R   U   S   S   I   A

Pskov

Dno

Riga

Novosokolniki

Northern front

Velikie Luki

Western front

Dvina R.

Nevel

Nieman R.

German
forces

Russian
forces

Polotsk

Kaunas

Vitebsk

Smolensk

E. PRUSSIA

Vilna

Dnieper R.

Minsk

Mogilev

POLAND

Brest-Litovsk

KORNILOV'S ADVANCE

0   50   100   150
Miles

➤ Advance of Kornilov's forces
┼┼┼ Key rail lines
▬▬▬ Front line following surrender of Riga
‐‐‐ Line of demarcation between fronts
◉ Provisional Government
▣ General Staff Headquarters

H. Faye

Narva and Iamburg, and the First Don Cossack Division on the Warsaw line between Pskov and Luga.

Units of the Savage Division posed the most immediate threat to the capital. On the evening of August 28 elements of the Ingushsky and Cherkessky regiments reached Vyritsa, only thirty-seven miles from the capital. But rail workers there had blocked the right of way with lumber-filled railway cars and had torn up the track for miles beyond. Not only were the troops unable to progress further by rail, it was impossible for them to communicate effectively with other elements of the division or with General Krymov, Stavka, or Petrograd. While the division's officers fumed helplessly, the soldiers were harangued by a stream of agitators, among whom were emissaries from the Committee for Struggle, several Petrograd district soviets, and a number of Petrograd factories, as well as from garrison military units then digging in for battle outside Tsarskoe Selo further north. Also on hand were a team of nearly a hundred agitators selected by Tsentroflot (the Central Executive Committee of the Navy) from among sailors in the Second Baltic Fleet Crew who previously had been attached to the Savage Division as machine gunners, and a smaller, all-Moslem, delegation, dispatched by the Executive Committee of the Union of Moslem Soviets, which included a grandson of the legendary Shamil.

At times, echelons of the Savage Division were encircled by local workers and peasants who berated them for betraying the revolution. The troops had not been told the real reason for their movement northward, and, as it turned out, most had little sympathy for Kornilov's objectives and no desire to oppose the Provisional Government and the Soviet. On August 30 the troops hoisted a red flag inscribed "Land and Freedom" over their headquarters and arrested the headquarters commandant when he protested. They then formed a revolutionary committee to prevent any further movement toward Petrograd, to inform other units in the division about how they were being "used" by the counterrevolution, and to organize a meeting of representatives of all units in the division. When such a meeting, attended by the Moslem delegation, was convened the next day, it voted to send a delegation to Petrograd at once with a pledge of loyalty to the Provisional Government.[45]

The Ussuriisky Mounted Division found itself in a similar situation. On August 28 railway workers in Narva delayed its forward progress for some seven hours. Late that night lead elements of the division reached Iamburg but could go no further, since the track beyond had been blocked and wrecked. On August 29 and 30 crowds of agitators from the Narva and Iamburg soviets and from factories, military units, and mass organizations in Petrograd, as well as a delegation from the Committee for Struggle led by Tsereteli, circulated among the troops. As in the case of the Savage Division, the Ussuriisky soldiers were quickly persuaded not to obey their officers' orders and to pledge loyalty to the Provisional Government; all that was necessary to win over some unit committees was a reading of Kerensky's initial public proclamations of Kornilov's treachery.[46]

Probably the most difficult force to neutralize was the First Don Cossack Division, with which General Krymov and his staff were traveling. Elements of the division had reached Luga the night of August 27, but here, too, speedy measures by railway workers, acting in concert with the Luga Soviet, stymied further advance by rail; the railway workers held back rolling stock, wrecked bridges and track, and effectively blocked communications between Krymov's forces. Subsequently, the trains carrying the First Don Cossack Division were surrounded by soldiers from the twenty-thousand-man Luga garrison. Deputies from the Luga Soviet and the Petrograd City Duma, as well as worker-soldier representatives from the capital, swarmed around the wagons, haranguing the occupants through the train windows. Officers in the division protested the presence of Bolshevik agents, but to no avail. Krymov, upon receiving orders from Kornilov to continue his advance on Petrograd regardless of the obstacles, weighed the possibility of marching his troops the remaining fifty-seven miles to the capital. He rejected this course when it became clear that the soldiers from the Luga garrison would resist such action by force and that the cossacks would not oppose the soldiers.

Actually, there were almost no skirmishes between Kornilov's forces and those on the government's side during the entire affair. In the case of the First Don Cossack Division, agitators were soon drawing the troops to mass rallies before Krymov's very eyes. With relatively little difficulty they won soldier-representatives in most units to their point of view, and by August 30 some cossacks were expressing their readiness to arrest Krymov. Finally, late on the afternoon of August 30, a government emissary, Colonel Georgii Samarin, invited Krymov to accompany him back to Petrograd for talks with Kerensky. Given firm assurances of his personal safety, Krymov reluctantly acquiesced.[47]

Krymov, who had just received word from Finisov and Desimeter that disorders would break out in the capital momentarily, seems to have left Luga with some hope that Kerensky might still turn to him for help in suppressing the left. His hope, however, was shortlived. Arriving in Petrograd by car the night of August 30–31, Krymov found the city altogether quiet; it was plain by now that the affair was all but over. The bulk of the army had remained loyal to the government and the Soviet. On the southwestern front the outspoken General Denikin had been incarcerated by his own troops. The aging commander of the northern front, General Klembovsky, who had disobeyed Kerensky's order to take Kornilov's place as supreme commander, quietly resigned and was soon replaced by the leftish General Cheremisov. Commanders of the other major Russian fronts now belatedly pledged their loyalty to the government. Kerensky named himself supreme commander, and the conservative General Alekseev emerged from retirement to become chief of staff.[48] Because of his former close association with Kornilov, Savinkov was stripped of his posts as governor-general and acting war minister; his replacement in the latter capacity was General Verkhovsky, the commander of the Moscow Military District. A high-level commission appointed by Kerensky, much like the body created several weeks earlier to hand up indictments in connection with the July uprising, was about to begin an investigation of the conspiracy.

The public figures who had hailed the "people's commander-in-chief" at the time of the Moscow Conference now hastened to put distance between themselves and Kornilov. Declared Rodzianko sanctimoniously: "All I know about the evils of the day is what I read in the papers. . . . To start internecine warfare and argument now is a crime against the motherland." Vladimir Lvov, still seemingly in a daze, expressed genuine pleasure at the outcome of the affair. On August 30, from his jail cell, he penned the following note to Kerensky: "My dear Alexander Fedorovich. From the bottom of my heart I congratulate you and am happy that I delivered a friend from Kornilov's clutches. Yours always and everywhere, V. Lvov."[49]

General Krymov met with Kerensky in the Winter Palace on the morning of August 31. According to all reports, their conversation was extremely heated, although information on precisely what transpired is contradictory. Krymov evidently insisted that his troops had not been directed against the Provisional Government, that his only object was and had always been to help facilitate the maintenance of order. Hearing this after he had read Krymov's August 26 order regarding the imposition of military rule in Petrograd, Kerensky grew livid and berated Krymov fiercely for his duplicity. For Krymov the experience was understandably trying. A courageous commander who took great pride in the traditional military virtues of patriotism, straightforwardness, and decisiveness, he had hoped since February to help halt the revolution and reestablish a strong central government, in the belief that otherwise Russia was doomed. Yet now he was forced to lie to save himself and his associates, accused of crimes against the state by a man who for some time had been privately voicing similar convictions. Ahead lay further interrogation, the necessity for more deception, and the ignominity of arrest, prosecution, and prison. Krymov, in despair, left Kerensky at around 2:00 P.M. with the understanding that he would appear at the Admiralty for further questioning later in the afternoon. From the Winter Palace, he went to the apartment of a friend, where, to no one in particular, he observed dejectedly, "The last card for saving the motherland has been beaten—life is no longer worth living." Then, retiring to a private room, ostensibly for a rest, he scribbled a brief message to Kornilov and shot himself once through the heart.[50]

·9·

THE QUESTION OF A NEW GOVERNMENT

The quick collapse of the Kornilov movement brought to the fore the thorny problem of what kind of government should replace the defunct second coalition. At the start of the Kornilov emergency a temporary understanding had been reached between Kerensky, who was bent on creating a strong Directory, and leaders of the Soviet, who, although uniformly opposed to the formation of such a government, were for the moment concerned primarily with shoring up the revolution's defenses. According to the political resolution passed by the All-Russian Executive Committees the night of August 27–28, Kerensky was to be given leave to form whatever government he wished, provided only that it remain fully dedicated to leading an all-out fight against Kornilov.[1]

On August 28, when it seemed likely that Krymov's forces would enter the capital and that a bloody clash between the forces of the right and the left would inevitably ensue, it appeared for a time that Kerensky might not act in accordance with the Executive Committees' resolution. At the height of the crisis, the Kadet Party leadership sought to forestall civil war by convincing Kerensky to yield his post to an authoritative figure with whom Kornilov would be willing to deal before Krymov's legions reached Petrograd.

The candidate selected by the Kadets as potentially acceptable to both Kornilov and Kerensky was General Alekseev. On the afternoon of the twenty-eighth, Miliukov offered his services to Kerensky as an intermediary between the government and the General Staff. Shortly afterward, another high-ranking Kadet, Nikolai Kishkin, sounded out Kerensky specifically on the question of his resignation in favor of Alekseev. That evening, a majority of Kerensky's acting ministers apparently agreed on the advisability of substituting Alekseev for Kerensky, and many of them made their views known to the prime minister. Allied representatives in Russia, led by

Britain's George Buchanan, also attempted to persuade Kerensky to negotiate with Kornilov. It is clear that Kerensky, under the weight of such pressure, came very close to yielding his post. But the leadership of the Soviet categorically opposed negotiation; upon its insistence, Kerensky, at the eleventh hour, rejected the course pushed by the Kadets.[2]

Of course, by the next day, August 29, the Kornilov bubble had burst. For Kerensky, there was no longer any question of coming to terms with the generals. One might have expected that at this point, having suffered so badly at the hands of the right and having witnessed the enormous power of the left, the prime minister would have taken pains to retain the support of the latter. Yet, obsessed more than ever by fear of the extreme left and still intent on somehow strengthening the war effort, Kerensky now behaved almost as if the Kornilov affair had not happened. To be sure, he insisted on Kornilov's arrest and on the immediate resignation of Savinkov, and he now proclaimed Russia a republic. But in a charge to the chairman of the commission set up to investigate the Kornilov conspiracy, Kerensky stipulated that the inquiry, as it pertained to the military establishment, should be limited as much as possible to the complicity of the main participants.[3] In addition, Kerensky appointed General Alekseev, the Kadet candidate for prime minister, to the post of chief-of-staff. In accepting his new position, Alekseev, whose views on the changes in the army brought about by the revolution coincided with those of Kornilov and Denikin, acknowledged privately that his primary motivation was to ease the fate of Kornilov and his supporters.[4] Most telling of all, as soon as the Kornilov threat subsided, Kerensky began laying plans to form an authoritarian government oriented toward law and order—a right-socialist–liberal coalition cabinet in which the influence of the Kadets would be stronger than ever.

Meanwhile, the exigencies of the struggle against Kornilov had pulled the moderate socialists leftward into conflict with the government and toward closer alliance with the extreme left. After the July days, most Mensheviks and SRs had actively supported Kerensky in his attempts to disarm workers and suppress the Bolsheviks; during the Kornilov emergency, on the other hand, the Committee for Struggle Against the Counterrevolution was forced to endorse and facilitate the formation of armed workers' detachments.[5] Although it is difficult to estimate how many workers first obtained arms and became organized for violent political action at this time, it is safe to say that whatever limited progress had been made earlier in pacifying the Petrograd masses was instantly undone.

One of the Bolsheviks' most insistent demands as the price of their participation in mutual defense organs (a plea echoed during the crisis by a myriad of mass organizations) was that Bolshevik leaders still in prison on suspicion of having been involved in the July uprising be released without further delay. On August 29, when a group of soldier-Bolsheviks broke out of their place of detention in the Second District Militia headquarters, evidently with the help of some sympathetic guards, the Committee for Struggle agreed that they should be allowed to remain free "in order to participate in the common struggle against the counterrevolution." Pressure to do something about the prisoner issue mounted when leftist officers held in the First District Militia headquarters issued a public demand to be allowed to help in the fight against Kornilov and emphasized their demand by proclaiming a hunger strike. Yielding to this pressure, which was strengthened by intervention on the prisoners' behalf by the Committee for Struggle, the authorities released a few Bolsheviks at the height of the Kornilov scare. Some other leftist leaders were freed in the first half of September. Thus on September 4 prison gates swung open for Antonov-Ovseenko and Dybenko. Trotsky was released the same day, his bail furnished by the Petrograd Soviet of Trade Unions.[6] Several of the Bolshevik officers involved in the hunger strike in the First District Militia headquarters, among them Military Organization leaders Krylenko, Dashkevich, Kudelko, and Ter-Arutuniants, won their freedom a week later. All of these liberated Bolsheviks were to play active roles in the subsequent development of the revolution.[7]

Preparing to combat Kornilov, officials of the Committee for Struggle became alarmed that officers in the headquarters of the Petrograd Military District, supposedly participating in the defense of the city, were surreptitiously trying to aid the general. There were numerous indications that these officers were dragging their feet in mobilizing, arming, and properly provisioning garrison units; upon their directives, some of the units ultimately dispatched were deployed so as to be sitting ducks for the attacking forces. When the sabotage by the military staff became apparent, the Committee for Struggle sent its own commissars to oversee the staff's operations.[8]

On August 28, when Kerensky had appeared on the verge of stepping down in favor of General Alekseev, the moderate socialists had brought pressure to bear upon Kerensky to prevent such a step. In the aftermath of the Kornilov experience many prominent Mensheviks and SRs were cool to Kerensky's aim of forming another coalition with the Kadets. This was partly because the Kadets were now a symbol of antirepublican, antireform, and prowar sentiment, and hence popular opinion in Petrograd was hostile to continued Kadet participation in the government. It was also because of genuine concern among the Menshevik and SR leaders themselves about the Kadet role in the Kornilov conspiracy.

A joint plenary meeting of the All-Russian Executive Committees, primarily to consider the government question, was quickly scheduled for the evening of August 31, soon after Kerensky's political intentions became known. Meanwhile, a hastily assembled emergency meeting of the Menshevik Central Committee adopted a resolution stating that "participation in the government of elements that had sympathized with the counterrevolution or whose intention had been to paralyze the fight against the counter-revolution was impermissible." As to the status of the Kadets, the resolution declared specifically that they could not longer be included in the Provisional Government.[9] A meeting of the SR Central Committee adopted an analogous position. These views were conveyed immediately to Kerensky, who at this juncture temporarily shelved plans to construct another coalition and instead announced the formation of a "caretaker" five-man Directory from which Kadets were excluded. Headed by Kerensky, the Directory was made up of Tereshchenko, still handling foreign affairs; two younger, relatively progressive military officers, Admiral Dmitrii Verderevsky and General Verkhovsky, heading the naval and war ministries respectively; and Aleksei Nikitin, an undistinguished right Menshevik who had been minister of labor in the second coalition, as minister of post and telegraph.

In formulating a stance on the government issue, the moderate socialists were faced with a situation reminiscent in many ways of the July days. At that time massive numbers of workers and soldiers had taken to the streets to protest the policies of the Provisional Government and to demand that the Soviet assume power; their cry had been "Down with the Ten Minister-Capitalists!" "All Power to the Soviets!" Now, in the first flush of their triumph over Kornilov, the local-level mass organizations and the factory workers, soldiers, and sailors who had joined in the anti-Kornilov movement expressed their views regarding the nature, makeup, and program of the future government in a torrent of letters, resolutions, and political declarations; these revealed that at bottom the demands of the masses at this time differed little from what they had been two months earlier.

Some representative examples will serve to convey the tenor of these appeals. Workers from the machine shop of the Petrograd pipe factory, after discussing "the current moment" on August 28, declared: "In view of the emerging bourgeois counterrevolutionary movement, as well as the attacks on freedom and on all the democratic gains of the Russian proletariat by former tsarist *oprichniki* [police thugs], all power must be transferred to the soviet of workers', soldiers', and peasants' deputies."[10] The same day eight thousand workers in the Metallist factory approved a declaration of no confidence in the "minister-socialists," presumably for their willingness to cooperate with the bourgeoisie. These workers demanded the immediate creation of a "forceful revolutionary government." On the twenty-ninth an angry meeting of several thousand workers in the mammoth Putilov factory agreed that "the future government has to be composed solely of representatives of the revolutionary classes," adding that "any negotiations regarding the creation of a coalition government at a time when the bourgeoisie and its representative Kornilov are making war on the people will be considered treachery to the cause of freedom." Meanwhile, employees of the Novo-Admiralteisky shipbuilding plant, after considering the existing political

Factory workers gathered for a political meeting.

situation, insisted that "state power must not remain in the hands of the counterrevolutionary bourgeoisie a minute longer. It must be put into the hands of the workers, soldiers, and poorer peasantry and be responsible to the soviets of workers', soldiers', and peasants' deputies."[11]

Public declarations adopted in the wake of the Kornilov affair by virtually all units of the Petrograd garrison were similarly explicit. Thus at an emergency meeting on August 28, twenty-five hundred soldiers from four key military units based in the capital—the Preobrazhensky, Litovsky, and Volynsky guards regiments, and the Sixth Engineer Battalion—passed a resolution insisting that the government be drawn exclusively from representatives of the revolutionary classes. On August 31 the same soldiers, after reasserting the call for a government made up representatives of the workers and poorer peasants, proclaimed bluntly than "any coalition . . . will be fought by all loyal sons of the people just as they fought Kornilov." No less outspoken were the soldiers of the Second Machine Gun Regiment, who the same day expressed their views about Kornilov and the immediate tasks of a new government in the following terms:

> We brand Kornilov and his supporters traitors. . . . We haven't had any confidence in Kornilov since April 21, when that "brave" general directed artillery to be rolled out on the Palace Square to quiet our comrade workers. . . . This conspiracy must be crushed with all possible severity and we machine gunners place ourselves completely at the disposal of the Central Executive Committee. . . . We insist on the immediate arrest and trial of the counterrevolutionary commanding staff and the abolition of capital punishment, to become effective after the execution of General Kornilov and his supporters. We demand the restoration of revolutionary regiments that have been broken up and the dissolution of counterrevolutionary shock battalions, the Union of Saint George Cavaliers, the Union of Officers of the Army and Navy, the Military League, etc. . . . The only way out of the present situation lies in transferring power into the hands of the working people.
>
> We demand the immediate liberation of our comrades arrested on July 3–5 and their replacement [in prison] by the conspirators, for example: Guchkov, Purishkevich, and the counterrevolutionary officers. As regards foreign affairs, we insist on a decisive break with both Russian and allied imperialism and a campaign for peace without annexations and indemnities on the basis of the self-determination of nations. Soldiers' pay should be increased to twenty rubles. . . . The necessary funds should be obtained by confiscating excess profits from plant and factory owners. We will fight for all of these revolutionary measures to the last machine gunner, and the government that carries them out will have our full support.[12]

On September 1, two hundred soldiers assigned to the Electro-Technical Officers' School resolved that "the replacement of Kornilov with Alekseev changed nothing" and that "the politics of compromise with the bourgeoisie and landowners must and did lead inevitably to the Kornilov conspiracy." In order to avert another counterrevolutionary attack, these soldiers insisted on the necessity of transferring all power to "representatives of the workers, soldiers, and peasants under the control of their elected organizations." A mass meeting of soldiers from the Petrogradsky Guards Regiment two days later called for the creation of a new cabinet "made up exclusively of socialists who have suffered in prisons for the people's cause and who have wasted the best years of their lives in far-off Siberia." Like the Second Machine Gun Regiment, the soldiers from the Electro-Technical School and the Petrogradsky Guards Regiment also demanded death for Kornilov and his followers.[13]

Not surprisingly, bitterness toward Kerensky and the desire for an immediate change in government after the Kornilov experience were nowhere stronger than among the radicalized Baltic sailors. On August 30 the crew of the *Petropavlovsk*, who had voted earlier to execute officers refusing to pledge loyalty to the revolution, agreed that "death is the most appropriate punishment for Kornilov." The resolution they adopted asserted that "only the democracy, in the person of its finest representatives—the Executive Committees of the Soviets of Workers', Soldiers', and Peasants' Deputies —can save the country; consequently, all power must be transferred into the hands of the soviets. Experience has shown," the resolution continued, "that coalitions of responsible ministries of any kind are incapable of leading the country out of the critical situation in which it finds itself. It is the direct responsibility of the Soviet to take power into its hands, and we will gladly submit to such a government and obey all its orders with pleasure."

Distinctly more critical of the moderate socialists was a resolution on "the current moment" adopted overwhelmingly at a joint meeting of the Helsingfors Soviet; the Regional Executive Committee of the Army, Fleet, and Workers in Finland; and representatives of army and ship committees from the Helsingfors area on September 2. Concluded the resolution: "Up to now, not only has the Central Executive Committee neglected to pursue a policy of furthering the revolution—by supporting the politics of compromise with the bourgeoisie, it has strengthened the position of the counterrevolution. This kind of behavior must cease. We emphatically insist that the Central Executive Committee refrain from pledging confidence to any coalition ministry (with the bourgeoisie) and that it immediately convene the Second All-Russian Congress of Workers', Soldiers', and Peasants' Deputies," i.e., to create a soviet regime.[14]

To register their protest against Kerensky's proclamation of a nondemocratic republic while forming a Directory and conducting negotiations with the bourgeoisie, members of nineteen Baltic Fleet ship's committees, meeting jointly on September 6, recommended that ships of the fleet fly red battle flags "until the promulgation of all reforms associated with a democratic form of government." Tsentrobalt endorsed this method of protest the following day, after which the red flags were raised.[15] The mood of the Baltic sailors at this time was also expressed in a lead editorial entitled "Enough of Past Errors," by V. Maslenikov, in *Izvestiia Kronshtadtskogo soveta*.

> The politics of compromise with the bourgeoisie is what has brought us to this tragic pass. The compromisers had faith in people who wailed hypocritically about the impending ruin of the country and who did everything according to their own recipe. . . . All the warnings of the proletariat and of the parties which did not abandon it proved justified . . .

[yet] it turns out that this is not enough. . . . What is this—political blindness or a conscious attack on the revolution? . . . This cannot be. Our task now is to say emphatically: "We have had quite enough compromise! All power to the working people."[16]

On August 29 the Kronstadt Soviet adopted a set of demands to be presented in the Central Executive Committee by Kronstadt's representative there. Drawn up by the Bolsheviks and immediately endorsed by the SR- and Menshevik-Internationalists (the main SR and Menshevik factions in Kronstadt), these demands were patterned after the moderate resolution "On the Current Moment," which Lunacharsky had introduced at the Executive Committees meeting the night of August 27–28 and which had called for a decisive rupture with the capitalists; the transfer of power into the hands of revolutionary workers, peasants, and soldiers; and the creation of a democratic republic.

Kronstadt's ideal remained a democratic soviet government in which all socialist groups would work together effectively in pursuit of a revolutionary program, precisely as the socialists had been doing locally, in the Kronstadt Soviet, since March. The Kronstadt sailors were heartened by the prospect that the Kornilov experience might serve to bring the moderate socialist leadership of the All-Russian Executive Committees back into the revolutionary fold. This hopeful attitude was expressed by deputies to the Kronstadt Soviet in their response to a report on the latest developments in Petrograd presented to them by Kolbin on August 29. After lashing out at Kerensky for indecisiveness in combatting Kornilov, Kolbin, in the course of his account, related that when Tsereteli had declared to the Central Executive Committee that this was a time not for compromise but for strong military action, Chernov had embraced him in a gesture of solidarity. The Kronstadt deputies greeted with stormy applause this sign of moderate socialist unity in defense of the revolution.[17]

It is worth noting that even workers in industrial plants that heretofore had been Menshevik and SR strongholds, as well as soldiers in some of the more politically restrained regiments of the garrison—for example, those which initially had remained neutral and subsequently had taken the lead in helping to suppress the July uprising—now turned against the government. What is more, even some of the military personnel rushed from the front to the capital after the July days now joined the ranks of the opposition.

The political resolutions passed at this time were inspired by no single party or organization. Some were proposed by Bolsheviks, others by Menshevik-Internationalists or Left SRs, and still others by individuals or representatives of interest groups with no identifiable political affiliation. These statements varied greatly in regard to specifics. Some called for the creation of a government representing workers, soldiers, and peasants; others, perhaps a majority, insisted on transfer of power to the soviets or creation of a revolutionary government responsible to the Soviet, often coupling such demands with a call for another national Congress of Soviets. However, common to virtually all were concern that Kornilov and his supporters be dealt with harshly so as to avoid further attacks by the "counter-revolution," aversion to political collaboration with the propertied classes in any form, and attraction for the immediate creation of some kind of exclusively socialist government which would bring an end to the war. It is evident that to many, including Bolsheviks, the swift defeat of Kornilov appeared to confirm the immense potentialities of all socialist groups working together. Such a large representative number of statements are available for study, either in the contemporary press or in published document collections, and they are corroborated so strongly by other kinds of evidence, that it is fair to conclude that among Petrograd workers and soldiers and Baltic sailors who expressed themselves politically in any way, these sentiments were by now nearly universally shared.

Such were the pressures under which members of the All-Russian Executive Committees labored as they assembled to consider the government question late on the afternoon of August 31. This session, which with adjournments lasted until the early morning of September 2, merits consideration as one of the most important meetings of the Soviet leadership between February and October 1917. Prior to the October days, at any rate, this seems to have been the moment when the Mensheviks and SRs came closest to breaking with the liberals and adopting much more radical policies, which might significantly have altered the revolution's course.

Early in the discussion Kamenev proposed that the deputies adopt a broad policy statement, "On the Government Question," which, while relatively moderate in content and tone, nonetheless constituted a fundamental, decisive break with previous Soviet policy.[18] Kamenev himself had composed the statement, and it had been endorsed at an earlier caucus of Bolshevik Central Committee members with representatives of the Bolshevik fractions in the All-Russian Executive Committees and the Petrograd Soviet. It began with a forthright repudiation of the politics of "compromise" and "irresponsibility," which "made it possible for the military high command and the institutions of government to become breeding grounds for the instrument of a conspiracy against the revolution." The statement called for the exclusion from the government of the Kadets and all representatives of propertied elements, and affirmed that the only viable course open to the democracy was to create a national government made up of "representatives of the revolutionary proletariat and peasantry," whose first task would be to proclaim a *democratic republic.*" Other basic tasks of this new government would be confiscation of manorial lands without compensation and their transfer to peasant committees in advance of the Constituent Assembly, proclamation of workers' control over industrial production, nationalization of key branches of industry, and the proposal of a universal democratic peace. Among measures for immediate implementation, the resolution called for an end to all repression directed against the working class and its organizations, abolition of capital punishment at the front and restoration of full freedom for political agitation and activity on the part of democratic organizations in the army, a purge of the counterrevolutionary commanding staff within the military, recognition of the right to self-government of minority nationalities living in Russia, immediate convocation of the Constituent Assembly, and abolition of all class privileges.

The resolution's emphasis on the formation of a revolutionary government to create a democratic republic, rather than a dictatorship of the proletariat and poorer peasantry, was obviously Kamenev's work and represented an accurate reflection of programmatic views regarding the development of the revolution consistently held by Bolshevik moderates.[19] At the same time, Kamenev's statement was a succinct and powerful formulation of the political aspirations of Petrograd workers and soldiers as expressed in the wake of the Kornilov experience. In presenting the resolution to the Executive Committees, Kamenev appealed for the maintenance of the unified revolutionary front which had emerged in the course of the struggle against Kornilov. Placing particular emphasis on the crucial role of the soviets, which had served as "the mortar binding all fundamentally democratic forces" during the crisis, he contended that "no one can say that there exists at the present time any organization more powerful than the soviets."

It is extremely important to note that while the policy statement proposed by Kamenev was universally interpreted as an appeal for transfer of political power to the soviets, Kamenev himself did not insist on this, evidently envisioning the possibility of a socialist cabinet which would include representatives of such "democratic" institutions as the trade unions, zemstvos, municipal dumas, and cooperatives which were not nominally part of the Soviet. As he observed toward the close of his remarks: "The Bolshevik fraction is concerned not with the purely technical aspects of forming a government but rather with the elements to be included in such a government—are they of like mind in their understanding of the immediate tasks and will they be able to march in step with the democracy?"[20]

Because of a conflict with a previously scheduled session of the Petrograd Soviet, the Executive Committees meeting was adjourned at 7:30 P.M. without having voted on the Kamenev resolution; further discussion of the government question was tabled until the following evening.

Kamenev's resolution was next presented at the late-night meeting of the Petrograd Soviet on August 31,[21] the first meeting of that body in ten days. Political attitudes in the Petrograd Soviet had been shifting leftward throughout the month of August; this was a reflection both of the growing misgivings on the part of incumbent deputies regarding the existing political situation and of the changing composition of the Soviet, as moderately inclined deputies elected in March and April were recalled and replaced by

A meeting of the Petrograd Soviet of Workers' and Soldiers' Deputies.

factory and garrison representatives with more militant views.[22] This transformation was immediately apparent on August 31. The agenda opened with reports on the latest political developments. Boris Bogdanov, a Menshevik, brought the deputies up to date on the work of the Committee for Struggle Against the Counterrevolution. Responding to the anger and impatience of his listeners, Bogdanov focused on the committee's efforts to strengthen and unite the left and to prevent the government from coming to terms with Kornilov. At each indication of forcefulness on the committee's part, both in counteracting Kornilov and in dealing with Kerensky, the deputies burst into applause.

On the question of a new government, Tsereteli publicly acknowledged, for the first time, the difficulty of including Kadets in the cabinet; however, he defended in the strongest terms coalition with representatives of other bourgeois groups. The democracy by itself would be helpless to deal with economic disintegration, he argued, and this situation would play into the hands of the counterrevolution.

Tsereteli's remarks were frequently interrupted by vociferous protests and jeers which prompted the chairman, Chkheidze, finally to blurt: "The Soviet still has enough power to throw disrupters out the door." Kamenev, by contrast, was spiritedly cheered when he presented his policy statement and repeated the attack on coalition politics that he had made earlier to the Executive Committees. Steklov also brought the deputies to their feet when he expressed solidarity with Kamenev. The SR spokesman Boldyrev broke with previous moderate socialist policy by proposing that the Executive

Committees construct a new cabinet. Boldyrev introduced a resolution which provided that such a government might include representatives of some bourgeois groups, although not the Kadets, and that it would be responsible to a "Provisional Revolutionary Parliament." But even this compromise was coolly received.

After several hours of further heated debate on the pros and cons of creating an exclusively socialist government, at about 5:00 A.M., September 1, the deputies rejected the resolution of the SRs and adopted as a political platform the statement offered by Kamenev. The vote on the Kamenev proposal was 279 deputies in favor, 115 opposed, with 51 abstentions. In assessing the significance of this Bolshevik success, it is important to note that the number of deputies present and voting on this occasion constituted a relatively small fraction of the Petrograd Soviet's total membership. This was at least partly because many military representatives were still on duty with their regiments, defending the capital against Kornilov. It is also true that many rank-and-file left Mensheviks and SRs with no organizational loyalty to the Bolsheviks sided with the Bolsheviks on this issue. Nonetheless, as suggested earlier, the vote of the Petrograd Soviet on August 31 reflected a gradual, although by no means negligible, leftward shift in the deputies' orientation.

It is worth recalling in this connection that on March 2 a Bolshevik resolution opposing assumption of power by the Provisional Government received a mere 19 votes in the Petrograd Soviet, while a resolution sponsored jointly by the Mensheviks and SRs pledging qualified support for the government attracted 400 votes. On April 2, when membership in the Petrograd Soviet more nearly approximated its full strength, a Bolshevik resolution opposing endorsement of the liberty loan drive—in effect, a referendum on the war—received 112 votes, while a Menshevik-SR resolution supporting the drive received 2,000 votes. In the wake of the April crisis a month later, when the deputies had to adopt a position on socialist participation in the cabinet, 100 deputies voted for a Bolshevik resolution which opposed participation, while Menshevik-SR strength held firm at 2,000. Popular support for the Bolshevik program rose on the eve of the July days, and this was reflected, to a limited extent, in the Petrograd Soviet; thus on June 20 a moderate socialist resolution endorsing the Kerensky offensive received 271 negative votes, with 39 abstentions.[23] But the August 31 session marked the first occasion on which a clear majority of the deputies present voted with the Bolsheviks on any political issue.

Adoption of the Kamenev resolution, which embodied a fundamental reorientation of priorities and goals, necessitated reorganization of the entire Petrograd Soviet leadership, a factor of immense subsequent importance to the development of the revolution. In the short run, however, inasmuch as the direct authority of the Petrograd Soviet was limited to the capital, the still uncertain decision of the All-Russian Executive Committees on the government question was naturally of more far-reaching significance. Responsibility for the immediate fate of the government was in their hands.

The All-Russian Executive Committees resumed their discussion of the government question late on the evening of September 1, at about the time Kerensky announced the creation of a Directory.[24] Yet, despite the popular desire for a reorientation of Soviet politics which passage of the Bolshevik resolution in the Petrograd Soviet represented, and the fact that Kerensky, in announcing the formation of the Directory, had presented the Executive Committees with a *fait accompli,* the continuing reluctance of the moderate socialists to break altogether with the existing regime was established from the outset. A procession of leading Mensheviks and SRs, among them Skobelev and Bogdanov, spoke against the Bolshevik position and urged that the existing government be supported, at least until the Democratic State Conference.

The right Menshevik Mark Liber ridiculed the very notion that the democracy could go it alone, declaring: "The Kadets have been thrown from the chariot, but let us take heed lest we end up in it by ourselves." Avksentiev actually hailed the Directory and asked that it be supported in every way possible. Chernov declared emphatically that no SR would join a government which included Kadets; he did not, however, dismiss the possibility of forming a coalition with representatives of other bourgeois circles. Sergei Znamensky, on behalf of the Trudoviks, also defended the principle of coalition, insisting: "We should not create a purely socialist ministry. . . . There are social and political groups apart from the Kadets that can walk arm in arm with us."

Besides the Bolsheviks, only Martov adopted a significantly more radical stance; he espoused the creation of an all-socialist ministry responsible to a democratic parliament.

Riazanov and Kamenev attempted to rebut the moderate socialists. With reference to a comment made earlier by Skobelev, Riazanov remarked:

> It has been argued there that the mood in Petrograd is not representative of the rest of Russia. But people in the provinces watch what is going on in Petrograd closely . . . and when we tighten the noose around the neck of the counterrevolution, there is no doubt we will find broad support among them. . . . If one rejects coalition with the Kadets, we are left with the commercial, industrial, and banking circles, which, as is now evident, nourished the yellow press. . . . It is high time to take into consideration the fact that the soviets represent the majority of the Russian people. . . . Let the soviets select a Provisional Government responsible to them which would lead the country to a quick convocation of the Constituent Assembly. Only the Constituent Assembly can conclude peace, enact necessary reforms, and bring us closer to a socialist restructuring of society.

For his part, Kamenev, referring to the announcement of a Directory, complained acidly that the Executive Committees "have been hit with another blow from Kerensky. Their significance has been reduced to nothing. . . . I would hope," he continued, "that you will repel this blow as you repelled Kornilov's attack. . . . Political duty demands that we declare that this government is not intended to serve the needs of the democracy but of Kerensky. . . . We see in what has occurred the consequences of a regime based on personal dictatorship and total irresponsibility. The proletariat, peasantry, and army must state that there is no place for this in the Russian revolution."

Tsereteli attempted to counter these arguments with the comment that "we are convening a broad democratic conference . . . and if it turns out that apart from us there are no other vital elements in the country, we will take power into our own hands." This was as close as Tsereteli and his supporters were to come toward acknowledging the possibility of forming an exclusively socialist government.

In the early-morning hours of September 2 the exhausted deputies voted upon and rejected the declarations of both the Bolsheviks and Menshevik-Internationalists and adopted, instead, a resolution sponsored jointly by the Mensheviks and SRs. The approved resolution endorsed the early convocation of a Democratic State Conference to arrive at a final decision on the government question and, in the meantime, called for continued support of the existing regime as formed by Kerensky.[25]

Although in retrospect the Executive Committees' decision to go along, temporarily, with the Directory appears to have been a particularly fateful step, it would obviously have been very difficult for the moderate socialists to have acted otherwise. Support for the course proposed by the Bolsheviks would have required the Mensheviks and SRs to repudiate their policies of the preceding six months and abandon their ideal of creating a democratic government representing all classes. It would have signified willingness on their part to form a new political regime and to take full responsibility for maintaining civil order, administering the economy, providing essential food and fuel supplies and services, and satisfying mounting mass demands for immediate social reform and peace; further, adoption of the Bolshevik resolution would have indicated the moderate socialists' readiness to attempt these tasks without the help of, indeed faced with certain opposition from, liberal political leaders, industrialists, and large landowners, as well as the military command. Finally, for the Mensheviks and SRs to have united with the Bolsheviks, as Kamenev and Riazanov eloquently advocated, would have meant forming an alliance with elements of dubious reliability whose political goals were often less compatible with their own than were those of the liberal bourgeoisie. If one takes into consideration the Bolsheviks' past behavior, coupled with the German military threat and the prevailing economic and social chaos, it is perhaps not so difficult to understand why the main body of Mensheviks and SRs, despite their by now almost universal disdain for Kerensky, resisted popular pressures for an immediate change in government.

The political effects of the Kornilov experience were enormous. For the time being, the rightist movement was, of course, shattered. Kornilov, the darling of the right, was under house arrest in Mogilev. Because of their behavior both before and during the crisis, the Kadets were widely suspected, to some extent unfairly, of having been in league with Kornilov. In the aftermath of the affair, they were temporarily excluded from the cabinet, much maligned, and deeply demoralized. Miliukov and Kokoshkin departed for the Crimea "as if fleeing arrest," Maklakov became ambassador to France, and numerous other Kadets retreated to their summer homes in the country. Kadet politics virtually ground to a half.[26]

Because of internal disputes in regard to the nature and makeup of the future government, the Mensheviks and SRs were scarcely in better shape. Fundamental differences of opinion on the key political issues of the day among leading Mensheviks emerged with particular clarity at a meeting of the Bureau of the Central Executive Committee on September 4. In the course of an acrimonious debate on the goals of the Democratic State Conference, scheduled to open in mid-September, the defensist Bogdanov joined the Menshevik-Internationalists Martov and Sukhanov in arguing the case for the formation of an exclusively "democratic" regime. The coming conference must be turned into a Constituent Assembly for the democracy, insisted Bogdanov, and the government formed there made responsible to the conference.

Such ideas seemed preposterous to Chkheidze, the Central Executive Committee chairman. Along with Liber, he underscored the importance of including at least some representatives of propertied elements in any future government, as well as at the Democratic State Conference. Dan and Tsereteli took a middle position between the Bogdanov and Chkheidze factions, acknowledging that the primary purpose of the conference was to arrive at a definitive solution to the government question and expressing readiness to abide by the conference's decision on the matter, whatever it might be. Tsereteli, who personally preferred a coalition, voiced regret that an assembly of all the "democratic" groups to be represented at the conference had not been convened earlier, adding that "if the vote is for a soviet regime, then we can risk it."[27]

Similar arguments were also tearing the SRs apart at this time. Thus, while a still-influential conservative SR faction headed by Avksentiev insisted on the necessity of preserving a broadly representative coalition government including Kadets, the former minister of agriculture, Chernov, wanted nothing more to do with the Kadets. Yet Chernov was equally opposed to the idea of an exclusively socialist government, sharing with many right Mensheviks the hope of attracting into the cabinet representatives of the bourgeoisie, excepting the Kadets, who would be willing to cooperate with socialists in realizing a meaningful reform program.[28] Meanwhile, well to the left of Chernov was an increasingly vocal and powerful Left SR faction, now almost an independent party, which adamantly rejected any kind of coalition with the bourgeoisie. During the second week in September, the Left SRs gained control of the local SR committee in Petrograd;[29] simultaneously they launched a campaign for the convocation of a national Congress of Soviets and the creation of a homogeneous socialist government responsible to the democracy.[30] The SR organization, to use Oliver Radkey's words, "had entered the final stage of disintegration."[31]

Not surprisingly, the Kornilov affair also made a shambles of whatever modest success Kerensky had achieved since early July in restoring governmental authority and strengthening the army. The soviets, now distinctly more radical in outlook, emerged from the crisis with their popularity among the masses immeasurably enhanced. Revolutionary Russia was more widely saturated than ever before with competing grass roots political organizations and revolutionary committees. Workers had become more militant and better organized, and significant numbers of them had obtained weapons. At the same time, democratic committees in the army, by virtue of their leading role in organizing soldiers against the Kornilov movement, were rejuvenated. Within the Petrograd garrison, control of many regimental committees passed from more moderate elements into the hands of the Bolsheviks.[32] Whatever moral authority officers still possessed among the troops was badly damaged by the Kornilov experience. During the first half of September a second purge of officers suspected of harboring counterrevolutionary sentiments was carried out in many units, and, in the meantime, the execution of even the simplest orders became very difficult.[33]

The government endeavored to reverse these developments. On September 1, for instance, Kerensky issued a directive to all military commanders, commissars, and army organizations to put a halt to political activity among the troops, but the order seems to have had no discernible impact. Three days later Kerensky published a decree dissolving all ad hoc revolutionary committees established during the Kornilov crisis, which included the Committee for Struggle Against the Counterrevolution.[34] The decree served merely to exacerbate relations between Kerensky and the Soviet leadership. No sooner had the order become public than the Committee for Struggle went into session (this in itself an act of civil disobedience) and adopted a carefully worded resolution expressing confidence that, in view of the still-threatening situation, all local revolutionary committees would continue to operate with their previous energy and restraint.[35]

While the government strived in vain to cope with these difficulties, the disintegration of the economy continued apace. In Petrograd the problems of unemployment, food and fuel shortages, and inflation now became significantly more acute. During these days as well, Kerensky's personal reputation was virtually destroyed. To the defeated right, it appeared that because of either personal ambition or lack of courage Kerensky had betrayed Kornilov. Meanwhile, to the left and to the masses of Petrograd workers and soldiers, it appeared that Kerensky was part and parcel of the counterrevolution. In a valuable unpublished memoir, Woytinsky, then commissar of the northern front, focused attention on this factor, recalling that every soldier knew that the conflict between Kerensky and Kornilov had been preceded by negotiations between them, and that discussed in these negotiations were the imposition of capital punishment, the curbing of soldiers' committees, the return of power to officers, in short, a return to the ways of the "old regime." Consequently, to the average soldier, the *Kornilovshchina* appeared as a conspiracy against himself and against the revolution on the part of the military high command *and* Kerensky.[36]

Among the competitors for power in 1917, then, it is clear that the winners in the Kornilov affair were the Bolsheviks. The defeat of Kornilov testified to the great potential power of the left and demonstrated once again the enormous attraction of the Bolshevik program. Yet it seems questionable to argue, as some do, that Kornilov's defeat made Lenin's victory inevitable. The mass mood was not specifically Bolshevik in the sense of reflecting a desire for a Bolshevik government. As the flood of post-Kornilov political resolutions revealed, Petrograd soldiers, sailors, and workers were attracted more than ever by the goal of creating a soviet government uniting all socialist elements. And in their eyes the Bolsheviks stood for soviet power—for soviet democracy. In any case, the July uprising and the subsequent reaction had demonstrated the risks inherent in relying on the mood of the masses. Moreover, the entire history of the party from the February revolution on suggested the potential for programmatic discord and disorganized activity existing within Bolshevik ranks. So that whether the party would somehow find the strength of will, organizational discipline, and sensitivity to the complexities of the fluid and possibly explosive prevailing situation requisite for it to take power was, at this point, still very much an open question.

·10·

"ALL POWER TO THE SOVIETS!"

Through these last critical days of August Lenin remained underground in Helsingfors, the capital of Finland. In Finland, part of the Russian empire since 1809, national aspirations complicated and greatly intensified the ferment which followed the collapse of the tsarist regime. Helsingfors was also the main base of the Baltic Fleet, within which the Bolsheviks were especially active and influential. As elsewhere in Russia, political and social antagonism and popular support for extreme left programs rose sharply in Finland in the late summer and early fall of 1917. The Third Regional Congress of Soviets of the Army, Fleet, and Workers in Finland, which met in Helsingfors on September 9–12, elected a permanent executive committee (the Regional Executive Committee of the Army, Fleet, and Workers in Finland) made up almost exclusively of Bolsheviks and Left SRs. Under the chairmanship of the ultraradical Bolshevik Ivar Smilga, this committee proclaimed itself the highest political authority in Finland.

During his stay in Helsingfors, Lenin had some contact with local social democratic leaders. And it seems that the strength of the left and the increasingly explosive political situation in Finland helped to shape his thinking about the further development of the revolution generally. But for the most part Lenin remained absorbed by revolutionary politics in Petrograd. Shortly after the move from Razliv to Finland on August 9 he had been able to arrange fairly reliable communications with the Central Committee, as well as delivery of newspapers from Petrograd, which usually arrived toward evening the day after publication. Apart from devouring and reflecting on the news, he seems to have divided his time between completing *The State and Revolution* and writing political commentaries for the Bolshevik press.[1]

Lenin first learned of General Kornilov's threat to Petrograd on August 28. Not until late on the twenty-ninth did he obtain the previous day's papers containing initial substantial accounts of the developing crisis. Even then, he had not received copies of the Bolshevik *Rabochii*, so that he was almost completely in the dark regarding his party's behavior. Nonetheless, on the morning of the thirtieth, as he anxiously awaited further news from Petrograd, he drafted a letter formulating tactical recommendations to the Central Committee which foreshadowed a significant, albeit temporary, shift in outlook on the development of the revolution. Lenin's initial response to the threat of a rightist dictatorship was that the existing political situation had suddenly been fundamentally altered and that the tactics of the party would have to be revised accordingly. No longer did he dismiss rumors of a counterrevolutionary conspiracy as "a carefully thought out ploy on the part of the Mensheviks and SRs," as he had during the Moscow Conference. Instead, Lenin urged Bolsheviks to join in the fight against Kornilov. Remaining silent on the crucial question of how closely it was permissible for party members to cooperate with majority socialists in defense preparations, he cautioned merely that Bolsheviks ought neither to support Kerensky directly nor, for the time being, to seek to overthrow him. Rather, they were to use every opportunity to expose Kerensky's weaknesses and shortcomings and to apply pressure on the government to fulfill such "partial demands" as the arrest of Miliukov, the arming of workers, the summoning of naval forces to Petrograd, the dissolution of the State Duma, the legislation of land transfers to the peasants, and the introduction of workers' control in the factories.

Both the tacit acceptance of coordination with other groups to combat Kornilov and the emphasis on applying pressure for the fulfillment of "partial demands" were departures from Lenin's previous insistence that the Bolsheviks remain aloof from the Mensheviks and SRs and that the organization of the direct seizure of power by the proletariat at the earliest possible date was the party's primary task. As we have seen, this was precisely the position adopted during the last days of August by most party leaders in Petrograd. Lenin's unexpected approval of their course of action was reflected in a postscript which he added to his letter to the Central Committee late on the evening of the thirtieth, after receiving a new batch of papers from Petrograd, including copies of *Rabochii*. "Having read six issues of *Rabochii* after this was written," he appended, "I must say our views fully coincide."[2]

The shift in Lenin's thinking that followed the outbreak of the Kornilov affair was even more pronounced in an article, "On Compromises," which he wrote on September 1 and which was received in Petrograd two days later. Indeed, it is difficult to interpret this essay as anything other than a retreat from the major assumptions underlying Lenin's directives to the Sixth Congress—the demise of the soviets as revolutionary institutions, the irrevocable bankruptcy of the Mensheviks and SRs, and the absolute necessity for the seizure of power by force. Stimulated by Kerensky's obvious weakness and isolation, impressed by the power demonstrated by the soviets in the struggle against Kornilov, and intrigued by the apparent growth of hostility to further collaboration with the Kadets among Mensheviks and SRs, Lenin now endorsed the possibility of returning to the "peaceful" pre-July tactical program urged all along by party moderates. Specifically, he proposed a compromise with the majority socialists which went roughly as follows: For the time being the Bolsheviks would give up their demand for the transfer of power to a government made up of representatives of the proletariat and poorer peasantry and officially return to the pre-July slogan "All Power to the Soviets." In return, the Mensheviks and SRs would take power into their own hands and form a government responsible to the Soviet. Political power would be transferred to local soviets everywhere in Russia. The Bolsheviks would remain outside the government and would be guaranteed full freedom to campaign on behalf of their own program. In essence, "On Compromises" was an expression of readiness to forego the use of armed force and instead to compete for power within the soviets by political means if the Mensheviks and SRs broke with the bourgeoisie. Lenin now maintained that such a course "could in all probability secure the peaceful advance of the whole revolution, and provide exceptionally good chances for great strides in the world movement towards peace and the victory of socialism."

On September 3, as Lenin was about to send "On Compromises" to Petrograd, he learned of the creation of the Directory, of the fundamental reluctance of a majority of moderate socialists to sanction the formation of an exclusively socialist government, and, to the contrary, of their efforts to organize a new coalition cabinet with representatives of the bourgeoisie from outside the Kadet Party. Under the influence of these reports, Lenin added a brief postscript to "On Compromises" in which he observed pessimistically: "After reading today's [Sunday's] papers, I say to myself: perhaps it is already too late to offer a compromise. . . . Yes, to all appearances, the day when by chance the path of peaceful development became possible has already passed."[3]

Yet even now Lenin did not wholly abandon the idea of a peaceful course. During the first week and a half of September, his interest in a possible "compromise" was evidently kept at least partially alive by continuing, well-publicized wrangling within Menshevik and SR ranks regarding a future government, and festering antipathy between Kerensky and the moderate socialist leadership of the Soviet, as reflected, for example, in the stubborn resistance of the Committee for Struggle to government attempts at dissolving revolutionary committees created during the Kornilov crisis. At any rate, Lenin returned to the question of a possible compromise with the moderates and the nonviolent development of the revolution in three subsequent articles of this period: "The Tasks of the Revolution," "The Russian Revolution and Civil War," and "One of the Fundamental Questions of the Revolution."[4]

In "The Tasks of the Revolution," written around September 6 although not published until the end of September, Lenin elaborated in some detail on the political scheme that he had first proposed in "On Compromises." "By seizing full power," he contended, "the soviets could still today—and this is probably their last chance—insure the peaceful development of the revolution, peaceful elections of deputies by the people, and a peaceful struggle of parties inside the soviets."[5]

In "One of the Fundamental Questions of the Revolution," written a day or two later (but published on September 14), Lenin expounded upon the supreme importance of state power in the development of any revolution and the new significance which he attached to the immediate transfer of "all power to the soviets":

> The question of power cannot be evaded or brushed aside because it is the key question determining everything in a revolution's development. . . . The whole issue at present is whether the petty-bourgeois democrats have learned anything during these great, exceptionally eventful, six months. If not, then the revolution is lost, and only a victorious uprising of the proletariat can save it. If they have learned something, the establishment of a stable, unwavering power must be begun immediately. . . . Only soviet power could be stable and not be overthrown even in the stormiest months of the stormiest revolution. Only this power could insure a continuous and broad development of the revolution, a peaceful struggle of parties within the soviets.

Directing his attention to the Mensheviks and SRs Lenin went on to explain the meaning of the slogan "All Power to the Soviets" as he had resurrected it in "On Compromises":

> The slogan "Power to the Soviets" is very often incorrectly interpreted to mean a "cabinet of the parties of the Soviet majority." . . . [Not so.] "Power to the Soviets" means radically reshaping the entire old state apparatus, that bureaucratic apparatus which hampers everything democratic. It means removing this apparatus and substituting for it a new popular one, i.e., a truly democratic apparatus of soviets, i.e., the organized and armed majority of the people—the workers, soldiers, and peasants. It means allowing the majority of the people initiative and independence not only in the election of deputies, but also in state administration, in effecting reforms and various other changes.

Only a soviet regime, he suggested, would possess the courage and decisiveness to institute a grain monopoly, impose effective controls over production and distribution, restrict the issue of paper money, insure a fair exchange of grain for manufactured goods, etc.—all measures required by the unprecedented burdens and hardships of the war and the unparalleled economic dislocation and danger of famine. Such a government, "steering a firm course," he explained, would in effect be the "dictatorship of the proletariat and poorer peasantry" whose necessity he had pointed to in the

"April Theses." This government would deal forcefully with Kornilov and his cohorts and would complete the democratization of the army at once. Lenin assured his readers that two days after its creation, 99 percent of the army would be enthusiastic supporters of this dictatorship. It would give land to the peasants and full power to the local peasant committees, and hence would be certain of peasant support. Only a strong, popularly based government, Lenin contended, would be capable of smashing the resistance of the capitalists, displaying truly supreme courage and determination in the exercise of power, and securing the enthusiastic, selfless, and heroic support of the masses both in the army and among the peasants. Immediately transferring power to the soviets, he insisted, was the only way to make further progress gradual, peaceful, and smooth.[6]

In "The Russian Revolution and Civil War," the last essay of the series, probably completed on September 9 (and published on September 16), Lenin sought to allay the fears of the moderate socialists that breaking with the bourgeoisie would precipitate a bloody civil war, arguing that, to the contrary, the growing indignation and bitterness of the masses insured that further dalliance in the creation of a soviet government would make inevitable a workers' uprising and a civil war which, while bloody and to be avoided if at all possible, would in any case result in the triumph of the proletariat. "Only the immediate transfer of all power to the soviets would make civil war in Russia impossible," he explained. "A civil war begun by the bourgeoisie against an alliance of the Bolsheviks with the Socialist Revolutionaries and Mensheviks, against the soviets of workers', soldiers', and peasants' deputies, is inconceivable: such a 'war' would not last even until the first battle." In support of this line of reasoning, Lenin pointed to the helplessness of the bourgeoisie during the Kornilov affair. At that time, he declared, the alliance of Bolsheviks, SRs and Mensheviks "scored a victory over the counterrevolution with an ease heretofore never achieved in any revolution."[7]

It is indicative of the spirit of freewheeling debate within the Bolshevik organization in 1917 that even Lenin's new moderation was not accepted without opposition. By the time "On Compromises" was received by Bolshevik leaders in Petrograd, the All-Russian Executive Committees had formally rejected the Bolsheviks' August 31 declaration. To the editors of *Rabochii put'*, the kind of "compromise" envisioned by Lenin seemed impracticable. One member of the editorial board, Grigorii Sokolnikov, later recalled that "On Compromises" was initially rejected for publication. Upon Lenin's insistence, the decision was reconsidered, and the article was published on September 6.[8]

Objections to the views expressed in "On Compromises" also emerged among members of the consistently militant Bolshevik Moscow Regional Bureau[9] and among some of the more radical leaders of the Petersburg

Committee, who, having rallied to Lenin's side on the question of breaking with the moderate socialists entirely and preparing for an eventual independent armed seizure of power at the Sixth Congress little more than four weeks earlier, were clearly dumbfounded by this latest abrupt shift in Lenin's outlook. Such a reaction on the part of some local leaders in Petrograd emerged during an evaluation of the "current moment" by the Petersburg Committee on September 7, the day after the publication of "On Compromises."[10]

Representing the Petersburg Committee's Executive Commission, the outspoken Slutsky opened this discussion. While accepting Lenin's contention that the masses and the moderate socialists had been pushed leftward and that to some extent even the soviets had been rejuvenated by the Kornilov experience, he rebelled at the thought of *rapprochement* with the Mensheviks and SRs, arguing that the party's main tasks were to restrain the masses from premature action and to prepare to use the soviets as combat centers in the seizure of power.[11] Later in the discussion, responding to arguments upholding Lenin's point of view, Slutsky again took the floor. "As in the factories, so among the poverty-stricken peasants, we see movement leftward," he declared. "For us to consider compromise now is ludicrous. No compromises! . . . Our revolution is not like those which occurred in the West. Ours is a proletarian revolution. Our task is to clarify our position and to prepare unconditionally for a military clash." In a similar vein, G. F. Kolmin, an independent thinker who had been among the party's hotheads in July, rejected the idea that the soviets and the Mensheviks and SRs had somehow been fundamentally transformed by the Kornilov affair. "Their leftward swing," he insisted, "does not give us reason to believe the soviets will take a revolutionary path. Our position should stay the same. Our goal is not to go arm in arm with the Soviet leaders, but to try to tear more revolutionary elements away from them and mobilize them behind us." Interestingly, the remarks of the Central Committee's representative to the Petersburg Committee, Bubnov, seemed closer to the sentiments of Slutsky and Kolmin than to the ideas expressed by Lenin in "On Compromises."

It is difficult to gauge the extent of such feelings among members of the Petersburg Committee at this time because the discussion of the current moment at the September 7 meeting ended without the adoption of a resolution. In any case, as in the pre-July period, a peaceful course was compatible in the short run with the programmatic views both of right Bolsheviks like Kamenev—who considered Russia unprepared for a socialist revolution, and for the time being looked no further than to the construction of a broadly based, exclusively socialist coalition government, including Bolsheviks, creation of a democratic republic, and the convocation of the Constituent Assembly—and of those like Lenin, Trotsky, and local-level Bolshevik leaders in Petrograd, to whom transfer of power to the soviets and a

Menshevik-SR government were seen as a transitory stage in the development of the socialist revolution, one which would quickly lead to the establishment of a dictatorship of the proletariat and poorer peasantry. It is clear
that among a majority of the Central Committee the course proposed by
Lenin struck a responsive chord. And, under the Central Committee's direction, the Petrograd Bolsheviks during the first weeks in September concentrated less on deepening the gulf between them and the moderates, or preparing the masses for an early armed seizure of power in the spirit of
Lenin's directives to the Sixth Congress, than on tasks consistent with the
possibility of a peaceful development of the revolution. In particular, they
devoted their energies to winning the support of still-wavering elements in
the Menshevik-SR camp to the principle of breaking completely with the
bourgeoisie, further expanding and consolidating the party's influence in
mass organizations (most importantly in the Petrograd Soviet), and assuring
the largest possible party representation in the coming Democratic State
Conference, now scheduled for mid-September and designated by the Mensheviks and SRs as the forum in which the question of coalition and the
nature of a new government would be finally settled.

For the Bolsheviks, competition for influence in the Petrograd Soviet required particular attention. Less than half of those eligible to vote in the
Soviet had been present for the sensational August 31 session at which a
majority voted support for the Bolshevik political program. A high percentage of the absent deputies were soldiers (among whom SR influence had
been very great heretofore), then still occupying defensive positions outside
the capital. Thus it is not surprising that the moderate socialists played
down the import of the August 31 Bolshevik triumph and looked to its early
reversal.

The issue that SR-Menshevik strategists picked for a direct test of relative
strength in the soviet was the future makeup of the Petrograd Soviet's Presidium. From its inception in March, the Presidium had been composed
exclusively of Mensheviks and SRs. Among its members were Chkheidze,
Tsereteli, Chernov, Dan, Skobelev, Gots, and Anisimov—the moderates'
best known and most authoritative public figures. These luminaries now
declared their intention of resigning en masse if the vote of August 31 was
not formally repudiated and the old leadership given a vote of confidence.
This strategy put the Bolsheviks in a perilous position because it was possible, even likely, that they could not command enough votes to win such a
contest of personal prestige. Yet a reversal of the August 31 vote and a
pledge of confidence in the Mensheviks and SRs would mean a serious setback in the party's recently successful drive for broader mass support.

To avoid the possibility of such a defeat, the Bolsheviks attempted to
diffuse the political significance of the vote on the Presidium by focusing
attention on procedural matters. Specifically, they argued that it was unfair
for the Presidium to be composed, as it had been in the past, exclusively of
representatives of the majority. Instead of choosing between opposing polit-

ical programs and in effect letting the winners form the Presidium, as the moderates proposed, the Bolsheviks suggested that the democratic procedure would be to reconstruct the Presidium on a proportional basis, adding an appropriate number of members from previously unrepresented groups. This plan appeared quite reasonable to the many deputies who leaned to the left but who might be reluctant to side with the Bolsheviks at the cost of wholly repudiating their own leaders.[12] In a effort to appeal to these wavering deputies, Kamenev, arguing before the Petrograd Soviet in favor of proportional representation, declared: "If coalition with the Kadets was acceptable to the Mensheviks and SRs at the Moscow State Conference, surely they can engage in coalition politics with the Bolsheviks in this organ."

The crucial test vote on procedures for the reorganization of the Presidium took place at the start of the Petrograd Soviet session on September 9. The Bolshevik position received a narrow majority.[13] Lenin was subsequently to criticize the Bolshevik leadership in the Soviet for championing proportional representation in the elections to the Presidium, viewing their action as merely another instance of his followers accepting an unnecessary degree of cooperation with other socialist groups at the expense of their own goals. The soundness of the proportional representation tactic, however, was borne out later at the same session when debate on another Bolshevik proposal revealed that the Bolsheviks did not yet have a dependable majority in the Petrograd Soviet. In this case, changes proposed by the Bolsheviks in the basis upon which soldiers were to be represented in the Soviet were opposed by a majority, and the Bolsheviks were forced to withdraw their resolution at the last minute to avoid its certain defeat.[14]

Ultimately the party's sensitive strategy in the Petrograd Soviet worked to Bolshevik advantage. When the results of the September 9 vote on proportional representation were announced, the majority socialists who had comprised the old Presidium walked out in a huff, and on September 25 the leadership of the Petrograd Soviet was completely reorganized. Making up the new Presidium were two SRs, one Menshevik, and four Bolsheviks (Trotsky, Kamenev, Rykov, and Fedorov); Trotsky replaced Chkheidze as chairman.[15]

Concurrently, the Bolshevik leadership was also devoting considerable attention to preparations for the Democratic State Conference. In a cable of September 4 to thirty-seven subordinate party committees throughout the country and in a follow-up letter the next day, the party leadership had underlined the significance of a strong representation at the conference; Bolsheviks were advised to become thoroughly familiar with the makeup of the conference and, wherever possible, to work for the election of party members. All delegates elected with Bolshevik support were to report to the headquarters of the Bolshevik Soviet fraction at Smolny for orientation immediately upon arrival in the capital.[16]

Hopes that the Democratic State Conference would repudiate coalition politics and initiate steps to form a new, exclusively socialist government were dealt a blow with the announcement of the conference's composition. Workers', soldiers', and peasants' soviets; municipal dumas; army committees; trade unions; and a dozen lesser institutions were to be represented at the conference by some 1,198 delegates. But the proportion of seats allotted to urban workers' and soldiers' soviets and trade unions, institutions in which the Bolsheviks were strongest, was low in comparison with the representation given rural peasant soviets, zemstvos, and cooperatives, still dominated by the moderates.

Even so, the Bolsheviks did not completely give up the hope that the conference might create a socialist government. At a meeting on September 13 the Central Committee assigned Trotsky, Kamenev, Stalin, Miliutin, and Rykov to draw up an appropriate platform for presentation to the conference.[17] Based in part on Lenin's writings of early September, the resulting platform was predicated on the assumption that a peaceful development of the revolution was still possible and that a revolutionary government could and should be created by the conference.[18] Like Lenin's "On Compromises," the Bolshevik platform for the Democratic State Conference was basically an appeal to previous supporters of coalition politics to break definitively with the bourgeoisie, and an expression of faith in the soviets as organs of revolutionary government. The platform declared bluntly that the Bolsheviks had not tried to take power against the organized will of the majority of the working masses and would not. In language similar to Lenin's, it was affirmed that with full freedom of agitation and the continuous renovation of the soviets from below, the struggle for influence and power would take place within the soviets.[19] At the same time the platform differed from "On Compromises" in not specifically excluding the possibility that the Bolsheviks would participate in a soviet government;[20] this appears to have been the result of Kamenev's influence.

On the eve of the Democratic State Conference it became apparent that the extreme left's apprehension regarding the probable composition of the conference was well founded. Of the arriving delegates willing to declare a political preference, 532 turned out to be SRs (of whom 71 were Left SRs), 530 were Mensheviks (of whom 56 were Internationalists), 55 were Popular Socialists, and 17 affirmed that they had no specific party affiliation. Only 134 were Bolsheviks.[21]

Still, in preliminary discussions at individual party caucuses and at meetings of delegates by institutional affiliation it was immediately revealed that on the crucial question of further coalition with nonsocialist parties there was no consensus among the moderates; the major divisions over this issue which had first appeared in the wake of the Kornilov crisis had, if anything, deepened. The uneasiness of many Menshevik and SR leaders previously loyal to the Provisional Government was voiced by the Menshevik Bogdanov, who commented on the opening day of the conference: "At this terrible time we must recognize without equivocation that we don't have a governmental authority; we have had a continuous reshuffling of the cabinet, governmental leapfrog in no way distinguishable from that of tsarist times. The result of these never-ending ministerial switches has been total ineffectiveness, for which we ourselves are responsible. . . . It is painful for me as a supporter of coalition to say so, but I must acknowledge that the main cause of this governmental paralysis has been the coalition character of the cabinet."[22]

Thus, as the Democratic State Conference got underway, there were at least a few encouraging signs for Bolshevik leaders in Petrograd who still held out hope that a majority of delegates might vote to break with Kerensky and create a homogeneous socialist government. This lingering hope was voiced by Zinoviev in a front-page editorial titled "Our Triumph and Our Tasks," published in the September 13 issue of *Rabochii put'* and no doubt circulated among the arriving delegates:

> The chief question now confronting every revolutionary is whether or not there remain possibilities for the peaceful development of the revolution and what needs to be done to strengthen these possibilities. And it is necessary to answer that any such possibilities hinge on the adoption of a specific compromise, a definite agreement between the working class, once and for all following our party, and the masses who make up the petty bourgeois democracy and who follow the SRs and Mensheviks. . . . An agreement with the petty bourgeois democracy is desirable and, under conditions which are well known, possible! . . . The All-Russian Conference convening shortly could still open the way for such a peaceful outcome.[23]

The Democratic State Conference opened in the Alexandrinsky Theater, now the Pushkin Theater, on the night of September 14. The famous old hall, its loges, orchestra, and balconies crammed with delegates from all over Russia, took on an appearance quite unknown in tsarist days. The red plush upholstery of the seats and boxes blended with the crimson sea of revolutionary banners. Onstage the curtains were raised to reveal a set depicting a large hall with several doors flanked by artificial junipers and palms. The conference presidium was seated behind a long, narrow table extending across the stage; before the table stood a lectern draped with red bunting and bearing a sign cautioning, "No Smoking!"

The Bolsheviks' hopes for the creation of a new government at the Democratic State Conference were voiced in the formal opening address made in the party's behalf by Kamenev at the first conference session and in comments by Trotsky to a caucus of the Bolshevik delegation the following afternoon. In his lengthy speech, Kamenev declared that the record achieved by the various cabinets over the preceding six months made it impossible to retain any confidence in the policies proposed by Kerensky.

Kamenev insisted that conditions had deteriorated to such a tragic state that time for further experiments with coalition government had run out. The government's failure to squelch the counterrevolutionary movement in the army, as well as actions taken in regard to agriculture, food supply, and the conduct of foreign affairs, he argued, were errors not of this or that minister-socialist, but of the political influence of the bouregoisie as a class:

> There has not been a single revolution in which the realization of the ideals of the workers did not provoke the terror of counterrevolutionary forces. . . . If the democracy is unwilling to take power now, it must honestly tell itself: "We don't have confidence in our own powers and so you Burishkins and Kishkins[24] must come and take charge of us, we don't know how to do it.". . . You can write a program to satisfy the working democracy but it is pure utopianism to believe that such a program would be pursued genuinely and honestly by the bourgeoisie. . . . The only possible course is for state power to be transferred to the democracy—not to the Soviet of Workers' and Soldiers' Deputies, but to that democracy which is well enough represented here. We must establish a new government and an institution to which that government must be responsible.[25]

Trotsky, in his orientation to Bolshevik delegates alone, explained that in so far as possible, their primary aim should be to convince the conference to reject coalition with the privileged classes and to take the organization of a new government into its own hands; if successful, this would be the first step in the transfer of power to the soviets.[26]

It is worth noting that while Kamenev was speaking out for the creation of a broad, democratic coalition government (reflective of the various groups invited to the Democratic State Conference) and against an exclusively soviet regime, Trotsky urged the transfer of full power to the soviets. This important distinction bespoke fundamentally different views on the development of the Russian revolution which were soon to erupt into one of the bitterest and most important internal controversies in the history of Bolshevism. In the context of the present discussion, however, the crucial point is that both Kamenev and Trotsky, along with most Petrograd Bolsheviks, viewed positively the work of the Democratic State Conference and the prospects for peaceful development of the revolution.

In view of the Bolsheviks' prevailing moderation at this time, and considering that since early September Lenin himself had been lending encouragement to such an approach, one can imagine the shock experienced by the top Bolshevik leadership when, on September 15, they received two letters written by Lenin between September 12 and 14 in which he completely abandoned the moderate positions embodied in "On Compromises" and summoned the Bolsheviks to take upon themselves the preparation of an immediate armed uprising.

There appear to have been a number of mutually supporting reasons for this outwardly dramatic shift. On the one hand, factors such as the strong position of the extreme left in Finland, the winning of majority support for the Bolshevik program in the Petrograd and Moscow soviets and in a number of other regional soviets, the massive expansion of social upheaval among land-hungry peasants in the countryside, the continuing disintegration of the army at the front and the soldiers' increasingly insistent demands for immediate peace, and signs of revolutionary unrest in the German Fleet seem to have encouraged Lenin to hope that seizure of power by the Bolsheviks would have strong support in the cities and would no longer be solidly opposed by the provinces and the front, and that the creation of a genuinely revolutionary government in Russia would serve as a catalyst for mass rebellions in other European countries. And, of course, as Lenin began to sense the possibility of a quick resolution to the problem of creating an extreme left government, his interest in "compromise" with the moderate socialist parties cooled. On the other hand, somewhat contradictorily, Lenin also seems to have become genuinely alarmed that the government might somehow still manage to deflate the revolution by negotiating a separate peace, surrendering Petrograd to the Germans, manipulating elections to the Constituent Assembly, or provoking a disorganized popular insurrection. He also seems to have worried that if the party delayed too long, it would begin to lose influence among the masses and become powerless to halt Russia's slide into complete anarchy.

The first of Lenin's two explosive letters, this one addressed to the Central, Petersburg, and Moscow committees, began: "The Bolsheviks, having obtained a majority in the soviets of workers' and soldiers' deputies in both capitals, can and *must* take state power into their own hands. They can because the active majority of revolutionary elements in the two chief cities is large enough to carry the people with it, to overcome the opposition's resistance, to smash it, and to gain and retain power." The Democratic State Conference, he insisted, "represents *not* a majority of the revolutionary people, but *only the compromising upper strata of the petty bourgeoisie.*" Why was it necessary for the Bolsheviks to assume power "*at this very moment*"? Because, affirmed Lenin, "the impending surrender of Petrograd will make our chances a hundred times less favorable." Selecting the precise moment for the start of an uprising would be up to local leaders on the spot; what the top Bolshevik leadership had to do at once was to take advantage of the presence in Petrograd of what amounted to a party congress to set the task of organizing an "armed uprising in Petrograd and Moscow, the seizure of power, and the overthrow of the government." By taking power in Moscow and Petrograd at once (it didn't matter to him which came first), Lenin concluded, "we shall win absolutely and unquestionably."[27]

In his second letter, which bore the title "Marxism and Insurrection" and was addressed to the Central Committee alone, Lenin argued that "treating

insurrection as an art" was not Blanquism, as alleged by "present-day op-
portunists," but a fundamental tenet of Marxism. To be successful, he
wrote, insurrection had necessarily to rely not upon conspiracy or upon a
party, but upon the proletariat, and it had to be based on a revolutionary
upsurge of the people. A final condition was that a successful insurrection
had to be timed to occur when the activity of the advanced ranks was at its
height, while, on the other hand, vacillations within the enemy camp were
strongest. Affirming that refusal to treat insurrection as an art once these
preconditions existed was a "betrayal of Marxism and of the revolution,"
Lenin went on to explain why an immediate insurrection was the "order of
the day." He contrasted the existing situation with conditions prevailing
in July, observing that at that time the Bolsheviks had still lacked the support of the proletariat; now, as a result of the persecution of the Bolsheviks
and the Kornilov experience, the party had majorities in the soviets in both
Moscow and Petrograd. In July there had been no countrywide revolutionary upsurge, but such an upsurge had followed the Kornilov revolt. Finally, earlier there had not been serious wavering among the Bolsheviks'
enemies, while now there was a significant degree of vacillation. "We could
not have retained power politically on July 3–4," Lenin concluded,
"because *before the Kornilov revolt*, the army and the provinces could and
would have marched against Petrograd. Now the picture is entirely different. . . . All the objective conditions exist for a successful insurrection."

Toward the end of "Marxism and Insurrection," Lenin demanded that
the Central Committee consolidate the Bolshevik group at the Democratic
State Conference—"without fearing to leave the waverers in the waverers'
camp." It was to draw up a brief declaration ("the briefer and the more
trenchant the better") "emphasizing in no uncertain manner the irrelevance
of long speeches and of 'speeches' in general, the need for immediate action
to save the revolution, the absolute necessity for a complete break with the
bourgeoisie, for the removal of the present government in its entirety . . .
and for the immediate transfer of all power to *revolutionary democrats, headed
by the revolutionary proletariat.*" The Bolsheviks, "having read this declaration, and having appealed for decisions and not talk, for action and not
resolution-writing," were to dispatch their "entire group to the *factories and
barracks.*" At the same time, treating insurrection in a Marxist way, as an
art, and without losing a single moment, the Bolsheviks were to "organize a
headquarters of insurgent detachments, distribute forces, move the reliable
regiments to the most important points, surround the Alexandrinsky Theater, occupy the Peter and Paul Fortress, [and] arrest the General Staff and
the government." They were to "mobilize the armed workers and call them
to fight the last desperate fight, occupy the telegraph and telephone exchanges, establish headquarters in the central telephone exchange, and con-
nect it by telephone with all the factories, regiments, and points of armed
conflict."[28]

Not surprisingly, the initial response of Bolshevik leaders in Petrograd to these messages was strongly reminiscent of the one which had been accorded Lenin's earlier "Letters from Afar." "We were all aghast," Bukharin was to recall a few years later.[29] Hastening from the Alexandrinsky Theater to their own headquarters, members of the Central Committee met in emergency secret session the evening of September 15 to discuss the letters. Present were not only those Central Committee members normally in Petrograd and responsible for the day-to-day direction of the party (that is, Bubnov, Dzerzhinsky, Ioffe, Miliutin, Sverdlov, Sokolnikov, Stalin, and Uritsky), but also Kamenev, Kollontai, and Trotsky (this was Trotsky's second Central Committee meeting since his release from jail); the Moscow Bolsheviks Bukharin, Lomov, Nogin, and Rykov; and Stepan Shaumian, Central Committee representative of the Bolshevik organization in the Caucasus. Copies of Lenin's letters had been distributed to most of those in attendance prior to their deliberations.[30] The published protocol of the ensuing discussion is extremely fragmentary.[31] The committee agreed on the advisability of scheduling an early meeting specifically devoted to tactical questions. A suggestion by Stalin that Lenin's letters be circulated was rejected, despite the fact that the first letter was specifically addressed to the Petersburg and Moscow committees, as well as to the Central Committee. To the contrary, most of those present were apparently concerned above all that they be quietly destroyed. Bukharin later maintained that the Central Committee considered burning the letters and, indeed, unanimously agreed to do so.[32] According to the official protocol, the committee voted to preserve only one copy of each letter and to take steps to prevent a movement into the streets.

Lomov later pointed to one of the Central Committee's overriding concerns at this time: "We are apprehensive about what would happen if the letters reached the Petrograd workers . . . and the Petersburg and Moscow committees because this would have immediately introduced enormous discord into our ranks. . . . We were afraid that if Lenin's words reached the workers, many would doubt the correctness of the position adopted by the whole Central Committee."[33] As an additional safeguard, the Central Committee concluded its discussion on September 15 by charging members assigned to working with the Military Organization and the Petersburg Committee (Sverdlov and Bubnov respectively) with responsibility for insuring that no appeals for immediate action along the lines demanded by Lenin were made in barracks and factories.

For the time being, then, Lenin's appeals for the overthrow of the Provisional Government were unceremoniously turned aside. Virtually the only change in the public behavior of the Bolsheviks at the Democratic State Conference after receipt of Lenin's messages was that Trotsky, for one, began to play down the possibility of the conference's forming a government as the first step toward the transfer of power to the soviets. Instead, he now categorically insisted on the transfer of political power directly to the soviets. This subtle but important shift was reflected at a caucus of conference delegates from workers' and soldiers' soviets on September 18. There Trotsky got into a heated argument with Martov, who spoke in favor of the creation by the conference of a broad socialist government including representatives of all the major groups invited to the Democratic State Conference. Countering Martov, Trotsky contended that the composition of the Democratic State Conference was such that endowing it with complete governmental power would be a rash step; rather, it was absolutely necessary to transfer power to the soviets, which had fully proved themselves to be a powerful, constructive political force.[34]

Bolshevik efforts to prevail upon conference delegates to break with the bourgeoisie and take the first steps toward the creation of a revolutionary government were not terminated. The party's formal statement on the government question, the platform which had been authorized by the Central Committee on September 13 and which, as we have seen, was modeled in part after Lenin's "On Compromises," was formally read to a session of the conference on September 18. That night, in response to Bolshevik appeals, 150 delegates from Petrograd factories and military units staged a demonstration outside the Alexandrinsky Theater in support of the creation of an exclusively socialist government. Thus, instead of withdrawing from the conference and going to the masses with a call to rise, as Lenin advised, the party was mobilizing workers and soldiers to apply pressure on the Democratic State Conference to pursue a more radical course.[35]

For Lenin, the presentation of the Bolshevik platform to the Democratic State Conference was an unmistakable sign of the party leadership's rejection of the assumptions contained in his mid-September letters. No doubt Lenin was even more disturbed upon reading the September 16 edition of *Rabochii put'*, which featured his earlier essay, "The Russian Revolution and Civil War," with its author identified. Not only had the Central Committee taken steps to insure that the party at large would not be influenced by his appeals for an immediate uprising, but it also was circulating his more moderate views of the previous week, inevitably conveying the impression that they constituted his thinking at the moment.

At this point Lenin decided to return at once to Petrograd despite the fact that the Central Committee had expressly forbidden him to do so, ostensibly out of fear for his safety. On September 17 or shortly thereafter, without the Central Committee's authorization,[36] Lenin traveled from Helsingfors to Vyborg, within eighty miles of the capital, and advised Krupskaia and Sverdlov, although not the Central Committee, of his determination to return to Petrograd.[37]

Meanwhile, at the Democratic State Conference, delegates had spent the better part of four days (September 14–18) in group meetings, party gatherings, and official sessions turning over all questions relating to the nature of the future government. A formal vote on this issue was held on September 19, and it turned out to be a complete fiasco for everyone concerned. According to procedures worked out in advance by the conference presidium, the delegates were first to register their views on coalition in principle. Next, they were asked to vote on two proposed amendments: (1) that elements of the Kadet Party and other groups which had been involved in the Kornilov affair be excluded from participation in the coalition; and (2) that the entire Kadet Party be excluded. Finally, the delegates were to vote on the entire resolution as amended.

In an initial roll call vote which lasted five hours, the principle of coalition with the bourgeoisie was accepted by a count of 766 in favor, 688 opposed, with 38 abstentions. This vote confirmed Bolshevik apprehensions regarding the makeup of the conference; representatives of workers' and soldiers' soviets and trade unions had voted overwhelmingly against coalition, but they were overpowered by large majorities of the more numerous deputies from peasant soviets, military committees, zemstvos, and cooperatives, who supported coalition.[38] Next, the conference acted on the two proposed amendments. On behalf of the Bolsheviks, Trotsky spoke in support of both, as did Martov for the Menshevik-Internationalists and Boris Kamkov for the Left SRs. To the dismay of many, though obviously not all, of those who favored coalition in principle, both amendments were passed. The entire resolution as amended—that is, the acceptance of coalition in principle but with the exclusion of the Kadet Party as well as other groups that had supported Kornilov—satisfied almost no one. The Bolsheviks, of course, opposed the resolution; they were joined by large numbers of coalition supporters who simply could not imagine the creation of a viable coalition government *without* the Kadets. Only 183 delegates voted for the resolution as amended, with 813 opposed and 80 abstentions.[39]

Thus four days of the most intense discussion and debate had fully revealed the fundamental difference of opinion among "democratic groups" but had settled absolutely nothing regarding the makeup of the future government. The relationship of the socialists to the government was, if anything, more confused than it had been before the contradictory voting of September 19. That such a situation could not continue was abundantly clear to the Presidium of the Democratic State Conference; upon its insistence, before adjournment of the session of September 19, conference delegates resolved not to disperse until mutually acceptable conditions for the formation, functioning, and program of a new government were somehow agreed upon.

The following day the Presidium scheduled formal discussions aimed at breaking the existing impasse. Participating in this gathering were Presidium members and representatives of the various parties and groups attending the Democratic State Conference. Their bitter debates on the

government issue lasted from morning until early evening. Tsereteli, pointing to the deep divisions which had emerged within the democracy the
previous day in regard to the question of coalition, argued that the democracy by itself could not organize a viable government. He was joined by
Gots and Avksentiev, who stressed once again the importance of maintaining some kind of political alliance with the bourgeoisie. Kamenev was the
Bolsheviks' chief spokesman at this meeting. Contending unconvincingly
that the formation of a coalition government had been decisively rejected
the previous day, he pressed the case for a "homogeneous democratic ministry." To calm the fears of the moderates in regard to what the Bolsheviks'
attitude toward such a government might be, he added categorically: "We
will not overthrow such a government. We will support it insofar as it
pursues a democratic policy and leads the country to the Constituent Assembly." After the delegates had talked themselves hoarse, a formal vote
was taken on the question of coalition: fifty delegates voted in favor; sixty
were opposed.

In view of this continuing, almost even, split, Tsereteli suggested a
somewhat different tack. He proposed that an attempt be made to come to a
consensus regarding the political program to be pursued by the future government and to leave the precise character of the cabinet to the discretion of
a permanent representative body which would be selected by the conference and to which the government would be responsible until the convocation of the Constituent Assembly. This course was subsequently adopted.
With regard to the program to be pursued by a new government, most
delegates expressed solidarity with the Soviet's "August 14 program";[40]
only the Bolsheviks voiced opposition. But the Bolsheviks joined the rest of
the participants in this meeting in supporting the creation of a permanent
representative body.[41]

Kamenev hoped that this new institution would be "homogeneous," that a
significant proportion of its membership would come from workers' and
soldiers' soviets, and hence that it would be less resistant to breaking with
the bourgeoisie than the Democratic State Conference. It became clear almost immediately, however, that any such hope was ill-founded. With the
Bolsheviks again alone in opposition, the participants in this meeting went
on to agree that the new permanent body (it was initially christened the
"Democratic Council" but was referred to more often as the "Preparliament") should include both representatives of groups at the conference and
propertied elements. This was a direct reversal of the previous day's voting
pattern. At the September 19 session the delegates had begun by approving
coalition in principle and then had eliminated any practical possibility of
actually creating a coalition government by rejecting Kadet participation.
Then, on September 20, an ad hoc meeting of delegates, after initially rejecting coalition, adopted a resolution indirectly reintroducing the possibil-

ity of political cooperation with representatives of the bourgeoisie, not excluding the Kadets.[42]

Proponents of coalition were quick to seize upon this opportunity. At a
conference plenum late the same night, September 20, Tsereteli introduced
a resolution, subsequently passed, which shifted responsibility for a final
decision on the government question to the Preparliament. Among other
things, this resolution provided that the future government would work to
realize the program of August 14, that it would pursue an energetic foreign
policy aimed at concluding a general peace, and that it would be responsible
and accountable to a permanent representative body which, pending convocation of the Constituent Assembly, would reflect the popular will. The
resolution specified that this representative body, the Preparliament, was to
be made up of delegates to the Democratic State Conference. The resolution contained nothing specific about the participation of the bourgeoisie in
either the Preparliament or the future government; however, it tacitly endorsed the possibility of another coalition with the vague statement that if
bourgeois elements were to be drawn into the government, the permanent
representative body would be enlarged by the inclusion of bourgeois
groups. The resolution specified that under those circumstances, the pre-
dominance of democratic elements would have to be maintained. Finally,
the resolution provided for the selection of five conference delegates (this
figure was later doubled) to begin negotiations aimed at facilitating the construction of a government in accordance with these provisions. These delegates were to report to the Democratic Council on the results of their efforts, which were to be subject to confirmation by the council.[43] Thus the
long-anticipated Democratic State Conference ended in what amounted to
an evasion: a few as-yet-unnamed representatives were to be made responsible for somehow devising an acceptable solution to the cabinet crisis
which more than a thousand delegates to the conference from all over Russia had been unable to resolve.

In part because opponents of further cooperation with the bourgeoisie
would have no part of formal discussions with Kerensky, the conference
negotiating team was inevitably dominated by prominent proponents of coalition politics from the Soviet—people like Tsereteli, Avksentiev, Gots,
and Chkheidze—along with representatives of cooperative and zemstvo
groups who viewed the participation of authoritative segments of the
bourgeoisie in the government as absolutely essential for Russia's survival.
This delegation met in acrimonious bargaining sessions with Kerensky,
other cabinet ministers, representatives of the Kadet Central Committee,
and business and industrial figures from Petrograd and Moscow on September 22–24. As was to be expected, spokesmen for the bourgeoisie were
unwilling to accept the Soviet's program of August 14 as the basis for government policy; while not totally opposed to the idea of a Preparliament,

they insisted that legally only the Provisional Government had the authority to create such an organ, and that, in any case, under no circumstances could a new cabinet be responsible to the Preparliament—in other words, that the latter could be no more than an advisory body. At the same time, Kerensky was absolutely adamant on the need to form another coalition cabinet.

For practical purposes, then, members of the delegation from the Democratic State Conference were faced with the choice of backing down on the more controversial planks in the August 14 program and tacitly acknowledging the government's primacy over and independence of the Preparliament, or breaking with Kerensky and giving up the prospect of bringing representatives of the bourgeoisie into the government. Predictably, they opted for the first alternative. In a sense, the tactics that Tsereteli's delegation pursued in the complex political negotiations of September 22–24 were the opposite of those employed by Tsereteli at the Democratic State Conference. At the conference, Tsereteli had managed to gain an agreement that allowed for the possibility of a coalition by putting aside the question of the precise makeup of the cabinet and focusing attention on the program to be pursued by the government irrespective of its composition. Now, in the face of firm resistance both to the August 14 program as the basis for policy and to the responsibility of the government to the Preparliament, Tsereteli was forced to deemphasize these considerations and, instead, to stress the critical importance of an alliance between the democracy and the bourgeoisie as the only possible basis for solving Russia's ills.

During the last phase of the negotiations of September 22–24 the August 14 program was revised and softened so as to make it palatable to the Kadets. At this time, it was agreed that the government would quickly prepare and issue a decree formally establishing the Preparliament, and that this institution, now renamed the Council of the Republic but still referred to most often as the Preparliament, would be composed of the 367 delegates already selected from the Democratic State Conference plus up to 150 representatives of the propertied classes. It was also understood that legally this would be a purely advisory body and, most important, that it would have no formal jurisdiction over the government.[44]

Late on the night of September 23, the Preparliament, as originally formed at the close of the Democratic State Conference, met and handily rejected a Bolshevik declaration presented by Trotsky repudiating the Tsereteli delegation's negotiations as a betrayal of the will of the masses and calling for the creation of a "genuinely revolutionary government." Instead, by a narrow margin, the Preparliament passed a resolution introduced by Dan tacitly endorsing the new arrangements. Having done this, the delegates adjourned to await formal reconstitution by the Provisional Government of an expanded assembly. The way was now open for Kerensky to name formally a new coalition cabinet, and he did so on September 25. The new cabinet included the Kadets Alexander Konovalov, Kishkin, Sergei Smirnov, and Anton Kartashev. While technically a majority of the ministers were socialists, the key Foreign Ministry remained in the hands of Tereshchenko, Konovalov was named deputy prime minister and minister of industry, and Kerensky stayed on as head of the government and commander-in-chief of the army.[45]

On September 21, the day after the Democratic State Conference adopted Tsereteli's resolution sanctioning discussions with Kerensky on the formation of a new government (but before the results of these negotiations were known), the Bolshevik Central Committee met to consider the party's immediate political course. What was perhaps most striking about this meeting was that even now, in the face of the Democratic State Conference's failure to break with the politics of coalition, Lenin's recommendation that the urban masses be called to arms was given absolutely no consideration.[46] To be sure, this was probably due partly to the influence of right Bolsheviks such as Kamenev, Rykov, and Nogin. But the fact remains that even party officials who fully shared Lenin's fundamental assumptions regarding the necessity and feasibility of an early socialist revolution in Russia were skeptical of successfully mobilizing the masses behind the "immediate bayonet charge" envisioned by Lenin. In part because of their continuing interaction with workers and soldiers, leaders like Trotsky, Bubnov, Sokolnikov, and Sverdlov possessed what appears to have been a realistic appreciation of the limits of the party's influence and authority among the masses, and of the latter's attachment to the soviets as legitimate democratic organs in which all genuinely revolutionary groups would work together to fulfill the revolution. Also, as a result of the Kornilov experience they were much less concerned than Lenin about Kerensky's capacity to damage the left. Consequently, they now began to associate the seizure of power and the creation of a new government with the convocation in the near future of a national Congress of Soviets—this to take advantage of the legitimacy of the soviets in the eyes of the masses.

It should be added that in the wake of the Democratic State Conference, right Bolsheviks also supported the early convocation of a Congress of Soviets and paid lip service to the slogan "All Power to the Soviets." The essential difference between "Leninists in spirit," like Trotsky, and right Bolsheviks, like Kamenev, was that while the former looked to a soviet congress to transfer power to a government of the extreme left pledged to immediate peace and a radical program of internal change, the latter viewed a Congress of Soviets as a vehicle for building a broader, stronger alliance of "democratic groups," which might, at the most, form a caretaker all-socialist coalition government, pending convocation of the Constituent Assembly.

Hence the central issue that divided the party leadership in Petrograd as the Democratic State Conference drew to a close was not the organization of an immediate popular uprising, which everyone in the coterie of high Bolsheviks privy to Lenin's most recent recommendations seems to have rejected categorically, or the immediate convocation of a Congress of Soviets, which all accepted. Rather, it was whether to stage a formal walk-out from the Democratic State Conference and whether to participate in the Preparliament, the former in its last hours and the latter in the process of formation and scheduled to open on September 23. To the Kamenev faction, taking advantage of the end of the Democratic State Conference and the proceedings of the Preparliament to discredit coalition politics and to maintain alliances with wavering elements in the Menshevik-SR camp was an essential counterpart to the consolidation, at the coming Congress of Soviets, of the strongest possible broad socialist bloc. Meanwhile, to party leaders of Trotsky's persuasion, demonstratively withdrawing from the Democratic State Conference and boycotting the Preparliament constituted the necessary prelude to utilizing a Congress of Soviets to break decisively with conciliatory groups, transfer power to the soviets, and strike out anew on a revolutionary path with whatever other genuinely revolutionary groups were willing to go along.

At its morning meeting on September 21, the Bolshevik Central Committee adopted something of a compromise on the question of the Democratic State Conference: it was decided not to pull out of the conference formally but rather to register a protest against the actions of the coalitionists by recalling the Bolshevik members of the conference Presidium. Then, the Central Committee voted nine to eight not to participate in the Preparliament. Because of the almost even split on this issue, it was agreed that a final decision regarding a boycott of the Preparliament would be left to the discretion of a joint meeting of the Central Committee with the Bolshevik delegation to the Democratic Conference, to be held as soon as the delegates could be gathered.

This assembly, in size roughly equivalent to a party congress, met later the same day. Trotsky acted as spokesman for those in favor of a boycott and Rykov for those opposed. Stalin, among others, sided with Trotsky; Kamenev, Nogin, and Riazanov supported Rykov. Trotsky later remembered that the ensuing debate was long and extremely heated. When the matter came to a vote, the earlier Central Committee decision was reversed—a major setback for the left. The assembled party representatives from all over Russia voted seventy-seven to fifty in favor of participation in the Preparliament; the decision was immediately confirmed by the Central Committee.[47]

Two days later, on September 23, under prodding from the Bolsheviks, the Central Executive Committee met with delegates to the Democratic State Conference from provincial soviets, and it was agreed to convene a nationwide Congress of Soviets in Petrograd on October 20. With the Congress of Soviets now scheduled, the Bolsheviks adopted a major policy statement setting forth the relationship of the party's activities in the Preparliament to the campaign underway for transfer of power to the soviets at the coming congress. According to this statement, adopted on September 24 at a joint meeting of the Central Committee, representatives of the Petersburg Committee, and the Bolshevik Preparliament delegation, just formed, the primary task of the party in the prevailing situation was to mobilize the broad masses in support of the transfer of power to the soviets and to strengthen and expand the political authority of the soviets to the point where it rivaled that of the government. In this connection, party members were to focus attention on strengthening ties among local soviets; firming up contacts with other worker, soldier, and peasant revolutionary organs; arranging the reelection of national and local soviet executive organs still controlled by moderates, holding regional soviet congresses; and, of course, insuring that the All-Russian Congress of Soviets would, indeed, be held. Activity in the Preparliament, the statement emphasized, was to be strictly subordinate to the requirements of this mass struggle.[48]

Meanwhile, developments in the Petrograd Soviet reflected the degree to which the formation of the third coalition cabinet, together with worsening economic conditions, was working to the advantage of the extreme left. On September 25, the new Bolshevik-dominated Presidium officially took office. To roars of approval, Trotsky again assumed leadership of the Petrograd Soviet, the position he had held in 1905 when he had first distinguished himself as a powerful revolutionary tribune. In accepting the post of chairman, Trotsky harked back to those earlier days, recalling that then

> the Petrograd Soviet was experiencing a moment of crisis which ended in defeat. Now we feel distinctly stronger. Yet the list of new ministers published in the evening papers . . . attests to the fact that the revolution has reached [another] critical point. We are certain that the work of the new Presidium will be accompanied by a new rise in the development of the revolution. We belong to different parties and have our own work to conduct, but in directing the work of the Petrograd Soviet we will observe the individual rights and complete freedom of all fractions: the arm of the Presidium will never be used to stifle a minority.[49]

Not long after Trotsky's pledge to direct the work of the Petrograd Soviet in a democratic spirit, the Bolsheviks put before the deputies a resolution authored by Trotsky expressing the unwillingness of Petrograd workers and soldiers to support the new coalition. Passed immediately by an overwhelming vote, the resolution expressed certainty that the entire revolutionary democracy would greet the formation of the new government with the demand "Resign!" Sustained by this unanimous voice of the genuine democracy, the All-Russian Congress of Soviets would replace the coalition with a genuinely revolutionary government.[50]

This basic orientation toward the creation of a new government at the Congress of Soviets was to shape the Bolsheviks' activity throughout the latter part of September. This was the line taken, for example, by *Rabochii put'* during this period; beginning on September 27, each day's edition carried the banner headline "Prepare for the Congress of Soviets on October 20! Convene Regional Congresses Immediately!" Zinoviev expressed this outlook in a front-page editorial on September 26, condemning the newly announced coalition government—the so-called September bloc: "In our view the all-powerful authority over the Russian land is the Congress of Soviets opening on October 20. By the time the congress convenes, if it is able to meet at all, the experience with this new coalition will have failed and wavering elements will at long last associate themselves with our slogan, 'All Power to the Soviets.' Each day will witness a growth in our force, each step of the September bloc will demonstrate the validity of our point of view."[51]

The party's new tactical course was neatly reflected in an appeal to workers and soldiers published in *Rabochii put'* on September 30 (it had evidently been written by Zinoviev and formally discussed and endorsed by the entire Central Committee). Titled "Before the Congress of Soviets," this appeal warned that the counterrevolution would go to any lengths to prevent the convocation of the nationwide soviet congress and the Constituent Assembly. In these circumstances workers and soldiers were to be vigilant, at the same time making every effort to insure the selection of congress delegates opposed to coalition:

> Be on your guard, comrades! Don't rely on anyone but yourselves. Don't waste even an hour, start getting ready for the Congress of Soviets. Convene regional congresses. Take care to see that enemies of coalition are sent to the congress. . . . Don't become involved in any kind of separate direct action! Let's concentrate all our energies on preparations for the Congress of Soviets; it alone will assure that the Constituent Assembly will be convened and carry forth its revolutionary work. . . .
>
> Central Committee of the RSDRP[52]

LENIN'S CAMPAIGN
FOR AN INSURRECTION

Judging by proceedings in the Petrograd Soviet and by the tenor of political resolutions appearing in the left press at the end of September, Petrograd workers and soldiers responded enthusiastically to the idea of an early congress of soviets to create a revolutionary government. The same cannot be said of Lenin, who was convinced that the party leadership in Petrograd was letting slip the last golden moments when the Provisional Government could be overthrown with ease. First from Vyborg and subsequently from the apartment of Margarita Fofanova (on the northernmost edge of the Vyborg District, just off the rail line from Finland),[1] where he was living secretly, he delivered a series of slashing rebukes to his followers in the capital. These were coupled with ever more insistent demands that the Provisional Government be overthrown without further delay.

The first of these verbal assaults took the form of an essay intended for publication in *Rabochii put'* entitled "Heroes of Fraud and the Mistakes of the Bolsheviks." It began with a scathing denunciation of the Democratic State Conference, the majority socialists, and Kerensky, and ended with a thoroughgoing critique of the Bolsheviks themselves. Wrote Lenin:

> The Bolsheviks should have walked out [of the Democratic State Conference]. Ninety-nine percent of the Bolshevik delegation should have gone to the factories and barracks. . . . The Bolsheviks, it turned out, had an erroneous attitude toward parliamentarianism in moments of revolutionary (and not constitutional) crisis and a mistaken attitude toward the Socialist Revolutionaries and Mensheviks. . . . Comrade Zinoviev made a mistake in writing about the Commune ambiguously, to say the least, so that it appeared that the Commune, although victorious in Petrograd, might be defeated, *as in France in 1871.*[2] This is absolutely untrue. If the Commune were victorious in Petrograd, *it would be victorious* throughout Russia. . . . It was [also] a mistake on his part to write that the Bolsheviks did

right in proposing proportional representation in the Presidium of the Pet-rograd Soviet. . . . [And] Comrade Kamenev was wrong in delivering the first speech at the conference in a purely "constitutional" spirit when he raised the foolish question of confidence or no-confidence in the government.[3]

Written as the Democratic State Conference drew to a close, "Heroes of Fraud and the Mistakes of the Bolsheviks" was published in *Rabochii put'* on September 24 under the title "Heroes of Fraud," and with all direct criti-cism of the Bolsheviks edited out.

Between September 22 and 24, Lenin worked on another newspaper essay, "From a Publicist's Diary," which took the form of a daily journal. A portion of the entry for September 22 reads:

> The more one reflects on the meaning of the so-called Democratic Con-ference . . . the more firmly convinced one becomes that our party com-mitted a mistake in participating in it. . . . We must boycott the Prepar-liament. We must leave it and go to the Soviet of Workers', Soldiers', and Peasants' Deputies, to the trade unions, to the masses in general. We must call *them* to the struggle. We must give *them* a correct and clear slogan: disperse Kerensky's Bonapartist gang with its fake Preparliament. . . . The Mensheviks and Socialist Revolutionaries, even after the Kornilov re-volt, refused to accept our compromise of peacefully transferring power to the soviets. . . . They have again sunk into the morass of mean and filthy bargaining with the Kadets. Down with the Mensheviks and Socialist Revolutionaries! . . . Ruthlessly expel them from all revolutionary organi-zations. No negotiations, no communications with these friends of the Kishkins, the friends of the Kornilovite landowners and capitalists.

The next day, September 23, Lenin recorded:

> Trotsky was for the boycott. Bravo, Comrade Trotsky! Boycottism was defeated in the Bolshevik group at the Democratic Conference. Long live the boycott! We cannot and must not under any circumstances reconcile ourselves to participation. A group at one of the conferences is not the highest organ of the party and even the decisions of the highest organs are subject to revision on the basis of experience. We must strive at all cost to have the boycott question solved at a plenary meeting of the Central Committee and at an extraordinary party congress. . . . There is not the slightest doubt that there are noticeable vacillations at the top of our party that may become *ruinous.*[4]

The editorial board of *Rabochii put'*, composed of Sokolnikov, Trotsky, Kamenev, Stalin, and Volodarsky, suppressed "From a Publicist's Diary" entirely, and instead on September 26 began publication of "The Tasks of the Revolution," one of the articles written during Lenin's period of moderation in early September, when he had been seriously considering the possibility of compromise with the moderates.

Lenin's patience was nearing the breaking point. On September 27 he wrote a long letter to Smilga giving vent to his frustrations and encouraging Smilga to take the initiative in preparing the overthrow of the government:

> Kerensky is obviously entering into an understanding with the Kornilovites to use troops to put down the Bolsheviks. And what are we doing? We are only passing resolutions. . . . It is necessary to agitate inside the party for an earnest attitude towards an armed uprising. . . . This letter should be typed and delivered to comrades in Petrograd and Moscow. . . . Take advantage of your high position [i.e., as chairman of the Regional Executive Committee of the Army, Fleet, and Workers in Finland]. . . . Devote exclusive attention to the military preparation of the troops in Finland plus the fleet for the impending overthrow of Kerensky. . . . Why should we tolerate three more weeks of war and Kerensky's "Kornilovite preparations"?[5]

Lenin returned to this theme two days later (very likely the day of his return to Petrograd) in an essay, "The Crisis Has Matured." Here he propounded the thesis that developments in all the major European countries indicated that the worldwide proletarian revolution was at hand, that the advantageous circumstances in which the Bolsheviks in Russia found themselves placed a special burden upon them, and that the Bolsheviks would be "miserable traitors to the proletarian cause" if they delayed seizing power any longer. In the last part of the essay, directed to members of the Bolshevik Central, Moscow, and Petersburg committees but not intended for publication, Lenin penned his most withering critique of the policies being pursued by his party's leadership. He even tendered his resignation from the Central Committee. He wrote:

> We must admit that there is a tendency . . . among the leaders of our party which favors *waiting* for the Congress of Soviets, [and] is *opposed* to taking power immediately. . . . That tendency must be overcome or the Bolsheviks will cover themselves with eternal *shame* and *destroy themselves* as a party. . . . "To wait" for the Congress of Soviets is idiocy, for the congress *will give nothing* and can give nothing. . . . We have thousands of armed workers and soldiers in Petrograd who could at once seize the Winter Palace, the General Staff building, the telephone exchange and the large printing presses. If we were to attack at once, suddenly, from three points, Petrograd, Moscow, and the Baltic fleet, the chances are a hundred to one that we would succeed with smaller sacrifices than on July 3–5.

In submitting his resignation, Lenin offered the following explanation:

In view of the fact that the Central Committee has *even left unanswered* the persistent demands I have been making for such a policy [the overthrow of the government] ever since the beginning of the Democratic Conference; in view of the fact that the central newspaper is deleting from my articles all references to such glaring errors on the part of the Bolsheviks as the shameful decision to participate in the Preparliament, the admission of the Mensheviks to the Presidium of the Soviet, etc., etc., I am compelled to regard this as a "subtle" hint at the unwillingness of the Central Committee even to consider this question, a subtle hint that I should keep my mouth shut, and as a proposal for me to retire.

I am compelled *to tender my resignation from the Central Committee,* which I hereby do, reserving for myself freedom to campaign among the *party rank and file* and at the party congress.

For it is my profound conviction that if we "wait" for the Congress of Soviets and let the present moment pass, we will *ruin* the revolution.[6]

There is no evidence that this resignation was ever formally considered by the Central Committee, and, as we shall see, Lenin was soon to participate in the deliberations of that body as if it had never been submitted.

Lenin's campaign for support within the party at large began two days later (October 1) with a letter addressed jointly to the Central, Moscow, and Petersburg committees, and also to Bolshevik members of the Petrograd and Moscow soviets. Lenin pointed to repression by the government of revolutionary unrest among the peasantry, mutinies in the German navy and the apparent beginnings of widespread revolutionary disturbances there, Bolshevik victories in local elections in Moscow and increases in Bolshevik support among soldiers, and major labor disputes involving railway and postal workers, as evidence that "procrastination is positively criminal," that "the Bolsheviks have no right to wait for the Congress of Soviets and must *take power at once.*" By so doing they would "save the world revolution," "save the Russian revolution," and "save the lives of hundreds of people at the front."[7]

At the same time, Lenin prepared an appeal "To Workers, Peasants, and Soldiers," obviously intended for the broadest mass circulation; it read in part:

. . . Comrades! Look around you, see what is happening in the countryside, see what is happening in the army, and you will realize that the peasants and soldiers cannot tolerate it any longer. . . .

Kerensky is again negotiating with the Kornilovite generals and officers to *lead troops against the soviets* of workers' and soldiers' deputies, *to prevent the soviets from obtaining power!*

. . . Go to the barracks, go to the cossack units, go to the working people and explain the *truth* to them.

If power is in the hands of the soviets . . . there will be *a workers' and peasants' government* in Russia; it will *immediately*, without losing a single day, *offer a just peace to all belligerent peoples*. . . .

If power is in the hands of the soviets, *the landowners' estates will immediately* be declared the *inalienable property of the whole people*. . . .

No, not *one more day* are the people willing to suffer postponement. . . .

Down with the government of Kerensky, who is conniving with the Kornilov-ite landowning generals to suppress the peasants, to fire on the peasants, to drag out the war!

All power to the soviets of workers' and soldiers' deputies![8]

Indications that the Central Committee could no longer successfully contain the dissemination of Lenin's appeals—indeed, that they were already having an impact on lower party organizations—appeared in the first days of October. One of Lenin's appeals for action had come into the possession of the Moscow Regional Bureau, firmly controlled by the militant wing of the Bolshevik organization in the Moscow area, at the end of September. At a meeting of the Central Committee on October 3, Lomov, a member of the bureau and a candidate member of the Central Committee, delivered a formal report on behalf of the bureau aimed at bringing pressure to bear on the Central Committee to initiate preparations for the seizure of power. Lomov expressed concern that in the Moscow area the mood was extremely tense, that the Bolsheviks had majorities in many soviets, and that the masses were insistent on concrete action; meanwhile, party members were simply marking time. The Central Committee heard Lomov out but declined to discuss his report.[9]

At roughly the same time (on October 3 or 4) several of Lenin's appeals also reached militant leaders of the Bolshevik Petersburg Committee.[10] In the pre-July period, the leadership of the Petersburg Committee frequently had stood significantly to the left of the Central Committee on issues relating to the development of the revolution and on occasion had acted quite independently in deciding major policy questions. This had led to friction between the Petersburg Committee and the Central Committee, and in the aftermath of the July uprising the two organs apparently had reached a tacit understanding of sorts: the Petrograd organization would not make decisions potentially affecting the entire country without first obtaining the consent of the Central Committee, while, for its part, the Central Committee would attempt to ascertain the Petersburg Committee's views before making major policy decisions. To facilitate coordination between the two committees, Bubnov had been delegated to represent the Central Committee in the Petersburg Committee.[11]

Upon receipt of Lenin's letters, the leadership of the Petersburg Committee learned for the first time that the Central Committee had grossly violated this tacit agreement. Not only had it rejected Lenin's proposal to organize an armed uprising without consulting the Petersburg Committee, it had actively endeavored to conceal and misrepresent Lenin's views throughout the second half of September. As it turned out, the Petersburg Committee's nine-man Executive Commission was divided between a strong majority responsive to Lenin's appeals and a vocal minority that considered them premature. Nonetheless, the Central Committee's censorship of Lenin's views enraged Executive Commission members to a man.[12] The commission's initial response was a formal request to the Central Committee for an immediate meeting between the Central Committee and representatives from Petersburg and Moscow to discuss the party's future tactical course.[13]

This request, dispatched on October 5, no doubt played a role in prompting the Central Committee to reassess its policies. Within the Central Committee itself, however, a shift in outlook regarding strategy and tactics was already taking place. The Preparliament, now thoroughly restructured, was due to reconvene on October 7, and at a meeting of the Central Committee on October 5 proponents of a boycott insisted that the question of participation be reconsidered. Now that the Preparliament contained propertied elements and, in any case, had little political power, only Kamenev, of those present on October 5, could find any merit in taking part. By a vote of all against one it was agreed that the party would stage a walkout from the Preparliament at its opening session.[14]

Naturally appalled at this decision, Kamenev immediately submitted a formal memorandum to the Central Committee contending that "withdrawal from the first session oriented the party's tactics in an extremely dangerous direction" and requesting to be relieved of all responsibility for representing the party in the Soviet Central Executive Committee and other political organs.[15] Quite likely at Kamenev's insistence, the boycott issue was discussed further at a meeting of the arriving Bolshevik Preparliament delegation, on the afternoon of October 7. As on September 21, arguments in this assembly of Bolshevik representatives from subordinate party organizations throughout the country dragged on interminably and were at times extremely heated. Trotsky again presented the main case for a boycott. In opposition, members of the more conciliatory wing of the party, Kamenev and Riazanov among them, no longer advocated participation in the Preparliament but urged merely that a withdrawal be postponed until the emergence of a serious issue which would provide clear justification for a walkout. In the end, however, by a very narrow margin, the delegation endorsed an immediate boycott.[16]

Meanwhile, without waiting for a response from the Central Committee, the Executive Commission called together the full Petersburg Committee expressly to discuss Lenin's letters.[17] This meeting was convened on October 5 at the Petersburg Committee's regular Narva District meeting-place at the same time as the Central Committee, gathered at Smolny, was debating a boycott of the Preparliament. The Executive Commission had agreed that this session should be closed to all but regularly elected district representatives; hence improperly accredited party members were preliminarily asked to leave. Lenin's letter of October 1 calling for the immediate overthrow of the government was then read aloud, after which Iukka Rakhia[18] took the floor on behalf of the Executive Commission to deliver a formal report on the current moment.

Rakhia had been among the Petersburg Committee's ultraradicals on the eve of the July uprising and was one of those imprisoned in its aftermath. He now acted as spokesman for the Executive Commission majority sympathetic to Lenin's appeals. In arguing the case for an immediate insurrection, Rakhia focused particular attention on conditions in his native Finland. The mood of the troops in Finland, he declared, was solidly Bolshevik; political power was effectively in the hands of the Bolshevik Regional Committee. The Regional Committee was at war with the Provisional Government, and the situation was such that it had to either surrender its position or go further. There were rumors regarding the disarmament of Kronstadt, he added, and an explosive situation was developing there. For these reasons he insisted that the party was in a life-or-death situation and urged that discussion focus exclusively on Lenin's recommendations and on technical matters connected with the preparation of an insurrection.

The intense but always sober and pragmatic Volodarsky rose next, to voice the concerns of the Executive Commission minority, which remained skeptical of the efficacy of immediate action. Volodarsky urged his listeners to weigh their steps carefully. "We have a responsibility to the working class," he argued. "At present the army gets 80 percent of the bread, nine-tenths of the meat, etc. And no measures can help this." In Volodarsky's estimate, the demoralization of the army at the front was also reason for pause. "At the front," he declared, "there is nothing but tiredness. . . . The soldiers want an end to the war. . . . We say that if our peace terms are not accepted, we will fight the imperialists . . . [but] the army will not take part in a revolutionary war." Volodarsky also expressed doubt regarding the party's concrete military support both locally and in the country at large. "Petrograd and Finland are not all of Russia, and yet even here we do not have sufficient strength compared with what can be mobilized against us from the front. If we could just hope to have bread for ten to fifteen days, if we could raise allowances, this would increase our influence and allow for the possibility of rousing the army. But the way things stand, we would not be able to do this. These are the toughest months for procuring food supplies. . . . Even if the entire countryside supported us and agreed to furnish bread, we would still have no means of transporting it."

Volodarsky asserted that the revolutionary situation abroad was another factor that called for delay. "Only revolutionary outbreaks in the West can save us," he declared. "The revolutionary movement is growing among Western European workers and if we do not force developments, this ally will only increase in strength." While recommending caution, Volodarsky took pains to disassociate himself from the policies advocated by the party's right and to suggest that his differences with Lenin centered upon tactics rather than goals. "Even at the Democratic Conference," he observed, "I was against participation in the Preparliament. We made an unpardonable error. The correct revolutionary path is to reject compromises but not to force developments . . . at the same time building up fighting strength so that power can be taken when it is inevitable and unavoidable." The hard thing, he contended, was not to seize power, but to keep it. "We must show the masses that our path, the course along which we came to power, is the only right one," he concluded. "We must understand that taking power, we will be forced to lower wages, to increase unemployment, to institute terror. . . . We do not have the right to reject these methods, but there is no need to rush into them."

Mikhail Lashevich, the only other member of the Executive Commission who can be identified definitively as sharing Volodarsky's views, now rose to support his colleague. Since 1906 Lashevich had been immersed almost totally in revolutionary activity. He had been drafted in 1915, and the mid-summer of 1917 found him attached to the rebellious First Machine Gun Regiment. On the eve of the July days, he was perhaps the only Bolshevik activist among the machine gunners who was genuinely alarmed about the prospect of an early insurrection. Lashevich had devoted much of his time to work in the Petrograd Soviet, where he was elected chairman of the Bolshevik fraction. At the Sixth Bolshevik Party Congress, along with Volodarsky, he was among those staunchly defending the soviets as revolutionary institutions, against the attacks of the Leninists. On the present occasion, he was similarly forthright, articulating practical concerns which subsequent events showed to have been shared by others but which at this point relatively few were willing to voice.

Lashevich acknowledged that the revolution had reached a critical moment, but warned his listeners against trying to move too far too fast. "We have heard reports from all regions and because of this the situation facing Russia is clear to us," he said, referring to reports made in the Petrograd Soviet and at the Democratic State Conference.

It has become apparent that the Russian economy—both industry and food production—is close to ruin. The Mensheviks themselves have acknowledged that revolutionary measures will be required to check this rush into disaster. Even the immediate conclusion of peace will not prevent the crash. Power is coming to us, this is a fact. We must accept it even though there is a 98 percent chance that . . . we will be defeated. . . . But must we take power now? I believe we ought not force matters. . . . By taking power now we will turn elements against us that are bound to come our way later. . . . Wavering elements are increasingly coming to recognize the necessity of revolutionary measures which we began advocating two months ago. Lenin's strategic plan limps on all four legs. . . . Let's not fool ourselves. We will not be able to furnish bread. The likelihood is great that we will not be able to provide peace. While the war is going on, I don't expect a revolution in Germany. . . . An immediate decree transferring land to the peasants would probably raise the spirit of the masses, but even then they probably would not go to fight. We must coolly take cognizance of all this when we make our decision. Lenin hasn't given us a sufficient explanation of why it is necessary to seize power now, before the Congress of Soviets. . . . The Congress of Soviets will provide an apparatus and if the delegates are in favor of taking power, it will be a different question. . . . I agree with Rakhia that we must prepare. We stand on a volcano. I wonder as I wake up each morning—has it already erupted?

Boky, the secretary of the Petersburg Committee, now interrupted the discussion to read aloud five theses written by Lenin a day or two earlier (they were intended primarily for consideration at a city party conference scheduled to open on October 7). In the theses Lenin had outlined his argument against participating in the Preparliament and tying the overthrow of the government to the Congress of Soviets, and had reiterated the necessity of organizing an armed uprising as quickly as possible. Under the influence of Lenin's militant stand several speakers rose to attack the views of Volodarsky and Lashevich and to defend those of Lenin. Kharitonov commented sarcastically: "Volodarsky and Lashevich have been infected by the atmosphere at Smolny. . . . As a political party we are aiming for power and I think we have come to a time when we can realize this aim."

Rakhia took the floor once again. "I thought all of us were revolutionaries," he declared, "but when I heard Volodarsky and Lashevich I began to wonder." Taking issue with the claim that a Bolshevik government would founder because of inability to maintain industrial production and provide essential food supplies, Rakhia expressed the opinion that much of Russia's economic distress resulted from the sabotage of industrialists, a problem that would be eliminated by a revolutionary government. Moreover, he insisted that in delaying the seizure of power, the Bolsheviks were alienating, rather than acquiring, support.

The Petersburg Committee's discussion had by now been going on for many hours. At the conclusion of the Central Committee meeting, which had taken place simultaneously, Bubnov, Sokolnikov, and Smilga went at once to the Petersburg Committee meeting, still in progress upon their arrival. All three were, of course, much closer to Lenin than to Kamenev in political sentiment, a fact which they immediately made clear. Indeed, their primary concern was to ascertain how local-level leaders in closest touch with workers and soldiers felt the masses would respond to the Bolshevik boycott of the Preparliament, which the Central Committee had just decided upon, and how and when, in their view, power might most easily be seized.

If any participants in this meeting, apart from Volodarsky and Lashevich, were inclined to argue against an immediate insurrection, the militancy of Bubnov, Sokolnikov, and Smilga probably inhibited them from taking the floor. Although no member of the Petersburg Commitee suggested initiating an uprising at once, as Lenin seemed to have been recommending, many of the most influential Petersburg Committee members, among them Latsis, Kalinin, Molotov, and Grigorii Evdokimov, spoke in support of a militant course. The indefatigable Latsis pointed to Russian naval defeats in the Baltic and expressed fear that the destruction of the Baltic Fleet was imminent—a development which would make the seizure of power significantly more difficult. Kalinin insisted somewhat ambiguously that the question of seizing power was now before the party and all that remained was the difficult question of ascertaining the proper moment for attack. Molotov spoke in a similar vein: "Presently we are on the eve of an overturn. . . . Our task now is not to restrain the masses but to select the most opportune moment for taking power into our own hands." Finally, Evdokimov, a member of the Central Soviet of Factory-Shop Committees, asserted that the soldiers' great thirst for peace was yet another argument for early action against the government since "a second Kornilov might appear with peace as his slogan and then we will be strangled."

Towards the close of the meeting, Rakhia proposed that, before adjourning, the Petersburg Committee should attempt to arrive at a decision regarding preparation of an uprising. However, Volodarsky advised that passage of a formal resolution be delayed until the convocation two days hence of the much larger citywide party conference. This proposal was apparently acceptable to the majority, for the published record breaks off abruptly at this point.[19]

Not long after the full Petersburg Committee had dispersed, however, the Executive Commission made a start at implementing Lenin's recommendations. As Latsis later explained, while it was necessary to be ready for serious combat, so far no systematic preparations had been made.[20] The Executive Commission now delegated three of its members—Iakov Fenikshtein, Ivan Moskvin, and Latsis—to initiate an evaluation of the party's military strength and, in general, to prepare district committees for action against the government. All this, records Latsis, was undertaken without informing the Central Committee.[21]

Word of what the Executive Commission was up to did not take long to reach the Central Committee, whose members, it will be recalled, had been apprehensive about the potentially explosive reaction of radically inclined local-level leaders from the time they had received Lenin's mid-September letters. The committee met at once to discuss the problem. The published record of this meeting on October 7 is brief, indicating only that Bubnov reported the formation by the Executive Commission of a bureau to ascertain the mood of the masses and to establish close contact between them and party centers, and that after considering and discussing the importance of proper coordination and precise information, it was decided to create a bureau attached to the Central Committee "for information concerning the struggle against the counterrevolution." Trotsky, Sverdlov, and Bubnov were designated as the Central Committee's representatives in this bureau.[22] Nevsky and Podvoisky from the Military Organization and Latsis and Moskvin from the Petersburg Committee were subsequently named to the bureau as well.[23] There is no evidence that the bureau functioned actively; for the time being the Central Committee's primary objective in establishing such a body seems to have been to undercut the operation initiated by the Executive Commission.

On the evening of October 7 Kerensky and his cabinet, representatives of the Allied diplomatic corps, nearly five hundred delegates from all parts of Russia, and a large contingent of journalists gathered in the stately white and crimson hall of the Mariinsky Palace, the former meeting-place of the Imperial State Council, for the ceremonial opening of the Preparliament. Befitting the times, the imperial crest over the speaker's tribune and a centennial portrait of the State Council by Repin were discreetly concealed behind red draperies. Most of the audience was in place when the fifty-three Bolshevik delegates arrived, directly from their heated deliberations at Smolny. This first session was given over largely to patriotic declarations and appeals to law and order by Kerensky; by the aging populist Ekaterina Breshko-Breshkovskaia, as senior member of the Preparliament; and by Avksentiev, its chairman. As the session drew to a close Trotsky demanded the floor for an emergency announcement.

Mounting the speaker's platform, Trotsky launched into a denunciation of the Provisional Government and the Preparliament as tools of the counterrevolutionary bourgeoisie, and warned that the revolution was on the verge of being crushed. Obviously choosing his words more for the benefit of Petrograd workers and soldiers than for his immediate audience, he sounded a ringing battle cry: "At a time when Wilhelm's troops are threatening Petrograd, the government of Kerensky and Konovalov is preparing to flee Petrograd. . . . Leaving the Provisional Council, we are appealing to workers, soldiers, and peasants of all Russia for vigilance and fortitude." "Petrograd is in danger," he roared, struggling to be heard over a storm of protests from the center and right. "The revolution and the people are in danger! The government is intensifying this threat and the ruling parties are helping it! Only the people can save themselves and the country! We turn to the people! All power to the soviets! All land to the people! Long live an immediate, just, democratic peace! Long live the Constituent Assembly!" The Bolshevik delegates now rose from their seats and filed out of the hall to the accompaniment of hoots and jeers. "Bastards!" someone shouted. "Go to your German trains!" hollered another in the audience, as the last of the Bolsheviks disappeared through the door.[24]

Predictably, Trotsky's inflammatory declaration and the Bolsheviks' demonstrative walkout from the Preparliament created a sensation, touching off a wave of speculation regarding the party's next move. "Literally everywhere," noted a reporter for *Novaia zhizn'* on October 8, "in long queues, among people casually congregating in the streets, in trolleys—rumors are circulating about an uprising being prepared by the Bolsheviks."

Still, it is unlikely that anyone took special notice when, on the evening of October 10, members of the Bolshevik Central Committee, bundled in heavy coats against the late fall chill and a drizzly rain, slipped out of Smolny, one by one, to attend a strategy session in a secret meeting-place across the Neva, far out on the Petersburg side. This was to be Lenin's first direct confrontation with the Central Committee since his return from Finland; it had been carefully organized by Sverdlov at Lenin's behest. By an ironic twist of fate the gathering was to be held in the apartment of the left Menshevik Sukhanov, that unsurpassed chronicler of the revolution who had somehow managed to turn up at almost every important political meeting in Petrograd since the February revolution. But on this occasion Sukhanov was not in attendance. His wife, Galina Flakserman, a Bolshevik activist since 1905 and in 1917 a member of the staff of *Izvestiia* and an aide in the Central Committee secretariat, once had offered Sverdlov the use of the Sukhanov flat, should the need arise. It was a roomy apartment with several entrances, so the comings and goings of a large number of people would not attract particular attention. Sverdlov had decided to make use of this location for the October 10 meeting. For her part, Flakserman insured that her meddlesome husband would remain away on this historic night. "The weather is wretched, and you must promise not to try to make it all the way back home tonight," she had counseled solicitously as he departed for work early that morning.[25]

At the start of the October 10 Central Committee meeting, while a few latecomers straggled in, Sverdlov disposed of routine business and also passed on some disturbing late reports filtering into the party's offices of counterrevolutionary plots allegedly being hatched on the northern front and at western front headquarters in Minsk. Sverdlov noted that these rumors had not yet been confirmed and suggested that one feasible way of dealing with any incipient plots in Minsk was to seize military headquarters there. He added that pro-Bolshevik troops in Minsk were also available for dispatch to Petrograd.

Lenin soon appeared. "Clean-shaven and wearing a wig, he looked every bit like a Lutheran minister," Kollontai later recalled. By 10:00 P.M. at least a dozen of the Central Committee's twenty-one members, including Lenin,

Bubnov, Dzerzhinsky, Zinoviev, Kamenev, Kollontai, Lomov, Sokolnikov, Stalin, Trotsky, Uritsky, and Iakovleva, were seated around the Sukhanovs' dining room table in the dim illumination provided by a hanging lamp. Their attention soon turned to the main item of business—"the current moment."

Lenin began the discussion with an impassioned plea for immediate action which lasted nearly an hour. At the outset, he reproached his associates for "indifference toward the question of an uprising." The party, he charged, should have concerned itself with the technical side of this problem long ago. In support of his claim that time was of the essence, Lenin again expressed certainty that the government was about to surrender Petrograd to the Germans as a means of stifling the revolution. (Apparently, unfounded rumors that Kerensky was contemplating giving up Petrograd without a fight circulated widely at this time, but it is difficult to say whether Lenin actually believed such a step likely or was merely trying to make the strongest possible case for immediate action.) Referring to other vague rumors of a possible peace settlement at Russia's expense and indications of revolutionary unrest abroad, he also insisted that the international situation provided another reason for the Bolsheviks to take the initiative at once.

Echoing the arguments advanced in some of his earlier letters, Lenin went on to compare the prevailing situation with the time of the abortive July uprising, concluding that in the intervening period the Bolsheviks had made gigantic strides in building up support. The indifference of the masses to revolutionary action could be explained by their boredom with words and resolutions. "The majority is with us now," Lenin insisted, and "the political situation is fully ripe for the transfer of power." It was now crucial to discuss the technical aspect of the overthrow of the government. Yet instead, like the defensists, the Bolsheviks were inclined to think of the systematic preparation of an uprising as something akin to a political sin. To wait for the Constituent Assembly, which obviously won't "be with us," said Lenin, was senseless and would only complicate the task. Lenin wound up his remarks with some concrete suggestions about how and when the insurrection against the government should start: the party must use the Northern Region Congress of Soviets opening at Smolny the next morning, as well as the proposed offer of soldiers from Minsk and the raid of military headquarters there, for the beginning of decisive action.

The official published account of the debate following Lenin's appeal is brief and very incomplete. The remarks of Kamenev and Zinoviev, Lenin's main opponents, are not reflected in the official record at all.[26] References to this meeting in other contemporary documents and descriptions in several published memoirs reveal that the discussion was "passionate and tense," that it lasted through the night and into the early morning, and that eventually virtually everyone present spoke. Lomov and Iakovleva appar-

ently reported on the tactical views of Bolshevik leaders in Moscow and on
the political situation in the Moscow area generally. Uritsky voiced grave
concern about the party's reliable military strength in Petrograd, yet asserted somewhat contradictorily that if the Bolsheviks were bent on an uprising then it was necessary to begin making definite preparations for it.
Sverdlov, drawing upon information flowing into the Central Committee
Secretariat, reported on conditions elsewhere in Russia and evidently
strongly supported the idea of an insurrection.

Late at night, the assembled leaders were badly shaken by an insistent
knock at the door. The caller turned out to be Flakserman's brother Iurii, a
military school cadet and also a Bolshevik, who had come to help with the
samovar. Not long after this momentary fright, Kamenev and Zinoviev, the
latter sporting an unaccustomed beard and with his curly hair clipped
short, tried their best to counter Lenin's arguments, attacking the idea of an
armed uprising on both theoretical and practical grounds. As he had at the
April Conference, Kamenev, now joined by Zinoviev, underlined the importance of the petty bourgeoisie in the development of the Russian revolution. As the two put it in a summation of their arguments which they later
prepared,[27] the Russian working class, by itself, could not complete the
present revolution. "We simply cannot lose sight of the fact that between us
and the bourgeoisie there is an enormous third camp, that of the petty
bourgeoisie. This camp joined with us during the Kornilov affair and
brought us victory. It will ally with us again more than once . . . , but for
the time being it is closer to the bourgeoisie than to [the Bolsheviks]."

Kamenev and Zinoviev also voiced skepticism regarding Lenin's assumptions that a majority of the Russian population now backed the Bolsheviks
and that the international proletariat was in the main for the Bolsheviks. In
their view, a majority of Russian workers and a significant percentage of
soldiers supported the Bolsheviks—"but everything else is questionable."
They suggested, for example, that if elections to the Constituent Assembly
were held in the prevailing circumstances, a majority of peasants would
vote for the SRs. As for the soldiers who now supported the Bolsheviks,
they would "run away" should the Bolsheviks be forced to conduct a revolutionary war. Granting some validity to Lenin's argument that it would
be more difficult for the German government to fight against a revolutionary Russia which proposed a democratic peace, they nonetheless considered it unlikely that such a handicap would deter the Germans.

At the same time, as far as Kamenev and Zinoviev were concerned, the
idea that the Bolsheviks in Russia could count on significant aid from revolutionary workers abroad was without foundation. While conceding that
there were important signs of growing revolutionary unrest in Germany
and Italy, they insisted that it was a long way from this to any kind of
active support for a proletarian revolution in a Russia which had declared
war on the entire bourgeois world. Moreover, if the Bolsheviks in Russia

were to suffer defeat, the revolutionary movement abroad would be dealt a major blow. The outbreak of serious revolutions in Europe would make it obligatory for Bolsheviks in Russia to take power at once, they argued. Only after the beginning of this upheaval abroad would the success of a proletarian revolution in Russia be assured. Such a time was coming, they acknowledged, but it most definitely had not yet arrived.

Finally, Kamenev and Zinoviev contended that Lenin's assessment of Bolshevik strength and of the government's isolation and weakness in Petrograd was vastly exaggerated. Neither workers nor soldiers were bursting for a fight, while, in any case, the military troops at the government's disposal were far stronger than those supporting the revolution. Moreover, supported by the Central Executive Committee, the Provisional Government would almost certainly request help from the front. In view of this, the party would be forced to fight in circumstances very different from those at the time of the struggle against Kornilov. Then the party had fought alongside the SRs and Mensheviks and even some close allies of Kerensky. Now it would be necessary to take on "the Black Hundreds, plus the Kadets, plus Kerensky and the Provisional Government, plus the Central Executive Committee and the SRs and Mensheviks." For the party, the consequences of such a struggle would be inevitable defeat.

As an alternative to the immediate uprising advocated by Lenin, Kamenev and Zinoviev urged that the party adhere to a nonviolent political course, "a defensive posture" aimed at acquiring the strongest possible representation for the masses at the Constituent Assembly. Countering Lenin's contention that if allowed more time, the government would successfully torpedo the Constituent Assembly, they expressed certainty that the bourgeoisie was too weak to implement its counterrevolutionary objectives, or even to effectively manipulate elections to the Constituent Assembly. Maintained Kamenev and Zinoviev: "Through the army, through the workers, we have a revolver pointed at the temple of the bourgeoisie. If it even considered attempting to do away with the Constituent Assembly, it would again push the petty bourgeois parties to us and the revolver would be triggered." Sympathy for the Bolsheviks would continue to grow while the Kadet-Menshevik-SR bloc would gradually disintegrate. Support for the party in the Constituent Assembly, working in conjunction with the soviets, would be so strong that the Bolsheviks' enemies would be forced to make concessions at every step or risk the creation of a majority bloc of Bolsheviks, Left SRs, nonparty peasant representatives, and the like that would put through the party's program. The only way such a scenario might be disrupted, Zinoviev and Kamenev concluded, would be if the party initiated an untimely insurrection such as that proposed by Lenin, thereby subjecting the proletariat to attack from the entire counterrevolution allied with the petty bourgeois democracy.

In sum, these were the arguments advanced by Kamenev and Zinoviev.

Perhaps in a broader party forum, such as that assembled in Petrograd during the Democratic State Conference, they might even now have attracted strong support. But such potential sympathizers as Nogin and Rykov were not present at the historic gathering of October 10, and everyone else sided with Lenin. Apart from Kamenev and Zinoviev, differences among Central Committee members on this occasion no longer revolved around fundamental theoretical issues or the question of whether or not to overthrow the Provisional Government and transfer power to the soviets, but centered on how soon and in what manner this might be done and whether or not it was necessary to associate an uprising with the Congress of Soviets. In the resolution which Lenin proposed at the close of the October 10 meeting these issues were somewhat blurred. Hastily scratched out with the gnawed end of a pencil on a sheet of paper torn from a child's notebook, it read in part:

> The Central Committee acknowledges that the international situation as it affects the Russian revolution . . . as well as the military situation . . . and the fact that the proletarian party has gained majorities in the soviets—all this, coupled with the peasant insurrection and the swing of popular confidence to our party, and finally, the obvious preparations for a second *Kornilovshchina* . . . makes armed insurrection the order of the day.
>
> Recognizing that an armed uprising is inevitable and the time fully ripe, the Central Committee instructs all party organizations to be guided accordingly and to consider and decide all practical questions from this standpoint (the Northern Region Congress of Soviets, the withdrawal of troops from Petrograd, the action of [comrades] in Moscow and Minsk, etc).

This call to arms was adopted by a vote of ten to two. Kollontai remembered that as soon as the vote was taken, the prevailing tension evaporated and everyone suddenly felt starved. Iurii Flakserman produced the samovar, along with some cheese, sausage, and black bread, and the hungry group immediately pounced on the food. Arguments continued for a bit, Kollontai recalled, but they were now interspersed with humor—and good-natured gibes at Kamenev and Zinoviev.[28]

Thus ended this historic meeting between Lenin and the Bolshevik Central Committee. Historians in the Soviet Union frequently have viewed the night of October 10 as the moment when doubts about a militant revolutionary course within the Central Committee were, for practical purposes, eliminated, after which Bolshevik organizations everywhere set about energetically preparing a popular armed uprising along the lines urged by Lenin. This interpretation does not accurately describe the circumstances. The Central Committee resolution of October 10, which left the exact character and timing of an insurrection to the discretion of subordinate Bolshevik organizations, did not resolve the very profound differences of opin-

The first page of the resolution endorsing an insurrection hastily scribbled by Lenin on October 10 for adoption by the Central Committee.

ion regarding revolutionary tactics that still existed between Lenin and other party leaders more acutely attuned to the specific political situation prevailing in Petrograd. As we shall see, these tactical divergences were to have great significance in the subsequent development of the revolution.

This is not to suggest that the Central Committee meeting of October 10 was unimportant. The October 10 resolution on "the current moment" made the seizure of power "the order of the day." For the Bolsheviks, this constituted a major advance over the corresponding resolution at the Sixth Congress (which had merely acknowledged the necessity of an armed uprising) as well as a formal reversal of the orientation toward a peaceful development of the revolution which had shaped the party's policies throughout September. While Kamenev and Zinoviev now watched in dismay, word of the Central Committee's decision and call to arms was spread to key party committees around the country. Looking back over the period between the Kornilov affair and the decision of October 10, one can see that, as in April, chief responsibility for this drastic transformation in the outlook of the party's top hierarchy belongs to Lenin. It was Lenin who, over a period of several weeks, alternately cajoled, pressured, and threatened his colleagues, and who, by force of argument and personal authority, ultimately succeeded in turning a majority of the Central Committee toward an insurrectionary course. This major personal victory of Lenin's should be borne in mind as we turn to a consideration of political developments in Petrograd and intraparty disputes over tactics between October 10 and the Bolshevik seizure of power. Few modern historical episodes better illustrate the sometimes decisive role of an individual in historical events.

·12·

OBSTACLES TO
AN UPRISING

The Bolshevik Central Committee's bitterly debated decision to make the seizure of power the order of the day was not reflected at once in *Rabochii put'*, the party's main newspaper. The banner headline "Comrade Workers, Soldiers, and Peasants—Prepare for the Congress of Soviets Opening October 20," displayed beside the paper's masthead daily since September 27, was for the time retained. This does not mean, however, that the October 10 resolution was without immediate effect; behind the scenes, Bolsheviks supporting the party's new, ultramilitant course now mounted a concerted effort to prepare an armed uprising at the earliest possible moment.

Attention was initially centered chiefly on the Northern Region Congress of Soviets, which met in Petrograd from October 11 to 13. As Latsis later recorded: "The plan was that it [the Northern Congress] would declare itself the government, and this would be the start."[1] One of the many regional assemblies of soviets convened in various parts of Russia in preparation for the coming All-Russian Congress, the Northern Region Congress brought together ninety-four delegates representing army and navy committees and local soviets, primarily from northwestern Russia.[2] Chaired by Krylenko and solidly leftist, the congress included among its participants fifty-one Bolsheviks, twenty-four Left SRs, four Maximalists (a small terrorist offshoot of the SR Party), one Menshevik-Internationalist, and only ten SRs (four Mensheviks had departed the congress shortly after it opened). It was this apparent strength of the extreme left that led Lenin and other party leaders to view the congress as a suitable institution around which to organize Kerensky's overthrow.

Apparently the Bolshevik-led Regional Executive Committee of the Army, Fleet, and Workers in Finland, which scheduled the Northern Region Congress and arranged for it to be held in Petrograd rather than Helsingfors, also viewed the congress as an appropriate institution for the initiation and legitimization of an insurrection. Plans for the congress were made after the Regional Executive Committee's chairman, Smilga, received Lenin's letter of September 27 in which he had been urged to personally take the initiative in preparing the overthrow of the government. In an article on the Northern Congress published in *Rabochii put'* on October 8 and in the Kronstadt *Proletarskoe delo* two days later, Smilga declared that the congress "would in all likelihood have to assume a tremendously important role in the political life of the country." "It is no secret to anyone," he went on to assert, "that defensists of all varieties are conducting a furious campaign against the All-Russian Congress of Soviets . . . [and] that if we passively await the twentieth, there will be no congress. It is necessary to rebuff the onslaught of the defensists, not only with words but with deeds. The crisis is growing with extraordinary speed. The current status can last only for a few days. . . . In this moment the regional congress can have enormous significance."[3]

On October 7, even before the Central Committee agreed to prepare an insurrection, participants in a citywide conference of Petrograd Bolsheviks were primed for the possibility that the Northern Region Congress would initiate action against the government.[4] Subsequently, on the morning of the eleventh, Kollontai informed conference participants of the resolution passed by the Central Committee, pointing, no doubt, to the key role envisioned for the Northern Region Congress.[5]

In a message of October 8 to Bolsheviks participating in the Northern Region Congress, Lenin insisted that delegates would be "traitors to the International" if they limited themselves to "mere resolutions." "We must not wait for the All-Russian Congress of Soviets, which the Central Executive Committee may put off until November," Lenin inveighed; "only the immediate movement of troops from Finland and the Baltic Fleet . . . can save the Russian and world revolutions. . . . [These forces] can and must march on Petrograd, smash the Kornilovite regiments, rouse both capital cities, initiate mass agitation for a government which will immediately give land to the peasants and make proposals for peace, overthrow Kerensky's government and establish such a government. Procrastination would be fatal."[6] Two days later, at the October 10 meeting of the Central Committee, Lenin had urged the party to make use of the Northern Region Congress of Soviets for the beginning of decisive action.

Word of the Central Committee's decision to organize an uprising was conveyed to Bolshevik delegates at the Northern Region Congress upon their arrival at Smolny the morning of October 11; indeed, it appears that during the early sessions of the congress, these delegates were led to believe that directives to start an insurrection could be expected momentarily.[7] One of the secretaries of the congress, the Kronstadt Bolshevik Boris Breslav, later remembered that as the congress opened, many of its participants assumed that it would become the center for an uprising: "They were under the impression that the Central Committee's signal to come out would be received at any minute."[8]

Such thinking was encouraged by Sokolnikov in a report on the current moment delivered on behalf of the Central Committee at an initial meeting of the party's fraction at the Northern Congress on the morning of October 11. Sokolnikov's message boiled down to the following: "The moment when it is necessary to go into battle for the triumph of the soviets throughout the country has arrived. . . . It is no accident that the congress has been moved to Petrograd, for it may be that it will have to be the organization that will start an uprising."[9]

The atmosphere at the Northern Region Congress of Soviets became greatly heated early in the proceedings when Antonov-Ovseenko announced that political prisoners still in the Crosses Prison had begun a hunger strike. In response, the delegates passed an appeal to the prisoners: "Halt your hunger strike and marshal your strength because the hour of your liberation is close at hand."[10] Yet, despite this beginning, the Bolshevik leadership held back from actually summoning the delegates to help organize the overthrow of Kerensky. Instead, the congress adjourned late on October 13 after passage of a fairly moderate joint Bolshevik–Left SR resolution which in effect tied the creation of a soviet government to the All-Russian Congress of Soviets.[11]

The failure of the Northern Region Congress to trigger an uprising can be explained by several related factors. For one thing, Bolshevik Military Organization leaders, who since April had had chief responsibility for preparing the seizure of power, raised what in retrospect seem to have been justified doubts regarding the party's readiness for an armed uprising. During the preceding weeks and months, as we have seen, the Bolsheviks had directed their attention almost entirely to activities consistent with the peaceful development of the revolution. Relatively little effort had been devoted, in either the barracks or the factories, to the kind of careful technical preparation needed to support a party-organized insurrection. Bolshevik control in units of the Petrograd garrison involved in the July days had not yet been restored.[12] Many of the worker Red Guard units created during the Kornilov crisis had since disintegrated; not until mid-October was an effort begun to coordinate and train Red Guard units on a citywide basis. Then too, nothing had yet been done to assure the cooperation of rail workers so that the capital would not be immediately cut off from the rest of the country in the event of an insurrection.

Nevsky had such problems in mind when, in a candid early memoir, he wrote that "educated by the bitter experience of the July days," the Military Organization at this time "delayed and carefully considered its actions. There was much that was not yet prepared, much that had to be adjusted, much to be corrected, and here and there, we found flagrant deficiencies."

Nevsky went on to acknowledge that, for these reasons, he and Podvoisky firmly insisted that the start of any uprising be delayed for about two weeks.[13] Elsewhere he later commented, "We had to pour cold water on all those ardent comrades who were straining for a fight, not having an idea of all the difficulties connected with an uprising"[14]—an assessment applicable most of all to Lenin.

A second factor impelling Bolshevik Party strategists to delay an insurrection against the Provisional Government was that local leaders in closest day-to-day contact with the masses now voiced similarly grave concern about the possibility of mobilizing sufficient numbers of Petrograd workers and soldiers in support of an armed uprising in advance of the Congress of Soviets, which since September 23 had been trumpeted with increasing volume, by Bolsheviks, Left SRs, and Menshevik-Internationalists alike, as the appropriate forum for the legitimate settlement of the government question. Particularly strong reservations along this line appear to have emerged at the citywide Bolshevik conference on October 10, at a conference of party representatives from Petrograd Province (that is, from outlying towns) on October 1, and at a meeting between members of the Military Organization Bureau and representatives from units of the Petrograd garrison which took place during the second week of October. According to the recollections of Alexander Shotman, an official of the provincial organization and a confidant of Lenin who had been active in the Russian social democratic movement from the days of the Petersburg Union of Struggle, majorities at all three gatherings opposed an uprising before the Second Congress of Soviets.[15]

Actually, the staunchly radical complexion of the Northern Region Congress notwithstanding, by the evening of October 12 it was probably evident that winning majority support for an immediate insurrection would be virtually impossible even there. In the first place, while Trotsky, Sokolnikov, and other supporters of the Central Committee's October 10 resolution were exploring how this decision might best be implemented, Kamenev and Zinoviev were working desperately to prevent the initiation of an uprising, certain that an immediate, party-organized insurrection could end only in a far more serious disaster than that following the July uprising, and believing, not unjustifiably, that a majority of party leaders in the country might well support this view. After the Central Committee meeting on October 10 they dispatched a summary of their arguments against the seizure of power to major party committees throughout the country and to the Bolshevik fractions in the Central Executive Committee, the Petrograd Soviet, and the Northern Region Congress of Soviets. "We are deeply convinced," they wrote, "that to declare an armed uprising now would be to risk the fate not only of the party but of the world revolution. There is no doubt that there are times in history when the downtrodden class must acknowledge that it is better to be defeated than to surrender without a struggle. Is the Russian working class in this kind of position now? No and a thousand times no!"[16]

In Petrograd, Kamenev and Zinoviev personally lobbied for postponement of precipitous revolutionary action among local party leaders generally and among deputies to the Northern Region Congress of Soviets in particular.[17]

At the Northern Region Congress, the Left SRs, who shared in full the reservations of Kamenev and Zinoviev regarding an armed uprising, also actively opposed use of the congress to overthrow the government.[18] At this time, the Left SRs were interested most of all in facilitating the creation of a broadly representative, exclusively socialist government at the coming Second All-Russian Congress of Soviets. As was the case with *Rabochii put'*, every issue of the Left SR newspaper *Znamia truda* from September 27 on carried the banner headline "Comrades, Prepare for the All-Russian Congress of Soviets."[19] Unlike *Rabochii put'*, however, the editors of *Znamia truda* consistently coupled this message with the sternest warnings against early armed action against the Provisional Government. Sergei Mstislavsky expressed this message in a lead editorial on October 13: "A coming-out by the workers and soldiers would be a monstrous crime . . . an attack not on the Provisional Government, but on the soviets. . . . And because of this, those who appeal to the masses for action, for the seizure of power, deceive. Their appeal is a cry not for the triumph of the people's will, but for its self-destruction."

Mstislavsky's colleague Boris Kamkov later explained the policies pursued by Left SRs in the capital at this time:

> In the wake of the Democratic State Conference, after it became clear that the defensists were unwilling to break with the politics of coalition, we looked to the All-Russian Congress of Soviets to assume the task of organizing a new government. In our agitation in military barracks and factories we emphasized the necessity of being prepared to provide organized armed support to the All-Russian Congress of Soviets in case the Kerensky regime did not recognize the authority of the newly organized socialist government. A few days before the All-Russian Congress, however, it became clear to those of us working in factories and barracks that the Bolsheviks were mobilizing their forces not simply to defend the government established by the congress, but rather to seize power in advance of the congress. And in this matter we departed very drastically from the Bolsheviks. Their course seemed to us both dangerous and senseless. After coalition had so bankrupted itself, after it had become an empty shell and the very word *coalition* had become a term of abuse in worker and soldier circles, and when among workers and peasants it was impossible to find a single solid group which would defend coalition government, it seemed to us that it would be possible to rid ourselves painlessly of this skeleton by action of the All-Russian Congress of Soviets. At the same time, we be-

lieved that if this were done in another way, say by means of the seizure of power in Petrograd before the congress, this might appear to be adventurist—as the seizure of power not by the soviets, but by one political party. It seemed to us that this would immediately complicate the situation and make it impossible to avoid civil war.[20]

The difficulties which the lobbying efforts of Kamenev and Zinoviev, coupled with the opposition of the Left SRs, posed for Bolshevik leaders seriously exploring the possibility of organizing an insurrection at the Northern Region Congress of Soviets can be easily understood if one bears in mind that the Left SRs, together with the SRs and Menshevik-Internationalists, could probably count on close to thirty-five of the ninety votes in the congress. Thus Kamenev and Zinoviev had only to sow reservations about the wisdom of an uprising among less than a dozen of the remaining fifty-five Bolshevik and Maximalist delegates to prevent immediate action—and there is no doubt that had the matter come to a vote, they would have had little difficulty in doing so.

Actually, as the Northern Region Congress drew to a close, what seems to have worried its participants most was the possibility that the Central Executive Committee might manage to have the All-Russian Congress postponed or cancelled altogether on the grounds that it was interfering with preparations for the Constituent Assembly. Consequently, one of its last acts was to adopt an appeal to the masses emphasizing the importance of the All-Russian Congress and its assumption of power as the sole means of assuring that a properly elected Constituent Assembly would be convened without further delays.[21]

The deputies also created a permanent executive committee. There is no doubt that some Bolshevik members of this committee viewed it primarily as an insurrectionary organ; thus, Antonov later recalled reaching an agreement with Smilga immediately after the Northern Congress to the effect that Smilga would return to Helsingfors to organize detachments of sailors, infantry, and artillerymen for the support of an uprising, while Antonov would direct the committee's work in Petrograd. According to Antonov, the forces mobilized by Smilga were to be dispatched to Petrograd upon receipt of a telegram reading "Send the regulations." Antonov makes it clear, however, that these arrangements were made privately.[22] The ostensible purpose of the permanent committee set up by the Northern Congress of Soviets was to organize and prepare military forces for the defense and support of the coming All-Russian Congress of Soviets; hence, even the Left SRs agreed to take part in its work.

As it turned out, the Northern Region Congress was for the most part a thundering, highly visible expression of ultraradical sentiment. Moreover, while the congress was in session, Bolshevik agitators were circulating throughout the working-class districts of Petrograd, energetically seeking, with mixed success, to whip up the hostility of workers and soldiers toward the existing government in preparation for a momentary call to arms. Yet from the party's point of view, for the time being this activity, following upon the heels of the Bolsheviks' departure from the Preparliament, had the largely negative effect of heightening the apprehension of government supporters in regard to Bolshevik intentions.[23] Virtually all of Petrograd's daily papers were now filled with speculation about Bolshevik plans and activities. The lead editorial in Gorky's *Novaia zhizn'* on October 15, for example, reported that the Bolsheviks were conducting widespread agitation for an uprising. "The mood of the masses is not uniform," wrote the editorialist, "A portion is apparently ready to act, another is not particularly inclined toward combat and is leaning more toward refraining from active steps, and there are also groups who are either hostile or completely passive toward a coming out."

Similarly, *Gazeta-kopeika* informed its readers on October 14 that "there is definite evidence that the Bolsheviks are energetically preparing for a coming out on October 20." A few days later, under the headline "The Bolsheviks Are Coming Out," the rightist *Zhivoe slovo* announced that "the vile and bloody events of July 3–5 were only a rehearsal. Now the Bolsheviks are preparing to give the performance itself. . . . In factories and barracks everywhere, Bolsheviks are appealing to workers and soldiers to come out into the streets of Petrograd with weapons in hand at the first signal, to overthrow the government and massacre the bourgeoisie." All writers coupled their alarms with dire warnings regarding the consequences of revolutionary action and/or insistent appeals that the government take decisive measures against the left before it was too late. A writer for *Birzhevye vedomosti* declared on the morning of October 14 in an editorial titled "It Is Time to Act": "The Bolsheviks talk about an early coming out of the masses ever more precisely and definitely. . . . Yet all this is patiently tolerated by the government and the democracy without counteraction. . . . The moment which the government must use for the firm defense of revolutionary Petrograd from anarchy has arrived."

Of course, moderate socialist leaders at Smolny and the cabinet ministers in the Winter Palace were now equally attuned to the likelihood of an early Bolshevik-led insurrection. At a plenary session of the All-Russian Executive Committees on October 14, Dan, referring to the flood of reports of extremist agitation and apparent Bolshevik preparations for an insurrection, declared: "We must ask the comrade Bolsheviks candidly, what is the purpose of their politics? . . . The Bolsheviks must announce from this podium whether or not they are calling upon the revolutionary proletariat to come out. . . . I want a yes-or-no answer." From the floor came Riazanov's far from reassuring reply: "We demand peace and land." Significantly, at the close of this session even Martov, for the Menshevik-Internationalists, and Livshits, for the Left SRs, rose to support a resolution proposed by Dan appealing to workers, soldiers, and peasants to maintain calm and branding a "coming out" of any kind completely impermissible.[24]

To judge by press reports, a significant portion of each daily session of Kerensky's cabinet at this time was devoted to discussion of the Bolshevik menace. At a meeting on October 17, Kishkin, minister of the interior, reported that the force at the disposal of the government would be sufficient to put down disturbances once they broke out, but too weak to initiate action against the left. According to information in the government's hands, he added, an uprising had originally been planned for October 18 but had been postponed until the twenty-third because of insufficient preparation.[25]

The cabinet weighed various countermeasures. Yet, conscious of the complexities of the prevailing situation, it limited itself to directing the commander of the Petrograd Military District, General Georgii Polkovnikov, to ready the government's defenses, and to issuing daily appeals for order; clearly the ministers hoped the Bolsheviks would compromise themselves by making the first move. As the war minister, General Verkhovsky, declared realistically: "We have a plan—it is necessary to await the action of the other side. Bolshevism has infected the Soviet and there is not enough strength to disperse it."[26] Departing from a cabinet meeting on the night of October 13, the date the Northern Region Congress of Soviets closed, an unidentified minister commented to waiting reporters somewhat more brashly: "At present the government is not in the least desirous of a clash. But what are we to do? If the Bolsheviks act, we will carry out a surgical operation and the abscess will be extracted once and for all."[27]

In the wake of the Northern Region Congress, Lenin continued to press for an immediate rising, while, for their part, Kamenev and Zinoviev campaigned just as vigorously to prevent a precipitous insurrection and to allay the apprehension of the Bolsheviks' opponents regarding this possibility. Meanwhile, local party activists with close ties to the garrison, factories, and mass organizations went on exploring practical possibilities for implementing the Central Committee's October 10 resolution. The difficulties which they encountered in preparing an insurrection before the All-Russian Congress of Soviets surfaced clearly at two important party strategy sessions which followed the Northern Region Congress—the first, an October 15 emergency meeting of the Petersburg Committee, and the second, a hastily arranged conference between the Central Committee and representatives of the Petersburg Committee, Military Organization, Petrograd Province Bolshevik Committee, Petrograd Soviet, and trade union and factory-shop committee leadership the following night.[28]

The Petersburg Committee meeting of October 15 was attended by thirty-five representatives of Bolshevik committees from the districts of Petrograd. The primary business of the evening, discussion of preparations for an insurrection, opened with a formal report on the current moment by Bubnov, the Central Committee's man on the Petersburg committee. Bubnov made a strong plea for action against the government, declaring: "We are drawing ourselves into a clash. . . . We stand at the brink of a 'coming out.' " Maintaining that all the elements for an uprising were at hand, he insisted: "We must prepare all our forces for action. . . . We must gather all our agitators. . . . If we are to save the revolution, we must follow an offensive as well as a defensive policy."

No sooner had Bubnov finished, however, than Nevsky rushed forward to present the case for a substantial delay in the organization of an uprising. The enormous impact of the July experience on Military Organization leaders is clearly reflected in Nevsky's carefully phrased speech on this occasion. "I must turn the assembly's attention to the myriad of difficulties we have encountered," he insisted at the start. "The Military Organization has just become rightist." Warning that absolutely nothing had been done to prepare the provinces for the overthrow of the Provisional Government and that the Bolsheviks were in fact just beginning to gain a foothold in the countryside, he asserted that peasants in several regions had declared that in the event of an uprising they would withhold bread. He added that the party could not hope to achieve victory if it ignored the mood of the masses. Nevsky went on to point out that such vital factors as the support of railroad workers and the cooperation of the Fifth Army on the northern front had not been secured. In general, technical preparations for an uprising had not been initiated; as matters stood, there was no assurance that the Bolsheviks would have that initial preponderance of strength necessary for victory over the Provisional Government. For all these reasons Nevsky concluded that the Central Committee's resolution of October 10 was premature.

Following Nevsky's address, evidently in response to a request from the floor, Boky, the Petersburg Committee secretary, read aloud in their entirety both the Central Committee's October 10 resolution and the long Kamenev-Zinoviev memorandum. The blunt warnings of Kamenev and Zinoviev, coming on the heels of those of Nevsky, clearly had a profound impact on the assembled local party officials, for it was now agreed that the Central Committee's resolution should be considered "broadly," that is, from the standpoint of both its basic feasibility and the prospects for its implementation.

With this in mind, the committee listened to reports on the prevailing situation in each district. For the most part, these served to reinforce apprehensions regarding the wisdom of immediate action. To be sure, it would be misleading to suggest that the reports were uniformly pessimistic. For example, the indefatigable Latsis lavished praise on preparations for the seizure of power being made by workers in the crucial Vyborg District and expressed confidence that they could be depended upon. Vinokurov, the representative of the Nevsky District, who, unlike Latsis, was not given to exaggeration, vouchsafed, "The mood favors us—the masses are beginning to prick up their ears." And Iukka Rakhia, speaking for the Finns, declared that their attitude toward an uprising was "the sooner the better."

On the other hand, the general picture of the state of affairs in the factories and barracks was often so unpromising that it could not but have had a dampening effect on the mood of party members. Perhaps the most alarming factor brought out at this discussion was the apparent lethargy of large numbers of Petrograd workers and soldiers. It should be borne in mind that at issue here was not whether workers and soldiers were sympathetic to transfer of power to the soviets—that the Bolshevik program was broadly supported by the masses was acknowledged by all—but whether or not they would risk loss of work, immediate shipment to the front, imprisonment, or even death in response to a Bolshevik call for an uprising on the very eve of the Congress of Soviets. And in this regard, of nineteen district representatives who reported on the situation in their localities, only eight felt the masses were in a fighting mood and ready to rise at once, six appear to have viewed the prevailing spirit as indefinite and inclined toward waiting, while five referred explicitly to the absence of any desire to come out.[29]

Kalinin, the future president of the Soviet state, observed that in the Lesnovsky subdistrict (part of the large Vyborg District), things were moving badly for the moment. Savva Ravich of the Moscow District, a dentist, expressed the view that the masses would come out if directed by the Soviet, but that few would respond at the behest of the party. Sergei Prokhorov, a carpenter by trade and representative of the Petersburg District, reported that "where our influence is strong, there is a wait-and-see mood; where this is not the case, the mood is apathetic. . . . Even if the Soviet issues a call to come out, some factories, mine for example, will not act." Alexander Akselrod of the Rozhdestvensky District, and Naum Antselovich, who represented the Petrograd Trade Union Soviet and was also chairman of the electricians' union, agreed that the mood of the masses was such that if they were attacked by the counterrevolution a rebuff would be given, but that the masses would not attack by themselves. Akselrod added that the mood was deflated because of layoffs connected with the evacuation of factories. Representing the Petrograd provincial party organization, Kharitonov, summarizing reports made at the Petrograd provincial conference two weeks earlier, was similarly pessimistic. He said the consensus there was that the masses were dispirited. "Out of five thousand of our supporters in Krasnoe Selo," he asserted, "only five hundred would come here [to participate in an insurrection]; the rest would wait it out in Krasnoe Selo." He added that in Kronstadt the mood had fallen sharply and that there was widespread drunkenness, even among Bolsheviks.

Apparent mass apathy was by no means the only important problem contributing to the pessimistic picture emanating from lower party levels on the eve of the proposed Bolshevik seizure of power. The local reports of October 15 also revealed widespread concern about a general absence of technical preparations for an insurrection; indeed, there were few speakers who did not take note of serious organizational problems in connection with the Red Guards or critical shortages of arms and ammunition, and from the reports taken together, it is clear that no insurrectionary organs had been created as yet. S. M. Gessen, of the Narva District, observed drily that since there were no combat centers, fighting forces, presumably those created during the Kornilov crisis, had broken up. Vinokurov, who had been optimistic about the mood of workers in the Nevsky District, acknowledged that the district had no Red Guard units and that it could not boast about its organizational apparatus. Prokhorov declared directly, "Things are bad as regards the Red Guards. . . . In general the district is in a state of complete disintegration." The representative of the Shlusselburg District noted that a Red Guard unit had been organized but that people were reluctant to enroll because there were few arms.

Clearly appalled by the turn of the discussion, Bubnov demanded to be heard out of turn to remind Petersburg Committee members that the Central Committee went ahead with a consideration of the current moment on October 10 under prodding from the Petersburg Committee. He implored his listeners to focus their attention on practical measures. Shortly afterward, the assembled local party representatives agreed, among other things, to call a conference of party agitators to explain slogans, to organize the publication of an evening newspaper, to improve communications, to strengthen contacts with rail and postal-telegraph workers, and to speed up the instruction of workers in the use of weapons. Most Petersburg Committee members who voted for such steps were perhaps more hopeful that they would achieve quick results than was Kalinin, who, having listened to the district reports, commented: "The resolution of October 10 is one of the best resolutions the Central Committee has ever passed . . . but when this uprising will take place is uncertain—perhaps in a year." Still, clearly implicit in the measures adopted by the Petersburg Committee on the night of October 15 was the assumption that the party was not yet ready for immediate battle.

The hastily organized Central Committee conference the following night had as its purpose reassessment of the party's strategy in the face of the difficulties that had developed in implementing the call for an immediate insurrection. The meeting, attended by roughly twenty-five Bolshevik leaders, was held in the headquarters of the Lesnoi District Duma, far out on the northern outskirts of the capital, under arrangements worked out by Shotman and Kalinin, the latter then chairman of the Lesnoi District Duma. Sverdlova recalls that until the last minute participants did not know where the meeting would be held; they were given a password and a rendezvous, and when assembled, they were led, a few at a time, to the

Duma building. One of the last to arrive was Lenin, who hastily doffed his wig before entering the two connecting rooms where the rest of the participants were gathered. There were few chairs; most people simply sat on the floor.[30] Lenin settled on a hassock in a corner, drew some notes from his pocket, and began to inspect them. By habit, he raised his hand to pat down his wig, then caught himself and smiled.[31]

A young Bolshevik, Ekaterina Alekseeva, who worked in the Lesnoi District Duma building straightening up and doing other odd jobs, recorded her vivid recollections of this occasion. Alekseeva's greatest fear was that some suspicious outsider would call the authorities. Until the very last party official had departed in the wee hours of the morning, she was frantic with worry, listening for strange sounds and keeping a close watch on neighboring buildings to assure herself that all was quiet. She recalls that each arrival was greeted by a loud howl from a neighbor's restless Saint Bernard, and that when she was not keeping watch at the windows or firing up the samovar, she spent a good deal of time calming the dog. The meeting, which began around 8:00 P.M., broke up at 3:00 A.M. the next morning, by which time a slushy snow, one of the season's first, had begun to fall. The participants, recalls Alekseeva, left behind a big mess.[32]

The October 16 meeting opened with Lenin delivering a strong defense of the Central Committee's decision to organize an immediate insurrection. Responding at the outset to lingering interest on the part of Bolshevik moderates in working with the Mensheviks and SRs, he emphasized that every effort had already been made to achieve a compromise with them; but by the time the impossibility of reaching an understanding with the moderate socialists had become clear, it had also become evident that the masses followed the Bolsheviks. Lenin went on to minimize the significance of the apparent deflation in the mood of the masses which had emerged so strongly in the reports of local party activists the previous evening, insisting that "we cannot govern ourselves according to the mood of the masses since it fluctuates and is difficult to appraise. . . . The masses have given the Bolsheviks their trust and demand from them not words but deeds, decisive policies both in the fight against the war and in the struggle with economic dislocation." Toward the close of his remarks, Lenin outlined his reasons for believing that the situation was propitious for a socialist revolution in Russia, concluding that "acting now we will have the entire European proletariat on our side." He ended by articulating his apprehension regarding the plans of the government, arguing that "the bourgeoisie is intent on surrendering Petrograd as a means of crushing the revolution, and the only way of avoiding this is by taking the defense of the capital into our own hands. . . . It follows that the most decisive political action possible is now required—which can only mean an armed uprising." "Power must be seized immediately, at once," he repeated again and again; "Every day lost could be fatal. History will not forgive us if we do not take power now!"[33]

In 1924, Shotman, who had heard Lenin speak frequently both before and after the October revolution, recalled this as one of his best addresses.[34] At the October 16 meeting, Shotman commented with justification that at earlier gatherings where the feasibility of a coming out had been discussed, the mood among participants had been much more pessimistic than it seemed now. This was a reflection, no doubt, of Lenin's legendary persuasiveness. Even so, following Lenin's speech, Nikolai Krylenko, on behalf of the Military Organization, reaffirmed that it was the impression of the Military Organization leadership that the revolutionary mood of the soldiers was subsiding, and that a majority believed that the party "should not force the issue." Reporting on the attitudes of the deputies in the Petrograd Soviet, Volodarsky, who, after Trotsky, was perhaps the party's most effective and popular spokesman there, voiced the general impression that "nobody is tearing into the streets, but everybody would respond to a call by the Soviet." Vasilii Shmidt, a leading figure in the Petrograd Trade Union Soviet, and Alexander Shliapnikov, chairman of the metalworkers' union and also a high official in the Trade Union Soviet, attempted to characterize the political attitude of trade union members. Shmidt contended that while everyone demanded transfer of power to the soviets, active steps on the part of Petrograd's more than 500,000 trade unionists could not be expected, primarily because of widespread fear of dismissals and layoffs. Shliapnikov added that in the metalworkers' union the party's influence was predominant, but a Bolshevik coming-out was not popular. Rumors of such action had even triggered panic.

At the start of the October 16 meeting, Kamenev and Zinoviev had turned down the opportunity to reply to Lenin immediately. Bolstered by such negative reports, Zinoviev took the floor at this point to insist that "there are fundamental doubts about whether the success of an uprising is assured." He ticked off a string of arguments against an uprising and urged that, if possible, the Central Committee resolution of October 10 be reconsidered. Kamenev declared that the experience of trying to organize an uprising confirmed that the conditions for one did not exist. The party's preparations, he urged, served only to cause the government to strengthen its defenses. Echoing Kamenev, Volodarsky made the point that if the Central Committee's resolution had been intended as an order, then it was already unfulfilled. "If the question of a coming out is posed as a question for tomorrow," he went on to affirm, "then we have to acknowledge that we are not ready. I have been making public appeals daily and must report that the masses are puzzled by our appeal."

Lenin nonetheless insisted on a formal endorsement of the Central Committee's October 10 resolution, leaving the precise form and timing of an insurrection up to the Central Committee, and to the party leadership in the Petrograd Soviet and in the All-Russian Executive Committee. Zinoviev countered Lenin's proposal by recommending adoption of a resolution prohibiting the actual organization of an uprising before consultation with the Bolshevik fraction at the Second Congress of Soviets. When the resolutions were voted upon, nineteen participants in the meeting supported Lenin's resolution, with two opposed and four abstentions; the vote on Zinoviev's resolution was six in favor, fifteen opposed, and three abstentions. The latter vote indicates, it would seem, that a fairly large minority of nine of the party leaders present—that is, more than a third of those who took part in the voting—had strong enough reservations about the preparation of an immediate insurrection either to favor consultation or to abstain from taking sides on this question.[35] Beyond this, comparison of these figures with individual speeches at the meeting suggests that even some of those party officials who still harbored reservations about the wisdom of trying to organize an armed uprising before the Congress of Soviets probably voted in favor of Lenin's resolution and against Zinoviev's. For implicit in the comments of several speakers who ostensibly supported Lenin's motion was the assumption that conditions were not yet ripe for a party-organized insurrection, and that the October 10 resolution was an affirmation of intent to overthrow the government at the first suitable opportunity, rather than a policy directive for immediate implementation.

At the October 16 meeting, Miliutin articulated the view just described most openly and directly; while Trotsky did not attend the meeting, he clearly shared this outlook. Historians in the Soviet Union often attribute these attitudes to timidity—or "constitutional illusions," to use Lenin's phrase—and tend to equate them with the positions of Kamenev and Zinoviev. More accurately, however, the position taken by Trotsky and others of like mind seems to have been based on a realistic appraisal of available evidence regarding the prevailing mood and correlation of forces in Petrograd, the provinces, and the front.

In any case, it is important to note that the controversy raging within the Bolshevik leadership over the preparation of an uprising was by no means silenced by this endorsement of the October 10 resolution. At the conclusion of the October 16 meeting, Kamenev, declaring that he could not defend the point of view reflected in the Central Committee's latest decisions and believing that this position would lead to the defeat of the party and the proletariat, submitted his resignation from the Central Committee. At the same time, Kamenev joined Zinoviev in formally demanding the immediate convocation, by telegraph, of a Central Committee plenum. Three other moderates—Nogin, Miliutin, and Rykov—tried unsuccessfully to have *Rabochii put'* publish an appeal, the substance of which has never come to light.[36] Unable to get a hearing in the Bolshevik press, Kamenev aired his arguments against an insurrection in Gorky's paper, *Novaia zhizn'*, on October 18. After the appearance of Kamenev's statement, even Lenin, to judge by his letters, momentarily feared that the opportunity to strike might have been lost. Beside himself with fury, he now declared war on

Kamenev and Zinoviev and launched an effort to have them ousted from the party.[37] At a meeting on October 20, however, the Central Committee stubbornly resisted Lenin's demands, and limited its action to accepting Kamenev's resignation from the party leadership and admonishing Kamenev and Zinoviev not to make public statements of any kind counter to the decisions of the Central Committee.[38]

On October 18, the evening that Kamenev's declaration against an uprising appeared in *Novaia zhizn'*, the intraparty controversy also erupted openly at a gathering of some two hundred Bolshevik activists at Smolny, called expressly to coordinate preparations for the seizure of power. Here the Bolshevik moderates Riazanov and Larin took the floor to attack preparations for an uprising. Also speaking out in this vein was Grigorii Chudnovsky, freshly arrived in the capital from the southwestern front to attend the Congress of Soviets. Drawing on his experience among troops on the southwestern front, where the Bolsheviks did not have a firm foothold, Chudnovky proclaimed with great passion that an insurrection organized by the Bolsheviks was destined for certain defeat.[39]

·13·

THE GARRISON CRISIS AND THE MILITARY REVOLUTIONARY COMMITTEE

Among Bolshevik leaders who shared Lenin's impatience to have done with the Provisional Government, reactions to the obstacles connected with an immediate armed uprising were varied. In the face of continuing concern that the insurrectionary organs, weapons, and trained personnel for an organized insurrection were not yet ready; that seizure of power by the Bolsheviks alone would be opposed by all other major political parties, by the peasants in the provinces and the soldiers at the front, indeed perhaps even by such mass democratic institutions as the soviets and trade unions, as well as by elements within the Bolshevik Party itself; and finally, that even workers and soldiers in Petrograd were unresponsive to calls for a rising before the Congress of Soviets—some Bolshevik officials counseled simply that the start of an insurrection be postponed pending further preparation. As we have seen, this was the response of the Military Organization chiefs, Podvoisky and Nevsky, who consistently viewed the seizure of power in purely military terms.[1]

Another approach which gradually suggested itself to tactically cautious Bolsheviks, often those most active in the soviets or in other local representative institutions and hence particularly attuned to the prevailing mass mood, ran along the following lines: (1) that the soviets (because of their stature in the eyes of workers and soldiers), and not the organs of the party, should be employed for the overthrow of the Provisional Government; (2) that for the broadest support, any attack on the government should be masked as a defensive operation on behalf of the soviets; (3) thus that action should be delayed until a suitable excuse for giving battle presented itself; (4) that to undercut potential resistance and maximize the probability of success, every opportunity should be utilized to subvert the Provisional

Government's power peacefully; and (5) that the formal overthrow of the government should be linked with and legitimized by the decisions of the Second All-Russian Congress of Soviets.[2] While this was, in many respects, an extension of the politics and outlook of the Bolshevik left before October 10, these tactics were now to be pursued much more aggressively. It should be borne in mind as well that most Bolsheviks holding these views either in full or in part were confident that a majority at the coming Congress of Soviets would support a transfer of power to the soviets. Their most influential spokesman was Trotsky. But his outlook was shared by a significant number of other top Bolsheviks, including Stalin.

Framed against this background, the Provisional Government's sudden announcement, in the second week of October, of plans to move the bulk of the Petrograd garrison to the front came as a godsend to the Bolsheviks. It provided a perfect immediate cause around which a decisive struggle with the Kerensky regime could be initiated.

Outwardly, the Russian cabinet's decision regarding disposition of garrison units was tied to German military moves in the Baltic. It will be recalled that on August 20 German forces had occupied the key seaport of Riga; it had seemed that, for the first time in the long war, the enemy might attempt an early advance on Petrograd itself. It should also be remembered that on the eve of the Kornilov affair, Kerensky had used the possibility of a further German advance to justify transfer of sizable numbers of Bolshevized garrison troops to the northern front.

Concern about an enemy attack on Petrograd again mounted sharply in the first week of October when German air and amphibious forces carried out a brilliantly successful sneak attack, capturing the small but strategically important islands of Ösel and Moon, at the entrance to the Gulf of Riga, and Dago, at the mouth of the Gulf of Finland. As a result, the entire Russian Baltic Fleet was driven back into the Finnish Gulf.[3] Appraising the significance of these setbacks, the chief of staff of the Russian army, General Nikolai Dukhonin, declared in the Preparliament that "with the loss of these islands, which for us are keys to the Baltic in the full sense of the term, we are in effect back to the age of Tsar Aleksei Mikhailovich, our outlets to the sea controlled by Germany."[4]

In Petrograd news of these most recent military disasters gave rise to a storm of mutual recriminations. The government, along with liberal and conservative circles, implied that the unruly Baltic sailors were primarily to blame. Even before the German assault was well underway, Kerensky himself had helped to fuel these charges, demanding in a message immediately released to the press that the sailors put an end to "consciously or unconsciously playing into the hands of the enemy." He asserted: "The Kronstadters have already succeeded in seeing to it that in this critical hour, not all of our defenses are in place."[5] After the islands had fallen, Kerensky, at a closed meeting of a Preparliament committee for defense matters, contended that fully adequate military planning for the protection of the islands had come to naught because of the cowardice, lack of discipline, and demoralization of the naval units charged with their defense.[6]

On the other hand, the extreme left spoke up for the sailors, accusing the government and the General Staff of intentionally mismanaging Russia's defenses in order to justify political repression, resurrecting claims first raised against top civil and military authorities after the unexpected Russian retreat from Riga. Such accusations quickly helped intensify popular fears that Kerensky was preparing to surrender Petrograd in order to stifle the revolution. Apprehension in this regard reached fever pitch in the wake of rumors (later substantiated) that the Provisional Government was making preparations for a hasty move to Moscow, and a sensational, widely publicized speech by Mikhail Rodzianko, the well-known, formerly powerful president of the State Duma. Addressing the possibility that the Germans might take Petrograd, Rodzianko declared directly: "Petrograd appears threatened. . . . I say, to hell with Petrograd. . . . People fear our central institutions in Petrograd will be destroyed. To this, let me say that I should be glad if these institutions are destroyed because they have brought Russia nothing but grief."[7]

There is no direct evidence that the Provisional Government ever seriously entertained the idea of surrendering Petrograd to the Germans without a fight. Moreover, Russian military leaders do not appear to have considered an early German attack on Petrograd likely in the fall of 1917.[8] What does seem to be true is that, as in late August, the embattled Kerensky perceived the apparent German threat as an excellent excuse to rid the capital once and for all of the more unruly elements in the garrison.[9]

At this time, the Provisional Government's commissar on the northern front, Woytinsky, was assigned the task of facilitating the removal from the capital of the more unreliable garrison regiments, replacing them with less "corrupt" units from the army in the field.[10] Simultaneously, on October 5, the government directed General Polkovnikov, commander of the Petrograd Military District, to prepare his troops for transfer to the front, and the following day Polkovnikov issued preliminary instructions to key commanders.[11]

According to Woytinsky, Cheremisov himself had little taste for such an operation, feeling that the transfer of troops from Petrograd would only increase problems at the front. This is confirmed by a classified telegram which Cheremisov sent to the War Ministry on October 17, clarifying his attitude toward the receipt of garrison troops: "The initiative for dispatch of garrison troops to the front came from you, not from me. . . . When it became apparent that garrison units . . . were incapable of fighting, I said that from an operational point of view they were of little need to us. . . . We have enough such units as it is. In view of the desire you have expressed to send them to the front, however, I do not reject them, if you consider their movement from Petrograd necessary."[12] Despite his reservations, on October 9 Cheremisov issued a supplementary order, drafted by Woytinsky, endorsing Polkovnikov's directives and justifying them on the grounds that such action was absolutely vital to the defense of the capital from the Germans.

Soldiers in Petrograd reacted to news of these orders with predictable vehemence. In unison, garrison troops proclaimed their lack of confidence in the Provisional Government and demanded the transfer of power to the soviets. As in the aftermath of the Kornilov crisis, all the major garrison regiments that had been reluctant to follow the Bolsheviks during the July uprising now repudiated the Provisional Government and pledged support to the Petrograd Soviet. Moreover, those units of which the government was most confident—for example, cossack forces and front soldiers who had been rushed to Petrograd following the July days—either affirmed their neutrality in the struggle now developing over disposition of the garrison between the Petrograd Soviet and military authorities, or sided openly with the Soviet.

Typical of the avalanche of antigovernment resolutions adopted by garrison units at this time was one passed at a mass protest meeting of soldiers from the Egersky Guards Regiment on October 12. It affirmed:

> The pulling out of the revolutionary garrison from Petrograd is needed only by the privileged bourgeoisie as a means of stifling the revolution, dispersing the Congress of Soviets, and subverting the convocation of the Constituent Assembly. As long as governmental power remains in the hands of obvious counterrevolutionaries, Kornilovites, and semi-Kornilovites, we will carry on a firm struggle against the transfer of the revolutionary garrison from Petrograd, the center of the revolution. . . . We declare to all who listen that, while refusing to leave Petrograd, we will nonetheless heed the voice of the genuine leaders of the workers and poorer peasantry, that is, the Soviet of Workers' and Soldiers' Deputies. We will believe in and follow it because everything else is pure treachery and open mockery of the world revolution.[13]

In the foregoing resolution, the soldiers of the Egersky Regiment underlined their loyalty and support for the Soviet, rather than the Bolsheviks or any other single political party. This attitude, which, as mentioned earlier, had been observed by local Bolshevik leaders, was expressed in many of the political statements adopted by worker, soldier, and sailor organizations at this time. It was vividly reflected, for instance, at a mass meeting of personnel from the Petrograd-based Second Baltic Fleet Detachment on October 19 called in the wake of persistent rumors that the Bolsheviks were organizing an armed uprising to take place the next day.[14] The government commissar in the unit, Krasnovsky, opened the meeting by reading an appeal for patience and order from the day's *Izvestiia*. Subsequently, Avgust

Loos, a military clerk who was not formally affiliated with any political party but whose revolutionary credentials are established by the fact that he was a member of the Tsentrobalt delegation imprisoned following the July uprising, also called on the sailors to refrain from coming out in the near future because "such action before elections to the Constituent Assembly might damage the support which left parties now enjoy among a broad segment of the population."

At this point, a Bolshevik, Nikolai Nevarovsky, took the floor, and, upon identifying himself as a Kronstadt sailor, was greeted by loud applause. Nevarovsky berated Krasnovsky for citing *Izvestiia*, which, he claimed, had outlived its time and did little to defend the interests of the laboring classes; nonetheless Nevarovsky also argued that it was necessary to refrain from any coming out. Next, the chairman of the unit sailor committee, Volodin, one guesses a Bolshevik as well, spoke up to say he had information regarding "a coming-out of thirty thousand workers whose patience with the Provisional Government has reached the limit." Volodin expressed hope that the men of the Second Baltic Fleet Detachment would not confine themselves merely to the passage of resolutions. Yet this is precisely what the sailors did. The meeting ended with the adoption of a formal statement specifically repudiating "separate disorganized armed action," but at the same time declaring the readiness of the sailors to "come out" if such action was specifically sanctioned by the Petrograd Soviet. The resolution concluded: "As ardent enemies of the coalition Provisional Government who believe the policies of this government to be disastrous for democracy . . . we await with great impatience the portentous opening of the Congress of Representatives of the Soviets of Workers' and Soldiers' Deputies, in which we have faith, and which we invite to take power. We propose that it create an organ which will give the people bread and arrange a peace based on the principles proclaimed by the laboring democracy."

The new crisis involving the garrison, which surfaced publicly on Monday, October 9, did not reach its peak until the following week. Throughout this time, the Bolsheviks exploited it to the fullest. In the press, in the Petrograd Soviet, and, most importantly, in factories and barracks, the Bolsheviks trumpeted the slogan, "the All-Russian Congress is in danger," fanning fears of a second Kornilov affair. Thus on October 11 the lead editorial in *Rabochii put'* ridiculed the argument that garrison forces were being ordered out of Petrograd for strategic reasons, contending that ostensibly the offensive of June 18 had been "organized in the name of strategic necessity; yet later leading SRs and Mensheviks had openly acknowledged that the offensive was initiated for political reasons—in order to take the army in hand." The same pattern, *Rabochii put'* implied, had been repeated in August.

> The Kornilov "reforms," capital punishment, and the suppression of army organizations had been justified by the need to raise the fighting capacity

of the army to combat the foreign enemy. Yet later it became clear to everyone that all of Kornilov's strategy had been aimed at fighting the revolution. Before the Kornilov uprising the conspirators demanded the transfer of a whole group of regiments from Petrograd, for strategic necessity, of course. The Bolsheviks had told soldiers, you are being destroyed. But the soldiers still trusted the SR and Menshevik windbags—they left to dig trenches and the revolution nearly fell into the pit being dug for it by Kornilov.

The government attempted to counter these arguments by presenting the dangers of a German attack in ever more alarming terms. Among the most important allies the government could look to in its conflict with the garrison were embittered front soldiers, impatient to move to the rear, and front committees, many of them still in the hands of moderates. Consequently, military authorities attempted to employ pressure from army front committees to force garrison regiments to accept transfer. On October 14 major garrison regiments received urgent telegrams from the headquarters of the Petrograd Military District, endorsed by General Cheremisov, ordering them to select delegates for a conference with front commanders and representatives of front army committees to be held at northern front headquarters in Pskov the next day; the purpose of this meeting was to brief garrison units on the conditions necessitating their withdrawal from the capital and to acquaint them with the attitudes of front army organizations on this question.[15]

During these same days, front pressure on the garrison was exerted through the government and the moderate socialist press, which published numerous resolutions and letters from front committees demanding that garrison regiments "do their revolutionary duty." Thus on October 17 *Golos soldata* printed in full, on its front page, a strongly worded resolution passed by the Executive Committee of the Twelfth Army Soviet of Soldiers' Deputies. The resolution declared that only by "helping to defend the front could garrison regiments save the revolutionary capital" and it concluded with a demand for "submission to revolutionary duty and unqualified sacrifice" so that "brothers in the trenches would not be destroyed." An analogous declaration dispatched by the soldiers' committee of the First Army, which appeared in *Golos soldata* two days later, was even more emphatic; it bitterly attacked soldiers in the rear for having allowed "liberty to deteriorate into anarchy and revolution into pogroms" and expressed full readiness to make garrison units move to the front by force of arms if they were unwilling to do so voluntarily.[16]

In his memoirs, Woytinsky suggests that by this time the gap in outlook between the radicalized, peace-hungry soldiers in the trenches and the more moderate, defensist front committees was so great that perhaps only on the issue of front troops being replaced by soldiers from the rear were the two in agreement.[17] Nonetheless, for the Bolsheviks the apparent resentment of trench soldiers toward troops in the rear which emerged over the issue of transfers was a matter of considerable concern, serving to increase the possibility that, as in July, front units might be mobilized successfully by Kerensky to pacify the capital.

That the policies of Bolshevik leaders in the Petrograd Soviet were fully attuned to this danger is yet another sign of the degree to which the Bolsheviks were sensitive to, and, in their overall behavior, very much influenced by, the prevailing mass mood. On October 15, the Bolshevik leadership in the Petrograd Soviet arranged an early-morning meeting of garrison representatives designated to go to Pskov. The purpose of this gathering was to formulate a common response to the demands of the front committees. In this connection, the representatives readily accepted the argument of the Bolsheviks that inasmuch as the question of garrison transfers was a central political issue, the resolution of which was the prerogative of the Executive Committee of the Petrograd Soviet, the dispatch of representatives to Pskov should be delayed pending its review.

Army committees on the northern front responded to this temporary rebuff with a declaration that only a joint conference of front and garrison representatives, and not the Petrograd Soviet or garrison alone, had the right to decide the legitimacy of transfers. The front declaration demanded that representatives of the garrison present themselves for such a conference on October 17.[18] Meanwhile, the Petrograd Soviet Executive Committee hurriedly considered the question of what to do about the demand for a conference in Pskov; ultimately, it authorized dispatch of a delegation, but drastically altered its character and composition. As provided for by the Executive Committee, the delegation of garrison representatives was to be expanded by the addition of an even larger contingent of soviet deputies who shared the point of view of the Petrograd Soviet in regard to Petrograd's revolutionary defense. A plenary session of the Petrograd Soviet on October 16 endorsed this procedure, stipulating that the delegation was empowered only to gather and exchange information.[19]

Of course the Petrograd Soviet's action effectively destroyed any possibility that the Pskov conference would work to the advantage of the Provisional Government. Convened on the afternoon of October 17, it acted as a sounding board for differing points of view, but nothing more. Cheremisov and his fellow officers, surrounded by battle maps, outlined the military situation on the northern front and in the Baltic. Woytinsky contends that Cheremisov spoke without enthusiasm, conveying the distinct impression that at bottom it made no difference to him whether or not Petrograd regiments moved to the front, and that he did not wish to become involved in the matter. A succession of embittered front representatives described, graphically, the impossible situation of the front soldiers and the latter's resentment of garrison troops, whom they believed to be lounging comfortably in the rear, unwilling to support the common defense effort.

In response, the Petrograd delegation pointed to the purported sacrifices already made by most garrison soldiers in the interests of the revolution and of Russia's defense. To Woytinsky's frustration, the subsequent discussion was concerned as much with the need for transfer of power to the soviets, for peace, and for the long-suffering front-line soldier to return home, as it was with the question of getting new regiments into the trenches. Toward the close of the meeting, the Bolshevik Military Organization leader and chairman of the Military Section of the Petrograd Soviet, Andrei Sadovsky, who had played a prominent role in the writing of "Order Number One" at the time of the February revolution, read a formal statement on behalf of the Petrograd delegation. Composed by Sverdlov, the message voiced the left's apprehension that counterrevolutionary motives were behind efforts to withdraw the garrison. For his part, Woytinsky sought to obtain a pledge from the visitors that they would work to obtain the garrison's voluntary compliance with requests for troop support. Leaning on their limited mandate, the delegates from Petrograd refused to enter into such an agreement and even demurred from endorsing an oral résumé of their discussion.[20]

Actually, mistrust of the Provisional Government's intentions at this time was so widespread that even the moderate socialists were forced to recognize that garrison troops could not be expected to respond to relocation orders not in some way controlled by the Petrograd Soviet. On the morning of October 9, not long after Cheremisov's directive to the garrison became public, the Executive Committee of the Petrograd Soviet considered the question of the capital's military defense and the suspicions of garrison troops in regard to the government's motives; at least by implication, all of the participants in this discussion acknowledged that the fears of the soldiers were justified. The Menshevik Mark Broido put before the deputies a joint Menshevik-SR resolution which, while calling on garrison soldiers to begin preparations for movement to the front, at the same time sought to calm them by providing for the creation of a special committee to evaluate defense needs and to prepare military defense plans that would inspire popular confidence. At bottom, the intent of the resolution was to facilitate cooperation between the Petrograd Soviet and the government in the interest of the war effort.[21]

The Bolsheviks countered this proposal with a significantly more militant one, hastily scratched out by Trotsky, repudiating the Kerensky government as the ruination of the country and proclaiming that Russia's sole hope of salvation lay in immediate peace.[22] The resolution embodying this proposal accused the bourgeoisie, along with Kerensky, of preparing to turn over Petrograd, "the main fortress of the revolution," to the Germans. Affirming that the Petrograd Soviet could in no way take responsibility for the government's military strategy and, in particular, the withdrawal of troops from Petrograd, it insisted that the way to assure survival was to transfer power to the soviets. Like the moderate socialist resolution, the

Bolshevik proposal called on the garrison to come to battle readiness; even now, popular determination to resist the foreign foe was too strong for the Bolsheviks to ignore completely. By implication, however, these preparations were intended as much to defend the revolution from the government and the right as from the Germans. The Bolshevik resolution specifically provided for the creation of a "revolutionary defense committee" (the future Military Revolutionary Committee), the primary purpose of which was to become fully familiar with all information relating to the defense of the capital and to take all possible steps to arm workers in order to "facilitate the revolutionary defense of Petrograd and the safety of the people from the attacks being openly prepared by military and civil Kornilovites." The proposed committee appeared to be modeled after the Committee for Struggle Against the Counterrevolution organized by the Soviet leadership at the time of the Kornilov affair. Yet there was a fundamental difference between the two institutions: while the defense committee established in late August had been formally committed to the protection of the Provisional Government against the onslaught of the counterrevolution, for the committee proposed by the Bolsheviks one of the main enemies was the Provisional Government itself.

The surprising thing about the October 9 vote on the Menshevik-SR and Bolshevik resolutions in the Petrograd Soviet Executive Committee, now commonly assumed to be completely controlled by the Bolsheviks, was that the Menshevik-SR resolution was passed. A narrow majority of deputies present were evidently sympathetic to the moderates' argument that the Bolshevik resolution, by creating an independent military headquarters alongside that of the government, would severely cripple defense efforts. However, both resolutions were subsequently put before an unusually crowded and lively plenary session of the Petrograd Soviet late the same evening (a reporter later commented that the mood of the meeting was reminiscent of the first days of the revolution); here the militant Bolshevik motion clearly struck the more responsive chord, receiving the support of an overwhelming majority of factory and barracks representatives.[23]

Such, in brief, was the original conception of the Military Revolutionary Committee, the institution used by the Bolsheviks in the following days to subvert and overthrow the Provisional Government. Histories of the October revolution written in the Soviet Union in Stalin's time conveyed the impression that the creation of the Military Revolutionary Committee was a direct result of the Bolshevik Central Committee's decision of October 10 to organize an armed uprising, and that from the outset the organization of an insurrection was the committee's primary purpose.[24] Indeed, this view was implicit even in the valuable three-volume collection of documents concerning the Military Revolutionary Committee published by the Soviet Academy of Sciences in the mid-1960s.[25] This interpretation is obviously misleading.[26] At no time during the first half of October was the question of forming a nonparty institution like the Military Revolutionary Committee ever raised in the Central Committee; indeed, the Military Revolutionary Committee was conceived on October 9, that is, the day before the Central Committee's decision regarding preparation of an uprising.

An organizational plan for the Military Revolutionary Committee was considered by leaders of the Military Section of the Petrograd Soviet on October 11. This plan was overwhelmingly endorsed at meetings of the Executive Committee of the Petrograd Soviet on October 12 and the Soldiers' Section on October 13, and it was officially ratified by the full Petrograd Soviet on the night of October 16, at the same session that endorsed the Executive Committee's plans for the Pskov conference. As the organizational plan for the Military Revolutionary Committee emerged on October 16, it provided for the creation of a committee to determine the minimum military force required in Petrograd itself (and hence not available for transfer), to make a precise accounting of all garrison personnel and reserves of provisions and weapons, and to formulate a working plan for the defense of the capital. The enabling act which set up the Military Revolutionary Committee also provided for the creation of a "garrison conference," primarily an assembly of representatives from all units of the garrison which would meet on a regular basis to facilitate communications between the Military Revolutionary Committee and the garrison, and among the individual regiments themselves.[27]

It is worthy of note that this plan was significantly less provocative than the proposal that had been first rejected by the Executive Committee and later adopted by the full Petrograd Soviet on October 9; the plan adopted on October 16 said nothing about arming workers or about defense against internal, as well as external, threats to the revolution. To be sure, this was in part the result of practical parliamentary considerations; still, there is no reason to doubt that, initially, even most Bolsheviks viewed the new committee's chief purpose as the prevention of government attempts to ship the Bolshevized Petrograd garrison to the front and, in general, the defense of the left from attack, rather than the overthrow of the government. As we have seen, during these days, Lenin and other Bolshevik militants looked not to the Petrograd Soviet, but to the Bolshevik Military Organization and the Northern Region Congress of Soviets to organize an insurrection. Not until after the Northern Congress had ended (at the time of the October 15 and 16 party strategy sessions when the crucial importance of tying any moves against the government prior to the Congress of Soviets to the defense of the soviets and the congress was perceived) did party leaders begin to look at the Military Revolutionary Committee as something more than an organ of mutual self-defense. Relevant in this respect is the fact that at the October 15 Petersburg Committee meeting, local party leaders were uncertain of how the Military Revolutionary Committee just then taking shape related to their own planning for an insurrection; Latsis merely took note of the committee's creation and pointed to the necessity of determining an official attitude toward it. The Petersburg Committee considered simply dispatching representatives to the Military Revolutionary Committee, but concluded by agreeing to seek a clarification of the latter's status from the Central Committee before doing so.[28]

The Central Committee, at its meeting on October 16, after reconfirming the October 10 decision, selected a "Military-Revolutionary Center" composed of Sverdlov, Stalin, Bubnov, Uritsky, and Dzerzhinsky. It then specified that this center was to "become part of the Soviet Revolutionary Committee," thereby suggesting for the first time the possibility that the Military Revolutionary Committee might become the directing body for the seizure of power.[29] Not until October 20, however, did the Military Revolutionary Committee hold an organizational meeting; at this time it selected a five-man leadership bureau composed of three Bolsheviks (Antonov, Podvoisky, and Sadovsky) and two Left SRs (Lazimir and Sukharkov). Before this, it had been conceivable that the Mensheviks and SRs might be prominently represented in the committee; hence it was only after the actual composition and leadership of the Military Revolutionary Committee became clear that the Bolshevik strategists could fully relate it to their own planning with any degree of confidence.

Significantly, between October 9 and 22 the formation and initial activities of the Military Revolutionary Committee, which were major news topics in all other newspapers including *Rabochii put'*, were virtually ignored in *Soldat*, reflecting the fact that the leadership of the Military Organization was still jealously guarding its primacy in matters relating to the garrison. On October 19 or 20, the Military Organization sent a memorandum to the Central Committee (its text has not been published) evidently insisting on the critical importance of leaving the direction of an armed uprising in the hands of the Military Organization rather than regular party organs or the Petrograd Soviet.[30] On October 20, however, most likely after the first organizational session of the Military Revolutionary Committee, the Central Committee rejected the Military Organization's arguments, asserting that "all Bolshevik organizations can become part of the revolutionary center organized by the [Petrograd] Soviet and discuss within the Bolshevik fraction all questions which concern them."[31]

It is important to note that by this time Lenin had also come to see the potential importance of the Military Revolutionary Committee as an ostensibly nonparty insurrectionary organ, although, in contrast to Trotsky and many other top party strategists, he remained absolutely adamant on the need to seize power by means of an armed uprising and, equally important, to do so before the Second Congress of Soviets, which on October 18 had been rescheduled to open on October 25. Late one evening, probably between October 20 and 23,[32] at Lenin's insistence, the chiefs of the Military Organization, Podvoisky and Nevsky, along with Antonov (as head of the

Executive Committee created by the Northern Region Congress of Soviets) were summoned from Smolny to a small apartment in the Vyborg District for an urgent consultation. To judge by the recollections of this meeting by Podvoisky, Nevsky, and Antonov, at this point the Military Organization leadership, like Lenin, still tended to envision the seizure of power primarily in military terms, that is, as a properly organized armed uprising against the existing government. Podvoisky attempted to obtain Lenin's endorsement of the Military Organization's primacy in preparations for the overthrow of the Provisional Government—but to no avail. Rather, echoing the earlier decision of the Central Committee, Lenin insisted not only that the Military Organization work through the Military Revolutionary Committee, but that it not attempt to dictate the latter's policies, that the membership of the Military Revolutionary Committee be made as broad as possible, and that individual initiatives be encouraged, as long as they were consistent with the party's objectives.[33]

According to Nevsky, Lenin's chief purpose in calling this meeting was to "eradicate the last vestiges of stubbornness" within the Military Organization in regard to an uprising.[34] For, even now, Military Organization leaders were divided and, on the whole, pessimistic about the wisdom of initiating an insurrection without significant further preparation. At this late-night confrontation with Lenin, Antonov reported on the revolutionary situation in Finland, observing that the artillerists in Sveaborg were still under the influence of Mensheviks and SRs, and that the political attitudes of Kuban Cossacks stationed in Finland were cause for concern. In regard to the assistance that the Bolsheviks could expect from revolutionary elements in the Baltic region, Antonov expressed certainty that the fleet would respond positively to a call for an insurrection. He minimized the significance of the actual immediate military support that could be counted upon from the sailors, however, warning that "the depth of the channels would be prohibitive, that sailors on the more radical big ships would be fearful of submarines and cruisers, and, finally, that the sailors would be unwilling to expose the front." To this Lenin retorted, "The sailors must understand that the revolution is in greater danger in Petrograd than on the Baltic." Responded Antonov: "They don't understand. The most I can guarantee are two or three gunboats to be brought up the Neva and a defensive detachment of three thousand or so sailors and workers from Vyborg." "Not enough," growled Lenin.[35]

When it was their turn to report, both Nevsky and Podvoisky argued for a delay of ten to fifteen days in the start of an uprising. Nevsky reemphasized the difficulty of moving radicalized elements of the fleet to the capital in time to be of any use, while Podvoisky pleaded for further time to coordinate preparations for an insurrection at the front and in provincial garrisons. As far as Podvoisky was concerned, time was on the Bolsheviks' side, and the danger lay in premature action.

To all these reservations Lenin turned a deaf ear; Podvoisky remembered that he became "restless and impatient" at the very mention of delay. "Time is on the side of the government," not the Bolsheviks, Lenin argued. Waiting would "only give the government more time to destroy the Bolsheviks with loyal troops brought in from the front."[36] Over and over Lenin reiterated the absolute necessity of overthrowing the Provisional Government before the Congress of Soviets so that "the congress, irrespective of its composition, would be confronted with a situation in which the seizure of power by the workers is an actual fact."[37] Antonov recalled that he and Nevsky were greatly influenced by Lenin's arguments, but that Podvoisky remained skeptical. At any rate, their discussion ended with the Military Organization leaders agreeing to work within the Military Revolutionary Committee and, in general, to intensify their preparation to maximum degree.[38]

Meanwhile, both the Military Revolutionary Committee and the garrison conference, which had been approved formally by the Petrograd Soviet on October 16, had begun to function. The garrison conference was the first of the two to start operations, representatives of most major military units in Petrograd and its suburbs responding positively to requests from the Military Section of the Petrograd Soviet to send delegates to Smolny for the conference's first session on October 18. The main purpose of this initial gathering was to obtain a clearer sense of the extent to which individual units would go in supporting the Petrograd Soviet and, in particular, in opposing the government on the issue of withdrawing the bulk of the garrison from the capital. Each of the assembled representatives characterized the political position of his unit and, specifically, its attitude toward taking arms against the Provisional Government. From the government's point of view, the results of this informal sounding, capturing the leftward swing among the soldiers caused by the threat of shipment to the front, were thoroughly disquieting. All but three of the eighteen representatives whose reports were recorded proclaimed lack of confidence in the Provisional Government and firm support for transfer of power to the soviets. At the same time, these reports were not wholly reassuring to the Bolsheviks. Roughly half the spokesmen affirming support for a soviet government were noncommittal in regard to armed action, while the remainder either directly or implicitly made it clear that they would countenance a "coming-out" only if it were organized by the Petrograd Soviet or, in one case, the All-Russian Congress of Soviets. Said the representative of the Egersky Guards Regiment, "We would support an uprising only in response to an order from the Petrograd Soviet; but [in such a case] we would take action in an organized way and would demand the immediate overthrow of the government and transfer of power to the soviets."[39]

In the wake of this meeting, Mensheviks and SRs in the Central Executive Committee were fully alert to the danger that the Bolsheviks might successfully exploit the crisis over the garrison to mobilize soldiers for an insurrection. Seeking to dissuade the troops from such a course, they arranged an independent gathering of garrison representatives for the following day. In addition to spokesmen for Petrograd-based units, they invited to this meeting moderately inclined military personnel supposedly representing army committees from the front. Yet despite such maneuvering, this gathering proved no less alarming to government supporters than the preceding one.

Early in the session, Dan appealed to the soldiers to devote their energies to preparations for the Constituent Assembly and to organize for the struggle against "the Germans, the counterrevolution, and insurrection of any kind." But, as it happened, the audience was distinctly more receptive to Trotsky's argument that the most effective way of supporting the Constituent Assembly was to bring about transfer of power to the soviets; the soviets would then insure that the broad masses of soldiers, rather than the more conciliatory army committees, would be strongly represented in the Constituent Assembly. A succession of garrison representatives jumped up to affirm faith in the Petrograd Soviet and willingness to act in its behalf. Indeed, even the supposedly loyalist visitors from the front combined expressions of opposition to an armed uprising in the prevailing circumstances with enthusiastic declarations of support for transfer of power to the soviets, an immediate armistice, and land for the peasants. The meeting's sponsors were dealt a further blow when a majority agreed not to vote on any formal resolutions since they had been called together by the Central Executive Committee without approval from the Petrograd Soviet.[40]

The Military Revolutionary Committee took concrete shape between October 16 and 21. Included among its members, which until the overthrow of the Provisional Government probably numbered no more than a few dozen, were Bolsheviks, Left SRs, and a few anarchists (the Mensheviks had completely washed their hands of the committee at the start), as well as delegates from the Petrograd Soviet; the Soviet of Peasants' Deputies; Tsentrobalt; the Regional Executive Committee of the Army, Fleet, and Workers in Finland; factory-shop committees; and trade unions. As noted earlier, at the outset a Military Revolutionary Committee bureau made up of Bolsheviks and Left SRs was formed to help direct the committee's day-to-day work. With Bolshevik approval, the formal chairman of the bureau and of the Military Revolutionary Committee as a whole was a Left SR, Pavel Lazimir (a senior military medical aide and chairman of the Soldiers' Section of the Petrograd Soviet); this furthered the committee's ostensibly nonparty character. However, during the most critical days of the October revolution in Petrograd, that is, between October 21 and 25, Podvoisky, Antonov-Ovseenko, and Trotsky acted in the capacity of Military Revolutionary Committee chairman almost as often as did Lazimir.

Members of the Military Revolutionary Committee. Bottom row, left to right: F. E. Dzerzhinsky, V. A. Antonov-Ovseenko, A. D. Sadovsky, M. S. Uritsky. In the center: N. I. Podvoisky. First group photograph, left to right: A. A. Ioffe, K. A. Mekhonoshin, V. I. Nevsky. Second group photograph, left to right: L. D. Trotsky, Ia. M. Sverdlov, I. S. Unshlikht, S. I. Gusev, S. S. Pestkovsky, Iu. M. Kotsiubinsky. Third group photograph, left to right: N. A. Skrypnik, M. M. Lashevich, G. I. Chudnovsky, K. S. Eremeev, P. E. Dybenko, V. M. Molotov, G. I. Boky, F. F. Raskolnikov, B. A. Breslav, N. V. Krylenko.

From its inception, the Military Revolutionary Committee was housed in a few rooms, always crowded and bustling, on the third floor of Smolny; here leftist leaders in constantly changing numbers discussed late-breaking developments. The committee as a whole met rarely, and at the most critical moments the committee's tactics were evidently determined by whichever members happened to be on the scene, acting in accordance with their varying perceptions of the prevailing situation and their views on the development of the revolution in general.[41]

In part because of the great preponderance of Bolsheviks in the Military Revolutionary Committee, Western historians have tended to view the organ as merely a front organization closely controlled by the Bolshevik Central Committee or the Military Organization.[42] Yet such an assessment is inaccurate. Bolsheviks played the leading role within the committee; however, they were not its only active members, and even the Bolshevik participants were by no means united in their conception of the committee's tasks. Further, the published record of the Central Committee's activities during these days reveals that at its meetings, scant attention was paid to the operations of the Military Revolutionary Committee; the Central Committee now devoted most of its time to internal party matters such as the appropriate action to be taken against Kamenev and Zinoviev and the formulation of positions for the coming Congress of Soviets. For its part, at least until the culmination of the seizure of power, the leadership of the Military Organization abided by the Central Committee's ruling of October 20 and worked within the Military Revolutionary Committee's outwardly nonparty institutional framework.

At its first organizational meeting on October 20, the Military Revolutionary Committee seems to have been concerned above all with strengthening the defenses of the Petrograd Soviet against attack and further solidifying its status among units of the garrison. Members of the committee were particularly uneasy at this point about possible trouble on Sunday, October 22. That date had been formally designated by the Petrograd Soviet leadership as "Petrograd Soviet Day," a time for concerts and speech-making, intended originally to raise funds for the Soviet and, more recently, as yet another opportunity to gauge mass support for the Petrograd Soviet's radical political program. However, October 22 also happened to be the 105th anniversary of Moscow's liberation from Napoleon; in celebration of that event the Soviet of the Union of Cossack Military Forces announced plans for a midday religious procession. Leftist leaders were fearful, with apparent justification, that in the inflamed atmosphere, the cossack march might be utilized by the extreme right to provoke an armed clash.[43] As it turned out, at the eleventh hour the cossacks canceled their procession. But on October 20, one of the Military Revolutionary Committee's first actions was to dispatch representatives to key combat units and weapons depots as a precaution against possible counterrevolutionary moves.[44]

Before adjourning on October 20, the Military Revolutionary Committee scheduled another session of the garrison conference for the following morning; at this gathering and at others on October 22 and 23 firm links were forged between the newly created Military Revolutionary Committee and individual garrison units. The October 21 garrison conference session opened with a rousing speech by Trotsky, who, in an evident reference to the cossack religious march, warned of "approaching threatening events" and appealed to workers and soldiers to rally around the Petrograd Soviet, to support the Military Revolutionary Committee, and to aid the soviets in the struggle for power. An observer for the Menshevik-SR organ, *Golos soldata*, captured the audience's response:

> After Trotsky's speech, a whole series of people spoke out in regard to the necessity of immediately transferring power to the soviets; moreover, the auditorium became so electrified that when the soldier Goldberg appeared on the tribune to say that the subject under discussion was not fully clear to the audience, not only did the assembly break out in shouts of "Away!" and "Go to hell!"; it completely prevented the speaker from explaining what he had in mind.
>
> The representative of the Fourth Don Cossack Regiment informed the assembly that his regimental committee had decided against participation in the next day's religious procession.
>
> The representative of the Fourteenth Don Cossack Regiment caused a sensation when he declared that his regiment not only would not support counterrevolutionary moves, irrespective of whence they came, but would fight the counterrevolution with all its strength. "In this sense," [he said,] "I shake hands with my comrade cossack from the Fourth Don Cossack Regiment." (At this the orator bent down and shook hands with the cossack from the Fourth Regiment.) And, in response, the assembly exploded in a roar of enthusiastic approval and thunderous applause which did not die down for a long time.

The gathering concluded with the passage of resolutions drafted by Trotsky relating to the Military Revolutionary Committee, Petrograd Soviet day, and the tasks of the All-Russian Congress of Soviets. Taken together, these resolutions illustrate both the increased aggressiveness of the Petrograd garrison under the threat of shipment to the front and the committee's strategy of utilizing the defense of the revolution to mobilize support for the Petrograd Soviet and the seizure of power. The resolution on the Military Revolutionary Committee passed by the garrison conference on October 21 hailed the committee's birth and promised it full support "in all steps aimed at tying the front more closely to the rear in the interests of the revolution." The resolution dealing with Petrograd Soviet day warned "brother cossacks" against being victimized by the enemies of the revolution and invited them to participate instead in the rallies planned by the left; at the same time it warned that any attempts by Kornilovites and the bourgeoisie to inject confusion and dissension into the ranks of the revolution would be met with a merciless rebuff. Finally, in its resolution on the Congress of Soviets, the garrison conference endorsed all the political decisions of the Petrograd Soviet, called on the coming All-Russian Congress to "take power in its hands and provide peace, land, and bread for the people," and pledged all the resources at the command of the garrison to the fulfillment of these demands.[45]

Buttressed by these assurances of support, the Military Revolutionary Committee now embarked on a decisive confrontation with the government over ultimate control of the garrison. First, it began dispatching its own commissars to replace those supporting the government in all units of the garrison and in all weapons and munitions depots. Then, late on the night of October 21, it sent a group of representatives (including Lazimir, Sadovsky, and Mekhonoshin) to General Staff headquarters to formally assert the committee's claim to prior command authority over garrison units. Arriving around midnight, the group was ushered into General Polkovnikov's office. Sadovsky came straight to the point. "Henceforth," he proclaimed, "orders not signed by us are invalid."[46] Polkovnikov retorted that the garrison was his responsibility. Referring to the commissar from the Central Executive Committee already working with him, he added: "We know only the [commissar of the] Central Executive Committee. We won't recognize your commissars. If they break the law we will arrest them."[47] At this, the group returned to Smolny.

Returning to Military Revolutionary Committee headquarters, Lazimir, Sadovsky, and Mekhonoshin rounded up Antonov, Sverdlov, and Trotsky; together they mapped out plans to exploit the Petrograd Military District's uncooperative stance.[48] Most importantly, Trotsky drafted for endorsement by the garrison conference and circulation to all units later in the day what was to become one of the seminal documents of the October revolution in Petrograd—a formal declaration that amounted to a categorical repudiation of the Provisional Government's authority over garrison troops. Wrote Trotsky:

> At a meeting on October 21 the revolutionary garrison united around the Military Revolutionary Committee as its directing organ. Despite this, on the night of October 21–22 the headquarters of the Petrograd Military District refused to recognize the Military Revolutionary Committee, rejecting work in association with the representatives of the Soldiers' Section of the [Petrograd] Soviet. In so doing, the headquarters breaks with the revolutionary garrison and the Petrograd Soviet of Workers' and Soldiers' Deputies. . . . The headquarters becomes a direct weapon of counterrevolutionary forces. . . . The protection of revolutionary order from counterrevolutionary attacks rests with the revolutionary soldiers directed by the Military Revolutionary Committee. No directives to the garrison not signed by the Military Revolutionary Committee should be considered

valid. . . . The revolution is in danger. Long live the revolutionary garrison.[49]

A few years later Trotsky mused aloud about whether Lazimir, in cooperating in the work of the Military Revolutionary Committee, recognized that he was taking part in a conscious plan to overthrow the Provisional Government or whether his outlook simply reflected the "formless revolutionary spirit of the Left SRs."[50] Trotsky concluded the latter to be the case, and this may indeed be true. There is little doubt, however, that in the minds of Sadovsky, Mekhonoshin, Sverdlov, and, of course, Trotsky himself, the politics of the Military Revolutionary Committee were part of a conscious, gradual subversion of the government.

Largely because of current political considerations, most historians in the Soviet Union consider the October insurrection to have begun some time on October 24. Yet this interpretation ignores the crucial significance of the steps taken by the Military Revolutionary Committee on October 21–22. To cite the knowledgeable contemporary Czech specialist on the Russian revolution Michael Reiman: "Already on October 21 and 22 the Military Revolutionary Committee, in effect, took upon itself authority over the garrison. Its actions, from both a practical and a juridical standpoint, would be considered by any nation a clear case of mutiny and insurrection."[51]

On Sunday, October 22—Petrograd Soviet Day—the Bolsheviks' most popular orators, Trotsky, Volodarsky, Lashevich, Kollontai, Raskolnikov, and Krylenko among them, took to the stump at mass political rallies in factories and public meeting-halls throughout the capital. Even Kamenev participated prominently in the speech-making; ignoring the Central Committee's specific ban on speaking out publicly counter to its decisions, he made use of this opportunity to ridicule once again the possibility of the party's involvement in an insurrection before the Congress of Soviets.[52]

Typical of the highly successful rallies staged on behalf of the Petrograd Soviet on October 22 was one held in the House of the People, on the right bank of the Neva. Well before the start of the program a massive crowd of factory workers, soldiers, and a smattering of lower-middle-class townspeople filled the colossal opera house, primarily to see and hear the legendary Trotsky, the featured speaker. Trotsky's address contained little not already repeated by the Bolsheviks ad infinitum. Warning that Petrograd was on the verge of being surrendered to the Germans, he proclaimed that the workers and soldiers themselves would take responsibility for defending the approaches to the capital. The revolutionary fire kindled by the new government to be selected by the Congress of Soviets, he went on to say, would be so intense as to engulf not only all Russia, but the entire world. And having taken power, the Soviet would bring immediate peace; it would also eliminate private property, confiscating grain hidden away by large landowners and excess money, clothing, and footwear in the hands of the bourgeoisie, and distributing land to the peasants as well as money, bread, clothing, and footwear to all those in need.[53]

Perhaps because of the apparent imminence of these shattering developments, or as a result of Trotsky's oratorical skill, or a combination of both, the audience was unusually stimulated by his words. A reporter for *Rech'* who was on the scene observed with consternation that after Trotsky asked for a pledge of support to the Soviet when it moved from words to deeds, the huge audience threw up its hands and chanted, "We swear it!" Another of Trotsky's listeners was Sukhanov, who subsequently recorded:

> All around me was a mood bordering on ecstasy. It seemed as if the crowd, spontaneously and of its own accord, would break into some religious hymn. Trotsky formulated a brief and general resolution. . . .
> Who was for? The crowd of thousands, as one man, raised its hands. . . .
> Trotsky went on speaking. The innumerable crowd continued to hold up its hands. Trotsky rapped out the words: "Let this vote of yours be your vow—with all your strength and at any sacrifice to support the Soviet that has taken on itself the glorious burden of bringing the victory of the revolution to a conclusion and of giving land, bread, and peace!"
> The vast crowd was holding up its hands. It agreed. It vowed. . . .[54]

While these rallies were in progress, military officials launched efforts to deal with the Military Revolutionary Committee. In the early-morning hours, General Polkovnikov invited representatives of garrison regimental and brigade committees, as well as officials of the All-Russian Executive Committees and the Petrograd Soviet, to an immediate meeting at General Staff headquarters, obviously with an eye toward applying pressure on the Military Revolutionary Committee to back off from its insistence on veto power over the regular military command. Even before Polkovnikov's meeting got underway, however, a hastily convened session of the garrison conference at Smolny voted formally to endorse Trotsky's declaration of the preceding night. Shortly afterward, an invitation was received from Polkovnikov to send representatives to the meeting at General Staff headquarters. In response, a garrison conference delegation headed by Dashkevich put in a brief appearance at the meeting. On the garrison conference's behalf, Dashkevich at once reasserted that henceforth all the military command's directives had to be countersigned by the Military Revolutionary Committee. The delegation then departed.[55] Indicative of the weakness of the Petrograd Military District in the prevailing situation was the fact that Polkovnikov reacted to this *démarche* with a fresh effort to settle the conflict over authority in the garrison peacefully; he now issued an invitation to the Military Revolutionary Committee to meet with him the next day for the purpose of discussing Soviet representation at headquarters.

On and off through the day and night of October 22–23 Kerensky conferred with his chief advisers in regard to the developing crisis. From all parts of the city came reports of the massive public support for the left exhibited at the huge rallies organized by the Bolsheviks, this on top of news of the Military Revolutionary Committee's direct challenge to the government's authority in the garrison. In the early evening the Petrograd Military District chief of staff, General Iakov Bagratuni, requested army headquarters on the northern front to prepare an infantry brigade, a cavalry regiment, and an artillery battery for rapid shipment to the capital. Woytinsky responded from the northern front that readying these detachments in advance, without knowledge of the purposes for which they were to be used, was out of the question, one must suppose because the soldiers would become suspicious and resist such a step.[56] Somewhat later, Kerensky dispatched an urgent appeal to General Cheremisov to come to Petrograd, presumably to discuss the problem of getting loyalist troops to the capital in a hurry. Moreover, to his fellow ministers Kerensky proposed dispatching available forces to arrest members of the Military Revolutionary Committee and to liquidate the committee without further delay, but he was temporarily dissuaded from this course by Polkovnikov. The Petrograd Military District commander expressed the hope that in discussions the next day the Military Revolutionary Committee might be prevailed upon to retract its declaration. The prime minister thereupon ordered General Bagratuni to present the Soviet with a firm ultimatum: either it rescind the October 22 declaration immediately or military authorities would take whatever steps were necessary to restore law and order.[57]

Meanwhile, the process begun by the Military Revolutionary Committee on October 21 of substituting commissars of its own choosing for those of the government throughout the city was intensified. Most of the new commissars were well-known members of the Bolshevik Military Organization only recently released from jail; almost everywhere they were greeted with enthusiasm. As the appointment of the new commissars neared completion on October 23, the Military Revolutionary Committee issued an order endowing its commissars with unlimited veto power over military orders, thus to some extent making control over operations at district headquarters superfluous. This order, immediately published in the leftist press and circulated throughout the capital, informed the population that in the interest of defense of the revolution and its achievements from encroachments on the part of the counterrevolution, Military Revolutionary Committee commissars had been appointed to military units and especially important points in the capital and its suburbs, and stipulated that orders and directives sent to these points were to be fulfilled only if confirmed by them.[58]

The continuing drastic decline of the Provisional Government's military position in the capital was also reflected on October 23 in the Military Revolutionary Committee's winning of the strategically crucial Peter and Paul Fortress and the adjoining Kronwerk Arsenal, a central storehouse of arms and munitions. One of the Military Revolutionary Committee's few setbacks in its campaign for authority over the Petrograd garrison had occurred at the fortress on October 19, when committees representing units garrisoned there had passed a resolution opposing a "coming-out." When the Military Revolutionary Committee sent a commissar to the fortress three days later, it was feared that he might be arrested by hostile soldiers.[59] Particularly worrisome in connection with the fortress was the attitude toward the left of several thousand cyclists from the front based there since the July days.

The Military Revolutionary Committee, with Trotsky, Podvoisky, Antonov, and Lashevich, among others, in attendance, had considered the problem of the Peter and Paul Fortress initially on October 22. Antonov subsequently recalled that at this discussion he strongly urged sending some Bolshevized troops from the Pavlovsky Regiment to capture the old fortress; however, Trotsky, still concerned with appearances, persuaded the committee to make an attempt to take the fortress from within. "It cannot be that the troops there would not be sympathetic to us," Trotsky reportedly declared.[60]

In an effort to take the fortress by persuasion, the Military Revolutionary Committee arranged a mass meeting with the cyclists and all other soldiers to begin at midday, October 23, on the fortress's main square.[61] Lashevich recalls that arriving for this meeting, he found a host of right SR and Menshevik luminaries, as well as the fort commander, on hand to contest the Bolsheviks for the allegiance of the troops. After the meeting had been underway for several hours, with Lashevich and Chudnovsky leading the fight for the Military Revolutionary Committee, Trotsky arrived to test his persuasive powers on the soldiers. Wrote Lashevich later: "During Chudnovsky's speech, there was an abrupt, deafening roar of hurrahs and applause. Chudnovsky peered down from the tribune trying to catch the cause of the commotion. Suddenly his face lit up with a pleased smile. 'I yield my place to Comrade Trotsky,' he loudly proclaimed. Trotsky mounted the tribune. . . . Finally it became still, and there followed not so much a speech as an inspirational song."[62]

The mass meeting on the fortress square dragged on long after Trotsky had finished speaking; when it grew dark the soldiers moved outside the fortress to the nearby Cirque Moderne. In the end, most of the soldiers voted to support transfer of power to the soviets and to obey the directives of the Military Revolutionary Committee. As Lashevich remembered: "At 8:00 P.M., in an atmosphere of extreme tension, the question was put to a vote. . . . All those who supported the Military Revolutionary Committee moved to the left, those against to the right. With cries of hurrah, an overwhelming majority rushed to the left. Remaining in opposition to the Military Revolutionary Committee was a small group of officers and intellectuals from among the cyclists."[63]

Control of the Peter and Paul Fortress, whose cannon overlooked the Winter Palace, was a victory of immense psychological and strategic importance. Moreover, with the securing of the Kronwerk Arsenal, virtually all major weapons stores in the capital were at the disposal of the Military Revolutionary Committee, which now funneled massive stocks of arms and ammunition to its supporters. Yet counterbalancing these unexpectedly easy victories was the fact that the Left SRs continued stubbornly to resist all moves to generate the support of mass organizations for the overthrow of the government before the Congress of Soviets.[64] In addition, late reports on political attitudes at the front were highly contradictory; while a flood of telegrams suggested that the mood of the average front soldier was not much different from that of his garrison counterpart, many front delegates arriving in the capital for the Congress of Soviets gave the impression that if an insurrection were to break out in the capital before the congress, many large front-line units would respond to an appeal for help from the Central Executive Committee. Actually, Bolshevik strategists in Petrograd were still not confident of the degree to which they could count on workers and soldiers in the capital to support immediate direct military action against the government. Nor could they ignore the possibility that an independent, ultramilitary course would be resisted by provincial party officials, strongly represented in the Bolshevik congress fraction. Resistance of this sort had already occurred in early summer, when the Bolshevik fraction at the First All-Russian Congress of Soviets helped pressure the Central Committee into aborting the armed demonstration planned for June 10;[65] at the time of the Sixth Congress, when delegates from outside the capital heaped criticism on the Central Committee for its behavior in connection with the July uprising; and, more recently, in the aftermath of the Democratic State Conference, when the Bolshevik conference fraction reversed the Central Committee's narrow decision to boycott the Preparliament.

On the other hand, there was every hope that if the party waited for the government to attack, whether this occurred before the opening of the congress or after the congress' proclamation of a soviet government, it would be able to count on the support of the Left SRs, the soldiers at the front and rear, a united Bolshevik Party, and a broad front of mass organizations, from the Petrograd Soviet to the factory-shop committees. Blame for whatever bloodshed ensued would then fall on the Kerensky regime, and the prospects for retention of power by the left would be increased immeasurably. Such a course might well lead to the creation of a socialist coalition government, including moderates, rather than a government of the extreme left alone. It appears that Lenin was one of the very few top Bolshevik leaders to whom the risks of an independent, ultraradical course were outweighed by impatience to create an exclusively leftist regime at once.

Hence, despite its successes, no doubt for the preceding reasons and others as well, the Military Revolutionary Committee did not cross the Rubicon between moves that could be justified as defensive and steps which would appear to have usurped the prerogatives of the congress. At a plenary meeting of the Petrograd Soviet the night of October 23, Antonov-Ovseenko, in a major report on the activities of the Military Revolutionary Committee, carefully described and justified each of the committee's early moves as a defense of the revolution, the Congress of Soviets, and the Constituent Assembly. Following his address, an overwhelming number of deputies supported a Bolshevik-sponsored resolution endorsing the measures taken by the Military Revolutionary Committee and whatever steps of a similar character the developing situation might require. The phrasing of the resolution captures the spirit of the tactics still pursued by the left: "The Petrograd Soviet considers that due to the energetic work of the Military Revolutionary Committee, the ties of the Petrograd Soviet to the revolutionary garrison are strengthened, and expresses confidence that only continuation of efforts in the same direction will insure the possibility of free and unimpeded work by the All-Russian Congress of Soviets now opening. . . ."[66]

The continuing tactical caution of the Military Revolutionary Committee was demonstrated even more strikingly later the same night, when the committee suddenly announced acceptance of the Petrograd Military District's ultimatum to rescind its declaration of October 22.[67] Information as to how this came about is fragmentary. Apparently, the Menshevik moderates Gots and Bogdanov personally intervened in the committee's deliberations in an attempt to persuade committee members to withdraw their insistence on absolute control over the military command. Gots and Bogdanov must have been dissatisfied with the initial response to this appeal, because subsequently they issued an announcement that the Central Executive Committee was breaking relations with the Military Revolutionary Committee and departing from Smolny.[68] The only published memoir account of this meeting is by Antonov; while obviously confused in some details, his recollection suggests that after Gots and Bogdanov left the meeting, the Military Revolutionary Committee did, in fact, rescind its declaration at the firm insistence of the Left SRs (who evidently threatened to withdraw from the committee if it did not) and Bolshevik moderates, led by Riazanov.[69]

If caution remained the watchword at Smolny, such was not the case in the Winter Palace, where Kerensky had by now decided that direct action to suppress the left could be delayed no longer. Receiving word of the Military Revolutionary Committee's apparent readiness to reach agreement with the Petrograd Military District, he dismissed the announcement as a tactic to delay temporarily a head-on military clash with the government, as indeed it was. Obviously underestimating the degree to which potential military support for the government in the capital had disintegrated, and, at any rate, counting on rapid reinforcements from the front, Kerensky announced his intention of arresting at once the entire membership of the Military Revolutionary Committee. But, as on the previous night, cooler heads prevailed upon Kerensky not to attempt quite so drastic a step. Rather, the cabinet agreed to initiate formal criminal proceedings against members of the Military Revolutionary Committee for circulating appeals for civil disobedience and activity against the lawful government. More immediately, they resolved to return to jail those Bolsheviks accused of participation in the July uprising who, while free on bail, had conducted antigovernment agitation of any kind; implementation of this plan would have rounded up many of the left's top leaders, among them Trotsky. The cabinet also ordered the shutdown of *Rabochii put'* and *Soldat*, and, evidently as a demonstration of impartiality, the extreme right papers, *Zhivoe slovo* and *Novaia Rus'*, were decreed closed as well. The editors of these papers, along with the authors of articles calling for insurrection, were to be prosecuted on criminal charges.[70]

The headquarters of the Petrograd Military District was now instructed to take all measures required to implement these objectives; General Bagratuni issued orders to cadets from the Pavlov, Vladimir, and Konstantinov military schools in Petrograd and the officers' training schools in Peterhof and Gatchina, a battery of horse artillery from Pavlovsk, a rifle regiment of war-wounded from Tsarskoe Selo, and the First Petrograd Women's Shock Battalion from Levashova to report for duty on the Palace Square.[71]

Anticipating a negative reaction to these measures from democratic circles, Kerensky accepted the recommendations of his colleagues that he appear personally to justify and clarify them in the Preparliament the next day. But the Provisional Government's direct attack on the extreme left did not wait. Before daybreak on October 24 a detachment of cadets and militiamen raided the Trud printing press, publishers of *Rabochii put'*, and officially shut it down. Several thousand fresh copies of the day's *Rabochii put'* were seized and some matrices were destroyed. Entrances to the building were thereupon sealed and a permanent guard was posted to prevent the press from reopening.

·14·

ON THE EVE

Well after midnight on October 23–24, after a tense day of strategy meetings and discussions, Lomov and Rykov, along with several other provincial Bolshevik leaders newly arrived in Petrograd for the Second All-Russian Congress of Soviets, bedded down on heaps of books and pamphlets in the Bolshevik-operated Priboi publishing house, not far from Smolny. A scant three or four hours later, Lomov was awakened by the persistent ringing of the telephone. He waited briefly for someone else to brave the predawn chill, then roused himself, fumbled in the dark for the phone, and heard Trotsky's thundering voice summoning him and his comrades to Military Revolutionary Committee headquarters: "Kerensky is on the offensive. . . . We need everyone at Smolny!"[1]

Trotsky barely had had time to savor his success in helping to win control of the Peter and Paul Fortress when the first disjointed reports of Kerensky's call for loyal troops from outside the capital and rumors of the government's crackdown on the extreme left began to trickle into Smolny. Soon Military Revolutionary Committee contacts in the suburbs began phoning in word of alarming activity among troop units in their localities, and workers from the Trud printing press arrived with news of the raid on *Rabochii put'*. Between phone calls to the dwellings and offices of party officials, Military Revolutionary Committee leaders already at Smolny (Trotsky, Lazimir, Sverdlov, Antonov, Podvoisky, and Lashevich among them) drew up and dispatched an alert to regimental committees and commissars in military units and installations throughout the Petrograd area. Titled "Directive Number One," this order read: "The Petrograd Soviet is in direct danger; counterrevolutionary conspirators have attempted to bring cadets and shock battalions from the suburbs to Petrograd during the night. The newspapers *Soldat* and *Rabochii put'* have been closed. You are hereby directed to bring your regiment to battle readiness [and to] await further instructions. Any procrastination or interference in executing this order will be considered a betrayal of the revolution."[2]

To bring insurgent forces to battle readiness was one thing; to decide what direct military action, if any, to take in response to the apparent government attack was quite another. Only a few hours earlier the Military Revolutionary Committee had backed away from the brink of a military clash with the government, still justifiably fearful of seriously weakening its base of support. By the morning of October 24, enough delegates to the Congress of Soviets had arrived in the capital to indicate that, with the Left SRs, a solid majority could be counted on to support the transfer of power to the soviets and the creation by the congress of an exclusively socialist government.[3] Kerensky's crackdown on the left, however, injected a major new element into the situation. If Kerensky were not rebuffed, if he succeeded in mobilizing a large loyalist military force and putting leftist leaders back behind bars, it was still possible that the Congress of Soviets would not meet at all. Even if the congress were not dispersed, the Military Revolutionary Committee's careful and, up to now, apparently successful effort to set the stage for the overthrow of the government, either immediately before or just after the opening of the congress, would be seriously undermined.

With such considerations in mind, some members of the Military Revolutionary Committee now spoke up for starting an armed uprising without further delay. However, a majority, led by Trotsky, insisted on a firm yet more restrained response. Trotsky quickly scratched out an order to soldier committees in two of the best organized, most revolutionary units in the garrison—the Litovsky Regiment and the Sixth Engineer Battalion—directing them to take charge of reopening the Trud press and insuring its security. "The Soviet of Workers' and Soldiers' Deputies cannot tolerate suppression of the free word," the order asserted. "For the people fighting off the attack of the pogromists, there must be assurance of an honest press."[4]

This directive was implemented at once; a company of Litovsky guards, armed with machine guns and led by Dashkevich, arrived at the building housing the Trud press at 9:00 A.M. Dashkevich, ignoring the Military Revolutionary Committee's announcement of the previous night, declared bluntly that "orders of the government not countersigned by the Military Revolutionary Committee are invalid." His troops overwhelmed loyalist militiamen and smashed government seals; within a couple of hours *Rabochii put'* was back in production. A reporter for *Birzhevye vedomosti*, describing these developments in the October 24 evening edition, observed that "the comrade soldiers made no similar effort to liberate *Zhivoe slovo*," which also had been shut down.

Meanwhile, at Smolny, Sverdlov had managed to convene a meeting of the party Central Committee. Present were Lomov, Dzerzhinsky, Sverdlov, Bubnov, Nogin, Miliutin, Ioffe, Uritsky, Trotsky, and Berzin, as well as Kamenev, whose earlier resignation from the committee seems to have been simply ignored.[5] In view of the developing crisis and the difficulty of rounding up Central Committee members in a hurry, it was agreed at the outset that for the rest of the day no members would leave Smolny without specific authorization. The first substantive issue that the committee discussed, interestingly enough, was—not the government's attack on the left, but the progress of negotiations between the Military Revolutionary Committee and General Polkovnikov on the nature of the Petrograd Soviet's influence over military operations; initially, committee members seem to have had the mistaken impression that the government's actions had been undertaken before the Military Revolutionary Committee's acceptance of the terms proposed by the Petrograd Military District. Only after Kamenev had reported on the earlier agreement did the Central Committee turn to the trouble at Trud, ultimately endorsing the dispatch of a guard to protect the press, as well as the adoption of whatever other steps were necessary to insure the publication of the next regular issues of the party's papers.

Apart from this, the Central Committee members seem to have been most concerned with the possibility that postal and telegraph workers and also railwaymen, among whom moderate socialist influence was still strong, might oppose the overthrow of the Provisional Government and respond to the transfer of power to the soviets by attempting to isolate the capital from the rest of the country. As political developments relating to the Congress of Soviets appeared to be reaching a climax and the creation of a revolutionary regime seemed imminent, they also worried about matters such as food supply and the maintenance of a close working relationship with the Left SRs. Thus Bubnov was made responsible for establishing contact with rail workers and Dzerzhinsky with postal and telegraph employees. At the same time, Miliutin was charged with organizing food supplies, and Kamenev and Berzin were designated to conduct negotiations with the Left SRs. At Trotsky's insistence, the Central Committee, before adjourning, agreed on one further precaution: a reserve headquarters was to be established in the newly won Peter and Paul Fortress, for use if Smolny should fall to the loyalists.

Actually, the historical importance of the Central Committee meeting of October 24 derives as much from what was not discussed there as from the issues that were in fact raised. On the morning of October 24, it has been noted, some Military Revolutionary Committee members advocated an immediate call for a mass rising. At roughly the same hour, the Bolshevik Petersburg Committee, assembled for the first time since October 15, responded to the latest developments by formally calling for the preparation of an insurrection "without any delay whatever."[6] Within the Central Committee, however, no doubt in part because of Lenin's absence, the crucial question of whether or not to attempt to do away with the Provisional Government at once, or at any rate before the Congress of Soviets, was apparently given no serious consideration. Rather, it appears that at this point most Central Committee members were absorbed with the task of neutralizing the actions of the enemy and retaining or consolidating the strength of the left, so as to maximize the possibility of utilizing the Congress of Soviets to settle scores, finally, with the government. Significant in this regard is a comment on the Central Committee's outlook made by Stalin on the afternoon of October 24 at a caucus of Bolshevik congress delegates. "Within the Military Revolutionary Committee," he said, "there are two points of view. The first is that we organize an uprising at once, and the second is that we first consolidate our forces. The Central Committee has sided with the second view."[7]

The continuing emphasis of the Bolshevik Central Committee and the Military Revolutionary Committee on the role of the Congress of Soviets in completing the task of subverting the Provisional Government and creating a revolutionary soviet regime was nowhere more clearly reflected than in the lead editorial prepared by Stalin for the edition of *Rabochii put'* that reached the streets sometime after midday on October 24. Capped by the headline "What We Need," the editorial called upon workers and soldiers to form delegations for the purpose of applying direct pressure on the Congress of Soviets to replace the Kerensky government with a revolutionary regime. Wrote Stalin:

> . . . The present impostor government, which was not elected by the people and which is not accountable to the people, must be replaced by a government recognized by the people, elected by the representatives of the workers, soldiers and peasants, and accountable to these representatives. . . .
>
> Do you want the present government of landlords and capitalists to be replaced by a new government, a government of workers and peasants?
>
> Do you want the new government of Russia to proclaim . . . the abolition of landlordism and to transfer all the landed estates to peasant committees without compensation?
>
> Do you want the new government of Russia to publish the tsar's secret treaties, to declare them invalid, and to propose a just peace to all belligerent nations?
>
> Do you want the new government of Russia to put a thorough curb on organizers of lockouts and profiteers who are deliberately fomenting famine and unemployment, economic disruption and high prices?
>
> *If you want this*, muster all your forces, rise as one man, organize meetings and elect your delegations and, through them, lay your demands before the Congress of Soviets which opens tomorrow at Smolny.

The tactical caution displayed by the national Bolshevik leadership was also reflected on October 24 in the Kronstadt Bolshevik paper, *Proletarskoe delo*, and in the new Bolshevik-controlled evening newspaper of the Petrograd Soviet, *Rabochii i soldat*. Dominating the front page of *Rabochii i soldat* on the evening of October 24 was the banner headline "The All-Russian Congress Will Begin on October 25"; this was followed by a full-page proclamation from the Military Revolutionary Committee:

To the Population of Petrograd

Citizens:

The counterrevolution has raised its treacherous head. The Kornilovites are mobilizing their forces to suppress the All-Russian Congress of Soviets and to break up the Constituent Assembly. At the same time pogromists may try to instigate disorders and massacres on the streets of Petrograd.

The Petrograd Soviet of Workers' and Soldiers' Deputies takes upon itself responsibility for the protection of revolutionary order from the counterrevolution and pogromist attacks.

The garrison of Petrograd will not permit any violence or disturbance. . . .

Citizens! We call upon you to maintain calm and self-control. The cause of order and of the revolution is in firm hands!

The Military Revolutionary Committee

This continuing orientation toward the Congress of Soviets was voiced in public pronouncements as well as in the press. In a speech to the afternoon caucus of the Bolshevik congress fraction at which Stalin had drawn attention to the Central Committee's tactical stance, Trotsky seemed anxious, above all, to dispel whatever fears the Bolshevik leaders, assembled from all over Russia, might have that the revolution was in imminent danger or that the actions of the Military Revolutionary Committee in any way usurped the functions of the congress. He declared:

The government is powerless; we are not afraid of it because we have sufficient strength. . . . Some of the comrades, for example Kamenev and Riazanov, do not agree with our assessment of the situation. However, we are leaning neither to the right nor to the left. Our tactical line has been determined by developing circumstances. We grow stronger every day. Our task is to defend ourselves and gradually to expand our sphere of authority so as to build a solid foundation for tomorrow's Congress of Soviets. The views of the entire country will be revealed tomorrow; and Petrograd will not be alone in responding to its summons.[8]

According to a letter written the following day by Mikhail Zhakov, a participant in this caucus, Trotsky, toward the end of his address, took pains to insist that the arrest of the Provisional Government was not planned as an independent task. "If the congress creates a government and Kerensky does not obey it, this would be a police and not a political problem," Trotsky is recorded as declaring. "It would be a mistake to use even one of the armored cars which now defend the Winter Palace to arrest the government. However, the Military Revolutionary Committee's decision to reopen the printing house of *Rabochii put'* and to entrust the valiant Litovsky Regiment, instead of cadets, to guard it, was no mistake. This is defense, comrades. This is defense." Zhakov noted that at this point Trotsky was interrupted by a storm of wild applause.[9]

At a session of the Petrograd Soviet a few hours later, Trotsky spoke out in a similar vein, insisting that "an armed conflict today or tomorrow, on the eve of the All-Russian Congress, is not in our plans." "We are confident that the congress will fulfill our slogan with great force and authority," he continued. "But if the government wants to make use of the twenty-four, forty-eight, or seventy-two hours which it still has and comes out against us, then we will respond with a counterattack, matching blow for blow, steel for iron."[10] Moreover, at close to this same hour, upon the insistence of the Left SRs, the Military Revolutionary Committee issued a press release in which it categorically denied that an uprising was in preparation: "Contrary to all kinds of rumors and reports, the Military Revolutionary Committee declares that it exists not to prepare and carry out the seizure of power, but exclusively for defense of the interests of the Petrograd garrison and the democracy from counterrevolutionary encroachments."[11]

While the Bolsheviks were working to consolidate support for their program in the Congress of Soviets and making preparations for the creation of a revolutionary government by the congress, Kerensky was feverishly attempting to implement his plans to curb the left and, equally important, to strengthen his defenses. He spent much of the morning of October 24 in the General Staff building trying to speed up the dispatch to the capital of loyal troops from the front. Orders were now issued for the immediate removal of all Military Revolutionary Committee commissars, and all troops of the garrison were strictly forbidden to leave their barracks without the specific authorization of Petrograd Military District headquarters.[12]

During the morning and early afternoon, it became evident that the vast majority of troops were responding to directives from the extreme left, not to those from the regular military command. The alacrity with which soldiers from the Litovsky Regiment fulfilled Trotsky's order to assist in reopening the Trud printing press has already been mentioned. The behavior of the more than five hundred-man crew of the cruiser *Aurora*, which was just completing a year of capital repairs at the Franco-Russian shipyard, was also typical. Recognizing that the *Aurora*'s radicalized crew would support the Military Revolutionary Committee, the regular naval command ordered the ship out to sea for engine tests. At the instigation of the Military Revolutionary Committee, however, Tsentrobalt countermanded this order, and, in response, the sailors rose against their officers and remained in Petrograd.[13]

As the hours wore on, it also became apparent to defenders of the government that, at best, the arrival of significant military help from outside

Personnel of the Women's Battalion on the Palace Square.

Petrograd would be seriously delayed. Some of the military units called out on the night of October 23–24 and the following day immediately declared their unwillingness to come to the government's aid, while others were prevented from doing so by local forces supporting the Military Revolutionary Committee. Then too, as at the time of the Kornilov affair, the movement of troops from the front was interrupted well outside the capital, most front soldiers readily pledging support to the Military Revolutionary Committee as soon as the struggle between the government and the Petrograd Soviet was explained to them.

About noon the Women's Shock Battalion from Levashova, less than two hundred strong, reported for duty at the Winter Palace. They were joined at 2:00 P.M. by a detachment of sixty-eight cadets from the Mikhailovsky Artillery School. Also either already at the palace or reporting there during the day and night of October 24, were 134 officers and roughly two thousand cadets from officer-training schools in Peterhof, Oranienbaum, and Gatchina. For the time being, this relatively meager force, a small fraction of what the Military Revolutionary Committee could draw on, was the best Kerensky could muster.[14] Utilizing some of these forces, Kerensky did his best to strengthen security around government offices, rail stations, the Neva bridges, and vital public-service institutions.

In the early afternoon the prime minister was driven to the Mariinsky Palace, where he sought to rally the Preparliament in support of the government and to obtain its endorsement for the measures already initiated to

suppress the left. Kerensky's rambling, emotion-charged speech on this occasion was to be his last public address in Russia. Frequently interrupted
by storms of applause from the right and boos and hoots from the left, the
speech, recently characterized by one historian as the "hysterical wail of a
bankrupt politician,"[15] lasted well over an hour. Kerensky began by accusing both the extreme right and the radical left of working to subvert the
convocation of a Constituent Assembly and the creation of a free, democratic system of government. The brunt of his criticism was reserved for the
Bolsheviks. To buttress his condemnation of the party, Kerensky quoted
extensively from the arguments for an immediate insurrection contained in
Lenin's "Letter to Comrades," serialized in *Rabochii put'* between October 19
and 21; he also catalogued what he termed "repeated Bolshevik appeals for
and armed uprising" voiced at public meetings and in the party's press.

Kerensky went on to contend that "by organizing an uprising" the Bolsheviks were assisting

> not the German proletariat but . . . the German ruling classes; they are
> opening Russia's front to the mailed fist of Wilhelm and his friends. . . .
> In full awareness of my responsibility, I proclaim from this platform that
> such actions by a Russian political party constitute treason and a betrayal
> of the Russian state. . . . A certain portion of the Petersburg population is
> in a state of insurrection. . . . Arrests have been ordered. . . . At the
> present time, when the state is imperiled by deliberate or unwitting be-
> trayal and is at the brink of ruin, the Provisional Government, myself in-
> cluded, prefers to be killed and destroyed rather than to betray the life,
> honor, and the independence of the State.

At this, members of the Preparliament, with the exception of the
Menshevik-Internationalists and Left SRs, rose from their seats and
gave Kerensky a prolonged, resounding ovation—a circumstance which
prompted a Kadet, Moisei Adzhemov, to rush to the left benches screaming,
"Let's have a photograph of the people sitting down!"[16]

After order was restored with some difficulty, Kerensky continued his
speech. Reading from the Military Revolutionary Committee's "Directive
Number One," which was then circulating throughout the city, he bel-
lowed: "This is an attempt to incite the rabble against the existing order.
. . . It is an attempt to block the Constituent Assembly and to expose the
front to the serried ranks of Wilhelm's concentrated forces." Turning to the
left, he insisted that "at the present time everyone must decide whether he
is on the side of the Republic, freedom, and democracy, or against these."
In conclusion, he roundly declared:

> I have come to call upon you for vigilance, for the defense of the gains of
> freedom won by the many sacrifices, by the blood and the lives of many
> generations of free Russian people. . . . All elements of Russian society,

those groups and those parties which have dared to raise a hand against the free will of the Russian people, threatening at the same time to expose the front to Germany, are subject to immediate, decisive, and total liquidation. . . . I demand that this very day the Provisional Government receive your answer as to whether or not it can fulfill its duty with the assurance of support from this exulted gathering.[17]

Kerensky subsequently remembered that he left the Mariinsky Palace after his speech at around 2:30 P.M., convinced that within a couple of hours he would receive a strong pledge of support from the Preparliament.[18] This was not to be. Preparliament deputies spent the rest of the afternoon and early evening of October 24 in acrimonious fractional meetings debating how best to respond to Kerensky's request for a vote of confidence. When the deputies reassembled at 7:00 P.M., the opposition of a significant portion of the Preparliament to granting Kerensky *carte blanche* for a wholesale crackdown on the left emerged sharply.

The initial speaker after the extended break was Kamkov, chief spokesman of the Left SRs. Four weeks later, in his speech to the First Left SR Congress, he would recall his anguish when Kerensky "demanded full powers to suppress the Bolshevik uprising and was completely oblivious to the fact that there was nobody to put down the uprising regardless of what sanctions he was granted." Kamkov explained then that "to those of us working among the lower classes of Petrograd, it was clear that in the Petrograd garrison Kerensky could not find a dozen people who would come out to defend him as head of the coalition government."[19] In the Preparliament on the evening of October 24, Kamkov declared:

> After the head of the government comes here and announces that some kind of rabble is rising and demands that this assembly aid him in dealing with it, overwhelming numbers of you may decide to grant this sanction. But I am uncertain that the Russian people, the revolutionary army, the proletariat, and the laboring peasantry will do the same. Let's not play hide and seek with each other. Is there anybody at all who would trust this government. . . ? It does not have the support of the revolutionary army, or the proletariat, and coming out against it is not the rabble but precisely the most politically conscious elements of the revolutionary democracy. If we are seriously interested in eliminating the soil in which the horrors of civil war are maturing, we must openly declare that the only way out of the present predicament is through the creation of a homogeneous, revolutionary, democratic government in which there will be no elements who organize demonstrations of homage to Kornilov.

Martov, who took the floor next on behalf of the Menshevik-Internationalists, was similarly critical of the existing government. As he appeared on the rostrum, someone on the right cried out, "Here is the minister of foreign affairs in the future cabinet"—to which Martov, peering in the direction of his critic, at once retorted, "I'm nearsighted and cannot tell if this is said by the minister of foreign affairs in Kornilov's cabinet." Declared Martov:

> The language of the prime minister, who permitted himself to speak of a rabble movement when what is at hand is a movement of a significant portion of the proletariat and the army, even if directed toward mistaken objectives, is a provocation for civil war. But I have not lost the hope that . . . [we] will not yield to the desires of those who seek to use the current situation to bring the revolution to a halt. The democracy must declare that it will not give the government any support if it does not immediately guarantee that it will fulfill the most urgent needs of the people. Repression cannot be substituted for satisfaction of the needs of the revolution. An announcement must be made immediately that Russia is pursuing a policy of immediate peace, that land committees will have control over alienated lands awaiting settlement, and that the democratization of the army will not be stopped. [And] if such declarations are impossible for the government in its present form, then the government must be reorganized.

There was nothing unexpected about these declarations by Kamkov and Martov; what was genuinely startling was the response to Kerensky's demands by representatives of the main body of Mensheviks and SRs, people like Dan and Gots, who had openly wavered in their support for coalition for the first time in the wake of the Kornilov affair. At the Preparliament session on the evening of October 24, their point of view was voiced by Dan. From the outset, Dan expressed total opposition and aversion to the behavior of the Bolsheviks. Yet, with equal emphasis, he insisted that if the conflict between the government and the left were not settled peacefully, the ultimate winners would be the extreme right. Moreover, he declared that the only way a disastrous bloodbath could be avoided was by responding, without further delay, to the aspirations of the masses who now followed the Bolsheviks. As Dan put it:

> Regardless of how the Bolshevik uprising ends tomorrow, if it is submerged in blood and order is restored by force of arms . . . practically speaking, this will be a triumph for that third force which will sweep away the Bolsheviks, the government, the democracy, and the revolution. If you want to remove the soil in which the Bolsheviks are growing like rotten mushrooms, we must turn to political measures. What is necessary is the clear enunciation by the government and the Council of the Republic of a platform in which the people will see their just interests supported by the government and the Council of the Republic and not the Bolsheviks. . . . The questions of peace and land and the democratization of the army must be framed in such a way that not a single worker or soldier will have the slightest doubt that our government is moving along this course with firm and resolute steps.[20]

In a memoir, Dan later recalled his reactions to Kerensky's speech and attempted to explain his thinking at the time.[21] From the very beginning of the Preparliament's deliberations in early October, he and other Menshevik and SR leaders with similar views had worked for the eventual creation of a leftist, democratic, exclusively socialist government, capable of quickly enacting a radical reform program. They had done this, Dan contended, in the belief that only through immediate, drastic political steps was there any hope of successfully combating the Bolsheviks. Dan maintained that in his wing of the Preparliament "it was axiomatic that to fight the Bolsheviks with strictly military means was useless, if only because the government did not possess such means." Dan indicated that this view was rejected by the Preparliament right, who erroneously believed that the military force at the government's disposal was sufficient to crush the Bolsheviks, and who consequently looked forward to "engaging them in open battle." After Kerensky's speech to the Preparliament on the afternoon of October 24, Dan and his colleagues considered it their duty to indicate to the government the only course they believed held out any hope of salvation, and to reemphasize that they were prepared to join the government in that course to the very end.

Toward the close of the Preparliament session on October 24, three resolutions were introduced: one, on behalf of cooperative organizations and the Kadet Party, pledged full support to the government in the adoption of decisive steps to suppress the revolt in the capital; the second, a much more inflammatory resolution put forward by the command of the cossacks, bitterly criticized the entire left, directly repudiated the Provisional Government for its weakness and even for "conniving with the Bolsheviks," and demanded that the government guarantee that "on this occasion it would in no way indulge the Bolsheviks"; the third resolution, drawn up by the Preparliament left and presented by Dan, explicitly criticized the Provisional Government for delays in the promulgation of urgent political and social reform and made the Preparliament's support dependent upon the immediate promulgation of a radical "land and peace" program and the creation of a "Committee of Public Safety," made up of representatives of municipal governments and the soviets, to work with the Provisional Government in restoring order. At 8:30 P.M., by the narrow margin of 123 votes to 102, with 26 abstentions, the resolution of the left, in effect a vote of "no confidence" in Kerensky, was adopted.[22]

Dan indicated in his memoir that, upon the passage of this resolution, he and Gots, dragging along the much more conservative president of the Preparliament, Avksentiev, hastened to a meeting of the cabinet in the Winter Palace to demand that the government adopt the Preparliament's recommendations. According to Dan, he and Gots fervently hoped that the government would acquiesce and that a momentous proclamation would be printed and plastered throughout the capital that very evening, announcing to the citizenry that the Provisional Government had formally proposed the immediate cessation of all military activity and the start of negotiations for universal peace, that land committees had been informed by phone that all manorial land holdings would be transferred to them, and that the convocation of the Constituent Assembly would be speeded up.

Dan and Gots apparently insisted to Kerensky that such action would bring about a shift in the mood of the masses and strengthen the hand of Bolshevik leaders opposed to an uprising. Not surprisingly, however, word of the Preparliament's action drove the prime minister into a blind rage. "Kerensky appeared then," Dan later wrote, "like a person approaching the last stages of exhaustion." At first he declared his intention of resigning the next morning; in the end, he simply dismissed Dan, Gots, and Avksentiev with the assertion that the government had "no need for admonitions and instructions and would cope with the rebellion by itself."[23]

This was a great blow to those who, like Dan, hoped to neutralize popular unrest and pull the rug from under the Bolsheviks by pressuring Kerensky to adopt a more radical reform program or, failing this, by forcing him to give way to a new, more responsive government. Still, efforts to achieve this goal were not halted. At an emergency joint meeting of the All-Russian Executive Committees, which began just after midnight and lasted until 4:00 A.M., October 25, centrist and left Mensheviks secured passage of a resolution which, while condemning the Bolsheviks and endorsing the creation of a Committee of Public Safety, nonetheless, reaffirmed the categorical demands for immediate reform adopted earlier by the Preparliament.[24]

Moreover, in a series of heated party strategy caucuses, the Left SRs and Menshevik-Internationalists now campaigned vigorously for the creation, by the Congress of Soviets, of an exclusively socialist coalition government. This campaign initially appeared to be bearing fruit. A meeting of the Menshevik congress fraction, which included both "defensists" and "internationalists," adopted a set of "theses" for incorporation in a political resolution to be presented to the congress, which constituted an even more significant departure from previous moderate socialist policies than did the resolution of the Preparliament. These theses called for the complete reconstruction of the cabinet and specifically stipulated that the new government be "homogeneous" and "democratic." While condemning the actions of the Bolsheviks, they called at the same time for the repudiation of the Provisional Government's policies, which were viewed as having provoked the Bolshevik insurrection. The theses also included a recommendation that attempts by the government to suppress the Bolshevik insurrection by armed force be given a "firm rebuff."[25]

Meanwhile, the Left SRs turned out to have a comfortable majority at a caucus of the SR congress fraction on the morning of October 25. A resolution offered there by the SR Central Committee was defeated by a vote of ninety-two to sixty, after which the majority agreed to "get in touch with the Menshevik-Internationalists," evidently to coordinate efforts for the creation of a "homogeneous" socialist government.[26] Equally significant, in the wake of this victory some Left SR leaders retained hope that at the congress the entire fraction might stick together behind the program of the left.[27]

To anyone analyzing political developments in Petrograd during the afternoon and early evening of October 24, the confidence voiced by Kerensky in his ability to deal independently with the left at this time seems utterly incomprehensible. The sketchy, sometimes confused eyewitness reports that filled the "Latest News" columns of Petrograd's newspapers on October 25–26 testified to the degree to which the government's position had deteriorated.

Not long after Kerensky's unfortunate appearance before the Preparliament, the anxiety of military officials at General Staff headquarters was heightened by reports of alarming numbers of armed workers and soldiers congregating around Smolny. Consequently, they now issued orders for the Liteiny, Troitsky, and Nikolaevsky bridges across the Neva to be drawn, and for strict government control of the only other Neva span, the Palace Bridge—this to interdict the flow of insurgents from working-class districts on the Neva's right bank to the center sections of the city.[28] Describing his reaction upon learning of the government's intentions in regard to the Neva bridges on October 24, the Bolshevik Military Organization leader Ilin-Zhenevsky subsequently wrote: "Involuntarily, I remembered the July days. . . . The drawing of the bridges appeared to me as the first step in another attempt to destroy us. Was it possible the Provisional Government would triumph over us once again?"[29]

On this occasion, there was no such danger. As soon as loyalist cadets from the Mikhailovsky Artillery School arrived at the Liteiny Bridge, they were challenged by an irate crowd of citizens, many of them carrying weapons. Forced to give up their arms, the cadets were escorted humiliatingly back to their academy; as nearly as can be determined, this action took place without any specific directives from the Military Revolutionary Committee. Similarly, as soon as the struggle for the bridges began, Ilin-Zhenevsky, also acting on his own, saw to it that garrison soldiers took control of the smaller Grenadersky and Samsonevsky bridges across the Bolshaia Nevka between the Vyborg District and the Petrograd side.[30]

The military district command gave a company of the First Petrograd Women's Shock Battalion responsibility for drawing the Troitsky Bridge; orders issued to the battalion specifically authorized the use of firearms to prevent movement on the bridge.[31] It appears that the women soldiers did not try seriously to execute this order, quite likely because machine guns mounted along the walls of the Peter and Paul Fortress were well within shooting range. After a brief struggle between cadets and Red Guards, the former were successful in drawing the Nikolaevsky Bridge connecting Vasilevsky Island with the center of the capital. For some time yet the Palace Bridge remained firmly controlled by cadets and personnel of the Women's Battalion. Still, by early evening it was apparent that the crucial "battle for the bridges" had been won by forces hostile to the government. Two of the four main Neva bridges were in their hands, as well as all the bridges over the Bolshaia Nevka and Malaia Neva.

At 4:00 P.M., the cyclists who had had primary responsibility for security around the Winter Palace from the time of their transfer to the capital following the July days suddenly announced that they would no longer remain at their posts. An hour later, upon orders from the Military Revolutionary Committee, one of its commissars, Stanislav Pestkovsky, took control of the central telegraph office. This first success in the contest for key communications facilities was obtained without a shot fired, this despite the fact that among the telegraph office's three thousand employees there was not a single Bolshevik. The important factor here was that on regular guard duty at the telegraph office at the time was a detachment of soldiers from the Keksgolmsky Regiment, which had long since pledged loyalty to the Military Revolutionary Committee. And with the support of their commander, Pestkovsky pressured the head of the postal-telegraph workers' union, a right SR, to recognize his authority.[32]

A detachment of cadets tried unsuccessfully to recapture the central telegraph office around 8:00 P.M.[33] Not long afterward, another Military Revolutionary Committee commissar, the Helsingfors Bolshevik Leonid Stark, accompanied only by twelve armed sailors, occupied and assumed supervision of the Petrograd Telegraph Agency, a news wire service. One of Stark's first acts was to stop the political resolution just then passed by the Preparliament from going out over the wire.[34] At about the same time, troops of the Izmailovsky Guards Regiment, the first major garrison unit to come to the government's aid in July, took control of the Baltic Station, rail terminus for loyalist reinforcements arriving from the seaboard along the Gulf of Finland and points west. The best Petrograd Military District headquarters could muster by way of a response was a telegraphed warning that "echelons loyal to the government and the Central Executive Committee are in transit from the front."[35]

Some of the ultimately most important steps taken by the left at this time were accomplished in secret and hence for the time being were not publicly evident. In the early evening of October 24, Dybenko, in Helsingfors, finally received the telegram agreed upon with Antonov during the Northern Congress of Soviets: "Send the regulations"—meaning "Dispatch sailors and ships to Petrograd."[36] Antonov also passed a handwritten request to a liaison man from the Kronstadt Soviet, the Bolshevik Aleksei Pronin, for the dispatch of Kronstadt sailors to the capital the next day.[37] Several hours later, on behalf of the Military Revolutionary Committee, Aleksei Baranov called Dybenko from Petrograd to confirm the dispatch of naval forces. "The atmosphere is tense," Baranov reported. "Can we count on your support?" "The cruisers will sail at dawn," responded Dybenko.[38]

Except for the individual garrison units and Red Guard contingents ordered by the Military Revolutionary Committee to carry out specific military tasks, most of the Petrograd area's well over half million workers, soldiers, and sailors remained in their factories and barracks during these initial skirmishes with government forces. Throughout the afternoon and evening of October 24, and on into the following day, a round of meetings was held in working-class districts of the capital and at the main bases of the Baltic Fleet. Almost invariably, these gatherings produced expressions of support for the Petrograd Soviet and its program. For the time being, there were almost no popular disturbances. Mass demonstrations like those of February and July, which it was commonly assumed would signal a final clash between the left and the government, were completely absent.

Toward midafternoon, when word of the drawing of the Neva bridges became known, students at primary and secondary schools and employees in government offices were dismissed for the day, banks and stores in the central sections of the city were closed, and streetcar service was curtailed. Still, the streets remained calm. In the evening fashionably dressed crowds promenaded on Nevsky Prospect, where the usual prostitutes continued to ply their trade. Restaurants, casinos, moving-picture houses, and theaters operated normally, although with decreased attendance—a revival by Meyerhold of Aleksei Tolstoi's *The Death of Ivan the Terrible* at the Alexandrinsky Theater and a performance of *Boris Godunov* at the Mariinsky Theater went on as scheduled. This state of affairs, coupled with the Military Revolutionary Committee's continuing disavowal of insurrection, was profoundly confusing to contemporary observers, giving an intense sense of unreality to the decisive developments then taking place in widely scattered sections of the capital.

Not surprisingly, no one appears to have been more confused and troubled by the tactics of the Military Revolutionary Committee than Lenin. Throughout this historically momentous time he had remained away from the scene of battle, at Fofanova's apartment on the outskirts of the capital. On October 20, evidently responding to rumors of Lenin's presence in Petrograd, the minister of justice had issued a new order for the Bolshevik leader's arrest, dispelling any hope that it might now be safe for him to come out of hiding. Between October 21 and 23 Lenin had rejoiced in the Military Revolutionary Committee's successes in the struggle with the Petrograd Military District for control of the Petrograd garrison. But, unlike Trotsky, he viewed these triumphs not as part of a gradual subversion of the Provisional Government's authority which, if all went well, might culminate in a relatively painless transfer of power to the soviets at the Congress of Soviets, but merely as the prelude to a popular armed uprising.

Workers in a Petrograd factory listen to a soldier speak.

And each passing day simply confirmed his long-held conviction that the prospects for creating a Bolshevik-dominated government would be maximized if power were seized by force at once; waiting for the congress, he felt, would simply allow the government more time to ready its forces and would needlessly risk the creation by an indecisive congress of, at best, a wishy-washy all-socialist coalition government. After learning of the last-minute cancellation of the cossack procession (on either October 22 or 23), Lenin wrote to Sverdlov: "The calling-off of the cossack demonstration is a gigantic *triumph!* Hurrah! Take to the attack with all forces and complete victory will be ours in a few days."[39]

In the morning papers on October 24 Lenin read of the Military Revolutionary Committee's decision to accept the "compromise" offered by the Petrograd Military District. Throughout the day, no doubt mostly through Fofanova, he had maintained contact with Smolny; thus he had learned almost at once of the government's crackdown on the left and of the efforts by some moderate socialists to force the government to adopt and immediately announce a more radical reform program.[40] News of these developments greatly upset him. Fofanova recalled that he sent her out several times during the day and evening with requests to the Central Committee for permission to go to Smolny. Each of these appeals was summarily rejected. Towards late afternoon, upon reading yet another of the Central Committee's noncommittal responses, Lenin crumpled the note and threw it on the floor. "I don't understand them. What are they afraid of?" he stormed. "Only the day before yesterday Podvoisky reported that this military unit was Bolshevik and this other one as well. . . . And now suddenly nothing is happening. Just ask them if they have one hundred loyal soldiers or Red Guardsmen with rifles. I don't need anything else!"[41]

Around 6:00 P.M. Lenin resolved, once again, to circumvent the Central Committee and to call on lower levels of the party, particularly the Petersburg Committee and the district Bolshevik committees, to take the completion of the revolution into their own hands. Quickly drafting the following appeal,[42] he commissioned Fofanova to deliver it to Krupskaia, "and no one else":

Comrades,
I am writing these lines on the evening of the twenty-fourth. The situation is critical in the extreme. In fact it is now absolutely clear that to delay the uprising would be fatal.
With all my might I urge comrades to realize that everything now hangs by a thread; that we are confronted by problems which are not to be solved by conferences or congresses (even congresses of soviets), but exclusively by peoples, by the masses, by the struggle of the armed people.
The bourgeois onslaught of the Kornilovites and the removal of Verkhovsky show that we must not wait. We must at all costs, this very evening, this very night, arrest the government, having first disarmed the officer cadets (defeating them, if they resist), and so on.
We must not wait! We may lose everything! . . .
Who must take power?
That is not important at present. Let the Military Revolutionary Committee do it, or "some other institution." . . .
All districts, all regiments, all forces must be mobilized at once and must immmediately send delegations to the Military Revolutionary Committee and to the Bolshevik Central Committee with the insistent demand that under no circumstance should power be left in the hands of Kerensky and Co. until the twenty-fifth—not under any circumstances; the matter must be decided without fail this very evening, or this very night.
History will not forgive revolutionaries for procrastinating when they could be victorious today (and they certainly will be victorious today), while they risk losing much tomorrow; in fact, they risk losing everything.
If we seize power today, we seize it not in opposition to the soviets but on their behalf.
The seizure of power is the task of the uprising; its political purpose will become clear after the seizure.
It would be a disaster, or a sheer formality, to await the wavering vote

of October 25. The people have the right and are in duty bound to decide such questions not by a vote, but by force; in critical moments of revolution, the people have the right and are in duty bound to give directions to their representatives, even their best representatives, and not to wait for them. . . .

The government is tottering. It must be *given the deathblow* at all costs. To delay action is fatal.[43]

A few hours after sending Fofanova out with this last appeal, Lenin was unable to restrain himself further. Leaving a note for his hostess on the kitchen table ("I have gone where you did not want me to go"), Lenin donned his wig and a battered cap and wrapped a bandage around his face. Then, violating a direct Central Committee ban on his movement for the second time in a month, accompanied by Eino Rakhia, he set off for Smolny.[44] The two traveled through the Vyborg District as far as the Finland Station in an almost empty streetcar, the frantic Lenin peppering the conductress with questions regarding late political developments; when Lenin discovered she was a leftist, he began filling her ears with practical advice on revolutionary action. As they approached Smolny on foot via Shpalernaia Street, where the unlucky Voinov had come to his end on July 6, the pair was forced to dodge a roving, mounted cadet patrol, scaring Rakhia half out of his wits. Finally, sometime before midnight, they safely reached their destination.

Smolny, upon Lenin's arrival, looked like a military camp on the eve of battle. Heavily armed patrols stood watch at adjacent streetcorners. Groups of soldiers and Red Guards huddled around glowing bonfires in the surrounding squares and side alleys. The courtyard inside the main gate reverberated with the din of trucks, automobiles, and motorcycles, constantly arriving and departing, and Smolny's massive façade was ablaze with lights. Machine guns had been emplaced at both sides of the central entry; here guards tried to control movement into the building, which John Reed likened to a "gigantic hive." Neither Rakhia nor Lenin had proper passes. Initially denied admission, they managed to lose themselves in an incoming crowd and so were able to squeeze by the guards.[45] Accidentally doffing his toupee along with his cap in the excitement, Lenin at once began upbraiding his closest associates, pressing them to get on with the business of finishing off the Provisional Government.

Accounts of the October revolution by writers in the Soviet Union, seeking to maximize Lenin's role in the Bolshevik seizure of power at the expense of Trotsky's, convey the impression that under the latter's influence, the party exaggerated Kerensky's strength and underestimated that of the left, and passively awaited a vote of the Congress of Soviets to create a revolutionary government. This interpretation is, of course, seriously dis-

Smolny Institute during the October days.

torted; as we have seen, the policies of the Military Revolutionary Committee between October 21 and 24 were directed toward effectively subverting the Provisional Government in advance of the congress, an objective already largely fulfilled by the night of October 24. Also, these tactics were dictated, more than anything else, by what seems to have been a realistic evaluation of the prevailing correlation of forces and popular mood.

Yet there is a measure of truth in the Soviet view that prior to Lenin's appearance at Smolny late on the night of October 24–25, a majority of the Military Revolutionary Committee, not to speak of the Central Committee, was still uneasy about the possibility of going too far too fast—of losing potentially crucial support, or perhaps even breaking up the congress, by appearing to usurp the functions of the Congress of Soviets. As we have seen, the Military Revolutionary Committee's initial efforts in the wake of the government's offensive against the left were aimed at alerting left forces and readying them for possible action, not calling the masses into the streets. And almost all of the Military Revolutionary Committee's subsequent military operations on October 24 can be interpreted as reactions to offensive moves by the government. Thus, garrison soldiers were sent to reopen *Rabochii put'* after the government had closed it, and Military Revolutionary Committee forces took control of the Neva bridges when the government set about interrupting movement over them. Similarly, forces supporting the Military Revolutionary Committee occupied the Baltic Station following reports that troops loyal to the government from Peterhof and the northern front were boarding trains bound for the capital.[46]

It is altogether likely that as Kerensky's helplessness in the prevailing situation became more obvious and as the hour of the congress's opening drew near, the pace of the Military Revolutionary Committee's operations would have quickened, whether or not Lenin appeared on the scene. But it must also be borne in mind that Lenin, in contrast to almost everyone else, attached decisive importance to overthrowing the Provisional Government in advance of the congress. His arrival at Smolny inevitably intensified pressure on the leadership of the left to act more boldly. At any rate, for whatever the reason, well before dawn on October 25 the actions of the Military Revolutionary Committee suddenly became much more aggressive. All pretense that the committee was simply defending the revolution and attempting most of all to maintain the status quo pending the expression of the congress's will was abruptly dropped. Instead, an open, all-out effort was launched to confront congress delegates with the overthrow of the Provisional Government prior to the start of their deliberations.

There is very little hard evidence regarding the circumstances of this decision. Latsis later wrote that "towards morning on the famous night when the question of a government was being decided and the Central Committee wavered, Illich ran to the office of the Petersburg Committee with the question: 'Fellows, do you have shovels? Will the workers of Piter go into the trenches at our call?'" Latsis recorded that the response was positive, adding that the decisiveness of Lenin and the Petersburg Committee affected the waverers, allowing Lenin to have his way.[47] From the subsequent complaints of top Left SR leaders, it appears clear that the Military Revolutionary Committee shifted its stance without their knowledge.[48]

In any case, the moment when this fundamental tactical change occurred can be pinpointed fairly closely. Thus on the evening of October 24, Osvald Dzenis, Military Revolutionary Committee commissar in the Pavlovsky Regiment, was ordered to take control of the Troitsky Bridge, between the Petersburg side and the War Memorial Field. He recalls that around 9:00 P.M., after taking the bridge, he detected a sharp increase in traffic to and from the Palace Square; on his own, he directed the erection of barricades, the establishment of checkpoints to and from the Winter Palace, and the arrest of government officials, the most important of whom were escorted to Smolny. A short time after initiating these measures, Dzenis received an urgent call from Podvoisky informing him that the arrested officials sent to Smolny by him were being released; that the kind of action he had undertaken was unauthorized and premature; and that while the Military Revolutionary Committee had not yet decided when more active operations would be initiated, it would not be before the next day. Podvoisky insisted that Dzenis stop detaining government officials and dismantle his checkpoints, an order which Dzenis asserts appeared so shortsighted that he did not implement it. A few hours later, evidently around 2:00 A.M., Dzenis received a new order; this time he was directed to reenforce his cordon of outposts and to strictly control all movement through it.[49]

About this time, that is, 2:00 A.M., October 25, the First Company of the Sixth Engineer Battalion occupied the Nikolaevsky Station, off Znamensky Square, then dominated by a massive bronze equestrian statue of Alexander III. One of the engineers later recalled the moment: "It was a freezing night. One could feel the north wind permeate the bones. On the streets adjacent to the Nikolaevsky Station groups of engineers huddled, shivering from the cold, and peered vigilantly into the shadowy night. The moonlight created a fantastic scene. The hulks of houses looked like medieval castles—giant shadows followed the engineers. At this sight, the next-to-the-last emperor appeared to rein in his horse in horror."[50]

Also around 2:00 A.M., a Military Revolutionary Committee commissar, Mikhail Faerman, took control of the Petrograd electric station. At his direction, electrical service to most government buildings was switched off. More or less simultaneously, insurgent soldiers occupied the main post office, where the Military Revolutionary Committee commissar Karl Kadlubovsky took charge. Sometime after midnight, the crew of the *Aurora* had been authorized to "use all means at its disposal" to restore traffic along the Nikolaevsky Bridge.[51] Because the ship's captain at first refused to have anything to do with this order, the Military Revolutionary Committee commissar Alexander Belishev and several sailors took over operation of the vessel themselves. Navigating the *Aurora* through the shallow, twisting Neva was a tricky business, however, and the captain soon gave in. Announcing that he could not "allow the *Aurora* to be run aground," he agreed to help bring the newly renovated ship to its destination. At 3:30 A.M. the *Aurora* moved to an anchorage next to the Nikolaevsky Bridge, the one Neva bridge still under government control. As the *Aurora*'s crew directed its searchlights on the bridge, the cadets responsible for guarding it fled into the night. Ship's electricians supervised the closing of the span. A short time later, when a thirty-two-man detachment of government shock troops sent to reopen the bridge arrived on the scene, they found it securely in the hands of some two hundred workers and sailors.[52]

A forty-man detachment of sailors occupied the State Bank at 6:00 A.M.; there was no resistance, as soldiers of the Semenovsky Regiment on regular guard there remained neutral. An hour later, a detachment of soldiers from the Keksgolmsky Regiment, accompanied by Lashevich and another Military Revolutionary Committee commissar, P. S. Kaliagin, occupied the main Petrograd telephone station, immediately shutting off most lines to military headquarters and the Winter Palace. Bloodshed during occupation of the telephone station was avoided, in part perhaps because the detachment of Keksgolmsky soldiers was commanded by one A. Zakharov, who,

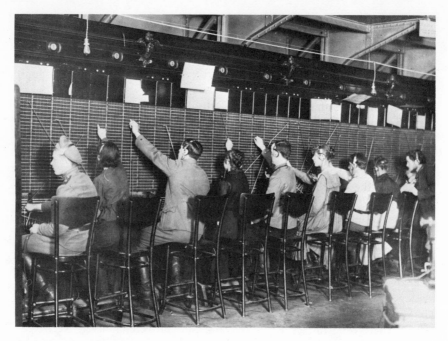

Garrison soldiers helping to operate the switchboard of the main Petrograd telephone station during the October days.

as a military school cadet, had often served on guard duty there. Familiar with security procedures at the telephone station, he supervised the quick isolation and disarmament of the cadets on guard.[53] Thus, by early morning, October 25, the government was for the most part without phones or lights. At 8:00 A.M., the last of Petrograd's three major rail terminals, the Warsaw Station, terminal point for rail lines connecting the capital with the northern front and army headquarters at Pskov, also fell to the Military Revolutionary Committee.

In the Winter Palace, a closed meeting of the cabinet devoted to consideration of further measures to deal with the left had broken up at 1:00 A.M. At 3:00 A.M. Kerensky received further alarming reports on the developing situation; accompanied by the deputy premier, Konovalov, he again hurried off to the General Staff building.[54] The reports he received there throughout the remainder of the night and early morning were uniformly bleak. One key point after another was passing rapidly into the Military Revolutionary Committee's hands. The military school cadets and soldiers of the Women's Battalion, the main forces in the Winter Palace, were now becoming understandably fidgety. Suddenly announcing their inability to fight soldiers of the garrison, they were temporarily calmed by what were, in retrospect, misleading assurances that troops from the front were expected momentarily.

At Kerensky's command, towards dawn a last desperate appeal was di-

Prime Minister Kerensky (second from right) and his aides in the Winter Palace. This is the last known photograph of Kerensky in Petrograd.

rected to cossack forces in the capital: "In the name of freedom, honor, and the glory of our native land, the commander-in-chief has ordered the First, Fourth, and Fourteenth Cossack regiments to act to aid the Soviet Central Executive Committee, the revolutionary democracy, and the Provisional Government, and to save the perishing Russian state."[55] In reply cossack spokesmen asked whether the infantry would also be "coming out." Receiving an unsatisfactory response, representatives of all but a relatively small number of cossacks let it be known they had no intention of "acting alone and serving as live targets."[56]

The text of a candid report from General B. A. Levitsky in Petrograd to General Mikhail Diterikhs at the front about developments in Petrograd on October 24 captures the prevailing situation. Levitsky brought Diterikhs up to date on the struggle for control of the garrison between the Military Revolutionary Committee and the Petrograd Military District headquarters, and on the former's directive, calling on garrison units not to obey the orders of the latter. Levitsky observed:

> This act yesterday forced the minister-president to explain clearly and precisely to the Council of the Republic [the Preparliament] the situation which had developed and to indicate the actions to be taken by the Provisional Government. . . . After this, units of the Petrograd garrison . . . went over to the side of the Bolsheviks. The bridges which had been

drawn open were once again closed. The entire city is covered by posts manned by garrison soldiers, but there has not been a mass coming out. The telephone station is in the garrison's hands. Those units in the Winter Palace are guarding it only in a strictly formal sense, since they have already agreed not to actively "come out." . . . It is as if the Provisional Government were in the capital of an enemy country.[57]

By the morning of October 25, the government's desperate situation had finally become obvious even to the hitherto obtusely confident commander of the Petrograd Military District, General Polkovnikov; he now drafted a report to Kerensky in which he evaluated the situation as "critical" and concluded that for practical purposes "the government had no troops at its disposal."[58] At this juncture, Kerensky's sole hope for survival appeared to rest with the successful mobilization of solid support from the army at the front. In view of this, at about 9:00 A.M. Kerensky left Konovalov in temporary charge of the cabinet and began to make arrangements for an immediate departure to Pskov.

A few hours earlier the Bolshevik Central Committee had met at Smolny. It appears that no protocol of this historically important assembly was ever recorded—at any rate, none has been published, and the existing bits and pieces of information about what took place there come from a few sketchy memoirs. The scene of the gathering was apparently the Central Committee's regular meeting-place, Room 36 on the first floor. Lenin was there and also, among others, Trotsky, Stalin, Smilga, Miliutin, Zinoviev, Kamenev, and Berzin. Rakhia tucked himself into a corner to wait for Lenin and to watch the proceedings. From time to time someone knocked at the door with reports on the course of the struggle for power in the streets outside. Lenin expressed satisfaction at each advance, at the same time pressing impatiently for the seizure of the Winter Palace and the arrest of the Provisonal Government. During a brief break in the deliberations, one of the Central Committee members suggested drawing up a list of the government to be submitted to the congress the next day. And immediately there arose the question of what to call the new government and its members. One memoirist recalls that to everyone the term *Provisional Government* sounded "outmoded" and that the term *ministers* for members of the government conveyed an unacceptable sense of "bureaucratic mustiness." It was Trotsky who quickly came forth with the idea of calling the new ministers "people's commissars," a suggestion which delighted all those present. "Yes, that's very good," Lenin interjected; "it smells of revolution. And we can call the government itself 'the Council of People's Commissars.' " Seizing pencil and paper, Miliutin prepared to accept suggestions for commissars. Still, the battle against the Provisional Government had not yet ended, and to some Central Committee members, drawing up a list of cabinet members seemed so premature that they treated it, at first, as a joke.[59]

·15·

THE BOLSHEVIKS
COME TO POWER

At the main bases of the Baltic fleet, activity began long before dawn on the morning of Wednesday, October 25. The first of three large echelons of armed sailors, bound for the capital at the behest of the Military Revolutionary Committee, departed Helsingfors by train along the Finnish railway at 3:00 A.M.; a second echelon got underway at 5:00 A.M., and a third left around midmorning. About the same time, a hastily assembled naval flotilla, consisting of a patrol boat—the *Iastrev*—and five destroyers—the *Metki, Zabiiaka, Moshchny, Deiatelny,* and *Samson*—started off at full steam for the roughly two hundred-mile trip to Petrograd, with the *Samson* in the lead flying a large banner emblazoned with the slogans "Down with the Coalition!" "Long Live the All-Russian Congress of Soviets!" and "All Power to the Soviets!"[1]

Activity of a similar kind was taking place at Kronstadt. Describing the night of October 24–25 in that center of revolutionary radicalism, Flerovsky was later to recall:

> It is doubtful whether anyone in Kronstadt closed his eyes that night. The Naval Club was jammed with sailors, soldiers, and workers. . . . The revolutionary staff drew up a detailed operations plan, designated participating units, made an inventory of available supplies, and issued instructions. . . . When the planning was finished . . . I went into the street. Everywhere there was heavy, but muffled traffic. Groups of soldiers and sailors were making their way to the naval dockyard. By the light of the torches we could see just the first ranks of serious determined faces. . . . Only the rumble of the automobiles, moving supplies from the fortress warehouses to the ships, disturbed the silence of the night.[2]

Shortly after 9:00 A.M. the sailors, clad in black pea jackets, with rifles slung over their shoulders and cartridge pouches on their belts, finished boarding the available vessels: two mine layers, the *Amur* and the *Khopor;* the former yacht of the fort commandant, the *Zarnitsa,* fitted out as a hospital ship; a training vessel, the *Verny;* a battleship, the *Zaria svobody,* so old that it was popularly referred to as the "flatiron" of the Baltic Fleet and had to be helped along by four tugs; and a host of of smaller paddle-wheel passenger boats and barges. As the morning wore on these vessels raised anchor, one after the other, and steamed off in the direction of the capital.[3]

At Smolny at this time, the leaders of the Military Revolutionary Committee and commissars from key locations about the city were completing plans for the capture of the Winter Palace and the arrest of the government. Podvoisky, Antonov-Ovseenko, Konstantin Eremeev, Georgii Blagonravov, Chudnovsky, and Sadovsky are known to have participated in these consultations. According to the blueprint which they worked out, insurrectionary forces were to seize the Mariinsky Palace and disperse the Preparliament; after this the Winter Palace was to be surrounded. The government was to be offered the opportunity of surrendering peacefully. If it refused to do so, the Winter Palace was to be shelled from the *Aurora* and the Peter and Paul Fortress, after which it was to be stormed. The main forces designated to take part in these operations were the Pavlovsky Regiment; Red Guard detachments from the Vyborg, Petrograd, and Vasilevsky Island districts; the Keksgolmsky Regiment; the naval elements arriving from Kronstadt and Helsingfors; and sailors from the Petrograd-based Second Baltic Fleet Detachment. Command posts were to be set up in the barracks of the Pavlovsky Regiment and the Second Baltic Fleet Detachment, the former to be directed by Eremeev and the latter by Chudnovsky. A field headquarters for overall direction of the attacking military forces, to be commanded by Antonov-Ovseenko, was to be established in the Peter and Paul Fortress.[4]

Even as these preparations for the seizure of the last bastions of the Provisional Government in Petrograd were being completed, Lenin, elsewhere at Smolny, was nervously watching the clock, by all indications most anxious to insure that the Kerensky regime would be totally eliminated before the start of the Congress of Soviets, now just a scant few hours away. At about 10:00 A.M. he drafted a manifesto "To the Citizens of Russia," proclaiming the transfer of political power from the Kerensky government to the Military Revolutionary Committee:

25 October 1917

To the Citizens of Russia!

The Provisional Government has been overthrown. State power has passed into the hands of the organ of the Petrograd Soviet of Workers' and Soldiers' Deputies, the Military Revolutionary Committee, which stands at the head of the Petrograd proletariat and garrison.

The cause for which the people have struggled—the immediate proposal of a democratic peace, the elimination of landlord estates, workers' control

Отъ Военно-Революціоннаго Комитета при Петроградскомъ Совѣтѣ Рабочихъ и Солдатскихъ Депутатовъ.

Къ Гражданамъ Россіи.

Временное Правительство низложено. Государственная власть перешла въ руки органа Петроградскаго Совѣта Рабочихъ и Солдатскихъ Депутатовъ — Военно-Революціоннаго Комитета, стоящаго во главѣ Петроградскаго пролетаріата и гарнизона.

Дѣло, за которое боролся народъ: немедленное предложеніе демократическаго мира, отмѣна помѣщичьей собственности на землю, рабочій контроль надъ производствомъ, созданіе Совѣтскаго Правительства — это дѣло обезпечено.

ДА ЗДРАВСТВУЕТЪ РЕВОЛЮЦІЯ РАБОЧИХЪ, СОЛДАТЪ И КРЕСТЬЯНЪ!

Военно-Революціонный Комитетъ при Петроградскомъ Совѣтѣ Рабочихъ и Солдатскихъ Депутатовъ.

25 октября 1917 г. 10 ч. утра.

Lenin's manifesto of October 25, 1917, "To the Citizens of Russia," proclaiming the transfer of political power from the Kerensky government to the Military Revolutionary Committee.

over production, the creation of a soviet government—the triumph of this cause has been assured.

Long live the workers', soldiers', and peasants' revolution!

> The Military Revolutionary Committee
> of the Petrograd Soviet
> of Workers' and Soldiers' Deputies[5]

The seminal importance Lenin attached to congress delegates being faced, from the very start, with a *fait accompli* as regards the creation of a soviet government is clearly illustrated by the fact that this proclamation was printed and already going out over the wires to the entire country even before the Military Revolutionary Committee strategy meeting described above had ended.

If October 25 began as a day of energetic activity and hope for the left, the same cannot be said for supporters of the old government. In the Winter Palace, Kerensky by now had completed arrangements to meet troops heading for the capital from the northern front. A striking indication of the isolation and helplessness of the Provisional Government at this point is the fact that the Military Revolutionary Committee's control of all rail terminals precluded travel outside of Petrograd by train, while for some time the General Staff was unable to provide the prime minister with even one automobile suitable for an extended trip. Finally, military officials managed to round up an open Pierce Arrow and a Renault, the latter borrowed from the American embassy. At 11:00 A.M., almost precisely the moment when Lenin's manifesto proclaiming the overthrow of the government began circulating, the Renault, flying an American flag, tailed by the aristocratic Pierce Arrow, roared through the main arch of the General Staff building, barreled past Military Revolutionary Committee pickets already forming around the Winter Palace, and sped southwestward out of the capital. Huddled in the back seat of the Pierce Arrow were the assistant to the commander of the Petrograd Military District, Kuzmin; two staff officers; and a pale and haggard Kerensky, on his way to begin a desperate hunt for loyal troops from the front, a mission that was to end in abject failure less than a week later.[6]

As Kerensky's entourage streaked by the Mariinsky Palace, the relatively few deputies to the Preparliament assembled there were exchanging news of the latest political developments, awaiting the start of the day's session. Within an hour, a large contingent of armed soldiers and sailors, under Chudnovsky's command, began sealing off adjacent streets and posting guards at all palace entrances and exits. The armored car *Oleg*, flying a red flag, clattered up and took a position at the western corner of the palace.

When these preparations were completed, an unidentified Military Revolutionary Committee commissar entered the palace, searched out Avksentiev, and handed him a directive from the Military Revolutionary Committee ordering that the Mariinsky Palace be cleared without delay. Meanwhile, some soldiers and sailors burst into the building, brandishing their rifles, and posted themselves along the palace's grand main staircase. While many of the frightened deputies dashed for their coats and prepared to brave the phalanx of armed soldiers and sailors, Avksentiev had the presence of mind to collect part of the Preparliament steering committee. These deputies hurriedly agreed to formally protest the Military Revolutionary Committee's attack, but to make no attempt to resist it. They also instructed Avksentiev to reconvene the Preparliament at the earliest practicable moment. Before they were permitted to leave the palace, the identity of each of the deputies was carefully checked, but no one was detained. For the time being, the Military Revolutionary Committee forces were apparently under instructions to limit arrests to members of the government.[7]

Elsewhere by this time, insurgent ranks had been bolstered by the liberation from the Crosses Prison of the remaining Bolsheviks imprisoned there since the July days. A Military Revolutionary Committee commissar simply appeared at the ancient prison on the morning of October 25 with a small detachment of Red Guards and an order for the release of all political prisoners; among others, the Bolsheviks Semion Roshal, Sakharov, Tolkachev, and Khaustov were immediately set free.[8] At 2:00 P.M. the forces at the disposal of the Military Revolutionary Committee were increased still further by the arrival of the armada from Kronstadt. One of the more than a thousand sailors crammed on the deck of the *Amur*, I. Pavlov, subsequently recalled the waters outside Petrograd at midday, October 25:

> What did the Gulf of Finland around Kronstadt and Petrograd look like then? This is conveyed well by a song that was popular at the time [sung to the melody of the familiar folk tune *Stenka Razin*]: "Iz za ostrova Kronshtadta na prostor reki Nevy, vyplyvaiut mnogo lodok, v nikh sidiat bol'sheviki!" [From the island of Kronstadt toward the River Neva broad, there are many boats a-sailing—they have Bolsheviks on board.] If these words do not describe the Gulf of Finland exactly, it's only because "boats" are mentioned. Substitute contemporary ships and you will have a fully accurate picture of the Gulf of Finland a few hours before the October battle.[9]

At the entrance to the harbor canal the *Zaria svobody*, pulled by the four tugs, dropped anchor; a detachment of sailors swarmed ashore and undertook to occupy the Baltic rail line between Ligovo and Oranienbaum. As the rest of the ships inched through the narrow channel, it occurred to Flerovsky, aboard the *Amur*, that if the government had had the foresight to lay a couple of mines and emplace even a dozen machine guns behind the parapet of the canal embankment, the carefully laid plans of the Kronstadters would have been wrecked. He heaved a sigh of relief as the motley assortment of ships passed through the canal unhindered and entered the Neva, where they were greeted by enthusiastic cheers from crowds of workers gathered on the banks. Flerovsky himself was in the cabin of the *Amur* ship's committee below decks, discussing where to cast anchor, when a mighty, jubilant hurrah rent the air. Flerovsky ran up on deck just in time to see the *Aurora* execute a turn in the middle of the river, angling for a better view of the Winter Palace.[10]

As the men on the *Aurora* and the ships from Kronstadt spotted each other, cheers and shouts of greeting rang out, the round caps of the sailors filled the sky, and the *Aurora*'s band broke into a triumphant march. The

Amur dropped anchor close by the *Aurora,* while some of the smaller boats continued on as far as the Admiralty. Moments later Antonov-Ovseenko went out to the *Amur* to give instructions to leaders of the Kronstadt detachment. Then, as students and professors at St. Petersburg University gawked from classroom windows on the embankment, the sailors, totaling around three thousand, disembarked, large numbers of them to join the forces preparing to besiege the Winter Palace. A member of this contingent later remembered that upon encountering garrison soldiers, some of the sailors berated them for their cowardliness during the July days. He recalled with satisfaction that the soldiers were now ready to repent their errors.[11]

Important developments were occurring in the meantime at Smolny. The great main hall there was packed to the rafters with Petrograd Soviet deputies and representatives from provincial soviets anxious for news of the latest events when Trotsky opened an emergency session of the Petrograd Soviet at 2:35 P.M.[12] The fundamental transformation in the party's tactics that had occurred during the night became apparent from the outset of this meeting, perhaps the most momentous in the history of the Petrograd Soviet. It will be recalled that less than twenty-four hours earlier, at another session of the Petrograd Soviet, Trotsky had insisted that an armed conflict "today or tomorrow, on the eve of the congress, is not in our plans." Now, stepping up to the speaker's platform, he immediately pronounced the Provisional Government's obituary. "On behalf of the Military Revolutionary Committee," he shouted, "I declare that the Provisional Government no longer exists!" To a storm of applause and shouts of "Long live the Military Revolutionary Committee!" he announced, in rapid order, that the Preparliament had been dispersed, that individual government ministers had been arrested, and that the rail stations, the post office, the central telegraph, the Petrograd Telegraph Agency, and the state bank had been occupied by forces of the Military Revolutionary Committee. "The Winter Palace has not been taken," he reported, "but its fate will be decided momentarily. . . . In the history of the revolutionary movement I know of no other examples in which such huge masses were involved and which developed so bloodlessly. The power of the Provisional Government, headed by Kerensky, was dead and awaited the blow of the broom of history which had to sweep it away. . . . The population slept peacefully and did not know that at this time one power was replaced by another."

In the midst of Trotsky's speech, Lenin appeared in the hall. Catching sight of him, the audience rose to its feet, delivering a thundering ovation. With the greeting, "Long live Comrade Lenin, back with us again," Trotsky turned the platform over to his comrade. Side by side, Lenin and Trotsky acknowledged the cheers of the crowd. "Comrades!" declared Lenin, over the din:

The workers' and peasants' revolution, the necessity of which has been talked about continuously by the Bolsheviks, has occurred. What is the significance of this workers' and peasants' revolution? First of all, the significance of this revolution is that we shall have a soviet government, our own organ of power without the participation of any bourgeois. The oppressed masses will form a government themselves. . . . This is the beginning of a new period in the history of Russia; and the present, third Russian revolution must ultimately lead to the victory of socialism. One of our immediate tasks is the necessity of ending the war at once.

We shall win the confidence of the peasantry by one decree, which will abolish landlord estates. The peasants will understand that their only salvation lies in an alliance with the workers. We will institute real workers' control over production.

You have now learned how to work together in harmony, as evidenced by the revolution that has just occurred. We now possess the strength of a mass organization, which will triumph over everything and which will lead the proletariat to world revolution.

In Russia we must now devote ourselves to the construction of a proletarian socialist state.

Long live the world socialist revolution.

Lenin's remarks were brief; yet it is perhaps not surprising that on this occasion most of his listeners did not trouble themselves with the question of how a workers' government would survive in backward Russia and a hostile world. After Lenin's remarks, Trotsky proposed that special commissars be dispatched to the front and throughout the country at once to inform the broad masses everywhere of the successful uprising in Petrograd. At this someone shouted, "You are anticipating the will of the Second Congress of Soviets," to which Trotsky immediately retorted: "The will of the Second Congress of Soviets has already been predetermined by the fact of the workers' and soldiers' uprising. Now we have only to develop this triumph."

The relatively few Mensheviks in attendance formally absolved themselves of responsibility for what they called "the tragic consequences of the conspiracy underway" and withdrew from the executive organs of the Petrograd Soviet. But most of the audience listened patiently to greetings by Lunacharsky and Zinoviev, the latter, like Lenin, making his first public appearance since July. The deputies shouted enthusiastic approval for a political statement drafted by Lenin and introduced by Volodarsky. Hailing the overthrow of the Provisional Government, the statement appealed to workers and soldiers everywhere to support the revolution; it also contained an expression of confidence that the Western European proletariat would help bring the cause of socialism to a full and stable victory.[13] The deputies then dispersed, either to factories and barracks to spread the glad

Barricades near St. Isaac's Cathedral on October 25.

tidings, or, like Sukhanov, to grab a bite to eat before the opening session of the All-Russian Congress.

Dusk was nearing, and the Winter Palace was still not in Bolshevik hands. As early as 1:00 P.M. a detachment of sailors commanded by Ivan Sladkov had occupied the Admiralty, a few steps from the Winter Palace, and arrested the naval high command. At the same time, elements of the Pavlovsky Regiment had occupied the area around the Winter Palace, bounded by Millionnaia, Moshkov, and Bolshaia Koniushennaia streets, and Nevsky Prospect from the Ekaterinsky Canal to the Moika. Pickets, manned with armored cars and anti-aircraft guns, were set up on bridges over the Ekaterinsky Canal and the Moika, and on Morskaia Street. Later in the afternoon, Red Guard detachments from the Petrograd District and the Vyborg side joined the Pavlovsky soldiers, and troops from the Keksgolmsky Regiment occupied the area north of the Moika to the Admiralty, closing the ring of insurrectionary forces around the Palace Square. "The Provisional Government," Dashkevich would subsequently recall, "was as good as in a mousetrap."[14]

Noon had been the original deadline for the seizure of the Winter Palace. This was subsequently postponed to 3:00 and then 6:00 P.M., after which, to quote Podvoisky, the Military Revolutionary Committee "no longer bothered to set deadlines."[15] The agreed-upon ultimatum to the govern-

Petrograd during the October days. Baltic sailors helping to unpack artillery shells.

ment was not dispatched; instead, loyalist forces gained time to strengthen their defenses. Thus in the late afternoon, insurgent troops watched impatiently while cadets on the Palace Square erected massive barricades and machine gun emplacements of firewood brought from the General Staff building.

By 6:00 P.M. it was dark, drizzly, and cold, and many of the soldiers deployed in the area around the palace hours earlier were growing hungry and restless. Occasionally, one of them would lose patience and open fire at the cadets, only to be rebuked with the stern command, "Comrades, don't shoot without orders." On the Petrograd side, the Bolshevik Military Organization leader Tarasov-Rodionov, for one, was beside himself worrying about what was happening in the center of the city. "I had the urge," he later wrote, "to drop everything—to rush to them [the Military Revolutionary Committee] to speed up this idiotically prolonged assault on the Winter Palace." During these hours, Lenin sent Podvoisky, Antonov, and Chudnovsky dozens of notes in which he fumed that their procrastination was delaying the opening of the congress and needlessly stimulating anxiety among congress deputies.[16]

Antonov implies in his memoirs that unexpected delays in the mobilization of insurgent soldiers, faulty organization, and other problems of a minor yet troublesome nature were the main reasons it took so long to launch the culminating offensive on the government.[17] In support of this view, there are indications that, for one reason or another, last-minute snags developed in connection with mobilizing some elements of the Preobrazhensky and Semenovsky regiments for the attack. More important, most of the sailor detachments from Helsingfors that the Military Revolutionary Committee was counting on for its assault did not arrive until late evening or even the following day. (In one case, a trainload of armed sailors was delayed in an open field outside Vyborg for many hours after the locomotive had burst its pipes; the Vyborg stationmaster, sympathetic to the government, had purposely provided the sailors with the least reliable locomotive available.[18])

The Military Revolutionary Committee did indeed encounter a number of minor difficulties which prompted concern at the time, but which in retrospect appear almost comical. When Blagonravov began checking out the cannon at the Peter and Paul Fortress in preparation for shelling the Winter Palace, he found that the six-inch guns on the walls of the fortress facing the palace had not been used or cleaned for months. Artillery officers persuaded him that they were not serviceable. Blagonravov then made soldiers in the fortress drag heavy three-inch training cannon some distance to where they could be brought into action, only to find that all of these weapons had parts missing or were genuinely defective. He also discovered that shells of the proper caliber were not immediately available. After the loss of considerable time, it was ascertained that making the six-inch guns work was not impossible after all.[19] Even more bizarre, by prior arrangement a lighted red lantern hoisted to the top of the fortress flagpole was to signal the start of the final push against the Winter Palace, yet when the moment for action arrived, no red lantern could be found. Recalls Blagonravov, "After a long search a suitable lamp was located, but then it proved extremely difficult to fix it on the flagpole so it could be seen."[20]

Podvoisky, in his later writings, tended to attribute continuing delays in mounting an attack on the Winter Palace to the Military Revolutionary Committee's hope, for the most part realized, of avoiding a bloody battle. As Podvoisky later recalled: "Already assured of victory, we awaited the humiliating end of the Provisional Government. We strove to insure that it would surrender in the face of the revolutionary strength which we then enjoyed. We did not open artillery fire, giving our strongest weapon, the class struggle, an opportunity to operate within the walls of the palace."[21] This consideration appears to have had some validity as well. There was little food for the almost three thousand officers, cadets, cossacks, and women soldiers in the Winter Palace on October 25. In the early afternoon the ubiquitous American journalist John Reed somehow wangled his way into the palace, wandered through one of the rooms where these troops were billeted, and took note of the dismal surroundings: "On both sides of the parqueted floor lay rows of dirty mattresses and blankets, upon which occasional soldiers were stretched out; everywhere was a litter of cigarette-

Military school cadets in the Winter Palace during the October days.

butts, bits of bread, cloth, and empty bottles with expensive French labels. More and more soldiers, with the red shoulder-straps of the Yunker-schools, moved about in a stale atmosphere of tobacco smoke and unwashed humanity. . . . The place was a huge barrack, and evidently had been for weeks, from the look of the floor and walls."[22]

As time passed and promised provisions and reinforcements from the front did not arrive, the government defenders became more and more demoralized, a circumstance known to the attackers. At 6:15 P.M. a large contingent of cadets from the Mikhailovsky Artillery School departed, taking with them four of the six heavy guns in the palace. Around 8:00 P.M. the two hundred cossacks on guard also returned to their barracks.

Representatives of the Military Revolutionary Committee participated in at least two attempts to convince other elements defending the government to leave peacefully. In the early evening, a representative of the Oranienbaum cadets persuaded Chudnovsky to accompany him to the palace to help arrange the peaceful withdrawal of his men. The cadets guaranteed Chudnovsky's safe conduct and kept their word. But Petr Palchinsky, an engineer and deputy minister of trade and industry who was helping to direct the defense of the government, insisted that Chudnovsky be arrested. The cadets protested, however, and forced Chudnovsky's release. Dashkevich had also slipped into the palace to try to win over some of the cadets; like Chudnovsky, he was detained and then allowed to leave. Partly as a result of the efforts of Chudnovsky and Dashkevich, more than half of the cadets guarding the Winter Palace left there at around 10:00 P.M.[23]

Whatever obstacles confronted the Military Revolutionary Committee in its assault on the Winter Palace on October 25 pale by comparison with the difficulties facing members of the Provisional Government, gathered in the grand Malachite Hall on the second floor of the palace. Here Konovalov convened a cabinet session at noon, an hour after Kerensky's hurried departure for the front. Present were all of the ministers except Kerensky and the minister of food supply, a distinguished economist, Sergei Prokopovich, who, having been temporarily detained by an insurgent patrol in the morning, was unable to reach the Winter Palace before it was completely sealed off in the afternoon. Fortunately for the historian, several of the participants in this ill-fated last meeting of Kerensky's cabinet penned detailed recollections of their final hours together; these tortured accounts bear witness to the almost complete isolation of the Provisional Government at this time, and to the ministers' resulting confusion and ever-increasing paralysis of will.[24]

Konovalov opened the meeting with a report on the political situation in the capital. He informed the ministers of the Military Revolutionary Committee's virtually unhampered success the previous night, of Polkovnikov's shattering early-morning status report, and of Kerensky's decision to rush to the front. For the first time, the full impact of the Petrograd Military District command's utter helplessness in dealing with the insurrection underway, and indeed of its inability even to furnish personal protection for the ministers, was felt by the cabinet as a whole. Responding to Konovalov's assessment, Admiral Verderevsky, the naval minister, observed coldly: "I don't know why this session was called. . . . We have no tangible military force and consequently are incapable of taking any action whatever." [25] He suggested it would have been wiser to have convened a joint session with the Preparliament, an idea that became moot moments later, when news was received of the latter's dispersal. At the start of their deliberations, however, most of the ministers did not fully share Verderevsky's pessimism. Tending, no doubt wishfully, to place most of the blame for the government's plight on Polkovnikov, they agreed to replace him with a "dictator" who would be given unlimited power to restore order and resolved that the cabinet would remain in continuous session in the Winter Palace for the duration of the emergency.

With periodic interruptions while Konovalov attempted unsuccessfully to bring more cossacks to the Winter Palace grounds, and while other ministers received disjointed reports on late-breaking developments and issued frantic appeals for help over the few phones still in operation to contacts elsewhere in the capital and over the direct wire to the front, the cabinet spent the better part of the next two hours engaged in a disorganized, meandering discussion of possible candidates for the post of "dictator." Ultimately, they displayed their insensitivity to the prevailing popular mood by settling on the minister of welfare, Kishkin. A physician by profession and a Muscovite, Kishkin had no prestige in Petrograd. Worst of all, he was a Kadet. Indeed, the selection of Kishkin was exactly the opposite of the more conciliatory course urged on Kerensky the preceding day by the Preparliament—a blatant provocation to democratic circles and an unexpected boon to the extreme left.

Kishkin formally assumed his new position as governor-general shortly after 4:00 P.M. After naming as his assistants Palchinsky and Petr Rutenberg, an assistant to the commander of the Petrograd Military District, he rushed off to military headquarters to direct the struggle against the insurrection. There Kishkin immediately sacked Polkovnikov, replacing him with the chief of staff, General Bagratuni. As nearly as one can tell, the main effect of this reshuffling of personnel was to increase significantly the chaos reigning at headquarters. For in protest to the treatment accorded Polkovnikov, all of his closest associates, including the quartermaster, General Nikolai Paradelov, immediately resigned in a huff. Some of these individuals packed off and went home. Others simply stopped work; from time to time, they could be seen peering out of the windows of the General Staff building at the clusters of insurgent soldiers, sailors, and workers advancing along the banks of the Moika and up Millionnaia Street.[26]

Meanwhile, in the Winter Palace, the rest of the cabinet occupied itself in preparing an appeal for support to be printed up for mass circulation. At 6:15 P.M. the ministers were informed of the departure of the cadets from the Mikhailovsky Artillery School; fifteen minutes later, they adjourned to Kerensky's third-floor private dining room, where a supper of borshch, fish, and artichokes—and more painful blows—awaited them.

By now, at the Peter and Paul Fortress, Blagonravov, under continual prodding from Smolny, had decided that the final stage of the attack on the government could be delayed no longer, this despite the fact that difficulties with the cannon and the signal lantern had not yet been fully surmounted. At 6:30 P.M. he dispatched two cyclists to the General Staff building, and in twenty minutes they arrived there armed with the following ultimatum:[27]

> By order of the Military Revolutionary Committee of the Petrograd Soviet, the Provisional Government is declared overthrown. All power is transferred to the Petrograd Soviet of Workers' and Soldiers' Deputies. The Winter Palace is surrounded by revolutionary forces. Cannon at the Peter and Paul Fortress and on the ships *Aurora* and *Amur* are aimed at the Winter Palace and the General Staff building. In the name of the Military Revolutionary Committee we propose that the Provisional Government and the troops loyal to it capitulate. . . . You have twenty minutes to

answer. Your response should be given to our messenger. This ultimatum expires at 7:10, after which we will immediately open fire. . . .

Chairman of the Military Revolutionary Committee Antonov
Commissar of the Peter and Paul Fortress G. B.

At the General Staff building when this message was delivered were, among others, Kishkin, General Bagratuni, General Paradelov, and Palchinsky and Rutenberg. They persuaded one of the cyclists to return to the fortress with a request for a ten-minute extension. Leaving Paradelov behind to receive the government's response by phone and pass it on to the remaining cyclist, Kishkin, Bagratuni, and the others rushed to the Winter Palace to consult with the cabinet.[28]

Along with the news of the Military Revolutionary Committee's ultimatum, the ministers also learned that large numbers of previously wavering cadets from Oranienbaum and Peterhof now intended to leave the palace. Besides, the original deadline set by Antonov was already close to expiration. The ministers hurried back to the Malachite Hall at once to consider the question of whether or not to surrender. Looking out at the crowded Neva and the Peter and Paul Fortress, one member of the cabinet wondered aloud, "What will happen to the palace if the *Aurora* opens fire?"

The cruiser *Aurora* on the Neva the night of October 25.

"It will be turned into a heap of ruins," replied Admiral Verderevsky, adding sanguinely: "Her turrets are higher than the bridges. She can demolish the place without damaging any other building." [29]

Still, all the ministers, including Verderevsky, were agreed that surrender in the prevailing circumstances was unthinkable. They resolved simply to ignore the ultimatum, and Kishkin, Gvozdev, and Konovalov immediately rushed off to coax the cadets to remain at their posts. In his diary, Minister of Justice Pavel Maliantovich attempted to explain the cabinet's decision. He suggested that although at this point the ministers had lost hope of holding out until the arrival of outside help, they believed strongly that legally the Provisional Government could hand over its authority only to the Constituent Assembly. They felt a solemn obligation to resist until the very last moment so that it would be clear beyond doubt that they had yielded only to absolutely overwhelming force. That moment had not yet come, Maliantovich affirmed, hence the cabinet's decision to give no reply to the Military Revolutionary Committee and to continue resistance. [30]

Ironically, at precisely the moment that the Military Revolutionary Committee's ultimatum was delivered to General Staff headquarters, General Cheremisov, in Pskov, was conferring on the direct wire with General Bagratuni. At the start of the communication, Cheremisov had asked for a report on the condition of the capital. Specifically, he inquired as to the whereabouts of the government, the status of the Winter Palace, whether order was being maintained in the city, and whether or not units dispatched from the front had reached Petrograd. Bagratuni was answering these questions, as best he could, when he was called away to receive the ultimatum. General Paradelov then got on the Petrograd end of the direct wire and passed on to Cheremisov his misgivings about Kishkin's appointment and behavior, stating quite directly his belief that the Provisional Government was doomed. Cheremisov, in turn, requested Paradelov to call the Winter Palace to obtain more information about the situation there. [31] Paradelov went off to do this but was interrupted by Bagratuni, just then leaving for the Winter Palace with the ultimatum. Paradelov was instructed to stand by to receive the government's telephoned response. As Paradelov waited for the message from the Winter Palace, insurgent soldiers and workers suddenly flooded the building; resistance was impossible. [32] Meanwhile, Cheremisov, still at the other end of the direct wire, inquired impatiently, "Where is Paradelov, and will he give me an answer soon?" In response, a military telegrapher barely managed to tap out: "We will find him. . . . The headquarters has been occupied by Military Revolutionary Committee forces. I am quitting work and getting out of here!"[33]

Word of the capture of the General Staff building reached General Bagratuni and the cabinet in the second-floor office of one of Kerensky's assistants, facing the palace courtyard, to which they had moved from the more vulnerable Malachite Hall. Bagratuni responded to the loss of his staff and headquarters by tendering his resignation. Soon after departing the palace, he was pulled from a cab and arrested by an insurgent patrol.

For their part, the ministers now dispatched the following radio-telegram to the Russian people:

> To All, All, All!
> The Petrograd Soviet has declared the Provisional Government over-thrown, and demands that power be yielded to it under threat of shelling the Winter Palace from cannon in the Peter and Paul Fortress and aboard the cruiser *Aurora*, anchored on the Neva. The government can yield power only to the Constituent Assembly; because of this we have decided not to surrender and to put ourselves under the protection of the people and the army. In this regard a telegram was sent to Stavka. Stavka an-swered with word that a detachment had been dispatched. Let the country and the people respond to the mad attempt of the Bolsheviks to stimulate an uprising in the rear of the fighting army.[34]

The ministers also managed to establish telephone contact with the mayor of Petrograd, Shreider, in the City Duma building. They informed him that the Winter Palace was about to be shelled from the *Aurora* and the Peter and Paul Fortress, and appealed to him to help mobilize support for the government. The previous day, deeply concerned by the actions of the Military Revolutionary Committee, the City Duma, in which the SRs and Kadets still had a majority, had dispatched a fact-finding mission to Smolny; subsequently, in spite of fierce opposition from its Bolshevik members, the Duma, like the Preparliament, had initiated steps to form a Committee of Public Safety to help maintain order in the city and to protect the popula-tion. Now, upon receipt of the Provisional Government's appeal, Shreider immediately convened the City Duma in emergency session. Announcing at the outset that "in a few minutes the cannon will begin to thunder . . . [and] the Provisional Government of the Russian Republic will perish in the ruins of the Winter Palace," he called upon the Duma to help the gov-ernment by all means possible. Inasmuch as the deputies had no military forces at their disposal, they agreed to dispatch emissaries to the *Aurora*, to Smolny, and to the Winter Palace immediately in an effort to halt the siege of the Winter Palace and to mediate differences between the government and the Military Revolutionary Committee.[35]

Meanwhile, at the Peter and Paul Fortress, cannon and signal-lantern difficulties having been overcome at last, Blagonravov and Antonov were preparing to commence the shelling of the Winter Palace. One further delay occurred when they received what turned out to be an erroneous report, evidently sparked by the surrender of General Staff headquarters, that the Winter Palace had capitulated. Blagonravov and Antonov drove across the Neva to check out the rumor themselves. At 9:40 P.M. Blagonravov finally returned to the fortress and signaled the *Aurora* to open fire. The *Aurora* responded by firing one blank round from its bow gun. The blast of a cannon shooting blanks is significantly greater than if it were using combat ammunition, and the ear-splitting reverberations of the *Aurora*'s first shot were felt throughout the capital. The blast impelled gawking spectators lined up on the Neva embankments to flop to the ground and crawl away in panic, and it contributed to the further thinning out of military forces inside the Winter Palace. (Many cadets finally abandoned their posts at this point and were followed shortly afterward by a number of the women soldiers.) Contrary to legend and to Verderevsky's prediction, the *Aurora*'s shot did no physical damage.

After the *Aurora*'s action the artillerists at the Peter and Paul Fortress allowed time for those forces who wished to do so to leave the palace. During this interim, the officer of the watch on the *Amur* spotted a string of lights at the mouth of the Neva and sounded the alarm: "Ships approaching!" As their silhouettes came into view, old deck hands on the *Amur* triumphantly identified the arriving vessels as the destroyers *Samson* and *Zabiiaka*, accompanied by some of the other ships from Helsingfors.[36]

At around 11:00 P.M. Blagonravov gave the order to commence shooting in earnest. Most of the shells subsequently fired exploded spectacularly but harmlessly over the Neva, but one shattered a cornice on the palace and another smashed a third-floor corner window, exploding just above the room in which the government was meeting. The blast unnerved the ministers and influenced at least a few of them to have second thoughts about the wisdom of further resistance. Meanwhile, from the walls of the Peter and Paul Fortress, Tarasov-Rodionov watched the spectacular fireworks, whose tremors momentarily drowned out the sound of the rifle and machine gun fire and the droning of lighted streetcars crawling single file across the Troitsky and Palace bridges, and wondered at the incredibility of it all, of "the workers' soviet overthrowing the bourgeois government while the peaceful life of the city continued uninterrupted."[37]

To City Duma deputies, it was by this time patently clear that their hopes of interceding between the Military Revolutionary Committee and the embattled ministers in the Winter Palace would not be realized. A Military Revolutionary Committee commissar refused to permit the representatives of the City Duma to go anywhere near the *Aurora*. The delegation sent to the Winter Palace was halted several times by the besiegers and, in the end, forced to scurry back to the City Duma building after being fired upon from upper-story windows of the Winter Palace. ("The cadets probably didn't see our white flag," a member of the delegation later said.) The City Duma emissaries who went to Smolny, Mayor Shreider among them, fared somewhat better. They managed to have a few minutes with Kamenev, who helped arrange for Molotov to accompany them to the Winter Palace. But this delegation, too, was unable to make it through the

narrow strip of no man's land which now separated the tight ring of insurrectionary forces from the barricades set up by defenders of the
government.[38]

About the time the City Duma was informed of these setbacks it also
received a bitter telephone message from Semion Maslov, the minister of
agriculture, and a right SR. The call was taken by Naum Bykhovsky, also
an SR, who immediately relayed Maslov's words to a hushed Duma. "We
here in the Winter Palace have been abandoned and left to ourselves," declared Maslov, as quoted by Bykhovsky. "The democracy sent us into the
Provisional Government; we didn't want the appointments, but we went.
Yet now, when tragedy has struck, when we are being shot, we are not
supported by anyone. Of course we will die. But my final words will be:
'Contempt and damnation to the democracy which knew how to appoint us
but was unable to defend us!' "[39]

Bykhovsky at once proposed that the entire Duma march in a body to the
Winter Palace "to die along with our representatives." "Let our comrades
know," he proclaimed, "that we have not abandoned them, let them know
we will die with them." This idea struck a responsive chord with just about
everyone, except the Bolsheviks. Reporters present noted that most deputies stood and cheered for several minutes. Before the proposal was actually voted upon, the City Duma received a request from a representative of
the All-Russian Executive Committee of Peasant Soviets that the leadership
of the peasant soviets be permitted to "go out and die with the Duma." It
also heard from the minister of food supply, Prokopovich, who tearfully
pleaded to be allowed to join the procession to the Winter Palace, "so that
he could at least share the fate of his comrades." Not to be outdone, Coun-
tess Sofia Panina, a prominent Kadet, volunteered "to stand in front of the
cannon," adding that "the Bolsheviks can fire at the Provisional Government over our dead bodies." The start of the march to the Winter Palace
was delayed a bit because someone demanded a roll call vote on
Bykhovsky's motion. During the roll call, most of the deputies insisted on
individually declaring their readiness to "die with the government," before
voting "Yes"—whereupon each Bolshevik solemnly proclaimed that he
would "go to the Soviet," before registering an emphatic "No!"[40]

While all this was going on, Lenin remained at Smolny, raging at every
delay in the seizure of the Winter Palace and still anxious that the All-
Russian Congress not get underway until the members of the Provisional
Government were securely behind bars. Andrei Bubnov later recorded that
"the night of October 25 . . . Ilich hurried with the capture of the Winter
Palace, putting extreme pressure on everyone and everybody when there
was no news of how the attack was going."[41] Similarly, Podvoisky later remembered that Lenin now "paced around a small room at Smolny like a
lion in a cage. He needed the Winter Palace at any cost: it remained the last

gate on the road to workers' power. V. I. scolded . . . he screamed . . . he was ready to shoot us." [42]

Still, the start of the congress had been scheduled for 2:00 P.M. By late evening, the delegates had been milling around for hours; it was impossible to hold them back much longer, regardless of Lenin's predilections. Finally, at 10:40 P.M., Dan rang the chairman's bell, formally calling the congress into session. "The Central Executive Committee considers our customary opening political address superfluous," he announced at the outset. "Even now, our comrades who are selflessly fulfilling the obligations we placed on them are under fire at the Winter Palace."[43]

John Reed, who had pushed his way through a clamorous mob at the door of the hall, subsequently described the scene in Smolny's white assembly hall as the congress opened:

> In the rows of seats, under the white chandeliers, packed immovably in the aisles and on the sides, perched on every windowsill, and even the edge of the platform, the representatives of the workers and soldiers of all Russia awaited in anxious silence or wild exultation the ringing of the chairman's bell. There was no heat in the hall but the stifling heat of unwashed human bodies. A foul blue cloud of cigarette smoke rose from the mass and hung in the thick air. Occasionally someone in authority mounted the tribune and asked the comrades not to smoke; then everybody, smokers and all, took up the cry "Don't smoke, comrades!" and went on smoking. . . .
>
> On the platform sat the leaders of the old Tsay-ee-kah [Central Executive Committee] . . . Dan was ringing the bell. Silence fell sharply intense, broken by the scuffling and disputing of the people at the door. . . .[44]

According to a preliminary report by the Credentials Committee, 300 of the 670 delegates assembled in Petrograd for the congress were Bolsheviks, 193 were SRs (of whom more than half were Left SRs), 68 were Mensheviks, 14 were Menshevik-Internationalists, and the remainder either were affiliated with one of a number of smaller political groups or did not belong to any formal organization.[45] The dramatic rise in support for the Bolsheviks that had occurred in the previous several months was reflected in the fact that the party's fraction was three times greater than it had been at the First All-Russian Congress of Soviets in June; the Bolsheviks were now far and away the largest single party represented at the congress. Yet it is essential to bear in mind that, despite this success, at the opening of the congress the Bolsheviks did not have an absolute majority without significant help from the Left SRs.

Because delegates, upon arrival at Smolny, were asked to fill out detailed personal questionnaires, we can ascertain not only the political affiliation of most of them, but also the character of each of the 402 local soviets represented at the congress and its official position on the construction of a new national government. Tabulation of these questionnaires reveals the striking fact that an overwhelming number of delegates, some 505 of them, came to Petrograd committed in principle to supporting the transfer of "all power to the soviets," that is, the creation of a soviet government presumably reflective of the party composition of the congress. Eighty-six delegates were loosely bound to vote for "all power to the democracy," meaning a homogeneous democratic government including representatives of peasant soviets, trade unions, cooperatives, etc., while twenty-one delegates were committed to support of a coalition democratic government in which some propertied elements, but not the Kadets, would be represented. Only fifty-five delegates, that is, significantly less than 10 percent, represented constituencies still favoring continuation of the Soviet's former policy of coalition with the Kadets.[46]

As a result of the breakdown in relative voting strength, moments after the congress opened fourteen Bolsheviks took seats in the congress Presidium alongside seven Left SRs (the Mensheviks, allotted three seats in the Presidium, declined to fill them; the Menshevik-Internationalists did not fill the one seat allotted to them but reserved the right to do so). Dan, Lieber, Broido, Gots, Bogdanov, and Vasilii Filipovsky, who had directed the work of the Soviet since March, now vacated the seats at the head of the hall reserved for the top Soviet leadership; amid thunderous applause their places were immediately occupied by Trotsky, Kollontai, Lunacharsky, Nogin, Zinoviev, Kamkov, Maria Spiridonova, Mstislavsky, and other prominent Bolsheviks and Left SRs.[47]

As if punctuating this momentous changeover, an ominous sound was heard in the distance—the deep, pounding boom of exploding cannon. Rising to make an emergency announcement, Martov, in a shrill, trembling voice, demanded that, before anything else, the congress agree to seek a peaceful solution to the existing political crisis; in his view, the only way out of the emergency was first to stop the fighting and then to start negotiations for the creation of a united, democratic government acceptable to the entire democracy. With this in mind, he recommended selection of a special delegation to initiate discussions with other political parties and organizations aimed at bringing to an immediate end the clash which had erupted in the streets.

Speaking for the Left SRs, Mstislavsky immediately endorsed Martov's proposal; more significantly, it was also apparently well received by many Bolsheviks. Glancing around the hall, Sukhanov, for one, noted that "Martov's speech was greeted with a tumult of applause from a very large section of the meeting." Observed a *Delo naroda* reporter, "Martov's appeal was showered with torrents of applause by a majority in the hall." Bearing in mind that most of the congress delegates had mandates to support the creation by the congress of a coalition government of parties represented in the Soviet and since Martov's motion was directed toward that very end, there is no reason to doubt these observations. The published congress proceedings indicate that, on behalf of the Bolsheviks, Lunacharsky responded to Martov's speech with the declaration that "the Bolshevik fraction has absolutely nothing against the proposal made by Martov." The congress documents indicate as well that Martov's proposal was quickly passed by unanimous vote.[48]

No sooner had the congress endorsed the creation of a democratic coalition government by negotiation, however, than a succession of speakers, all representatives of the formerly dominant moderate socialist bloc, rose to denounce the Bolsheviks. These speakers declared their intention of immediately walking out of the congress as a means of protesting and opposing the actions of the Bolsheviks. The first to express himself in this vein was Iakov Kharash, a Menshevik army officer and delegate from the Twelfth Army Committee. Proclaimed Kharash: "A criminal political venture has been going on behind the back of the All-Russian Congress, thanks to the political hypocrisy of the Bolshevik Party. The Mensheviks and SRs consider it necessary to disassociate themselves from everything that is going on here and to mobilize the public for defense against attempts to seize power." Added Georgii Kuchin, also an officer and prominent Menshevik, speaking for a bloc of moderately inclined delegates from army committees at the front: "The congress was called primarily to discuss the question of forming a new government, and yet what do we see? We find that an irresponsible seizure of power has already occurred and that the will of the congress has been decided beforehand. . . . We must save the revolution from this mad venture. In the cause of rescuing the revolution we intend to mobilize all of the revolutionary elements in the army and the country. . . . [We] reject any responsibility for the consequences of this reckless venture and are withdrawing from this congress."[49]

These blunt statements triggered a storm of protest and cries of "Kornilovites!" and "Who in the hell do you represent?" from a large portion of the assembled delegates. Yet after Kamenev restored a semblance of order, Lev Khinchuk, from the Moscow Soviet, and Mikhail Gendelman, a lawyer and member of the SR Central Committee, read similarly bitter and militantly hostile declarations on behalf of the Mensheviks and SRs respectively. "The only possible peaceful solution to the present crisis continues to lie in negotiations with the Provisional Government on the formation of a government representing all elements of the democracy," Khinchuk insisted. At this, according to Sukhanov "a terrible din filled the hall; it was not only the Bolsheviks who were indignant, and for a long time the speaker wasn't allowed to continue." "We leave the present congress," Khinchuk finally shouted, "and invite all other fractions similarly unwilling to accept responsibility for the actions of the Bolsheviks to assemble together to discuss the situation." "Deserters," came shouts from the hall. Echoed Gendelman: "Anticipating that an outburst of popular indignation will follow the inevitable discovery of the bankruptcy of Bolshevik promises . . . the Socialist Revolutionary fraction is calling upon the revolutionary forces of the country to organize themselves and to stand guard over the revolution. . . . Taking cognizance of the seizure of power by the Bolsheviks . . . , holding them fully responsible for the consequences of this insane and criminal action, and consequently finding it impossible to collaborate with them, the Socialist Revolutionary fraction is leaving the congress!"[50]

Tempers in the hall now skyrocketed; there erupted a fierce squall of foot-stamping, whistling, and cursing. In response to the uprising now openly proclaimed by the Military Revolutionary Committee, the Mensheviks and SRs had moved rightward, and the gulf separating them from the extreme left had suddenly grown wider than ever. When one recalls that less than twenty-four hours earlier the Menshevik and SR congress fractions, uniting broad segments of both parties, appeared on the verge of at long last breaking with the bourgeois parties and endorsing the creation of a homogeneous socialist government pledged to a program of peace and reform, the profound impact of the events of October 24–25 becomes clear. One can certainly understand why the Mensheviks and SRs reacted as they did. At the same time, it is difficult to escape the conclusion that by totally repudiating the actions of the Bolsheviks and of the workers and soldiers who willingly followed them, and, even more, by pulling out of the congress, the moderate socialists undercut efforts at compromise by the Menshevik-Internationalists, the Left SRs, and the Bolshevik moderates. In so doing, they played directly into Lenin's hands, abruptly paving the way for the creation of a government which had never been publicly broached before —that is, an exclusively Bolshevik regime. In his memoir-history of the revolution, Sukhanov acknowledged the potentially immense historical significance of the Menshevik-SR walkout. He wrote that in leaving the congress "we completely untied the Bolsheviks' hands, making them masters of the entire situation and yielding to them the whole arena of the revolution. A struggle at the congress for a united democratic front *might* have had some success. . . . By quitting the congress, we ourselves gave the Bolsheviks a monopoly of the Soviet, of the masses, and of the revolution. By our own irrational decision, we ensured the victory of Lenin's whole 'line'!"[51]

All this is doubtless more apparent in retrospect than it was at the time. At any rate, following the declarations of Kharash, Kuchin, Khinchuk, and Gendelman, several radically inclined soldier-delegates took the floor to assert that the views of Kharash and Kuchin in no way represented the thinking of the average soldier. "Let them go—the army is not with them," burst out a young, lean-faced soldier named Karl Peterson, representing the Latvian Rifle Regiment; his observation would soon be only too evident to all. At this the hall rocked with wild cheering. "Kuchin refers to the mobilization of forces," shouted Frants Gzhelshchak, a Bolshevik soldier from the Second Army at the front, as soon as he could make himself heard. "Against whom—against the workers and soldiers who have come out to defend the revolution?" he asked. "Whom will he organize? Clearly not the workers and soldiers against whom he himself is determined to wage war." Declared Fedor Lukianov, a soldier from the Third Army, also a Bolshevik, "The thinking of Kuchin is that of the top army organizations which we elected way back in April and which have long since failed to reflect the views and mood of the broad masses of the army."[52]

At this point Genrikh Erlikh, a representative of the Bund (the Jewish social democratic organization), interrupted to inform the congress of the decision of a majority of City Duma deputies, taken moments earlier, to march en masse to the Winter Palace. Erlikh added that the Menshevik and SR fractions in the Executive Committee of the All-Russian Soviet of Peasant Deputies had decided to join the Duma deputies in protesting the application of violence against the Provisional Government, and invited all congress delegates "who did not wish a bloodbath" to participate in the march. It was at this point that the Mensheviks, SRs, Bundists, and members of the "front group"—deluged by shouts of "Deserters!" "Lackeys of the bourgeoisie!" and "Good riddance!"—rose from their places and made their way out of the hall.

Soon after the departure of the main bloc of Mensheviks and SRs, Martov, still intent most of all on facilitating a peaceful compromise between the moderate socialists and the radical left, took the floor to present a resolution on behalf of the Menshevik-Internationalists. His resolution condemned the Bolsheviks for organizing a coup d'état before the opening of the congress and called for creation of a broadly based democratic government to replace the Provisional Government. It read in part:

> Taking into consideration that this coup d'état threatens to bring about bloodshed, civil war, and the triumph of a counterrevolution . . . [and] that the only way out of this situation which could still prevent the development of a civil war might be an agreement between insurgent elements and the rest of the democratic organizations on the formation of a democratic government which is recognized by the entire revolutionary democracy and to which the Provisional Government could painlessly surrender its power, the Menshevik [Internationalist] fraction proposes that the congress pass a resolution on the necessity of a peaceful settlement of the present crisis by the formation of an all-democratic government . . . that the congress appoint a delegation for the purpose of entering into negotiations with other democratic organs and all the socialist parties . . . [and] that it discontinue its work pending the disclosure of the results of this delegation's efforts.[53]

It is easy to see that from Lenin's point of view, passage of Martov's resolution would have been a disaster; on the other hand, the departure of the moderates offered an opportunity which could now be exploited to consolidate the break with them. Not long after Martov resumed his seat, congress delegates rose and cheered the surprise appearance of the Bolshevik City Duma fraction, members of which, pushing their way into the crowded hall, announced that they had come "to triumph or die with the All-Russian Congress!" Then Trotsky, universally recognized as the Bolsheviks' most forceful orator, took the platform to declare:

> A rising of the masses of the people requires no justification. What has happened is an insurrection, and not a conspiracy. We hardened the revolutionary energy of the Petersburg workers and soldiers. We openly forged the will of the masses for an insurrection, and not a conspiracy. The masses of the people followed our banner and our insurrection was victorious. And now we are told: Renounce your victory, make concessions, compromise. With whom? I ask: With whom ought we to compromise? With those wretched groups who have left us or who are making this proposal? But after all we've had a full view of them. No one in Russia is with them any longer. A compromise is supposed to be made, as between two equal sides, by the millions of workers and peasants represented in this congress, whom they are ready, not for the first time or the last, to barter away as the bourgeoisie sees fit. No, here no compromise is possible. To those who have left and to those who tell us to do this we must say: You are miserable bankrupts, your role is played out; go where you ought to go: into the dustbin of history!

Amid stormy applause, Martov shouted in warning, "Then we'll leave!" And Trotsky, without a pause, read a resolution condemning the departure of Menshevik and SR delegates from the congress as "a weak and treacherous attempt to break up the legally constituted all-Russian representative assembly of the worker and soldier masses at precisely the moment when their avant-garde, with arms in hand, is defending the congress and the revolution from the onslaught of the counterrevolution." The resolution endorsed the insurrection against the Provisional Government and concluded: "The departure of the compromisers does not weaken the soviets. Inasmuch as it purges the worker and peasant revolution of counterrevolutionary influences, it strengthens them. Having listened to the declarations of the SRs and Mensheviks, the Second All-Russian Congress continues its work, the tasks of which have been predetermined by the will of the laboring people and their insurrection of October 24 and 25. Down with the compromisers! Down with the servants of the bourgeoisie! Long live the triumphant uprising of soldiers, workers, and peasants!"[54]

This bitter denunciation of the Mensheviks and SRs and blanket endorsement of the armed insurrection in Petrograd was, of course, as difficult for the Left SRs, left Mensheviks, and Bolshevik moderates to swallow as Martov's resolution was for the Leninists. Kamkov, in a report to the First

Left SR Congress in November, when these events were still very fresh in mind, attempted to explain the thinking of the Left SRs at this moment, when the gulf dividing Russian socialists widened, when in spite of Left SR efforts the Military Revolutionary Committee had been transformed into an insurrectionary organ and had overthrown the Provisional Government, and when the moderate socialists had repudiated and moved to combat this development:

> As political leaders in a moment of decisive historical significance for the fate of not only the Russian but also the world revolution, we, least of all, could occupy ourselves with moralizing. As people concerned with the defense of the revolution we had first of all to ask ourselves what we should do today, when the uprising was a reality . . . and for us it was clear that for a revolutionary party in that phase of the Russian revolution that had developed . . . our place was with the revolution. . . . We decided not only to stay at Smolny but to play the most energetic role possible. . . . We believed we should direct all of our energies toward the creation of a new government, one which would be supported, if not by the entire revolutionary democracy, then at least by a majority of it. Despite the hostility engendered by the insurrection in Petrograd . . . knowing that included within the right was a large mass of honest revolutionaries who simply misunderstood the Russian revolution, we believed our task to be that of not contributing to exacerbating relations within the democracy. . . . We saw our task, the task of the Left SRs, as that of mending the broken links uniting the two fronts of the Russian democracy. . . . We were convinced that they [the moderates] would with some delay accept that platform which is not the platform of any one fraction or party, but the program of history, and that they would ultimately take part in the creation of a new government.[55]

At the Second Congress of Soviets session the night of October 25–26, loud cheers erupted when Kamkov, following Trotsky to the platform, made the ringing declaration: "The right SRs left the congress but we, the Left SRs, have stayed." After the applause subsided, however, tactfully but forcefully, Kamkov spoke out against Trotsky's course, arguing that the step Trotsky proposed was untimely "because counterrevolutionary efforts are continuing." He added that the Bolsheviks did not have the support of the peasantry, "the infantry of the revolution without which the revolution would be destroyed."[56] With this in mind, he insisted that "the left ought not isolate itself from moderate democratic elements, but, to the contrary, should seek agreement with them."

It is perhaps not without significance that the more temperate Lunacharsky, rather than Trotsky, rose to answer Kamkov:

> Heavy tasks have fallen on us, of that there is no doubt. For the effective fulfillment of these tasks the unity of all the various genuinely revolutionary

elements of the democracy is necessary. Kamkov's criticism of us is unfounded. If starting this session we had initiated any steps whatever to reject or remove other elements, then Kamkov would be right. But all of us unanimously accepted Martov's proposal to discuss peaceful ways of solving the crisis. And we were deluged by a hail of declarations. A systematic attack was conducted against us. . . . Without hearing us out, not even bothering to discuss their own proposal, they [the Mensheviks and SRs] immediately sought to fence themselves off from us. . . . In our resolution we simply wanted to say, precisely, honestly, and openly, that despite their treachery we will continue our efforts, we will lead the proletariat and the army to struggle and victory.[57]

The quarrel over the fundamentally differing views of Martov and Trotsky dragged on into the night. Finally, a representative of the Left SRs demanded a break for fractional discussions, threatening an immediate Left SR walkout if a recess were not called. The question was put to a vote and passed at 2:40 A.M., Kamenev warning that the congress would resume its deliberations in half an hour.[58]

By this time, the march of City Duma deputies to the Winter Palace had ended in a soggy fiasco. At around midnight Duma deputies, members of the Executive Committee of the Peasants' Soviets, and deputies from the congress who had just walked out of Smolny (together numbering close to three hundred people), assembled outside the Duma building, on Nevsky Prospect, where a cold rain had now begun to fall. Led by Shreider and Prokopovich (the latter carrying an umbrella in one hand and a lantern in the other), marching four abreast and singing the "Marseillaise," armed only with packages of bread and sausages "for the ministers," the motley procession set out in the direction of the Admiralty. At the Kazan Square, less than a block away, the delegation was halted by a detachment of sailors and dissuaded from attempting to proceed further. John Reed, who was standing by, described the scene:

> . . . Just at the corner of the Ekaterina Canal, under an arc-light, a cordon of armed sailors was drawn across the Nevsky, blocking the way to a crowd of people in column of fours. There were about three or four hundred of them, men in frock coats, well-dressed women, officers . . . and at the head white-bearded old Shreider, mayor of Petrograd, and Prokopovich, minister of supplies in the Provisional Government, arrested that morning and released. I caught sight of Malkin, reporter for the *Russian Daily News.* "Going to die in the Winter Palace," he shouted cheerfully. The procession stood still, but from the front of it came loud argument. Shreider and Prokopovich were bellowing at the big sailor who seemed in command. "We demand to pass!" . . . "We can't let you pass" [the sailor responded]. . . . Another sailor came up, very much irritated.

"We will spank you!" he cried, energetically. "And if necessary we will shoot you too. Go home now, and leave us in peace!"

At this there was a great clamor of anger and resentment, Prokopovich had mounted some sort of box, and, waving his umbrella, he made a speech:

"Comrades and citizens!" he said. "Force is being used against us! We cannot have our innocent blood upon the hands of these ignorant men! . . . Let us return to the Duma and discuss the best means of saving the country and the Revolution!"

Whereupon, in dignified silence the procession marched around and back up the Nevsky, always in column of fours.[59]

It was now well after midnight, and the situation of the cabinet in the Winter Palace was growing more desperate by the minute. The steady dwindling of loyalist forces had by this time left portions of the east wing almost completely unprotected. Through windows in this section of the building, insurgents, in increasing numbers, were able to infiltrate the palace. In their second-floor meeting-room, many of the ministers now slouched spiritlessly in easy chairs or, like Maliantovich, stretched out on divans, awaiting the end. Konovalov, smoking one cigarette after another, nervously paced the room, disappearing next door from time to time to use the one phone still in service. The ministers could hear shouts, muffled explosions, and rifle and machine gun fire as the officers and cadets who had remained loyal to them fought futilely to fend off revolutionary forces. Their moments of greatest apprehension occurred when the artillery shell from the Peter and Paul Fortress burst in the room above and, somewhat later, when two grenades thrown by infiltrating sailors from an upper gallery exploded in a downstairs hall. Two cadets injured in the latter incident were carried to Kishkin for first aid.

Every so often Palchinsky popped in to try to calm the ministers, each time assuring them that the insurgents worming their way into the palace were being apprehended, and that the situation was still under control. Maliantovich recorded one of these moments: "Around one o'clock at night, or perhaps it was later, we learned that the procession from the Duma had set out. We let the guard know. . . . Again noise. . . . By this time we were accustomed to it. Most probably the Bolsheviks had broken into the palace once more, and, of course, had again been disarmed. . . . Palchinsky walked in. Of course, this was the case. Again they had let themselves be disarmed without resistance. Again, there were many of them. . . . How many of them are in the palace? Who is actually holding the palace now: we or the Bolsheviks?"[60]

Contrary to most accounts written in the Soviet Union, the Winter Palace was not captured by storm. Antonov himself subsequently recounted that by late evening "the attack on the palace had a completely disorganized character. . . . Finally, when we were able to ascertain that not many cadets remained, Chudnovsky and I led the attackers into the palace. By the time we entered, the cadets were offering no resistance."[61] This must have occurred at close to 2:00 A.M., for at that time Konovalov phoned Mayor Shreider to report: "The Military Revolutionary Committee has burst in. . . . All we have is a small force of cadets. . . . Our arrest is imminent." Moments later, when Shreider called the Winter Palace back, a gruff voice replied: "What do you want? From where are you calling?"—to which Shreider responded, "I am calling from the city administration; what is going on there?" "I am the sentry," answered the unfamiliar voice at the other end of the phone. "There is nothing going on here."[62]

In the intervening moments, the sounds outside the room occupied by the Provisional Government had suddenly become more ominous. "A noise flared up and began to rise, spread, and draw nearer," recalled Maliantovich. "Its varying sounds merged into one wave and at once something unusual, unlike the previous noises, resounded, something final. It was clear instantly that this was the end. . . . Those sitting or lying down jumped up and grabbed their overcoats. The tumult rose swiftly and its wave rolled up to us. . . . All this happened within a few minutes. From the entrance to the room of our guard came the shrill, excited shouts of a mass of voices, some single shots, the trampling of feet, thuds, shuffling, merging into one chaos of sounds and ever-mounting alarm."[63]

Maliantovich adds that even then the small group of cadets outside the room where the ministers sat seemed ready to continue resistance; however, it was now apparent to everyone that "defense was useless and sacrifices aimless"—that the moment for surrender had finally arrived. Kishkin ordered the commander of the guard to announce the government's readiness to yield. Then the ministers sat down around the table and watched numbly as the door was flung open and, as Maliantovich described it, "a little man flew into the room, like a chip tossed by a wave, under the pressure of the mob which poured in and spread at once, like water, filling all corners of the room." The little man was Antonov. "The Provisional Government is here—what do you want?" Konovalov asked. "You are all under arrest," Antonov replied, as Chudnovsky began taking down the names of the officials present and preparing a formal protocol. The realization that Kerensky, the prize they sought most of all, was not in the room, drove many of the attackers into a frenzy. "Bayonet all the sons of bitches on the spot!" someone yelled. Maliantovich records that it was Antonov who somehow managed to prevent the cabinet from being lynched, insisting firmly that "the members of the Provisional Government are under arrest. They will be confined to the Peter and Paul Fortress. I will not allow any violence against them."[64]

The ministers were accompanied from the Winter Palace and through the Palace Square by a selected convoy of armed sailors and Red Guards and a swearing, mocking, fist-shaking mob. Because no cars were available, they were forced to travel to their place of detention on foot. As the procession neared the Troitsky Bridge, the crowd surrounding the ministers once again became ugly, demanding that they be beheaded and thrown into the Neva. This time, the members of the government were saved by the apparently random firing of a machine gun from an approaching car. At the sounds of the shots, machine gunners at the Peter and Paul Fortress, believing themselves under attack, also opened fire. Ministers, escorts, and onlookers scattered for cover. In the ensuing confusion, the prisoners were rushed across the bridge to the safety of the fortress.[65]

The ministers were led into a small garrison club-room, lighted only by a smoky kerosene lamp. At the front of the room they found Antonov, seated at a small table, completing the protocol which Chudnovsky had begun preparing at the Winter Palace. Antonov read the document aloud, calling the roll of arrested officials and inviting each to sign it. Thereupon, the ministers were led to dank cells in the ancient Trubetskoi Bastion not far from where former tsarist officials had been incarcerated since February. Along the way Konovalov suddenly realized he was without cigarettes. Gingerly, he asked the sailor accompanying him for one and was relieved when the sailor not only offered him shag and paper but, seeing his confusion about what to do with them, rolled him a smoke.[66] Just before the door of his cell banged shut, Nikitin found in his pocket a half-forgotten telegram from the Ukrainian Rada to the Ministry of Interior. Handing it to Antonov, he observed matter of factly: "I received this yesterday—now it's your problem."[67]

At Smolny, meanwhile, the Congress of Soviets session had by now resumed. Ironically, it fell to Kamenev, who had fought tooth and nail against an insurrection for a month and a half, to announce the Provisional Government's demise. "The leaders of the counterrevolution ensconced in the Winter Palace have been seized by the revolutionary garrison," he barely managed to declare before complete pandemonium broke out in the hall. Kamenev went on to read the roll of former officials now incarcerated—at the mention of Tereshchenko, a name synonymous with the continuation of the hated war, the delegates erupted in wild shouts and applause once more.

As if to assure the congress that there was no immediate threat to the revolution, Kamenev also announced that the Third Cycle Battalion, called to Petrograd from the front by Kerensky, had come over to the side of the revolution. Shortly after this encouraging news, the Military Revolutionary Committee's commissar from the garrison at Tsarskoe Selo rushed forward to declare that troops located there had pledged to protect the approaches to Petrograd. "Learning of the approach of the cyclists from the front," he reported, "we prepared to rebuff them, but our concern proved unfounded since it turned out that among the comrade cyclists there were no enemies of the All-Russian Congress [the protocols record that this comment triggered another extended burst of enthusiastic applause]. When we sent our commissars to them it became clear that they also wanted the transfer of all power to the soviets, the immediate transfer of land to the peasants, and the institution of workers' control over industry."[68]

No sooner had the commissars from the Tsarskoe Selo garrison finished speaking than a representative of the Third Cycle Battalion itself demanded to be heard. He explained the attitude of his unit in these terms:

> Until just recently, we served on the southwestern front. But a few days ago, upon receipt of orders by telephonogram, we were moved northward. In the telephonogram it was indicated that we were being moved to defend Petrograd, but from whom—this was not known to us. We were marching on the people blindfolded; we didn't know where we were being sent but we generally guessed what was up. Along the way we were bothered by the questions: Where? Why? At the station of Peredolsk we held a short meeting in association with the Fifth Cycle Battalion in order to clarify the situation. At this meeting it turned out that among all of the cyclists there could not be found one person who would agree to act against brothers and spill their blood. And we decided that we would not obey the Provisional Government. They, we said, are people who do not want to defend our interests but send us against our brothers. I declare to you concretely: No, we will not give power to a government at the head of which stand bourgeois and landowners!

A bit later, the unwillingness of front soldiers to defend the Provisional Government was further confirmed by Krylenko, who informed the congress of late reports from the northern front. A Military Revolutionary Committee had been formed there to counter attempts to send military forces supporting the old government to the capital. Krylenko also announced that General Cheremisov had already recognized the authority of this committee; that Kerensky's commissar on the northern front, Woytinsky, had resigned; and that, one after the other, delegations from those units already in transit to the capital were reporting to the Military Revolutionary Committee to announce their solidarity with the Petrograd garrison.[69]

Apparently at this point at least a portion of the Menshevik-Internationalist fraction reentered the hall, and its spokesman, Kapelinsky, tried to turn the delegates' attention to Martov's idea of recessing the congress while a delegation was sent to sound out all socialist organizations about the creation of a representative democratic government. Before long, many of the delegates who now either ignored or booed Kapelinsky would regain interest in seeking an accommodation with moderate groups. But for the moment, in their initial ecstasy over the apparently painless triumph over the Kerensky regime, they were in no mood to do so. For the Bolsheviks, Kamenev summarily dismissed Kapelinsky's plea with the claim that the moderate socialists had only themselves to blame for the fact that Martov's proposal to search for peaceful ways of dealing with the crisis had not been implemented. At the same time, he proposed that Trotsky's resolution condemning the Mensheviks and SRs be tabled, thus leaving the door partly open for the resumption of relations with them.

As the Menshevik-Internationalists again walked out of the hall, Lunacharsky rose to present, for the congress' immediate adoption, a manifesto written by Lenin "To All Workers, Soldiers, and Peasants," endorsing the Petrograd uprising; decreeing the transfer of supreme political authority into the hands of the congress and of local soviets everywhere in Russia; and, in the most general terms, outlining the immediate plan of the new soviet regime. This historic proclamation, ultimately the source of Soviet political authority, read:

To All Workers, Soldiers, and Peasants:

The Second All-Russian Congress of Soviets of Workers' and Soldiers' Deputies has opened. It represents the great majority of the soviets, including a number of deputies of peasant soviets. The prerogatives of the Central Executive Committee of the compromisers are ended.

Supported by an overwhelming majority of the workers, soldiers, and peasants, and basing itself on the victorious insurrection of the workers and the garrison of Petrograd, the congress hereby resolves to take governmental power into its own hands.

The Provisional Government is deposed and most of its members are under arrest.

The Soviet authority will at once propose a democratic peace to all nations and an immediate armistice on all fronts. It will safeguard the transfer without compensation of all land—landlord, imperial, and monastery—to the peasant committees; it will defend the soldiers' rights, introducing a complete democratization of the army; it will establish workers' control over industry; it will insure the convocation of the Constituent Assembly on the date set; it will supply the cities with bread and the villages with articles of first necessity; and it will secure to all nationalities inhabiting Russia the right of self-determination.

The congress resolves that all local authority shall be transferred to the soviets of workers', soldiers', and peasants' deputies, which are charged with the task of enforcing revolutionary order.

The congress calls upon the soldiers in the trenches to be watchful and steadfast. The Congress of Soviets is confident that the revolutionary army will know how to defend the revolution against all imperialistic attempts until the new government has concluded a democratic peace which it is proposing directly to all nations.

The new government will take every measure to provide the revolutionary army with all necessities, by means of a determined policy of requisition from and taxation of the propertied classes. Care will be taken to improve the position of the soldiers' families.

The Kornilovites—Kerensky, Kaledin, and others—are endeavoring to lead troops against Petrograd. Several regiments, deceived by Kerensky, have already joined the insurgents.

Soldiers! Resist Kerensky, who is a Kornilovite! Be on guard!

Railwaymen! Stop all echelons sent by Kerensky against Petrograd!

Soldiers, Workers, Employees! The fate of the revolution and democratic peace is in your hands!

Long live the Revolution!

> The All-Russian Congress of Soviets
> of Workers' and Soldiers' Deputies
> Delegates from the Peasants' Soviets[70]

The reading of this historic manifesto was interrupted again and again by thundering waves of delirious cheers. After Lunacharsky had finished and a semblance of order was restored, Kamkov announced that, with a minor change, the Left SRs would support its adoption. The change was immediately accepted. A spokesman for the tiny Menshevik–United Internationalist fraction declared that if the proclamation would be amended to provide for the immediate organization of a government based on the broadest possible elements of the population, he would vote for it as well; however, when this suggestion was ignored, he announced that his followers would abstain. Finally, at 5:00 A.M., October 26, the manifesto legitimizing the creation of a revolutionary government was voted on and passed by an overwhelming margin, only two deputies voting against and twelve abstaining. A misty gray dawn, typical of Petrograd in late fall, was breaking as congress delegates drifted slowly out of Smolny. Upstairs, exhausted Military Revolutionary Committee leaders stretched out on the floor of their crowded command post to catch some sleep, many of them for the first time in several days. Lenin had gone off to the nearby apartment of Bonch-Bruevich to rest and draft a decree on land reform for adoption at the next session of the congress. The Bolsheviks had come to power in Petrograd, and a new era in the history of Russia and of the world had begun.

·16·

EPILOGUE

About 9:00 P.M., October 25, a few hours before the capture of the Winter Palace by the Military Revolutionary Committee, Kerensky reached northern front headquarters in Pskov, 175 miles southwest of Petrograd. Earlier, the Pskov Soviet had passed a resolution forbidding the dispatch of front detachments to Petrograd to defend the Provisional Government; as Krylenko soon reported to jubilant deputies at the Second Congress of Soviets, a military revolutionary committee formed by the Pskov Soviet assumed control of local communications and transportation facilities and began monitoring the actions of the military high command. General Cheremisov, commander of the northern front, recognizing the futility of opposing the troops in the prevailing circumstances and cognizant of the Provisional Government's hopeless position, now revoked earlier directives authorizing the shipment of reinforcements from the front to Petrograd. He further ordered that troops already en route to the capital be halted. When Kerensky arrived, Cheremisov warned that he could not guarantee the prime minister's personal safety and urged him to leave Pskov at once.[1]

Later that night, Kerensky, still in Pskov, met with General Petr Krasnov, the late General Krymov's replacement as commander of the Third Corps, the sizable military force that had been moved toward Petrograd and slated for occupation duty there by General Kornilov in late August. Krasnov, an archreactionary in politics, disapproved of Cheremisov's decision to halt the transfer of front soldiers to Petrograd and was receptive to an attempt to mobilize his own cossacks for the pacification of the capital. At this time, however, Third Corps personnel were scattered over hundreds of miles and, by and large, were no more prone to support the Provisional Government than were most other troops on the northern front. Hence the force that Krasnov was able to muster on Kerensky's behalf was meager, consisting of twelve and a half seventy-man cossack squadrons, some light artillery, an armored train, and one armored car. On the morning of October 27 these units occupied Gatchina, where Kerensky established a headquarters; the troops then paused briefly in the vain hope of acquiring reinforcements and began preparations to launch an early assault on the capital.[2]

In Petrograd, meanwhile, the Second All-Russian Congress of Soviets had approved Lenin's decrees on peace and land. The peace decree promised an end to secret diplomacy and proposed immediate negotiations to secure a democratic peace "without annexations and without indemnities." The land decree, borrowed in its essentials from the popular agrarian program of the Left SRs, abolished private property in land and provided for the transfer of all private and church lands to land committees and soviets of peasants' deputies for distribution to the peasantry according to need. Prior to dispersing on the early morning of October 27, the deputies had also elected a new Central Executive Committee, to be chaired by Kamenev and consisting of sixty-two Bolsheviks, twenty-nine Left SRs, six Menshevik-Internationalists, and four representatives of minor leftist groups. The congress also endorsed the appointment of a provisional revolutionary government. Members of this new, at first exclusively Bolshevik, administration,[3] formally named the Council (Soviet) of People's Commissars, were Lenin, chairman; Trotsky, foreign affairs; Rykov, internal affairs; Miliutin, agriculture; Shliapnikov, labor; Nogin, industry and commerce; Lunacharsky, education; Antonov-Ovseenko, Krylenko, and Dybenko, army and navy; Lomov, justice; Ivan Skvortsov, finance; Ivan Teodorovich, food supply; Nikolai Avilov, post and telegraph; and Stalin, nationalities. Among the new commissars' first acts was an announcement that elections to the Constituent Assembly would be held on schedule on November 12.[4]

Initially fierce resistance to the Bolshevik regime coalesced around the so-called All-Russian Committee for the Salvation of the Country and the Revolution organized on October 26, primarily by Mensheviks and SRs in the Petrograd City Duma. This committee included representatives of the City Duma, the Presidium of the Preparliament, the old Central Executive Committee, the All-Russian Executive Committee of Peasant Soviets, the Menshevik and SR delegations that had left the Second Congress of Soviets; the railroad and postal and telegraph workers' unions, Tsentroflot, and the Menshevik and SR Central Committees. In the first days after the Bolsheviks came to power, the Committee for Salvation called on government employees and citizens generally to refrain from recognizing or obeying the Council of People's Commissars, claiming for itself the right to reconstitute a Provisional Government.

Leaders of the Committee for Salvation also drew up plans to coordinate an uprising in Petrograd with the entry into the capital of Krasnov's cossacks, expected momentarily. But their intentions became known to the Military Revolutionary Committee on the night of October 28, before Krasnov was ready to attack. Consequently, the Committee for Salvation was forced to initiate open military action against the Bolsheviks the next

В центре — В. И. ЛЕНИН
1-й ряд сверху — И. В. СТАЛИН, В. П. МИЛЮТИН,
А. И. РЫКОВ, А. Г. ШЛЯПНИКОВ, Н. П. АВИЛОВ
(ГЛЕБОВ). 2-й ряд — В. П. НОГИН, А. В. ЛУНА-
ЧАРСКИЙ. 3-й ряд — И. И. СКВОРЦОВ (СТЕПА-
НОВ), Л. Д. БРОНШТЕЙН (ТРОЦКИЙ). 4-й ряд —
Г. И. ОППОКОВ (А. ЛОМОВ), И. А. ТЕОДОРОВИЧ.
5-й ряд — Н. В. КРЫЛЕНКО, В. А. АНТОНОВ-
ОВСЕЕНКО, П. Е. ДЫБЕНКО.

СОВЕТ НАРОДНЫХ КОМИССАРОВ,
ИЗБРАННЫЙ НА ВТОРОМ ВСЕРОССИЙСКОМ СЪЕЗДЕ
СОВЕТОВ РАБОЧИХ И СОЛДАТСКИХ ДЕПУТАТОВ
26 октября ст. ст. 1917 г.

The First Council of People's Commissars. Center: V. I. Lenin. Top row, left to right: I. V. Stalin, V. P. Miliutin, A. I. Rykov, A. G. Shliapnikov, N. P. Avilov. Second row: V. P. Nogin, A. V. Lunacharsky. Third row: I. I. Skvortsov, L. D. Trotsky. Fourth row: G. Lomov, I. A. Teodorovich. Fifth row: N. V. Krylenko, V. A. Antonov-Ovseenko, P. E. Dybenko.

morning. Cadets from military schools in the capital seized the Petrograd telephone station, the Hotel Astoria, and the state bank. They then prepared to oust the Bolsheviks from Smolny. Among military personnel in Petrograd, however, only cadets joined the insurrection, and they were no match for the forces quickly mustered by the Military Revolutionary Committee. The points captured early on October 29 by the cadets were easily regained. The military schools involved in the insurrection were quickly isolated, blockaded, and, in one case, bombarded with artillery fire. Before nightfall, all the military schools had capitulated and the premature revolt had been effectively suppressed.[5]

Also actively opposed to retention of the exclusively Bolshevik government formed on the night of October 26–27 was the moderate-socialist–dominated All-Russian Executive Committee of the Union of Railway Workers (Vikzhel). Vikzhel now sought to act as an intermediary between the Military Revolutionary Committee and the Committee for Salvation, and to further the creation of a homogeneous socialist government including representatives of all socialist groups, from the People's Socialists on the right to the Bolsheviks on the extreme left. In pursuit of this objective, Vikzhel called a conference of socialist parties for October 29, threatening a nationwide rail walkout at midnight on October 29 if its efforts to obtain a ceasefire between the warring sides and to initiate negotiations regarding formation of a broader government were unsuccessful.[6] The threat of a railway strike was ominous; by interrupting communications between Petrograd and the rest of the country and by withholding food from the capital, Vikzhel could create an untenable situation for the new government. Partly for this reason, the Bolsheviks agreed to participate in the Vikzhel-sponsored conference, which began on schedule the evening of October 29.[7]

While successful in stimulating high-level political talks, Vikzhel was unable to bring about a ceasefire. The key battle between Krasnov's roughly one-thousand-man cossack force and a motley army approximately ten times larger, made up of workers' detachments, soldiers of the Petrograd garrison, and Baltic sailors, took place October 30 on the Pulkovo Heights north of Tsarskoe Selo, twelve miles from Petrograd. This struggle, aptly termed "the Valmy of the Russian revolution,"[8] was confused, disorganized, and bloody, with both sides suffering severe casualties. By late afternoon, the offensive of Krasnov's demoralized forces had been halted. The cossacks, running low on ammunition, were in danger of being outflanked and cut off from the rear. Forced to fall back on Gatchina, the cossacks agreed two days later to end their resistance and to turn over Kerensky for arrest and public trial on the condition that they be given amnesty and safe conduct home. Forewarned of the cossacks' capitulation, Kerensky, disguised in a sailor's uniform and automobile goggles, narrowly evaded capture and went into hiding.[9]

Under continued pressure from Vikzhel, whose appeals for compromise and an end to civil war were echoed by the Left SRs and Menshevik-Internationalists and by such mass organizations in the capital as the Petrograd Trade Union Soviet, the Central Soviet of Factory-Shop Committees, and several district soviets, discussions regarding the formation of a broad socialist government dragged on for several days. At the start of these talks, representatives of the Menshevik and SR central committees had been more concerned with mobilizing military support to defeat the Bolsheviks than with reaching an accommodation with them.[10] As initial confidence that the Bolsheviks would be overthrown with ease proved unfounded, moderate socialist leaders became somewhat more amenable to serving in a coalition cabinet with the Bolsheviks. They remained adamantly opposed, nonetheless, to participation in a government that included either Lenin or Trotsky. Additionally, the moderate socialists insisted on a variety of safeguards aimed at insuring that any future government would not be Bolshevik-dominated.[11]

Between October 29 and 31, when it seemed that Krasnov's forces might take the capital, and at a time when the new regime was encountering great difficulty in consolidating its authority in Moscow, the Bolshevik leadership appeared ready to make significant concessions on these fundamental issues.[12] During this period, Lenin and Trotsky, preoccupied with pressing logistical and military matters, did not attend either the party meetings at which the Bolshevik stand on the government issue was formulated or the sessions of the Central Executive Committee and the Vikzhel conference at which the character and program of a new government were discussed. In their absence, the views of Kamenev, Zinoviev, Rykov, Miliutin, and other Bolshevik moderates carried particular weight. Kamenev and his associates were firmly convinced that the only hope of defending and preserving the gains of the revolution and of achieving an early convocation of the Constituent Assembly and the conclusion of peace lay in the creation of a broad socialist coalition government, which had been their position all along. Hence, they insisted mainly that any new cabinet not include representatives of the propertied classes and that it be pledged to pursue the general political and social program endorsed by the Second Congress of Soviets.

It is ironic that at the time the Bolshevik Party leadership was inclined toward compromise, the Mensheviks and SRs displayed little interest in coming to terms with the Bolshevik regime. After Krasnov's defeat, when moderate socialists became more amenable to agreement with the Bolsheviks, the Bolshevik Central Committee repudiated the position of its more moderate members and adopted a significantly harder line in the Vikzhel negotiations. This was in part because the immediate danger to the survival of the new regime in Petrograd had passed and partly because Lenin and Trotsky now returned to the party's inner councils, where their outlook prevailed. Party representatives were instructed to participate in the Vikzhel talks solely to expose the impracticability of coalition with moderate socialist groups and to bring the talks quickly to an end.[13]

In public institutions such as the Central Executive Committee, Bolshevik moderates continued to press for the formation of a government in which all socialist parties would be represented, even after the moderate position had been voted down in the Central Committee. Indeed, on

November 3 Kamenev and Zinoviev secured the Central Executive Committee's endorsement of continued efforts to form such a government.[14] For Lenin, who a week and a half earlier had urged that Kamenev and Zinoviev be ousted from the party for their public opposition to an insurrection, the moderates' readiness to sabotage the party's work and once again to jeopardize the revolution was maddening. On November 3 Lenin drafted an ultimatum which was subsequently signed by nine other members of the Central Committee: either the "opposition" would observe party discipline and support the policies agreed upon by a majority, or steps would be taken to expel its members from the party.[15]

Lenin's ultimatum was presented formally on November 4, after which Kamenev, Zinoviev, Rykov, Nogin, and Miliutin resigned from the Central Committee in protest. Rykov, Nogin, and Miliutin, along with Teodorovich, also withdrew from the government. A few weeks later, the Vikzhel discussions having foundered, the Left SRs agreed to enter the Council of People's Commissars and several Left SRs subsequently accepted government portfolios.[16] Not long after the formation of the Bolshevik–Left SR coalition government, Kamenev and his associates ended their open opposition to the Bolshevik leadership. In time all reassumed positions of authority within the party and the government. The participation of the Left SRs in the Council of People's Commissars proved to be short-lived. In mid-March 1918 they resigned in protest against the signing of the onerous Treaty of Brest-Litovsk, which ended Russia's involvement in World War I.

Ahead for the Soviet regime lay a two-and-a-half-year civil war against anti-Bolshevik armies, domestic and foreign. This unprecedentedly bitter and devastating life-and-death struggle was followed by an economic and social crisis the dimensions of which far exceeded what Russia had gone through in 1917. During these tortured years, the democratic character of the Bolshevik Party was lost; the independence of the soviets was destroyed; an oppressive, centralized bureaucracy was reimposed throughout the country; and Russian political and economic life became harnessed to the dictates of the Bolshevik leadership.[17] These events, however, belong to another chapter in modern Russian history, no less portentous than the preceding one.

The central question of why the Bolsheviks won the struggle for power in Petrograd in 1917 permits no simple answer. To be sure, from the perspective of more than half a century, it is clear that the fundamental weakness of the Kadets and moderate socialists during the revolutionary period and the concomitant vitality and influence of the radical left at that time can be traced to the peculiarities of Russia's political, social, and economic development during the nineteenth century and earlier. The world war also inevitably had a good deal to do with the way the 1917 revolution in Petrograd turned out. Had it not been for the Provisional Government's commitment to pursue the war to victory, a policy which in 1917 enjoyed no broad support, it surely would have been better able to cope with the myriad problems that inevitably attended the collapse of the old order and, in particular, to satisfy popular demands for immediate fundamental reform.

As it was, a major source of the Bolsheviks' growing strength and authority in 1917 was the magnetic attraction of the party's platform as embodied in the slogans "Peace, Land, and Bread" and "All Power to the Soviets." The Bolsheviks conducted an extraordinarily energetic and resourceful campaign for the support of Petrograd factory workers and soldiers and Kronstadt sailors. Among these groups, the slogan "All Power to the Soviets" signified the creation of a democratic, exclusively socialist government, representing all parties and groups in the Soviet and committed to a program of immediate peace, meaningful internal reform, and the early convocation of a Constituent Assembly. In the late spring and summer of 1917, a number of factors served to increase support for the professed goals of the Bolsheviks, especially for transfer of power to the soviets. Economic conditions steadily worsened. Garrison soldiers became directly threatened by shipment to the front. Popular expectations of early peace and reform under the Provisional Government dwindled. Concomitantly, all other major political groups lost credibility because of their association with the government and their insistence on patience and sacrifice in the interest of the war effort. In the wake of the Kornilov affair, among the lower strata of the Petrograd population the desire for an end to coalition government with the Kadets became very nearly universal.

That in the space of eight months the Bolsheviks reached a position from which they were able to assume power was due as well to the special effort which the party devoted to winning the support of military troops in the rear and at the front; only the Bolsheviks seem to have perceived the necessarily crucial significance of the armed forces in the struggle for power. Perhaps even more fundamentally, the phenomenal Bolshevik success can be attributed in no small measure to the nature of the party in 1917. Here I have in mind neither Lenin's bold and determined leadership, the immense historical significance of which cannot be denied, nor the Bolsheviks' proverbial, though vastly exaggerated, organizational unity and discipline. Rather, I would emphasize the party's internally relatively democratic, tolerant, and decentralized structure and method of operation, as well as its essentially open and mass character—in striking contrast to the traditional Leninist model.

As we have seen, within the Bolshevik Petrograd organization at all levels in 1917 there was continuing free and lively discussion and debate over the most basic theoretical and tactical issues. Leaders who differed with the majority were at liberty to fight for their views, and not infrequently Lenin was the loser in these struggles. To gauge the importance of this tolerance of differences of opinion and ongoing give-and-take, it is enough to recall that throughout 1917 many of the Bolsheviks' most important resolutions and public statements were influenced as much by the outlook of right Bolsheviks as by that of Lenin. In addition, moderate Bolsheviks like Kamenev, Zinoviev, Lunacharsky, and Riazanov were among the party's most articulate and respected spokesmen in key public institutions such as the soviets and the trade unions.

In 1917 subordinate party bodies like the Petersburg Committee and the Military Organization were permitted considerable independence and initiative, and their views and criticism were taken into account in the formation of policy at the highest levels. Most important, these lower bodies were able to tailor their tactics and appeals to suit their own particular constituencies amid rapidly changing conditions. Vast numbers of new members were recruited into the party, and they too played a significant role in shaping the Bolsheviks' behavior. Among these newcomers were many of the leading figures in the October revolution, among them Trotsky, Antonov-Ovseenko, Lunacharsky, and Chudnovsky. The newcomers included tens of thousands of workers and soldiers from among the most impatient and dissatisfied elements in the factories and garrison who knew little, if anything, about Marxism and cared nothing about party discipline. This caused extreme difficulties in July when leaders of the Military Organization and the Petersburg Committee, responsive to their militant constituencies, encouraged an insurrection, against the wishes of the Central Committee. But during the period of reaction that followed the July uprising, in the course of the fight against Kornilov, and again during the October revolution, the Bolsheviks' extensive, carefully cultivated connections in factories, local workers' organizations, and units of the Petrograd garrison and the Baltic Fleet were to be a significant source of the party's durability and strength.

The importance to the Bolshevik success of the dynamic relationship that existed in 1917 within the top Bolshevik hierarchy, as well as between it, the ostensibly subordinate elements of the party, and the masses, was illustrated immediately after the July uprising. At the time, Lenin believed that the Provisional Government was effectively controlled by counterrevolutionary elements; overestimating the government's capacity to damage the left, he was convinced, moreover, that under the influence of the Mensheviks and SRs the existing soviets had been rendered powerless. Hence he demanded that the party abandon its orientation toward a possible peaceful transfer of power to the soviets and shift its attention toward preparations for an armed uprising at the earliest opportunity. Other leaders, many of whom had particularly close ties with workers and soldiers and were also active in the Central Executive Committee and the Petrograd Soviet, refused to discount completely the Mensheviks and SRs as potential allies and the soviets as legitimate revolutionary institutions. While the slogan "All Power to the Soviets" was officially withdrawn by the Sixth Congress in late July, this change did not take hold at the local level. Moreover, the congress did not deemphasize efforts to win the soviets, and they continued to be a major focus of party activity throughout the month of August.

As it turned out, the impact of the post–July days reaction against the left was not nearly as serious as originally feared. To the contrary, the repressive measures adopted by the government, as well as the indiscriminate persecution of leftist leaders and the apparently increasing danger of counterrevolution, served simply to increase resentment toward the Kerensky regime among the masses and stimulated them to unite more closely around the soviets in defense of the revolution. The Bolsheviks, working in cooperation with Mensheviks and SRs primarily through revolutionary committees created by the soviets, played a leading role in the quick defeat of Kornilov. In the capital, the Petrograd Soviet, distinctly more radical in composition and outlook, emerged from the Kornilov experience with its power and authority greatly enhanced. In response, the Bolsheviks in early September formally resurrected their main pre-July slogan, "All Power to the Soviets."

Probably the clearest example of the importance and value of the party's relatively free and flexible structure, and the responsiveness of its tactics to the prevailing mass mood, came during the second half of September, when party leaders in Petrograd turned a deaf ear to the ill-timed appeals of Lenin, then still in hiding in Finland, for an immediate insurrection. To be sure, on October 10 the Bolshevik Central Committee, with Lenin in attendance, made the organization of an armed insurrection and the seizure of power "the order of the day." Yet in the ensuing days there was mounting evidence that an uprising launched independently of the soviets and in advance of the Second Congress of Soviets would not be supported by the Petrograd masses; that the seizure of power by the Bolsheviks alone would be opposed by all other major political parties, by peasants in the provinces and soldiers at the front, and possibly even by such mass democratic institutions as the soviets and trade unions; and that in any case the party was technically unprepared for an offensive against the government. In these circumstances tactically cautious party leaders in Petrograd, headed by Trotsky, devised the strategy of employing the organs of the Petrograd Soviet for the seizure of power; of masking an attack on the government as a defensive operation on behalf of the Soviet; and, if possible, of linking the formal overthrow of the government with the work of the Second Congress of Soviets.

On October 21–23, using as an excuse the government's announced intention of transferring the bulk of the garrison to the front and cloaking every move as a defensive measure against the counterrevolution, the Military Revolutionary Committee of the Petrograd Soviet took control of most

Petrograd-based military units, in effect disarming the Provisional Government without a shot. In response, early on the morning of October 24, Kerensky initiated steps to suppress the left. Only at this point, just hours before the scheduled opening of the Congress of Soviets and in part under continuous prodding by Lenin, did the armed uprising that Lenin had been advocating for well over a month actually begin.

The argument has been made that the belated uprising of October 24–25 was of crucial historical importance because, by impelling the main body of Mensheviks and SRs to withdraw from the Second Congress of Soviets, it prevented the creation by the congress of a socialist coalition government in which the moderate socialists might have had a strong voice. In so doing, it paved the way for the formation of a soviet government completely controlled and dominated by the Bolsheviks. The evidence indicates that this was indeed the case. A more crucial point, however, is that only in the wake of the government's direct attack on the left was an armed uprising of the kind envisioned by Lenin feasible. For it bears repeating that the Petrograd masses, to the extent that they supported the Bolsheviks in the overthrow of the Provisional Government, did so not out of any sympathy for strictly Bolshevik rule but because they believed the revolution and the congress to be in imminent danger. Only the creation of a broadly representative, exclusively socialist government by the Congress of Soviets, which is what they believed the Bolsheviks stood for, appeared to offer the hope of insuring that there would not be a return to the hated ways of the old regime, of avoiding death at the front and achieving a better life, and of putting a quick end to Russia's participation in the war.

Notes

Dates of newspaper citations are for 1917 unless otherwise specified. Full citations are given in the bibliography. The following abbreviations are used in the notes:

KL: *Krasnaia letopis'*

PSS: V. I. Lenin, *Polnoe sobranie sochinenii*, 55 vols., 5th ed. (Moscow, 1958–1965)

PR: *Proletarskaia revoliutsiia*

Introduction

1. Oliver H. Radkey, *The Agrarian Foes of Bolshevism* (New York, 1958); William G. Rosenberg, *Liberals in the Russian Revolution: The Constitutional Democratic Party, 1917–1921* (Princeton, 1974); Ronald G. Suny, *The Baku Commune, 1917–1918* (Princeton, 1972); Marc Ferro, *La Revolution de 1917: La chute du tsarisme et les origines d'octobre* (Paris, 1967); George Katkov, *Russia 1917: The February Revolution* (New York, 1967); Rex A. Wade, *The Russian Search for Peace: February–October 1917* (Stanford, 1969).

2. William Henry Chamberlin, *The Russian Revolution, 1917–1921*, 2 vols. (New York, 1935).

3. After the outbreak of World War I the official name of the Russian capital was hastily changed from the German-derived "St. Petersburg" to the Russianized "Petrograd."

4. S. P. Melgunov, *The Bolshevik Seizure of Power* (Santa Barbara, 1972). This is an edited and abridged translation of the same author's *Kak bol'sheviki zakhvatili vlast'* (Paris, 1953).

5. Robert V. Daniels, *Red October* (New York, 1967).

6. Lenin expressed his views on the tasks and organization of the Russian Social Democratic Workers' Party in the essay "What Is to Be Done?" compiled in 1902. Lenin, *PSS*, vol. 6, pp. 3–192.

7. Ibid., vol. 27, pp. 299–426. The important writings of Lenin cited here are available in English in Robert C. Tucker, *The Lenin Anthology* (New York, 1975).

8. Lenin, *PSS*, vol. 31, pp. 1–74. In this connection see V. I. Startsev, *Ocherki po istorii Petrogradskoi krasnoi gvardii i rabochei militsii* (Moscow, 1965), pp. 18–19, and

Akademiia nauk SSSR, Institut istorii, Leningradskoe otdelenie, *Oktiabr'skoe voo-ruzhennoe vosstanie*, ed. S. N. Valk, 2 vols. (Leningrad, 1967), vol. 1, pp. 184–85.

9. N. I. Podvoiskii, *God 1917* (Moscow, 1925), p. 23.

10. After his return from abroad on May 4, 1917, Trotsky headed his own small social democratic organization, the Interdistrict Committee. By the immediate pre-July period he and many of his associates were working closely with the Bolsheviks. At the Bolshevik Sixth Congress in late July the Interdistrict Committee formally merged with the Bolsheviks and Trotsky became a member of the Bolshevik Central Committee.

11. As a gesture of opposition to the war, the Petersburg Committee retained its name after St. Petersburg was renamed "Petrograd."

12. The Bolshevik Military Organization was created in March 1917 by the Petrograd party organization for the purpose of conducting revolutionary activities in the Petrograd garrison and at the Kronstadt naval base. In April the organization was placed directly under the Central Committee and given the task of winning the support of the armed forces at the front and in the rear and of organizing them into a reliable, disciplined revolutionary force.

13. The fullest and most candid account of Bolshevik behavior at this time by a Soviet historian is contained in E. N. Burdzhalov, "O taktike bol'shevikov v marte–aprele 1917 goda," *Voprosy istorii*, 1956, no. 4, pp. 38–56. The Czech historian Mikhail Reiman makes the important point that in several Russian cities there existed united Bolshevik-Menshevik organizations: "The impulse toward unification was very strong throughout the party, even reaching the Central Committee. This impulse was so strong that it often obscured fundamental differences which actually made unification an impossibility." Reiman, *Russkaia revoliutsiia, 23 fevralia–25 oktiabria 1917*, 2 vols. (Prague, 1968), vol. 2, p. 162.

14. These discussions were held in conjunction with a national *conference* of soviets which met in Petrograd from March 29 to April 3.

15. Lenin, *PSS*, vol. 31, pp. 113–18.

16. Institut marksizma-leninizma pri TsK KPSS, *Sed'maia (Aprel'skaia) Vserossii-skaia konferentsiia RSDRP (bol'shevikov): Petrogradskaia obshchegorodskaia konferentsiia RSDRP (bol'shevikov), aprel' 1917 goda: Protokoly* (Moscow, 1958), pp. 290–91. The minutes of Petersburg Committee meetings for 1917 are contained in Vsesoiuznaia Kommunisticheskaia partiia (bol'shevikov), Leningradskii istpart, *Pervyi legal'nyi Peterburgskii komitet bol'shevikov v 1917 godu: Sbornik materialov i protokolov zasedanii Peterburgskogo komiteta RSDRP(b) i ego Ispolnitel'noi komissii za 1917 g.*, ed. P. F. Kudelli (Moscow and Leningrad, 1927).

17. *Sed'maia konferentsiia*, pp. 241–45.

18. Included in the Central Committee elected at the April Conference were the moderates Kamenev, Viktor Nogin, Vladimir Miliutin, and Grigorii Zinoviev, alongside Lenin, Stalin, Iakov Sverdlov, and Ivar Smilga.

19. No reference was made, for example, to Lenin's controversial motion that the bourgeois democratic revolution had ended in Russia and that power should be transferred to the proletariat and poorer peasantry. A resolution on the "current moment" described the Russian revolution as "merely the first stage of the first revolution that would inevitably result from the war" and asserted that conditions for unified revolutionary action by workers in different countries were gradually developing. The same resolution explained that because the Russian proletariat op-

erated in one of the most backward states in Europe, it could not achieve a socialist reconstruction of society; still, the proletariat could work on such practical steps on the road to socialism as nationalization of land, imposition of state control over banks, and other measures aimed at a more equal distribution of property.

This emphasis on Russia's backwardness and on specific economic gains reflects Kamenev's thinking. Lenin would have preferred to focus exclusive attention on the factors facilitating the consummation of a workers' revolution in Russia: he was opposed to encouraging hopes for partial reform since this would divert the proletariat from the main task of preparing for the transfer of power to the soviets. *Sed'maia konferentsiia*, pp. 241–60.

20. This subject was to have been thrashed out during a scheduled debate connected with the adoption of a new party program to replace the outdated program of 1903. However, evidently because of substantial opposition to the changes proposed by Lenin and lack of sufficient time in which to deal with the matter, conference delegates merely adopted some guidelines for revising the program and authorized the Central Committee to prepare a draft program for the consideration of subordinate party organizations. In view of the urgency of this matter, it was agreed that a special congress to adopt a new program would be convened within two months.

21. P. V. Volobuev, *Proletariat i burzhuaziia Rossii v 1917 godu* (Moscow, 1964), pp. 90–100.

22. Ibid., pp. 124–38; Z. V. Stepanov, *Rabochie Petrograda v period podgotovki i provedeniia oktiabr'skogo vooruzhennogo vosstaniia* (Moscow and Leningrad, 1965), p. 54. *Oktiabr'skoe vooruzhennoe vosstanie*, vol. 1, pp. 390–450, contains a useful discussion of the Petrograd economy in the first half of 1917.

23. In addition, Order Number One placed control of all weapons in the hands of elective committees, announced that orders of the Provisional Government should be obeyed only if they did not conflict with orders of the Soviet, and proclaimed full rights to soldiers when not on duty.

24. Alexander Rabinowitch, "The Petrograd Garrison and the Bolshevik Seizure of Power," in *Revolution and Politics in Russia: Essays in Memory of B. I. Nicolaevsky*, ed. Alexander and Janet Rabinowitch with Ladis K. D. Kristof (Bloomington, 1972), pp. 172–74. The most useful studies of the Petrograd garrison in the revolutionary period are M. I. Akhun and V. A. Petrov, *Bol'sheviki i armiia v 1905–1917 gg.* (Leningrad, 1929); A. K. Drezen, "Petrogradskii garnizon v iiule i avguste 1917 g.," *KL*, 1927, no. 3 (24), pp. 191–223; O. N. Chaadaeva, "Soldatskie massy petrogradskogo garnizona v podgotovke i provedenii oktiabr'skogo vooruzhennogo vosstaniia," *Istoricheskie zapiski*, 1955, no. 51, pp. 3–44; V. M. Kochakov, "Sostav petrogradskogo garnizona v 1917 g.," *Uchenye zapiski Leningradskogo gosudarstvennogo universiteta*, 1956, vyp. no. 205, pp. 60–86; V. M. Kochakov, "Bol'shevizatsiia petrogradskogo garnizona v 1917 godu," in Akademiia nauk SSSR, Institut istorii, Leningradskoe otdelenie, *Oktiabr'skoe vooruzhennoe vosstanie v Petrograde* (Moscow and Leningrad, 1957), pp. 142–83. A valuable collection of documents is A. K. Drezen, ed., *Bol'shevizatsiia petrogradskogo garnizona: Sbornik materialov i dokumentov* (Leningrad, 1932).

25. Rabinowitch, "The Petrograd Garrison and the Bolshevik Seizure of Power," p. 175.

26. A valuable analysis of the revolutionary situation prevailing in urban Rus-

sia just before the start of the war is contained in Leopold Haimson, "The Problem of Social Stability in Urban Russia, 1905–1917," *Slavic Review*, vol. 23, no. 4 (1964), pp. 620–42, and vol. 24, no. 1 (1965), pp. 1–22.

27. Elected factory-shop committees were formed in virtually all Petrograd industrial enterprises immediately after the February revolution. Initially created primarily to represent the interests of workers in negotiations with management and governmental and other public institutions, such committees often became prominently involved in factory administration. Between early May and mid-October, representatives of factory-shop committees in Petrograd held four citywide conferences. They also formed a permanent executive body, the Central Soviet of Factory-Shop Committees. A national conference of factory-shop committees was held in Petrograd October 17–22.

28. *Pravda* was a daily newspaper published by the Bolshevik Central Committee. Shut down after the July days, it was replaced by *Proletarii* (August 13), *Rabochii* (August 25), and *Rabochii put'* (September 3). *Soldatskaia pravda* was put out by the Military Organization; banned in early July, it was replaced by *Rabochii i soldat* (July 23) and *Soldat* (August 13). *Rabotnitsa* was a journal for women workers published by the Central Committee two or three times a month.

29. Alexander Rabinowitch, *Prelude to Revolution: The Petrograd Bolsheviks and the July 1917 Uprising* (Bloomington, 1968), pp. 229–31.

30. Ibid., pp. 102–6.

31. *Pervyi vserossiiskii s"ezd Sovetov rabochikh, soldatskikh i krest'ianskikh deputatov* (Leningrad, 1930), p. xxvii. See also M. S. Iugov, "Sovety v pervyi period revoliutsii," in *Ocherki po istorii oktiabr'skoi revoliutsii*, ed. M. N. Pokrovskii, 2 vols. (Moscow and Leningrad, 1927), vol. 2, p. 222.

32. On the relationship at the local level between anarchists and Bolsheviks, and on the behavior of the latter during the April crisis, see Rabinowitch, *Prelude to Revolution*, pp. 43–45, 61–64.

33. Ibid., pp. 74–75, 94.

34. Ibid., pp. 121–22, 131–32.

35. V. D. Bonch-Bruevich, *Na boevykh postakh fevral'skoi i oktiabr'skoi revoliutsii* (Moscow, 1931), pp. 72–73.

1 · *The July Uprising*

1. Bonch-Bruevich, *Na boevykh postakh*, pp. 72–73; M. A. Savel'ev, "Lenin v iiul'skie dni," *Pravda*, July 17, 1930, p. 2; *Birzhevye vedomosti*, July 7, evening edition, p. 2. See also N. N. Maslov, ed., *Lenin i revoliutsiia, 1917 god* (Leningrad, 1970), pp. 216–17, 222–23.

2. *Izvestiia*, July 4, p. 5.

3. This crisis grew out of claims to autonomy for the Ukraine by the Ukrainian Central Rada in Kiev. Socialist members were more willing to make immediate concessions to the Rada than were Kadet ministers. At the end of June, Kerensky, Tsereteli, and Tereshchenko negotiated a compromise with the Rada which represented a substantial victory fot the Ukrainians. At a late-night cabinet meeting on July 2, the Kadets A. I. Shingarev, A. A. Manuilov, V. A. Stepanov, and D. I. Shakhovsky refused to approve the agreement, and, upon instructions from their Central Committee, tendered their resignations. The remaining Kadet, N. V. Ne-

krasov, favored the compromise and resigned from the Kadet Party rather than leave the government.

4. *Rech'*, July 4, p. 1. See also *Birzhevye vedomosti*, July 4, morning edition, p. 3.

5. *Den'*, July 4, p. 3.

6. *Izvestiia*, July 4, p. 2.

7. *Birzhevye vedomosti*, July 4, morning edition, p. 2.

8. Bonch-Bruevich, *Na boevykh postakh*, p. 73.

9. *Rech'*, July 4, p. 3.

10. Ibid.; *Den'*, July 4, p. 2.

11. *Den'*, July 4, p. 4.

12. *Rech'*, July 4, p. 2.

13. *Birzhevye vedomosti*, July 4, morning edition, p. 3; *Izvestiia*, July 4, pp. 4–5.

14. *Rech'*, July 4, p. 2; *Den'*, July 4, pp. 1, 5; *Novaia zhizn'*, July 4, p. 2; *Birzhevye vedomosti*, July 4, morning edition, p. 1.

15. *Den'*, July 4, p. 2; *Izvestiia*, July 4, p. 6.

16. *Okopnaia pravda* was an organ of the Bolshevik Military Organization. It was published in Riga and was widely circulated among soldiers on the northern front.

17. A. Shliapnikov, *Semnadtsatyi god*, 4 vols. (Moscow and Petrograd, 1923), vol. 2, pp. 190–92; *Pervyi legal'nyi Peterburgskii komitet*, pp. 7, 39–40.

18. A member of the Executive Commission of the Bolshevik Petersburg Committee and a masterful political agitator, Bagdatiev was one of the most tactically radical Petrograd Bolsheviks. He was formally removed from membership in the Petersburg Committee after the April crisis when, without authorization, he circulated a leaflet in the name of the Petersburg Committee calling for the overthrow of the government. According to some sources, he did the same during the July days.

19. The son of a poor artisan, Volodarsky joined the Bund (the Jewish social democratic organization) in 1905 and subsequently became a Menshevik. During the war he emigrated to Philadelphia, where he joined the American Socialist Party and the International Ladies' Garment Workers' Union, and became active in the American antiwar movement. After the February revolution he returned to Petrograd, at first becoming associated with Trotsky's Interdistrict Committee. However, he quickly gravitated to the Bolsheviks, distinguishing himself as an effective leader in such institutions as the Petrograd Soviet and the Petersburg Committee. In addition, among fellow Bolsheviks he was generally reputed to be one of the party's most effective and popular mass orators.

20. N. Avdeev, *Revoliutsiia 1917 goda: Khronika sobytii* (Moscow and Leningrad, 1923), vol. 2, pp. 115–16; *Pervyi legal'nyi Peterburgskii komitet*, pp. 208–9.

21. M. Kedrov, "Iz krasnoi tetradi ob Il'iche," in *Vospominaniia o Vladimire Il'iche Lenine* (Moscow, 1956), vol. 1, p. 485.

22. Lenin, *PSS*, vol. 34, pp. 21–22; A. M. Liubovich, "3–5 iiulia," *Leningradskaia pravda*, July 16, 1925, p. 3.

23. In this connection see Podvoisky's recollections of a meeting with Lenin on June 18, in N. I. Podvoiskii, "Voennaia organizatsiia TsK RSDRP(b) i voenno-revoliutsionnyi komitet 1917 g.," *KL*, 1923, no. 6, p. 76.

24. Rabinowitch, *Prelude to Revolution*, pp. 164–66.

25. Kalinin, *Krasnaia gazeta*, July 16, 1920, p. 2; see also Rabinowitch, *Prelude to Revolution*, p. 184.

26. In a long editorial in *Pravda* on June 22, Kamenev had specifically warned against premature revolutionary action. "Uncoordinated demonstrations by individual regiments attempting to eliminate the unavoidable petty bourgeois stage by means of sabotage are foolish and inexpedient," he wrote. "The proletariat will prepare for the new stage in the revolution not by anarchistic demonstrations and partial endeavors, but through renewed organizational work and unity." Viktor Nogin took every opportunity to speak out in a similar vein at this time. For example, see his impassioned appeal for constraint at a plenary meeting of the Moscow Regional Bureau on June 28, in Akademiia nauk SSSR, Institut istorii, et al., *Revoliutsionnoe dvizhenie v Rossii v mae–iiune 1917 g.: Iiun'skaia demonstratsiia*, ed. D. A. Chugaev, et al. (Moscow, 1959), pp. 116–17. When word of the demonstrations reached Kamenev on the afternoon of July 3, he immediately ordered party leaders in Kronstadt to oppose participation by the sailors and, with Zinoviev, drafted an appeal to workers and soldiers to halt their protests. Late on the night of July 3 Kamenev tried to persuade his colleagues not to support continuation and expansion of the demonstrations the next day but rather to attempt to organize peaceful rallies in the districts.

27. L. D. Trotskii, *Sochineniia*, vol. 3, part 1: *Ot fevralia do oktiabria* (Moscow, 1925), pp. 165–66; Rabinowitch, *Prelude to Revolution*, pp. 157–74.

28. M. Ia. Latsis, "Iiul'skie dni v Petrograde: Iz dnevnika agitatora," *PR*, 1923, no. 5 (17), pp. 104–5; *Pervyi legal'nyi Peterburgskii komitet*, p. 164.

29. V. I. Nevskii, "Voennaia organizatsiia i oktiabr'skaia revoliutsiia," *Krasnoarmeets*, 1919, nos. 10–15, p. 40.

30. B. Nikitin, *Rokovye gody* (Paris, 1937), p. 121.

31. The issue of German subventions to the Bolsheviks is explored in George Katkov, *Russia 1917: The February Revolution;* George Katkov, "German Political Intervention in Russia During World War I," in *Revolutionary Russia: A Symposium*, ed. Richard Pipes (Cambridge, 1968), pp. 80–112; Michael Futrell, *The Northern Underground* (London, 1963); S. P. Mel'gunov, *Zolotoi nemetskii kliuch k bol'shevistskoi revoliutsii* (Paris, 1940); W. B. Scharlau and Z. A. B. Zeman, *Merchant of Revolution: A Life of Alexander Helphand* (London and New York, 1965); Stephen Possony, *Lenin: The Compulsive Revolutionary* (Chicago, 1964), Michael Pearson, *The Sealed Train* (New York, 1975). Related documents are contained in Z. A. B. Zeman, *Germany and the Revolution in Russia 1915–1918: Documents from the Archives of the German Foreign Ministry* (London and New York, 1958).

32. On this point see Alexander Dallin's comment on "German Political Intervention in Russia during World War I" by George Katkov, in *Revolutionary Russia*, p. 117, and I. G. Tsereteli, *Vospominaniia o fevral'skoi revoliutsii*, 2 vols. (Paris, 1963), vol. 2, pp. 336–41.

33. See Pereverzev's letter to the editor in *Birzhevye vedomosti*, July 9, evening edition, p. 7.

34. *Rech'*, July 9, p. 3.

35. Tsereteli, *Vospominaniia*, vol. 2, pp. 332–33. Tsereteli recalls that the charges released by Aleksinsky and Pankratov were most striking for their superficial and frivolous character. Nekrasov, for one, was enraged by Pereverzev's action. At the time a rumor circulated that he had challenged the minister of justice to a duel. Pereverzev was forced to resign a few days later. See *Zhivoe slovo*, July 7, p. 2.

36. Tsereteli, *Vospominaniia*, vol. 2, pp. 333–34.
37. *Izvestiia*, July 7, p. 3.

2 · *The Bolsheviks Under Fire*

1. Lenin, *PSS*, vol. 32, p. 416.
2. These essays—"Where Is State Power and Where Is Counterrevolution?" ("Gde vlast' i gde kontrrevoliutsiia?"), "Foul Slander by Ultrareactionary Newspapers and Aleksinsky" (Gnusnye klevety chernosotennykh gazet i Aleksinskogo"), "Slander and the Facts" ("Zloslovie i fakty"), and "A New Dreyfus Case?" ("Novoe delo Dreifusa?")—were all published in *Listok pravdy*, July 6, pp. 1–2. (See Lenin, *PSS*, vol. 32, pp. 410–22.)
3. *Izvestiia*, July 6, p. 6; *Gazeta-kopeika*, July 6, p. 2.
4. *Edinstvo*, July 9, p. 1. *Edinstvo* was the organ of a group of right social democrats headed by Plekhanov. Its editorial policy strongly supported the Provisional Government and the Russian war effort.
5. *Petrogradskaia gazeta*, July 7, p. 2; *Petrogradskii listok*, July 7, p. 1.
6. *Rech'*, July 6, p. 1.
7. This reticence was reflected most clearly in the aftermath of the abortive June 10 demonstration. At that time several prominent moderate socialists, headed by Tsereteli, urged that sanctions be applied against the Bolsheviks and their sympathizers—most importantly, that military regiments and worker detachments under Bolshevik influence immediately be disarmed. A majority of the Soviet leadership, however, refused to sanction such action. See Rabinowitch, *Prelude to Revolution*, pp. 81–84.
8. Akademiia nauk SSSR, Institut istorii, et al., *Revoliutsionnoe dvizhenie v Rossii v iiule 1917 g.: Iiul'skii krizis*, ed. D. A. Chugaev, et al. (Moscow, 1959), pp. 295–97. During the last years of the tsarist regime, the State Council was the upper house of the Russian legislature; the Duma was the lower house.
9. *Rech'*, July 16, p. 1; July 18, p. 2; Rosenberg, *Liberals in the Russian Revolution*, pp. 178–85.
10. *Rech'*, July 11, p. 2. On the German counterattack see Robert S. Feldman, "The Russian General Staff and the June 1917 Offensive," *Soviet Studies*, April 1968, pp. 540–42.
11. *Izvestiia*, July 8, p. 4.
12. Ibid., July 11, pp. 3–4, 6; *Golos soldata*, July 11, p. 3. The same day, July 9, the Bureau of the Central Executive Committee formally waived the right of its members to immunity from arrest, provided that the committee be informed of such arrests within twenty-four hours and that it be given the opportunity of keeping a close watch on the disposition of these cases.
13. *Izvestiia*, July 11, p. 1.
14. *Delo naroda*, July 11, p. 2; *Izvestiia*, July 12, p. 7; *Sotsial-Demokrat*, July 11, p. 3.
15. *Rabochaia gazeta*, July 19, p. 3.
16. *Izvestiia*, July 18, p. 5.
17. *Novoe vremia*, July 25, pp. 2–3; Rosenberg, *Liberals in the Russian Revolution*, pp. 191–95; Kh. M. Astrakhan, *Bol'sheviki i ikh politicheskie protivniki v 1917 godu* (Leningrad, 1973), pp. 285–86; Wade, *The Russian Search for Peace*, pp. 92–95;

Oktiabr'skoe vooruzhennoe vosstanie, vol. 1, pp. 379–80; P. N. Miliukov, *Istoriia vtoroi russkoi revoliutsii*, 3 parts (Sofia, 1921–1924), part 2, pp. 19–20, 36.

18. *Malenkaia gazeta*, July 6, p. 1; *Volia naroda*, July 6, p. 3; G. Shidlovskii, "Razgrom redaktsii *Pravdy* v iiule 1917 g.," *KL*, 1927, no. 1 (22), pp. 48–50.

19. Rabinowitch, *Prelude to Revolution*, pp. 208–9, 213–14.

20. *Golos soldata*, July 7, p. 2. During the July days, for security reasons, meetings of the cabinet were held in the General Staff building. Beginning around July 11 the government moved its permanent headquarters from the Mariinsky Palace to the Winter Palace. At this time the Winter Palace also became Kerensky's residence.

21. Ibid.

22. Russia, 1917, Provisional Government, *Zhurnaly zasedanii Vremennago pravitel'stva* (Petrograd, 1917), meeting of July 6, 1917, p. 1.

23. *Vestnik Vremennago pravitel'stva*, July 7, p. 1.

24. *Revoliutsionnoe dvizhenie: Iiul'skii krizis*, p. 290.

25. Alexander Kerensky, *Russia and History's Turning Point* (New York, 1965), p. 290.

26. V. Vladimirova, *Revoliutsiia 1917 goda: Khronika sobytii*, vol. 3, *Iiun'–iiul'* (Moscow, 1923), p. 156.

27. *Gazeta-kopeika*, July 7, p. 3; *Edinstvo*, July 7, p. 3.

28. *New York Times*, July 25, p. 1.

29. *Zhurnaly zasedanii Vremennago pravitel'stva*, meeting of July 7, 1917, p. 4; *Revoliutsionnoe dvizhenie: Iiul'skii krizis*, pp. 73–74; Akademiia nauk SSSR, Institut istorii, et al., *Baltiiskie moriaki v podgotovke i provedenii velikoi oktiabr'skoi sotsialisticheskoi revoliutsii*, ed. P. N. Mordvinov (Moscow and Leningrad, 1957), pp. 131–32.

30. *Revoliutsionnoe dvizhenie: Iiul'skii krizis*, pp. 290, 293, 298–303; *Razlozhenie armii v 1917 godu*, ed. Ia. A. Iakovlev (Moscow and Leningrad, 1925), pp. 96–98. Capital punishment was originally abolished by order of the Provisional Government on March 12, 1917.

31. *Revoliutsionnoe dvizhenie: Iiul'skii krizis*, pp. 302, 304, 564.

32. Vladimirova, *Khronika sobytii*, vol. 3, p. 161.

33. *Malenkaia gazeta*, July 6, p. 3; *Birzhevye vedomosti*, July 6, morning edition, p. 3.

34. *Zhivoe slovo*, July 11, p. 3; *Birzhevye vedomosti*, July 10, morning edition, p. 4. Khaustov had been jailed on June 9 for inflammatory articles he wrote for *Okopnaia pravda* condemning the forthcoming offensive.

35. *Baltiiskie moriaki*, p. 131; I. N. Kolbin, "Kronshtadt ot fevralia do kornilovskikh dnei," *KL*, 1927, no. 2 (23), pp. 153–54; *Proletarskoe delo*, July 14, p. 1.

36. F. F. Raskol'nikov, "V tiur'me Kerenskogo," *PR*, 1923, no. 10 (22), p. 135.

37. A. M. Kollontai, "V tiur'me Kerenskogo," *Katorga i ssylka*, 1927, no. 7 (36), pp. 25–32.

38. *Izvestiia*, July 19, p. 5.

39. *Novaia zhizn'*, July 13, p. 2.

40. *Gazeta-kopeika*, July 25, p. 3; Raskol'nikov, "V tiur'me Kerenskogo," p. 139. A close friend of Trotsky's, Larin was formally a Menshevik-Internationalist at this time. At the Sixth Congress shortly afterward he became associated with the Bolsheviks.

41. *Petrogradskaia gazeta*, July 9, p. 2; M. Ul'ianova, "Poiski Il'icha v pervye dni iiulia 1917 g.," in *O Lenine* (Moscow, 1927), pp. 35–40. For Nikitin's recollection of this episode see *Rokovye gody*, p. 152.

42. Lenin spent the night of July 5 at the apartment of Maria Sulimova, a Military Organization secretary. After the government's early-morning raid on the Kshesinskaia mansion, he spent a few hours each at the quarters of a Vyborg District factory worker, V. N. Kaurov, and the apartment of a close friend of Krupskaia's, Margarita Fofanova. On the night of July 6 he stayed at the apartment of Nikolai Poletaev, a former Social Democratic Duma deputy, moving in with the Alliluevs on the morning of July 7. See Institut marksizma-leninizma pri TsK KPSS, *Vladimir Il'ich Lenin: Biograficheskaia khronika*, vol. 4, *Mart-oktiabr' 1917* (Moscow, 1973), pp. 275–82.

43. S. Ordzhonikidze, "Il'ich v iiul'skie dni," *Pravda*, March 28, 1924, p. 4.

44. Institut marksizma-leninizma pri TsK KPSS, *Shestoi s"ezd RSDRP (bol'shevikov), avgust 1917 goda: Protokoly* (Moscow, 1958), pp. 32–33.

45. A. G. Shliapnikov, "Kerenshchina," *PR*, 1926, no. 7 (54), p. 35.

46. *Shestoi s"ezd*, pp. 28–36.

47. N. K. Krupskaia, "Vospominaniia o Lenine," in Institut marksizma-leninizma pri TsK KPSS, *Vospominaniia o Vladimire Il'iche Lenine*, 5 vols. (Moscow, 1968), vol. 1, p. 471.

48. Lenin, *PSS*, vol. 49, p. 445.

49. Ordzhonikidze, "Il'ich v iiul'skie dni," p. 4.

50. Lenin, *PSS*, vol. 34, pp. 8–9.

51. *Vladimir Il'ich Lenin: Biograficheskaia khronika*, vol. 4, pp. 287–88.

52. G. Zinov'ev, "Lenin i iiul'skie dni," *PR*, 1927, nos. 8–9 (67–68), p. 70.

53. A. Shotman, "Lenin nakanune oktiabria," in Institut Lenina pri TsK RKP(b), *O Lenine: Sbornik vospominanii*, 4 vols. (Leningrad, 1924–1925), vol. 1, pp. 112–24; Zinov'ev, "Lenin v iiul'skie dni," pp. 67–69. Lenin wrote most of *The State and Revolution*, originally titled "Marxism and the State," in January and February 1917 while in Zurich. Recently characterized by Robert C. Tucker as "Lenin's most important contribution to Marxist political theory" (*The Lenin Anthology*, p. 311), it was left behind in Stockholm when Lenin returned to Russia in April 1917 and was delivered to him at Emelianov's in late July.

54. This account of the All-Russian Executive Committees meeting of July 13 is based on reports in *Izvestiia*, July 14, pp. 3–4; *Novaia zhizn'*, July 14, p. 2; and *Den'*, July 14, p. 2.

55. The Trudovik (Toiler) group was a caucus of nonaligned populist-oriented socialists active in the State Duma. In the Fourth Duma Kerensky was the chief Trudovik spokesman.

56. Lisy Nos, literally "bald nose," is a point a few miles northwest of Petrograd which juts into the Finnish Gulf toward nearby Kronstadt.

57. N. Emel'ianov, "Tainstvennyi shalash," in *O Lenine*, ed. M. L. Meshcheriakov, vol. 1 (Moscow and Leningrad, 1924), p. 109.

58. M. I. Sulimova, "Iiul'skie dni," in *K godovshchine smerti V. I. Lenina*, ed. A. F. Il'in-Zhenevskii (Leningrad, 1925), pp. 136–38; M. I. Sulimova, "O sobytiiakh 1917 goda," in Institut marksizma-leninizma pri TsK KPSS, *Velikaia oktiabr'skaia sotsialistcheskaia revoliutsiia: Sbornik vospominanii* (Moscow, 1957), p. 120; *Leninskii sbornik*, vol. 4 (Leningrad, 1925), p. 319.

59. Shotman, "Lenin nakanune oktiabria," pp. 114–15.
60. Zinov'ev, "Lenin i iiul'skie dni," pp. 68–70.

3 · Petrograd During the Reaction

1. The following were consulted in preparing this account of the cossacks' funeral: *Izvestiia*, July 14, p. 2; July 15, pp. 1–2; and July 16, p. 4; *Golos soldata*, July 16, p. 1; *Zhivoe slovo*, July 16, p. 1; *Rech'*, July 16, pp. 1–2; *Volia naroda*, July 16, p. 4; *Delo naroda*, July 15, p. 4; July 16, p. 3.
2. *Rech'*, July 7, p. 1.
3. V. Voitinskii, "Gody pobed i porazhenii, 1917 god" (Nicolaevsky archives, Hoover Institution, Stanford, California), p. 209.
4. *Golos soldata*, July 7, p. 1; *Izvestiia*, July 7, p. 1; Vladimirova, *Khronika sobytii*, vol. 3, p. 161.
5. *Izvestiia*, July 19, p. 5; *Gazeta-kopeika*, July 19, p. 2.
6. See, for example, *Groza*, August 20, pp. 1–2; August 27, pp. 1–2.
7. *Petrogradskii listok*, July 27, p. 1.
8. Tat'iana Graf, "V iiul'skie dni 1917 g.," KL, 1928, no. 2 (26), p. 47, *Novaia zhizn'*, July 21, p. 3.
9. Vladimirova, *Khronika sobytii*, vol. 3, pp. 149, 165, 319–20.
10. Graf, "V iiul'skie dni 1917 g.," pp. 69–73; *Golos soldata*, July 12, p. 3.
11. A. Il'in-Zhenevskii, "Bol'sheviki v tiur'me Kerenskogo," *KL*, 1928, no. 2 (26), p. 47.
12. *Izvestiia*, July 6, p. 7; *Den'*, July 6, p. 3.
13. *Gazeta-kopeika*, July 8, p. 4; July 11, p. 3; *Golos soldata*, July 12, p. 3; *Izvestiia Moskovskogo soveta rabochikh deputatov*, July 13, p. 1.
14. This account of the July 18 meeting of the Provisional Committee is based on A. Drezen, ed., *Burzhuaziia i pomeshchiki v 1917 godu: Chastnye soveshchaniia chlenov Gosudarstvennoi dumy* (Moscow and Leningrad, 1932), pp. 192–205.
15. A. Il'in-Zhenevskii, *Ot fevralia k zakhvatu vlasti: Vospominaniia o 1917 g.* (Leningrad, 1927), p. 87.
16. I. P. Flerovskii, "Iiul'skii politicheskii urok," *PR*, no. 7 (54), pp. 83–84.
17. *Proletarskoe delo* was published by the Bolshevik fraction in the Kronstadt Soviet beginning July 14, 1917, as a replacement for *Golos pravdy*, just then banned by the authorities.
18. L. Trotskii, *Sochineniia*, vol. 3, part 1, *Ot fevralia do oktiabria* (Moscow and Leningrad, 1925), pp. 206–11.
19. Institut istorii partii Leningradskogo obkoma KPSS, *Geroi oktiabria, biografii aktivnykh uchastnikov podgotovki i provedeniia oktiabr'skogo vooruzhennogo vosstaniia v Petrograde*, 2 vols. (Leningrad, 1967), vol. 1, pp. 239–40. As the only party member killed in attacks on the Bolsheviks after the July days, Voinov was made a hero after the October revolution. The street where he was assaulted was renamed Voinov Street.
20. Il'in-Zhenevskii, *Ot fevralia k zakhvatu vlasti*, p. 93.
21. Il'in-Zhenevskii, "Bol'sheviki v tiur'me Kerenskogo," p. 48.
22. Ibid., p. 51; Raskol'nikov, "V tiur'me Kerenskogo," p. 137. To judge by a memoir by Tatiana Graf, a young member of the Bolshevik Petrograd District Committee, among party members thrown into prison in the aftermath of the July

days, those in the Nikolaevsky Military Hospital seem to have had the most lenient regime. Graf recalls her astonishment when, visiting the hospital to deliver food and clothing to three Bolsheviks there, she could not locate these inmates. She later learned that guards at the hospital, acting without authorization, permitted prisoners to go into town on a regular basis, sometimes for several days at a time. Graf, "V iiul'skie dni 1917 g.," p. 75.

23. Kollontai, in the women's prison, was also held in solitary confinement. For several weeks she was not permitted to leave her cell; she was denied contact with other prisoners and not allowed reading materials. What tidbits of news she managed to pick up were all bad. Apprehension for the fate of the party became an obsession. Eventually she fell seriously ill. When Maxim Gorky and Leonid Krasin launched a protest in the press against her harsh treatment, *Zhivoe slovo* countered with an expose of what Kollontai's life in prison was "really" like. According to this fanciful account, Kollontai was so pleased with prison borshch and kasha that when a sympathizer brought her a large basket of sardines, cheese, sprats, and fried goose, she gave it all away to fellow prisoners. Kollontai was released from prison on August 19. Kollontai, "V tiur'me Kerenskogo," pp. 37–41; *Zhivoe slovo*, August 13, p. 4.

24. Raskol'nikov, "V tiur'me Kerenskogo," pp. 138, 142, 144–45, 155.

25. *Rabochii i soldat*, July 29, p. 1.

26. *Soldat*, August 20, p. 3.

27. Il'in-Zhenevskii, "Bol'sheviki v tiur'me Kerenskogo," pp. 51–52.

28. Raskol'nikov, "V tiur'me Kerenskogo," p. 149.

29. Il'in-Zhenevskii, "Bol'sheviki v tiur'me Kerenskogo," pp. 55–58; *Izvestiia Kronshtadtskogo soveta*, August 8, p. 3.

4 · *The Ineffectiveness of Repression*

1. *Zhivoe slovo*, July 8, p. 2.

2. *Rech'*, July 7, p. 1.

3. Vsesoiuznaia Kommunisticheskaia partiia (bol'shevikov), *Vtoraia i Tret'ia petrogradskie obshchegorodskie konferentsii bol'shevikov v iiule i oktiabre 1917 goda: Protokoly* (Moscow–Leningrad, 1927). *Novaia zhizn'*, July 21, p. 3.

4. *Izvestiia*, July 12, p. 4.

5. Ibid., July 12, p. 5; July 13, p. 3; Vladimirova, *Khronika sobytii*, vol. 3, p. 175.

6. Vladimirova, *Khronika sobytii*, vol. 3, pp. 180–81.

7. See, for example, I. Tobolin, ed., "Iiul'skie dni v Petrograde," *Krasnyi arkhiv*, 1927, no. 4 (23), pp. 1–63, and no. 5 (24), pp. 3–70.

8. *Izvestiia*, July 22, p. 7.

9. *Novaia zhizn'*, July 23, p. 1; see also A. S. Farfel, *Bor'ba narodnykh mass protiv kontrrevoliutsionnoi iustitsii vremennogo pravitel'stva* (Minsk, 1969), p. 98.

10. G. E. Zinov'ev, *Sochineniia*, 16 vols. (Moscow, 1923–1929), vol. 7. For a useful analysis of Zinoviev's activity in 1917, see Myron Hedlin, "Zinoviev's Revolutionary Tactics in 1917," *Slavic Review*, vol. 34, no. 1 (1975), pp. 19–43.

11. A new Central Committee was elected at the Sixth Congress. Its members were Ia. A. Berzin, A. S. Bubnov, N. I. Bukharin, F. E. Dzerzhinsky, L. B. Kamenev, A. M. Kollontai, N. N. Krestinsky, V. I. Lenin, V. P. Miliutin, M. K.

Muranov, V. P. Nogin, A. I. Rykov, F. A. Sergeev, S. G. Shaumian, I. T. Smilga, G. Ia. Sokolnikov, I. V. Stalin, Ia. M. Sverdlov, L. D. Trotsky, M. S. Uritsky, and G. E. Zinoviev.

12. A. F. Il'in-Zhenevskii, "Nakanune oktiabria," *KL*, 1926, no. 4 (19), pp. 15–16.

13. See below, pp. 72–74.

14. Institut marksizma-leninizma pri TsK KPSS, *Perepiska sekretariata TsK RSDRP(b) s mestnymi partiinymi organizatsiiami: Sbornik dokumentov*, vol. 1, *Mart-oktiabr' 1917 g.* (Moscow, 1957), p. 22.

15. Among the approximately fifteen top party officials attending this meeting were Sverdlov and Nogin from the Central Committee; Gleb Boky, Viacheslav Molotov, Saveliev, and Volodarsky from the Petersburg Committee; and Bubnov, Olminsky, Sokolnikov, Bukharin, and Aleksei Rykov from Moscow.

16. These appear under the title "Politicheskoe polozhenie (Chetyre tezisa)," in Lenin, *Sochineniia*, vol. 34, pp. 1–5; for the background and an interpretation of these theses, see A. M. Sovokin, "Rasshirennoe soveshchanie TsK RSDRP(b) 13–14 iiulia 1917 g.," *Voprosy istorii KPSS*, 1959, no. 4, pp. 130–31.

17. S. Ordzhonikidze, "Il'ich v iiul'skie dni," *Pravda*, March 28, 1924, p. 4. This statement by Lenin has been edited out of some editions of Ordzhonikidze's memoirs. See, for example, S. Ordzhonikidze, *Put' bol'shevika* (Moscow, 1956).

18. According to Podvoisky, Lenin spoke to him about the necessity of preparing the masses for an armed uprising immediately after the June 18 demonstration. Lenin also appears to have discussed his views on this subject with Kamenev, Zinoviev, and Stalin at Fofanova's on the evening of July 6.

19. See especially *Vtoraia i Tret'ia petrogradskie obshchegorodskie konferentsii*, pp. 75, 85.

20. L. A. Komissarenko, "Deiatel'nost' partii bol'shevikov po ispol'zovaniiu vooruzhennykh i myrnikh form bor'by v period podgotovki i provedeniia velikoi oktiabr'skoi sotsialisticheskoi revoliutsii" (Candidate dissertation, Leningrad State University, Leningrad, 1967), p. 23.

21. Sovokin, Rasshirennoe soveshchanie," p. 132.

22. *Vtoraia i Tret'ia petrogradskie obshchegorodskie konferentsii*, p. 85. An interesting analysis of this conference is contained in Komissarenko, "Deiatel'nost' partii bol'shevikov," pp. 22–23. On the Central Committee's rejection of Lenin's advice in the post-July period, see G. Sokol'nikov, "Kak podkhodit' k istorii oktiabria," in *Za leninizma* (Moscow and Leningrad, 1925), p. 165.

23. *Vtoraia i Tret'ia petrogradskie obshchegorodskie konferentsii*, p. 84.

24. Ibid., pp. 144–45.

25. See Olminsky's comments at an expanded meeting of the Moscow Committee on July 15 in *Revoliutsionnoe dvizhenie: Iiul'skii krizis*, p. 186.

26. Lenin, *Sochineniia*, vol. 34, pp. 10–17; Sovokin, "Rasshirennoe soveshchanie," p. 134.

27. E. A. Fedosikhina, "Bol'shevistskie partiinye konferentsii nakanune VI s"ezda partii" (Candidate dissertation, Moscow State University, Moscow, 1969), pp. 65–67, 87, 92.

28. *Vtoraia i Tret'ia petrogradskie obshchegorodski konferentsii*, p. 56.

29. M. Ia. Latsis, "Iiul'skie dni v Petrograde: Iz dnevnika agitatora," *PR*, 1923, no. 5 (17), p. 115.

30. *Pervyi legal'nyi Peterburgskii komitet*, pp. 210–14.

31. *Izvestiia*, July 16, p. 7; Latsis, "Iiul'skie dni v Petrograde," p. 116; *Petrogradskii listok*, July 19, p. 1.

32. *Vtoraia i Tret'ia petrogradskie obshchegorodskie konferentsii*, pp. 64–68.

33. Ibid., pp. 69–70.

34. Ibid., pp. 70–71; 75–76.

35. Ibid., pp. 71–72.

36. Ibid., pp. 74–75.

37. Ibid., p. 78.

38. Ibid., pp. 78–88.

39. Ibid., p. 88; Komissarenko, "Deiatel'nost' partii bol'shevikov," pp. 41–42. Less than a week later Slutsky attempted to get the Petersburg Committee to reevaluate "the current moment." See the minutes for the Petersburg Committee meeting of July 12 in *Pervyi legal'nyi Peterburgskii komitet*, p. 216.

40. See Il'in-Zhenevskii, "Nakanune oktiabria," pp. 10–12, for personal recollections of a purge by fellow officers in his military unit.

41. *Golos soldata*, July 12, p. 4.

42. V. I. Nevskii, "V oktiabre," *Katorga i ssylka*, 1932, nos. 11–12 (96–97), p. 28; A. Minchev, "Boevye dni," *KL*, 1924, no. 9, p. 9. Lingering resentment toward the Military Organization on the part of district representatives frequently surfaced at meetings of the Petersburg Committee. For example, see the hostile references to the Military Organization at the Petersburg Committee meeting of August 17 in *Pervyi legal'nyi Peterburgskii komitet*, pp. 227–29.

43. *Vtoraia i Tret'ia petrogradskie obshchegorodskie konferentsii*, pp. 57–61, and *Shestoi s"ezd*, pp. 59–66. On this point see S. E. Rabinovich, "Bol'shevistskie voennye organizatsii v 1917 g.," *PR*, 1928, nos. 6–7 (77–78), pp. 187–89.

44. *Shestoi s"ezd*, p. 289; B. Shumiatskii, "Shestoi s"ezd partii i rabochii klass," in *V dni velikoi proletarskoi revoliutsii: Epizody bor'by v Petrograde v 1917 godu* (Moscow, 1937), p. 92.

45. Il'in-Zhenevskii, "Nakanune oktiabria," p. 7.

46. Ibid., p. 9.

47. Institut marksizma-leninizma pri TsK KPSS, *Protokoly Tsentral'nogo komiteta RSDRP(b): Avgust 1917–fevral' 1918* (Moscow, 1958), p. 4.

48. Ibid., p. 24.

49. Ibid., p. 20.

50. The All-Russian Bureau was formed at the All-Russian Conference of Bolshevik Military Organizations in June; its members were Nevsky, Podvoisky, E. F. Rozmirovich, and Lazar Kaganovich, all of whom escaped arrest in July, and Flavian Khaustov, I. Ia. Arosev, Nikolai Krylenko, Konstantin Mekhonoshin, and I. I. Dzevaltovsky, all of whom were jailed.

51. *Protokoly Tsentral'nogo komiteta*, pp. 23–25.

52. Il'in-Zhenevskii, *Ot fevralia k zakhvatu vlasti*, p. 98.

53. Nevskii, "V oktiabre," pp. 28–30.

54. Ibid., p. 29.

55. *Protokoly Tsentral'nogo komiteta*, pp. 22–23. Two weeks later, on the heels of the Kornilov affair, Sverdlov presented a very favorable progress report to the Central Committee on the state of the Military Organization. He declared that the Military Organization was "not an independent political organization but a military

commission under the Central Committee. Simultaneously," he went on, "the work of the Military Organization is being supervised by the Central Committee. Comrade Bubnov is working with the staff of *Soldat*, and [Military Organization] work in general is being supervised by Dzerzhinsky and Sverdlov." Ibid., p. 64.

56. *Perepiska sekretariata TsK*, vol. 1, p. 23.

57. *Soldat*, August 20, p. 6.

58. Ibid., September 13, p. 4.

59. Ibid., September 2, p. 4.

60. Ibid., September 13, p. 4.

61. Akademiia nauk SSSR, Institut istorii, Leningradskoe otdelenie, *Raionnye sovety Petrograda v 1917 godu: Protokoly, rezoliutsii, postanovleniia obshchikh sobranii zasedanii ispolnitel'nykh komitetov*, 3 vols. (Moscow and Leningrad, 1964–1966). For worthwhile descriptions and analyses of these materials, see Theodore H. Von Laue's review essay in *Kritika*, vol. 4, no. 3 (Spring 1968), pp. 33–57, and Rex A. Wade, "The Raionnye Sovety of Petrograd: The Role of Local Political Bodies in the Russian Revolution," *Jahrbücher für Geschichte Osteuropas*, vol. 20 (1972), pp. 226–40.

62. On this point see Wade, "Raionnye Sovety," p. 240.

63. *Raionnye sovety Petrograda*, vol. 3, pp. 248–50. The fullest study of the Interdistrict Conference is M. L. Lur'e, "Petrogradskoe mezhraionnoe soveshchanie v 1917 godu," *KL*, 1932, no. 3 (48), pp. 13–43, and no. 4 (49), pp. 30–50.

64. This independence was mirrored in the action taken by the conference in response to an appeal for funds on the part of the Central Executive Committee. The Bolsheviks apparently opposed such aid while the majority socialists obviously favored it. In its resolution on the matter, the Interdistrict Conference, while endorsing donations for the Soviet's upkeep, pointedly declared that if the central Soviet organs were experiencing difficulties obtaining funds in the districts of Petrograd, it was only because of the disappointment of the Petrograd proletariat with the policies of the Central Executive Committee leadership. Until the politics of the Central Executive Committee majority were altered in a fundamental way, the district soviet representatives warned, the Central Executive Committee was bound to encounter passivity on the part of the proletariat toward all aspects of its work requiring mass support, finances included. *Raionnye sovety Petrograda*, vol. 3, pp. 283–84.

65. Ibid., p. 88.

66. Ibid., p. 201. District soviet documents do not include any protocols for meetings of the Porokhovsky and Obukhovsky district soviets for the period just after the July days; to judge by their behavior in June and August, one would surmise that their positions were close to those of the Okhtinsky and Rozhdestvensky district soviets.

67. Ibid., vol. 1, p. 143.

68. Ibid., vol. 3, pp. 268–70.

69. Ibid., vol. 1, pp. 32–33.

70. Ibid., vol. 3, pp. 70–71.

71. Ibid., vol. 2, pp. 224–28.

72. Ibid., vol. 3, pp. 203–4.

73. Ibid., pp. 268–72.

74. Ibid., pp. 272–79. The district soviet deputies were received by the Bureau

of the Central Executive Committee later the same day, but there is no evidence that the mission had any effect.

75. Ibid., vol. 1, pp. 144–45.

76. Ibid., vol. 3, pp. 279–80.

77. Ibid., vol. 2, p. 46.

5 · *The Bolshevik Resurgence*

1. An initial edition of the Sixth Congress protocols appeared in 1919 (Izdatel'stvo Kommunist). It was obviously incomplete, quite likely more than anything else a reflection of the difficult circumstances under which the congress met. According to Soviet sources, the secretarial record of the congress was then lost, as a result of which the original 1919 edition has been the basis of all subsequent editions of the Sixth Congress protocols. These appeared in 1927, 1934, and, most recently, 1958.

2. *Shestoi s"ezd*, pp. 27–36, 270.

3. *Revoliutsionnoe dvizhenie: Iul'skii krizis*, p. 326.

4. *Shestoi s"ezd*, pp. 109, 423–24.

5. Il'in-Zhenevskii, *Ot fevralia k zakhvatu vlasti*, p. 96.

6. *Shestoi s"ezd*, pp. 69–70.

7. Il'in-Zhenevskii, *Ot fevralia k zakhvatu vlasti*, p. 96.

8. *Shestoi s"ezd*, p. 7.

9. I. P. Flerovskii, "Lenin i kronshtadtsy," in *O Vladimire Il'iche Lenine* (Moscow, 1963), p. 276; I. P. Flerovskii, "Na putiakh k oktiabriu," in Institut marksizma-leninizma pri TsK KPSS, *Velikaia oktiabr'skaia sotsialisticheskaia revoliutsiia: Sbornik vospominanii uchastnikov revoliutsii v Petrograde i Moskve* (Moscow, 1957), p. 105.

10. *Shestoi s"ezd*, p. 28.

11. Ibid., p. 122.

12. Ibid., pp. 111–12.

13. Not included, apparently intentionally, in any editions of the Sixth Congress protocols and materials, this draft resolution was published shortly after the congress in the August 13 issue of the Kiev Bolshevik paper, *Golos sotsial-demokrata*. From some notations made by Lenin before his departure for Finland, it appears clear that he prepared a draft resolution "On the Current Moment" specifically for the congress. For these notations see *Leninskii sbornik*, vol. 21 (Moscow, 1933), pp. 81–82. The resolution itself was finally republished in A. M. Sovokin, *V preddverii oktiabria* (Moscow, 1973), pp. 336–41. Heretofore most Soviet sources suggested that the text of this resolution had never been found.

14. On this point see *Oktiabr'skoe vooruzhennoe vosstanie*, vol. 2, p. 96. More fundamental theoretical questions relating to the very possibility of a socialist revolution in Russia were raised by only three delegates: Nogin, Evgenii Preobrazhensky, and N. S. Angarsky.

15. *Shestoi s"ezd*, pp. 116–18.

16. Ibid., pp. 119–20.

17. Ibid., pp. 124–25; for a valuable view of the revolution in Baku, see Suny, *The Baku Commune 1917–1918*.

18. *Shestoi s"ezd*, pp. 134–36.

19. Ibid., pp. 114–42.

20. Ibid., pp. 125–28.

21. Ibid., pp. 131–32.

22. Ibid., pp. 133–32.

22. Ibid., pp. 133–39.

23. For the text of this resolution, see Institut marksizma-leninizma pri TsK KPSS, Institut istorii parti MK i MGK KPSS, *Podgotovka i pobeda oktiabr'skoi revoliutsii v Moskve* (Moscow, 1957), pp. 202–4.

24. *Shestoi s"ezd*, pp. 144–45.

25. A. M. Sovokin, "Razrabotka V. I. Leninym novoi taktike partii posle iiul'skikh sobytii 1917 g.," (Candidate dissertation, Institute of Marxism-Leninism, Moscow, 1962), p. 185; *Shestoi s"ezd*, p. 251.

26. *Shestoi s"ezd*, pp. 225–27.

27. Akademiia nauk SSSR, Institut istorii, et al., *Revoliutsionnoe dvizhenie v Rossii v avguste 1917 g.: Razgrom kornilovskogo miatezha*, ed. D. A. Chugaev, et al. (Moscow, 1959), p. 46.

28. On this point see *Oktiabr'skoe vooruzhennoe vosstanie*, vol. 1, p. 385.

29. Thus participants in a gathering of local SR officials on August 23, reviewing developments since mid-July, worried aloud about significant membership losses to the Bolsheviks. Only a very few representatives of SR district party committees were able to say that support for the SRs in their areas was undiminished. *Oktiabr'skoe vooruzhennoe vosstanie*, vol. 1, pp. 387–88.

30. At the end of July, in elections to the Kronstadt Duma, the Bolshevik list, headed by Raskolnikov, received 10,214 votes of the 28,154 votes cast, second only to the SRs, with 10,900 votes.

Early August elections to the powerful Kronstadt Soviet provided an even more striking sign of support for the Bolsheviks: ninety-six Bolsheviks took seats in the new soviet alongside ninety-six nonaffiliated candidates, seventy-three SRs, thirteen Mensheviks, and seven anarchists. (Of 280 deputies in the first Kronstadt Soviet formed in March, only sixty were Bolsheviks. The second Kronstadt Soviet, elected in early May, contained ninety-three Bolsheviks, ninety-one SRs, forty-six Mensheviks, and sixty-eight nonaffiliated deputies.) Nonetheless, even now the Bolsheviks did not have a majority in the Kronstadt Soviet; an SR, Konstantin Shugrin, was elected chairman. *Petrogradskii listok*, July 30, p. 2; *Izvestiia Kronshtadtskogo soveta*, August 13, p. 1; S. S. Khesin, *Oktiabr'skaia revoliutsiia i flot* (Moscow, 1971), pp. 74–75, 153, 299.

31. A. M. Andreev, *Sovety rabochikh i soldatskikh deputatov nakanune oktiabria* (Moscow, 1967), pp. 255–59; L. F. Karamysheva, *Bor'ba bol'shevikov za Petrogradskii sovet* (Leningrad, 1964), p. 136.

32. Vladimirova, *Khronika sobytii*, vol. 4, p. 24.

33. *Novaia zhizn'*, August 8, p. 3.

34. See below, pp. 110–15.

35. *Rech'*, August 15, p. 1.

36. *Pervyi legal'nyi Peterburgskii komitet*, pp. 223–26, 232–33.

37. *Soldat*, August 19, p. 1; *Proletarii*, August 19, p. 1.

38. *Soldat*, August 19, p. 1; *Proletarii*, August 20, p. 1.

39. For a valuable analysis of the vote, see William G. Rosenberg, "The Russian Municipal Duma Elections of 1917: A Preliminary Computation of Returns," *Soviet Studies*, XXI (1969), pp. 152–63.

40. *Rech'*, August 23, p. 1. According to this writer, the actual vote totals didn't mean much because (1) absenteeism had been highest in areas of greatest Kadet strength, and (2) the SR and Bolshevik figures were swelled by the votes of thousands of soldiers who were only temporary residents of the capital. To him, the most essential point was that 40 percent of the total vote *minus* soldiers was Kadet.

41. *Novaia zhizn'*, August 23, p. 1.

42. *Rabochaia gazeta*, August 23, p. 1.

43. *Rabochaia gazeta*, August 24, p. 1.

6 · *The Rise of Kornilov*

1. On August 11 an uncontrolled fire in the Malaia Okhta District totally destroyed four factories and a large quantity of shells. Three days later fire ravaged a gunpowder plant and ammunition depot in Kazan; spectacular incendiary explosions there went on for three days. Moreover, on August 16 yet another major industrial fire leveled the sprawling Westinghouse factory in Petrograd.

2. Shortages of bread, meat, fish, vegetables, dairy products, and other essential foodstuffs increased dramatically at the end of the summer and in the early fall. Most seriously affected by these shortages were citizens with low incomes, unable to deal in the black market which now flourished everywhere, or even to afford the somewhat lower albeit rapidly rising prices in legitimate produce shops. Simultaneously, the supply of fuel for home and industrial use also became critical; in early August government officials were warning that by midwinter 50 percent of Petrograd factories would be forced to shut down for lack of fuel. *Oktiabr'skoe vooruzhennoe vosstanie*, vol. 2, pp. 5–16, 69–86.

3. J. D. White, "The Kornilov Affair: A Study in Counterrevolution," *Soviet Studies*, vol. XX (1968), pp. 188–89.

4. See Rosenberg, *Liberals in the Russian Revolution*, pp. 196–200.

5. Ibid.

6. Made up primarily of conservatively inclined army officers, the Union of Officers, the Military League, and the Union of Saint George Cavaliers were originally formed shortly after the February revolution to help arrest the deterioration in the position of officers and the breakdown of traditional discipline in the armed forces, and, in general, to further the cause of "war to victory." In addition to maintaining a central headquarters at Mogilev, the Main Committee of the Union of Officers had representatives scattered on the various Russian fronts. Membership in the Union of Saint George Cavaliers was limited to holders of the Cross of Saint George, awarded for heroism in battle. Like other ultrapatriotic pressure groups, the Union of Officers, the Military League, and the Union of Saint George Cavaliers were hostile to the soviets and rabidly anti-Bolshevik.

7. White, "The Kornilov Affair," p. 187.

8. V. Ia. Laverychev, "Russkie monopolisty i zagovor Kornilova," *Voprosy istorii*, 1964, no. 4, p. 36.

9. N. Ia. Ivanov, *Kornilovshchina i ee razgrom* (Leningrad, 1965), pp. 34–37.

10. E. I. Martynov, *Kornilov: Popytka voennogo perevorota* (Leningrad, 1927), pp. 11–17.

11. Ibid., pp. 16–18.

12. Ibid., p. 20.

13. Akademiia nauk SSSR, Institut istorii, et al., *Revoliutsionnoe dvizhenie v Ros-*

sii posle sverzheniia samoderzhaviia, ed. D. A. Chugaev, et al. (Moscow, 1957), pp. 409–10.

14. Martynov, *Kornilov*, p. 18.

15. P. N. Miliukov, *Rossiia na perelome*, 2 vols. (Paris, 1927), vol. 2, p. 67.

16. I. G. Tsereteli, *Vospominaniia o fevral'skoi revoliutsii*, 2 vols. (Paris, 1963), vol. 1, pp. 91–92.

17. The group had its own weekly journal, *Freedom in Struggle*.

18. Laverychev, "Russkie monopolisty," pp. 34–35; White, "The Kornilov Affair," pp. 187–88. It appears that Zavoiko was acting on behalf of his own organization, grouped around *Freedom in Struggle*, rather than on behalf of the Society for the Economic Rehabilitation of Russia, as is suggested by Laverychev and White.

19. Zavoiko was the son of an admiral who had distinguished himself in the Crimean War. At the turn of the century, Zavoiko, then in his twenties, managed to acquire a large personal fortune through some highly questionable real estate transactions while serving as a district marshal of the nobility in Poland. (Martynov, *Kornilov*, pp. 20–21.) After the 1905 revolution he became active in oil industry management and in high industrial finance. He was also involved in political journalism; during World War I he served as copublisher of an extreme right newspaper, *Russkaia volia*, and in April 1917, prior to his departure for the front, he was editor and publisher of *Freedom in Struggle*.

20. P. N. Miliukov, *Istoriia vtoroi russkoi revoliutsii*, 2 vols. (Sofia, 1921–1924), vol. 1, part 2, p. 60.

21. Martynov, *Kornilov*, p. 20.

22. W. S. Woytinsky, *Stormy Passage* (New York, 1961), p. 333.

23. See above pp. 22–23.

24. See *Rabochaia gazeta*, July 29, p. 3; N. Bukhbinder, "Na fronte v predoktiabr'skie dni," *KL*, 1923, no. 6, pp. 32–34.

25. Bukhbinder, "Na fronte v predoktiabr'skie dni," p. 34.

26. Rosenberg, *Liberals in the Russian Revolution*, p. 207.

27. Martynov, *Kornilov*, p. 25.

28. Ibid., p. 29.

29. General Nikolai Ruzsky was commander of the northern front at the time of the February revolution, a post which he held until April. General Mikhail Alekseev was commander-in-chief of the Russian army from early March until May 21, 1917. At the time of the Stavka conference, both officers were still awaiting reassignment.

30. Bukhbinder, "Na fronte v predoktiabr'skie dni," p. 39. This source contains full protocols of the July 16 Stavka conference, excerpts of which have been translated into English in R. P. Browder and A. F. Kerensky, eds., *The Russian Provisional Government 1917*, 3 vols. (Stanford, 1961), vol. 2, pp. 989–1010.

31. Bukhbinder, "Na fronte v predoktiabr'skie dni," pp. 21–27. The Declaration of Soldiers' Rights was a statement of democratic rights initially published by the Petrograd Soviet on March 15 and issued in revised form by War Minister Kerensky on May 11.

32. D. V. Lehovich, *White against Red: The Life of General Anton Denikin* (New York, 1974), p. 104.

33. M. V. Alekseev, "Iz dnevnika generala Alekseeva," *Russkii istoricheskii arkhiv*, vol. 1 (Prague, 1929), p. 41.

34. Martynov, *Kornilov*, pp. 32–33; Bukhbinder, "Na fronte v predoktiabr'skie dni," p. 31.

35. A. I. Denikin, *Ocherki russkoi smuty*, vol. 1, part 2 (Paris, 1921), p. 188.

36. Bukhbinder, "Na fronte v predoktiabr'skie dni," p. 31; see also Ivanov, *Kornilovshchina i ee razgrom*, p. 39.

37. *Miatezh Kornilova: Iz belykh memuarov* (Leningrad, 1928), p. 202. See also B. Savinkov, "General Kornilov: Iz vospominanii," *Byloe*, 1925, no. 3 (31), pp. 188–90.

38. A. F. Kerensky, *The Catastrophe* (New York, 1927), p. 114.

39. A. F. Kerensky, *Prelude to Bolshevism: The Kornilov Rising* (New York, 1919), pp. xiii, 13–14.

40. On this point, see White, "The Kornilov Affair," pp. 196–97.

41. Ivanov, *Kornilovshchina i ee razgrom*, p. 41.

42. Soviet historians have speculated with good reason that this was less because of reservations about Cheremisov's abilities as a military leader than because of his reputation for "leftism" and concern about him as a potential political rival. For example, see Martynov, *Kornilov*, p. 40.

43. V. Vladimirova, *Kontr-revoliutsiia v 1917 g. (Kornilovshchina)* (Moscow, 1924), p. 48.

44. General Denikin was now appointed commander of the southwestern front.

45. Martynov, *Kornilov*, p. 45; Ivanov, *Kornilovshchina i ee razgrom*, p. 53.

46. Martynov, *Kornilov*, p. 48.

47. For example, see *Izvestiia*, August 5, p. 3.

48. *Novaia zhizn'*, August 8, p. 3; see above, pp. 90–91.

49. *Izvestiia*, August 4, p. 4; see also *Novaia zhizn'*, August 4, p. 3.

50. See below, pp. 110–15.

51. *Revoliutsionnoe dvizhenie v Rossii: Razgrom kornilovskogo miatezha*, p. 360; for an illuminating analysis of Kadet behavior at the conference, see Rosenberg, *Liberals in the Russian Revolution*, pp. 210–18.

52. M. F., "K istorii Kornilovshchiny," *KL*, 1924, no. 1 (10), pp. 207–17, contains the full text of this revised proposal. See also Ivanov, *Kornilovshchina i ee razgrom*, pp. 57–58, and Vladimirova, *Khronika sobytii*, vol. 4, pp. 36–37.

53. This occurred between August 10 and 17.

54. Vladimirova, *Kontr-revoliutsiia v 1917 g.*, p. 61.

55. A. F. Kerenskii, *Delo Kornilova* (Moscow, 1918), pp. 52–53.

56. White, "The Kornilov Affair," p. 200.

57. Ivanov, *Kornilovshchina i ee razgrom*, pp. 59–60. At the insistence of the Kadets the cabinet considered the military aspects of the program on August 11, approving them in principle but requesting further discussion.

58. Martynov, *Kornilov*, p. 48.

59. On this point, see *Oktiabr'skoe vooruzhennoe vosstanie*, vol 2, p. 133.

60. Martynov, *Kornilov*, p. 56.

61. A. S. Lukomskii, *Vospominaniia*, 2 vols. (Berlin, 1922), vol. 1, p. 227.

62. On this point, see White, "The Kornilov Affair," pp. 197–99.

63. Lukomskii, *Vospominaniia*, vol. 1, p. 227.

7 · Kornilov versus Kerensky

1. Ariadna Tyrkova-Williams, *From Library to Brest Litovsk: The First Year of the Russian Revolution* (London, 1919), p. 167.

2. *Gosudarstvennoe soveshchanie*, ed. M. N. Pokrovskii and Ia. A. Iakovlev (Moscow and Leningrad. 1930), p. 508.

3. *Izvestiia*, August 13, p. 2.

4. *Protokoly Tsentral'nogo komiteta*, pp. 6–7.

5. Vladimirova, *Khronika sobytii*, vol. 4, p. 35.

6. Martynov, *Kornilov*, p. 64.

7. A. F. Rasstrigin, "Revoliutsionnye komitety avgustskogo krizisa 1917 g." (Candidate dissertation, Leningrad State University, Leningrad, 1969), p. 90.

8. *Revoliutsionnoe dvizhenie v Rossii: Razgrom kornilovskogo miatezha*, pp. 20, 379–80.

9. Ibid., p. 392.

10. N. Sukhanov, *Zapiski o revoliutsii*, 7 vols. (Berlin, Petersburg, and Moscow, 1922–1923), vol. 5, pp. 155–56; Vladimirova, *Khronika sobytii*, vol. 4, p. 45.

11. Sukhanov, *Zapiski o revoliutsii*, vol. 5, p. 156.

12. Vladimirova, *Khronika sobytii*, vol. 4, p. 45.

13. *Gosudarstvennoe soveshchanie*, p. 133.

14. Ibid., pp. 74–76.

15. Ibid., pp. 112–17.

16. Subsequently this platform was referred to as the "August 14 Program."

17. See Vladimirova, *Kontr-revoliutsiia v 1917 g.*, p. 88, for differences between the Provisional Government's declaration of July 8 and the more conservative August 14 program.

18. *Gosudarstvennoe soveshchanie*, p. 4.

19. Miliukov, *Istoriia vtoroi russkoi revoliutsii*, vol. 1, part 2, pp. 127–28.

20. *Novoe vremia*, August 13, p. 1.

21. Vladimirova, *Kontr-revoliutsiia v 1917 g.*, p. 84.

22. A. I. Verkhovskii, *Rossiia na Golgofe* (Petrograd, 1918), p. 107.

23. Miliukov, *Istoriia vtoroi russkoi revoliutsii*, vol. 1, part 2, pp. 174, 183.

24. *Posledniia novosti*, January 20, 1937, p. 2; Laverychev, "Russkie monopolisty," p. 40.

25. White, "The Kornilov Affair," p. 200.

26. Z. Gippius, *Siniaia kniga: Peterburgskii dnevnik, 1914–1918 gg.* (Belgrade, 1929), p. 174.

27. In the Russian press, the disaster at Riga quickly became the source of great controversy, in part because it came without much warning. The generals, at once echoed by liberal and conservative opinion, insisted that the defeat was further evidence of the chaos reigning in the armed forces. At the time this appears to have been Kerensky's view. To the left, on the other hand, it seemed that the General Staff had intentionally failed to provide properly for Riga's defense in order to buttress their demands for repressive measures.

28. Martynov, *Kornilov*, pp. 74–75. Savinkov, in turn, delegated the actual preparation of these decrees to an ad hoc commission in the War Ministry under General Apushkin.

29. The Tenth Cavalry Division, technically part of the Third Corps, remained at its regular station.

30. *Oktiabr'skoe vooruzhennoe vosstanie*, vol. 2, pp. 131–32; Martynov, *Kornilov*, pp. 56–59; Ivanov, *Kornilovshchina i ee razgrom*, pp. 78–83. Included in the Savage Division (Kavkazskaia Tuzemnaia Divisiia) were the Kabardinsky, Dagestansky, Tatarsky, Cherkessky, and Ingushsky Cavalry regiments, the Osetinsky Foot Brigade, and the Eighth Don Cossack Artillery Division.

31. *Revoliutsionnoe dvizhenie v Rossii: Razgrom kornilovskogo miatezha*, pp. 439, 629.

32. *Oktiabr'skoe vooruzhennoe vosstanie*, vol. 2, p. 132.

33. Martynov, *Kornilov*, pp. 77–78.

34. *Revoliutsionnoe dvizhenie v Rossii: Razgrom kornilovskogo miatezha*, pp. 420, 452–53.

35. Radkey, *The Agrarian Foes of Bolshevism*, pp. 386–87.

36. Ibid., and A. F. Kerensky, *Russia and History's Turning Point* (New York, 1965), pp. 341–42.

37. Savinkov's reconstruction of the first of these talks is contained in *Revoliutsionnoe dvizhenie v Rossii: Razgrom kornilovskogo miatezha*, pp. 421–43. Lukomsky, General I. P. Romanovsky, Colonel V. L. Baranovsky, and Filonenko sat in on parts of the second discussion on the evening of July 23. Vladimirova, *Kontr-revoliutsiia v 1917 g.*, pp. 206–9, contains a summary of this part of the talks signed by Kornilov, Lukomsky, and Romanovsky.

38. *Revoliutsionnoe dvizhenie v Rossii: Razgrom kornilovskogo miatezha*, pp. 421–23; see also Savinkov's statement to the press in *Birzhevye vedomosti*, September 12, p. 1, and Martynov, *Kornilov*, pp. 80–82.

39. *Revoliutsionnoe dvizhenie v Rossii: Razgrom kornilovskogo miatezha*, p. 432.

40. Ibid., p. 421.

41. Martynov, *Kornilov*, p. 80; O. Chaadaeva, *Kornilovshchina* (Moscow and Leningrad, 1930), pp. 90–91.

42. Martynov, *Kornilov*, p. 78.

43. Kerensky, *Delo Kornilova*, p. 82.

44. Kerensky, *Prelude to Bolshevism*, pp. 214–15.

45. *Revoliutsionnoe dvizhenie v Rossii: Razgrom kornilovskogo miatezha*, pp. 432, 629.

46. Ibid., pp. 433–34; see also *Oktiabr'skoe vooruzhennoe vosstanie*, vol. 2, pp. 133–34.

47. *Revoliutsionnoe dvizhenie v Rossii: Razgrom kornilovskogo miatezha*, pp. 434–35; 439–40.

48. Kerensky, *Russia and History's Turning Point*, p. 342.

49. Browder and Kerensky, *The Russian Provisional Government*, vol. 3, pp. 1561–62.

50. Martynov, *Kornilov*, p. 84; see also *Revoliutsionnoe dvizhenie v Rossii: Razgrom kornilovskogo miatezha*, p. 444, and Kerensky, *Delo Kornilova*, pp. 100–3.

51. Significantly, in testimony to government investigators at the time, Lvov did not mention any offer by Kerensky to resign. See *Revoliutsionnoe dvizhenie v Rossii: Razgrom kornilovskogo miatezha*, pp. 425–28.

52. This was the strong impression received by the progressive General Ver-

khovsky, who was in Mogilev on August 24 and spoke with Kornilov soon after Lvov's visit. In his diary, Verkhovsky recorded that Kornilov appeared to attach great importance to acting in concert with the government and that he had just received assurance from Lvov that this would be the case. Verkhovskii, *Rossiia na Golgofe*, p. 110.

53. Browder and Kerensky, *The Russian Provisional Government*, vol. 3, pp. 1564–65; *Revoliutsionnoe dvizhenie v Rossii: Razgrom kornilovskogo miatezha*, pp. 428, 450; Martynov, *Kornilov*, pp. 87–88.

54. Martynov, *Kornilov*, p. 88.

55. *Revoliutsionnoe dvizhenie v Rossii: Razgrom kornilovskogo miatezha*, pp. 441–42; Kerensky, *Delo Kornilova*, pp. 105–106; Martynov, *Kornilov*, pp. 96–97.

56. *Revoliutsionnoe dvizhenie v Rossii: Razgrom kornilovskogo miatezha*, p. 443; Kerensky, *Delo Kornilova*, pp. 108–9; Browder and Kerensky, *The Russian Provisional Government*, vol. 3, p. 1571.

57. F. F. Kokoshkin and N. M. Kishkin, reports to the Kadet City Committee in Moscow, August 31, 1917 (a copy of which is in the Nicolaevsky Archive, Hoover Institution, Stanford, California), pp. 8–10; *Revoliutsionnoe dvizhenie v Rossii: Razgrom kornilovskogo miatezha*, p. 444; Miliukov, *Istoriia vtoroi russkoi revoliutsii*, vol. 1, part 2, pp. 218–20; Rosenberg, *Liberals in the Russian Revolution*, pp. 229–30.

58. *Revoliutsionnoe dvizhenie v Rossii: Razgrom kornilovskogo miatezha*, p. 448.

59. Ibid., pp. 448–52.

60. Vladimirova, *Khronika sobytii*, vol. 4, p. 101.

61. *Revoliutsionnoe dvizhenie v Rossii: Razgrom kornilovskogo miatezha*, p. 445.

62. Gippius, *Siniaia kniga*, p. 179.

63. Browder and Kerensky, *The Russian Provisional Government*, vol. 3, p. 1573.

64. *Oktiabr'skoe vooruzhennoe vosstanie*, p. 137.

65. Vladimirova, *Khronika sobytii*, vol. 4, p. 104; see also Lehovich, *White against Red*, p. 124.

66. Vladimirova, *Khronika sobytii*, vol. 4, p. 110.

67. Browder and Kerensky, *The Russian Provisional Government*, vol. 3, pp. 1573–74.

68. Woytinsky, *Stormy Passage*, pp. 350–51.

69. Sukhanov, *Zapiski o revoliutsii*, vol. 5, p. 217.

8 · *The Bolsheviks and Kornilov's Defeat*

1. In September Smolny became the meeting-place for the Bolshevik Central Committee, and by the time of the October revolution it was the hub of Bolshevik Party activity in Petrograd.

2. *Novaia zhizn'*, August 29, p. 2; Rasstrigin, "Revoliutsionnye komitety avgustskogo krizisa," p. 130; *Revoliutsionnoe dvizhenie v Rossii: Razgrom kornilovskogo miatezha*, pp. 476–77.

3. *Izvestiia*, August 28, p. 3; August 29, p. 1; *Novaia zhizn'*, August 29, pp. 1–2; *Rabochaia gazeta*, August 29, pp. 2–3.

4. *Izvestiia*, August 29, pp. 1–2; Sukhanov, *Zapiski o revoliutsii*, vol. 5, p. 293.

5. Sukhanov, *Zapiski o revoliutsii*, vol. 5, pp. 291–92.

6. Lenin, *PSS*, vol. 34, pp. 119–21.

7. *Shestoi s" ezd*, pp. 255–57; 169–70.

8. Lenin, *PSS*, vol. 34, pp. 73–78. Although they were not published at the time, these materials had made the rounds of the top party leaders in Petrograd by August 27.

9. See above, pp. 111–12.

10. The only Soviet historian who has candidly discussed Lenin's misjudgments in regard to the threat of a rightist coup in August 1917 is V. I. Startsev. See his "V. I. Lenin v avguste 1917 godu," *Voprosy istorii*, 1967, no. 8, pp. 124–27.

11. *Protokoly Tsentral'nogo komiteta*, p. 32; V. V. Anikeev, *Deiatel'nost' TsK RSDRP(b) v 1917 godu: Khronika sobytii* (Moscow, 1969), p. 267.

12. Two separate protocols of this meeting appear, side by side, in the volume of Petersburg Committee documents published in 1927 (*Pervyi legal'nyi Peterburgskii komitet*, pp. 237–54). Both variants are cryptic and incomplete, no doubt most of all a reflection of the prevailing tension. For the most part they supplement and reinforce each other; hence I have drawn upon both versions in attempting to reconstruct the discussion.

13. An invaluable analysis of the behavior of Moscow Bolsheviks in 1917 and of differences in outlook between younger Bolsheviks strongly represented in the Moscow Regional Bureau and more moderate, senior party officials concentrated in the municipal Moscow Committee is contained in Stephen F. Cohen's extraordinarily valuable biography of Bukharin, *Bukharin and the Bolshevik Revolution* (New York, 1973), pp. 45–53.

14. See below, pp. 216–17.

15. On Bubnov's "leftism" at this time, see Komissarenko, "Deiatel'nost' partii bol'shevikov," pp. 185–86.

16. The extra edition is dated Tuesday, August 28, clearly a slip. August 28 was a Monday, and internal evidence indicates that this issue could not have been published before the early morning of August 20. *Soldat* did not normally appear on Monday, and, in contrast to *Rabochii*, there was no *Soldat* extra on Monday, August 28. Thus the regular issue and extra of *Soldat* on August 29 were the Military Organization's first press responses to the Kornilov affair.

17. *Soldat*, August 29, p. 4.

18. Significantly, apart from some leaflets produced wholly or in part by the Military Organization, Drezen, *Bol'shevizatsiia petrogradskogo garnizona*, and the more recent *Revoliutsionnoe dvizhenie v Rossii: Razgrom kornilovskogo miatezha*, contain only two items relating to the organization's activity between August 27 and 30: the text of the resolution passed at the meeting of Military Organization representatives on August 28 (*Bol'shevizatsiia petrogradskogo garnizona*, pp. 242–43; *Revoliutsionnoe dvizhenie v Rossii: Razgrom kornilovskogo miatezha*, pp. 482–83) and the responses of the Moscow-Narva District Bolshevik Committee to a Military Organization questionnaire about the state of the local Red Guard (*Revoliutsionnoe dvizhenie v Rossii: Razgrom kornilovskogo miatezha*, pp. 510–11).

19. *Perepiska sekretariata TsK RSDRP(b)s mestnymi partinymi organizatsiiami*, vol. 1, p. 31.

20. Rasstrigin, "Revoliutsionnye komitety avgustskogo krizisa," p. 112.

21. See below, p. 153.

22. The Military Section has been referred to variously in the literature as the Provisional Military Committee, the Operations Section, the Military Committee, and even the Military Revolutionary Committee; it should not be confused with the

Provisional Revolutionary Committee originally formed by the Executive Committees to investigate the July uprising or the more radical Military Section of the Petrograd Soviet.

23. *Kornilovskie dni: Biulleteni vremennago voennago komiteta pri TsIK s 28 avgusta po 4 sentiabria 1917 g.* (Petrograd, 1917); A. Anskii, ed., *Protokoly Petrogradskogo soveta professional'nykh soiuzov za 1917 g.* (Leningrad, 1927), p. 70.

24. See above, p. 77.

25. *Raionnye sovety Petrograda*, vol. 3, p. 292; *Protokoly Petrogradskogo soveta professional'nykh soiuzov*, p. 58.

26. *Raionnye sovety Petrograda*, vol. 3, pp. 292–93.

27. *Revoliutsionnoe dvizhenie v Rossii: Razgrom kornilovskogo miatezha*, pp. 498–99.

28. See Iu. S. Tokarev, *Narodnoe pravotvorchestvo nakanune velikoi oktiabr'skoi sotsialisticheskoi revoliutsii (mart–oktiabr' 1917 g.)* (Moscow and Leningrad, 1965), pp. 144–46, and B. D. Gal'perina, "Raionnye sovety Petrograda v 1917 godu" (Candidate dissertation, Institute of History, USSR Academy of Sciences, Leningrad, 1968), pp. 228–38, for discussions of the important role of the Interdistrict Conference and district soviets in preparations to fight Kornilov.

29. This committee was composed of three representatives elected from the Peterhof Soviet; one representative each from five party organizations; one representative from each of the three commissariats in the district; and one representative each from the Putilov factory committee, the Putilov docks, the district board, the company of soldiers stationed at the Putilov factory, the district trade union bureau, and small enterprises in the district.

30. *Raionnye sovety Petrograda*, vol. 2, pp. 251–53; *Revoliutsionnoe dvizhenie v Rossii: Razgrom kornilovskogo miatezha*, p. 496; Tokarev, *Narodnoe pravotvorchestvo*, pp. 145–46.

31. Formed in March 1917, the Petrograd Trade Union Soviet was at this time made up of elected delegates from nearly fifty trade unions in the capital. It was headed by an executive commission. For a valuable account of the Petrograd Trade Union Soviet's activities in 1917, see A. Anskii, "Petrogradskii sovet professional'nykh soiuzov v 1917 g.," in *Professional'noe dvizhenie v Petrograde v 1917 g.*, ed. A. Anskii (Leningrad, 1928), pp. 45–77.

32. *Izvestiia*, August 29, p. 6.

33. This commission was evidently later absorbed by the Committee for Struggle Against the Counterrevolution.

34. *Protokoly Petrogradskogo soveta professional'nykh soiuzov*, pp. 57–72; *Revoliutsionnoe dvizhenie v Rossii: Razgrom kornilovskogo miatezha*, pp. 500–1; Anskii, "Petrogradskii sovet professional'nykh soiuzov v 1917 g.," p. 53.

35. Vladimirova, *Kontr-revoliutsiia v 1917 g.*, p. 167; Z. V. Stepanov, *Rabochie Petrograda v period podgotovki i provedeniia oktiabr'skogo vooruzhennogo vosstaniia* (Moscow and Leningrad, 1965), p. 173. See also A. G. Egorova, *Partiia i profsoiuzy v oktiabr'skoi revoliutsii* (Moscow, 1970), p. 160.

36. At this time Vikzhel was made up of forty members—fourteen SRs, seven Mensheviks, three Popular Socialists, two Interdistrict Committee representatives, two Bolsheviks, one Bolshevik sympathizer, and eleven nonparty individuals, many of whom supported the Kadets.

37. A. P. Taniaev, *Ocherki po istorii dvizheniia zheleznodorozhnikov v revoliutsii 1917 goda (fevral'-oktiabr')* (Moscow and Leningrad, 1925), p. 95; Vladimirova, *Kontr-revoliutsiia v 1917 g.*, pp. 161–62; Kerenskii, *Delo Kornilova*, pp. 153–54, 156.

38. V. I. Startsev, the most knowledgeable specialist on the development of armed workers' militias in revolutionary Petrograd, estimates conservatively that thirteen thousand to fifteen thousand workers now became organized for military action. V. I. Startsev, *Ocherki po istorii Petrogradskoi krasnoi gvardii i rabochei militsii* (Moscow and Leningrad, 1965), p. 164.

39. The Petrograd Soviet had two main sections, the Workers' and Soldiers' sections, composed of factory and garrison representatives respectively. Headed by a large executive commission, the Soldiers' Section concerned itself with problems of special interests to military troops.

40. Ivanov, *Kornilovshchina i ee razgrom*, pp. 156–57; Drezen, *Bol'shevizatsiia petrogradskogo garnizona*, pp. 253–64; Kochakov, "Bol'shevizatsiia petrogradskogo garnizona v 1917 godu," pp. 174–77.

41. *Izvestiia Kronshtadtskogo soveta*, September 6, p. 1; September 8, p. 1; Akademiia nauk SSSR, Institut istorii, et al., *Baltiiskie moriaki v podgotovke i provedenii velikoi oktiabr'skoi sotsialisticheskoi revoliutsii*, ed. P. N. Mordvinov (Moscow and Leningrad, 1957), pp. 186–89; Akademiia nauk SSSR, Institut istorii, et al., *Protokoly i postanovleniia Tsentral'nogo komiteta Baltiiskogo flota*, ed. D. A. Chugaev (Moscow and Leningrad, 1963), pp. 150–58; V. V. Petrash, *Moriaki Baltiiskogo flota v bor'be za pobedu oktiabria* (Moscow and Leningrad, 1966), pp. 200–16; Ivanov, *Kornilovshchina i ee razgrom*, pp. 156–57; A. K. Drezen, "Baltiiskii flot ot iiulia k oktiabriu 1917 g.," *KL*, 1929, no. 5 (32), pp. 191–99.

42. *Razlozhenie armii v 1917 g.*, ed. M. N. Pokrovskii and Ia. A. Iakovlev (Moscow and Leningrad, 1925), p. 116; *Protokoly i postanovleniia Tsentral'nogo komiteta Baltiiskogo flota*, pp. 167–72; Ivanov, *Kornilovshchina i ee razgrom*, p. 63.

43. Interview with Finisov by Nicholas Vakar in *Posledniia novosti*, March 6, 1937, p. 3.

44. For conflicting recollections of this episode and the reasons for the inaction of Petrograd rightist groups, see G. Vinberg, *V plenu u obez'ian* (Kiev, 1918), pp. 104–8; interviews with A. I. Putilov and P. N. Finisov by Nicholas Vakar in *Posledniia novosti*, January 24, 1937, p. 5, and March 6, 1937, p. 3; L. P. Desimeter, "Zagovor Kornilova: Pis'mo v redaktsiiu," *Posledniia novosti*, May 28, 1937; Kerensky, *Russia and History's Turning Point*, p. 381; Denikin, *Ocherki russkoi smuty*, vol. 2, pp. 64–65; and Miliukov, *Vtoraia russkaia revoliutsiia*, vol. 1, part 2, pp. 258–59.

45. The fullest account of these developments, based largely on unpublished materials in Soviet archives, is contained in Ivanov, *Kornilovshchina i ee razgrom*, pp. 174–79. See also *Bol'shevizatsiia petrogradskogo garnizona*, p. 257; Martynov, *Kornilov*, pp. 142–46; Vladimirova, *Khronika sobytii*, vol. 4, pp. 107–45, 241–49; *Revoliutsionnoe dvizhenie v Rossii: Razgrom kornilovskogo miatezha*, p. 531–32, 633.

46. Ivanov, *Kornilovshchina i ee razgrom*, pp. 180–81; Vladimirova, *Khronika sobytii*, vol. 4, pp. 134, 349; Martynov, *Kornilov*, pp. 147–49; *Revoliutsionnoe dvizhenie v Rossii: Razgrom kornilovskogo miatezha*, p. 535.

47. Ivanov, *Kornilovshchina i ee razgrom*, pp. 170–74; Vladimirova, *Khronika sobytii*, vol. 4, pp. 343–50; Martynov, *Kornilov*, pp. 135–42.

48. Alekseev was replaced, in turn, by Dukhonin on September 10.

49. Martynov, *Kornilov*, pp. 155–71; Vladimirova, *Khronika sobytii*, vol. 4, pp. 124–32.

50. Browder and Kerensky, *The Russian Provisional Government*, vol. 3, pp. 1586–89. The text of Krymov's message to Kornilov is unknown.

9 · The Question of a New Government

1. See above, p. 131.

2. Rosenberg, *Liberals in the Russian Revolution*, pp. 230–32, provides a persuasive reconstruction of the Kadet role in this episode. See also Kokoshkin report, pp. 11–12, 15; Miliukov, *Istoriia vtoroi russkoi revoliutsii*, vol. 1, part 2, pp. 249–54; Vladimirova, *Khronika sobytii*, vol. 4, p. 138.

3. Kerensky, *Delo Kornilova*, p. 174.

4. Ivanov, *Kornilovshchina i ee razgrom*, p. 207.

5. *Kornilovskie dni*, p. 152.

6. *Protokoly Petrogradskogo soveta professional'nykh soiuzov*, p. 76.

7. Il'in-Zhenevskii, "Bol'sheviki v tiur'me Kerenskogo," pp. 59–62; Vladimirova, *Khronika sobytii*, vol. 4, p. 162; Institut istorii partii pri Leningradskom obkome KPSS, Filial Instituta marksizma-leninizma pri TsK KPSS, *Bol'sheviki Petrograda v 1917 godu: Khronika sobytii* (Leningrad, 1957), p. 478.

8. *Golos soldata*, September 5, p. 1.

9. N. Ruban, *Oktiabr'skaia revoliutsiia i krakh men'shevizma* (Moscow, 1968), p. 272, quoting from an unpublished protocol of this meeting in the Soviet archives.

10. Often such calls for transfer of power to the Soviet were initiated by Bolsheviks—a clear sign of the degree to which the decisions of the Sixth Congress regarding slogans failed to influence the behavior of local party representatives at the time of the Kornilov crisis. See, for example, Skrypnik's comments at the joint meeting of the Trade Union Soviet and the Central Soviet of Factory-Shop Committees on August 29 (*Protokoly Petrogradskogo soveta professional'nykh soiuzov*, p. 70). On September 4 a meeting of eight hundred pipe factory workers, including representatives of all twenty thousand plant employees, reaffirmed this position, demanding the creation of a "Provisional Revolutionary Government" made up of representatives of the proletariat and peasantry and responsible only to revolutionary organs.

11. *Revoliutsionnoe dvizhenie v Rossii: Razgrom kornilovskogo miatezha*, pp. 487, 489, 501, 541–42. This source contains numerous other examples of such resolutions. They can be found in most socialist papers of the time, although they appeared most prominently in the Bolshevik papers *Rabochii*, *Rabochii put'*, and *Soldat*, and the Left SR daily *Znamia truda*. Incomplete lists of factories passing such resolutions were published periodically in *Rabochii put'*.

12. Drezen, *Bol'shevizatsiia petrogradskogo garnizona*, pp. 256–57.

13. Ibid., pp. 251–57, 265–68. This source, as well as all issues of *Soldat* during the last days of August and the first half of September, contain large collections of such resolutions. Virtually all key elements of the garrison seem to be represented. See also A. K. Drezen, "Petrogradskii garnizon v oktiabre," *KL*, 1927, no. 2 (23), pp. 106–7.

14. *Baltiiskie moriaki*, pp. 203, 207–8.

15. *Baltiiskie moriaki*, pp. 210–11; *Protokoly i postanovleniia Tsentral'nogo komiteta Baltisskogo flota*, pp. 192, 445–46; Drezen, "Baltiiskii flot," pp. 200–1. The flags were lowered several days later in deference to the Democratic State Conference.

16. *Izvestiia Kronshtadtskogo soveta*, August 29, pp. 2–3.

17. Ibid., August 30, p. 1.

18. *Protokoly Tsentral'nogo komiteta*, pp. 37–38. The fullest accounts of this meeting are contained in *Delo naroda*, September 1, p. 2, and September 3, pp. 2–3;

and in *Izvestiia*, September 1, p. 2; September 2, p. 4; September 3, p. 7. See also Vladimirova, *Khronika sobytii*, vol. 4, pp. 140–42, and 149–50, and *Oktiabr'skoe vooruzhennoe vosstanie*, vol. 2, pp. 171–81.

19. In this connection, it is interesting that at a late-evening meeting on August 31 the Bolshevik Central Committee, by itself, voted to make another discussion of "the current moment" the first item of business at a Central Committee plenum scheduled for September 3, evidently to further air differing assessments of the proper course to be followed in the prevailing situation. Stalin, for the left, and Kamenev, for the right, were specifically assigned the task of presenting opposing arguments. There is no information on whether or not such a meeting actually took place. *Protokoly Tsentral'nogo komiteta*, pp. 39–40, 72.

20. *Izvestiia*, September 1, p. 2; *Delo naroda*, September 1, p. 2.

21. For accounts of this meeting, see *Rech'*, September 1, p. 4; September 2, p. 3; *Delo naroda*, September 2, p. 2; *Birzhevye vedomosti*, September 1, morning edition, pp. 3–4; see also Vladimirova, *Khronika sobytii*, vol. 4, pp. 138–39.

22. See above, p. 90.

23. M. N. Potekhin, *Pervyi sovet proletarskoi diktatury* (Leningrad, 1966), p. 23.

24. The fullest accounts of this portion of the discussion are contained in *Izvestiia*, September 2, pp. 3–4; September 3, pp. 5–7; *Delo naroda*, September 3, pp. 2–3; *Birzhevye vedomosti*, September 3, morning edition, p. 3; *Rech'*, September 2, p. 3, and September 3, p. 3. See also Vladimirova, *Khronika sobytii*, vol. 4, pp. 149–50.

25. *Izvestiia*, September 3, p. 7.

26. Rosenberg, *Liberals in the Russian Revolution*, pp. 236–39.

27. *Delo naroda*, September 5, pp. 3–4. For Dan's recollections of his views at this time, see F. Dan, "K istorii poslednikh dnei Vremennogo pravitel'stva," *Letopis' revoliutsii*, book 1, 1923, pp. 163–75. Interestingly, a meeting of the Menshevik Central Committee on September 5 was evenly divided between proponents and opponents of coalition. (*Oktiabr'skoe vooruzhennoe vosstanie*, vol. 2, p. 186, citing an unpublished protocol in Soviet archives.)

28. See, for example, an account of a meeting of the SR Soviet fractions on September 6 in *Delo naroda*, September 7, p. 3. On internal SR Party factions at this time, see Radkey, *The Agrarian Foes of Bolshevism*, pp. 402–8.

29. *Delo naroda*, September 12, p. 2; *Znamia truda*, September 12, pp. 1–2.

30. See *Znamia truda*, September 12, p. 1, and all immediately succeeding issues.

31. Radkey, *The Agrarian Foes of Bolshevism*, p. 403.

32. A. L. Khokhriakov, "Iz zhizni petrogradskogo garnizona," *KL*, 1926, no. 2 (17), pp. 36–37.

33. See Drezen, *Bol'shevizatsiia petrogradskogo garnizona*, pp. 258–63, for protocols of garrison meetings during which such purges were conducted. For an interesting discussion of the Kornilov affair's impact on the average soldier, see S. E. Rabinovich, *Bor'ba za armiiu v 1917 g.* (Leningrad, 1930), p. 44.

34. *Revoliutsionnoe dvizhenie v Rossii: Razgrom kornilovskogo miatezha*, pp. 470–71.

35. Akademiia nauk SSSR, Institut istorii, et al., *Revoliutsionnoe dvizhenie v Rossii v sentiabre 1917 g.: Obshchenatsional'nyi krizis*, ed. D. A. Chugaev, et al. (Moscow, 1961), pp. 148–49, 553.

36. V. Voitinskii, "Gody pobed i porazhenii, 1917 god," pp. 295–99.

10 · *"All Power to the Soviets!"*

1. G. S. Rovio, "Kak Lenin skryvalsia u gel'singforsskogo 'politsmeistera,' " in Institut marksizma-leninizma pri TsK KPSS, *Lenin v 1917 godu, vospominaniia* (Moscow, 1967), pp. 148–56; Startsev, "V. I. Lenin v avguste 1917 goda," pp. 121–30; Startsev, "O nekotorykh rabotakh V. I. Lenina pervoi poloviny sentiabria 1917 g.," in A. L. Fraiman, ed., *V. I. Lenin v oktiabre i v pervye gody sovetskoi vlasti* (Leningrad, 1970), pp. 30–31; Kh. M. Astrakhan, et al., *Lenin i revoliutsiia 1917 g.* (Leningrad, 1970), pp. 277–84; Norman E. Saul, "Lenin's Decision to Seize Power: The Influence of Events in Finland," *Soviet Studies*, April 1973, pp. 491–505; M. M. Koronin, "V. I. Lenin i finskie revoliutsionery," *Voprosy istorii*, 1967, no. 10, pp. 11–17.

2. Lenin, *PSS*, vol. 34, pp. 119–21.

3. Ibid., pp. 133–39.

4. Western historians have ignored these writings almost entirely. Among historians in the Soviet Union, who have sought to elucidate the evolution of Lenin's views with minute accuracy, they have been the subject of great confusion and, on occasion, bitter dispute. This is partly a result of the fact that candid discussions of Lenin's professed interest in a peaceful development of the revolution in September 1917 and of the relationship between Lenin's views in this respect and those of the party leadership in Petrograd have been considered taboo. It is also in part because of the time lag between the writing of these essays and their publication; apparently only very recently was a careful attempt made to ascertain the precise date of their preparation. For differing points of view, see A. M. Sovokin, "O vozmozhnosti mirnogo razvitiia revoliutsii posle razgroma kornilovshchiny," *Voprosy istorii KPSS*, 1960, no. 3, pp. 50–64; B. I. Sandin, "Lenin o sootnoshenii mirnogo i vooruzhennogo putei razvitiia revoliutsii posle razgroma kornilovshchiny," *Uchenye zapiski Leningradskogo gosudarstvennogo pedagogicheskogo instituta*, vol. 195, vyp. 2 (1958), pp. 213–32; S. N. Frumkin, "V. I. Lenin o vozmozhnosti mirnogo razvitiia revoliutsii," *Uchenye zapiski Riazanskogo gosudarstvennogo pedinstituta*, vol. 19 (1958), pp. 29–51; Startsev, "O nekotorykh rabotakh V. I. Lenina pervoi poloviny sentiabria 1917 g.," pp. 28–38; N. Ia. Ivanov, "Nekotorye voprosy krizisa 'praviashchikh verkhov' i taktika bol'shevikov nakanune oktiabr'skogo vooruzhennogo vosstaniia," in I. I. Mints, *Lenin i oktiabr'skoe vooruzhennoe vosstanie v Petrograde: Materialy Vsesoiuznoi nauchnoi sessii sostoiavsheisia 13–16 noiabria 1962 g. v Leningrade* (Moscow, 1964), pp. 202–14. In all but the most recent edition of Lenin's collected works, these essays were included in the order of their publication date, that is, between September 14 and 27. A definitive analysis of internal evidence has led V. I. Startsev to conclude that all three passages were written much earlier than was generally believed (i.e., between September 6 and 9).

5. Lenin, *PSS*, vol. 34, pp. 229–38.

6. Ibid., pp. 200–7.

7. Ibid., pp. 214–28.

8. Sokol'nikov, "Kak podkhodit' k istorii oktiabria," p. 165; *Oktiabr'skoe vooruzhennoe vosstanie*, vol. 2, p. 188.

9. See *Perepiska sekretariata TsK RSDRP(b) s mestnymi partiinymi organizatsiiami*, vol. 1, pp. 186–87.

10. Protocols of this meeting are contained in *Pervyi legal'nyi Peterburgskii komitet*, pp. 259–70.

11. Slutsky presented an Executive Commission resolution which has not been published, evidently embodying this position.

12. On this point see Trotskii, *Sochineniia*, vol. 3, part 1, pp. 435–36.

13. The vote was 519 for the Bolshevik plan to 414 for the moderate socialist resolution, with 67 abstentions.

14. Every unit in the Petrograd garrison, regardless of size, was permitted at least one representative to the Petrograd Soviet, while factory workers were allowed representation in the Soviet according to a norm of one deputy per thousand workers. In practice, this resulted in a great imbalance in representation between soldiers, among whom the SRs had been relatively strong, and workers, among whom the Bolsheviks had particularly great influence. Beginning in August, the Bolsheviks had sought unsuccessfully to eliminate this disadvantage by providing for the election of one representative for every thousand soldiers, as in the case of workers.

15. Vladimirova, *Khronika sobytii*, vol. 4, p. 269.

16. *Perepiska sekretariata TsK RSDRP(b) s mestnymi partiinymi organizatsiiami*, vol. 1, p. 35; Komissarenko, "Deiatel'nost' partii bol'shevikov," p. 300.

17. *Protokoly Tsentral'nogo komiteta*, p. 49.

18. On this point, see V. I. Startsev, "Iz istorii priniatiia resheniia ob organizatsii vooruzhennogo vosstaniia," in *Lenin i oktiabr'skoe vooruzhennoe vosstanie v Petrograde*, p. 472.

19. *Protokoly Tsentral'nogo komiteta*, pp. 49–54; Trotskii, *Sochineniia*, vol. 3, part 1, pp. 293–98; 351–57; see also *Oktiabr'skoe vooruzhennoe vosstanie*, vol. 2, pp. 196 and 206.

20. On this point see Reiman, *Russkaia revoliutsiia*, vol. 2, p. 271.

21. *Izvestiia*, September 17, p. 7.

22. *Soldat*, September 17, p. 3.

23. *Rabochii put'*, September 13, pp. 1–2.

24. A. A. Burishkin was a Moscow industrialist and Kishkin was the Moscow Kadet; at this time both participated in conversations with Kerensky about a future government.

25. Press accounts of Kamenev's speech differ considerably. See *Rabochii put'*, September 17, pp. 2–3; *Izvestiia*, September 15, p. 5; *Novaia zhizn'*, September 15, p. 5.

26. *Izvestiia*, September 16, p. 5.

27. Lenin, *PSS*, vol. 34, pp. 239–41.

28. Ibid., pp. 242–47.

29. N. I. Bukharin, "Iz rechi tov. Bukharina na vechere vospominanii v 1921 g.," *PR*, 1922, no. 10, p. 319.

30. E. D. Stasova, "Pis'mo Lenina v TsK partii," in *Vospominaniia o V. I. Lenine*, 5 vols. (Moscow, 1969), vol. 2, p. 454.

31. *Protokoly Tsentral'nogo komiteta*, p. 55.

32. Bukharin, "Iz rechi tov. Bukharina na vechere vospominanii," p. 319.

33. G. Lomov, "V dni buri i natiska," *PR*, 1927, no. 10 (69), p. 166.

34. *Novaia zhizn'*, September 19, p. 5.

35. *Oktiabr'skoe vooruzhennoe vosstanie*, vol. 2, pp. 208–9.

36. A. Shotman, "Lenin nakanune oktiabria," in *O Lenine*, 4 vols. (Moscow and Leningrad, 1925), vol. 1, p. 116.

37. N. Krupskaia, "Lenin v 1917 godu," in *O Vladimire Il'iche Lenine: Vospominaniia 1900–1922* (Moscow, 1963), p. 208; K. T. Sverdlova, *Iakov Mikhailovich Sverdlov* (Moscow, 1960), p. 283.

38. *Izvestiia*, September 20, p. 6; *Soldat*, September 20, p. 3.

39. *Izvestiia*, September 20, p. 7.

40. I.e., the platform coupling reform with firm government that was worked out by the All-Russian Executive Committees and presented to the Moscow State Conference on August 14. See above, pp. 112–13.

41. *Izvestiia*, September 21, p. 2.

42. *Delo naroda*, September 21, p. 2; Vladimirova, *Khronika sobytii*, vol. 4, pp. 245–46.

43. *Izvestiia*, September 21, pp. 2–4.

44. *Delo naroda*, September 24, p. 2, and September 26, p. 2; *Rech'*, September 23, pp. 3–4, and September 24, pp. 3–4; *Izvestiia*, September 24, p. 2.

45. *Protokoly Tsentral'nogo komiteta*, p. 68; Vladimirova, *Khronika sobytii*, vol. 5, pp. 263–64, 275.

46. *Protokoly Tsentral'nogo komiteta*, p. 65. In a speech in 1920 Stalin declared that after the October revolution Lenin acknowledged that the party leadership in Petrograd had been right in rejecting his tactics at this time. See Leon Trotsky, *The Stalin School of Falsification*, translated by John G. Wright (New York, 1962), pp. 200–1.

47. *Protokoly Tsentral'nogo komiteta*, pp. 65, 261–62. Trotskii, *Sochineniia*, vol. 3, part 1, pp. 301–2, 359, 441–42; Komissarenko, "Deiatel'nost' partii bol'shevikov," pp. 332–33.

48. *Rabochii put'*, September 29, p. 3; *Revoliutsionnoe dvizhenie v Rossii v sentiabre: Obshchenatsional'nyi krizis*, pp. 74–75.

49. *Izvestiia*, September 26, p. 5; *Rabochii put'*, September 27, p. 3.

50. Ibid.; also Trotskii, *Sochineniia*, vol. 3, part 1, pp. 317–18.

51. *Rabochii put'*, September 26, pp. 1–2.

52. *Rabochii put'*, September 30, p. 1. On September 23 right Bolshevik strength in the Central Committee was augmented by the addition of Zinoviev, who became a regular participant in Central Committee meetings. At the same time, for nearly a week beginning September 28, Trotsky, chief spokesman for the party left, did not participate in the work of the Central Committee or the Petrograd Soviet because of illness. *Protokoly Tsentral'nogo komiteta*, pp. 67–75; Reiman, *Russkaia revoliutsiia*, vol. 2, p. 287.

11 · *Lenin's Campaign for an Insurrection*

1. Among historians and memoirists in the Soviet Union, there is no unanimity about the exact date of Lenin's return to Petrograd from Vyborg. While the officially accepted date is October 7, some writers indicate that Lenin returned to the Russian capital on October 20. Others claim that the date was significantly earlier—September 22 according to some, September 29 according to others. Confusion over the correct date is the result of the deception and secrecy that naturally surrounded Lenin's movements in the fall of 1917, extensive tampering with histori-

cal sources that occurred in Stalin's time, and present-day political and ideological requirements.

The late P. N. Mikhrin contended that Lenin returned to Petrograd on a Friday in late September, most probably September 29. His case for this date is based on careful analysis of memoirs by Krupskaia, Margarita Fofanova (in whose apartment Lenin stayed after his return), and Alexander Shotman and Eino Rakhia (who were in close contact with Lenin during these days); the personal testimony of Elena Stasova (the chief Central Committee secretary in September and October); Lenin's writings of this period; and archival documents unavailable to me. Having sifted through the available literature on this issue, I find Mikhrin's case in support of a date in late September very convincing. Mikhrin's arguments appear in I. I. Mints, ed., *Lenin i oktiabr'skoe vooruzhennoe vosstanie v Petrograde*, pp. 119–24.

2. Here Lenin referred to Zinoviev's essay "Chto ne delat' " *(Rabochii,* August 30, p. 2), written during the Kornilov crisis. Zinoviev had warned that a workers' uprising in Petrograd would end in defeat, as in Paris in 1871.

3. Lenin, *PSS,* vol. 34, pp. 248–56.

4. Ibid., pp. 257–63.

5. Ibid., pp. 264–68.

6. Ibid., pp. 280–83.

7. Ibid., pp. 340–41. In view of what was to come, it is worth noting that towards the end of this letter Lenin suggested that in the prevailing circumstances "it might be that power could be seized without an armed uprising." Moreover, he asserted, there was no reason that action against the government could not be initiated in Moscow. In what subsequently proved to be a particularly blatant misjudgment he added: "In Moscow our victory is assured and there is nobody to fight."

8. Lenin, *PSS,* vol. 34, pp. 284–86.

9. *Protokoly Tsentral'nogo komiteta,* p. 74.

10. M. Ia. Latsis, "Rol' Petrogradskogo komiteta v oktiabre," *Petrogradskaia pravda,* November 5, 1922, p. 2.

11. M. Ia. Latsis, "Nakanune oktiabr'skikh dnei," *Izvestiia,* November 6, 1918. p. 2.

12. Ibid. See also M. Ia. Latsis, "Iz oktiabr'skikh vospominanii," *Bakinskii rabochii,* Nobember 1, 1927, p. 3.

13. *Perepiska sekretariata TsK RSDRP(b) s mestnymi partiinymi organizatsiiami,* vol. 1, p. 315.

14. *Protokoly Tsentral'nogo komiteta,* pp. 75–76. It is worth noting that members of the Central Committee, such as Rykov, Zinoviev, and Nogin, who would have sided with Kamenev, were absent from the October 5 meeting. At this meeting the Central Committee took one other step which reflected the possibility that a major change in policy might be imminent. A Congress of Soviets of the Northern Region was scheduled to open in Petrograd on October 10, and at Stalin's behest the committee agreed to organize a conference of Central Committee members and party representatives from Petrograd and Moscow in conjunction with this congress, presumably for a thoroughgoing reassessment of goals and tactics. *Protokoly Tsentral'nogo komiteta,* p. 76.

15. Ibid., p. 76.

16. Trotskii, *Sochineniia*, vol. 3, part 1, p. 456; Sukhanov, *Zapiski o revoliutsii*, vol. 6, pp. 247–48.

17. Latsis, *Izvestiia*, November 6, 1918, p. 2. The minutes of this meeting are contained in *Pervyi legal'nyi Peterburgskii komitet*, pp. 296–306.

18. Iukka Rakhia was the brother of Eino Rakhia, who served as a liaison between Lenin and the Central Committee.

19. *Pervyi legal'nyi Peterburgskii komitet*, p. 303. Komissarenko ("Deiatel'nost' partii bol'shevikov," p. 369) reaches the same conclusion.

20. Latsis, *Bakinskii rabochii*, November 1, 1927, p. 3.

21. Latsis, *Izvestiia*, November 6, 1918, p. 2; Latsis, *Petrogradskaia pravda*, November 5, 1922, p. 2.

22. *Protokoly Tsentral'nogo komiteta*, p. 80.

23. Latsis, *Petrogradskaia pravda*, November 5, 1922, p. 2.

24. *Rech'*, October 8, p. 3; Miliukov, *Vtoraia russkaia revoliutsiia*, vol. 1, part 2, pp. 123–28; Sukhanov, *Zapiski o revoliutsii*, vol. 6, pp. 248–51.

25. Sukhanov, *Zapiski o revoliutsii*, vol. 7, p. 33; Iu. N. Flakserman, "10 oktiabria 1917 goda," in *Petrograd v dni velikogo oktiabria: Vospominaniia uchastnikov revoliutsionnykh sobytii v Petrograde v 1917 godu* (Leningrad, 1967), p. 266.

26. *Protokoly Tsentral'nogo komiteta*, pp. 83–86. Iakovleva, who was responsible for taking notes, subsequently indicated she was instructed to be cryptic for security reasons.

27. Fortunately for the historian, Kamenev and Zinoviev prepared a detailed résumé of their arguments for broad circulation immediately following the October 10 meeting (see below, pp. 212–13). The complete résumé is contained in *Protokoly Tsentral'nogo komiteta*, pp. 87–92.

28. *Protokoly Tsentral'nogo komiteta*, pp. 83–92; G. Lomov, "V dni buri i natiska," *Bakinskii rabochii*, November 5, 1927, p. 4; V. Iakovleva, "Podgotovka oktiabr'skogo vosstaniia v moskovskoi oblasti," *PR*, 1922, no. 10 (22), pp. 305–6; A. Kollontai, "Ruka istorii," *Krasnoarmeets*, 1919, nos. 10–15, p. 69; Flakserman, "10 oktiabria," pp. 264–69.

12 · *Obstacles to an Uprising*

1. Latsis, *Izvestiia*, November 6, 1918, p. 2.

2. V. Breslav, *Kanun oktiabria 1917 goda* (Moscow, 1934), p. 17; a special delegation from Moscow also participated.

3. *Rabochii put'*, October 8, p. 2; *Proletarskoe delo*, October 10, p. 1; Breslav, *Kanun oktiabria*, p. 19.

4. See Rakhia's speech at the opening session in *Vtoraia i Tret'ia petrogradskie obshchegorodskie konferentsii*, p. 108.

5. Ibid., p. 132; *Oktiabr'skoe vooruzhennoe vosstanie*, vol. 2, p. 132.

6. Lenin, *PSS*, vol. 34, pp. 385–90.

7. On this point see V. I. Startsev, "O vybore momenta dlia oktiabr'skogo vooruzhennogo vosstaniia," in *Lenin i oktiabr'skoe vooruzhennoe vosstanie v Petrograde*, p. 71.

8. Breslav, *Kanun oktiabria*, pp. 18–22; see also *Oktiabr'skoe vooruzhennoe vosstanie*, vol. 2, p. 250.

9. Breslav, *Kanun oktiabria*, pp. 21–22.

10. Ibid., pp. 31–32.

11. On this point see *Oktiabr'skoe vooruzhennoe vosstanie*, vol. 2, p. 253.

12. See Podvoisky's observations in this regard in *Vtoraia i Tret'ia petrogradskie obshchegorodskie konferentsii*, p. 114.

13. V. I. Nevskii, "Dve vstrechi," *KL*, 1922, no. 4, pp. 142–43.

14. V. I. Nevskii, "Istoricheskoe zasedanie Peterburgskogo komiteta RSDRP (bol'shevikov) nakanune oktiabr'skogo vosstaniia," *KL*, 1922, nos. 2–3, p. 318.

15. Shotman writes: "I remember well that arguments at [these conferences] revolved around the central question: Should power be seized at once or put off until the convocation of the Second Congress of Soviets. . . . All three conferences came out for the seizure of power in the near future. Not a single voice was raised against this. A majority of speakers were against seizing power right away, where-upon majorities at the three conferences voted against the immediate seizure of power." Shotman, "Lenin nakanune oktiabria," p. 119.

16. *Protokoly Tsentral'nogo komiteta*, pp. 86–92.

17. Thus, Raskolnikov, who rushed to the opening session of the congress after his release from jail the morning of the eleventh, learned of the party's decision regarding preparation of an armed uprising and was handed a copy of the Kamenev-Zinoviev memorandum immediately upon arrival at Smolny. Moments later, he was taken aside by Kamenev, who explained his reservations regarding the party's tactics and his reasons for feeling that an uprising would be an unmitigated disaster. F. F. Raskol'nikov, *Kronshtadt i Piter v 1917 godu* (Moscow and Leningrad, 1925), pp. 203–4. Similarly, Ilin-Zhenevsky of the Military Organization recalls riding with Kamenev to a political meeting on October 12; during the drive, Kamenev carefully outlined his point of view, arguing that, apart from anything else, the Military Organization itself was a long way from ready for immediate battle. Il'in-Zhenevskii, "Nakanune oktiabria," p. 25.

18. See Breslav's complaints about this in the Kronstadt Soviet as recorded in *Izvestiia Kronshtadtskogo soveta*, October 26, pp. 3–4.

19. Beginning October 3, *Znamia truda*'s editors, in response to accusations that the congress was intended to circumvent the Constituent Assembly, added the phrase, "Prepare for the Constituent Assembly."

20. From a speech delivered by Kamkov at the First All-Russian Congress of Left SRs in late November 1917; see *Protokoly pervago s"ezda partii levykh sotsialistov-revoliutsionerov (internatsionalistov)* (Moscow, 1918), pp. 38–39.

21. Breslav, *Kanun oktiabria*, pp. 68–69.

22. V. A. Antonov-Ovseenko, "Baltflot v dni kerenshchiny i krasnogo oktiabria," *PR*, 1922, no. 10, p. 122.

23. On this point see *Oktiabr'skoe vooruzhennoe vosstanie*, vol. 2, p. 253.

24. K. Riabinskii, *Revoliutsiia 1917 goda: Khronika sobytii*, vol. 5 (Moscow, 1926), pp. 88–89; *Izvestiia*, October 15, p. 3.

25. P. V. Volobuev, "Iz istorii bor'by Vremennogo pravitel'stva s revoliutsiei," *Istoricheskii arkhiv*, 1960, no. 5, pp. 83–85.

26. Ibid., p. 84. For follow-up directives from Polkovnikov's staff to military units in and around Petrograd, see Akademiia nauk SSSR, Institut istorii, et al., *Velikaia oktiabr'skaia sotsialisticheskaia revoliutsiia: Oktiabr'skoe vooruzhennoe vosstanie v Petrograde: Dokumenty i materialy*, ed. G. N. Golikov, et al. (Moscow, 1957), pp. 263–74.

27. *Birzhevye vedomosti*, October 14, evening edition, p. 2.

28. *Pervyi legal'nyi Peterburgskii komitet*, pp. 307–19; *Protokoly Tsentral'nogo komiteta*, pp. 93–105.

29. These are Nevsky's figures; they do not seem exaggerated. Nevskii, "Istoricheskoe zasedanie Peterburgskogo komiteta RSDRP (bol'shevikov) nakanune oktiabr'skogo vosstaniia," p. 38.

30. Sverdlova, *Iakov Mikhailovich Sverdlov*, p. 287.

31. Shotman, "Lenin nakanune oktiabria," p. 121.

32. E. A. Alekseeva, "Na vsiu zhizn'," in *Petrograd v dni velikogo oktiabria*, pp. 270–82.

33. *Protokoly Tsentral'nogo komiteta*, p. 94; Shotman, "Lenin nakanune oktiabria," p. 122.

34. Shotman, "Lenin nakanune oktiabria," p. 122.

35. On this point, see the comments of A. L. Sidorov in *Lenin i oktiabr'skoe vooruzhennoe vosstanie v Petrograde*, pp. 109–10.

36. *Protokoly Tsentral'nogo komiteta*, p. 105.

37. See Lenin's letters in this regard to the party at large and to the Central Committee, dated October 18 and 19 respectively. Lenin, *PSS*, vol. 34, pp. 419–27.

38. *Protokoly Tsentral'nogo komiteta*, pp. 106–7.

39. S. I. Avvakumov, "Bor'ba Petrogradskikh bol'shevikov za osushchestvlenie leninskogo plana oktiabr'skogo vosstaniia," in *Oktiabr'skoe vooruzhennoe vosstanie v Petrograde*, pp. 54–56; Sverdlova, *Iakov Mikhailovich Sverdlov*, pp. 289–91.

13 · *The Garrison Crisis and the Military Revolutionary Committee*

1. The Military Organization's tactical orientation is reflected clearly in issues of *Soldat* at this time.

2. For Trotsky's later assessment of the crucial significance of not seizing power independently of the Petrograd Soviet and of timing an uprising to coincide with the deliberations of the Second All-Russian Congress of Soviets, see L. D. Trotsky, *Lenin* (New York, 1971), pp. 92–93.

3. For a detailed analysis of this novel and complex operation, see Fon Chishvits, *Zakhvat baltiiskikh ostrov germaniei v 1917 g.* (Moscow, 1937).

4. S. S. Khesin, *Oktiabr'skaia revoliusiia i flot* (Moscow, 1971), pp. 414–15.

5. *Izvestiia*, October 1, p. 1.

6. Khesin, *Oktiabr'skaia revoliutsiia i flot*, pp. 411–12.

7. *Soldat*, October 15, p. 1.

8. Riabinskii, *Khronika sobytii*, vol. 5, p. 67; *Gazeta kopeika*, October 12, p. 1; October 13, p. 2.

9. Voitinskii, "Gody pobed i porazhenii, 1917 god," pp. 319–22.

10. Ibid.; Woytinsky, *Stormy Passage*, p. 367.

11. O. N. Chaadaeva, "Soldatskie massy petrogradskogo garnizona v podgotovke i provedenii oktiabr'skogo vooruzhennogo vosstaniia," *Istoricheskie zapiski*, 1955, no. 51, p. 14.

12. Riabinskii, *Khronika sobytii*, vol. 5, p. 111.

13. *Soldat*, October 14, p. 4. For similar resolutions, see Riabinskii, *Khronika sobytii*, vol. 5, pp. 53–73 passim; Drezen, *Bol'shevizatsiia petrogradskogo garnizona*, pp.

297–302; *Oktiabr'skoe vooruzhennoe vosstanie v Petrograde: Dokumenty i materialy*, pp. 155–68, 217–19.

14. A protocol of this meeting is contained in A. K. Drezen, *Baltiiskii flot v oktiabr'skoi revoliutsii i grazhdanskoi voine* (Moscow and Leningrad, 1932), pp. 6–8.

15. Riabinskii, *Khronika sobytii*, vol. 5, p. 90; "Vospominaniia ob oktiabr'skom perevorote," *PR*, 1922, no. 10, pp. 44–93.

16. *Golos soldata*, October 19, p. 1.

17. Voitinskii, "Gody pobed i porazhenii," pp. 320–21, 324.

18. *Izvestiia*, October 18, p. 4.

19. Ibid., October 17, pp. 5–6. The delegation was to consist of twenty-five representatives of the new Soviet majority and fifteen garrison representatives.

20. Voitinskii, "Gody pobed i porazhenii," pp. 322–24; *Rabochii i soldat*, October 22, pp. 2–3.

21. On this point see E. D. Orekhova, "K izucheniiu istochnikov o sozdanii Petrogradskogo voenno-revoliutsionnogo komiteta," in D. A. Chugaev, ed., *Istochnikovedenie istorii sovetskogo obshchestva*, vypusk 2 (Moscow, 1968), p. 15. The text of Broido's resolution is contained in Riabinskii, *Khronika sobytii*, vol. 5, pp. 237–38.

22. According to some writers, the full text of this resolution has not been found. Judging by press accounts of the October 9 Petrograd Soviet Executive Committee meeting, it was probably nearly identical to a Bolshevik resolution presented later the same day to a plenary session of the Petrograd Soviet. The complete text of the latter is contained in Riabinskii, *Khronika sobytii*, vol. 5, p. 238.

23. *Birzhevye vedomosti*, October 10, morning edition, p. 4. The fullest analysis of the creation of the Military Revolutionary Committee and of the relevant primary sources is Orekhova, "K izucheniiu istochnikov o sozdanni Petrogradskogo voenno-revoliutsionnogo komiteta."

24. See, for example, *History of the Communist Party of the Soviet Union (Bolsheviks): Short Course* (New York, 1939), pp. 205–6.

25. Akademiia nauk SSSR, Institut istorii, et al., *Petrogradskii voenno-revoliutsionnyi komitet: Dokumenty i materialy*, ed. D. A. Chugaev, et al., 3 vols. (Moscow, 1966). See in particular the editors' introduction to vol. 1, pp. 5–6.

26. This is acknowledged by some present-day historians in the Soviet Union; see for example the statement of Iu. S. Tokarev in *Lenin i oktiabr'skoe vooruzhennoe vosstanie*, vol. 2, p. 168. After recounting accurately the Military Revolutionary Committee's evolution, Tokarev adds: "All these facts were certainly well known earlier, but in the conditions prevailing during the cult of personality, historians could not criticize any of the *Short Course*'s interpretations and were forced to follow them."

27. *Petrogradskii voenno-revoliutsionnyi komitet*, vol. 1, pp. 40–41.

28. *Pervyi legal'nyi Peterburgskii komitet*, p. 318.

29. *Protokoly Tsentral'nogo komiteta*, p. 104.

30. Ibid., pp. 106–8. On this point, see Orekhova, "K izucheniiu istochnikov o sozdanii Petrogradskogo voenno-revoliutsionnogo komiteta," pp. 25–26.

31. *Protokoly Tsentral'nogo komiteta*, p. 108.

32. The exact date of this meeting has not been established. The conflicting evidence and differing points of view on this matter are analyzed by E. D. Orekhova and A. S. Pokrovskii, "O datirovke vstrech V. I. Lenina s rukovoditeliami Voennoi organizatsii bol'shevikov i Petrogradskogo VRK v oktiabre 1917

g.," in D. A. Chugaev, ed., *Istochnikovedenie istorii sovetskogo obshchestva*, vypusk 2 (Moscow, 1968), pp. 56–78. Having studied the available published evidence, I believe that this meeting could not have occurred prior to October 20, and that it probably took place between the latter date and the twenty-third.

33. N. I. Podvoiskii, "O voennoi deiatel'nosti V. I. Lenina," *Kommunist*, 1957, no. 1, p. 37.

34. V. I. Nevskii, "Voennaia organizatsiia i oktiabr'skaia revoliutsiia," *Krasnoarmeets*, 1919, nos. 10–15, pp. 42–43.

35. Antonov-Ovseenko, "Revoliutsiia pobedila," *Krasnaia gazeta*, November 7, 1923, p. 3.

36. Podvoiskii, "O voennoi deiatel'nosti V. I. Lenina," p. 35.

37. N. I. Podvoiskii, "Voennaia organizatsiia TsK RSDRP(b) i voenno-revoliutsionnyi komitet 1917 g.," *KL*, 1923, no. 8, p. 16.

38. Nevskii, "Voennaia organizatsiia i oktiabr'skaia revoliutsiia," p. 43; Antonov-Ovseenko, "Baltflot v dni kerenshchiny i krasnogo oktiabria," pp. 122–25. In this connection Nevsky was now hurriedly dispatched to Helsingfors to help coordinate the mobilization of revolutionary forces there.

39. *Rabochii put'*, October 20, p. 2.

40. *Delo naroda*, October 20, p. 4; *Novaia zhizn'*, October 20, p. 3; *Golos soldata*, October 20, p. 5.

41. While information relating to the functioning of the committee is fragmentary, there appears to have been no definite operating procedure prior to the October revolution.

42. I have made this error myself. See Rabinowitch, "The Petrograd Garrison and the Bolshevik Seizure of Power," in *Revolution and Politics in Russia*, p. 188.

43. In this regard, see Ia. P. Birzhal, "Krestnyi khod," in *Petrograd v dni velikogo oktiabria*, pp. 287–89.

44. *Petrogradskii voenno-revoliutsionnyi komitet*, vol. 1, pp. 55–56.

45. *Golos soldata*, October 21, p. 3; *Oktiabr'skoe vooruzhennoe vosstanie v Petrograde: Dokumenty i materialy*, pp. 169–70; Trotskii, *Sochineniia*, vol. 3, part 2, pp. 36–37.

46. "Vospominaniia ob oktiabr'skom perevorote," *PR*, 1922, no. 10, p. 87; K. A. Mekhonoshin, "Shtab oktiabr'skoi revoliutsii (beseda s tov. Mekhonoshinym)," *Agit-Rosta*, October 26, 1919, p. 1.

47. E. F. Erykalov, *Oktiabr'skoe vooruzhennoe vosstanie v Petrograde* (Leningrad, 1966), p. 298; see also *Golos soldata*, October 24, p. 3.

48. Mekhonoshin, *Agit-Rosta*, October 26, 1919, p. 1; S. Piontkovskii, "Voenno-revoliutsionnyi komitet v oktiabr'skie dni," *PR*, 1927, no. 10, pp. 114–15.

49. *Petrogradskii voenno-revoliutsionnyi komitet*, vol. 1, p. 63.

50. "Vospominaniia ob oktiabr'skom perevorote," p. 53.

51. Reiman, *Russkaia revoliutsiia*, vol. 2, p. 385.

52. *Rech'*, October 24, p. 5.

53. Ibid.

54. Sukhanov, *Zapiski o revoliutsii*, vol. 7, pp. 90–91.

55. *Golos soldata*, October 24, p. 3; *Rech'*, October 24, p. 3.

56. *Oktiabr'skoe vooruzhennoe vosstanie v Petrograde: Dokumenty i materialy*, p. 277.

57. Riabinskii, *Khronika sobytii*, vol. 5, pp. 151–52.

58. *Petrogradskii voenno-revoliutsionnyi komitet*, vol. 1, pp. 67–68.

59. Antonov-Ovseenko, *Krasnaia gazeta*, November 7, 1923, p. 3.

60. Antonov-Ovseenko, *V semnadtsatom godu* (Moscow, 1933), p. 133.

61. *Rech'*, October 24, p. 3.

62. M. Lashevich, "Pervyi voenno-revoliutsionnyi komitet," *Krasnaia gazeta*, November 7, 1920, p. 4.

63. M. Lashevich, "Oktiabr'skie dni v Petrograde," *Politrabotnik Sibiri*, 1922, no. 11, p. 5.

64. See, for example, Kamkov's impassioned arguments against an uprising at the First All-Russian Conference of Factory-Shop Committees, which took place in Petrograd October 17–22 (*Rabochii i soldat*, October 22, p. 5). Following debate on "the current moment," the conference adopted a relatively innocuously worded Bolshevik statement, which affirmed that the survival of the revolution and the achievement of the goals of the laboring classes lay in transfer of power to the soviets, but which remained silent about how and when such a transfer would come about. See Komissiia po izucheniiu istorii professional'nogo dvizheniia v SSSR, *Oktiabr'skaia revoliutsiia i fabzavkomy: Materialy po istorii fabrichno-zavodskikh komitetov*, 2 vols. (Moscow, 1927), vol. 2, p. 167.

65. Rabinowitch, *Prelude to Revolution*, pp. 76–77.

66. *Petrogradskii voenno-revoliutsionnyi komitet*, vol. 1, p. 74.

67. Riabinskii, *Khronika sobytii*, vol. 5, p. 160.

68. Erykalov, *Oktiabr'skoe vooruzhennoe vosstanie v Petrograde*, p. 312.

69. Antonov-Ovseenko, "Oktiabr'skaia buria," *Pervyi narodnyi kalendar' na 1919 g.* (Petrograd, 1919), p. 102. On continuing Left SR threats to leave the committee, see Mekhonoshin, *Agit-Rosta*, October 26, 1919, p. 1.

70. *Izvestiia*, October 25, p. 7; Riabinskii, *Khronika sobytii*, vol. 5, p. 161.

71. *Oktiabr'skoe vooruzhennoe vosstanie v Petrograde: Dokumenty i materialy*, pp. 281–82.

14 · On the Eve

1. G. Lomov, "V dni buri i natiska," *Izvestiia*, November 6, 1918, p. 4; G. Lomov, "V dni buri i natiska," *PR*, 1927, no. 10 (69), pp. 169–70.

2. *Petrogradskii voenno-revoliutsionnyi komitet*, vol. 1, p. 86; M. Lashevich, "Vosstanie," *Petrogradskaia pravda*, November 5, 1922, p. 8; Antonov-Ovseenko, "Oktiabr'skaia buria," *Izvestiia*, November 6, 1918, pp. 3–4.

3. *Izvestiia*, October 25, p. 7; *Izvestiia Kronshtadtskogo soveta*, November 5, pp. 3–4.

4. *Petrogradskii voenno-revoliutsionnyi komitet*, vol. 1, p. 85; Trotskii, *Sochineniia*, vol. 3, part 2, p. 51.

5. *Protokoly Tsentral'nogo komiteta*, pp. 119–21.

6. B. Elov, "PK nakanune 25-go oktiabria," *Petrogradskaia pravda*, November 5, 1922, p. 2. *Oktiabr'skoe vooruzhennoe vosstanie v Petrograde: Dokumenty i materialy*, p. 287.

7. "Vospominaniia ob oktiabr'skom perevorote," *PR*, 1922, no. 10, p. 92.

8. *Den'*, October 25, p. 1.

9. "Vospominaniia ob oktiabr'skom perevorote," *PR*, 1922, no. 10, p. 90.

10. *Izvestiia*, October 25, p. 7.

11. *Novaia zhizn'*, October 25, p. 3.

12. *Oktiabr'skoe vooruzhennoe vosstanie v Petrograde: Dokumenty i materialy*, pp. 327–28.

13. Polenov, "Vystrel s 'Avrory,' " *Leningradskaia pravda*, November 6–7, 1927, p. 6; Riabinskii, *Khronika sobytii*, vol. 5, pp. 166–67.

14. The most precise and accurate count of loyalist forces is contained in Erykalov, *Oktiabr'skoe vooruzhennoe vosstanie v Petrograde*, p. 435.

15. Ibid., p. 318.

16. Sukhanov, *Zapiski o revoliutsii*, vol. 7, p. 131; *Izvestiia*, October 25, pp. 2–3.

17. *Izvestiia*, October 25, pp. 2–3; *Rech'*, October 25, p. 2; a translation of Kerensky's speech appears in Browder and Kerensky, *The Russian Provisional Government*, vol. 3, pp. 1772–78.

18. Kerensky, *Russia and History's Turning Point*, p. 435.

19. *Protokoly pervago s"ezda partii levykh sotsialistov-revoliutsionerov (internatsionalistov)*, p. 40.

20. *Izvestiia*, October 25, pp. 3–4.

21. See F. Dan, "K istorii poslednikh dnei Vremennogo pravitel'stva," *Letopis' revoliutsii*, vol. 1 (1923), pp. 163–75.

22. *Izvestiia*, October 25, p. 4; see also N. F. Slavin, "Oktiabr'skoe vooruzhennoe vosstanie i predparlament," in *Lenin i oktiabr'skoe vooruzhennoe vosstanie*, pp. 224–28.

23. Dan, "K istorii poslednikh dnei Vremennogo pravitel'stva," pp. 172–75.

24. *Rabochaia gazeta*, October 26, p. 2.

25. Italics mine. In some published versions of this resolution, the adjective "friendly" is substituted for "firm." The version cited appeared in *Rabochaia gazeta*, October 25, p. 2.

26. *Novaia zhizn'*, October 26, p. 2.

27. S. Mstislavskii, *Piat' dnei* (Berlin, 1922), p. 122–23; *Vtoroi vserossiiskii s"ezd sovetov R. i S. D.*, ed. M. N. Pokrovskii and Ia. A. Iakovlev (Moscow and Leningrad, 1928), p. 162. Mstislavskii recalls sadly that by the time he reached Smolny the evening of October 25, the SRs and Left SRs "were already sitting in different rooms."

28. *Izvestiia*, October 25, p. 7.

29. Il'in-Zhenevskii, "Oktiabr'skaia revoliutsiia," *KL*, 1926, no. 5 (20), p. 37.

30. Ibid.

31. *Oktiabr'skoe vooruzhennoe vosstanie*, vol. 2, pp. 303–4; *Oktiabr'skoe vooruzhennoe vosstanie v Petrograde: Dokumenty i materialy*, p. 332.

32. S. Pestkovskii, "Ob oktiabr'skikh dniakh v Pitere," *PR*, 1922, no. 10, pp. 95–96; *Oktiabr'skoe vooruzhennoe vosstanie*, vol. 2, p. 308.

33. A. M. Liubovich, "Revoliutsionnoe zaniatie petrogradskogo telegrafa," *Pochtovotelegrafnyi zhurnal*, 1918, no. 9–12, pp. 35–41.

34. *Rech'*, October 26, p. 2.

35. *Oktiabr'skoe vooruzhennoe vosstanie v Petrograde: Dokumenty i materialy*, p. 338.

36. P. E. Dybenko, "Baltflot v oktiabr'skie dni," in *Velikaia oktiabr'skaia sotsialisticheskaia revoliutiutsiia: Sbornik vospominanii uchastnikov revoliutsii v Petrograde i Moskve* (Moscow, 1957), p. 305; Petrash, *Moriaki Baltiiskogo flota v bor'be za pobedu oktiabria*, p. 251.

37. A. G. Pronin, "Podgotovka k zakhvatu vlasti," *Bakinskii rabochii*, November 7, 1927, p. 4.

38. Dybenko, "Baltflot v oktiabr'skie dni," p. 305.

39. Lenin, *PSS*, vol. 34, p. 434.

40. M. V. Fofanova, "Il'ich pered oktiabrem 1917 goda," in *Vospominaniia o Vladimire Il'iche Lenine*, vol. 2, p. 448.

41. M. V. Fofanova, "Poslednee podopol'e," in *Ob Il'iche: Vospominaniia pitertsev* (Leningrad, 1970), p. 348.

42. During the Stalin period this letter was ignored, evidently because it reflected continuing differences between the Central Committee and Lenin in regard to the development of the revolution. The letter does not contain an addressee, and headings in the post-Stalin fourth and fifth editions of Lenin's writings indicate that it was directed to the Central Committee. As a few contemporary scholars in the Soviet Union have acknowledged, however, from the content of the letter it is obvious that it was directed to lower levels of the party and was intended to stimulate them to apply pressure on the top party leadership and the Military Revolutionary Committee to arrest the members of the Provisional Government before the opening of the Congress of Soviets. On this point, see the comments of E. N. Gorodetskii and S. I. Shul'ga in *Lenin i oktiabr'skoe vooruzhennoe vosstanie v Petrograde*, pp. 189, 478–82.

43. Lenin, *PSS*, vol. 34, pp. 435–36.

44. Fofanova, "Poslednee podpol'e," p. 349; E. Rakh'ia, "Poslednee podpol'e Vladimira Il'icha," *KL*, 1934, no. 58, pp. 89–90; E. A. Rakh'ia, "Moi vospominaniia o Vladimire Il'iche," in *Vospominaniia o Vladimire Il'iche Lenine*, vol. 2, p. 434.

45. E. Rakh'ia, "Moi predoktiabr'skie i posleoktiabr'skie vstrechi s Leninym," *Novyi mir*, 1934, no. 1, pp. 35–36.

46. On this point, see *Oktiabr'skoe vooruzhennoe vosstanie*, vol. 2, pp. 292–307. There is some indication that the Military Revolutionary Committee took control of the telephone and electrical stations only after people at Smolny began experiencing difficulties with phones and lights. The one Military Revolutionary Committee action that does not quite fit this pattern was the taking of the telegraph facilities.

47. Latsis, *Petrogradskaia pravda*, November 5, 1922, p. 2.

48. See, for example, Kamkov's comments in *Protokoly pervago s"ezda partii levykh sotsialistov-revoliutsionerov*, pp. 40–41.

49. O. P. Dzenis, "Kak my brali 25 okt. zimnii dvorets," *Pravda*, November 6–7, 1921, p. 7; O. P. Dzenis, "Pod zimnim dvortsom," in *Velikaia oktiabr'skaia sotsialisticheskaia revoliutsiia: Sbornik vospominanii*, p. 270.

50. A. Ignat'ev, "V noch' na 25 oktiabria 1917 goda," *KL*, 1923, no. 6, p. 314.

51. *Baltiiskie moriaki v podgotovke i provedenii velikoi oktiabr'skoi sotsialisticheskoi revoliutsii*, p. 259; P. Kurkov, "Kreiser 'Avrora,' " *KL*, 1923, no. 6, p. 360.

52. Ibid.

53. *Oktiabr'skoe vooruzhennoe vosstanie*, vol. 2, pp. 324–35.

54. Riabinskii, *Khronika sobytii*, vol. 5, p. 175.

55. Ibid., pp. 175–76.

56. *Izvestiia*, October 26, p. 3; some two hundred cossacks of the Fourteenth Cossack Regiment reported to the Winter Palace; however, this token detachment was not enough to alter the government's situation.

57. *Oktiabr'skoe vooruzhennoe vosstanie v Petrograde: Dokumenty i materialy*, p. 340.

58. A. V. Liverovskii, "Poslednie chasy Vremennogo pravitel'stva: Dnevnik ministra Liverovskogo," *Istoricheskii arkhiv*, 1960, no. 6, p. 41.

59. V. Miliutin, *O Lenine* (Leningrad, 1924), pp. 4–5; Rakh'ia, "Moi predoktiabr'skie i posleoktiabr'skie vstrechi s Leninym," p. 36; see also Reiman, *Russkaia revoliutsiia*, vol. 2, p. 332.

15 · The Bolsheviks Come to Power

1. *Oktiabr'skoe vooruzhennoe vosstanie v Petrograde: Dokumenty i materialy*, pp. 348–50; "Baltflot v dni kerenshchiny i krasnogo oktiabria," pp. 123–24.

2. I. P. Flerovskii, "Kronshtadt v oktiabr'skoi revoliutsii," *PR*, 1922, no. 10, pp. 136–37.

3. *Baltiiskie moriaki*, p. 270.

4. *Oktiabr'skoe vooruzhennoe vosstanie*, vol. 2, p. 330; K. Eremeev, "Osada zimnego," *Bakinskii rabochii*, November 7, 1927, p. 9. See also Dzenis, "Kak my brali 25 okt. zimnii dvorets," p. 7, and G. I. Blagonravov, "Oktiabr'skie dni v petropavlovskoi kreposti," *PR*, 1922, no. 4, p. 33.

5. Lenin, *PSS*, vol. 35, p. 1.

6. V. I. Startsev, "Begstvo Kerenskogo," *Voprosy istorii*, 1966, no. 11, pp. 204–5; for Kerensky's version of this episode, see *Russia and History's Turning Point*, pp. 437–39.

7. *Rech'*, October 26, p. 2; *Novaia zhizn'*, October 26, p. 2; *Izvestiia*, October 26, pp. 3–4.

8. Riabinskii, *Khronika sobytii*, vol. 5, p. 177.

9. I. Pavlov, "Avral'naia rabota 25-go oktiabria 1917 goda," *Krasnyi flot*, 1926, nos. 10–11, p. 25.

10. Flerovskii, "Kronshtadt v oktiabr'skoi revoliutsii," p. 139.

11. Ibid., pp. 139–40; Pavlov, "Avral'naia rabota 25-go oktiabria 1917 goda," p. 25.

12. Riabinskii, *Khronika sobytii*, vol. 5, pp. 179–80; *Izvestiia*, October 26, p. 7; October 27, pp. 4–5.

13. Ibid.

14. P. V. Dashkevich, "Oktiabr'skie dni," *Leningradskaia pravda*, November 7, 1924, p. 11.

15. "Vospominaniia ob oktiabr'skom perevorote," *PR*, 1922, no. 10, pp. 84–85.

16. A. Tarasov-Rodionov, "Pervaia operatsiia," *Voennyi vestnik*, 1924, no. 42, p. 12; "Vospominaniia ob oktiabr'skom perevorote," *PR*, 1922, no. 10, pp. 78–79.

17. V. A. Antonov-Ovseenko, "Baltflot v dni kerenshchiny i krasnogo oktiabria," pp. 124–29; Antonov-Ovseenko, "Revoliutsiia pobedila," *Krasnaia gazeta*, November 7, 1923, p. 3.

18. Kostiukov, "Kak my opozdali ko vziatiiu zimnego dvortsa," *Krasnyi balteets*, 1920, no. 6, p. 36.

19. *Oktiabr'skoe vooruzhennoe vosstanie*, vol. 2, p. 346.

20. Blagonravov, "The Fortress of Peter and Paul, October 1917," in *Petrograd October 1917* (Moscow, 1957), p. 206.

21. "Vospominaniia ob oktiabr'skom perevorote," *PR*, 1922, no. 10, p. 79.

22. John Reed, *Ten Days That Shook the World* (New York, 1960), p. 116.

23. G. Chudnovskii, "V zimnem dvortse pered sdachei," *Pravda*, November 21, 1917, p. 2; P. V. Dashkevich, "Oktiabr'skie dni," *Leningradskaia pravda*, November 7, p. 11.

24. See, in particular, Liverovskii, "Poslednie chasy Vremmenogo

pravitel'stva"; P. N. Maliantovich, "V zimnem dvortse 25–26 obtiabria 1917 goda," *Byloe*, 1918, no. 12, pp. 111–41; P. N. Pal'chinskii, "Dnevnik," *Krasnyi arkhiv*, 1933, no. 56, pp. 136–38; A. M. Nikitin, "Rasskaz A. M. Nikitina," *Rabochaia gazeta*, October 28, p. 2; "Kak zaniali zimnii dvorets," *Delo naroda*, October 29, pp. 1–2; A. Sinegub, "Zashchita zimnego dvortsa," *Arkhiv russkoi revoliutsii*, 1922, no. 4, pp. 121–97. The most useful secondary source on the final hours of the Provisional Government is V. I. Startsev, "Poslednii den' Vremennogo pravitel'stva," in *Iz istorii velikoi oktiabr'skoi sotsialisticheskoi revoliutsii i sotsialisticheskogo stroitel'stva v SSSR* (Leningrad, 1967), pp. 99–115.

25. Liverovskii, "Poslednie chasy Vremennogo pravitel'stva," pp. 42–43.

26. Startsev, "Poslednii den' Vremennogo pravitel'stva," p. 101.

27. The text of this ultimatum is contained in Liverovskii, "Poslednie chasy Vremennogo pravitel'stva," p. 45.

28. *Edinstvo*, October 27, p. 3.

29. Maliantovich, "V zimnem dvortse," p. 120.

30. Ibid., p. 121.

31. *Oktiabr'skoe vooruzhennoe vosstanie v Petrograde: Dokumenty i materialy*, pp. 407–8.

32. *Edinstvo*, October 27, p. 3.

33. *Oktiabr'skoe vooruzhennoe vosstanie*, vol. 2, p. 343; *Oktiabr'skoe vooruzhennoe vosstanie v Petrograde: Dokumenty i materialy*, pp. 395–96, 407–8. For Cheremisov, this conversation was apparently the last straw, helping to confirm his conviction that the Provisional Government was totally bankrupt. Much more than most other top military leaders, Cheremisov had been sensitive and responsive to revolutionary sentiment in the army throughout 1917. Initially antagonized by Kerensky in late July at the time of Kornilov's appointment as chief of staff, during the first weeks of October Cheremisov gave only reluctant and half-hearted support to Kerensky's attempts to involve front-line forces in support of the Provisional Government. Now, on the night of October 25, learning firsthand of Kishkin's appointment, of the military shakeup in Petrograd, and of the occupation of General Staff headquarters, he issued an order immediately halting the movement of troops to Petrograd, significantly undercutting Kerensky's hopes of mobilizing help at the front.

34. *Oktiabr'skoe vooruzhennoe vosstanie v Petrograde: Dokumenty i materialy*, pp. 414–15.

35. Erykalov, *Oktiabr'skoe vooruzhennoe vosstanie v Petrograde*, pp. 314–17 and 444, drawing upon the journals of the Petrograd City Duma and the stenographic accounts of its proceedings, August 20, 1917, convocation; see also I. Milchik, "Petrogradskaia tsentral'naia gorodskaia duma v fevrale–oktiabre 1917 goda," *KL*, 1927, no. 2 (23), p. 201.

36. Flerovskii, "Kronshtadt v oktiabr'skoi revoliutsii," pp. 141–42.

37. Tarasov-Rodionov, "Pervaia operatsiia," p. 13.

38. Erykalov, *Oktiabr'skoe vooruzhennoe vosstanie v Petrograde*, pp. 445–46; V. M. Molotov, "Smolnyi i zimnii," *Pravda*, November 7, 1924, p. 9.

39. Erykalov, *Oktiabr'skoe vooruzhennoe vosstanie v Petrograde*, pp. 450–51.

40. *Rech'*, October 26, p. 3; Milchik, "Petrogradskaia tsentral'naia gorodskaia duma v fevrale-oktiabre 1917 goda," p. 202.

41. Bubnov, "Lenin v oktiabr'skie dni," *Bakinskii rabochii*, November 7, 1927, p. 3.

42. "Vospominaniia ob oktiabr'skom perevorote," *PR*, 1922, no. 10, p. 79.

43. *Vtoroi vserossiiskii s"ezd sovetov*, p. 33.

44. Reed, *Ten Days That Shook the World*, p. 124.

45. *Oktiabr'skoe vooruzhennoe vosstanie*, vol. 2, p. 353. Figures published in the press on the total size and composition of the congress vary somewhat; those cited here appeared in *Pravda* on October 29.

46. *Vtoroi vserossiiskii s"ezd sovetov*, pp. 144–53; A. F. Butenko and D. A. Chugaev, eds., *Vtoroi vserossiiskii s"ezd sovetov rabochikh i soldatskikh deputatov: Sbornik dokumentov* (Moscow, 1957), pp. 386–98.

47. *Vtoroi vserossiiskii s"ezd sovetov*, pp. 2–3, 33.

48. Ibid., pp. 4, 34–35; Sukhanov, *Zapiski o revoliutsii*, vol. 7, p. 199; *Delo naroda*, October 27, p. 2.

49. *Vtoroi vserossiiskii s"ezd sovetov*, pp. 34–35.

50. Ibid., pp. 37–38; Sukhanov, *Zapiski o revoliutsii*, vol. 7, p. 200.

51. Sukhanov, *Zapiski o revoliutsii*, vol. 7, pp. 219–20; on this point see Leonard Schapiro, *Origins of the Communist Autocracy* (New York, 1965), pp. 66–68.

52. *Vtoroi vserossiiskii s"ezd sovetov*, pp. 38–39.

53. Ibid., pp. 41–42.

54. Ibid., pp. 43–44.

55. *Protokoly pervago s"ezda partii levykh sotsialistov-revoliutsionerov (internatsionalistov)*, pp. 41–43.

56. *Delo naroda*, October 27, p. 2.

57. *Vtoroi vserossiiskii s"ezd sovetov*, pp. 45–46.

58. *Rech'*, October 26, p. 3; see also *Izvestiia*, October 26, p. 6.

59. Reed, *Ten Days That Shook the World*, pp. 136–37; See also Sukhanov, *Zapiski o revoliutsii*, vol. 7, p. 208.

60. Maliantovich, "V zimnem dvortse," p. 129.

61. Antonov-Ovseenko, "Oktiabr'skaia buria," p. 104.

62. Erykalov, *Oktiabr'skoe vooruzhennoe vosstanie v Petrograde*, p. 456.

63. Maliantovich, "V zimnem dvortse," pp. 129.

64. Ibid., p. 130.

65. "Rasskaz K. A. Gvozdeva ob ego areste," and "Rasskaz A. M. Kishkina," in *Rabochaia gazeta*, October 28, p. 2.

66. I. Kolbin, "Storming the Winter Palace," in *Petrograd 1917*, p. 321.

67. Antonov-Ovseenko, "Oktiabr'skaia buria," p. 104.

68. *Vtoroi vserossiiskii s"ezd sovetov*, pp. 47–50.

69. Ibid., p. 52.

70. *Vtoroi vserossiiskii s"ezd sovetov*, pp. 53–54; translation from Browder and Kerensky, *The Russian Provisional Government*, vol. 3, pp. 1797–98.

16 · *Epilogue*

1. A. L. Fraiman, *Forpost sotsialisticheskoi revoliutsii* (Leningrad, 1969), p. 19; I. S. Lutovinov, *Likvidatsiia miatezha Kerenskogo-Krasnova* (Moscow and Leningrad, 1965), p. 7.

2. *Oktiabr'skoe vooruzhennoe vosstanie*, vol. 2, p. 376.

3. The Left SRs were invited to joint the governmemt but refused, believing that by remaining outside they would be able to mediate between the Bolsheviks and their adversaries in the interest of forming a broad socialist government.

4. *Izvestiia*, October 28, p. 2. The elections took place as promised on November 12–14. The Bolsheviks, while triumphant in Petrograd, ran second to the SRs in the balloting throughout the country and even with the Left SRs did not have a majority. The Constituent Assembly opened in Petrograd on January 5, 1918, but the deputies refused to endorse the changes brought about by the October revolution and were forcibly dispersed after just one session.

5. *Novaia zhizn'*, October 30, p. 3; Melgunov, *The Bolshevik Seizure of Power*, pp. 141–42.

6. I. N. Liubimov, *Revoliutsiia 1917 goda: Khronika sobytii* (Moscow, 1930), vol. 6, pp. 436–37; *Oktiabr'skoe vooruzhennoe vosstanie*, vol. 2, p. 403.

7. Liubimov, *Khronika sobytii*, vol. 6, pp. 436–37; *Oktiabr'skoe vooruzhennoe vosstanie*, vol. 2, pp. 403–5.

8. Daniels, *Red October*, p. 206.

9. *Izvestiia*, November 3, p. 5; for Kerensky's version of these events see *Russia and History's Turning Point*, pp. 443–46.

10. *Oktiabr'skoe vooruzhennoe vosstanie*, vol. 2, p. 406.

11. The moderate socialists demanded, among other things, that key ministerial posts be held by non-Bolsheviks, that no single party have a majority in the government, that ministers enter the government as individuals rather than as representatives of their respective parties, and that the government be responsible not to the Central Executive Committee but to a broader representative assembly constructed along the lines of the Democratic State Conference, in which the likelihood of a Bolshevik majority would be minimal.

12. *Novaia zhizn'*, November 3, p. 2.

13. *Protokoly Tsentral'nogo komiteta*, p. 130.

14. The government's adoption of stricter press controls at this time strengthened the resolve of the moderates to continue the fight for a more broadly representative government. Such limitations of freedom appeared to them the inevitable consequence of rule by the Bolsheviks alone.

15. *Protokoly Tsentral'nogo komiteta*, pp. 133–34.

16. Gusev, *Krakh partii levykh eserov*, pp. 107–8.

17. See Cohen, *Bukharin and the Bolshevik Revolution*, pp. 66–106, for a valuable analysis of the impact of the civil war on Soviet politics and society.

Selected Bibliography

1 · Chronologies

Akhun, M. I., and Petrov, V. A. *1917 god v Petrograde: Khronika sobytii i bibliografiia.* Leningrad: Lenpartizdat, 1933.

Anikeev, V. V. *Deiatel'nost' TsK RSDRP(b) v 1917 godu: Khronika sobytii.* Moscow: Mysl', 1969.

Avdeev, N. *Revoliutsiia 1917 goda: Khronika sobytii.* Vol. 1, *Ianvar'–aprel'.* Vol. 2, *Aprel'–mai.* Moscow: Gosizdat, 1923.

Institut istorii partii pri Leningradskom obkome KPSS. *Bol'sheviki Petrograda v 1917 godu: Khronika sobytii.* Leningrad: Lenizdat, 1957.

Institut marksizma-leninizma pri TsK KPSS. *Vladimir Il'ich Lenin: Biograficheskaia khronika, 1870–1924.* Vol. 4, *Mart–oktiabr' 1917*, edited by G. N. Golikov, et al. Moscow: Politizdat, 1973.

———. *Lenin v 1917 godu: Daty zhizni i deiatel'nosti.* Moscow: Politizdat, 1957.

Konstantinov, A. P. *Bol'sheviki Petrograda v 1917 godu: Khronika sobytii.* Leningrad: Lenizdat, 1957.

Liubimov, I. N. *Revoliutsiia 1917 goda: Khronika sobytii.* Vol. 6, *Oktiabr'–dekabr'.* Moscow: Gosizdat, 1930.

Riabinskii, K. *Revoliutsiia 1917 goda: Khronika sobytii.* Vol. 5, *Oktiabr'.* Moscow: Gosizdat, 1926.

Vladimirova, V. *Revoliutsiia 1917 goda: Khronika sobytii.* Vol. 3, *Iiun'–iiul'.* Moscow: Gosizdat, 1923. Vol. 4, *Avgust–sentiabr'.* Leningrad: Gosizdat, 1924.

2 · Documentary Materials

Akademiia nauk SSSR, Institut istorii, et al. *Baltiiskie moriaki v podgotovke i provedenii velikoi oktiabr'skoi sotsialisticheskoi revoliutsii.* Edited by P. N. Mordvinov. Moscow and Leningrad: Izdatel'stvo Akademii nauk SSSR, 1957.

———. *Ekonomicheskoe polozhenie Rossii nakanune velikoi oktiabr'skoi sotsialisticheskoi revoliutsii.* Edited by A. L. Sidorov, et al. 2 vols. Moscow and Leningrad: Izdatel'stvo Akademii nauk SSSR, 1957.

———. *Petrogradskii voenno-revoliutsionnyi komitet: Dokumenty i materialy.* Edited by D. A. Chugaev. 3 vols. Moscow: Nauka, 1966.

————. *Protokoly i postanovleniia Tsentral'nogo komiteta Baltiiskogo flota.* Edited by D. A. Chugaev. Moscow and Leningrad: Izdatel'stvo Akademii nauk SSSR, 1963.

————. *Revoliutsionnoe dvizhenie v Rossii posle sverzheniia samoderzhaviia.* Edited by D. A. Chugaev, et al. Moscow: Izdatel'stvo Akademii nauk SSSR, 1957.

————. *Revoliutsionnoe dvizhenie v Rossii v aprele 1917 g.: Aprel'skii krizis.* Edited by L. S. Gaponenko, et al. Moscow: Izdatel'stvo Akademii nauk SSSR, 1958.

————. *Revoliutsionnoe dvizhenie v Rossii v avguste 1917 g.: Razgrom kornilovskogo miatezha.* Edited by D. A. Chugaev, et al. Moscow: Izdatel'stvo Akademii nauk SSSR, 1959.

————. *Revoliutsionnoe dvizhenie v Rossi v iiule 1917 g.: Iiul'skii krizis.* Edited by D. A. Chugaev, et al. Moscow: Izdatel'stvo Akademii nauk SSSR, 1959.

————. *Revoliutsionnoe dvizhenie v Rossii v mae–iiune 1917 g.: Iiun'skaia demonstratsia.* Edited by D. A. Chugaev, et al. Moscow: Izdatel'stvo Akademii nauk SSSR, 1959.

————. *Revoliutsionnoe dvizhenie v Rossii v sentiabre 1917 g.: Obshchenatsional'nyi krizis.* Edited by D. A. Chugaev, et al. Moscow: Izdatel'stvo Akademii nauk SSSR, 1961.

————. *Velikaia oktiabr'skaia sotsialisticheskaia revoliutsiia: Oktiabr'skoe vooruzhennoe vosstanie v Petrograde. Dokumenty i materialy.* Edited by G. N. Golikov, et al. Moscow: Izdatel'stvo Akademii nauk SSSR, 1957.

Akademiia nauk SSSR, Leningradskoe otdelenie instituta istorii. *Raionnye sovety Petrograda v 1917 godu: Protokoly, rezoliutsii, postanovleniia obshchikh sobranii zasedanii ispolnitel'nykh komitetov.* 3 vols. Moscow and Leningrad: Nauka, 1964–1966.

Anskii, A., ed. *Protokoly Petrogradskogo soveta professional'nykh soiuzov za 1917 g.* Leningrad: Izdatel'stvo Leningradskogo gubprofsoveta, 1927.

Belkov, A. K., and Verevkin, B. P., eds. *Bol'shevistskaia pechat': Sbornik materialov.* Vol. 4. Moscow: Vysshaia partiinaia shkola, 1960.

Browder, Robert P., and Kerensky, Alexander F., eds. *The Russian Provisional Government 1917: Documents.* 3 vols. Stanford: Stanford University Press, 1961.

Bukhbinder, N. "Na fronte v predoktiabr'skie dni." *Krasnaia letopis',* 1923, no. 6, pp. 9–63. Protocols of July 16 emergency council at Stavka.

Bunyan, J., and Fisher, H. H. *The Bolshevik Revolution, 1917–1918.* Stanford: Stanford University Press, 1934.

Butenko, A. F., and Chugaev, D. A., eds. *Vtoroi vserossiiskii s"ezd sovetov rabochikh i soldatskikh deputatov: Sbornik dokumentov.* Moscow: Gospolitizdat, 1957.

Chaadaeva, O., ed. *Soldatskie pis'ma 1917 goda.* Moscow: Gosizdat, 1927.

Drezen, A. K., ed. *Baltiiskii flot v oktiabr'skoi revoliutsii i grazhdanskoi voine.* Moscow and Leningrad: Partizdat, 1932.

————. *Bol'shevizatsiia petrogradskogo garnizona: Sbornik materialov i dokumentov.* Leningrad: Lenoblizdat, 1932.

————. *Burzhuaziia i pomeshchiki v 1917 godu: Chastnye soveshchaniia chlenov Gosudarstvennoi dumy.* Moscow and Leningrad: Partiinoe Izdatel'stvo, 1932.

Elov, B., ed. "Petrogradskaia organizatsiia RSDRP(b) nakanune iiul'skikh sobytii." In *3–5 iiulia 1917 g.,* pp. 53–74. Petrograd, 1922. Incomplete protocols of pre–July days sessions of the Second Citywide Conference of Petrograd Bolsheviks.

————. "Posle iiul'skikh sobytii." *Krasnaia letopis',* 1923, no. 7, pp. 95–127. Incomplete protocols of the post–July days sessions of the Second Citywide Conference.

Gaponenko, L. S., ed. *Revoliutsionnoe dvizhenie v Russkoi armii*. Moscow: Nauka, 1968.

Golder, Frank A., ed. *Documents of Russian History, 1914–1917*. New York: Century, 1927.

Institut Marksa-Engel'sa-Lenina-Stalina pri TsK KPSS. *Kommunisticheskaia Partiia Sovetskogo Soiuza v rezoliutsiiakh i resheniiakh s"ezdov, konferentsii i plenumov TsK, 1898–1954*. 4 vols. 7th ed. Moscow: Gospolitizdat, 1954.

Institut marksizma-leninizma pri TsK KPSS. *Doneseniia komissarov Petrogradskogo voenno-revoliutsionnogo komiteta*. Moscow: Gospolitizdat, 1957.

———. *Listovki petrogradskikh bol'shevikov*. Vol. 3. Leningrad: Lenizdat, 1957.

———. *Perepiska sekretariata TsK RSDRP(b) s mestnymi partiinymi organizatsiiami: Sbornik dokumentov*. Vol. 1, *Mart–oktiabr' 1917 g*. Moscow: Gospolitizdat, 1957.

———. *Protokoly Tsentral'nogo komiteta RSDRP(b): Avgust 1917–fevral' 1918*. Moscow: Gospolitizdat, 1958.

———. *Sed'maia (Aprel'skaia) Vserossiiskaia konferentsiia RSDRP (bol'shevikov); Petrogradskaia obshchegorodskaia konferentsiia RSDRP (bol'shevikov), aprel' 1917 goda: Protokoly*. Moscow: Gospolitizdat, 1958.

———. *Shestoi s"ezd RSDRP (bol'shevikov), avgust 1917 goda: Protokoly*. Moscow: Gospolitizdat, 1958.

Institut marksizma-leninizma pri TsK KPSS, Institut istorii partii MK i MGK KPSS. *Podgotovka i pobeda oktiabr'skoi revoliutsii v Moskve*. Moscow: Moskovskii rabochii, 1957.

Kerenskii, A. F. *Delo Kornilova*. Moscow: Zadruga, 1918. Edited stenogram of Kerensky's testimony to the official commission investigating the Kornilov conspiracy, with commentary by Kerensky.

Kerensky, A. F. *Prelude to Bolshevism: The Kornilov Rising*. New York: Dodd, Mead and Company, 1919. English translation of *Delo Kornilova*.

Kokoshkin, F. F., and Kishkin, N. M. "Po otchetu o zasedanii moskovskogo gorodskogo komiteta k.-d. partii, 31 avg. 1917 g." Typescript in Nicolaevsky archive, Hoover Institution, Stanford, California.

Komissiia po izucheniiu istorii professional'nogo dvizheniia v SSSR. *Oktiabr'skaia revoliutsiia i fabzavkomy: Materialy po istorii fabrichno-zavodskikh komitetov*. 2 vols. Moscow: Izdatel'stvo VTsSPS, 1927.

Kommunisticheskaia Partiia Sovetskogo Soiuza. *Protokoly s"ezdov i konferentsii Vsesoiuznoi kommunisticheskoi partii (bol'shevikov): Shestoi s"ezd, 8–16 avgusta 1917*. Edited by A. S. Bubnov. Moscow: Gosizdat, 1927.

Kornilovskie dni: Biulleteni vremennogo voennogo komiteta pri TsIK s 28 avgusta po 4 sentiabria 1917 g. Petrograd: Soiuz sotsialistov narodnoi armii, 1917.

Leningrad. Sovet deputatov trudiashchikhsia. *Petrogradskii Sovet rabochikh i soldatskikh deputatov: Protokoly zasedanii Ispolnitel'nogo komiteta i Biuro Ispolnitel'nogo komiteta*. Moscow: Gosizdat, 1925.

Leninskii sbornik. Vol. 21. Edited by V. V. Adoratsky, et al. Moscow: Partiinoe Izdatel'stvo, 1933. Miscellaneous Lenin documents relating to the period between January 1917 and the end of 1918.

Liverovskii, A. V. "Poslednie chasy Vremennogo pravitel'stva: Dnevnik ministra Liverovskogo." *Istoricheskii arkhiv*, 1960, no. 6, pp. 38–48.

M. F. "K istorii kornilovshchiny." *Krasnaia letopis'*, 1924, no. 1 (10), pp. 201–17. Contains the text of April 23 memorandum by Kornilov to War Minister Guchkov and the full text of Kornilov's August 10 proposal to Kerensky.

"Nakanune oktiabr'skogo perevorota: Vopros o voine i mire; ochety o sekretnykh zasedaniiakh komissii vremennogo soveta Rossiiskoi respubliki." *Byloe*, 1918, no. 6, pp. 3–41.

Nikolaevskii, B. I. "Men'sheviki v dni oktiabr'skogo perevorota." Inter-university project on the history of the Menshevik movement, paper no. 8. New York, 1952.

Okun, S. D., ed. *Putilovets v trekh revoliutsiiakh: Sbornik materialov po istorii Putilovskogo zavoda.* Moscow and Leningrad: Ogiz, 1933.

Pal'chinskii, P. N. "Dnevnik." *Krasnyi arkhiv*, 1933, no. 56, pp. 136–38.

Pokrovskii, M. N., and Iakovlev, Ia. A., eds. *Gosudarstvennoe soveshchanie.* Moscow and Leningrad: Gosizdat, 1930.

———. *Pervyi vserossiiskii s"ezd sovetov rabochikh, soldatskikh i krest'ianskikh deputatov.* Moscow and Leningrad: Gosizdat, 1930.

———. *Rabochee dvizhenie v 1917 godu.* Moscow and Leningrad: Gosizdat, 1926.

———. *Razlozhenie armii v 1917 g.* Moscow and Leningrad: Gosizdat, 1925.

———. *Vtoroi vserossiiskii s"ezd sovetov R. i S. D.* Moscow and Leningrad: Gosizdat, 1928.

Protokoly pervago s"ezda partii levykh sotsialistov-revoliutsionerov (internatsionalistov). Moscow: Revoliutsionnyi sotsializm, 1918.

Protokoly VI s"ezda RSDRP (bol'shevikov) 26 iiulia–3 avgusta 1917 g. Moscow and Petrograd: Kommunist, 1919.

Russia. 1917 Provisional Government. *Zhurnaly zasedanii Vremennogo pravitel'stva.* Petrograd, 1917.

"Stavka 25–26 oktiabria 1917 g." *Arkhiv russkoi revoliutsii*, vol. 7 (1922), pp. 279–320. Transcripts of communications between officials of the Provisional Government in Petrograd and military leaders at the front during the October days.

Tobolin, I., ed. "Iiul'skie dni v Petrograde." *Krasnyi arkhiv*, 1927, no. 4 (23), pp. 1–63, and no. 5 (24), pp. 3–70. Valuable documents relating to the Provisional Government's investigation of the July uprising.

Velikii oktiabr': Aktivnye uchastniki i organizatsii, albom. Compiled by P. F. Kudelli and P. I. Kuliabko. Moscow and Leningrad: Gosizdat, 1927.

Volobuev, P. V. "Iz istorii bor'by Vremennogo pravitel'stva s revoliutsiei." *Istoricheskii arkhiv*, 1960, no. 6, pp. 83–85. Contains notes for a meeting of Kerensky's cabinet the evening of October 17.

Vsesoiuznaia Kommunisticheskaia partiia (bol'shevikov). *Vtoraia i Tret'ia petrogradskie obshchegorodskie konferentsii bol'shevikov v iiule i oktiabre 1917 goda: Protokoly.* Moscow and Leningrad: Gosizdat, 1927.

———. Leningradskii istpart. *Pervyi legal'nyi Peterburgskii komitet bol'shevikov v 1917 godu: Sbornik materialov i protokolov zasedanii Peterburgskogo komiteta RSDRP(b) i ego Ispolnitel'noi komissii za 1917 g.* Edited by P. F. Kudelli. Moscow and Leningrad: Gosizdat, 1927.

Zeman, Z. A. B., ed. *Germany and the Revolution in Russia, 1915–1918: Documents from the Archives of the German Foreign Ministry.* London: Oxford University Press, 1958.

3 · 1917 Newspapers

Bakinskii rabochii. Baku. Daily newspaper of the Baku Bolshevik Committee.

Birzhevye vedomosti. Petrograd. Nonparty liberal daily.

Delo naroda. Petrograd. Socialist-Revolutionary. Beginning July 1, organ of the SR Central Committee.

Den'. Petrograd. Right Menshevik paper edited by A. Potresov.

Edinstvo. Petrograd. Right socialist. Published by Edinstvo, G. V. Plekhanov's political organization.

Gazeta-kopeika. Petrograd. Popular "boulevard" daily.

Golos pravdy. Kronstadt. Kronstadt Bolshevik organ published March 15 to July 13. Resumed publication October 28.

Golos soldata. Petrograd. Moderate socialist daily initiated by the Petrograd Soviet in May, primarily for military troops. Became main military organ of the Central Executive Committee in July.

Golos sotsial-demokrata. Kiev. Bolshevik daily.

Izvestiia Kronshtadtskogo Soveta rabochikh i soldatskikh deputatov. Kronstadt. Kronstadt Soviet organ.

Izvestiia Moskovskogo Soveta rabochikh deputatov. Moscow. Main paper of the Moscow Soviet of Workers' Deputies.

Izvestiia Petrogradskogo Soveta rabochikh i soldatskikh deputatov. Daily newspaper of the Petrograd Soviet and, beginning in late June, of the Central Executive Committee. On August 1 the paper was renamed *Izvestiia Tsentral'nogo Ispolnitel'nogo Komiteta i Petrogradskogo Soveta rabochikh i soldatskikh deputatov*.

Listok pravdy. Petrograd. Bolshevik. Published on July 6 in place of *Pravda*.

Malenkaia gazeta. Petrograd. Right-wing daily.

New York Times.

Novaia zhizn'. Petrograd. Left Menshevik daily edited by Maxim Gorky.

Novoe vremia. Petrograd. Important liberal daily.

Petrogradskaia gazeta. Petrograd. Popular nonparty daily.

Petrogradskii listok. Petrograd. Popular nonparty daily.

Pravda. Petrograd. Central Bolshevik Party newspaper. Published March 2 to July 5. Resumed publication October 27.

Proletarii. Petrograd. Bolshevik. Published August 14 to August 24 in place of *Pravda*.

Proletarskoe delo. Kronstadt. Published by Bolshevik fraction in the Kronstadt Soviet July 14 to October 27, in place of *Golos pravdy*.

Rabochaia gazeta. Petrograd. Central Menshevik Party newspaper.

Rabochii. Petrograd. Bolshevik. Published August 25 to September 2 in place of *Pravda*.

Rabochii i soldat. Petrograd. Bolshevik. Published by Bolshevik Military Organization July 23 to August 9 as replacement for *Soldatskaia pravda*.

Rabochii put'. Petrograd. Bolshevik. Published September 3 to October 26 in place of *Pravda*.

Rabotnitsa. Petrograd. Magazine for women workers published by Bolshevik Central Committee two or three times a month beginning May 10, 1917. Ceased publication January 1918.

Rech'. Petrograd. Organ of the Constitutional Democratic Party.

Soldat. Petrograd. Published by the Bolshevik Military Organization between August 13 and October 26 as replacement for *Soldatskaia pravda.*

Soldatskaia pravda. Petrograd. Organ of the Bolshevik Military Organization. Published April 15 to July 5. Resumed publication October 27.

Sotsial-Demokrat. Moscow. Central organ of the Moscow Bolsheviks.

Vestnik Vremennogo pravitel'stva. Petrograd. Official daily organ of the Provisional Government.

Volia naroda. Petrograd. Organ of right SRs.

Volna. Helsingfors. Organ of the Helsingfors Bolshevik Committee.

Vpered. Petrograd. Interdistrict Committee newspaper.

Zhivoe slovo. Petrograd. Extreme rightist paper.

Znamia truda. Petrograd. Left SR daily. Published as official organ of the Left SR–controlled SR Petrograd Committee beginning August 23.

4 · *Memoirs and Other Works by Bolsheviks*

Alekseeva, E. A. "Na vsiu zhizn'." In *Petrograd v dni velikogo oktiabria: Vospominaniia uchastnikov revoliutsionnykh sobytii v Petrograde v 1917 godu*, pp. 270–82. Leningrad: Lenizdat, 1967.

Alliluev, S. "Kak skryvalis' tov. Lenin i tov. Zinov'ev v iiul'skie dni 1917 goda." In *O Lenine: Vospominaniia*, ed. I. L. Meshcheriakov, vol. 3, pp. 96–100. Moscow and Leningrad: Gosizdat, 1925.

Antonov-Ovseenko, V. A. "Baltflot v dni kerenshchiny i krasnogo oktiabria." *Proletarskaia revoliutsiia*, 1922, no. 10, pp. 118–29.

——. "Oktiabr'skaia buria." *Izvestiia*, November 6, 1918, pp. 3–4.

——. "Oktiabr'skaia buria." *Pervyi narodnyi kalendar' na 1919 g.* Petrograd: Izdatel'stvo Soiuza kommunistov severnoi oblasti, 1919.

——. "Podgotovka perevorota (beseda s tov. Antonovym-Ovseenko)." *Krasnoarmeets*, 1920, nos. 28–30, pp. 24–29.

——. "Revoliutsiia pobedila." *Krasnaia gazeta*, November 7, 1923, p. 3.

——. *Stroitel'stvo Krasnoi Armii v revoliutsii.* Moscow: Krasnaia nov', 1923.

——. *V semnadtsatom godu.* Moscow: Gosizdat, 1933.

——. *V revoliutsii.* Moscow: Gospolitizdat, 1957.

Ashkenazi, I. "Iz istorii iiul'skikh dnei." *Izvestiia*, November 6, 1918, p. 2.

Birzhal, Ia. P. "Krestnyi khod." In *Petrograd v dni velikogo oktiabria: Vospominaniia uchastnikov revoliutsionykh sobytii v Petrograde v 1917 godu*, pp. 285–97. Leningrad: Lenizdat, 1967.

Blagonravov, G. I. "Oktiabr'skie dni v petropavlovskoi kreposti." *Proletarskaia revoliutsiia*, 1922, no. 4, pp. 24–52.

——. "The Fortress of Peter and Paul, October 1917." In *Petrograd October 1917*, pp. 189–227. Moscow: Foreign Languages Publishing House, 1957.

——. "Zimnii vziat i nashi tam!" *Petrogradskaia pravda*, November 5, 1922, p. 8.

Bonch-Bruevich, V. *Na boevykh postakh fevral'skoi i oktiabr'skoi revoliutsii.* Moscow: Federatsiia, 1931.

——. "Ot iiulia k oktiabriu." *Proletarskaia revoliutsiia*, 1922, no. 10, pp. 105–10.

Breslav, V. "15 let tomu nazad." *Katorga i ssylka*, 1932, nos. 11–12 (96–97), pp. 46–59.

——. *Kanun oktiabria 1917 goda.* Moscow: Izdatel'stvo Politkatorzhan, 1934.

Bubnov, A. "Lenin v oktiabr'skie dni." *Bakinskii rabochii*, November 7, 1927, p. 3.

Bukharin, N. I. "Iz rechi tov. Bukharina na vechere vospominanii v 1921 g." *Proletarskaia revoliutsiia*, 1922, no. 10, pp. 316–22.

Chudnovskii, G. "V zimnim dvortse pered sdachei." *Pravda*, November 21, 1917, p. 2.

Dashkevich, P. V. "Oktiabr'skie dni." *Leningradskaia pravda*, November 7, 1924, p. 11.

———. "TsO partii v oktiabr'skie dni." *Krasnaia letopis'*, 1933, no. 1 (52), pp. 101–5.

Dybenko, P. E. "Baltflot v oktiabr'skie dni." In *Velikaia oktiabr'skaia sotsialisticheskaia revoliutsiia: Sbornik vospominanii uchastnikov revoliutsii v Petrograde i Moskve*, pp. 302–10. Moscow: Gospolitizdat, 1957.

———. *Iz nedr tsarskogo flota k velikomu oktiabriu: Iz vospominanii o revoliutsii*. Moscow: Voennyi vestnik, 1928.

Dzenis, O. P. "Kak my brali 25 okt. zimnii dvorets." *Pravda*, November 6–7, 1921, p. 7.

———. "Pod zimnim dvortsom." In *Velikaia oktiabr'skaia sotsialisticheskaia revoliutsiia: Sbornik vospominanii uchastnikov revoliutsii v Petrograde i Moskve*, pp. 268–73. Moscow: Gospolitizdat, 1957.

Emel'ianov, N. A. "Tainstvennyi shalash." In *O Lenine*, edited by M. L. Meshcheriakov, vol. 1, pp. 106–10. Moscow and Leningrad: Gosizdat, 1924.

Eremeev, K. "Iiul'skii pogrom 1917 goda." *Pravda*, July 17, 1927, p. 4.

———. "Osada zimnego." *Bakinskii rabochii*, November 7, 1927, p. 9.

Flakserman, Iu. N. "10 oktiabria 1917 goda." In *Petrograd v dni velikogo oktiabria: Vospominaniia uchastnikov revoliutsionnykh sobytii v Petrograde v 1917 godu*, pp. 264–69. Leningrad: Lenizdat, 1967.

Flerovskii, I. P. "Iiul'skii politicheskii urok." *Proletarskaia revoliutsiia*, 1926, no. 7 (54), pp. 57–90.

———. "Kronshtadt v oktiabr'skoi revoliutsii." *Proletarskaia revoliutsiia*, 1922, no. 10, pp. 130–50.

———. "Lenin i kronshtadtsy." In *O Vladimire Il'iche Lenine*, pp. 274–79. Moscow: Gosizdat, 1963.

———. "Na putiakh k oktiabriu." In *Velikaia oktiabr'skaia sotsialisticheskaia revoliutsiia: Sbornik vospominanii uchastnikov revoliutsii v Petrograde i Moskve*, pp. 83–102. Moscow: Gospolitizdat, 1957.

———. *V. Volodarskii*. Moscow: Gosizdat, 1922.

Fofanova, M. V. "Il'ich pered oktiabrem 1917 goda." In *Vospominaniia o Vladimire Il'iche Lenine*, edited by G. N. Golikov, et al., vol. 2, pp. 445–48. Moscow: Politizdat, 1969.

———. "Iz vospominanii o 1917 gody." *Pravda*, January 22, 1928, p. 3.

———. "Poslednee podpol'e." In *Ob Il'iche: Vospominaniia pitertsev*, pp. 344–50. Leningrad: Lenizdat, 1970.

———. "Poslednee podpol'e V. I. Lenina." *Istoricheskii arkhiv*, 1956, no. 4, pp. 166–72.

Graf, T. "V iiul'skie dni 1917 g." *Krasnaia letopis'*, 1928, no. 2 (26), pp. 66–75.

Iakovleva, V. "Podgotovka oktiabr'skogo vosstaniia v Moskovskoi oblasti." *Proletarskaia revoliutsiia*, 1922, no. 10 (22), pp. 302–6.

Ignat'ev, A. "V noch' na 25 oktiabria 1917 goda." *Krasnaia letopis'*, 1923, no. 6, pp. 313–14.

Il'in-Zhenevskii, A. F. "Bol'sheviki v tiur'me Kerenskogo." *Krasnaia letopis'*, 1928, no. 2 (26), pp. 43–65.

———., ed. *K godovshchine smerti V. I. Lenina, 1924–21 ianvaria 1925 g.* Leningrad: Gosizdat, 1925.

———. "Nakanune oktiabria." *Krasnaia letopis'*, 1926, no. 4 (19), pp. 5–26.

———. "Oktiabr'skaia revoliutsiia." *Krasnaia letopis'*, 1926, no. 5 (20), pp. 32–54.

———. *Ot fevralia k zakhvatu vlasti: Vospominaniia o 1917 g.* Leningrad: Priboi, 1927.

———. "Voennaia organizatsiia RSDRP i *Soldatskaia pravda.*" *Krasnaia letopis'*, 1926, no. 1 (16), pp. 57–73.

Institut marksizma-leninizma pri TsK KPSS. *Lenin v 1917 godu: Vospominaniia.* Moscow. Politizdat, 1967.

Itkina, A. M. "Oplot bol'shevizma." In *Narvskaia zastava v 1917 godu v vospominaniiakh i dokumentakh*, edited by M. I. Protopopov, et al., pp. 145–58. Leningrad: Lenizdat, 1960.

Izmailov, N. F., and Pukhov, A. S. *Tsentrobalt.* Kaliningrad: Kaliningradskoe knizhnoe izdatel'stvo, 1967.

Kalinin, M. I. "Vladimir Il'ich o dvizhenii." *Krasnaia gazeta*, July 16, 1920, p. 2.

Kaurov, V. "Oktiabr'skie ocherki." *Proletarskaia revoliutsiia*, 1925, no. 7 (42), pp. 134–55.

Kedrov, M. "Iz krasnoi tetradi ob Il'iche." In *Vospominaniia o Vladimire Il'iche Lenine*, vol. 1, pp. 475–85. Moscow: Gosizdat, 1956.

———. "Iz krasnoi tetradi ob Il'iche." *Proletarskaia revoliutsiia*, 1927, no. 1 (60), pp. 36–69.

Khaustov, F. "V oktiabre." *Krasnaia letopis'*, 1933, no. 2 (53), pp. 188–95.

Khokhriakov, A. (Bonner, S.) "Iz zhizni petrogradskogo garnizona v 1917 godu." *Krasnaia letopis'*, 1926, no. 2 (17), pp. 29–50.

Khovrin, N. A. *Baltiitsy idut na shturm.* Moscow: Voennoe izdatel'stvo, 1968.

Kolbin, I. N. "Kronshtadt organizuetsia, gotovitsia k boiu." In *Oktiabr'skii shkval: Moriaki Baltiiskogo flota v 1917 g.*, edited by P. F. Kudelli and I. V. Egorov, pp. 23–50. Leningrad: Krasnaia gazeta, 1927.

———. "Kronshtadt ot fevralia do kornilovskikh dnei." *Krasnaia letopis'*, 1927, no. 2 (23), pp. 134–61.

———. "Storming the Winter Palace." In *Petrograd 1917*, pp. 318–21. Moscow: Foreign Languages Publishing House, 1957.

Kollontai, A. "Ruka istorii." *Krasnoarmeets*, 1919, nos. 10–15, pp. 61–71.

———. "V tiur'me Kerenskogo." *Katorga i ssylka*, 1927, no. 7 (36), pp. 25–53.

Kostiukov. "Kak my opozdali ko vziatiu zimnego dvortsa." *Krasnyi balteets*, 1920, no. 6, pp. 25–46.

Krupskaia, N. K. *Lenin i partiia.* Moscow: Gospolitizdat, 1963.

———. "Lenin v 1917 godu." In *O Vladimire Il'iche Lenine: Vospominaniia 1900–1922*, pp. 203–11. Moscow: Gosizdat, 1963.

———. "Vospominaniia o Lenine." In Institut marksizma-leninizma pri TsK KPSS, *Vospominaniia o Vladimire Il'iche Lenine*, vol. 1, pp. 219–592. Moscow: Politizdat, 1968.

Kudelli, P. F., ed. *Leningradskie rabochie v bor'be za vlast' sovetov 1917 g.* Leningrad: Gosizdat, 1924.

Kurkov, P. "Kreiser 'Avrora.'" *Krasnaia letopis'*, 1923, no. 6, pp. 359–61.

Lashevich, M. "Oktiabr'skie dni v Petrograde." *Politrabotnik Sibiri*, 1922, no. 11, p. 5.

Lashevich, M. "Pervyi voenno-revoliutsionnyi komitet." *Krasnaia gazeta*, November 7, 1920, p. 4.

———. "Vosstanie." *Petrogradskaia pravda*, November 5, 1922, p. 8.

Latsis, M. Ia. "Iiul'skie dni v Petrograde: Iz dnevnika agitatora." *Proletarskaia revoliutsiia*, 1923, no. 5 (17), pp. 102–16.

———. "Iz oktiabr'skikh vospominanii." *Bakinskii rabochii*, November 1, 1927, p. 3.

———. "Nakanune oktiabr'skikh dnei." *Izvestiia*, November 6, 1918, p. 2.

———. "Rol' Petrogradskogo komiteta v oktiabre." *Petrogradskaia pravda*, November 5, 1922, p. 2.

Leningradskie rabochie v bor'be za vlast' sovetov: Sbornik statei, vospominanii i dokumentov. Leningrad: Gosizdat, 1924.

Lenin, V. I. *Polnoe sobranie sochinenii.* 55 vols. 5th ed. Moscow: Gospolitizdat, 1958–1965.

———. *Sochineniia.* 3rd ed. 30 vols. Moscow: Gosizdat, 1928–1929.

Lenin v 1917 godu: Vospominaniia. Moscow: Politizdat, 1967.

Liubovich, A. M. "Revoliutsionnoe zaniatie petrogradskogo telegrafa." *Pochtovotelegrafnyi zhurnal*, 1918, nos. 9–12, pp. 35–41.

———. "3–5 iiulia." *Leningradskaia pravda*, July 16, 1925, p. 3.

Lomov, G. "V dni buri i natiska." *Bakinskii rabochii*, November 5, 1927, p. 4.

———. "V dni buri i natiska." *Izvestiia*, November 6, 1918, p. 4.

———. "V dni buri i natiska." *Proletarskaia revoliutsiia*, 1927, no. 10 (69), pp. 166–82.

Lunacharsky, A. V. *Revolutionary Silhouettes.* Translated and edited by Michael Glenny. London: Allen Lane, The Penguin Press, 1967.

Mekhonoshin, K. A. "Shtab oktiabr'skoi revoliutsii (beseda s tov. Mekhonoshinym)." *Agit-rosta*, October 26, 1919, p. 1.

Miliutin, V. *O Lenine.* Leningrad: Gosizdat, 1924.

———. "Kak proizoshlo nazvanie Narodnyi Komissar." *Izvestiia*, November 6, 1918, p. 2.

Minchev, A. "Boevye dni." *Krasnaia letopis'*, 1924, no. 9, pp. 5–10.

Molotov, V. M. "Petrogradskaia organizatsiia RKP nakanune oktiabr'skoi revoliutsii." *Petrogradskaia pravda*, November 5, 1922, p. 2.

———. "Smolnyi i zimnii." *Pravda*, November 7, 1924, p. 9.

Nevskii, V. I. "Dve vstrechi." *Krasnaia letopis'*, 1922, no. 4, pp. 142–46.

———. *Istoriia RKP(b): Kratkii ocherk.* Leningrad: Priboi, 1926.

———. "Istoricheskoe zasedanie Peterburgskogo komiteta RSDRP (bol'shevikov) nakanune oktiabr'skogo vosstaniia." *Krasnaia letopis'*, 1922, nos. 2–3, pp. 316–32.

———. "Narodnye massy v oktiabr'skoi revoliutsii." *Rabotnik prosveshcheniia*, 1922, no. 8, pp. 20–22.

———. "Organizatsiia mass." *Krasnaia gazeta*, July 16, 1922, p. 3.

———. *V bure deianii: Petrograd za piat' let sovetskoi raboty.* Moscow and Petrograd: Gosizdat, 1922.

———. "V oktiabre." *Katorga i ssylka*, 1932, nos. 11–12 (96–97), pp. 27–45.

———. "Voennaia organizatsiia i oktiabr'skaia revoliutsiia." *Krasnoarmeets*, 1919, nos. 10–15, pp. 34–44.

Ob Il'iche: Sbornik statei, vospominanii, dokumentov, i materialov. Leningrad: Priboi, 1926.

Ob Il'iche: Vospominaniia pitertsev. Leningrad: Lenizdat, 1970.

O Lenine: Vospominaniia. Edited by I. L. Meshcheriakov. 4 vols. Moscow and Leningrad: Gosizdat, 1924–1925.

Ordzhonikidze, S. "Il'ich v iiul'skie dni." *Pravda*, March 28, 1924, p. 4.

———. *Put' bol'shevika*. Moscow: Gosizdat, 1956.

Ot fevralia k oktiabriu (iz anket uchastnikov velikoi oktiabr'skoi sotsialisticheskoi revoliutsii). Moscow: Gospolitizat, 1957.

O Vladimire Il'iche Lenine: Vospominaniia 1900–1921. Moscow: Gosizdat, 1963.

Pavlov, I. "Avral'naia rabota 25-go oktiabria 1917 goda." *Krasnyi flot*, 1926, nos. 10–11, pp. 25–26.

Pestkovskii, S. "Ob oktiabr'skikh dniakh v Pitere." *Proletarskaia revoliutsiia*, 1922, no. 10, pp. 94–104.

Petrograd, October 1917. Moscow: Foreign Languages Publishing House, 1957.

Petrograd v dni velikogo oktiabria: Vospominaniia uchastnikov revoliutsionnykh sobytii v Petrograde v 1917 godu. Leningrad: Lenizdat, 1967.

Polenov. "Vystrel s 'Avrory.' " *Leningradskaia pravda*, November 6–7, 1927, p. 6.

Podvoiskii, N. I. *God 1917*. Moscow: Gospolitizdat, 1958.

———. "Iiul'skie dni: Tri momenta." *Pravda*, July 18, 1925, p. 2.

———. "Kak proizoshla oktiabr'skaia revoliutsiia." *Izvestiia*, November 6, 1918, p. 3.

———. *Krasnaia gvardiia v oktiabr'skie dni*. Moscow and Leningrad: Gosizdat, 1927.

———. "O voennoi deiatel'nosti V. I. Lenina." *Kommunist*, 1957, no. 1, pp. 31–46.

———. "Voennaia organizatsiia TsK RSDRP(b) i voenno-revoliutsionnyi komitet 1917 g." *Krasnaia letopis'*, 1923, no. 6, pp. 64–97, and no. 8, pp. 7–43.

Pronin, A. G. "Podgotovka k zakhvatu vlasti." *Bakinskii rabochii*, November 7, 1927, p. 4.

Rakh'ia, E. "Moi predoktiabr'skie i posleoktiabr'skie vstrechi s Leninym." *Novyi mir*, 1924, no. 1, pp. 24–39.

———. "Moi vospominaniia o Vladimire Il'iche." In *Vospominaniia o Vladimire Il'iche Lenine*, vol. 2, pp. 432–36. Moscow: Politizdat, 1969.

———. "Poslednee podpol'e Vladimira Il'icha." *Krasnaia letopis'*, 1934, no. 58, pp. 79–90.

Raskol'nikov, F. F. *Kronshtadt i Piter v 1917 godu*. Moscow and Leningrad: Gosizdat, 1925.

———. "Kronshtadt v iiul'skie dni." *Pravda*, July 16, 1927, p. 3.

———. *Na boevykh postakh*. Moscow: Voenizdat, 1964.

———. "V tiur'me Kerenskogo." *Proletarskaia revoliutsiia*, 1923, no. 10 (22), pp. 133–65.

———. "Zasedaniia pervogo legal'nogo Peka." *Proletarskaia revoliutsiia*, no. 8, 1922, pp. 48–54.

Rovio, G. S. "Kak Lenin skryvalsia u gel'singforsskogo 'politsmeistera.' " In *Lenin v 1917 godu: Vospominaniia*, pp. 148–56. Moscow: Politizdat, 1967.

Savel'ev, M. "Lenin v iiul'skie dni." *Pravda*, July 17, 1930, p. 2.

Shidlovskii, G. "Razgrom redaktsii *Pravdy* v iiule 1917 g." *Krasnaia letopis'*, 1927, no. 1 (22), pp. 48–54.

Shliapnikov, A. "Iiul'skie dni v Petrograde." *Proletarskaia revoliutsiia*, 1926, no. 4 (51), pp. 46–89, and no. 5 (52), pp. 5–60.

———. "Kerenshchina." *Proletarskaia revoliutsiia*, 1926, no. 7 (54), pp. 9–56, and no. 8 (55), pp. 5–53.

———. "K oktiabriu." *Proletarskaia revoliutsiia*, 1922, no. 10, pp. 3–42.

Shliapnikov, A. *Semnadtsatyi god*. 4 vols. Petrograd: Gosizdat, 1923.

Shotman, A. "Lenin nakanune oktiabria." In Institut Lenina pri TsK RKP(b), *O Lenine: Sbornik vospominanii*, edited by L. B. Kamenev, vol. 1, pp. 112–24. Leningrad: Gosizdat, 1925.

Smirnov, A. M. "Kratkie zametki iz zhizni samokatchikov 3-go batal'ona v oktiabr'skie dni 1917 goda." *Krasnaia letopis'*, 1922, no. 2–3, pp. 155–57.

Shumiatskii, B. "Shestoi s"ezd partii i rabochii klass." In *V dni velikoi proletarskoi revoliutsii: Epizody bor'by v Petrograde v 1917 godu*, edited by I. P. Tovstukha, pp. 88–95. Moscow: Ogiz, 1937.

———. "Nakanune oktiabria." *Leningradskaia pravda*, November 6–7, 1927, p. 14.

Sokol'nikov, G. "Kak podkhodit' k istorii oktiabria." In *Za leninizma*, pp. 157–67. Moscow and Leningrad: Gosizdat, 1925.

Stalin, I. V. *Sochineniia*. 13 vols. Moscow: Gospolitizdat, 1946–1951.

Stasova, E. D. "Pis'mo Lenina v TsK partii." In *Vospominaniia o V. I. Lenine*, vol. 2, pp. 454–55. Moscow: Politizdat, 1969.

———. *Stranitsy zhizni i bor'by*. Moscow: Gosizdat, 1957.

Sulimova, M. "Eto budet poslednii i reshitel'nyi boi." In *Letopis' velikogo oktiabria*, edited by A. Iu. Krivitskii, pp. 101–7. Moscow: Sovetskaia Rossiia, 1958.

———. "Iiul'skie dni." In *K godovshchine smerti V. I. Lenina*, edited by A. F. Il'in-Zhenevskii. Leningrad: Gosizdat, 1925.

———. "O sobytiiakh 1917 goda." In Institut marksizma-leninizma pri TsK KPSS, *Velikaia oktiabr'skaia sotsialisticheskaia revoliutsiia: Sbornik vospominanii uchastnikov revoliutsii v Petrograde i Moskve*, pp. 112–22. Moscow: Gospolitizdat, 1957.

Sverdlova, K. T. *Iakov Mikhailovich Sverdlov*. Moscow: Molodaia gvardiia, 1960.

Tarasov-Rodionov, A. "Pervaia operatsiia." *Voennyi vestnik*, 1924, no. 42, pp. 10–13.

Trotskii, L. D. *Oktiabr'skaia revoliutsiia*. Moscow and Petrograd: Kommunist, 1918.

———. *Sochineniia*. Vol. 3, part 1, *Ot fevralia do oktiabria*. Moscow: Gosizdat, 1925.

Trotsky, Leon. *The History of the Russian Revolution*. Translated by Max Eastman. 3 vols. Ann Arbor: University of Michigan Press, 1957.

———. *Lenin*. New York: Capricorn, 1971.

———. *My Life*. New York: Grosset & Dunlap, 1960.

———. *Stalin*. New York: Stein & Day, 1967.

———. *The Stalin School of Falsification*. Translated by John G. Wright. New York: Pioneer, 1962.

Tucker, Robert C., ed. *The Lenin Anthology*. New York: W. W. Norton, 1975.

Ul'ianova, M. "Poiski Il'iche v pervye dni iiulia 1917 g." In *O Lenine*, pp. 35–40. Moscow: Pravda, 1927.

Velikaia oktiabr'skaia sotsialisticheskaia revoliutsiia: Sbornik vospominanii uchastnikov revoliutsii v Petrograde i Moskve. Moscow: Politizdat, 1957.

V ogne revoliutsionnykh boev: Raiony Petrograda v dvukh revoliutsiiakh 1917 g. Sbornik vospominanii starykh bol'shevikov-piertsev. Edited by F. N. Petrov, et al. 2 vols. Moscow: Mysl', 1967–1971.

"Vospominaniia ob oktiabr'skom perevorote." *Proletarskaia revoliutsiia*, 1922, no. 10, pp. 44–93.

[Institut marksizma-leninizma pri TsK KPSS.] *Vospominaniia o Vladimire Il'iche Lenine*. 3 vols. Moscow: Gospolitizdat, 1956–1957.

[Institut marksizma-leninizma pri TsK KPSS.] *Vospominaniia o Vladimire Il'iche Lenine*. Edited by G. N. Golikov, et al. 5 vols. Moscow: Politizdat, 1968–1969.

Za leninizma: Sbornik statei. Moscow and Leningrad: Gosizdat, 1925.

Zinov'ev, G. "Lenin i iiul'skie dni." *Proletarskaia revoliutsiia,* 1927, nos. 8–9 (67–68), pp. 55–72.

———. *Sochineniia.* Vol. 7, 2 parts. Moscow and Leningrad: Gosizdat, 1925.

5 · *Non-Bolshevik Memoirs*

Abramovich, Raphael R. *The Soviet Revolution, 1917–1939.* New York: International Universities Press, 1962.

Alekseev, M. V. "Iz dnevnika generala M. V. Alekseeva." In *Russkii istoricheskii arkhiv,* vol. 1, pp. 11–56. Prague: Izdatel'stvo Russkogo zagranichnogo istoricheskogo arkhiva v Prage, 1929.

Brusilov, A. A. *Moi vospominaniia.* Moscow: Voennoe izdatel'stvo, 1963.

Buchanan, Sir George. *My Mission to Russia and Other Diplomatic Memoirs.* 2 vols. London: Cassell, 1923.

Chernov, V. M. *The Great Russian Revolution.* Translated and abridged by Philip E. Mosely. New Haven: Yale University Press, 1936.

Chishvits, fon. *Zakhvat baltiiskikh ostrov germaniei v 1917 g.* Moscow: Gosvoenizdat, 1937.

Dan, F. "K istorii poslednikh dnei Vremennogo pravitel'stva." *Letopis' revoliutsii,* vol. 1, 1923, pp. 163–75.

Denikin, A. I. *Ocherki russkoi smuty.* 5 vols. Paris: J. Povolozhky & Cie., 1921–1926.

Desimeter, L. P. "Zagovor Kornilova: Pis'mo v redaktsiiu." *Posledniia novosti,* May 28, 1937.

Gippius, Z. *Siniaia kniga: Peterburgskii dnevnik, 1914–1918 gg.* Belgrade: Komissia Palata Akademii nauk, 1929.

Haimson, Leopold H., ed. *The Mensheviks: From the Revolution of 1917 to the Second World War.* Chicago: University of Chicago Press, 1974.

Iarchuk, E. *Kronshtadt v russkoi revoliutsii.* New York: Izdanie Ispolnitel'nogo komiteta professional'nykh soiuzov, 1923.

Krasnov, P. N. "Na vnutrennem fronte." In *Arkhiv russkoi revoliutsii,* vol. 1, pp. 97–190. Berlin: Slovo, 1922.

Kerensky, A. F. *Russia and History's Turning Point.* New York: Duell, Sloan & Pearce, 1965.

———. *The Catastrophe: Kerensky's Own Story of the Russian Revolution.* New York: Appleton-Century-Crofts, 1927.

Kshesinskaia, M. F. *Dancing in Petersburg: The Memoirs of Kschessinska.* Translated by Arnold Haskell. London: Victor Gollancz, 1960.

Lukomskii, A. S. *Vospominaniia.* 2 vols. Berlin: Otto Kirchner, 1922.

Maliantovich, P. N. "V zimnem dvortse 25–26 oktiabria 1917 goda." *Byloe,* 1918, no. 12, pp. 111–41.

Miatezh Kornilova: Iz belykh memuarov. Leningrad: Krasnaia gazeta, 1928.

Miliukov, P. N. *Istoriia vtoroi russkoi revoliutsii.* 3 vols. Sofia: Rossiisko-Bolgarskoe knigoizdatel'stvo, 1921–1924.

———. *Rossiia na perelome.* 3 vols. Paris: Imprimerie d'art Voltaire, 1927.

———. *Vospominaniia, 1859–1917.* New York: Izdatel'stvo imeni Chekhova, 1953.

Mstislavskii, S. *Piat' dnei.* Berlin: Grzhebin, 1922.

Nabokov, Vladimir. "Vremennoe pravitel'stvo." *Arkhiv russkoi revoliutsii*, vol. 1, pp. 9–96. Berlin: Slovo, 1922.

Nikitin, B. V. *Rokovye gody*. Paris: Le Polonais en France, 1937. English translation, *The Fatal Years*. London: William Hodge, 1938.

Pal'chinskii, P. I. "Poslednie chasy Vremennogo pravitel'stva v 1917 god." *Krasnyi Arkhiv*, 1933, no. 1 (56), pp. 136–38.

Polovtsev, P. A. *Dni zatmeniia*. Paris: Vozrozhdenie, n.d.

Price, M. Philips. *My Reminiscences of the Russian Revolution*. London: Allen & Unwin, 1921.

Robien, Louis de. *The Diary of a Diplomat in Russia 1917–1918*. Translated by Camilla Sykes. New York: Praeger, 1970.

Reed, John. *Ten Days That Shook the World*. New York: Vintage Books, 1960.

Savinkov, B. "General Kornilov: Iz vospominanii." *Byloe*, 1925, no. 3 (31), pp. 182–98.

Sinegub, A. "Zashchita zimnego dvortsa," *Arkhiv russkoi revoliutsii*, 1922, no. 4, pp. 121–97.

Stankevich, B. V. *Vospominaniia 1914–1919 gg.* Berlin: I. P. Ladyzhnikov, 1920.

Sukhanov, N. N. *The Russian Revolution, 1917*. Edited, abridged, and translated by Joel Carmichael. 2 vols. New York: Harper & Row, 1962.

———. *Zapiski o revoliutsii*. 7 vols. Berlin, Petersburg, Moscow: Z. I. Grzhebin, 1922–1923.

Tsereteli, I. G. *Vospominaniia o fevral'skoi revoliutsii*. 2 vols. Paris: Mouton, 1963.

Tyrkova-Williams, Ariadna, *From Liberty to Brest Litovsk: The First Year of the Russian Revolution*. London: Macmillan, 1919.

Vakar, Nicholas. Interviews with A. I. Putilov and P. N. Finisov. *Posledniia novosti*, January 24, 1937, and March 6, 1937.

Verkhovskii, A. I. *Rossiia na Golgofe*. Petrograd: Delo naroda, 1918.

Vinberg, G. *V plenu u obez'ian*. Kiev: Tipografiia gubernskogo pravleniia, 1918.

Voytinskii, V. S. "Gody pobed i porazhenii: 1917." Berlin, 1922. Typescript, Nicolaevsky archive, Hoover Institution, Stanford, California.

Williams, Albert Rhys. *Journey into Revolution: Petrograd 1917–1918*. Chicago: Quadrangle, 1969.

Woytinsky, W. S. *Stormy Passage*. New York: Vanguard Press, 1961.

6 · *Dissertations*

Fedosikhina, E. A. "Bol'shevistskie partiinye konferentsii nakanune VI s"ezda partii." Candidate dissertation, Moscow State University, Moscow, 1969.

Feldman, R. "Between War and Revolution. The Russian General Staff, February–July 1917." Doctoral dissertation, Indiana University, Bloomington, Indiana, 1967.

Gal'perina, B. D. "Raionnye sovety Petrograda v 1917 g." Candidate dissertation, Institute of History, USSR Academy of Sciences, Leningrad, 1968.

Hasegawa, Tsuyoshi. "The February Revolution of 1917 in Russia." Doctoral dissertation, University of Washington, Seattle, 1969.

Il'ina, I. V. "Bor'ba partii bol'shevikov protiv proiavlenii 'levizny' v period podgotovki oktiabr'skoi revoliutsii." Candidate dissertation, Moscow State University, Moscow, 1965.

Kabardin, G. M. "Bol'shevistskie fraktsii stolichnykh sovetov v period podgotovki i pobedy oktiabr'skogo vooruzhennogo vosstaniia (iiul'–oktiabr' 1917)." Candidate dissertation, Moscow State University, Moscow, 1967.

Komissarenko, L. A. "Deiatel'nost' partii bol'shevikov po ispol'zovaniiu vooruzhennykh i myrnikh form bor'by v period podgotovki i provedeniia velikoi oktiabr'skoi sotsialisticheskoi revoliutsii." Candidate dissertation, Leningrad State University, Leningrad, 1967.

Kornoukhov, E. M. "Bor'ba partii bol'shevikov protiv melkoburzhuaznoi revoliutsionnosti i avantiurizma anarkhistov v period podgotovki pobedy oktiabr'skoi revoliutsii (mart–oktiabr' 1917 goda)." Candidate dissertation, Moscow State University, Moscow, 1966.

Likhachev, M. "Ministerstvo prodovol'stviia Vremennogo pravitel'stva." Candidate dissertation, Moscow State University, Moscow, 1968.

Rasstrigin, A. F. "Revoliutsionnye komitety avgustskogo krizisa 1917 g." Candidate dissertation, Leningrad State University, Leningrad, 1969.

Sovokin, A. M. "Razrabotka V. I. Leninym novoi taktike partii posle iiul'skikh sobytii 1917 g." Candidate dissertation, Institute of Marxism-Leninism, Moscow, 1962.

7 · Soviet Secondary Sources

Adibek-Melikan, E. A. *Revoliutsionnaia situatsiia v Rossii nakanune oktiabria.* Erevan: Izdatel'stvo Aiastan, 1967.

Akademiia nauk SSSR, Institut istorii, et al. *Ocherki istorii Leningrada.* Edited by V. M. Kochakov, et al. 4 vols. Moscow and Leningrad: Izdatel'stvo Akademii nauk SSSR, 1955–1964.

Akademiia nauk SSSR, Institut istorii, Leningradskoe otdelenie. *Oktiabr'skoe vooruzhennoe vosstanie.* Edited by S. N. Valk, et al. 2 vols. Leningrad: Nauka, 1967.

Akhun, M. I., and Petrov, V. A. *Bol'sheviki i armiia v 1905–1917 gg.* Leningrad: Krasnaia gazeta, 1929.

Andreev, A. M. *Sovety rabochikh i soldatskikh deputatov nakanune oktiabria.* Moscow: Nauka, 1967.

Anskii, A. "Petrogradskii sovet professional'nykh soiuzov v 1917 g." In *Professional'noe dvizhenie v Petrograde v 1917 g.*, edited by A. Anskii, pp. 45–77. Leningrad: Izdatel'stvo Leningradskogo oblastnogo soveta profsoiuzov, 1928.

Astrakhan, Kh. M. *Bol'sheviki i ikh politicheskie protivniki v 1917 godu.* Leningrad: Lenizdat, 1973.

Avvakumov, S. I. "Bor'ba petrogradskikh bol'shevikov za osushchestvlenie leninskogo plana oktiabr'skogo vosstaniia." In Akademiia nauk SSSR, Institut istorii, Leningradskoe otdelenie, *Oktiabr'skoe vooruzhennoe vosstanie v Petrograde.* Moscow and Leningrad: Nauka, 1957, pp. 7–61.

Baranov, M. A. "V. I. Lenin o vozmozhnosti mirnogo razvitiia revoliutsii posle razgroma kornilovshchiny." *Uchenye zapiski Moskovskogo oblastnogo pedagogicheskogo instituta*, no. 58, Trudy kafedry istorii KPSS. Moscow, 1957.

Bogdanov, A. V. *Moriaki-baltiitsy v 1917 g.* Moscow: Voennoe izdatel'stvo, 1955.

Burdzhalov, E. N. "O taktike bol'shevikov v marte–aprele 1917 goda." *Voprosy istorii*, 1956, no. 4, pp. 38–56.

Burdzhalov, E. N. *Vtoraia russkaia revoliutsiia: Vosstanie v Petrograde*. Moscow: Nauka, 1967.

Central Committee of the CPSU. *History of the Communist Party of the Soviet Union (Bolshevik): Short Course*. New York: International Publishers, 1939.

Chaadaeva, O. *Kornilovshchina*. Moscow and Leningrad: Molodaia gvardiia, 1930.

————. "Soldatskie massy petrogradskogo garnizona v podgotovke i provedenii oktiabr'skogo vooruzhennogo vosstaniia," *Istoricheskie zapiski*, 1955, no. 51, pp. 3–44.

Drezen, A. K. "Baltiiskii flot ot iiulia k oktiabriu 1917 g." *Krasnaia letopis'*, 1929, no. 5 (32), pp. 157–212.

————. "Petrogradskii garnizon v iiule i avguste 1917 g." *Krasnaia letopis'*, 1927, no. 3 (24), pp. 191–223.

————. "Petrogradskii garnizon v oktiabre." *Krasnaia letopis'*, 1927, no. 2 (23), pp. 101–33.

Egorova, A. G. *Partiia i profsoiuzy v oktiabr'skoi revoliutsii*. Moscow: Mysl', 1970.

Elov, B. "PK nakanune 25-go oktiabria." *Petrogradskaia pravda*, November 5, 1922, p. 2.

Erykalov, E. F. *Oktiabr'skoe vooruzhennoe vosstanie v Petrograde*. Leningrad: Lenizdat, 1966.

Farfel, A. S. *Bor'ba narodnykh mass protiv kontrrevoliutsionnoi iustitsii Vremennogo pravitel'stva*. Minsk: Izdatel'stvo BGU imeni V. I. Lenina, 1969.

Fraiman, A. L. *Forpost sotsialisticheskoi revoliutsii*. Leningrad: Nauka, 1969.

Frumkin, S. N. "V. I. Lenin o vozmozhnosti mirnogo razvitiia revoliutsii." *Uchenye zapiski Riazanskogo gosudarstvennogo pedinstituta*, vol. 19 (1958), pp. 29–51.

Gaponenko, L. S. *Rabochii klass Rossii v 1917 godu*. Moscow: Nauka, 1970.

Geroi Oktiabria. 2 vols. Leningrad: Lenizdat, 1967.

Golikov, G. N. "Oktiabr'skoe vooruzhennoe vosstanie v Petrograde." *Istoriia SSR*, 1957, no. 4, pp. 40–63.

————. *Revoliutsiia, otkryvshaia novuiu eru*. Moscow: Politizdat, 1967.

Golub, P. *Partiia, armiia i revoliutsiia*. Moscow: Politizdat, 1967.

Gorev, B. I. *Anarkhizm v Rossii*. Moscow: Molodaia gvardiia, 1930.

Gorodetskii, E. N. "Iz istorii oktiabr'skogo vooruzhennogo vosstaniia i II vserossiiskogo s"ezda sovetov." *Voprosy istorii*, 1957, no. 10, pp. 23–48.

Grunt, A. Ia. *Zagovor obrechennykh (razgrom kornilovshchiny)*. Moscow: Gosizdat, 1962.

————. "Mogla li Moskva nachat'? V. I. Lenin o vozmozhnosti nachala vosstaniia v Moskve v 1917 g." *Istoriia SSSR*, 1969, no. 2, pp. 5–28.

Gusev, K. *Krakh partii levykh eserov*. Moscow: Sotsekgiz, 1963.

Gusev, K., and Eritsan, Kh. A. *Ot soglashatel'stva k kontrrevoliutsii*. Moscow: Mysl', 1968.

Iaroslavskii, E. E. *Partiia bol'shevikov v 1917 godu*. Moscow: 1927.

Ignat'ev, A. V. *Vneshniaia politika Vremennogo pravitel'stva*. Moscow: Nauka, 1974.

Institut istorii partii pri Leningradskom obkome KPSS. *Geroi oktiabria: Biografii aktivnykh uchastnikov podgotovki i provedeniia oktiabr'skogo vooruzhennogo vosstaniia v Petrograde*. 2 vols. Leningrad: Lenizdat, 1967.

————. *Ocherki istorii Leningradskoi organizatsii KPSS*. Part 1, *1883–oktiabr' 1917 gg.* Leningrad: Lenizdat, 1962.

Ioffe, A. A. "V noch' na 25-e oktiabria." *Krasnoarmeets*, 1925, no. 78, pp. 5–7.

Iugov, M. S. "Sovety v pervyi period revoliutsii." In *Ocherki po istorii oktiabr'skoi revoliutsii*, edited by M. N. Pokrovskii, vol. 2, pp. 113–253. Moscow-Leningrad: Gosizdat, 1927.

Ivanov, N. Ia. *Kornilovshchina i ee razgrom*. Leningrad: Izdatel'stvo Leningradskogo universiteta, 1965.

———. "Nekotorye voprosy krizisa 'praviaschchikh verkhov' i taktika bol'shevikov nakanune oktiabr'skogo vooruzhennogo vosstaniia." In *Lenin i oktiabr'skoe vooruzhennoe vosstanie v Petrograde: Materialy Vsesoiuznoi nauchnoi sessii sostoiavsheisia 13–16 noiabria 1962 g. v Leningrade*, edited by I. I. Mints. Moscow: Nauka, 1964.

Kapustin, M. I. *Zagovor generalov: Iz istorii kornilovshchiny i ee razgrom*. Moscow: Mysl', 1968.

Karamysheva, L. F. *Bor'ba bol'shevikov za Petrogradskii sovet: Mart–oktiabr' 1917 g.* Leningrad: Lenizdat, 1964.

Khesin, S. S. *Oktiabr'skaia revoliutsiia i flot*. Moscow: Nauka, 1971.

Kirillov, V. S. *Kurs podtverzhdennyi zhizn'u: K istorii ekonomicheskoi platformy bol'shevikov*. Moscow: Mysl', 1972.

Kniazev, S. P., ed. *Petrogradskie bol'sheviki v oktiabr'skoi revoliutsii*. Leningrad: Lenizdat, 1957.

Kochakov, V. M. "Bol'shevizatsiia petrogradskogo garnizona v 1917 godu." In Akademiia nauk SSSR, Institut istorii, Leningradskoe otdelenie, *Oktiabr'skoe vooruzhennoe vosstanie v Petrograde*, pp. 142–83. Leningrad: Nauka, 1957.

———. "Sostav petrogradskogo garnizona v 1917 g." *Uchenye zapiski Leningradskogo gosudarstvennogo universiteta*, 1956, vypusk 24, no. 205, pp. 60–86.

Koronin, M. M. "V. I. Lenin i finskie revoliutsonery." *Voprosy istorii*, 1967, no. 10, pp. 3–17.

Kostrikin, V. I. *Zemel'nye komitety v 1917 godu*. Moscow: Nauka, 1975.

Kulikova, I. S., ed. *Zhenshchiny russkoi revoliutsii*. Moscow: Politizdat, 1968.

Laverychev, V. Ia. *Po tu storonu barrikad*. Moscow: Mysl', 1967.

———. "Russkie monopolisty i zagovor Kornilova." *Voprosy istorii*, 1964, no. 4, pp. 32–44.

Lebedev, V. V. *Mezhdunarodnoe polozhenie Rossii nakanune oktiabr'skoi revoliutsii*. Moscow: Nauka, 1967.

Leningradskii ordena Lenina gosudarstvennyi universitet, Kafedra istorii KPSS. *Lenin, partiia, oktiabr'*. Leningrad: Izdatel'stvo Leningradskogo universiteta, 1967.

Lidak, O. A., ed. *Oktiabr' v Petrograde*. Leningrad: Lenizdat, 1933.

———. *1917 god. Ocherki istorii oktiabr'skoi revoliutsii*. Moscow and Leningrad: Partizdat, 1932.

Lur'e, M. L. "Petrogradskoe mezhraionnoe soveshchanie v 1917 godu." *Krasnaia letopis'*, 1932, no. 3 (48), pp. 13–43, and no. 4 (49), pp. 30–40.

Lutovinov, I. S. *Likvidatsiia miatezha Kerenskogo-Krasnova*. Moscow: Voenizdat, 1965.

Martynov, E. I. *Kornilov: Popytka voennogo perevorota*. Leningrad: Gosvoenizdat, 1927.

Maslov, N. N., ed. *Lenin i revoliutsiia, 1917 god*. Leningrad: Lenizdat, 1970.

Milchik, I. "Petrogradskaia tsentral'naia gorodskaia duma v fevrale–oktiabre 1917 goda." *Krasnaia letopis'*, 1927, no. 2 (23), pp. 189–218.

Miller, V. I. *Soldatskie komitety russkoi armii v 1917 g: Vozniknovenie i nachal'nyi period deiatel'nosti*. Moscow: Nauka, 1974.

Mints, I. I. *Istoriia velikogo oktiabria*. 3 vols. Moscow: Nauka, 1967–1972.

―――, ed. *Lenin i oktiabr'skoe vooruzhennoe vosstanie v Petrograde: Materialy Vsesoiuznoi nauchnoi sessii, sostoiavsheisia 13–16 noiabria 1962 g.v Leningrade*. Moscow: Nauka, 1964.

Nevskii, V. I. *Ocherki po istorii Rossiiskoi kommunisticheskoi partii*. 2d. ed. Leningrad: Priboi, 1925.

Ocherki istorii Leningradskoi organizatsii KPSS. 2 vols. Leningrad: Lenizdat, 1962–1968.

Orekhova, E. D. "K izucheniiu istochnikov o sozdanii Petrogradskogo voenno-revoliutsionnogo komiteta." In *Istochnikovedenie istorii sovetskogo obshchestva*, vypusk 2, edited by D. A. Chugaev, pp. 9–55. Moscow: Nauka, 1968.

―――. "O sostave Petrogradskogo voenno-revoliutsionnogo komiteta." *Istoriia SSSR*, 1971, no. 2, pp. 118–30.

Orekhova, E. D., and Pokrovskii, A. S. "O datirovke vstrech V. I. Lenina s rukoviditeliami voennoi organizatsii bol'shevikov i Petrogradskogo VRK v oktiabre 1917 g." In *Istochnikovedenie istorii sovetskogo obshchestva*, vypusk 2, edited by D. A. Chugaev, pp. 56–78. Moscow: Nauka, 1968.

Pershin, P. N. *Agrarnaia revoliutsiia v Rossii*. 2 vols. Moscow: Nauka, 1966.

Petrash, V. V. *Moriaki Baltiiskogo flota v bor'be za pobedu oktiabria*. Moscow and Leningrad: Nauka, 1966.

Petrov, I. F. *Strategiia i taktika partii bol'shevikov v podgotovke pobedy oktiabr'skoi revoliutsii*. Moscow: Politizdat, 1964.

Piontkovskii, S. "Voenno-revoliutsionnyi komitet v Pitere v oktiabr'skie dni." *Proletarskaia revoliutsiia*, 1927, no. 10 (69), pp. 110–37.

Pokrovskii, M., ed. *Ocherki po istorii oktiabr'skoi revoliutsii*. 2 vols. Moscow and Leningrad: Gosizdat, 1927.

Popov, A. L. *Oktiabr'skii perevorot: Fakty i dokumenty*. Petrograd: Izdatel'stvo Novaia epokha, 1918.

Potekhin, M. N. *Pervyi sovet proletarskoi diktatury*. Leningrad: Lenizdat, 1966.

Rabinovich, S. E. "Bol'shevistskie voennye organizatsii v 1917 g." *Proletarskaia revoliutsiia*, 1928, nos. 6–7 (77–78), pp. 179–98.

―――. *Bor'ba za armiiu 1917 g*. Leningrad: Gosizdat, 1930.

―――. "Rabota bol'shevikov v armii v 1917 g." *Voina i revoliutsiia*, 1927, no. 6, pp. 96–108.

Ruban, N. *Oktiabr'skaia revoliutsiia i krakh menshevizma*. Moscow: Gospolitizdat, 1968.

Sandin, B. I. "Lenin o sootnoshenii mirnogo i vooruzhennogo putei razvitiia revoliutsii posle razgroma kornilovshchiny." *Uchenye zapiski Leningradskogo gosudarstvennogo pedagogicheskogo instituta*, vol. 195, vypusk 2, 1958, pp. 213–32.

Sobolev, G. L. *Revoliutsionnoe soznanie rabochikh i soldat Petrograda v 1917 godu*. Leningrad: Nauka. 1973.

Soboleva, P. I. *Oktiabr'skaia revoliutsiia i krakh sotsial-soglashatelei*. Moscow: Izdatel'stvo Moskovskogo universiteta, 1968.

Sovokin, A. M. "O vozmozhnosti mirnogo razvitiia revoliutsii posle razgroma kornilovshchiny." *Voprosy istorii KPSS*, 1960, no. 3, pp. 50–64.

―――. "Rasshirennoe soveshchanie TsK RSDRP(b), 13–14 iiulia 1917 g." *Voprosy istorii KPSS*, 1959, no. 4, pp. 125–38.

―――. "VI s"ezd partii i istoricheskie istochniki." *Voprosy istorii KPSS*, 1967, no. 7, pp. 39–49.

————. *V preddverii oktiabria*. Moscow: Mysl', 1973.

Startsev, V. I. "Begstvo Kerenskogo." *Voprosy istorii*, 1966, no. 11, pp. 204–6.

————. "Iz istorii priniatiia resheniia ob organizatsii vooruzhennogo vosstaniia." In *Lenin i oktiabr'skoe vooruzhennoe vosstanie v Petrograde*, edited by I. I. Mints, pp. 469–75. Moscow: Nauka, 1964.

————. "Nekotorye voprosy istorii podgotovki i provedeniia oktiabr'skogo vooruzhennogo vosstaniia v Petrograde." In *Sovetskaia istoriografiia klassovoi bor'by i revoliutsionnogo dvizheniia v Rossii*, part 2, pp. 53–71. Leningrad: Izdatel'stvo LGU, 1967.

————. "O nekotorykh rabotakh V. I. Lenina pervoi poloviny sentiabria 1917 g." In *V. I. Lenin v oktiabre i v pervye gody sovetskoi vlasti*, edited by A. L. Fraiman, pp. 28–37. Leningrad: Nauka, 1970.

————. *Ocherki po istorii Petrogradskoi krasnoi gvardii i rabochei militsii*. Moscow and Leningrad: Nauka, 1965.

————. "Poslednii den' Vremennogo pravitel'stva." In *Iz istorii velikoi oktiabr'skoi sotsialisticheskoi revoliutsii i sotsialisticheskogo stroitel'stva v SSSR*, pp. 99–115. Leningrad: Izdatel'stvo Leningradskogo universiteta, 1967.

————. "V. I. Lenin v avguste 1917 godu." *Voprosy istorii*, 1967, no. 8, pp. 124–27.

Stepanov, Z. V. *Rabochie Petrograda v period podgotovki i provedeniia oktiabr'skogo vooruzhennogo vosstaniia*. Moscow and Leningrad: Nauka, 1965.

Taniaev, A. P. *Ocherki po istorii dvizheniia zheleznodorozhnikov v revoliutsii 1917 goda (fevral'–oktiabr')*. Moscow and Leningrad: Izdatel'stvo TsK Zheleznodorozhnikov, 1925.

Tokarev, Iu. S. *Narodnoe pravotvorchestvo nakanune velikoi oktiabr'skoi sotsialisticheskoi revoliutsii (mart–oktiabr' 1917 g.)*. Moscow and Leningrad: Nauka, 1965.

Tsukerman, S. I. "Petrogradskii raionnyi komitet bol'shevikov v 1917 g." *Krasnaia letopis'*, 1932, nos. 5–6 (51–52), pp. 213–40.

Velikaia oktiabr'skaia sotsialisticheskaia revoliutsiia: Malenkaia entsiklopediia. Edited by G. N. Golikov, et al. Moscow: Izdatel'stvo Sovetskaia entsiklopediia, 1968.

Vladimirova, V. "Iiul'skie dni 1917 goda." *Proletarskaia revoliutsiia*, 1923, no. 5 (17), pp. 3–52.

————. *Kontrrevoliutsiia v 1917 g. (Kornilovshchina)*. Moscow: Krasnaia nov', 1924.

Volobuev, P. V. *Ekonomicheskaia politika Vremennogo pravitel'stva*. Moscow: Izdatel'stvo Akademii nauk, 1962.

————. *Proletariat i burzhuaziia Rossii v 1917 godu*. Moscow: Mysl', 1964.

Zlokozov, G. I. *Petrogradskii sovet rabochikh i soldatskikh deputatov v period mirnogo razvitiia revoliutsii*. Moscow: Nauka, 1969.

Znamenskii, O. N. *Iiul'skii krizis 1917 goda*. Moscow and Leningrad: Nauka, 1964.

8 · *Non-Soviet Secondary Sources*

Anin, D. *Revoliutsiia 1917 goda glazami ee rukovoditelei*. Rome: Edizioni aurora, 1971.

Anweiler, Oskar. *The Soviets: The Russian Workers', Peasants', and Soldiers' Councils, 1905–1921*. Translated by Ruth Hein. New York: Pantheon, 1974.

Aronson, Grigorii. *Rossiia nakanune revoliutsii*. New York: Novoe Russkoe Slovo, 1962.

————. *Rossiia v epokhu revoliutsii*. New York: Walden Press, 1966.

Ascher, Abraham. "The Kornilov Affair." *Russian Review*, October 1953, pp. 235–52.

Asher, Harvey. "The Kornilov Affair." *Russian Review*, July 1970, pp. 286–300.

Avrich, Paul. "Russian Factory Committees in 1917." *Jahrbücher für Geschichte Osteuropas*, 1963, no. 11, pp. 161–82.

———. "The Bolshevik Revolution and Workers' Control in Russian Industry." *Slavic Review*, March 1963, pp. 47–63.

———. *The Russian Anarchists*. Princeton: Princeton University Press, 1967.

Avtorkhanov, A. *Proiskhozhdenie partokratii*. 2 vols. Frankfurt: Posev, 1973.

Baron, Samuel H. *Plekhanov: The Father of Russian Marxism*. Stanford: Stanford University Press, 1963.

Boyd, John R. "The Origins of Order No. 1." *Soviet Studies*, January 1968, pp. 359–72.

Carr, Edward H. *The Bolshevik Revolution, 1917–1923*. 3 vols. New York: Macmillan, 1951–1953.

Chamberlin, W. H. *The Russian Revolution, 1917–1921*. 2 vols. New York: Macmillan, 1935.

Cohen, Stephen F. *Bukharin and the Bolshevik Revolution*. New York: Alfred A. Knopf, 1973.

Cross, Truman B. "Purposes of Revolution: Victor Chernov and 1917." *Russian Review*, October 1967, pp. 351–60.

Curtiss, John S. *The Russian Revolutions of 1917*. Princeton: D. Van Nostrand, 1957.

Daniels, Robert V. *Red October*. New York: Scribners, 1967.

———. *The Conscience of the Revolution*. Cambridge: Harvard University Press, 1960.

Deutscher, Isaac. *Stalin: A Political Biography*. London and New York: Oxford University Press, 1949.

———. *The Prophet Armed*. New York: Oxford University Press, 1954.

Fainsod, Merle. *How Russia Is Ruled*. Cambridge: Harvard University Press, 1958.

Feldman, Robert S. "The Russian General Staff and the June 1917 Offensive." *Soviet Studies*, April 1968, pp. 526–43.

Ferro, Marc. *La Revolution de 1917: La chute du tsarisme et les origines d'octobre*. Paris: Aubier, 1967.

———. "The Russian Soldier in 1917: Undisciplined, Patriotic, and Revolutionary." *Slavic Review*, September 1971, pp. 483–512.

Fischer, Louis. *The Life of Lenin*. New York: Harper & Row, 1964.

Florinsky, Michael T. *The Fall of the Russian Empire*. New York: Collier, 1961.

Frankel, Jonathan. "Lenin's Doctrinal Revolution of April 1917." *Journal of Contemporary History*, April 1969, pp. 117–42.

Futrell, Michael. *Northern Underground*. London: Faber & Faber, 1963.

Geyer, Dietrich. *Die Russische Revolution: Historische Probleme und Perspektiven*. Stuttgart: W. Kohlhammer Verlag, 1968.

Getzler, Israel. *Martov: A Political Biography of a Russian Social Democrat*. London: Cambridge University Press, 1967.

Golovin, N. N. *The Russian Army in the World War*. New Haven: Yale University Press, 1931.

Haimson, Leopold. "The Problem of Social Stability in Urban Russia, 1905–1917." *Slavic Review*, vol. 23, no. 4, 1964, pp. 620–42, and vol. 24, no. 1, 1965, pp. 1–22.

Hedlin, Myron. "Zinoviev's Revolutionary Tactics in 1917." *Slavic Review*, vol. 34, no. 1, 1975, pp. 19–43.

Katkov, George. "German Political Intervention in Russia during World War I." In

Revolutionary Russia: A Symposium, edited by Richard Pipes, pp. 80–112. Cambridge: Harvard University Press, 1968.

———. *Russia 1917: The February Revolution*. New York: Harper & Row, 1967.

Keep, John. "1917: The Tyranny of Paris Over Petrograd." *Soviet Studies*, July 1968, pp. 22–45.

Kennan, George F. "The Russian Revolution—Fifty Years After: Its Nature and Consequences." *Foreign Affairs*, October 1967, pp. 1–21.

Kochan, Lionel. *Russia in Revolution, 1890–1918*. London: Weidenfeld & Nicolson, 1966.

———. "Kadet Policy in 1917." *Slavonic and East European Review*, January 1967, pp. 183–92.

Liebman, Marcel. *The Russian Revolution*. New York: Vintage, 1970.

Lehovich, Dimitry V. *White Against Red: The Life of General Anton Denikin*. New York: W. W. Norton, 1974.

Longley, D. A. "Divisions in the Bolshevik Party in March 1917." *Soviet Studies*, July 1972, pp. 61–76.

Medlin, Virgil. "Tseretelli and the Mensheviks, 1917." *Rocky Mountain Social Science Journal*, January 1972, pp. 51–59.

Mel'gunov, S. P. *Kak bol'sheviki zakhvatili vlast'*. Paris: Editions la Renaissance, 1953.

———. *The Bolshevik Seizure of Power*. Santa Barbara: Clio, 1972.

———. *Zolotoi nemetskii kliuch k bol'shevistskoi revoliutsii*. Paris: Dom knigi, 1940.

Meyer, Alfred, G. *Leninism*. New York: Praeger, 1957.

Nikolaevskii, Boris I. "I. G. Tsereteli i ego vospominaniia o 1917 g." *Sotsialisticheskii vestnik*, 1962, nos. 7–8, pp. 110–14, and no. 9–10, pp. 132–36.

———. "I. G. Tsereteli (stranitsy biografii)." *Sotsialisticheskii vestnik*, 1959, no. 6, pp. 119–22; no. 7, pp. 141–43; no. 8–9, pp. 159–63; no. 10, pp. 196–200; no. 11, pp. 219–23; no. 12, pp. 243–45; and 1960, no. 1, pp. 49–52.

Pethybridge, Roger. *The Spread of the Russian Revolution: Essays on 1917*. London: Macmillan–St. Martin's Press, 1972.

Pipes, Richard, ed. *Revolutionary Russia: A Symposium*. Cambridge: Harvard University Press, 1968.

Possony, Stephen. *Lenin: The Compulsive Revolutionary*. Chicago: Henry Regnery, 1964.

Rabinowitch, Alexander. *Prelude to Revolution: The Petrograd Bolsheviks and the July 1917 Uprising*. Bloomington: Indiana University Press, 1968.

———. "The Petrograd Garrison and the Bolshevik Seizure of Power." In *Revolution and Politics in Russia: Essays in Memory of B. I. Nicolaevsky*, edited by Alexander and Janet Rabinowitch with Ladis K. D. Kristof, pp. 172–91. Bloomington: Indiana University Press, 1972.

Radkey, Oliver H. *The Agrarian Foes of Bolshevism*. New York: Columbia University Press, 1958.

Reiman, Mikhail. *Russkaia revoliutsiia, 23 fevralia–25 oktiabria 1917*. 2 vols. Prague: Institut istorii sotsializma, 1968.

Riha, Thomas. *A Russian European: Paul Miliukov in Russian Politics*. South Bend: University of Notre Dame Press, 1969.

Rosenberg, William G. *Liberals in the Russian Revolution: The Constitutional Democratic Party, 1917–1921*. Princeton: Princeton University Press, 1974.

———. "The Russian Municipal Duma Elections of 1917: A Preliminary Computation of Returns." *Soviet Studies*, vol. 21, 1969, pp. 131–63.

Saul, Norman E. "Lenin's Decision to Seize Power: The Influence of Events in Finland." *Soviet Studies*, April 1973, pp. 491–505.

Schapiro, Leonard. *Origins of the Communist Autocracy*. New York: Praeger, 1965.

———. *The Communist Party of the Soviet Union*. New York: Random House, 1959.

Scharlau, W. B., and Zeman, Z. A. B. *Merchant of Revolution: A Life of Alexander Helphand*. London and New York: Oxford University Press, 1965.

Shub, David. *Lenin*. New York: Mentor, 1948.

Smith, C. Jay, Jr. *Finland and the Russian Revolution, 1917–1922*. Athens: University of Georgia Press, 1958.

Strakhovsky, Leonid. "Was There a Kornilov Rebellion? A Reappraisal of the Evidence." *Slavonic and East European Review*, June 1955, pp. 378–95.

Suny, Ronald G. *The Baku Commune, 1917–1918*. Princeton: Princeton University Press, 1972.

Treadgold, Donald W. *Twentieth-Century Russia*. Chicago: Rand McNally, 1959.

Tucker, Robert C. *Stalin as Revolutionary, 1879–1929: A Study in History and Personality*. New York: W. W. Norton, 1973.

Ulam, Adam B. *The Bolsheviks*. New York: Macmillan, 1965.

Vishniak, M. "I. G. Tsereteli." *Sotsialisticheskii vestnik*, 1959, no. 6, pp. 119–22.

Von Laue, Theodore H. "Of the Crisis in the Russian Polity." In J. S. Curtiss, ed., *Essays in Russian and Soviet History, in Honor of Geroid Tanquary Robinson*, pp. 303–22. New York: Columbia University Press, 1963.

———. Review of *Raionnye sovety Petrograda v 1917 godu. Kritika*, vol. 4, no. 3, Spring 1968, pp. 33–57.

———. "Westernization and the Search for a Basis of Authority: Russia in 1917." *Soviet Studies*, October 1967, pp. 155–80.

———. *Why Lenin? Why Stalin?* Philadelphia: J. B. Lippincott, 1964.

Wade, Rex A. "The Raionnye Sovety of Petrograd: The Role of Local Political Bodies in the Russian Revolution." *Jahrbücher für Geschichte Osteuropas*, vol. 20, 1972, pp. 226–40.

———. *The Russian Search for Peace, February–October 1917*. Stanford: Stanford University Press, 1969.

———. "Why October? The Search For Peace In 1917." *Soviet Studies*, July 1968, pp. 36–45.

Warth, Robert D. *The Allies and the Russian Revolution*. Durham: Duke University Press, 1954.

White, J. D. "The Kornilov Affair: A Study in Counterrevolution." *Soviet Studies*, vol. 20, 1968, pp. 188–89.

Wildman, Allan. "The February Revolution in the Russian Army." *Soviet Studies*, July 1970, pp. 3–23.

Wolfe, Bertram D. *Three Who Made a Revolution*. Boston: Beacon Press, 1948.

Index

Adzhemov, Moisei, 256
Akselrod, Alexander, 218
Alekseev, Gen. Mikhail, 96, 100, 101
  and defeat of Kornilov, 114, 146, 149–50, 152
  in formation of new government (Aug.), 151–53, 156
  on Kornilov, 97
  and rise of Kornilov, 106, 332n
Alekseeva, Ekaterina, 220
Aleksei I (Tsar), 225
Aleksinsky, Grigorii, 15, 17–19, 21, 320n
Alexandra (Empress), 97
Alliluev, Sergei, 32
All-Russian Bolshevik Party Conference (April Conference), xx, xxiv–xxv, 9, 60, 62, 134
All-Russian Committee for the Salvation of the Country and the Revolution, 306–8
All-Russian Congress of Peasants' Deputies, see All-Russian Executive Committees; Central Executive Committee; First All-Russian Congress of Soviets; Second All-Russian Congress of Soviets
All-Russian Congress of Workers' and Soldiers' Deputies, see All-Russian Executive Committees; Central Executive Committee; First All-Russian Congress of Soviets; Second All-Russian Congress of Soviets
All-Russian Executive Committees (soviets), xxiii, 52, 109, 172
  criticized (July), 45, 46
  and defeat of Kornilov, 129–34, 137, 138, 143, 148
  district soviets differ with, 77
  dominant elements in, 76
  in formation of new government (Aug.), 151, 153, 157–64
  in garrison crisis, 240–41, 243
  and ineffectiveness of repression, 53, 78
  in July uprising, 2, 12–13, 15–16, 29
  Kornilov affair and Lenin's shift on, 170
  and Kornilov-Kerensky dispute, 108, 110–13
  and Lenin's arrest (July), 33
  military dictatorship and, 95
  and new Soviet government (Oct.), 306
  and October uprising, 260
  and preparation for uprising, 213, 215, 221
  and reaction to July days, 17–18, 20–25, 34–35, 43, 63–64
All-Russian Union of Trade and Industry, 95
Amur (mine layer), 274, 277, 278, 285, 289
Anarchists, 10, 237
Angarsky, N. S., 329n
Anisimov, V. A., 34, 77, 174
Antonov-Ovseenko, Vladimir, 30, 48, 153, 312
  in garrison crisis, 234–37, 241, 247
  in Military Revolutionary Committee, 245
  in new Soviet government, 306
  in October uprising, 249, 262
  in preparation for uprising, 211, 214, 234
  in seizure of power, 274, 278, 281, 286, 288, 299–301
Antselovich, Naum, 218
April Conference (Seventh All-Russian Bolshevik Party Conference), xx, xxiv–xxv, 9, 60, 62, 134, 316n
"April Theses" (Lenin), xxiv, 171–72
Apushkin, General, 334n
Arosev, I. Ia., 327n

"August 14 Program," 112–13, 184, 334n
Aurora (cruiser), 144, 254, 269, 274, 277–78, 285, 286, 288, 289
Avilov, Nikolai, 306
Avksentiev, Nikolai, 55, 68
  and Democratic State Conference, 184, 185
  and new government (Aug.), 163, 165
  and October uprising, 259
  and Preparliament, 201
  and seizure of power, 276–77
Azev, Evno, 18

Bagdatiev, Sergei, 9, 30, 319n
Bagratuni, Gen. Iakov, 244, 248, 285–88
Baltic Fleet, see Russian naval units
Baluev, General, 127
Baranov, Aleksei, 262–63
Baranovsky, Col. V. L., 335n
"Before the Congress of Soviets" (Zinoviev), 190
Belishev, Alexander, 269
Berzin, Ia. A., 250, 251, 272, 325n
Bethmann-Holweg, Moritz August von, 5
Birzhevye vedomosti (newspaper), 3, 36, 215, 250
Black Hundreds, 26, 27, 42–43, 79, 97, 205
Blagonravov, Georgii, 274, 282, 285–86, 288–89
Bogdanov, Boris, 161, 163
  and Congress of Soviets, 292
  at Democratic State Conference, 176–77
  and garrison crisis, 247
  and new government (Aug.), 165
Bogdanov, Mikhail, 140
Boky, G. I., 199, 217, 326n
Boldyrev (SR spokesman), 161–62
Bolshevik Central Committee, 8–9, 316n, 325n
  conference of (July 13–14), 59–62, 66–70
  and Congress of Soviets, 188–89, 344n
  debates over July policy of, 48, 49
  and defeat of Kornilov, 134–38, 336n
  and demonstrations (April, June), xxx–xxxii
  division within (Sept.), 174, 187–88
  and formation of new government (Aug.), 159
  in garrison crisis, 234, 235, 239, 242, 246
  and ineffectiveness of government repression, 57–59
  in July uprising, xxxii, 11–13, 16
  lack of control by, xx
  Lenin and, during Kornilov affair, 169
  and Lenin's call to insurrection (Sept.–Oct.), 179–82, 313

in Lenin's campaign for insurrection, 193–210, 345n
Military Organization and, 72–74; see also Bolshevik Military Organization
and Military Revolutionary Committee, 232–33, 239
moderates control, xxiv–xxv
and Moscow State Conference, 110–11
new coalition government (Sept.) and, 187, 341n
and new Soviet government, 309–10
in October uprising, 250–52, 265–67, 272, 353n
and preparation for uprising, 210–23
and reaction to July days, 64, 66
and Sixth Congress, 83, 84
Bolshevik Military Organization, xx–xxi, xxxii–xxxiii, 233, 312, 316n
  arrest of top leaders of, 47
  charges of insurrection against members of, 54
  damaged by July days, 70–76
  and defeat of Kornilov, 135–38, 142, 143, 337n
  in garrison crisis, 231, 234–36, 244, 348n
  and ineffectiveness of government repression, 57, 59, 327n
  in July uprising, 8–13
  and Lenin's call to insurrection (Sept.), 181
  and Lenin's campaign for insurrection, 201
  in October uprising, 261
  in preparation for uprising, 211, 212, 216, 217, 221, 224, 347n
  in seizure of power, 281
  and Sixth Congress, 83, 84
  soldiers in, xxviii, xxx
Bolshevik Moscow Regional Bureau, 88, 89, 111, 135, 195
Bolshevik Party
  and alliance with left parties, xxiii–xiv
  attacks on offices of (July), 43, 44, 53
  and defeat of Kornilov, 132, 139
  and district soviets, 77, 81
  gains made by, among workers, xxvii–xxx
  German funds for, 14–15
  ineffectiveness of attempt to repress, 51–54
  internal organization of, xxi, 310–13
  Military Organization criticized by, 71–72
  origin of, xvii–xviii
  and reaction to July days, 17–19, 26–38
  resurgence of (after July), 83–93, 111–12
  Sixth Congress of, xx, 62, 83–90, 132, 134, 173, 174, 198, 313

support for goals of, xvii
takes over Kshesinskaia mansion, 8–9
Bolshevik Petersburg Committee, xx, xxiv,
  xxxii, 50, 73, 312, 316n
  and Congress of Soviets, 189
  and defeat of Kornilov, 134–36, 138, 337n
  and garrison crisis, 233–34
  and ineffectiveness of government repres-
    sion, 57, 62–70, 327n
  in July uprising, 8–12
  and Lenin's call to insurrection, 179, 181
  in Lenin's campaign for insurrection,
    193–200
  Lenin's moderation (Sept.) and, 172–73
  Military Organization criticized by, 71
  in October uprising, 265, 268
  and preparation for uprising, 216–19
  and reaction to July, 62–70
  and Sixth Congress, 83
Bonch-Bruevich, Vladimir M., xxxiii, 1, 3, 7,
  44
Bregman, Lazar, 144
Breshko-Breshkovskaia, Ekaterina, 201
Breslav, Boris, 210–11
Brest-Litovsk, Treaty of (1918), 310
Broido, Mark, 231, 292
Brusilov, Gen. Aleksei, 96, 97, 99–103, 106
Bubnov, Andrei, 57, 74, 325n, 326n, 328n
  and Congress of Soviets, 187
  and defeat of Kornilov, 135, 136
  and Lenin's call for insurrection, 181
  and Lenin's campaign for insurrection, 195,
    199–201, 203
  and Lenin's shift in September, 173
  in October uprising, 250, 251
  and preparation for uprising, 216–17, 219,
    234
  in seizure of power, 290
  at Sixth Congress, 88–90
Buchanan, George, 40, 152
Bukharin, Nikolai, 57, 72, 87, 88, 181, 325n,
  326n
Bulat, A. A., 36
Burishkin, A. A., 343n
Burtsev, Vladimir, 19
Bykhovsky, Naum, 290

Cadets (in defense of Winter Palace), 274, 278,
  280–91, 295, 298–301, 305
Capital punishment issue, 77–81, 91, 100–106
Central Committee, *see* Bolshevik Central
  Committee

Central Executive Committee (soviets), xxiii,
  196, 306
  capital punishment and, 91
  and defeat of Kornilov, 142
  district soviets and, 81–82
  and garrison crisis, 236–37, 241
  and ineffectiveness of repression, 54, 56–57,
    328n
  and July uprising, 15–16
  and Lenin's campaign for insurrection, 205
  and new government (Aug.), 158, 165
  and new Soviet government, 309–10, 357n
  and October uprising, 271
  and preparation for uprising, 212, 214
  and reaction to July days, 17–20, 24–25, 31,
    33–35, 39, 49–50, 321n
  Sixth Congress and, 87
Chamberlin, William Henry, xvi
Cheremisov, Gen. Vladimir
  army reform and, 102–5
  and defeat of Kornilov, 149, 333n
  in garrison crisis, 226–27, 229–31, 244
  and seizure of power, 287, 302, 305, 355n
Chernov, Viktor, xxvii, 22, 26, 27, 174
  and new Provisional Government (Aug.),
    158, 163, 165–66
Chkheidze, Nikolai, 7, 35, 112, 174, 175
  and Democratic State Conference, 185
  and new Provisional Government (Aug.),
    16, 165
Chudnovsky, Grigorii, 223, 312
  in garrison crisis, 245
  in seizure of power, 274, 276, 281, 283–84,
    300, 301
City Duma, *see* Duma, Petrograd City
Club Pravda, 9, 70
Committee for Struggle Against the Counterrevolution, 132, 138–41, 148, 149,
  152–53, 161, 166, 170, 232, 337n–38n
Congress of Soviets, *see* First All-Russian Congress of Soviets; Second All-Russian Congress of Soviets
Constituent Assembly, xx, xxvii, 173, 201–2,
  311
  Congress of Soviets and, 214
  and Democratic State Conference, 184, 185
  elections for, xxi, 4, 22, 37, 190, 306, 357n
  and garrison crisis, 227, 228, 237, 247
  and insurrection, 203–5, 256, 260
  and July uprising, 4
  Kornilov affair and, 131
  new Provisional Government (Aug.) and,
    159, 160, 163, 165

Constituent Assembly (*continued*)
  and new Soviet government, 309
  and seizure of power, 287, 288, 347*n*
Council of People's Commissars, 306–7
Council of the Republic, *see* Preparliament
"Crisis Has Matured, The" (Lenin), 193

Dan, Fedor, 23–24, 35, 90, 194
  in Congress of Soviets, 292
  in Democratic State Conference, 186
  and garrison crisis, 237, 243
  and new Provisional Government (Aug.),
    165, 341*n*
  in October uprising, 258–60
  and preparation for uprising, 215, 216
  and seizure of power, 291
Daniels, Robert V., xvi
Dashkevich, Petr, 47, 153, 250, 280, 283–84
"Declaration of Principles" (July 8), 21, 23–25
Declaration of Soldiers' Rights (March), 101
Delo naroda (newspaper), 292
Democratic State Conference (Sept.), 164,
    165, 174–88, 191, 192, 198, 213
Den' (newspaper), 19
Denikin, Gen. Anton I., 100–104, 127, 149,
    333*n*
Desimeter, Col. L. P., 96, 146, 149
"Directive Number One" (Oct.), 249, 256
Directory, 125, 130–31, 157, 170
District soviets, *see* Petrograd district soviets
Diterikhs, Gen. Mikhail, 271
Dolgorukov, Gen. A. M., 117
Dostoevsky, Fedor, 99
Dubrovin, Dr., 27
Dukhonin, Gen. Nikolai, 225
Duma, Petrograd City, 39, 43
  and defeat of Kornilov, 141, 149
  elections for, 91–93
  and new Soviet government, 306
  and seizure of power, 288–90, 295, 296,
    298–99
Duma, State, xxii, 22, 76, 110
  Provisional Committee of, 39, 44–46, 80
Dybenko, Pavel, 30, 48, 153, 262–63, 306
Dzenis, Osvald, 47, 268–69
Dzerzhinsky, Felix, 57, 74, 75, 325*n*, 328*n*
  in October uprising, 250, 251
  and preparation for insurrection, 181, 203,
    234
Dzevaltovsky, I. I., 327*n*
Dzhaparidze, Alesha, 86–88

Economy, the
  Bolshevik power and, 198, 199

factories, 6–8, 53–54, 63–64, 66, 169, 303,
    331*n*
food shortage, xxv, 3–4, 94, 167, 331*n*
fuel shortage, xxv, 4, 167, 331*n*
workers' situation in, xxv–xxvi
Edinstvo (newspaper), 19
Efremov, Ivan, 55, 60
Elizarova, Anna, 32
Emelianov, Nikolai, 34
Eremeev, Konstantin, 274
Erlikh, Genrikh, 295
Ermolenko, Lieutenant, 14
Executive Commission, *see* Bolshevik Peters-
    burg Committee
Executive Committee (All-Russian Congress
    of Peasants' Deputies), xxiii, 110, 295,
    298; *see also* All-Russian Executive Com-
    mittees
Evdokimov, Grigorii, 200

Factories, 6–8, 53–54, 63–64, 66, 169, 303,
    331*n*
Factory-shop committees, xxviii, 136, 140,
    216, 237, 246
  Central Soviet of, 141, 308
Fadeev, Aleko, 46–47
Faerman, Mikhail, 269
February revolution (1917), xviii–xix, xxv–
    xxvi
Fedorov, G. F., 175
Fenikshtein, Iakov, 200
Ferro, Marc, xvi
Filipovsky, Vasilii, 292
Filonenko, Maximilian, 99–104, 106, 107,
    335*n*
Finisov, P. N., 146, 149
Finland, 1, 34, 144, 168, 179, 197, 235
Finland, Regional Executive Committee of
    Army, Fleet, and Workers in, 168, 193,
    197, 209–10, 237
First All-Russian Congress of Soviets (June),
    xxx–xxxi, 21, 23, 291; *see also* All-Russian
    Executive Committees; Central Executive
    Committee; Executive Committee; Sec-
    ond All-Russian Congress of Soviets
First City Conference (Bolshevik; Petrograd),
    xxiv
Flakserman, Galina, 202
Flakserman, Iurii, 204, 206
Flerovsky, Ivan, 46, 273, 277
Fofanova, Margarita, 191, 263–66, 323*n*, 345*n*
Food shortage, xxv, 3–4, 94, 167, 331*n*
Francis, David, 40
Freedom in Struggle (newspaper), 332*n*

"From a Publicist's Diary" (Lenin), 192–93
Fuel shortage, xxv, 4, 167, 331*n*

Ganetsky, Iakov, 17
Garrison conference, 233, 236–37, 240–41
Gazeta-kopeika (newspaper), 36, 215
Gendelman, Mikhail, 293–94
Gessen, S. M., 219
Gippius, Zinaida, 126
Gogol, Nikolai, 7
Goldberg (soldier), 240
Golos pravdy (newspaper), 29, 324*n*
Golos soldata (newspaper), 19, 20, 39, 229, 240
Gorin, Alexander, 77, 81, 139
Gorky, Maxim, 19, 215, 325*n*
Gots, A. R., 90, 174
 and Congress of Soviets, 292
 and Democratic State Conference, 184, 185
 and garrison crisis, 247
 and October uprising, 258–60
Government, *see* Constituent Assembly;
 Council of People's Commissars; Preparliament; Provisional Government; Soviets
Groza (newspaper), 43
Guchkov, Alexander, xxi, xxvii, 96, 156
Gvozdev, K. A., 287
Gzhelshchak, Frants, 295

Helsingfors, 30, 143, 146, 157, 168, 273
"Heroes of Fraud and the Mistakes of the
 Bolsheviks" (Lenin), 191–92
Holy Russia, 43

Iakovleva (Bolshevik), 203–4, 346*n*
Ilin-Zhenevsky, Alexander F., 46, 47, 72
 on Central Committee (post-July), 57–58
 in October uprising, 261, 347*n*
 at Sixth Congress, 84–85
Interdistrict Committee, 77, 81, 83, 84, 316*n*
Interdistrict Conference of Soviets, 77, 78,
 80–84, 138–40, 328*n*
Ioffe, A. A., 181, 200
Iudenich, Gen. Nikolai, 106
Iurenev, Konstantin, 86, 88
Iurenev, Petr, 115, 125
Ivanov, Vasilii, 67
Ivashin, Anton, 47
Izvestiia (newspaper), 202, 227, 228
 and July uprising, 3
 and Kornilov, 105, 111, 129
 and reaction to July days, 19–20, 43, 45
Izvestiia Kronshtadtskogo soveta (newspaper), 157

July uprising, 1–82
 ineffectiveness of repression following,
 51–82
 reaction to, 17–50
June 10 demonstration, xxx, 3
June 18 demonstration, xxx–xxxi

Kadets (Constitutional Democrats; Party of
 People's Freedom), xxi, 170, 175, 192, 310
 district soviets and, 82
 in elections to City Duma, 91, 93
 general policy position of, 95
 in July uprising, 2–3, 318*n*–19*n*
 and Kornilov, 103–5, 112, 139, 333*n*
 and Lenin's campaign for insurrection, 200,
 205
 and October uprising, 259
 in Provisional Government, 25, 151–54,
 159, 162–66, 183–86
 and reaction to July days, 19, 21, 22
 and a Soviet government, 292
Kadlubovsky, Karl, 269
Kaganovich, Lazar, 327*n*
Kaledin, Gen. Aleksei, 106, 112, 114, 304
Kaliagin, P. S., 269
Kalinin, Mikhail, 12, 135, 136, 218, 219
Kamenev, Lev, xxiii, 239, 312, 325*n*
 at April Conference, xxiv, 316*n*
 and Congress of Soviets, 187, 188, 293, 298,
 301, 306
 and defeat of Kornilov, 132, 134
 and Democratic State Conference, 176–78,
 184, 188
 and garrison crisis, 242
 general views of, xx, 173, 317*n*, 320*n*
 and Lenin's call for insurrection, 181, 187
 and Lenin's campaign for insurrection,
 192–93, 196, 199, 203–8, 345*n*, 346*n*
 Military Organization and, 72
 and new Provisional Government (Aug.),
 159–65, 341*n*
 in new Soviet government, 309, 310
 in October uprising, 250–51, 272
 and preparation for uprising, 212–14, 216,
 217, 221–23, 347*n*
 on Presidium of Petrograd Soviet, 175
 and reaction to July days, 30–33, 37, 47–49,
 57
 in seizure of power, 289, 303
 Sixth Congress and, 83, 85
 Stalin compared with, 66
Kamkov, Boris, 183
 and Congress of Soviets, 292, 296–97, 304

Kamkov, Boris (*continued*)
  and October uprising, 257, 258, 351*n*
  and preparation for uprising, 213–14
Kapelinsky (Menshevik-Internationalist), 302, 303
Karinsky, N. S., 29, 32, 55–57
Kartashev, Anton, 187
Katkov, George, xvi
Kaurov, V. N., 323*n*
Kedrov, Mikhail, 72
Kerensky, Alexander F., xvi, 5, 44
  becomes prime minister, 21, 25–28, 55, 322*n*
  and defeat of Kornilov, 129–50
  and Democratic State Conference, 177–78, 185–86
  fall of, 274–78, 284, 287, 300–6, 308, 314, 355*n*
  in formation of a new government (Aug.), 151–67
  and funeral of cossacks, 40–41
  and garrison crisis, 225–31, 244
  ineffectiveness of repression under, 76
  internal policies of, 51, 52
  and July uprising, 2
  Kornilov vs., 110–28, 334*n*
  Lenin and, during Kornilov affair, 169–70
  and Lenin as German agent, 14, 28
  and Lenin's campaign for insurrection, 191–95, 201, 203, 205
  military dictatorship and, 99
  new coalition government under (Sept.), 186–87, 343*n*
  and October uprising, 249, 253–61, 265, 266, 268, 270–72
  preparation to overthrow, 210, 211, 216–17
  in Provisional Government (April), xxii, xxvii
  and reaction to July days, 30, 68, 323*n*
  and rise of Kornilov, 100–108
  seeks soviet's support, 35
  social disintegration alarms (Aug.), 94–95
  soldiers and reintroduction of death penalty by, 75
Kharash, Iakov, 293, 294
Kharitonov, Moisei, 67, 68, 199, 218
Khaustov, Flavian, 30, 48, 277, 327*n*
Khinchuk, Lev, 293–94
Khopor (mine layer), 274
Khovrin, Nikolai, 30, 48
Kishkin, Nikolai, 216
  in formation of new government (Aug.), 151, 343*n*, 355*n*
  during seizure of power, 285–87, 299, 300
Klembovsky, General, 100, 120, 127, 149

Kokoshkin, F. F., 125, 165
Kolchak, Adm. Aleksandr, 96
Kolbin, I. N., 158
Kollontai, Alexandra, 202
  and Congress of Soviets, 292
  and Lenin's call for insurrection, 181
  in Lenin's campaign for insurrection, 203, 206
  and preparation for uprising, 210
  during reaction to July days, 30–31, 48, 55–56, 325*n*
  Sixth Congress and, 83
Kolmin, G. F., 173
Konovalov, Alexander, 187, 201
  and rise of Kornilov, 106
  and seizure of power, 270, 284, 287, 299–301
Kornilov, Gen. Lavr, 90, 305
  biography of, 96–100
  defeat of, 129–52, 183, 187, 312, 313, 355*n*
  effects of defeat of, on Lenin, 132–35, 167–71, 173, 180, 204, 205
  formation of new government following defeat of, 159–67, 340*n*
  garrison crisis compared with affair involving, 228–29
  Kerensky vs., 110–28, 335*n*, 336*n*
  on Lenin, 109
  rise of, 94–109
Kotsiubinsky, Iurii, 47
Kozlovsky, Mechislav, 17
Krasnov, Gen. Petr, 305, 306, 308, 309
Krasnovsky (commissar), 227
Krestinsky, N. N., 325*n*
Kronstadt naval base, xxvi, 28, 273–74
Kronstadt sailors, *see* Sailors
Kronstadt Soviet, 30, 90, 144, 158, 262, 330*n*
Krupskaia, Nadezhda, 32, 182, 265, 345*n*
Krylenko, Nikolai, 47, 153, 209, 327*n*
  and Congress of Soviets, 305
  in garrison crisis, 242
  in new Soviet government, 306
  and preparation for uprising, 221
  in seizure of power, 302
Krymov, General, 109, 305
  and defeat of Kornilov, 131, 142, 146, 148–51
  removal of, 118
  and rise of Kornilov, 116, 120, 128
Kshesinskaia, Mathilde, 8–9, 35
Kshesinskaia mansion, 8–9, 26, 27, 53, 62
Kuchin, Georgii, 293–95
Kudelko, I. U., 47, 153
Kuzmin, A. I., 26, 276

Land reform, 4–5, 22, 169, 172, 303, 306
Larin, Iurii, 84–85, 223, 322*n*
Lashevich, Mikhail
  in garrison crisis, 242
  in Lenin's campaign for insurrection, 198–200
  and Military Revolutionary Committee, 245
  in October uprising, 249, 269
Latsis, Martin
  and defeat of Kornilov, 135
  in July uprising, 13
  and Lenin's campaign for insurrection, 200, 201
  and Military Revolutionary Committee, 233–34
  and obstacles to an uprising, 209, 217–18
  in October uprising, 268
  and reaction to July days, 63–66
Lazimir, Pavel, 234, 237, 241, 242, 249
Lebedev, Vladimir, 5, 6
Left Socialist Revolutionaries, 24, 168, 209
  and Congress of Soviets, 291–93, 296–98, 304
  and Democratic State Conference, 176, 183
  and district soviets, 77
  in garrison crisis, 246, 247
  and Lenin's campaign for insurrection, 205
  in Military Revolutionary Committee, 237
  and new Soviet government, 308–10, 356*n*
  in October uprising, 250, 251, 254, 257–61, 268, 352*n*
  in preparation for uprising, 213–15
  and reaction to July days, 24, 25
  and seizure of power, 306
Lenin, Vladimir Ilich, 233, 325*n*
  and Bolshevik competition for influence in Petrograd Soviet (Sept.), 175
  calls for insurrection (Sept.), 178–82, 187, 188, 313
  calls for revolution (April), xxi, xxiii, 316*n*–17*n*
  campaigns for insurrection, 191–208, 344*n*–45*n*
  charges against, 55–56
  and defeat of Kornilov, 132–35, 167–71, 173, 180, 204, 205, 337*n*
  and garrison crisis, 234–36
  as German agent, 14–19, 28, 31, 37–38
  and government crackdown on Bolshevik Party, 26, 27
  July theses of, 59–60, 66–70, 326*n*
  and July uprising, xxxiii, 1, 3, 6, 7, 9–14
  Kornilov on, 109
  leadership of, 311–12

  leftist regime sought by, 246–47
  manifesto by, as ultimate source of Soviet political authority, 303–4
  Martov and, 24
  Military Organization and, 75
  in new Soviet government, 306, 309, 310
  in October uprising, 251, 256, 263–67, 272, 353*n*
  party concept of, xxi
  political biography of, xvii–xx
  in preparation for uprising, 209–12, 216, 220–24
  and reaction to July days, 23, 30, 32–38, 44, 54, 57, 168, 312, 323*n*
  reactions of, to Central Committee conference of July 13–14, 61–62
  renews slogan "All Power to the Soviets," 169–74, 342*n*, 344*n*
  in seizure of power, 274–76, 278–81, 290–91, 294–96, 303, 306, 314
  situation confronting (April), xxiii–xxv
  Sixth Congress and, 83–90, 329*n*
  Stalin compared with, 66
"Letter to Comrades" (Lenin), 256
"Letters from Afar" (Lenin), xix, 181
Levitsky, Gen. B. A., 271–72
Liber, Mark, 44, 163, 165, 292
Listok pravdy (newspaper), 47
Livshits (Left SR), 215–16
Lomov, Georgii, 88
  and Lenin's call to insurrection, 181
  in Lenin's campaign for insurrection, 195, 203–4
  in new Soviet government, 306
  in October uprising, 249, 250
Loos, Avgust, 227–28
Ludendorff, Gen. Erich F. W., 5
Lukianov, Fedor, 295
Lukomsky, Gen. A. S., 109, 125, 335*n*
Lunacharsky, Anatolii, 312
  and Congress of Soviets, 292, 297–98, 303, 304
  and defeat of Kornilov, 131, 134
  and new Provisional Government (Aug.), 158
  in new Soviet government, 306
  and reaction to July days, 31–33, 46–48
  in seizure of power, 279
  Sixth Congress and, 83
  Stalin compared with, 66
Lvov, Georgii, xxi, xxii, 28
  and Bolsheviks receiving money from Germans, 15, 17
  resigns, 21, 22, 55

Lvov, Vladimir Nikolaevich, 121–26, 150, 335n, 336n

Maklakov, Vasilii, 40, 112, 126, 165
Malenkaia gazeta (newspaper), 18, 26, 30
Maliantovich, Pavel, 55, 287, 294, 300
Malkin (reporter), 298
Manuilov, Alexander, xxi, 318n
Manuilsky, Dmitrii, 33, 81, 87
Martov, Iulii, 24–25, 31, 56
  capital punishment opposed by, 90
  in Congress of Soviets, 292–96, 298, 302, 303
  and Democratic State Conference, 182, 183
  on directories, 130
  district soviets and, 82
  and new Provisional Government (Aug.), 163, 165
  and October uprising, 257–58
  and preparation for uprising, 215–16
  and seizure of power, 302, 303
  Sixth Congress and, 85
Martynov, Gen. E. I., 96–98
"Marxism and Insurrection" (Lenin), 179–80
Maslenikov, A. M., 45, 46, 80–81
Maslenikov, V., 157–58
Maslov, Semion, 290
Maslovsky, S. D., 67
Maximalists, 209, 214
Mekhonoshin, K. A., 241, 242, 327n
Melgunov, Sergei, xvi
Menshevik-Internationalists, 24, 176, 183, 209, 214
  in Congress of Soviets, 292, 304, 306
  in district soviets, 77
  and new Provisional Government (Aug.), 158, 159, 164
  and new Soviet government, 308–9
  in October uprising, 257–61
  in preparation for uprising, 215
Mensheviks, xviii, xxiii, xxiv, 192, 312, 313
  and Congress of Soviets, 291–96, 302, 314
  and defeat of Kornilov, 132–35
  and Democratic State Conference, 176
  in district soviets, 76, 77
  in elections to Petrograd City Duma, 93
  in garrison crisis, 231, 232, 245
  and July Central Committee resolution, 60–62
  and July uprising, 6, 13–14
  and Lenin's campaign for insurrection, 205
  Lenin's revised stand on (Sept.), 169–74

lose in Petrograd Soviet, 90
lose ground among workers, xxvii–xxviii
and new Provisional Government (Aug.), 153–54, 164–66, 341n
Menzhinskaia, L. R., 57, 75
Menzhinsky, V. R., 74
Metallist factory, 63–64, 154
Michaelis, George, 5
Mikhailov, Mikhail, 46–47
Military League, 95, 117, 156, 331n
Military Organization, *see* Bolshevik Military Organization
Military Revolutionary Committee, 232
  creation of, 232–34
  defends new Soviet government (Oct.), 306–8
  in garrison crisis, 236–48, 349n, 350n
  Military Organization and, 234–36
  in October uprising, 249–72, 353n
  in seizure of power, 273–304, 313–14
Miliukov, Pavel, xxi, xxvi–xxvii, xxxii, 40, 91
  drifts rightward, 95
  in formation of new government (Aug.), 151, 165
  on Kerensky, 113
  Kornilov and, 106, 112–15, 169
  and military dictatorship, 99
Miliutin, V. P., 74, 316n, 325n
  and Democratic State Conference, 176
  and Lenin's call for insurrection, 181
  in new Soviet government, 306, 309, 310
  in October uprising, 250, 272
  and preparation for uprising, 222
  at Sixth Congress, 88
Mogilev
  Kerensky in, 55, 100–2
  Kornilov in, 103, 105, 107, 108, 118–20, 122, 124
Molotov, Viacheslav, 326n
  in Lenin's campaign for insurrection, 200
  and Lenin's July theses, 60
  and reaction to July days, 67–69
  in seizure of power, 289
Moscow Bolsheviks, 60, 88, 89, 111, 133–34, 181, 203–4
Moscow Regional Bureau, *see* Bolshevik Moscow Regional Bureau
Moscow State Conference (Aug. 12–14), 110–17, 133–35, 175, 344n
Moskvin, Ivan, 200
Mstislavsky, Sergei, 213, 292, 352n
Muralov, Nikolai, 111
Muranov, M. K., 325n–26n

Nabokov, V. D., 91
Napoleon I, 96, 239
Narchuk, Viktor, 69–70
Nekrasov, Nikolai, xxi, 318n–19n
  and July uprising, 14, 15, 320n
  in Provisional Government, 26
  and rise of Kornilov, 108, 125
Nevarovsky, Nikolai, 228
Nevsky, Vladimir I.
  in garrison crisis, 234–36
  and July uprising, 13
  and Lenin's campaign for insurrection, 201
  in preparation for insurrection, 211–12, 217,
    224, 348n, 350n
  and repression, 72, 74, 75, 327n
New York Times, x–xi
Nicholas II (Tsar), xviii, xix, 8, 43, 99
Nikitin, Aleksei, 154, 301
Nikitin, Boris, 32
Nogin, Viktor, 316n, 320n, 326n
  and Congress of Soviets, 292
  and Democratic State Conference, 188
  fears coup (Aug.), 111
  and Lenin's call for insurrection, 181, 187
  and Lenin's campaign for insurrection, 206,
    345n
  opposes Lenin in July, 60
  in new Soviet government, 306, 310
  in October uprising, 250
  in preparation for uprising, 222
  and reaction to July days, 33–34, 36, 329n
  at Sixth Congress, 88
Northern Region Congress of Soviets, 209–16,
  233, 235, 345n
Noulens, Joseph, 40
Novaia Rus' (newspaper), 248
Novaia zhizn' (newspaper), 19, 56, 93, 133, 202,
  215, 222, 223
Novoe vremia (newspaper), 104

Officer corps, military dictatorship favored by,
  95, 96, 331n; *see also* Kornilov, Gen. Lavr
Okopnaia pravda (newspaper), 6, 29, 30
Olminsky, 326n
"On Compromises" (Lenin), 169–73, 176, 178,
  182
"On the Current Moment" (Stalin), 66, 158,
  329n
"On the Current Political Situation" (Stalin),
  85
"On the Government Question" (Kamenev),
  159–60
"On the Political Situation," 132

"On Slogans" (Lenin), 61, 69, 85, 88
"On Unification," 132, 133
"One of the Fundamental Questions of the
  Revolution" (Lenin), 170, 171
"Order Number One" (March 1), xxvi, 317n
Ordzhonikidze, Sergei, 33–35, 59
Osipov, Gavril, 70
Osipov, Ivan, 70
"Our Triumph and Our Tasks" (Zinoviev),
  177

Palchinsky, Petr, 283, 285, 286, 299
Panina, Sofia, 290
Pankratov, V., 15, 17–19, 21, 320n
Paradelov, Gen. Nikolai, 285–87
Pavlov, I., 277
Peasants
  and defeat of Kornilov, 148
  and preparation for uprising, 217
  Sixth Congress and, 87
  and socialism in Russia, xx
  Soviet regime (Sept.) and, 172
  See also Soviets
Pereverzev, Pavel, xxvii, 14, 15, 21, 55, 320n
Peshekhonov, Aleksei, xxvii, 3
Pestkovsky, Stanislav, 262
Peter the Great (Tsar), 7
Peter and Paul Fortress
  in July uprising, 2, 11, 26, 27
  reserve headquarters in, 251
  and seizure of power, 274, 282, 285, 286,
    288, 289, 299, 301
  taking of, 245–46, 249
Petersburg Committee, *see* Bolshevik Peters-
  burg Committee
Peterson, Karl, 294
Petrograd, 7–9, 315n
  effects of reaction to July days in, 42–45
  why study, xvi–xvii
Petrograd City Conference, *see* First City Con-
  ference; Second City Conference
Petrograd City Duma, *see* Duma
Petrograd district soviets, xxii–xxiii, xxviii,
  308
  and defeat of Kornilov, 138–40, 143
  and ineffectiveness of repression, 76–82
Petrograd garrison, *see* Garrison conference;
  Soldiers
Petrograd Soviet, 312
  Bolshevik competition for influence in
    (Aug.; Sept.), 90, 174–75
  capital punishment and, 105
  and defeat of Kornilov, 138, 139, 339n

Petrograd Soviet (*continued*)
district soviets and, 77, 80
dominant elements in, 76, 343*n*
emergence of, xxii–xxiii
extreme left strengthened in (Sept.), 189–90
and formation of new Provisional Government (Aug.), 159–63
and garrison crisis, 227, 228, 230–48, 348*n*, 349*n*
influence of (April), xxvi–xxvii
in July uprising, 2–5, 7, 9–13
Kornilov and, 97, 98
and Lenin's campaign for insurrection, 194, 198–99
and October uprising, 249, 250, 254–55, 263
and preparation for uprising, 212, 216, 221
and seizure of power, 274–76, 278, 279, 288, 313–14
Petrograd Trade Union Soviet, 83, 139, 141, 153, 218, 221, 308
Petrogradskaia gazeta (newspaper), 26–27, 32, 35, 36, 43
Petrogradskii listok (newspaper), 18
Petropavlovsk (battleship), 146, 157
Piskunov, Ivan, 47
Plehve, Viacheslav, 99
Plekhanov, Georgii, 18–19
Podvoisky, Nikolai, 71–72, 74, 326*n*, 327*n*
in garrison crisis, 234–37
in July uprising, 13
and Lenin's campaign for insurrection, 201
in Military Revolutionary Committee, 245
in October uprising, 249, 265, 268
and preparation for insurrection, 212, 224, 234
in seizure of power, 274, 280–82, 290–91
Poletaev, Nikolai, 323*n*
"Political Situation, The" (Lenin), 69
Polkovnikov, Gen. Georgii
and garrison crisis, 226, 241, 243, 244
and October uprising, 251, 272
and preparation for insurrection, 216
and seizure of power, 284, 285
Polovtsev, Gen. Petr, 2, 53, 54
Pravda (newspaper), xxiv, xxviii, 318*n*
closed, 29, 59, 72
and July uprising, 6, 12, 16
offices of, raided, 25, 53
and reaction to July days, 17, 19, 47, 66
Preobrazhensky, Evgenii, 329*n*
Preparliament (Council of the Republic)
function of, 185–86, 188, 189
and garrison crisis, 225–26, 246, 248

and Lenin's campaign for insurrection, 192, 196, 198–202
and new Soviet government, 306
in October uprising, 255–62, 271
and preparation for uprising, 215
in seizure of power, 274, 276–78, 284, 285
Prokhorov, Sergei, 218, 219
Prokopovich, Sergei, 284, 290, 298, 299
Proletarii (newspaper), 74, 91, 92, 318*n*
Proletarskoe delo (newspaper), 46–47, 210, 252, 324*n*
Pronin, Aleksei, 262
Provisional Government, xxiv
capital punishment issue and, 77–81, 91, 100–106, 322*n*
composition of, in Feb., xxi–xxii; in May, xxvii; in July, 26; in Sept., 186–87
and defeat of Kornilov, 130–50
and Democratic State Conference, 185–87
fall of, xv–xvii, 273–90, 293, 295, 296, 298–306, 310–14, 355*n*
formation of a new (Aug.), 151–67
garrison crisis undermining, 225–48
generals' demands made, 97, 101; *see also* Kornilov, Gen. Lavr
impotence of (Aug.), 94–95
ineffectiveness of repressive policies of (July–Aug.), 51–58
and July uprising, 2, 3, 10, 13–16
and land reform, 4–5
Lenin's call for insurrection against (Sept.–Oct.), 178–82
Lenin's campaign for insurrection against, 191–208
and Lenin's July theses, 59–60, 66–70
Moscow Conference and, 110–17, 133–35, 175
plans to overthrow (June), xxxii–xxxiii
prime ministers of, *see* Kerensky, Alexander F.; Lvov, Georgii
reaction to July days under, 20–41, 51, 52, 312, 322*n*
Sixth Congress and, 83–85
soldiers' and sailors' view of, xxvi
Soviet support for, xix, xx, xxiii, xxx–xxxi, 35, 36
Stalin's view of (July), 67
uprising against (Oct.), 249–72
Pskov, 55, 229, 230, 233, 271, 272, 305
Public Safety, Committee of, 288
Pulkovo Heights, 308
Purishkevich, Vladimir, 45–46, 80–81, 114, 156

Putilov, Aleksei, 96, 114, 115, 146
Putilov factory, 64, 83, 154

Rabochaia gazeta (newspaper), 93, 105
Rabochii (newspaper), 129, 169, 318*n*, 337*n*
Rabochii put' (newspaper), 318*n*
  and garrison crisis, 228–29, 234, 248, 249
  and Lenin's call for uprising, 172, 182
  and Lenin's campaign for insurrection, 190–92
  and preparation for insurrection, 209, 210, 213, 222
  and seizure of power, 250, 252, 254, 256, 267
Rabochii i soldat (newspaper), 72–74, 91, 252–53, 318*n*
Rabotnitsa (newspaper), xxviii, 318*n*
Radkey, Oliver H., xvi, 166
Rakhia, Eino, 35, 266, 272, 345*n*, 346*n*
Rakhia, Iukka, 197, 199, 200, 218, 272, 346*n*
Rappaport, Viktor, 81
Raskolnikov, Fedor, 330*n*, 347*n*
  charges against, 55–56
  in garrison crisis, 242
  and reaction to July days, 30–32, 47–49
Rasputin, Grigorii, 45
Ravich, Savva, 218
Rech' (newspaper), 3, 19, 42, 93, 243
Red Guards, 211, 219; *see also* Workers
Reed, John, 266, 282–83, 291, 298–99
Reiman, Michael, 242
Remnev, Afanasii, 30, 48
Republican Center, 96, 117
Riabushinsky, P. P., 106
Riazanov, David, 36, 312
  and Democratic State Conference, 188
  in garrison crisis, 247
  and Lenin's campaign for insurrection, 196
  and new Provisional Government (Aug.), 163, 164
  in preparation for insurrection, 215, 223
Riga, 83, 94, 119, 225
Rikhter, V. N., 130
Rodichev, Fedor, 40, 113–14
Rodzianko, Mikhail, 44, 150, 226
Romanovsky, Gen. I. P., 335*n*
Rosenberg, William G., xvi
Roshal, Semion, 30, 48, 49, 55–56, 277
Rozmirovich, E. F., 327*n*
"Rumors of a Conspiracy" (Lenin), 133, 134, 135
Russian army
  disintegration of, 98–100
  German offensive against, 22–23, 334*n*

halting political activity in (Sept.), 116
Kornilov reform of, 100–105; *see also* Kornilov, Gen. Lavr
  and Lenin's call to insurrection (Sept.), 180
  and Lenin's campaign for insurrection, 197
  offensives of, xxxii–xxxiii, 5–6
  a Soviet regime and (Sept.), 172
  steps to prevent disintegration of, 28–29
  See also Cadets; Officer corps; Soldiers
Russian military units
  armies
    First, 229
    Second, 295
    Third, 295
    Fifth, 5, 217
    Eighth, 98, 99, 103
    Eleventh, 22
    Twelfth, 229, 293
  corps
    First Cavalry, 117
    Third Cavalry, 116–18, 120, 124–27, 131, 146, 305, 335*n*
  divisions
    First Don Cossack, 116, 120, 127, 148, 149
    Fifth Cossack, 117
    Eighth Don Cossack Artillery, 335*n*
    Savage, 116–18, 120, 127, 136, 146, 148, 335*n*
    Tenth Cavalry, 335*n*
    Ussuriisky Mounted, 116, 120, 127, 146, 148, 149
  brigades
    Osetinsky Foot, 335*n*
  regiments
    Cherkessky, 148, 335*n*
    Dagestansky, 335*n*
    Egersky Guards, 227, 236
    First Don Cossack, 271
    First Machine Gun, 2, 48, 51–52, 198
    First Reserve Infantry, 70
    Second Machine Gun, 156
    Fourth Don Cossack, 240, 271
    Fourteenth Don Cossack, 240, 271, 353*n*
    Fourteenth Mistavsky Hussar, 27
    180th Infantry, 51–52
    Grenadier, 51–52
    Ingushsky, 148, 335*n*
    Izmailovsky Guards, 262
    Kabardinsky, 335*n*
    Keksgolmsky, 262, 269, 274, 280
    Latvian Rifle, 294
    Litovsky Guards, 71, 143, 154, 250, 254
    Pavlovsky, 245, 268, 274, 280

Russian military units (*continued*)
    Petrogradsky Guards, 26, 156
    Preobrazhensky Guards, 26, 32, 154, 282
    Semenovsky, 26, 269, 282
    Tatarsky, 335n
    Volynsky Guards, 26, 35, 154
battalions
    First Petrograd Women's Shock, 248, 255, 261, 262, 270
    Third Cycle, 301–2
    Fifth Cycle, 302
    Sixth Engineer, 143, 154, 250, 269
    Moscow Women's Battalion of Death, 113, 117
    Petrograd Carters', 143
companies
    First (Sixth Engineer Battalion), 269
miscellaneous
    Kuban Cossacks, 235
    Little Russian Dragoons, 27
    Second Baltic Fleet Detachment, 148, 227–28, 274
Russian naval units
fleets
    Baltic, 143, 168, 200, 225, 263, 273–74
    Black Sea, 26
Russian navy, *see* Russian naval units; Sailors; *specific ships*
"Russian Revolution and Civil War, The" (Lenin), 169, 172, 182
Russian Social Democratic Workers' Party, xviii; *see also* Bolshevik Party; Mensheviks
Ruzsky, Gen. Nikolai, 100, 332n
Rutenberg, Petr, 285, 286
Rykov, A. I., 326n
    and Democratic State Conference, 176, 188
    and Lenin's call for insurrection, 181, 187
    in Lenin's campaign for insurrection, 206, 345h
    in new Soviet government, 306, 309, 310
    in October uprising, 249
    opposes Lenin in July, 60
    in preparation for insurrection, 222
    on Presidium of Petrograd Soviet, 175

Sadovsky, Andrei, 231, 234, 241, 242, 274
Sailors
    Baltic defeats and, 225–26
    Bolshevik strength among, xxvii–xxx
    and defeat of Kornilov, 139, 143, 144, 146, 148
    and February revolution, xxvi
    in July uprising, 9–10, 13
    Kerensky condemns, 28
    and new Provisional Government (Aug.), 154, 157–59, 167
    in October uprising, 262–63, 269, 272–74
    political behavior of, xvii
    and reaction to July days, 28–30, 47
    and rise of Kornilov, 105
    in seizure of power, 274, 276–78, 282, 300–301
    See also Soviets
Sakharov, Vasilii, 47–48, 55–56, 70, 277
Samarin, Col. Georgii, 149
Saveliev, Maximilian, xxxiii, 1, 60, 67–69, 326n
Savinkov, Boris, 22–23, 99, 116
    Kornilov and, 106–8, 118–20, 122–26, 150, 334n, 335n
    and military dictatorship, 100
    resignation of, 152
Second All-Russian Congress of Soviets (Oct.)
    and basis for new government, 189–94, 199, 209–18, 313
    convocation of, 166, 187–89, 356n
    deliberations of, 292–98, 301–6
    and garrison crisis, 224–28, 233–36, 239, 242, 246, 247, 348n
    and October uprising, 250–54, 260, 263, 266–68, 273, 347n
    opens, 291–92
    and seizure of power, 274, 279, 290–91, 306, 314
    See also First All-Russian Congress of Soviets
Second City Conference (Petrograd; Bolsheviks), 63, 64, 66–70
Semenov, E. P., 98
Sergeev, F. A., 326n
Sergei (Grand Duke), 99
Seventh All-Russian Bolshevik Party Conference, *see* April Conference
Shakhovsky, D. I., 318n
Shaumian, Stepan, 181, 326n
Shcherbatov, General, 127
Shingarev, Andrei, xxi, 91, 318n
Shliapnikov, Alexander, 33, 221, 306
Shmidt, Vasilii, 141, 221
Shotman, Alexander, 34–35, 37, 212, 219, 221, 345n, 347n
Shreider, Grigorii, 39, 288, 289, 298, 300
Shugrin, Konstantin, 330n
Shumiatsky, Boris, 72
Sidorin, V. I., 146
Sixth Congress (Bolshevik Party; July

28–August 3), xx, 62, 83–90, 132, 134, 173, 174, 198, 313, 329*n*, 340*n*

Skobelev, Mikhail, xxvii, 5, 6, 163, 174

Skvortsov, Ivan, 306

Sladkov, Ivan, 280

Slavkin, Eliazar, 70

Slutsky, Anton, 67–69, 173, 327*n*, 343*n*

Smilga, Ivar, 13, 66, 74, 168, 316*n*, 326*n*
  in Lenin's campaign for insurrection, 193, 199, 200
  in October uprising, 272
  in preparation for uprising, 210, 214
  at Sixth Congress, 87–88

Smirnov, Sergei, 187

Smolny Institute, 129, 130, 266–67, 336*n*

Snodgrass, John Harold, xxii

Social Democratic Party, 36

Socialist Revolutionaries (SRs; Socialist Revolutionary Party), xxiii, xxvii, 192, 209, 312, 313, 357*n*
  Battle Organization of, 99
  Central Committee of, 117
  at Congress of Soviets, 291–95, 314
  and defeat of Kornilov, 132–35, 139, 141
  and Democratic State Conference, 176
  in district soviets, 76, 77
  in elections to Petrograd City Duma, 92–93
  in garrison crisis, 231, 232, 245
  and July Bolshevik Central Committee resolution, 60, 62
  and July uprising, 6, 13–14
  Kornilov affair and Lenin's shift in thinking about, 169–74
  and Lenin's campaign for insurrection, 204, 205
  and new Provisional Government (Aug.), 153, 158, 159, 161–66, 341*n*
  and new Soviet government, 306, 352*n*
  Petrograd Soviet and, 90, 174–75, 343*n*
  popular opinion (June) and, xxxi, 330*n*
  and reaction to July days, 20, 43–44, 59–61, 64
  See also Left Socialist Revolutionaries

Society for the Economic Rehabilitation of Russia, 96, 115, 146

Sokolnikov, Grigorii, 57, 74, 172, 326*n*
  and Congress of Soviets, 187
  and defeat of Kornilov, 130
  and Lenin's call for insurrection, 181
  in Lenin's campaign for insurrection, 192–93, 199, 200, 203
  in preparation for uprising, 211, 212
  at Sixth Congress, 87, 88

Soldat (newspaper), 74, 75, 91, 92, 136–37, 234, 248, 249, 318*n*, 337*n*, 340n

Soldatskaia pravda (newspaper), xxviii, 6, 29, 46, 70, 72, 318*n*

Soldiers
  Bolshevik strength among, xxvii–xxx, 90
  and defeat of Kornilov, 139, 143, 144, 146, 341*n*
  district soviets and, 78–82
  and February revolution, xxvi
  in garrison crisis, 225–48
  ineffectiveness of repression on, 52–53, 70–71
  in July uprising, 1–3, 5–7, 9–11, 13–14, 16
  Military Organization and, xxviii, xxx; *see also* Bolshevik Military Organization
  and new Provisional Government (Aug.), 154–56, 159, 160, 167
  in October uprising, 250, 254–55
  political behavior of, xvii, xx, 343*n*
  in preparation for insurrection, 215–19, 224
  and reaction to July days, 28–29, 51–53, 70–71, 75–76, 78
  and rise of Kornilov, 105–7
  in seizure of power, 276
  See also Soviets

Soviet, *see* All-Russian Executive Committees; Central Executive Committee; First All-Russian Congress of Soviets; Northern Region Congress of Soviets; Second All-Russian Congress of Soviets

Soviets, xxiv, 187, 340*n*
  defended (Sixth Congress), 198
  emergence of, xxiii
  future of (post–July days), 67–69
  in garrison crisis, 227, 231, 236, 245
  independence of, destroyed, 310
  influence of, xxvi–xxvii
  July resolution of Bolshevik Central Committee and, 60–62
  July uprising and power to, 2, 3
  Lenin on failure of (July), 62
  and Lenin's call to insurrection (Sept.), 181–82
  Lenin's shift on (Sept.), 169–74, 179
  Martov and power to, 24, 25
  and preparation for insurrection, 224–25
  and reaction to July days, 20, 59–60, 312–13
  Sixth Congress and future of, 85–90
  See also Petrograd Soviet; *and specific soviet institutions; for example:* All-Russian Executive Committees

Spiridonova, Maria, 292

Stalin, Iosif, 57, 60, 74, 92, 232, 316n, 326n, 344n, 353n
  at Democratic State Conference, 176, 188
  and Lenin's call for insurrection (Sept.), 181
  in Lenin's campaign for insurrection, 192–93, 203, 345n
  in new Soviet government, 306
  in October uprising, 252, 253, 272
  in preparation for insurrection, 225, 234, 341n
  and reaction to July days, 32, 33, 66–69
  at Sixth Congress, 85–89
Stark, Leonid, 262
Stasova, Elena, 345n
State Council, dissolved, 22
State and Revolution, The (Lenin), 35, 168, 323n
Steklov, Iurii, 44, 161
Stepanov, V. A., 318n
Strikes
  hunger, 50, 153, 211
  July, 5
  Moscow Conference and, 111
  political, 6–7
Sukhanov, N. N., 202
  and Congress of Soviets, 292–94
  on garrison crisis, 243
  and Kornilov, 128, 132, 137
  and new Provisional Government (Aug.), 165
  and seizure of power, 280
Sulimova, Maria, 36–37, 323n
Suny, Ronald G., xvi
Sverdlov, Iakov, 57, 59, 60, 74, 75, 316n, 326n
  and Congress of Soviets, 187
  in garrison crisis, 231, 241, 242
  and Lenin's call for insurrection, 181
  and Lenin's campaign for insurrection, 201, 202, 204
  and Lenin's return to Petrograd (Sept.), 182
  in October uprising, 249, 250, 264, 327n
  at Sixth Congress, 84
Sverdlova (Bolshevik), 219–20

"Tasks of the Revolution, The" (Lenin), 170, 171, 192–93
Tarasov-Rodionov, A., 281, 289
Teodorovich, Ivan, 306, 310
Ter-Arutuniants, Mikhail, 47, 153
Tereshchenko, Mikhail, xxi–xxii
  and July uprising, 14, 15
  in Provisional Government, 26, 154, 187
  and rise of Kornilov, 100, 101, 108, 127
  and seizure of power, 301

"To All Workers, Soldiers, and Peasants," 303–4
"To the Citizens of Russia" (Lenin), 274–75
"To Workers, Peasants, and Soldiers," 194–95
Tolkachev, A., 277
Tolstoi, Aleksei, 263
Tolstoy, Leo, 7
Tovarishch (newspaper), 28
Trade Union Soviet, see Petrograd Trade Union Soviet
Transport system, xxv
Tretiakov, S. N., 106
Trotsky, Lev D., xx, 153, 173, 234, 312, 316n, 322n, 326n
  at Congress of Soviets, 187, 292, 296–98, 303
  and defeat of Kornilov, 132
  and Democratic State Conference, 176–78, 183, 186, 188, 192
  during garrison crisis, 231–32, 237, 240–43, 248, 348n
  and July uprising, 12
  and Lenin's call for insurrection (Sept.), 181–82, 344n
  and Lenin's campaign for insurrection, 192–93, 196, 201, 203
  Military Organization and, 72
  in Military Revolutionary Committee, 240, 245
  in new Soviet government, 306, 309
  in October uprising, 249, 250–54, 263, 266–68, 272
  and Petrograd Soviet, 90, 175, 189, 313
  and preparation for insurrection, 212, 221, 222, 225
  and Preparliament, 201–2
  and reaction to July days, 19, 31–32, 47–50
  in seizure of power, 278, 279
  Sixth Congress and, 83, 85, 86
  Stalin compared with, 66
Trubetskoi, Prince Grigorii, 127–28
Tsentrobalt (Central Committee of the Baltic Fleet), 30, 48, 143, 157, 237, 306
Tsentroflot (Central Executive Committee of the Navy), 148
Tsereteli, Iraklii, 23, 36, 174
  and defeat of Kornilov, 131, 148
  and Democratic State Conference, 184–87
  and formation of new Provisional Government (Aug.), 158
  and Provisional Government, xxvii, 26, 55, 161, 164, 165, 320n
  and reaction to July days, 68, 321n

Turgenev, Ivan, 7
Tyrkova, Ariadna, 40, 91

Ulianov, Maria, xxxiii, 1, 33
Unemployment, shortages resulting in, 4
Union of Cossack Troops, 105
Union of Landowners, 95
Union of Metalworkers, 141, 221
Union of Officers of the Army and Navy, 95,
    105, 117, 119, 127, 156, 331*n*
Union of Railway Workers, 142; *see also* Vik-
    zhel
Union of Saint George Cavaliers, 95, 105, 156,
    331*n*
Uritsky, M. S., 181, 203, 204, 234, 250, 326*n*

Vainshtein, S. L., 130
Veinberg, Gavril, 67, 68
Verderevsky, Adm. Dmitrii, 154, 284, 287,
    289
Verkhovsky, Gen. A. I., 103, 114, 150, 154,
    216, 265, 335*n*–36*n*
Vikzhel, 142, 308–10
Vinokurov, Vasilii, 64, 217–19
Vishnegradsky, A. I., 106, 114, 115
Vishnevetsky, Nikolai, 47
Voinov, Ivan, 47, 266, 324*n*
Volia naroda (newspaper), 19, 20
Volodarsky, Moisei, 74, 77, 326*n*
    and garrison crisis, 242
    and ineffectiveness of government repres-
        sion, 64, 68, 69
    in July uprising, 9, 12–13, 319*n*
    leftists defended by, 90
    and Lenin's campaign for insurrection,
        192–93, 197–200
    opposes Lenin in July, 60, 61
    in preparation for insurrection, 221
    and reaction to July days, 33
    in seizure of power, 279
    at Sixth Congress, 86, 88
Volodin (chairman of sailors' committee), 228

Wade, Rex, xvi
Washington, George, xxii
"What We Need" (Stalin), 252
Wilhelm II (Kaiser of Germany), 27, 201, 256
Winter Palace, in October seizure of power,
    274, 278, 280–91, 295, 298–301, 305
Workers
    Bolshevik strength among, xxvii–xxx, 90
    defeat of Kornilov and Red Guards, 139–49,
        152, 339*n*
    district soviets and, 78–79, 81–82

economic situation of, xxv–xxvi
insurrection and Red Guards, 211, 219
in July uprising, 1–3, 5–7, 9–12
and new Provisional Government (Aug.),
    154–55, 159, 160, 166, 167, 340*n*
in October uprising, 261–63, 265, 266, 269
opposing new Soviet government, 306,
    308–9
political behavior of, xvii, xix–xx, 343*n*
in preparation for insurrection, 215–19, 224
rail, under martial law, 106
and reaction to July days, 28–30, 52–54,
    63–65, 70, 78
and rise of Kornilov, 105–7
in seizure of power, Red Guards, 274, 277,
    280, 300–301
See also Soviets
Workers' control, 169, 303, 318*n*
Workers' Section (Petrograd Soviet), 2, 90, 105
World War I, *see* Russian army; Russian mili-
    tary units; Russian naval units
Woytinsky, Vladimir, 42, 99, 167
    in garrison crisis, 226, 227, 229–31, 244
    in seizure of power, 302

Yagoda, Genrikh, 72

Zakharov, A., 269–70
Zarudny, Alexander, 55
Zavoiko, Vasilii, and rise of Kornilov, 98,
    100–104, 122–23, 126–27, 332*n*
Zhakov, Mikhail, 253, 254
Zhivoe slovo (newspaper), 17–18, 35, 36, 40,
    215, 248, 250, 325*n*
Zinoviev, Grigorii, 239, 312, 316*n*, 344*n*
    charges against, 55–56
    and Congress of Soviets, 190, 292
    and defeat of Kornilov, 132
    and Democratic State Conference, 177
    in July uprising, 12, 320*n*
    and Lenin's campaign for insurrection,
        191–92, 203–8, 345*n*, 346*n*
    in new Soviet government, 309, 310
    and October uprising, 272
    opposes Lenin in July, 60
    in preparation for insurrection, 212–14, 216,
        217, 221–23, 347*n*
    and reaction to July days, 19, 30–38, 44, 57
    and seizure of power, 279
    Stalin compared with, 66
Znamensky, Sergei, 163
Znamia truda (newspaper), 213, 347*n*

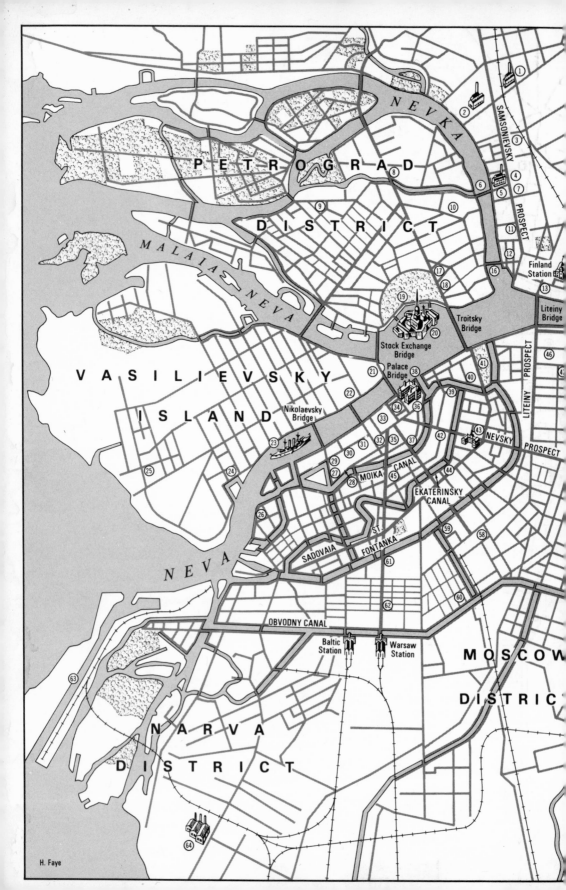

NEVKA

SAMSONIEVSKY

PETROGRAD

DISTRICT

PROSPECT

Finland
Station

Liteiny
Bridge

MALAIA NEVA

VASILIEVSKY

ISLAND

Nikolaevsky
Bridge

Stock Exchange
Bridge

Troitsky
Bridge

Palace
Bridge

LITEINY   PROSPECT

NEVSKY   PROSPECT

MOIKA   CANAL

EKATERINSKY
CANAL

ST.
SADOVAIA   FONTANKA

NEVA

OBVODNY CANAL

Baltic
Station

Warsaw
Station

MOSCOW

DISTRIC

NARVA

DISTRICT

H. Faye